# THE THREE WORLDS OF
# CAPTAIN JOHN SMITH

THE PORTRAICTUER OF CAPTAYNE IOHN SMITH ADMIRALL OF NEW ENGLAND.

Æ.14 37. A° 1616

These are the Lines that shew thy Face; but those
That shew thy Grace and Glory, brighter bee:
Thy Faire-Discoueries and Fowle-Overthrowes
Of Salvages, much Civilliz'd by thee
Best shew thy Spirit; and to it Glory Wyn;
So, thou art Brasse without, but Golde within.

CAPTAIN JOHN SMITH IN HIS THIRTY-SEVENTH YEAR

# THE THREE WORLDS

## of

# CAPTAIN

# John

# Smith

*by* PHILIP L. BARBOUR

*illustrated with* PHOTOGRAPHS *and* MAPS

HOUGHTON MIFFLIN COMPANY BOSTON

The Riverside Press Cambridge

MCMLXIV

TO THE CHERISHED MEMORY

OF

ABRAHAM VALENTINE WILLIAMS JACKSON

1862–1937

TEACHER AND FRIEND

*Praythee, take care, that tak'st*
*my book in hand,*
*To read it well: that is,*
*to understand.*
— BEN JONSON

# PREFACE

**W**HY set about writing yet another life of Captain John Smith?

Every school child knows that Captain Smith was a hero, a historian, and Pocahontas's sweetheart — or that he was a dastard, a liar and, so far as Pocahontas was concerned, an ingrate. It depends on whose life of Smith you read.

Praise or abuse — both unstinted — has been Smith's fate. Rarely has he been approached dispassionately, if ever. But what was he really like, this man who has stirred such conflicting emotions, and so little sober inquiry?

Here is the sole justification for my attempting a new life of Captain John Smith. In this book, for the first time, I believe, use has been made of the hints and clues that have long been lurking in insignificant sidelights, in documents which do not mention Smith directly, in the place-names strewn on his maps, honoring those from whom he had, or hoped to have, this, that or the other favor.

Ever since Thomas Fuller included a biography of John Smith among his "misshapen scraps, mixed with tattle and lies," over three hundred years ago, a certain hostility to Smith has been germinating, to burst into full bloom during the last century. Not bothering to look into the surviving, if faint, guides to Smith's career, imaginations livelier than Smith's own have worked almost ceaselessly to prove him so colossal a prevaricator that it is surprising that no one has come up with the suggestion that Smith himself was a fabrication.

This I make so bold as to state despite the obvious fact that

Charles Deane's first critical analysis of Smith's self-told tales was a sincere attempt to get at the truth, which can hardly be said of Henry Adams's "upside down" story. But Deane analyzed in a vacuum — that is, in almost total ignorance — and so have Smith's detractors (and most of his champions) to this day.

The chief trouble (the ignorance I have mentioned) has been that historians have studied Smith's career and Smith's writings without (or with little) reference to the atmosphere John Smith breathed. Even disregarding the improbable behavior known to have been characteristic of princes, prelates, and politicos, the whole *style* of the day was inflated — in writing and in living. The people were childish, "for all their gifts and all their ability." Attractive personalities were rare. (Sir John Hawkins has recently been singled out as "a reliable and modest character — unusual in that age.") Religious cleavages split society one way; a caste system cut across in another. Wealth could bridge gaps, to be sure, but that was acquired by cut-throat business, toadyism, blatant racketeering or piracy, when it was not inherited. Clearly, equal opportunity for all was a thought unfledged, if not unborn.

John Smith ranked but little higher in Elizabethan society than a Hindu "untouchable" in Akbar's India. Perhaps because of this, he was by disposition tolerant of everything but intolerance, and by this token he lacked both the background and the ruthlessness necessary to forge ahead in the field of money-making, or in his chosen field of building an English colonial empire. As a result, for all that he accomplished, he was a failure as a colonialist. This fact is of course remembered; that no man succeeded is forgotten. John Smith did not end in a blaze of glory as Sir John Smith (his surname gilded into Smythe), Governor General of Virginia and New England. This has condemned him to the petty cavil of less effective actors on the world's stage than himself.

But enough of defense! In presenting this study of Captain John Smith I have worked on what I believe may be called a scientific basis. To round out the story, I have added hypothetical explanation, without which it would be empty sequences of fact. The *persons* of the action would be but historical puppets. But by filling in with surmise and hypothesis where necessary, I trust I have explained the facts. New facts may refute my explanation in time, but that is part of the scientific process. Idle daydreaming, I trust, will not be found.

This approach has invited a grave shortcoming. In John Smith's egocentric yet curiously unrevealing writings, no hint exists of what made up his private life. Only in his *maps* are there clues, some of which lead to something, however little. Nevertheless, the most tantalizing of these clues is broken before we are out of the labyrinth. Another, in Smith's last will and testament, is equally futile. Both of these have reference to a lady. From the map, we know that someone named Abigail was dear to John Smith. From the will, we know of a Mrs. Tredway. Mrs. Tredway possibly cared for him in his last illness. But who was Abigail?

My indebtedness for help in digging out information for this book, over more than five years, is indeed vast. Space makes proper expression of gratitude all but impossible. Smith traveled far and wide, and this biographer had almost to follow his trail to be able to locate the information that was needed. It is therefore with some regret that I have to state that, for political reasons, I was unable to get any personal cooperation in Yugoslavia (although a visa was issued to me without trouble), and that Rumania ignored repeated requests for a visa. Thanks to the efforts of friends in Austria, some needed information was obtained indirectly from the People's Republics involved, but such searching as I carried out elsewhere in Europe was impossible where once upon a time I had been a welcome guest. My references in connection with John Smith's adventures in Eastern Europe are consequently sketchy. (Dr. Laura Polanyi Striker searched well in Hungary, but her objective was vindication rather than the truth.) The completion of this side of Smith's life consequently still needs diligent inquiry. Although I believe I have laid a sound foundation, more spadework is still needed.

Elsewhere, I have met with practically unexpected and cordial cooperation. My greatest debt is to Professor David Beers Quinn, of the University of Liverpool, who has gone over my manuscript with care and patience, giving me the benefit of his intimate knowledge of English colonial history. For further details of the English phase of Smith's career, I am indebted, among others, to Mr. R. A.

Skelton, of the British Museum; Mr. Derek Charman, County Archivist, Ipswich; Mr. F. G. Emmison, County Archivist, Chelmsford; Mrs. Joan Varley, Lincolnshire Archives Office, Lincoln; and Canon J. H. Adams, Landulph Rectory, Saltash, Cornwall.

Elsewhere, I want particularly to acknowledge the help and advice of Dr. C. T. McInnes, Emeritus Curator of Historical Records, and Mr. John Imrie, his successor, Curator, Edinburgh; Professor de la Fontaine Verwey, University Library, Amsterdam; Dr. Simon Hart, Gemeente-Archief, Amsterdam; Drs. N. M. Japikse, Algemeen Rijksarchief, The Hague; M. Marcel Delafosse, Archiviste de la Charente-Maritime, La Rochelle; M. Buffet, Directeur des Archives Départementaux, Rennes; M. Henri de la Villehuchet, Château de Plouër, Côtes-du-Nord; Dr. Josef Teschitel, S.J., Jesuit Archives, Rome; Professor Dr. Franz Babinger, Munich; Dr. F. von Mettnitz, Sauerlach, Bavaria; Dr. Gebhard Rath, Generaldirektor, Staatsarchiv, Vienna; Dr. Franz Pichler, Landesarchiv, Graz; Dr. Karl Dinklage, Landesarchiv, Klagenfurt; Dr. Karl Kurt Klein, Innsbruck; Dr. Hans Sokoll, Heraldisch-Genealogische Gesellschaft "Adler," Vienna; Dr. Tibor Halasi Kun, Columbia University, New York; Mr. Lewis M. Starke, Mr. Gerald D. McDonald, Mr. Archibald DeWeese, and Dr. Gerard L. Alexander, all of the New York Public Library, and their staffs; Dr. Lawrence C. Wroth, Librarian Emeritus of the John Carter Brown Library, Providence, and his successor, Mr. Thomas R. Adams; Dr. Frederick J. Dockstader, of the Museum of the American Indian, New York; Dr. William C. Sturtevant, Smithsonian Institution, Washington; Father Jean Lessard, O.M.I., Edmonton, Alberta; and Mr. Robert A. Logan, St. Paul, Minnesota.

Others, far too numerous to mention here, have provided bits of information, and still others have given me negative answers to inquiries which have directed my steps toward other solutions (notably in the case of Professor David Greene, of Dublin, Ireland). My debt to these is acknowledged in the Commentaries. I am of course also indebted to the staffs of a score of libraries in this country, not to mention another score across the Atlantic, whom space prevents naming.

To all these, I gladly give my thanks. They are responsible for contributing invaluable help. They are not to be blamed for the interpretation of their contributions, which is throughout mine alone.

It remains only to add that I have generally modernized the spelling of old accounts, except here and there where the flavor of the times ought especially to be preserved, or for some other specific reason.

PHILIP L. BARBOUR

Newtown, Connecticut
May-day. 1963

# CONTENTS

## PART III. PROMOTER

# ILLUSTRATIONS

The signature of John Smith on the front cover is reproduced from a letter by permission of The Huntington Library, San Marino, California.

## *frontispiece*

CAPTAIN JOHN SMITH IN HIS THIRTY-SEVENTH YEAR
From an engraving by Simon van de Passe. It appears in the upper left corner of the Map of New England included with Smith's *Description of New England* in 1616. The poem is by John Davies of Hereford. This is one of the best of many surviving prints. (Courtesy of the British Museum.)

## *following page 268*

ZSIGMOND BÁTHORY, PRINCE OF TRANSYLVANIA
From an anonymous engraving in *Ortelius Redivivus* (1665) by Hieronymus Ortelius. (Photograph by Herbert Wicks Studios, Danbury, Connecticut, from a copy in the author's possession.)

THE LIBERATION OF ALBA REGALIS (STUHLWEISSENBURG), SEPTEMBER 20, 1601
From an engraving in *Ortelius Redivivus*. (Photograph from a copy in the author's possession, by Herbert Wicks Studios.)

THE BATTLE OF TSCHARKA PASS, OCTOBER 15, 1601
From an original drawing in the *Haus-, Hof- und Staatsarchiv*. (By permission of the Direction.)

THE SIEGE OF NAGYKANIZSA

(Photograph by Herbert Wicks Studios from the author's copy of *Ortelius Redivivus.*)

KING JAMES I OF ENGLAND, FRANCE, SCOTLAND, AND IRELAND

Engraved in Cologne by Crispin van de Passe, father of the engravers who did so many portraits of James and his subjects. Crispin the elder may possibly have been in England in 1603 or 1604, but there is no record of his ever having seen King James. (Courtesy of the British Museum.)

SIR FRANCIS BACON, LORD KEEPER OF THE PRIVY SEAL

Engraved by Simon van de Passe. The titles point to the year 1617–1618. (Courtesy of the British Museum.)

SIR THOMAS SMYTHE, AGED ABOUT FIFTY-EIGHT

Engraved by Simon van de Passe. (Courtesy of the British Museum.)

FRANCES HOWARD, DUCHESS OF RICHMOND AND LENNOX,
AGED FORTY-FIVE

Engraved by Francis Delaram. This portrait was inserted in some copies of the *Generall Historie,* although an engraving by William van de Passe was more common. Both were made in 1623, and this has been chosen as the better portrait. (Courtesy of the British Museum.)

CAPTAIN SAMUEL ARGALL HARANGUES THE CHICKAHOMINIES

From *Americae Pars Decima* . . . by Johann-Theodore de Bry. (Courtesy of the New York Public Library.)

POWHATAN RECEIVES RALPH HAMOR

From De Bry's *Americae Pars Decima* . . . (Courtesy of the New York Public Library.)

IAPAZAWS AND HIS WIFE PERSUADE POCAHONTAS
TO VISIT CAPTAIN ARGALL'S SHIP

From *Americae Pars Decima* . . . (Courtesy of the New York Public Library.)

POCAHONTAS IN HER TWENTY-FIRST YEAR

From an engraving by Simon van de Passe done at about the same time as his picture of John Smith. This engraving, however, was made from an oil portrait by an unknown painter. It was apparently added to, or inserted in, Smith's *Generall Historie* after the book was originally issued. (Courtesy of the British Museum.)

CAPTAIN JOHN SMITH ESCAPES FROM HIS FRENCH CAPTORS
IN OCTOBER, 1615
This illustration, which is based on page 226 of Smith's *Works,* is also from De Bry's *Americae Pars Decima* . . . (Courtesy of the New York Public Library.)

DON DIEGO SARMIENTO DE ACUÑA, CONDE DE GONDOMAR
Engraved in 1622 by Simon van de Passe. (Courtesy of the British Museum.)

THE PERILS FACED BY THE DOUGHTY CAPTAIN
From Pieter van der Aa's *Naaukeurige versameling der gedenk-waardigste zee en land-reysen na Oost en West-Indien* . . . , Vol. 25. (By permission of the New York Public Library.)

# MAPS

# PART I

# Adventurer

# Adventurer

# CHAPTER 1

## JOHN SMITH, YEOMAN

ON SATURDAY, January 9, 1580, Cardinal Henry of Aviz, King of Portugal, summoned the Portuguese *Cortes* for the only time in his reign. He was carried in, partly because he was old and feeble, partly because he did not want to face his nobles. They had forced this action for patriotic reasons.

Cardinal-King Henry had been refused absolution from his vows so that he could marry. Unmarried, he could have no legitimate heir. And now he was so wasted in body that his sole article of diet (so it was said) was woman's milk. The Portuguese Crown was at stake, and with it the independence of the realm and its world-wide empire. It was imperative that Henry name a successor.

The nobles opted for King Philip II of Spain, a nephew of Cardinal-King Henry, for he was the most powerful monarch in Christendom, and a next-door neighbor. The clergy and the people wanted someone else — anyone else. Henry vacillated.

Whether it was the effect of the voice of his fellow servants of God, or the muffled voice of the people, or anemia, Henry had no successor to name. Appeals and protests alike were mere sound waves in the air. Sand trickled through the hourglass, while the future of Portugal gently slipped from the grasp of the Portuguese people. Then Cardinal-King Henry was borne from the audience as he had come, useless, sterile, even ominous.[1]

That same Saturday, a thousand and more miles away, a married couple proudly presented their first-born son at the baptismal font of the parish church of Willoughby by Alford, in the county of Lincolnshire, England. Their names were George and Alice Smith, and he at least was a relative newcomer in that region. His family home had been in Cuerdley, a parish fifteen or twenty miles up the Mersey from Liverpool — itself a small town in those days, and mainly a port for shipments to and from Ireland. George Smith was a freeman, not a "gentleman" in rank, and whether he himself had migrated from Lancashire, or whether an earlier generation of Smiths had sought new soil, George had acquired a small farm at Great Carlton, half a dozen miles east of Louth, and leased other property from Lord Willoughby de Eresby, lord of the manor of Willoughby by Alford.

George Smith had taken to wife Alice Rickard, descendant of the Rickards (variously spelled) of Great Heck, in the south of Yorkshire. Like John Shakespeare's wife, Alice was of slightly higher social standing than her husband, and she may not have been quite so much of a newcomer. There had been a branch of the Rickard family in Lincolnshire for several generations, but it is useless to attempt to trace from which branch she came. Her family was in any case an old one, and not without its "superior" connections, including at least one marriage with a knight, and a tie with an Archbishop of Dublin. The Smiths were, so far as anyone can tell, less honored in their connections, but had supplied a schoolteacher or two to the vicinity. It was enough to place George Smith and his wife a step above the total obscurity of the "mere" peasants.

That second Saturday in January, then, the eldest son of George and Alice was baptized, and given the name of John. George Smith, to judge by his will, had always been a shy and retiring, perhaps overhumble, man. Conceivably, he expected his son to take after him, since he metaphorically buried him at birth under the most anonymous of English names. If so, his shade, wandering about in the Great Beyond, must soon have been deeply distressed. For, from a John Smith who could be anybody — almost — the John Smith who was baptized on January 9, 1580, became a legend. Distinguished by the common title of Captain, he lived to become one of the famed men of English and American history.

The Smith family was a small one, and John eventually had but one brother and one sister who lived to maturity. Their worldly goods, if few, were ample for the simple life of farming toward the close of Queen Elizabeth's reign. And while their acreage was not great, the income from it was sufficient for George Smith to have amassed goods and chattels to the value of more than seventy-five pounds sterling by the time he died. In short, George (and John, after him) like enough was accounted a "yeoman"* in the loosening social categories of the time.

Life would possibly have continued for the Smiths as in the past, had not Cardinal-King Henry of Portugal died before John Smith was a month old. This set off a chain reaction of such international effect as to touch the lives even of ordinary people, like the Smiths and their baby John. *His* career grew out of the events thus provoked, and these events are therefore part of his story. Briefly, here is what happened.

As quickly as practicable after the Cardinal-King's death, Captain-General Fernando Álvarez de Toledo, Duke of Alba, marched on Lisbon at the behest of King Philip of Spain. Philip's first cousin, the Duke of Savoy, also a contender for the Portuguese Crown, was too far off and too weak in war potential to do anything to stop Philip, but the Portuguese people rallied around another first cousin who, although he was illegitimate, at least was Portuguese. This was Dom Antonio, the only child (apparently) of Henry's older brother, Dom Luiz, who had been made Prior of the seat of the Knights of Malta at Crato. Dom Antonio was proclaimed King at Santarem, but Alba soon swept all before him, and Dom Antonio took to his heels, encumbered only by the crown jewels of Portugal, which he believed might come in handy.

Philip of Spain was then "joyfully accepted" by the people of Portugal, while Alba's troops saw to it that no malcontents marred the general bliss — a procedure not unknown in the mid-twentieth century. In spite of Alba, however, it was eight months before Dom Antonio finally left his country, and more than a year before Philip went to Portugal to be invested as monarch. This personal union of Portugal with "All the Spains" produced a further magnification of Philip's empire that brought grave anxiety to the rest of Europe. Portugal itself was a valuable possession; but Brazil, the Azores and other Atlantic islands completed Philip's grip on the West and its wealth, while the chain of Portuguese outposts fringing Africa and India to China and the Moluccas gave him a

---

* "Yeoman: which worde now signifieth among us, a man well at ease and having honestlie to live, and yet not a gentleman."

*cordon sanitaire* around the wealth of the East. The possible economic and political consequences were, for the rest of Europe, horrific to contemplate.

England and France were understandably sensitive to this new accession to Spanish power, and Elizabeth kept toying — how seriously we do not know — with the idea of marrying the younger brother of the King of France. Meanwhile, there were rumors of an augmented Spanish fleet under construction, and a few hundred Spaniards and Italians arrived in Ireland (which "belonged" to Elizabeth) to support a couple of thousand Irish rebels who were fighting the English — under the Papal standard. Just about at that juncture, late in 1580, Sir Francis Drake returned from circumnavigating the globe, bringing a vast treasure robbed from Spanish vessels on the high seas. Relying on France for help, and playing off the Spanish troops in Ireland against Spanish Ambassador Mendoza's complaints about Drake, Elizabeth gradually turned the globe-encircling raid to her (and England's) advantage, and by the time Philip was crowned King of Portugal, Elizabeth had paid off her entire foreign debt with pilfered Spanish treasure.[3]

Such things as these were the elements of gossip around John Smith's ears from his babyhood. Don Bernardino de Mendoza was sent home as *persona non grata* before John's mind could understand the import of so drastic a move, but he was surely in school by the time the Spanish Armada struck terror and rage into the hearts of all Englishmen. Even before the summer of 1588, John Smith was almost certainly

> with his satchel
> And shining morning face, creeping like snail
> Unwillingly to school . . .*

at Alford, four miles from his home, across the fat and marshy land of eastern Lincolnshire.

The next year King Henry III of France was assassinated, leaving the crown, by deathbed will, to his brother-in-law and second cousin Henry, Protestant King of Navarre. The latter assumed the style Henry IV, King of France, but it was ten years before he was king in fact, as well as in name. The Catholic nobility could not, would not, accept a Protestant ruler.

---

* Shakespeare, *As You Like It,* II, vii, 145.

Elizabeth of England was only too happy to recognize the new monarch and to send him with startling speed some £20,000 (with more coming later) to help finance the campaigns that would have to be fought before Henry sat firmly in the royal palace of the Louvre. She also sent that valiant warrior Lord Willoughby de Eresby, whose tenant farmer George Smith was, to support Henry with a small army.

Willoughby landed in Normandy, met Henry, almost got to Paris with the loyal troops, retreated, saw him sworn King of France at Tours, and within the year returned to England. Willoughby had done his duty, so far as the limited, exceedingly limited, resources placed at his disposal permitted. But the problem was far beyond any such petty help. Henry had almost his entire kingdom to conquer by force of arms, and Catholic Brittany particularly set up strong resistance under the ex-governor, Philippe-Emmanuel of Vaudemont (and of Lorraine), Duke of Mercoeur, whose sister was the widow of the late not-much-lamented Henry III. Mercoeur's uncle Francis, Duke of Lorraine, had married Christina, daughter of the King of Denmark, and this brought relationship by marriage with Emperor Rudolph II, Philip II, Christian IV of Denmark (whose sister was Queen Anne of Scotland), and many other lesser notabilities, not to mention his own blood relationship (second cousin) with Mary Queen of Scots. As a staunch Catholic, Mercoeur felt obliged to call on his cousin Philip of Spain for help against his liege lord, Henry.

This was a double mistake, for it turned many a Breton against him, and at the same time really aroused Queen Elizabeth; for Philip cooperated to the extent of occupying part of Brittany, including the chief ports. Even devout Bretons preferred a French king to a Spaniard, regardless of religion.

In England, in the House of Commons, when the 1593 Parliament was called, men of such differing minds as Sir Robert Cecil, Sir Walter Ralegh, and Francis Bacon all spoke for increased taxes to equip a royal navy and army, to supplant King Philip in Brittany, and Lord Burghley declared in the Queen's name, before the House of Lords, that Philip had "become as a frontier enemy to all the west part of England." Nevertheless, 1593 passed before anything more tangible sallied forth from London than a rumor that Sir Francis Drake was going to sea again. Still, 1593 was a fateful year for John Smith. According to his own account, he made his first bid for adventure in that year.[4]

Sometime in the early 1620's, John Smith began writing a sketchy autobiography, interspersed with bits of historical and geographical information, and sailors' yarns. Any account of his life must be based on such of this autobiography as has survived (published in part in 1625, and in greater detail in 1629). But the account is not always clear, and long passages in it are extracted from various contemporary works. In spite of confusion and faulty sequence, however, the story of John Smith's early life can be recounted without any great demand on imagination or surmise, or any serious watering-down of passages originally written with characteristic Elizabethan flourish. Independently recorded history bears out all the main points. Reason can easily tie them together.

The first approximation of a date John Smith gives is the year 1593. The title page of his book reads: *The True Travels, Adventures, and Observations of Captaine John Smith, In Europe, Asia, Affrica, and America, from Anno Domini 1593 to 1629.* Inside, on page one, getting off to a bad start, he says that his "parent's dying when he was about thirteen years of age, left him a competent means, which he not being capable to manage, little regarded; his mind being even then set upon brave adventures," but that his "father's death stayed him." Meanwhile, he "sold his satchel, books, and all he had, intending secretly to get to sea." The truth of the matter appears to be that young John had left Alford to go to school in Louth (perhaps from 1592 to 1595) — and it is certain that his father did not die until 1596. Furthermore, his "parent's dying" and his "father's death" must refer to the same event, since his mother lived to marry a second time. What then?

In 1593 came the rumor from London that Drake was setting out on a punitive expedition against the Spaniards. Spaniards had haunted John Smith since the day he was born, so to speak. The rape of Portugal, the treachery of Ambassador Mendoza, the Invincible Armada, Drake's (unprofitable) raid on Lisbon in 1589 and Lord Willoughby's anti-Spanish command in France; then the capture of the great carrack *Madre de Dios,* with fabulous loot.* All

---

* Brought into Dartmouth on September 7, 1592, with booty valued at the time at £150,000. (Note that the total *double subsidy* of the last Parliament had been but £280,000.)

these events brought the name of Spain with ever-increasing persistence to John's ears, along with that of the formidable Sir Francis. With the rumor came news of the return of Captain John Davis from Brazil (in a wreck of a ship that barely made harbor) and word that Thomas Cavendish had surely passed the Straits of Magellan on *his* way around the world. What more would be needed than the cry that the incomparable Drake was off again, to stir the adventurous spirit of thirteen-year-old John Smith to action?

Obviously, the lad did not get very far. It was his father, not his father's death, that "stayed him," and his schooling (apparently under a relative named Robert Smith) continued for a year or two. Then, in 1595, young John was apprenticed to a merchant, Thomas Sendall, of King's Lynn, sixty miles away by the winding road south around The Wash. Sendall was known to Lord Willoughby, perhaps recommended by him. It is possible that John's father thought that in this way the restless boy could in time get a post as an overseas agent or factor, and make money and a name for himself besides.

But John's temperament was not suited to the painstaking drudgery of a countinghouse. A year of watching portly and pompous merchant princes strolling down the Old Chequer, of smelling wine from Spain and Portugal in Norfolk cellars, of hearing about barnacles and coal and wool, and the trifling difference in value between Spanish and Portuguese and Venetian ducats — trifling to him, but not to Thomas Sendall — was enough, and to spare. He might have wandered from filial duty once again, and soon, and more culpably, had not his father been summoned by the Recording Angel. On April 3, 1596, with John Smith respectfully in attendance we assume, George Smith was buried from the parish church in Willoughby by Alford. His will, painstakingly drawn, was dated only four days before.

His parent's death left John with some means, as he himself says, which were indirectly augmented in less than a year by the remarriage of his mother, to one Martin Johnson. According to the official inventory of the estate, made on February 19, 1597, George Smith's "goods and chattels" were valued at £77 16s. 2d.; and by virtue of the will as probated the farm where George Smith and his family had dwelt, held "by copy of Court Roll as the grant of the Right Honorable" Lord Willoughby, became John Smith's, along with the seven acres of pasture "within the territory of Charlton Magna." George Smith had foreseen his widow's marriage, as widows in those days seldom mourned for long.

John Smith was then sixteen, and under the guardianship of George Metham, a friend of his father's and in some remote way a connection of Lord Willoughby. Metham, according to John Smith's "autobiography," was more interested in guarding John Smith's estate than his person. On John's insistence, his apprenticeship was amicably terminated, and John "never saw his master in eight years after." And he added, now "he had liberty enough, though no means, to get beyond the sea."

John Smith's narrative is very confused at this point, and it is difficult to be sure of what he did immediately after repossessing his indenture. The only clue he provides is a reference to peace in France. If he is referring to the year 1596, the statement would seem justified. For by that year Henry IV had abjured his Protestantism, which opened the gates of Paris for him, had won the submission of Mercoeur and other stubborn rebels, had been granted pontificial absolution by Clement VIII, and had indeed brought peace to France in all but name. (A surprise attack on Amiens from nearby Doullens, Flanders, was the last flicker of the dying Spanish threat — at that time.)

John Smith can hardly have analyzed the situation in this form. Nevertheless, rumors were rife again, and we can reasonably surmise that he was referring to late 1596 or early 1597 when he wrote, "Peace being concluded in France, he went with Captain Joseph Duxbury into the Low Countries" — the Netherlands. Whether he meant 1596, soon after his father's death, or 1597, after the settlement of the little estate, is not clear. Neither is it clear how or where he picked up Duxbury. But the fact that a Duxbury was a captain under Sir Francis Vere at Nieuport in 1600 may not be entirely beside the point. Sir Francis was a first cousin of Lady Mary Willoughby, wife of the same Lord Willoughby whom John Smith had been charged and commanded by his father "to honour and love." Indeed, the strict moral and military principles of Sir Francis (and of his brother Sir Horatio, too) can be seen reflected in the clearest detail in John Smith's later life. This implies some sort of contact, however vague or remote, between young Smith and the famous "fighting Veres." Be that as it may, John Smith says he served under Captain Joseph Duxbury's colors for three or four years. It is immaterial whether the first of those years was 1596 or 1597. Documentary evidence shows that John Smith's next adventure began in 1599.* [5]

In the spring of the year before, while John Smith was with Duxbury, Lord Willoughby had been made governor of the border fortress of Berwick-upon-Tweed. By the end of that summer, if not before, his eldest son, Robert Bertie (Lord Willoughby's father had been Richard Bertie, Esq.), was in France completing his nobleman's-education. And in April, 1599, Robert wrote to his father that he hoped it would be agreeable to him to send his next younger brother, Peregrine, to France too, to accompany him "in his voyage," or more accurately his study-tour. Lord Willoughby acquiesced, the proper preparatory steps were taken, and on June 26, license was granted to Peregrine "to travel for 3 years, with his tutor, 2 servants, 2 horses, and £60." Such license was mandatory, it seems, for all English subjects down to the rank of gentlemen.

By that time, John Smith appears to have gotten back to England. How or when he got there is lost in the confused account already referred to; but it may have been during the lull in fighting in the Low Countries induced by the chilling combination of Philip II's death (his was the fire in the fight!) and the onrush of winter. Again, the details are foggy. But, "at last," he writes, "he found means to attend Master Peregrine Bertie into France." Apparently, one of Peregrine's "servants" was none other than John Smith, who by his own account took off from London with ten shillings of his own money in his pocket.

This need cast no reflection on young John, for all sorts of attendants on noblemen and their sons were called servants. On the contrary, the phrase "at last" seems to indicate that he had a little trouble being admitted to the party. But in the end, John was after all only three years older than Robert, was not experienced enough to be of much help, and Robert and his brother were both short of funds. Their father, despite his important post (in fact, largely because of it), was always hard pressed for ready cash.

* It was common practice to count both ends of such a period; in the New Testament, for example, Sunday is the third day after Friday — not the second.

Therefore, after a month or six weeks the brothers "sent him [Smith] back again to his friends." With him, they passed along a detailed personal message concerning their doings in France, and in recompense for the trouble caused him supplied John with money for the trip. The money, since they were having financial troubles all along, quite possibly came from the more ample resources of Lord Hume, a Scottish nobleman and friend of Lord Willoughby's who was then in Paris, more likely on some sort of business for James VI, King of Scots, than simply on pleasure bent. Wherever the money came from, however, for John Smith the return to England was "the least thought of his determination." Since his route from Orléans, where the Bertie brothers were, necessarily took him through Paris, John Smith clearly (though he does not say so) decided to look up the Hume family.

Lord Willoughby's friend Baron Hume was Alexander, sixth in descent from a Sir Alexander Hume who was a younger brother of Sir David Hume of Wedderburn. Sir David had a six-times-removed descendant, named for himself, who was also in Paris, and more of a fixture there than Lord Alexander. Distant-cousin David, twenty years the senior of John Smith, was a poet, an intellectual of the kind then called a "controversialist," and impecunious. In his search for the Humes John Smith ran across David, and it was not long before David, in John Smith's words, "making some use of his purse, gave him letters to his friends in Scotland to prefer [present] him to King James." This was not an unfair exchange, since the way to a royal court usually had some sort of a tollgate, and John Smith set out with a light heart (and bright prospects) for Rouen and some cross-Channel vessel.

On inspection, after leaving Paris, John Smith's purse proved as light as his heart — too light, indeed to get him very far. John "better bethinks himself," he wrote, lapsing into the vivid or historical present, so he aimed for Le Havre. There, he remembered, he first began to learn the life of a soldier, with Captain Duxbury.

Precisely what happened next is impossible to say. But somehow John Smith got to Holland, clearly by boat, to the town of Enkhuizen, then as now an important port for the North Sea herring fleets. At Enkhuizen he found a ship bound for the Port of Leith, which is only an hour's tramp from Holyrood Palace in Edinburgh. The

re, about that time. There is no reason, therefore, to doubt the
h of his service in the Netherlands, where many thousands of
ng Englishmen saw service, and thousands died.

short, on his return to Willoughby by Alford John was in all
bability the most-traveled member of the community, outside the
ily of the lord of the manor himself. This brought him a circle
iends and admirers, but it did not bring him further adventure.
with adventure in his blood, John Smith could not long rest in
amlet within walking distance of the sea, but astronomically
ote from the world.

o the same family leanings which produced Schoolmaster Smith
quite respectable marriages for a number of Rickard women-
may be attributed John Smith's next, at first glance romantic,
e. He had a logical, analytical mind, and he sought "good" but
flattering company. To escape the flatterers and to prepare him-
better for further adventure, John "retired himself into a little
dy pasture," as he put it, and dedicated himself to practical
ly. Being but twenty, and living in an age when a certain
unt of knighthood was still in flower, John acquired some local
in to be his "man," not only for hunting and companionship,
(which was even more important) to help him play-act his
isioned future role as a gentleman-adventurer (a knight, if you
), with his squire. But that this play-acting was more in the way
elf-education than of daydreaming is clear from the two books
ch John specifically mentions as his "study." These were Ma-
velli's *The Art of War* (which had been translated along with
rt of Vannoccio Biringuccio's *Pirotechnia* by Peter Whitehorne
y years before), and "Marcus Aurelius," by which John meant one
he two recent translations of Antonio de Guevara's *Dial of*
ces, or Book of Marcus Aurelius. These volumes were rather
ly for John Smith's limited resources, and it is not entirely out
he question that he may have borrowed them from Lord Wil-
ghby. That illustrious commander was certain to have Machia-
i in his library, and most likely had "Marcus Aurelius," a worth-
le volume for his sons.

he possibility that Smith borrowed his reading material from
d Willoughby hints at the great probability that at the time of
return from Scotland he presented his dutiful compliments to

North Sea appears to have been unwilling fo
royally received, however, and he was deposi
wreck of his fishing bark, on the sands of the
farne, less than a dozen miles from Berwic
loughby was seated as governor. John was eith
in the shipwreck, or taken very ill, for he ap
some time on the island. Nevertheless, he did
loughby, which seems to indicate that he got
Lord Willoughby had left for a visit to Lond
that lasted from early 1600 until mid-Septemb
off for Scotland when he was well, to deliver
Hume's kith and kin. Their general habitat w
two hours or so, on foot.

John stopped first at a place called Ripw
(more correctly) Redpath. This was, and is, a
name in the region, unfortunately, and it is
mine which of five suitable Redpaths he visi
Chirnside, nine miles west of Berwick, seems
most likely place.) From there he apparently
twenty or thirty miles to Dunbar, less than tw
lies the village and manor of Broxmouth.
stopped again, presenting his letter or letters.

Clearly "those honest Scots" were hospitable
they were frank enough to point out, or John
enough to see, that a yeoman farmer's son from
and sturdy though not unhandsome, was not cu
ners or pocketbook, for the life of a courtier.
table as they were, the Humes and their friend
the trouble of sponsoring young Smith themsel
some such "means" (sponsorship) were necess
gave up the idea. He returned, evidently nothin
shire.[6]

How much of the world John Smith had rea
he was twenty cannot be determined from his g
is no question that he had been in France with
acquaintance with microscopic points in Scotla
Scottish trip. The years 1596 to 1599 are obsc
later activities testify to practical military kno

his landlord, along with the long-delayed personal messages from sons Robert and Peregrine Bertie. Lord Willoughby, hearing of his adventures and hopes, like enough not only encouraged John's study of things martial and gentlemanly, but on John's request even gave him permission to camp out on one of the Willoughby estates and to hunt there. John Smith wrote that his food was more venison than anything else, but no charge of poaching was ever brought against him as was the case with his yeoman-born older contemporary, William Shakespeare. Perhaps the same guiding hand can also be seen in John Smith's next occupation.

Smith had a horse with him in his "little woody pasture" (an advantage not shared by Shakespeare in his pursuit of the hunt), and was practicing horsemanship. His friends, seeing this, persuaded an expert horseman to "insinuate into his woodish acquaintances," and give John suitable instruction — so he wrote in 1629. It can hardly be imagined that the friends were yokels, for the expert horseman was none other than the "Rider" (or riding master) to Henry Clinton, Earl of Lincoln, who lived at nearby Tattershall Castle. The Earl was one of the most disagreeable noblemen in all England, and it is doubtful if he would have permitted such nonsense had not some distinguished friend (Willoughby was a distant cousin) intervened. Furthermore, the Rider himself was a "difficult" person named Theodore Paleologue, a collateral descendant of Constantine XI, the last Greek Emperor of the Eastern Roman Empire.

Contact with Theodore Paleologue brought John Smith some knowledge of Italian (Theodore was an Italian by birth), and even more of those then legendary monsters, the Ottoman Turks. The "good discourse" he heard at Tattershall, where he stayed for a while, filled John Smith's fancies with further adventurous notions. A hundred and fifty years of history were swept away by the voice of one of the Emperor's own family, and the maturing farmerboy from Lincolnshire both lamented and repented, as he put it, having seen so many Christians slaughter one another in Europe (meaning the Netherlands), while the heathen Turks roamed at will in the East. Indeed, through Theodore Paleologue John Smith may have heard that the Grand Signior had once again broken the peace, but that the noble Christians had not long since freed several cities from his monstrous tyranny. (Since England for reasons of trade was officially somewhat neutral in this new war, the adverse tales John Smith heard must have come from prejudiced, non-English tongues. Such a tongue the Greek-Italian undoubtedly had.)

Summer was by then spent. John Smith grew restless, discontented with the pleasures of life at Tattershall and Willoughby by Alford. Collecting what resources he could, he once more set forth "upon brave adventures." This time, he wrote, it was not only to see more of the world. This time he would try his fortune against the Turks.[7]

# CHAPTER 2

## JOHN SMITH, CAPTAIN

O N JUNE 22, 1600, while John Smith was presumably tilting with Theodore Paleologue, one of history's minor decisive battles was fought in Flanders. This was the Battle of Nieuport, already casually mentioned, in which "Captain Duxbury" was killed. In it the combined Dutch and English forces roundly trounced the Spanish army, the first time the latter had been beaten in the field in the Dutch War of Independence. In the long run it was one of several battles which resulted in a free and independent Holland. In the short (and personal) run, Nieuport most probably decided John Smith's future. Twenty years before, the death of a distant cardinal-king had cast a shadow on that future. In 1600 a victory equally alien to John Smith's ambience gave it more substance.

There is nothing in Smith's writings which hints at the Battle of Nieuport. All he states is that he tired of languages and good discourse, and the exercise of riding, and returned again to the Low Countries. The date of his return there is unknown, but it must have been after June 22 (or July 2, as the new calendar would have it). Furthermore, what he did in the Low Countries is equally unknown. And it is only by inference that we know that he left before winter. So did a lot of other soldiers. For the Battle of Nieuport had amazingly exhausted both sides, and a period of wound-licking and stocktaking followed which released many troops. John Smith had been too late for *that* adventure. Characteristically, he sought — and found — another.[1]

Somewhere in Holland, Smith came across "four French Gallants," or fine gentlemen — probably with a touch of sarcasm. They had been soldiers, they said, and were out of a job now that (temporary) peace had come. In Hungary there was fighting, and they proposed to make their way to some place of recruitment for Emperor Rudolph's forces. John Smith admitted (or did he bring it up first?) that he too was seeking service against the paynim, and it was not long before they persuaded him to join them. They proposed to go to France, to the Duchess of Mercoeur, whose husband had been made General of Rudolph's Imperial Army, after Henry IV had liberated Brittany from him — largely with gold. The Duchess would surely give them letters to the Duke.

For the first time, young John saw clear prospects for fighting the Turks. He joined the Frenchmen and took ship around Spanish-held Belgium to France, "with such ill weather as winter affordeth." One night, after a sail of at least a hundred and fifty miles, the ship arrived off St.-Valery-sur-Somme, at the mouth of the river of that name. There the Gallants plotted with the ship's master to possess themselves of Smith's trunk and belongings, since they had already discovered that his simple demeanor concealed more tangible wealth than their own fripperies. On landing the Gallants first, therefore, the master took occasion to put Smith's trunk in the boat, and promised to send it back for Smith himself immediately.

Almost twenty-four hours had passed before the master returned, to inform Smith that the four had gone on to Amiens "where they would stay [wait for] his coming." Young John then knew that he had been done. So did the other soldiers and passengers. With characteristic sympathy for a cheated poor young man, outwitted by the pretending rich, they "had like to have slain the Master; and had they known how, would have run away with the ship."

One of the soldiers, whose name Smith distorted into "Curzianvere" and "Currianver," then told him that the seeming fine lord who headed the group was only the son of a lawyer, despite the fine title of "Lord Depreau" which he used, and that he came from Mortain, "in base Brittany," or rather lower Normandy. His attendants were "three young citizens [townfolk, and not "gentlemen"], as arrant cheats as himself," named Courcelles, Lanelly, and Montferrat. "Curzianvere" volunteered to accompany Smith to Mortain, and to find Depreau (or DePreau) for him. In addition, since Smith had on him but one "carralue" (cardecu, or *quart d'écu*, worth 18

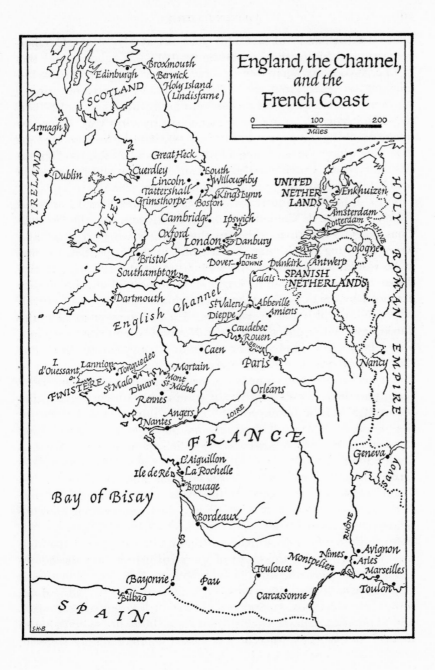

England, the Channel,
and the
French Coast

0        100        200
Miles

Armagh

IRELAND

Dublin

SCOTLAND

Edinburgh
Broxmouth
Berwick
Holy Island
(Lindisfarne)

WALES

Great Heck
Cuerdley
Lincoln
Louth
Willoughby
Tattershall
Grimsthorpe
King's Lynn
Boston
Cambridge
Ipswich
Oxford
London
Danbury
Bristol
THE DOWNS
Dover
Dunkirk
Antwerp
Cologne
Southampton
Calais
SPANISH
NETHERLANDS

UNITED
NETHER-
LANDS
Enkhuizen
Amsterdam
Rotterdam
RHINE

HOLY

Dartmouth

English   Channel

St Valery
Abbeville
Dieppe
Amiens

Caudebec
Rouen
SEINE

I.
d'Ouessant
Lannion
Torquedec
Mortain
Caen
Paris
Nancy

FINISTERE
St Malo
Dinan
Mont
St Michel
Rennes

Angers
LOIRE
Orléans

ROMAN

Nantes

F R A N C E

L'Aiguillon
Ile de Ré
La Rochelle
Brouage

Geneva
Savoy

Bay of Bisay

Bordeaux

RHÔNE

EMPIRE

Bayonne
Bilbao
Pau
Toulouse
Carcassonne
Montpelier
Nimes
Arles
Avignon
Marseilles
Toulon

S P A I N

S·H·B

pence sterling), and had to sell his cloak to pay his passage, Curzian-vere supplied him with whatever he needed.

The two ex-soldiers then set out across northern France to Dieppe, Caudebec, Honfleur, and Caen, where Curzianvere's friends welcomed them and even showed John Smith the tomb of William the Conqueror, which had been ruined nearly forty years before by image-smashing Huguenots. From there, Smith was escorted to Mortain, where the would-be Lord Depreau was found — "but to small purpose." Curzianvere was a "banished man, and durst not be seen," for reasons unclarified by John Smith. Smith's complaints were loud, however, and reached the ears of several local lords and ladies. Madame de Colombiers, Baron Larchamp, and the Sieur de Chasseguey, and others, came to the rescue of the stranded and wronged young Englishman, invited him to stay with them as long as he would, and supplied him with whatever he needed. (France did not differ greatly from England in respect of the hospitality extended by the owners of manors.)

But John Smith was ever restless. He had set out to fight the Turks, and he could not rest in Normandy and Brittany, and accept favors from kindly strangers. So off he started once more, this time down the Sélune River to the Bay of Saint-Michel, hoping to find a man-of-war (which need not be taken too literally) at one of the little ports. But ships generally seem to have been scarce in the bay, and before he found one John Smith ran out of what money the people of Mortain had given him. Somewhere not far beyond the famous Mont-St.-Michel Abbey, which then still housed Bene-dictine monks, he all but collapsed of "grief and cold." A wealthy farmer took pity on him, however, fed him, and gave him further financial relief, which lasted until — passing through a great grove of trees between Pontorson and Dinan — he came across none other than Monsieur Courcelles.

Smith, infuriated, drew his sword, and without a word they fell to. Farmers, hearing the clang of steel, rushed up, but not before Courcelles had had the worst of it. Smith was held by the men until Courcelles, perhaps under pressure, confessed to what he and his companions had done to Smith, and how the four cheats had after-wards fallen out among themselves — with himself finally being as cheated as Smith. With that the local inhabitants were satisfied, and let Smith continue on his way.

Somehow, either here or in Dinan, Smith learned that the lord of the Château of Plouër, a few miles down the Rance, had been brought up in England during the religious wars, and had returned to Brittany only recently. He was even then in residence.

It was a stroll of less than two hours from the great walled town, down steep streets and along a winding road, to the gray-stone mansion, nestling in the woods, with its barn, its chapel, and its decorative moat. John was soon admitted, and stood before the young Count, Amaury II Gouyon, not over three years the senior of John himself. Only the year before, Amaury had done proper homage to Henry IV and had his lordship over Plouër and the barony of la Moussaye confirmed. With him were his younger brothers, Charles, Viscount of Pommerit, and Jacques, Baron of Marcé. Charles had just celebrated his eighteenth birthday, and Jacques was less than two years younger.

Amaury's father, Charles Gouyon the elder, had been a page of King Charles IX but had turned Protestant. During the religious wars, he had undergone imprisonment, and had fought against the Duke of Mercoeur in company with English troops under General Sir John Norris, who in turn had served under (and quarreled with) Lord Willoughby. It appears that it was about that time that the Gouyon children went to England, although details of their stay are lacking. It may be that Norris was one of those who took care of them. Norris was related to the Earl of Lincoln by marriage, and it is therefore conceivable, though certainly not provable, that the boys were personally acquainted with Lincolnshire. But, whatever the cause, Amaury took John Smith in, entertained him, showed him the countryside and, when the time came for him to continue his travels, gave him such means that "he was better refurnished than ever." [2]

From Brittany, Smith turned south, hitchhiking (as we say today) his way to Bordeaux and Bayonne, and then across the south of France to Marseilles. Somewhere along the way he must have celebrated his twenty-first birthday, in fact or in spirit, and by the time he reached southern France the winter was over.

At Marseilles, he took passage for Italy — it being safer and cheaper to go by sea. But the ship he chose, apparently in coastwise trade, was not very serviceable and had to put in at Toulon, hardly more than fifty miles away. Setting out again, with little foresight, the master ran into foul spring weather which drove him to seek protection. Somewhere along the coast he anchored, near the shore and "under" a little island. John Smith states that this was the "Isle of S. Mary," opposite Nice in Savoy, and that it had no inhabitants beyond a few cows and goats. Although it is possible that this was some speck of land that has since been incorporated in the breakwaters protecting the old harbor at Nice, nothing exists that would hint at such an island today. Much more probably it was one of the Iles de Lérins, near Cannes. Sailors were by no means always sure where they were in those days — but in any case the matter is of relative unimportance.

What was important for John Smith was that the weather continued very adverse, and that not only were there many provincials aboard ship (with an ill-defined but nonetheless weighty burden of superstition), but also "a rabble of Pilgrims of divers Nations going to Rome," who saw in Smith a Huguenot, a pirate, and a vile subject of Queen Elizabeth (possibly with misplaced adjective), "his dread Sovereign." Fortunately for him, the pilgrims' passion brought them only to the point of heaving him overboard. It could have gone much harder with him.

But God and a knowledge of swimming brought him to the little isle, where he spent the night with unbiased domestic animals. At the same time, the tempest brought two other ships to the same shelter, and in the morning Smith and the newcomer-vessels spotted one another. He was taken aboard one of them, kindly treated and fed. One bit of chatter led to the discovery that the captain of the ship was one La Roche, of St.-Malo. Monsieur le Comte de Plouër was of necessity this gentleman's neighbor, and John Smith quickly became "his well respected friend." By the time the wind had changed, Smith had ephemerally abandoned his one-man crusade against the paynim Turk and associated himself in Mediterranean trade.

The first part of Captain La Roche's route is interesting, since not many Englishmen are known to have been in that region so early. At the same time, it was apparently commonplace for French captains. From the Riviera they sailed south past Corsica and Sardinia to Cape Bon, the northeastern tip of Tunisia. From there they went to Lampedusa, now Italian but then Tunisian, beyond which they steered east-southeast across the open sea, avoiding the coast and the pirates of Barbary, nearly seven hundred miles to Cape Ras-et-Tin (Smith calls it "Rosata") in Cyrenaica, then nominally under the control of the Sublime Porte. From there on the Mediterranean was better patrolled than in the West, and Captain La Roche could follow the arid coast to the Nile delta and Alexandria. Here they delivered their freight, whatever it was.

Thus lightened, the company sailed up to Alexandretta (*Iskanderun* in Arabic, and "Scanderoon" in John Smith), the port of Aleppo — then the most important European trading center in the Levant. Since this market was the scene of the keenest rivalry between English and French merchants, it was not without ulterior motives that La Roche went to "view what ships were in the [Scanderoon] roads." Smith, disinterested as he was in all aspects of mercantile competition, had no reason to take this inspection amiss.

It was time to return to France. Skirting the coast and the islands, the ship made its way to Greece, where a later reference hints that it took refuge from a storm — at Kalamata, an ancient town at the head of the gulf just west of the difficult Cape Matapan. Beyond this point the winds were less contrary, and they soon reached the island of Cephalonia, where they put in for a few days before continuing to Corfu for another few days.

Passing the Strait of Otranto on their way to Italy, Captain La Roche sighted an "argosy" from Venice. For unknown reasons Captain La Roche "desired to speak with them," but the argosy's answer was most "untoward." It came from a cannon, and it cost them a man.

La Roche was not the kind to stand for answers of this sort. Without waiting for further explanation, he fired back, first with a broadside, then with his stern pieces, then the other broadside, and finally his chase guns. The argosy, frightened, attempted to escape, but the shots from La Roche's smaller, faster ship wrought havoc with her sails and tackle. She was forced to stand to her defense. But La Roche "shot her so oft between wind and water, she was ready to sink," and the argosy surrendered.

La Roche's men boarded her and went to work in all directions, "some to stop the leaks, others to guard the prisoners that were chained, the rest to rifle her." John Smith writes, with enthusiasm, that what they unloaded in twenty-four hours "was wonderful." Silks, velvets, cloth of gold and tissue, all were stored on La Roche's ship, along with "piasters, chicqueenes [*zecchini*] and sultanies [from Turkey], which is gold and silver."

In addition to the experience in sea battle, the importance to John Smith of the meeting with the argosy was that La Roche was later able to set him ashore at Antibes with five hundred zecchini in his pocket "and a little box God sent him worth near as much more." [3]

This windfall altered John Smith's plans again. Again he postponed trying his fortune against the Turks, and again he set out for Italy, but this time with the definite intention "to better his experience." In other words, now that he had the money, he planned to travel like a gentleman and educate himself thereby, like a gentleman. With five hundred zecchini he could do this for as long as five years, depending on the style in which he lived, and of course barring the not infrequent unforeseen accidents which added zest to life in the early 1600's. His decision, furthermore, is all the more understandable when a reckoning of time elapsed reveals the season of the year. Spring had come.

At Antibes, John Smith embarked for Leghorn, a very busy port, and from there hiked or rode through the Grand Duchy of Tuscany to Siena. Somewhere in Sienese territory, to his patent surprise and pleasure, he ran across his friend Lord Willoughby's sons, Robert and Peregrine Bertie. Distressingly, they were both "cruelly wounded, in a desperate fray, yet to their exceeding great honor." Honor was a very serious matter in John Smith's day, and Peregrine Bertie's seems to have been peculiarly sensitive — in this instance, he may well have been the provocator. But whatever the cause, whatever was at stake, the chance meeting renewed the friendship between the Berties and Smith. It possibly also gave Smith a chance to show off a little, with his money from the Venetian argosy, and the little box "God sent him."

After leaving the Berties, evidently on their way to recovery, John Smith traveled south through Viterbo "and many other cities" to Rome. In Rome he saw Pope Clement VIII "creep up the holy Stairs" (the *Scala Santa*) and say mass in the cathedral church of

Saint John in Lateran. There, too, he visited the famous — to Protestants, infamous — English Jesuit, Father Robert Parsons, rector of the Catholic English College and renowned political agitator. The reason for the visit becomes clear as the gates of the future unfold.

Someone guided John Smith's later steps to "an English man and an Irish Jesuit" in Graz, capital of Austrian Styria. Who, considering John Smith's unquestioned Protestantism, would have been more likely to do this than Robert Parsons, S.J., in whose Roman nest so many plots were hatched? Indeed, the very brevity of Smith's remarks about Rome points to none other than Father Parsons as the real object of his going there. He concludes his account of the Eternal City: "Having saluted Father Parsons, that famous English Jesuit, and satisfied himself with the rarities of Rome, he went down the river of Tiber to Civitavecchia."

John Smith's steps to the proper people in Graz were anything but direct. Before he turned that way, he made a side excursion to Naples, after which he toured central Italy, Siena once again, and "that admired city of Florence." Then on to Venice — without so much as a further descriptive adjective for any of the stopping points on the way!

At Venice Smith found a ship sailing from the port of Malamocco on the Adriatic for Ragusa, Albania, and the Dalmatian Coast. This trip took "some time," but eventually he landed at Capo d'Istria, directly across the Gulf of Venice from his starting point. Then he took off overland for Graz and the Holy Roman Empire.

This roundabout approach to his Turkish adventures may not have been to see sights, as he writes, but may have been necessary because of the political situation — with which John Smith was none too familiar. For nearly a century, bands of Slavic Christian refugees from the Turks called *uskoks* ("refugees") had been carrying on guerrilla warfare by land and by sea. Venice considered herself mistress of the Adriatic, and was forced to take the side of the Ottoman Empire against the Christian outlaws in order to maintain this hegemony. The Holy Roman Empire on the other hand had more interest in annoying the Turks than in keeping a (wary) friendship with the Venetian Republic, and backed the uskoks. These then turned to outright piracy, using the Austrian port of

Trieste as one of their chief markets for loot. Result: The Venetian Admiral Giovanni Bembo was sent to blockade Trieste.

John Smith may simply have had difficulty getting into the Holy Roman Empire from Venice by any other means than circling the Adriatic to reach Graz. But once there, he met his "English man" and his "Irish Jesuit." He was a Protestant, to be sure, and the Empire was officially Catholic, but in the summer of 1601 the Empire needed soldiers. With the help of Father Parsons's friends, John Smith soon got acquainted with Austrian and Styrian petty noblemen and military leaders.[4]

Smith's first contact among these "brave Gentlemen of good quality" was one whose name he reports as "Lord Ebersbaught." Allowing for his lack of knowledge of German (not to mention the local variety of it), "Ebersbaught" can be taken to be Eibiswald (or Ybanswald; pronounced Ybisbald), the name of a prominent family of the Krain* — that borderland between Styria and Serbia which is now part of Yugoslavia and is called Slovenia. (John Smith's contact may even have been Sigismund, Freiherr von Eibiswald, who fought the Turks at Esztergom and Nagykanizsa in Hungary, and in Transylvania.) The Eibiswald in question, after some talk with John Smith, presented or sent him to Lieutenant Colonel Hanns Jakob Khissl (Smith's "Baron Kisell"), Chief of Artillery at Graz. Khissl was not only a connection of the Eibiswalds by marriage, but was also a member of the *Krainer Herrenstand,* or provincial "diet," along with Sigismund Eibiswald. Khissl in turn, whose approach to the religious problem was eminently practical, sent Smith to the Count of Modrusch, locally pronounced Mödritsch (Smith's "Earl of Meldritch"), who was a confirmed Protestant. Modrusch seems to have been forming a regiment (or a battalion) in Vienna. However it was, John Smith found his way to fight the Turks under Modrusch.

The family name of the Counts of Modrusch was Frankopan, and there were at least two Frankopans who fit in with John Smith's story — George and Nicholas — but specific identification is neither possible at the moment nor important. The significant fact is that the entire group of soldiers whom Smith met during his first two campaigns was made up of gentry or petty nobility from Slovenia,

* Compare the *Ukraine,* the "borderland" of southern Russia.

many of them interrelated by marriage. History has not preserved the detail of all their activities. Nevertheless, it is a matter of record that these families served in the Imperial Army in the places and at the time mentioned by Smith. Their very obscurity serves as confirmation of Smith's strange story, for he hardly could have *read* about them anywhere.[5]

Modrusch's first objective was the protection and relief of a fortified town which Smith calls Olumpagh or Olimpach. This can be no other than the place known in Latin as *Olimacum* and in German as *Limbach,* today called "Lower" Limbach. Although there was an "inhabitable fortress" named Upper Limbach thirty-odd miles to the north, in the mountains, the lower town was an important strategic point known to history since remote times. There can be no question which Limbach introduced John Smith to the art or science of fighting the Turks. The engagement in which he took part, to be sure, was too unimportant for either side to record or commemorate, in the great struggle between the two Empires — Holy Roman and Ottoman. But for John Smith it was the real beginning of his career. He determined to make the most of it.

Smith's reading in the "little woody pasture" in Lincolnshire had included, as has been said, Machiavelli's *Art of War,* with its supplement on pyrotechnics by Vannoccio Biringuccio, all translated by Peter Whitehorne. In addition, there was a work vaguely on the same subject by William Bourne (an author familiar to John Smith in later years), called *Inventions or Devices, Very Necessary for all Generals and Captains,* etc. In both the *Pyrotechnics* and the *Inventions* there were descriptions of devices whereby "you may cause your friends to write a letter" and make known your plans, secretly, over considerable distances, and even above the din of battle; in short, a signaling system for communication in time of war. The idea dated back to the days of Polybius, but the details in both books were English, with Italian inspiration. Given the obscurity of Bourne and Whitehorne, and the gibberish (English) in which the books were written, the signaling system which John Smith had learned had not reached the ears of the Provincial Chief of Artillery of the Imperial Army. It had reached Eibiswald's ears only through John Smith, who neither then nor later seems to have been shy about passing his knowledge on to others.

The opportunity for John Smith to make use of his learning, and simultaneously help in the problem before his battalion and promote himself, came up in this way. In late October, 1600, by wiles as much as by force, the Turkish army had acquired the key fort of Nagykanizsa. This brought the dreaded janissaries within fifty miles of the outposts of Styria, and left but a strip of Hungary that wide between Rudolph II and Mehmed III. Winter and spring and part of summer passed, and little happened to disturb the peaceful Turkish occupation of the place. Then the janissaries apparently got restless.

A raiding party was sent out (summer of 1601), and as the Christian troops were making their first maneuvers toward recapturing Nagykanizsa, succeeded, in the confusion, in surrounding Lower Limbach, which at that time seems to have been under Eibiswald's command. Eibiswald had interviewed John Smith, of course, perhaps with the aid of Latin or Italian, and had heard from him about Bourne and Whitehorne's signaling device. Smith found some way to get the ear of Khissl, and told him that he could send a message to Eibiswald if Khissl had any message to send. Since sending messages by signaling device was practically unheard of in those days, Khissl pricked up his ears, heard Smith out, and began to lay plans.

Within a day or so — Smith does not say how soon — Khissl evolved a strategy which he thought would liberate Lower Limbach, if he could get a message to Eibiswald. John Smith was then given guides to a hilltop and the necessary equipment, and soon showed three blazing torches, carefully spaced so many feet apart. Someone in Lower Limbach noticed this phenomenon and informed Eibiswald, who then remembered Smith's system and set up three corresponding torches above the beleaguered fort. Smith promptly began to transmit by combinations of lights, until Eibiswald received the Colonel's instructions: "On Thursday night I will charge on the east; at the alarm, sally!"

Khissl seems to have had qualms the moment he learned that his message had been sent *and* received. He was an artilleryman, not a captain of troops, and he expressed fears that even with the element of surprise his force was not large enough to inflict a decisive defeat. The guides and Smith together, however, assured him that the Turks were divided by the river, and Smith, remembering his studies, added brightly that a number of strings of ignited bits of tow to simulate the lighted "matches" of two or three thousand matchlock muskets could provide a diversion in the wrong direction, permitting Khissl's limited manpower to strike where least expected. This seems to have relieved the Colonel's anxiety, and everything was organized for the Thursday-night attack.

The scheme worked with clocklike precision. The lines of lighted tow were stretched by runners just as the alarm was sounded. The Turks grabbed their arms to dash off after these will-o'-the-wisps, while Eibiswald sallied from the town and Khissl attacked from another quarter. In the confusion, a third of the Turkish troops were caught between Khissl and Eibiswald, many who attempted to succor them were drowned, and the bulk of the army was out in the fields battling a web of lines and burning tow. Khissl thus managed to get two thousand more men into the town and to provision it with supplies from the camp of the deluded besiegers. When it was daylight and the Turkish commander could take stock of his losses and the enemy gains, he raised the siege and returned to Nagykanizsa.

Years after the event, Smith wrote that Khissl alone had ten thousand men at Limbach. That figure may be somewhere near the number involved on both sides — perhaps even including the peaceful inhabitants of the town itself. Between the proneness of the times to exaggeration, faulty memory, the natural human tendency to make the most of every event in which we are personally involved, *and* the carelessness of typesetters, scores of men became hundreds, and hundreds became thousands. But no matter how many troops were actually involved, the skirmish — it was certainly not a battle — was John Smith's real baptism of fire as a man. The relief of the siege of Limbach was therefore a critical juncture in his life. Its immediate aftermath underlined this.

Lieutenant Colonel Khissl marched his troops to Körmend, thirty-odd miles to the north — a strong point which had recently been proposed as the center of an array of defensive fortresses. Who was in command at Körmend at the moment is not known. John Smith relates, however, that Khissl was received with much honor. Thanks to Khissl's fairness, Smith got a good reward: he was promoted to be captain of 250 horse, under the command of Modrusch, the Protestant.[6]

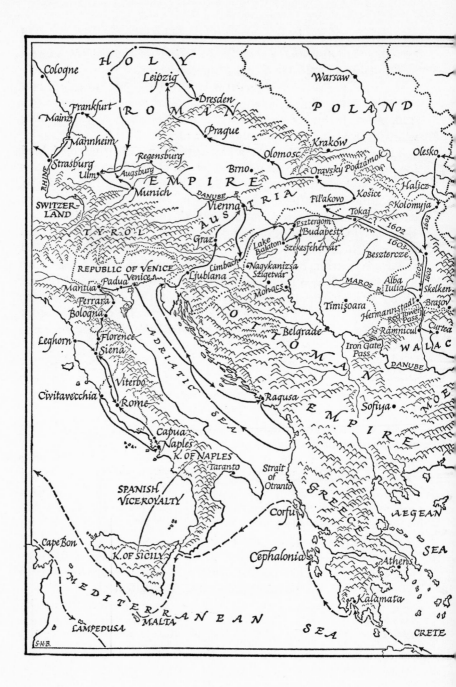

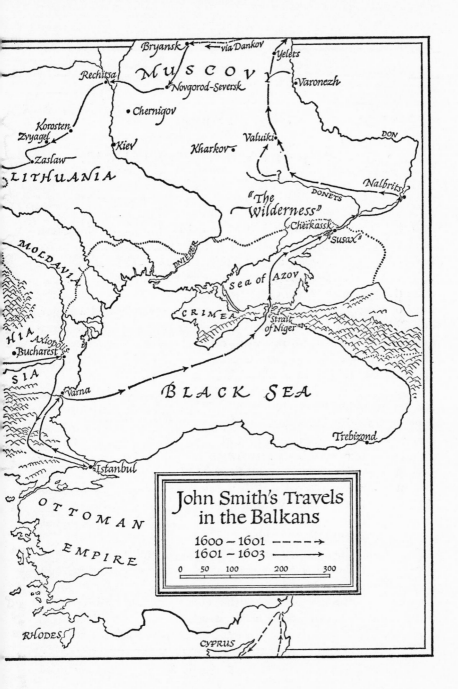

Bryansk ← via Dankov
Yelets
M U S C O V Y
Rechitsa
Novgorod-Seversk
Varonezh
Chernigov
Korosten
Zvyagel
DON
Kiev
Kharkov
Valuiki
Zaslaw
LITHUANIA
Nalbrits
DONETS
"The
Wilderness"
Cherkassk
"Susax"
MOLDAVIA
DNIEPER
Sea of AZOV
HIA
Axiopolis
Bucharest
CRIMEA
"Strait
of Niger"
SIA
Varna
B L A C K   S E A
Trebizond
Istanbul
O T T O M A N
**John Smith's Travels
in the Balkans**

1600 – 1601 ------→
1601 – 1603 ———→

0   50   100        200        300

E M P I R E

RHODES
CYPRUS

CHAPTER 3

# CAPTAIN JOHN SMITH, GENTLEMAN

LONG BEFORE John Smith first appeared on the plains of western
Hungary, Emperor Rudolph II had answered Turkish peace
feelers by calling for an all-out Christian offensive. The Catholic
rulers, with varying alacrity and some exceptions, responded. Despite the appeals of Pope Clement VIII, who sent a nephew at the
head of some auxiliaries, neither France nor Poland lifted a finger,
and Philip III of Spain was noticeably niggardly in his help. Elizabeth of England had no reason to collaborate, and the pugnacious
Doge of Venice, Marino Grimani, was practically hostile. Still, various Italian princes came through with all they could.

Basically, Rudolph's plan was simple — he wanted three armies,
for three specific tasks. The heads of these armies were to be his
brother Matthias, his cousin Ferdinand, and a relation-by-marriage
named Ferrante II Gonzaga, recently appointed Governor of High
Hungary (today's Slovakia). Matthias's right-hand man was none
other than Philippe-Emmanuel, Duke of Mercoeur, to whose Duchess the four French "Gallants" had promised John Smith an introduction. Ferdinand had Vincenzo Gonzaga, a cousin of Ferrante's,
for Imperial Lieutenant, while Ferrante himself had for Chief-of-
Staff one General Giorgio Basta.

John Smith had already unwittingly served under Ferdinand, at
Limbach — although Ferdinand's specific charge of retaking Nagykanizsa had not yet gotten under way. Later, Smith was to fight in
Transylvania, under Basta — without being aware of Ferrante's
higher authority. In between, he was marched off to Komárom
(today Komárno, in Czechoslovakia), where he was incorporated
with the rest of Modrusch's regiment, or battalion, into the Duke
of Mercoeur's army — by one of those quirks which could be called

Fate's jokes. In short, in his aim to fight the Turks, John Smith succeeded in fighting them on three out of three fronts.

The first of these armies to move, and with it Captain Smith, was Mercoeur's. His chief objective was Székesfehérvár, known in German as Stuhlweissenburg, and in Latin as Alba Regalis (or Alba Regia).* Seat of the Magyar kingdom more than once in the past, Alba Regalis (to use its most manageable name) was at the same time the Rheims and the Pantheon of the kings of Hungary, and its liberation from the Moslem infidels was of vast importance to other Catholics, as well as to the mostly Catholic Hungarian nation. Once this old capital was reconquered, after nearly sixty years of desecration, the new one (today's Budapest) would certainly be wrested from the Sultan without too great a struggle.

On September 3, 1601, Mercoeur gathered his troops for the march, and three days later set out. A detachment under Field Marshal Hermann Christof Graf von Russworm, Mercoeur's right-hand man, made a feint at Esztergom, while the Duke took the rest by a back road over the hills. Movement was slow, as always; news, quick. The Pasha of Buda, falling for the feint, sent his valuables to Alba Regalis and brought troops to Buda. But, to the bewilderment of the Pasha of Alba Regalis, Mercoeur appeared before *his* walls on September 9, having safely covered the fifty-one miles in a little over eighty hours. *No one* had seen the army! (Russworm arrived the next day.)

Alba Regalis then consisted of a fortified city surrounded by marshes through which the sluggish river Sárvíz ("Mud Water") made its way. Suburban villages formed a ring around it wherever islands emerged from the swamp. To the north and east there were hills, and there was hilly country to the west, across the Sárvíz. Alba Regalis had walls, and the suburbs toward the hills had walls and palisades, but the suburb of Sziget ("Island") on the west was virtually without defense because of the river and marshland that separated it from terra firma.

Mercoeur encamped northeast of the city and soon set up a relentless cannonading, to lead the defenders to think that he intended to weaken the defenses on that side and attempt an assault. Knowing the weakness of Sziget, he wanted to distract the enemy's

---

* "White Fortress" was an honored name (compare *Belgrade*, with the same meaning). This one was the capital, or royal White Fortress.

attention while he sent scouts to investigate the practicability of getting across the swamp and attacking the suburb. Reports were conflicting, and for the greater part discouraging, but he decided that such a move could be made anyway. Russworm offered to carry out the plan.

Meanwhile there were various sorties and skirmishes near the city proper. John Smith reports severe casualties among the Germans, "Bemers" (Bohemians), Hungarians, and French. The artillery retaliated, rather ineffectively. Then Modrusch, who had learned about some of Smith's pyrotechnical devices at Komárom and had watched him display his "fiery dragons" to the Imperial Chief of Artillery, Karl Ludwig Graf zu Sultz, called on him to add these to the bombardment. Smith was only too happy to contribute a touch of his own to a device of Whitehorne and Biringuccio, and sow death and terror behind the walls of Alba Regalis.

Taking earthenware pots to the number of forty or fifty, and sufficient gunpowder, pitch, brimstone, and turpentine, Smith fitted quartered musket-bullets to the pots with strong waxed cloth and inflammably impregnated woven hemp or cotton wick. Simple slings were then made, and when the time came the pots were ignited and lobbed over into the city. It was midnight, and Smith says that "it was a fearful sight to see the short flaming course of their flight in the air," and that when they had fallen "the lamentable noise of the miserable slaughtered Turks was most wonderful to hear."

About this time, Russworm was ready, and between two and three one morning he took a thousand men, each with a bundle of sedge and bound fagots to lend footing in the mud, and silently trudged, waded and half swam around the northern suburb to the unguarded rear of Sziget. Day was breaking when the sappers finally reached their objective. Russworm then ordered trumpets to sound and drums to roll as his men hastened to mop up what little resistance there was. This was the previously agreed on signal for Mercoeur to attack from the far side. The Turkish troops, caught between unexpected assailants from the rear and the lusty charge from the front, retreated into Alba Regalis proper. All the suburbs were soon in the hands of the Christians.

A few days later, on September 20, 1601 (new style), Mercoeur at last succeeded in breaching the main walls. Hand-to-hand fighting followed, broken now and then by the roar of exploding mines planted by the Turks. The carnage was revolting, the destruction almost fatal to the city. Even the graves of the Hungarian kings were plundered (by the Christians!), while the Pasha shut himself up with a bodyguard, determined to die rather than yield.

His resolution weakened, however, as all resistance collapsed, and he sent word to Mercoeur that he would surrender everything, in return for safe conduct for himself and his entourage. Modrusch, if John Smith is not just adding an extra honor badge to his hero, was appointed to convey that exalted captive through the mob of raging Imperial troops to Mercoeur's headquarters. (Once there, the Pasha was treated with honors becoming a prince — although no Christian historian seems to know his name — and some days later rode behind the Duke into Győr [Raab, Javarin], robed in cloth of gold.) Mercoeur then sent five thousand men out to occupy a crescent of five towns within a thirty-five-mile radius south of Alba Regalis, from the shore of Lake Balaton to the Danube. This, he apparently thought, would protect the half-destroyed city from a return attack.[1]

Within three weeks, however, an army of sixty thousand, according to Smith, had swarmed down from the northeast — from Budapest. Mercoeur's remaining troops, including Modrusch (and John Smith, of course) were encamped outside the city, somewhere in the neighborhood of shallow Velencze Lake. Alba Regalis could not accommodate troops because of the war damage, and the cold rainy weather forced them to a site where firewood was obtainable.

According to John Smith, the encampment was commanded by Russworm, aided by Kollnitz, Modrusch, Wild-Rheingraf, and Wagen von Wagensberg. Independent accounts mention Russworm and Kollnitz (and Wild-Rheingraf in another connection), but the *regimental* commanders are different. This merely underlines the likelihood that Modrusch (and Wagen) commanded battalions rather than regiments. As the Turkish army approached, there were skirmishes for several days. Inevitably, John Smith was involved in one of these:

> Here Earle *Meldritch* was so invironed amongst those halfe circuler Regiments of *Turkes,* they supposed him their Prisoner, and his Regiment lost; but his two most

couragious friends, *Vahan* and *Culnits,* made such a passage amongst them, that it was a terror to see how horse and man lay sprawling and tumbling, some one way, some another on the ground. . . .

Captain *Smith* had his horse slaine under him, and himselfe sore wounded; but he was not long unmounted, for there was choice enough of horses that wanted masters.

Such is Smith's vivid account of the engagement.

Then, on October 15, the Turkish *Kâhya* (Intendant) Mehmed, without consulting Mankirkouschi (Pasha or Governor of Buda), offered battle. The Christians accepted, led, according to John Smith, by Wild-Rheingraf, Kollnitz, and Modrusch. The location was a plain just at the mouth of Tscharka Gorge (pronounced roughly "charka," Smith's "Girke," pronounced "jerky"). The Turks had the worst of it, despite Mankirkouschi's attempt to bring help, and both he and the Kâhya were killed. According to Smith, there were "five or six thousand" casualties, among the Turks.

But both sides were ready to quit. The real victor was the rain and cold of oncoming winter. As the Christians retired toward Palota, on the other side of Alba Regalis, the Turks sent a dignitary who gave notice that they would recapture that city the next year (which they did), and returned to his camp. Mercoeur, who appears to have ridden the fifty-odd miles between Alba Regalis and Győr more than once, then divided his army in three parts for the winter. One he left to garrison Alba Regalis, one he sent under Russworm to join the second Imperial Army, then besieging Nagykanizsa, and the third he dispatched to the assistance of General Giorgio Basta in Transylvania. He himself went to Vienna and Prague, where he was acclaimed and *Te Deums* were chanted in his honor.

And Captain John Smith?

With the first Imperial Army's mission accomplished, for the moment at least, and with Russworm off to help the second in a campaign worthy of greater nobility of performance than it showed, Smith's career became involved in the third Army. That Army had a task which was basically more political than military, although it was confided to a drummerboy become general, whose conception of political moves seems to have been limited to employing assassins. In addition, even his military tactics were such a combination of blustering and ineffectiveness that his own behavior partakes somewhat of the same mutability of which his principal adversary (and problem) was accused. It is therefore not to be wondered that John Smith did not understand what "his" Army was supposed to accomplish, and his account of what he did in that Army seems confused and irrational as a result.[2]

John Smith begins his story with a two-paragraph explanation of where he went and why. To untangle the three confused sentences which make up the two paragraphs, and to fill in essential details omitted (because unknown) by Smith, it is necessary to summarize recorded history briefly. The story is rather typical of the Balkans.

East of the marshy central course of the Danube, the fertile Hungarian plain is cut off from eastern Europe by a crescent of mountains which enclose a province far more readily accessible from the west than from the east. This region is known as Transylvania. Just fifteen hundred years before John Smith arrived there, the Roman Emperor Trajan "united" it, so to speak, to the west. It is now part of Rumania.

More than a millennium after Trajan, when the Kingdom of Hungary had taken shape, Transylvania was virtually depopulated, from repeated barbarian inroads. Hungarians settled in the fertile central valleys, only to be generally wiped out by Batu's tidal wave of Mongols. When the wave retreated, the Hungarian King sent new colonists to join those who had survived — "Hungarians" to join the "Széklers" (old colonists of Hungarian stock). To these he added Germans, invited to help populate the land. They were called "Saxons," regardless of where they came from, and they were granted special privileges.

Out of this grew a modern political "Gaul" in three parts, which differed from Caesar's Gaul in that the three parts were inextricably mixed together within one geographical whole. Because of the geographical apartness of Transylvania, a prince or *voivode* (Slavic for "army leader") was appointed to rule in the name of the King of Hungary. Between 1520 and 1550 most Saxons became Protestants, but this added little to their already sharply defined separateness from the Hungarians and Széklers. The problem by then was not the threefold manner of men who lived in Transylvania, but the cancer that was gnawing at the kingdom itself. Incredible political discord permitted Sultan Suleyman the Lawgiver to inflict a disastrous defeat on the Hungarian army at Mohács in 1526. Hungarian King Louis II, hardly more than a boy, died on the battlefield, along with the flower of Hungarian nobility. Hungary became a kingdom in name only.

At that time John Zapolya, brother-in-law of Sigismund I, King of Poland and Grand Duke of Lithuania, was Voivode of Transylvania. Zapolya got himself elected King of Hungary, but soon had to call on Suleyman for backing. In a few years, one third of Hungary had — not illogically — become a Turkish pashalik. Then Zapolya died, "leaving" Hungary by his last will and testament to Ferdinand I, King of Bohemia and "of the Romans," and brother of the Emperor Charles V. Zapolya's own land, Transylvania, became a principality with his infant son as Prince, under the protection of Suleyman — a baby prince, independent in all but fact.

Zapolya's chief antagonist in 1526 had been Stephen Báthory, the third of that name, who was Palatine (virtually viceroy) of Hungary. Another Stephen Báthory, the fourth (possibly a grandson), meanwhile had served Zapolya as a captain, and as a reward succeeded Zapolya's son as Prince of Transylvania when the son died. He was confirmed in that position by Suleyman's son, Selim II, but a civil war broke out and it was a year before his opponents were quelled. Three years later, Stephen IV was elected Stephen I, King of Poland and Grand Duke of Lithuania.

Stephen persuaded the Transylvanian estates to elect his brother Christopher Báthory as Prince, and left for Poland. Christopher died while Stephen was gloriously fighting Ivan the Dread of Moscow, and in 1581 the reins of government came into the hands of his son Zsigmond, then eight years old. Zsigmond Báthory came to be the primary, if not the only, reason why the Duke of Mercoeur sent Modrusch and John Smith and many other soldiers into Transylvania under General Giorgio Basta.

Despite the unquestioned genius of Stephen IV, the Báthory family showed signs of mental imbalance. Zsigmond's older cousin,

Elizabeth, acquired gruesome fame a few years after John Smith had left the scene by trying to preserve her beauty by bathing in the blood of freshly murdered young women — the remains of some six hundred and fifty were found in her castle when the secret was finally out. His younger cousin, Gabriel, was less dangerous, but still met a violent death for his "licentious" life. Zsigmond himself was, as a contemporary put it, as unreliable as April weather. He is probably the only ruler in history who abdicated and was welcomed back to govern his country three times. He wanted to be a king, and when that failed made a fruitless effort to be made a cardinal. He married a sister of the Queen of Poland, who was also a first cousin of the Holy Roman Emperor, but the marriage was never consummated. This led to an investigation and another "primacy" for Zsigmond. He seems to be the only ruler in history whose impotence has been solemnly attributed to witchcraft, by a commission sitting in the Vatican itself. More wondrous than these Báthorys themselves, however, was the patience of the Transylvanian people with their prince.

Zsigmond abdicated for the first time in 1597, leaving Transylvania to his wife's cousin, the Emperor, and receiving in exchange the order of the Golden Fleece and a pair of Imperial fiefs in Silesia. In four months and ten days he was back again, welcomed by the people. Within a few months more he tired of ruling, and approached Rudolph II with a proposal to abdicate again if Rudolph would get his marriage annulled and a cardinal's hat in place of his wedding ring. Rudolph, who was slowly sinking into insanity himself, did nothing, and in March, 1599, Zsigmond abdicated by unilateral action, leaving Transylvania in the hands of his first cousin, Cardinal Andrew Báthory.

Andrew attempted to bring peace, but Michael the Brave, Voivode of Walachia, decided that his own strong arm could rule better, and marched in. Andrew was defeated, fled, and was captured by pious Székler peasants. They chopped his head off to send to Michael, and his finger to get his episcopal ring. Rudolph promptly recognized Michael as Councilor, Imperial Governor, and Commander-in-Chief in Transylvania. The date was November 20, 1599 (new style).

By the following April, the Transylvanians had had enough of

Michael. However much of a hero he may be in Rumanian history (Rumania was born of Walachia and Moldavia), Michael was the devil incarnate to Transylvania. The Transylvanians wanted Zsigmond back. Rudolph, to quell the disturbance, decided to send General Basta there. Basta, strictly a military man, came — with a determination to pacify the country even if that meant to slaughter all the inhabitants. Basta defeated Michael, with the help of Transylvanian troops under a General Csáki, in September. Michael fled. Basta, almost incomprehensibly, also left; he could not find winter quarters in Transylvania.

Thereupon Zsigmond, hearing of Transylvania's woes, collected an army, and was welcomed by the rejoicing populace early in 1601.

By then, Michael the Brave had made some sort of peace with the Emperor, and he and Basta joined troops to rid the country of Zsigmond. They were, not surprisingly, successful. Zsigmond escaped to Moldavia, to Bacău. Basta then, because of what we call today "a conflict of personalities," had Michael the Brave calmly murdered. Confident that he now had things under control, he even struck off some gold medals to commemorate this underhandedness. But Zsigmond showed up again at Brassó (Kronstadt, Braşov), in southeastern Transylvania, made himself welcome by bombarding his way in, and by October 2, 1601, had obtained forgiveness from the Transylvanians and an *atname* renominating him Prince of Transylvania from Mehmed III. Two weeks later a contingent of Turkish troops arrived to commemorate Zsigmond's control of things, and to help him keep it. Autumn floods prevented the Imperial man-in-control, Basta, from asserting himself, and by the end of 1601 Zsigmond was de facto master of most of the principality. Rudolph II roused himself then, enough to act — provoked to it perhaps by Mehmed's support of Zsigmond. He raised Basta to Commander-in-Chief of the Imperial Army in Transylvania on January 20, 1602, and ordered him to dethrone Zsigmond, preferably by persuasion but by force of arms if necessary.

Meanwhile, unbeknown to Basta, Zsigmond's uncle, Stephen Bocskay, had written Zsigmond from Prague, begging him to submit to the Emperor and permit a peaceful solution to Transylvania's harrowing troubles. The combination of the letter, Basta's increased authority, and the arrival of fresh troops — including Modrusch's battalion and John Smith — did the trick. Zsigmond began a "moral retreat," while desperately saving face.

On February 8, 1602, Chancellor Nicholas Bogáthy of Transylvania arrived at Basta's headquarters near Besztercze (Bistritz, Bistriţa), in northeastern Transylvania, with word that Zsigmond was willing to concede northwestern counties to Basta — which was not much of a concession, since Basta already held all northern Transylvania. Zsigmond sent the offer from Medgyes (Mediasch, Mediaş), seventy-five miles to the south. Basta granted a six-day truce as a starter, while he wrote privately to Prague asking for instructions and indicating his willingness to extend the truce.

The Chancellor rushed back to Medgyes, to find the Prince gone, of course. Zsigmond had retired to Brassó. A further wild ride through the winter brought Bogáthy the extra hundred miles to Zsigmond, and within a few days he was back again at Basta's encampment. Zsigmond demanded an additional two-week truce. Nevertheless, this seemed to indicate that, apart from the formalities, the end of the struggle was in sight.

But Zsigmond, for all his bewildering tacking about, knew the temper of his countrymen well. Peace was imperative, but peace without freedom was the peace of the grave. And the Transylvanians knew that peace under Basta almost amounted to that. The imperial general was autocratic, ruthless, intolerant of protestantism, and ignorant of the meaning of liberty in a political sense. If Zsigmond abdicated again, unless the ground were well prepared first, rebellion and reprisal would drench the land once more with blood.

John Smith's account of what he saw and heard at that very time is surprisingly penetrating, considering his position of mere Captain of Horse, his presumable unfluency in Latin, and his ignorance of Hungarian and two varieties of German: Austrian and Transylvanian. Despite a confusing situation, many of the details of which could not have been known to him, Smith's account of his adventures fits in well with recorded history (some of *that* being self-contradictory).

John Smith picks up the thread of his story, after the liberation of Alba Regalis and Mercoeur's departure, with his journey through the wintry cold from Hungary to Transylvania. After two or three months of rest, Modrusch and his men were apparently ordered into the field again not long after Basta's appointment to the command. According to John Smith they arrived at Besztercze after learning of the death of the Duke of Mercoeur, which took place February 17, 1602, in Nuremberg. With the aid of this known date, we can assign to early March the beginning of a new phase in Captain Smith's career. He had that military title, won in the field. Now he was determined to add to his experience and to his name. A turning in the military road came, and John Smith decided to go where risk and reward alike were greatest.[3]

The matter came up when General Basta suddenly announced his personal return to Hungary, taking with him the Imperial Army. Although his reasons are far from specific, or even straightforward, they may have been honest. Yet the move is puzzling. Basta was in contact with Zsigmond, through intermediaries, and with the Emperor by correspondence. Still, there seems to have been a vast amount of secret activity going on within and without that triangle. It has been suggested that Basta threw up his hands, unable to cope with so vacillating an opponent as Zsigmond and so undecided a backer as Rudolph. It has also been asserted that he could not control his Belgian Walloons or his "free hajdúk." * Certainly these were problems, but the sudden scuttling away of the Imperial Commander-in-Chief hints at something more serious. In any case, he and Zsigmond reached the desired truce, and Basta on his departure gave liberty to Zsigmond "to beat them [the hajdúk] out of the country." This exchange of responsibilities brought down the wrath of the ununderstanding Emperor on Basta's head, but those who possibly knew the true cause of all this were powerful enough to keep Basta robed in the majesty of the Supreme Command.

These tactics were naturally incomprehensible to Modrusch, not to mention John Smith. Modrusch had long been used to war, his father appears to have been killed by the Turks, and he had ties with, if not property in, Zsigmond's principality. In addition, he was a Protestant. Transylvania had been horribly ravaged by war. Murder, arson, wanton devastation ran amuck through town

---

* *Hajdúk* originally meant robbers, brigands, marauders. It was most appropriate for these mercenaries.

and field. Starvation brought men and women to eat cats and dogs, and children were seen devouring the emaciated corpses of their parents. This was the work of Basta's hajdúk, not of any Turk, and to Modrusch's mind even part of Basta's policy. To join Apollyon and his human-faced locusts on their retreat into Hungary was impossible. Modrusch harangued his men to stay with him and fight with Prince Zsigmond against these godless hajdúk, these "Turks" he called them in his rage — fight for Zsigmond, not for Basta. Basta was he that sat on the red horse of the Apocalypse, and he rode with Death, who sat on the pale horse. Basta was the enemy of the people and of their Prince.

The soldiers, including John Smith, were by the very nature of an army more devoted to their Captain and their Colonel than to their General. And in addition to Modrusch's words against Basta there was an inner voice that spoke: they were "worn out with those hard pays and travels," as Smith put it. "Upon hope to have free liberty to make booty upon what they could get possession of from the Turks," they were easily persuaded to follow him wherever he went.

That much accomplished, Modrusch sent word to Zsigmond that his twenty years of experience in the Emperor's service were now at *his* disposal, and that he "would spend the rest of his days for his country's defence in His Excellency's service." Modrusch's offer was accepted, undoubtedly with alacrity. Ancient and experienced soldiers were always welcome, and in appreciation Modrusch was made "Camp-master," perhaps a little more than an ordinary colonel. More to the point for the soldiers, arrangements were made for their regular pay in addition to being granted "what freedom they desired to plunder the Turks" — meaning rather the hajdúk.

Smith's story at this point bears every evidence of later rewriting for dramatic effect. A number of developments between 1602 and 1622 (when he finished the first draft for publication) made this romanticizing advisable, profitable. It is proper here only to try to get at the unvarnished facts. The story of the changes, the embellishments, belongs to Smith's later history.

One of the two or three contemporary Turkish histories states that Archduke Matthias's troops took Alba Iulia in Transylvania toward the end of winter in the Moslem year 1010, which corre-

lance; on each side, another leading his horse: where long
he stayed not, ere Smith with a noise of trumpets, only a
Page bearing his Lance, passing by him with a courteous
salute, took his ground with such good success, that at the
sound of the charge, he passed the Turk through the sight
of his Beaver [face guard], face, head, and all, that he fell
dead to the ground; where alighting and unbracing his
Helmet, [Smith] cut off his head, and the Turks took his
body; and so returned without any hurt at all.

Smith politely presented the head to General Székely, who
"kindly" accepted it, while the Christian army cheered. But Tur-
bashaw (Turk-bashi?) had friends, and before long one of these,
whom Smith calls Grualgo, more crazed than merely angered,
"directed a particular challenge to the Conqueror, to regain his
friend's head, or lose his own, with his horse and armor for advantage," or to boot.

John Smith dismisses this second challenge, which was fought the
next day, more briefly:

As before, upon the sound of the Trumpets, their Lances
flew in pieces upon a clear passage; but the Turk was near
unhorsed. Their Pistols were next, which marked Smith
upon the placard [reinforced breastplate]; but the next shot
the Turk was so wounded in the left arm, that being not
able to rule his horse, and defend himself, he was thrown to
the ground; and so bruised with the fall, that he lost his
head, as his friend before him; with his horse and Armor:
but his body and his rich apparel was sent back to the
Town.

With this second gentlemanly decollation, the besieged seemed
to lose interest in dueling. But John Smith, puffed up with jus-
tifiable pride, himself got restless. The siegeworks were not ready,
there was little to do, and furthermore, when you had fought two
such duels, custom really demanded a third. So he approached his
superiors "with so many incontradictable persuading reasons" that
they gave him permission to issue a challenge of his own. As he
embellished his proposal, he "obtained leave that the Ladies might

know he was not so enamored of their servants' heads, but if any Turk of their rank would come to the place of combat to redeem them, [he] should have his also upon like conditions, if he could win it." A Hector by the jaunty name of Bonny Mulgro accepted.

Smith's account of the third duel is the most detailed of all, and the most interesting. Catch-as-catch-can tactics were used that would probably have been ruled out in a "western" duel — but then, there was no umpire to stop the fight, and human heads were at stake.

The next day both the Champions entering the field as before, each discharging their Pistol (having no Lances, but such martial weapons as the defendant appointed), no hurt was done; their Battle-axes were next, whose piercing bills [spikes] made sometimes the one, sometimes the other to have scarce sense to keep their saddles: especially the Christian received such a blow that he lost his Battle-axe, and failed not much to have fallen after it; whereas the supposing conquering Turk had a great shout from the Ramparts. The Turk prosecuted his advantage to the uttermost of his power; yet the other, what by the readiness of his horse, and his judgement and dexterity in such a business, beyond all men's expectation, by God's assistance, not only avoided the Turk's violence, but having drawn his Falchion [curved broadsword], pierced the Turk so under the Culets [armorplates for the lower back] through back and body, that although he alighted from his horse, he stood not long ere he lost his head, as the rest had done.

What the ladies on the ramparts had to say by then is not recorded. But John Smith was conducted in triumph before General Moses Székely, with a guard of six thousand swarming around three Turkish horses before each of which the head of its quondam rider was borne aloft on a lance. Theodore Paleologue's training had not been in vain.

The General embraced Smith "in his arms," gave him yet another horse, with fine trappings, and threw in a scimitar and a belt worth three hundred ducats, for good measure. Modrusch in turn showed his appreciation by promoting John Smith to the rank of major — a title to which Smith never refers again.

Soon after these pastimes, Székely was ready for the serious business of the siege. Mounting all his ordnance above the plain, he succeeded in making two breaches in the walls in fifteen days. Clouds of gun smoke turned the day into night — but for the light "that proceeded from the murdering Muskets, and peace-making Cannon," John Smith intones.

Meanwhile, the "slothful Governor" lay in the fort. Székely commanded a general assault, but the slope proved more difficult than he had thought. Logs, bags of powder, and what not came tumbling down on the heads of the attackers, and every effort to dislodge the defenders came to nothing. Modrusch and two other colonels arrived, however, and turned the tide of battle. The Turks at last "retired and fled into the Castle, from whence by a flag of truce they desired composition" — terms of surrender, in modern English.

According to Smith's account, Modrusch was vengeful beyond description, and Székely's behavior after the surrender even pathologically bloodthirsty. Modrusch, "remembering his father's death," did his best to wipe the town off the face of the earth and put to the sword "all he found who could bear arms . . . and set their heads upon stakes round about the walls, in the same manner they had used the Christians, when they took it." As for Székely, he was "forced . . . to seek a further revenge," and took off to ravage towns down the Maros River, gathering up two thousand prisoners, "mostly women and children." Psychotic Zsigmond fortunately arrived in time to draw at least an entr'acte curtain over the "sound and fury."

Székely, his bloodthirst slaked, calmly reviewed his troops before his Prince, presenting him with his prisoners and thirty-six captured war ensigns. A religious service followed, with humble thanks offered to Almighty God "in triumph of those victories," and the heroes of the siege were received in audience. Among these was Captain John Smith.

Up to that time, John Smith's shield had been polished plain, or at best decorated with some conventional device. Armorial bearings (coats-of-arms) had to be won (or bought) — they could not be designed and etched or painted merely at the caprice of a soldier. Zsigmond stood ready to remedy this deficiency for John Smith. The novice had fought three duels in accordance with the laws of single combat — however crude these were on the Turkish frontier — and he was entitled to recognition. Zsigmond therefore authorized Captain John Smith from that date henceforward "to design and impress upon his shield three Turks' heads," in token of his feat. And he named John Smith "an English gentleman."

As an anticlimax, so far as Captain John Smith, Gentleman, was concerned, Zsigmond took his oath ever to wear the Three Turks' Heads in his colors, and gave him a medallion of himself set in a gold frame. And by way of financial reward, the generous Prince (about to abdicate for the fourth and last time) granted him an annual pension of three hundred ducats. The ladder of success looked shorter now.[5]

# CHAPTER 4

## SLAVE

GENERAL Giorgio Basta was not a man to give in easily. Defeated by a political, social, and patriotic climate he did not understand, he had retired to Vienna. Other motives there undoubtedly were, but the final upshot was that he got backing. Then he swept once more into Transylvania with fresh troops and an Imperial edict. Zsigmond was offered a choice between his already-granted Imperial fiefs and pension in Silesia, and "the flinty and steel couch of war." Even Zsigmond's most devoted followers now pressed him to give in.

Moses Székely, the Unitarian, got wind of this. *He* could not yield, not to the lackey of an emperor who was not only Catholic but also German. (That Rudolph was more than half insane was beside the point; his successor would be branded with the same two basic stigmata.) Therefore, well aware of Zsigmond's instability, Székely seems to have determined to keep him Prince of Transylvania by the neat move of ousting the Imperial Army. The project was simple, its realization chancy in the extreme. But Székely, as John Smith put it, "would do anything rather than come in subjection to the Germans." He assembled soldiers and "without any more ado marched to encounter Basta," who by then was on his way from Kolozsvár (Clausenburg, Cluj) to Alba Iulia.

The armies met at Tövis (Teiuş today), a dozen miles north of the latter city. There, on July 2, 1602 (new style), Moses Székely was soundly trounced. With the bare remnants of an army, he fled south and west, down the valley of the Maros, into the protecting arms of the Pasha of Temesvár (Timişoara today). On his flight he passed Zsigmond, who had moved to Déva, about a third of the way along the same road in the same direction. What Zsigmond really had in mind has never been known; what he did, is. He hustled a messenger off to Basta with a total disavowal of any responsibility for Székely's belligerence.

On July 8, Zsigmond met Basta near Alba Iulia and rode fifty miles with him to Nagyszeben (much better known as Hermannstadt, modern Sibiu), a metropolis then little smaller than Vienna. And from there he took his final leave of Transylvania on July 26. The Habsburgs had at last made good their claim to rule, at the price, in John Smith's words, of a Transylvania that was

> the very spectacle of desolation; their fruits and fields overgrown with weeds, their Churches and battered palaces and best buildings, as for fear, hid with moss and ivy.

Modrusch and John Smith and their companions no longer had any reason to stick by Prince Zsigmond. They and their men, and many another Transylvanian fighter with his men, offered their services to General Basta. Basta, finding no fault in their past conduct, accepted them — apparently gladly. News had reached him of further troubles which these experienced fighters might help him solve. These troubles were summed up in the person of one Jeremy Mogila, or Movila, a voivode set up by the Sublime Porte in Walachia in defiance of the voivode appointed by the Emperor, who was a Bessarabian by the name of Radul Şerban, or Sherban.

Thus John Smith came to ride off to war once again with his commander and friend Colonel Modrusch, as summer turned to brief autumn in the year 1602. The roster of commanders he names reads like a geographical gazetteer of Transylvania: "Veltuz" (Wöltz, near Medgyes), "Budendorf" (Szász-Buda, east of Sighişoara), "Becklefield" (Blechisfeld, near Grossau), "Oberwin" (Oberwinz, near Egerbegy), "Nederspolt" (Nieder-Apold, near Hermannstadt), "Zarvana" (Szászváros, near Déva) — a medley of Saxon, Magyar, and Székler names, all Transylvanians except for Modrusch.

John Smith reports that Jeremy Mogila assembled "an Army of forty thousand Turks, Tartars, and Moldavians" for his return to power in Walachia. The figure seems large, but in any case Radul bolted off — to Transylvania and Basta — with his ten-thousand-man army at his heels. He had not far to go, for Basta, unable to

billet his troops in the devastated north, was in the south — where
similar devastation seemed about to break out. (Again, Basta seemed
unable or unwilling to control his men. He even wrote to Prague
about it, as if the Emperor could do what the Commander-in-the-
Field could not!) Whatever the facts of the case, Basta was possibly
glad of an excuse to saddle somebody else with the responsibility
for a large segment of his army. Because of Radul's appeal for help,
in any event, the campaign was started which was to prove the
fourth and last in John Smith's sally to "try his fortune against the
Turks."

The Turks in the interim had reoccupied Alba Regalis and were
holding out in Nagykanizsa, but seemed to be losing strength in
Translyvania — what with their misplaced confidence in Zsigmond's
pertinacity. To get back the upper hand they sent for help to
Chancellor Zamoyski of Poland and to their "satellite," the Khan
of Crimea, Ghazi II Geray, nicknamed "Bora," which seems to
mean "The Drunken Camel." Ghazi Geray took longer to send help
than did Zamoyski, but when he moved, the countless sand hills of
the steppe turned horsemen to accompany him. Horde upon horde,
descendants of great Genghiz Khan's Mongolian riders rode westward with their Khan, Ghazi Geray. Zamoyski's troops, with bands
of Cossacks mingled in, were but a decoy; and Radul started south
from Hermannstadt to fight the decoy. He had no knowledge of
the peril that he ran.

The route of Radul's army lay along the Olt or Aluta River, a
tributary of the Danube which drains eastern Transylvania before
cutting through a narrow gorge into Walachia. Fifteen miles or so
from Hermannstadt they reached the great Red Tower which gave
the pass its name. Just beyond, scattered remnants of a gate built
by the Emperor Trajan lay unnoticed. Then the mountains closed
in.

Today, a railway and a road contend with the river for space.
In 1602, the road was hardly worthy of the name. It was rather a
track, with the Transylvanian Alps rising to nearly seven thousand
feet on one side of the river and over eight thousand on the other.
Over such terrain the army, thirty thousand strong according to
John Smith, must have advanced slowly.

Twenty-five miles beyond Red Tower Pass they came to a broad valley in the mountains, where the Lotru torrent pours into the Olt. There, if John Smith's "Raza" is the Brezoiu of today, they encamped. It was an ideal halting place, defended on the south by a savage but beautiful defile, and on the north by General Basta, less than a day's courier-ride away.

Jeremy Mogila meanwhile had dug in at Curtea de Argeş, not thirty miles below them in the plains of Piteşti. His Polonian-Cossack allies were already there, and he had only the promised Tatar reinforcements to wait for. Until they came he did not want to risk a real engagement, so he amused himself annoying Radul.

He sent small parties to the Olt Valley to reconnoiter and raid. Inevitably some of these were captured and their military careers quickly ended. Radul good-naturedly had them decapitated and sent the remains with reciprocal small parties to Jeremy, where in the night, as John Smith matter-of-factly reports, Radul "would cause their heads to be thrown up and down before the trenches." In retaliation, when seven of Radul's porters (human pack horses) were taken, Jeremy had them "flayed quick [alive]; and after hung their skins upon poles, and their carcasses and heads on stakes by them." Small wonder the Turks thought the Christians barbarous!

But Radul was getting impatient. He knew he had to draw Jeremy out of his trenches into battle before the arrival of the Crimean Tatars, and these (Radul had heard) were well on their way. The Turkish contingent of Jeremy's army had also got wind of the approaching aid and wanted to start something, but Jeremy was wise enough to refuse to be moved. Then Radul hit upon a scheme.

Marching toward Curtea de Argeş in full panoply of war, Radul burned and spoiled right and left, but suddenly, though he met with no resistance, turned and fled toward Râmnicul Vâlcea, on the Olt due west of Curtea, under cover of night. Jeremy was reluctantly persuaded to pursue Radul and was caught in a trap. After a battle, described in long and gory detail by John Smith, the victory was Radul's.

The date of this engagement (in which Smith does not mention his own name once) is surprisingly difficult to ascertain. Mentioned though it is in newsletters from Graz, Prague, and Istanbul, as well as in Knolles's *History*, it is possible to say only that the earliest date can have been September 23, 1602, and the latest, mid-October. Smith reports that twenty-five thousand were left dead on the field, a seemingly huge figure. Knolles limited himself to saying it was "a most terrible and bloody Battel." Thanks to it, in any event, "*Rodoll* was seated again in his Sovereignty," Smith declares, "and Walachia became subject to the Emperor." [1]

Radul reported his victory to General Basta, and then went about establishing some sort of government in the province. It was hopefully rumored that Jeremy had been slain, but his body was not found. On the other hand, as Smith writes, news came that Tatar stragglers were ravaging eastern Walachia near the Moldavian frontier, a hundred miles or so east of Red Tower Pass. Modrusch was promptly ordered off with eleven thousand men to cope with this new threat. John Smith went with him, as did Veltuz and other Transylvanians.

Modrusch had not gotten very far when he heard that the matter was much more serious than it had seemed. Jeremy had indeed escaped after the battle, and was now lying in ambush at Câm-pulung (German, Langenau), only twenty miles beyond Curtea, with fourteen or fifteen thousand. And Ghazi Geray, "the Drunken Camel," and his two war-bred sons were at that very moment sweeping through Moldavia at the head of thirty thousand Tatars. Modrusch beat a hasty retreat toward Red Tower Pass. But somewhere on the way, swift-riding enemy parties galloped around him, harassing and delaying his men. Skirmishes ensued. Foragers interfered. And soon Modrusch was all but trapped, in a wood.

Working by night, the encircled army cut trees to hinder attacks, chopped their way ahead, and finally surprised a body of two thousand pillagers groping their way through a thick early-morning fog. Loaded with plunder, the pillagers were driving two or three hundred horses and cattle before them. "Most of them were slain and taken prisoners," says John Smith, meaning "or." But the prisoners told them where Jeremy was lying, waiting for the main body of Tatars.

The prisoners were not entirely right. Ghazi's objective was the Iron Gate Pass on the Danube, and his main body would ride by some distance to the south. The season was advanced, and he wanted to reach Belgrade and distribute his horsemen for the winter.

But even so, a side wash of three or four Tatar "battalions" could be expected to surf up toward Jeremy — perhaps no more than that many thousand men, but doubly quadruplicated by the terror Tatar and Mongol armies inspired.

Modrusch, learning of the tidal danger that now threatened him, determined to get through to Red Tower Pass before he was engulfed. John Smith once more came through with an idea, a *stratagem* he calls it, which was no sooner suggested than put into practice. Smith supervised the filling of two or three hundred rocket cases with wildfire, such as he had used at Székesfehérvár, and while it was daylight attached these to as many lanceheads. Then, when night came, Modrusch ordered a charge, the men set fire to the rocket-headed lances, put spurs to their horses, and had a run at the enemy. Such a blazing and sparkling of rearing horses "amazed" not only the enemy horses, but their foot as well. The horses took panic, and in the confusion Modrusch and his men got through with little or no loss.

Even so, they still were not safe. With only three leagues (nine miles) yet to go before reaching the safety of the pass, Ghazi's Tatars caught them — "near forty thousand," Smith exaggerates. "They must either fight, or be cut in pieces flying."

Here the recollection of their plight and the slaughter that followed bursts out of John Smith's memory with a pent-up bitterness which must well reflect the hatred of the Habsburgs he found all around him. "Here Basta and the Emperor had their desire," he writes, "for the Sun no sooner displayed his beams, than the Tatar his colors; where at midday he stayed a while, to see the passage of a tyrannical and treacherous imposture, till the earth did blush with the blood of honesty, that the Sun for shame did hide himself from so monstrous sight of a cowardly calamity."

For a moment the gaudy picture of plumed knights in shining armor, with their lances and banners, enraptures Smith. But the mechanized gruesomeness of "modern" warfare interrupts. It is a "brave sight" only "till the silent expedition of the bloody blast from the murdering Ordnance, whose roaring voice is not so soon heard, as felt by the aimed at object, which made among them a most lamentable slaughter."

Thus caught at the entrance of Red Tower Pass, Modrusch lined his troops up as best he could, erected a screen of sharp stakes pointed at the Tatars, and dispersed chosen infantry in foxholes between and behind the stakes. In this way he formed a delaying trap, reinforced with a triple tier of short pikes firmly embedded in the ground. The infantry that manned this makeshift bulwark had instructions to harass and retire.

All was ready when the Tatars charged, "their Ensigns displaying, Drums beating, Trumpets and Hautboys sounding." Two cavalry units rushed at them in front of the stakes, forcing a momentary retreat. Then a larger body of Tatar horsemen rode wildly up, "darkening the skies with their flights of numberless arrows." This charge was resisted for over an hour until the superiority of the Tatar numbers drove the Christians back to take refuge behind the wall of stakes.

The Tatars, closing in for the kill, charged onto the unseen and unsuspected barrier. Horses were impaled and riders thrown, only to be hammered at and cut by Modrusch's infantry hidden alongside for that purpose. So great was the mangling of man and beast that the Christians raised a shout of *Victoria!* in good Latin so that the polyglot army could all understand. And the concealed infantry was recalled, while five or six field pieces began to pound the Tatars with devastating results.

The cry was premature. The Tatars still had thousands in reserve, and these surged up over the bodies of their comrades. Modrusch soon realized that he was lost. His only chance was to gather his men into a compact mass and make a dash for the river gorge.

For perhaps half an hour the bid for safety was successful, but it was made too late. Two more regiments, Turkish janissaries this time, overmatched and overthrew the Christian troops. Only the sudden fall of night saved the lives of a few. Modrusch, with thirteen or fourteen hundred horse, swam the Olt and escaped in the darkness.

To the historians of the time, this skirmish was a mere delaying action in the progress of the Tatar Khan to Hungary. Richard Knolles laconically observes that Ghazi's passage through Walachia was "not without great loss of their men (being fought with by the Valachians and free *Haiducks a whole day*)." But to John Smith it was infinitely painful. He writes:

And thus in this bloudy field, neere 30000. lay; some headless, armlesse, and leglesse, all cut and mangled: where breathing their last, they gave this knowledge to the world, that for the lives of so few, the Crym-Tartar never paid dearer.

Of the captains whose names Smith mentions, only Modrusch is stated to have gotten away. Of the men, Smith lists the names of eight Englishmen who were among the dead — Baskerfield (or Batchelor), Hardwicke, Thomas Milemer (or Milemay), Robert Mullineux, Thomas Bishop, Francis (or Roger) Compton, George Davison, Nicholas Williams, and one John, a Scot. And there were two Englishmen who escaped — Ensign ("Lieutenant") Thomas Carleton and Sergeant Edward Robinson. They lived to meet John Smith again in later years in London.[2]

As to John Smith himself, his own picturesque pen gives this picture of his plight:

But Smith, among the slaughtered dead bodies, and many a gasping soule, with toile and wounds lay groaning among the rest, till being found by the Pillagers hee was able to live; and perceiving by his armor and habit, his ransome might be better to them than his death, they led him prisoner with many others.

His captors cured his wounds, Smith does not say where, and somehow he reached Axiopolis, a market town which then stood on the banks of the Danube, a hundred miles due east of Bucharest. There John Smith and his fellow captives "were all sold for slaves, like beasts in a market-place; where every merchant, viewing their limbs and wounds, caused other slaves to struggle with them, to try their strength." Meanwhile, Ghazi Geray was resting for the winter, in Belgrade, writing poetry. "Wine and Coffee" were his subjects — Good and Evil was the name he gave his book. But for John Smith, there was no wine or coffee or good. There was only evil.

In the auction, John Smith

fell to the share of Bashaw Bogall, who sent him forthwith to Adrinopolis [Edirne], so for Constantinople to his faire Mistresse for a slave.

By twentie and twentie chained by the neckes, they
marched in file to this great Citie; where they were delivered to their severall Masters, and he to the young
Charatza Tragabigzanda.

How many months of pain and humiliation had slipped by it is
hazardous to guess. Yet certain facts may give us a clue. John
Smith later got from Zsigmond a document in which the date of
his capture is given as November 18. This fits in with the known
arrival of Ghazi Geray at Belgrade *after* November 2, by at least
a week, but before winter set in. Less than three months later, on
February 12, 1603 (new style), the month-long annual Moslem fast
of Ramadan began. It is doubtful in the extreme that slave
markets were in operation during that month, and it is equally
doubtful that John Smith could have been cured of his wounds
and marched at least two hundred (perhaps many more) miles, and
put on the market and sold, in eighty-five days. On the other hand,
Ramadan was followed by a three-day festival (March 14 to 16
that year, according to the Gregorian calendar) called *Küçük
Bayram*, during which the Sultan's subjects put on new clothes,
made official visits, paid respect to the dead, and gave presents to
friends. John Smith, by his own statement, was sent as a present.
What better time, then, for "Bashaw Bogall" to think of a gift
than Küçük Bayram? Especially with half a thousand miles separat-
ing him from his beloved!

However it was, John Smith arrived in Istanbul and at the home
of Charatza Trabigzanda (an extra syllable having crept into his
first account of her). He obviously thought it was her name, but
it was surely nothing but a description of who she was — in
Greek. She was a girl (in modern Greek *korítsi*) from Trebizond
(*tês Trapedzoûndos,* or some such form), probably a Greek herself,
and she was not ill-educated. To her, John Smith seems to have
been a novel slave. Indeed, in the end he was the object of her
sincere affection, if not her love.

Charatza — to call her by the only name we have — could speak
a little Italian. Once her curiosity was stimulated by the stocky,
straightforward, not bad-looking Englishman, she began to ask
questions. She wanted to know how Bogall had taken him prisoner,

and such things. And it was not long before she found out that her lover had not sent her, as he had claimed in a letter, "a Bohemian Lord conquered by his [own] hand," but a simple subject of Queen Elizabeth's most excellent Majesty, who had become a captain "only by his adventures" and had merely been bought in an open slave market by the doughty Bashaw Bogall.

Charatza regarded John Smith's story with true Greek skepticism. She called in friends who could speak and understand English, French, and Dutch, as well as Italian, and they subjected him to further questioning. When it was found out that all his accounts agreed, regardless of language of inquiry, and that English was his native language after all, Charatza "took (as it seemed) much compassion on him."

Apparently Charatza was not yet of age, for John Smith hints that she was afraid that her mother would sell him if she discovered this "compassion." He adds that "she had no use for him," which certainly means that she had no real need for a slave, and this may have been what she said to her mother, for she went on to suggest that it would be well if she sent him to her brother. Her brother was a petty official in charge of a *timar,* a sort of military fief, on the far side of the Black Sea. There he could learn the language, and "what it was to be a Turk, till time made her Master of her self." This somewhat obscure statement shows clearly enough that she and her brother were not Turks, and that she wanted him back when she came of age. By turning Turk, John Smith might eventually get a timar for himself.

Whatever thoughts he had in regard to his mistress's plans John Smith kept to himself. He may possibly have toyed with the idea, nebulously suggested in what he wrote, of returning to Istanbul to marry her. On the other hand, he may have accepted the scheme as offering a better hope of escape than continued slavery within the sturdy walls of the Turkish seat of empire. Or he may merely have yielded to persuasion, without giving much thought to what might happen next. In any case, Charatza sent him off to her brother.[3]

John Smith's route lay north through Rumelia and today's Bulgaria to Varna on the Black Sea. It was roughly the same route he had followed on his way down from Axiopolis, but this time the fields were green, and presumably he was a little freer — free at least to observe, if not to act. His narrative of the journey from Istanbul to the timar shows that John Smith had already begun to be a sharp observer.

From Varna, he crossed the Black Sea to "the Strait of Niger," today's Strait of Kerch. Beyond this he entered the Sea of Azov, which he calls "Mar delle Sabacche" after its current Italian name in those days. He notes that there were many shoals, beds of ooze, black rocks, and low islands; but for the most part all he saw was salt water "till they came betwixt Susax and Curuske, only two white towns at the entrance of the River Bruapo appeared."

Susax is evidently Turkish Azak, modern Azov in Russian, while Curuske must have been the trading post called Cherkassk by the Russians, named for the Circassians of the nearby Caucasus. The Bruapo (or Bruago, as he also writes it) seems almost necessarily to have been the Don,* since he sails on for six or seven days. During this time, he says,

> he saw four or five seeming strong castles of stone, with flat tops and battlements about them; but arriving at Cambia, he was (according to their custom) well used.*

There he was disembarked, two days journey from "Nalbrits" where Charatza's brother was then resident.

By this time, John Smith certainly did not know where he was. He may have asked and forgotten what he was told, or he may never have known. But in the quiet of a library in England, years later, he found a place called Nalbrits on a map, and this place was near the spot where he must have been. No such name was known in that region in 1603, but that did not matter — it would have been silly to write that he did not know where he went. So he went on with his story. At Nalbrits, wherever precisely that was, John Smith found the "Tymor Bashaw," as he calls the brother (whose correct title would have been "timariot," possibly plus "bashi"), in residence. The place was

> a great vast stony Castle with many great Courts about it, invironed with high stone walls, where was quartered their

* The names Bruapo (or Bruago) and Cambia (also written Cambria) were apparently contrived in London, years later. See the Commentaries.

Arms, when they first subjected those Countries: which only live to labor for those tyrannical Turks.

This statement can be taken as but little exaggerated.

John Smith presented his letter. It said that he should "sojourn" there, which clearly meant temporarily only, to learn the language, and other things which Charatza had hinted to Smith. The brother understood much too much, and quickly. He "diverted all this to the worst of cruelty," which was not surprising under the circumstances, and within an hour John Smith was "slave of slaves to them all" — that is, to the other Christian slaves, and to "near an hundred *Forsados* [usually "galley slaves"] of Turks and Moors." He was stripped naked, his hair and beard shaved off, and an iron ring riveted around his neck. Then he was given a coat made of coarse wool, with a strip of undressed leather for a belt.

Life was grim there, as Smith describes it, "for the best was so bad, a dog could hardly have lived to endure [it]." Beaten and reviled, the slaves were half starved as well. While the timariot and other local magnates ate pilau of rice and chick-peas, beef or mutton or horse-meat kebabs, and drank their coffee, John Smith and his fellow beasts-of-labor got but the remnants of a gruel of boiled millet, with the entrails of horses and wild sheep, baked or stewed, to enrich it.

John Smith recounts how his fellow Christians often discussed with him how they might flee. Old-timer slaves mumbled their confused thoughts. But all were soggily agreed on the hopelessness of their situation. Around them were impassable deserts and endless stretches of steppe — the *Dikoye Polye,* the Wilderness, where the Nogai Tatars roamed, descendants of Nogai and Genghiz Khan. They lived in hordes, and subsisted on raw horse meat and kumiss. Through their domain — and all the wide frontier was theirs — escape indeed seemed impossible.

But, as John Smith adds, "God beyond man's expectation or imagination helpeth his servants." Threshing time came, and Smith was made a thresher "at a grange in a great field, more than a league from the Tymor's house." The "Tymor," Charatza's brother, on one occasion went to the fields alone on an inspection tour. Coming across Smith, for some reason he took occasion to belabor, kick, and abuse that Christian dog in such fashion that reason took wing. The slave of slaves "beat out the Tymor's brains with his threshing bat, for they have no flails." (What Smith would have done with a flail is not stated.) Then, preferring voluntary death to the refinements of Turkish legal retribution, John Smith dressed himself in Charatza's brother's clothes, stuffed the corpse under some straw, filled his knapsack, shut the barn doors, mounted the brother's horse, and galloped off into the waste, "at all adventure." [4]

For two or three days he ambled, anxiously but aimlessly, in the Great Nowhere, miles from any settlement, until he chanced on the caravan route from Poland to Astrakhan and the Orient. It was a mere track, but here and there it was marked with symbols: a crescent for the road to Crimea, a cross for Muscovy, a sun . . . (for China, John Smith imagined). Whatever the other signs meant, the cross most surely meant some Christian land. John Smith took the route it indicated.

For sixteen days he followed the track across the steppe, ever fearful of being met and caught, to suffer slavery again, or something worse. But all roads have their goals, and in the end Smith came to a wooden-palisaded Muscovite outpost which he later identified as "Aecopolis." * There, whatever outpost it was, the resident governor or commandant took pity on him, had the chains struck from his neck, "and so kindly used him, he thought himself new risen from death." The governor's wife took pity, too. She "largely supplied all his wants," and John Smith shows his gratitude by giving her a name which hardly can have been hers. He called her *Callamata,* for the port in southern Greece that lay athwart his course with Captain La Roche, two years and more before. The knight who fought duels to the death could not forget the lady's name — nor could he admit he never knew it.

But soon a convoy was ready to carry news and other more tangible items across the hostile steppe toward Moscow. The governor offered Smith a place in the convoy, along with a certificate of how he had come to him, and letters to other officials along the route. John Smith was eager to be gone, and therefore soon was jogging along the primitive trail to Chernava. The governor of that post

---

* Again, no such name was known in the region at the time. See the Commentaries.

received him courteously, heard his story, saw his letter, and added a safe-conduct of his own to Smith's credentials.

The rest of John Smith's odyssey is briefly told. With kindnesses and further recommendations bestowed on him everywhere, he traveled north to Yelets and Dankov, and then ever west across the boundless plains of Lithuania and Poland to the confines of the Holy Roman Empire once again. Throughout this vast domain, he writes, "in all his life he seldom met with more respect, mirth, content, and entertainment: and not any Governor where he came, but gave him somewhat as a present, besides his charges [food and shelter]; seeing themselves as subject to the like calamity." Smith's tribute to these people who lived in the knowledge of the precariousness of human happiness is all the more touching when we remember that within months futile battles raged in their very midst, as the "Time of Troubles" lowered over Muscovy.

Once he was within the Imperial boundaries, Smith turned southward into Transylvania once again, to seek out his friends and companions-in-arms in Hermannstadt. By then he must have heard for the first time of the death of "the Old Queen." And having heard, he must have longed for further news from home. In short, his "native Country" called, as he writes. Off he rode once more, northward and westward — "glutted with content, and near drowned with joy." [5]

CHAPTER 5

# AFTERMATH: PIRATE

J OHN SMITH's route home seems to have been planned with an
eye to finding Zsigmond Báthory. Zsigmond had given him the
right to wear the Three Turks' Heads on his shield, but he had
nothing to prove it, and Zsigmond had promised him three hundred ducats a year pension. If he could not collect the latter, perhaps at least the former might be obtainable. And in any event
Zsigmond's whereabouts, uncertain though they were, lay somewhere across his path toward England. He had to go to the north
to avoid the Turks.

Zigzagging through "high Hungaria" (mostly Slovakia), the care-
free rider went to "Fileck" (Fil'akovo, Slovakia), Tokaj (back in
Hungary), and Košice (Smith's Cassovia), whence he made his way
northwest and west through the Slovakian mountains to "Underoro-
way," which must be Oravský Podzámok, the village under Orava
Castle. This was the last, and one of the strongest, of the Hungarian castles along the Polish frontier. It commanded the direct
route from Budapest to Kraków. That Smith rode up to this out-
of-the-way spot (he can hardly have started for England on foot)
hints that either he was interested in seeing so famous a fortress or
expected to get to Zsigmond at Ratibor or Oppeln through Poland.
Sight-seeing was always a weakness of John's, but if this was the
motive, it is strange that he did not mention the fortress as he mentioned Bayonne's "strength." On the other hand, it is difficult to
known what turned him back at the very gate of Poland, unless it
was some religious upheaval at the moment of his arrival. (There
was a general repression of Protestantism in Silesia around 1600.)
Whatever it was, Smith struggled with more mountains to the west

until he came to Olomouc, then capital of Moravia and famed for halting the Mongols' westward course in 1241. From Olomouc to Prague was just a pleasant canter of much less than two hundred miles, especially after he got across the last mountain ridges.

At Prague someone must have told him where to find Zsigmond the Changeable, ex-Prince of Transylvania.* That restless pension-naire of the Holy Roman Emperor had been scudding from anchor-age to moorings over the sea of empire, and was at the moment, Smith was told, in Leipzig, where the twenty-year-old Elector Christian II was strengthening Protestantism — a policy frowned on by the devoutly Catholic Emperor. Although winter was setting in, Smith boldly attacked the Erzgebirge, rode over tortuous if scenic trails, and out onto the Saxon plain. Leipzig was not then far, and there without any reported difficulty he was rewarded with a document which he kept with him the rest of his life. It was a *laissez-passer*, a "Passe" Smith calls it, "intimating the service he had done, and the honours he had received" — a cross between a passport and a certificate of discharge. It was couched in a Latin worthy, if not of Cicero, at least of the Báthory prince, for whom all Europe, in a better day, had not been "enough to satisfy his desires."

John Smith was justly puffed up over the terms of his document. He was referred to as "an English gentleman" (*Anglo generoso*, in the dative case to fit the sentence structure), he was confirmed in his past command (*250 militum Capitaneo*), he was authorized to wear three Turks' heads on his shield (*in Sigillum illius tria Turcia Capita designare et deprimere concessimus*), his dutiful return to his troops was celebrated (*ad suos Commilitones revertit*), he was relieved of further duty (*ex quibus ipsum liberavimus*), and the lords of all the lands through which he might pass on his way home were requested to permit him to pass freely, and without hindrance (*Rogamus ergo omnes . . . ut . . . permittatur Capitaneus libere sine obstaculo omniversari*). In addition to this formidable paper, he was presented with fifteen hundred ducats of gold "to repair his losses" — well over £500 at the lowest valuation for the ducat. The coin was a valuable addition to his purse; the document was an invaluable addition to his prestige. He may have *been* a "gentle-man" since Székely gave him the right to wear the Three Turks'

* Transylvania was without a Prince at the moment.

Heads, but only Zsigmond's inflated testimonial *proved* that he was. Leipzig had been worth visiting.

John Smith ran across Modrusch also in Leipzig. Modrusch's presence there was less surprising perhaps than Zsigmond's especially if he was the Protestant noble he seems to have been. In fact, Smith may have seen Modrusch before he got an audience with Zsigmond, and Modrusch may have gotten the document for Smith. (Modrusch gets his share of praise in it.) However it was, with this document dated December 9, 1603, in his possession, Modrusch and Zsigmond, Hungary and Transylvania, and the Turkish war, all slipped from his mind, while his ambitious young brain set to work on further adventures of potential profit to his name, his incipient social status, and his eventual standing at home.[1]

Lack of money, along with a vague sense of homesickness, may have had to do with Smith's decision to leave the pleasures of Hermannstadt and "rejoice himself . . . in his native Country." Now, with so much money jingling in his pocket (how unexpectedly is not known), he changed his mind about going to Lincolnshire. He was not a weather vane like Zsigmond, but after all there was no hurry. Why not make a tour of Germany? There were many "fair Cities" there.

So he started out by going to Dresden, the capital of Saxony. Since he has left no word as to how he traveled, we can only guess that he used horses for the longer stretches, and perhaps got a seat in a coach in Germany on occasion. It was not at all difficult to buy or sell a horse, and coach travel was not only expensive but usually extremely uncomfortable. Hiring a horse was not much cheaper, and at times became very complicated. The alternatives were tramping, hitchhiking, and river travel by barge. But only on one occasion does Smith bother to describe what means of locomotion he used.

Even John Smith's route is uncertain, due to obvious confusion in the printer's shop. Nevertheless, on the basis of places he names, it is possible to reconstruct his tour with considerable probability. From Dresden, about which he has nothing to say, he seems to have taken a boat down the Elbe, going as far as Magdeburg. On the way it seems he stopped at Wittenberg, "the cradle of the Reformation," where he visited the university. (This interest in a university belies the not infrequent claim that John Smith loathed learning, ran away from school, and remained at a low level of literacy for the rest of his life.) Then veering west at Magdeburg, a forty-mile ride brought him to Brunswick.

At Brunswick, Smith turned south, passing through Kassel in Hessen on his way to Ulm, Augsburg, and Munich. He may have visited Württemberg, although he does not mention Stuttgart, but his confused account makes it impossible to know. Munich was certainly his last objective before partly retracing his steps, and Augsburg evidently impressed him. But he seems to have dallied little. On he went to Hanau and Frankfurt-am-Main, the coronation city of the Holy Roman Emperors. It was at Frankfurt that the greatest book fairs in Europe were held, and the first book catalogues in the history of printing were published there. What John Smith knew about this side of Frankfurt's activities, he does not say. Fynes Moryson, his better "educated" contemporary says nothing about it, either.

After Frankfurt, Smith went to Mainz, where Gutenberg had plucked the idea of printing from the air and made it practical, and up the Rhine to Worms and Speyer — the one where Luther defended his doctrines before the Emperor Charles V, the other where the name "Protestant" was born.

John Smith's tour through Germany brought him in contact with the fountainhead of resistance to Papal authority, and with the first home of printing. The effect of this combination on his future life was to be great. Something of the soldier remained in him always, to be sure; yet only a very few years were to pass before John Smith's sword and shield were cast aside, and a sturdy pen taken up — dipped always in a well of protesting, if not "Protestant," ink.

Seventy miles up the Rhine, the fledgling gentleman came to Strassburg, an eminently Protestant city, after which he crossed "the Cardinalship" to Nancy, then capital of Lorraine. Soon he was back in France, after three years.

Cutting cross-country to Paris, then southwest to Orléans, Smith "went down the river of Loire, to Angers, and embarked himself at Nantes in Brittany, for Bilbao in Biskay." This, for once, indicates definitely what sort of means of conveyance he used. His stop at Angers, however, is unexplained, unless it was to see the famous feudal castle there, or because of its importance as a Huguenot center. Whatever the reason of his halt — if indeed it had any other reason than rest — it is apparent that Smith had by then determined to go on south to Spain. Nantes, where he took ship, was only fifty-odd miles beyond Angers.[2]

This was in a way a remarkable decision, for none of the casual Anglo-Protestant travelers of the day seem to have set foot within that monolithic Catholic state. The Spanish Inquisition was a fearful thing to brave, and not even authorized merchants always succeeded in keeping themselves safe outside its grasp. Yet John Smith calmly took passage across the Bay of Biscay, landed at Bilbao, traveled a zigzag course across the kingdom stopping at every significant town or city en route, and safely sailed from Gibraltar with no incident or observation worthy of his pen but that the Escorial (where Philip II had died five years before) was an "admired monastery." So uneventful a pilgrimage for a heretic to have enjoyed points not only to John Smith's ability to take care of himself, but also to the changed atmosphere since James I had succeeded Elizabeth I — and Philip III, Philip II.

By the beginning of 1604, twenty years after Elizabeth had peremptorily dismissed Ambassador Mendoza from England, both sides were war-weary. By then also James had been on the throne long enough to begin preliminary negotiations toward peace. (There had been abortive talks even under Elizabeth, in 1600.) News of these doings may have been circulated in Paris as early as April, by which time it can be assumed that John Smith had arrived there, and he probably heard rumblings of "secret" negotiations. Prospects of peace would in any case make travel less dangerous than it had been, encouraging Smith to visit His Catholic Majesty's dominions, uninvited. His education, his learning-by-travel, continues.[3]

At Gibraltar, a Spanish rock then, John Smith took ship for Ceuta, the other "Pillar of Hercules," which had been incorporated into the Spanish Empire after the death of Cardinal-King Henry along with all the rest of what had once been Portuguese. The spirit of adventure was again upon him, and he sailed out into the Atlantic, at first only to Tangier. Then he went on to Safi, at the time the most important port of the Kingdom of Morocco and less than a hundred miles from Marrakesh, the capital. The anchorage there was then protected on the north only, leaving the roadstead open to sudden and strong squalls from the southwest. This notwithstanding, not only did John Smith's coastwise vessel anchor there, but also a French man-of-war, along with other ships. John Smith, possibly remembering his attempts to find such a man-of-war in the Gulf of St.-Malo, got acquainted with the captain.

Perhaps with some vague notion of a little more soldiering in mind, perhaps merely as an adventure, he determined to go inland, to the capital, "to see the ancient monuments of that large renowned City." To go alone was impractical, if not foolhardy, however — even for so courageous a captain as John Smith. He therefore approached his friend, the French captain, and the two of them, with a dozen more (sailors, perhaps) made the trip.

But Marrakesh was but a shadow of the proud, populous metropolis it had been a few centuries before, and as for fighting, as Smith wrote, whatever there might have been was obviously "perfidious, treacherous, bloody murders rather than war." They did not stay long, but returned to Safi, where Smith accepted an invitation "to try some other conclusions at sea."

What expectations John Smith's restless soul envisioned beyond the horizon of the future when he took ship for Safi, when he rode up to Marrakesh, and when he temporarily cast his lot with the French captain, are secrets which lie buried with his body. Perhaps he had no clear idea himself and was trusting to luck to toss something his way. Perhaps the captain was going back to France after trying the "conclusions." All Smith says is that "he was animated by some friends." Elsewhere, he intimates that, had the moral climate been purer, he might have fought with the "right" side (of course!) against the "wrong" in the struggle for power between three brothers, with the throne of Morocco as prize. The only clear, although unsubstantiated, fact is that John Smith "and two or three more" accepted the invitation of the French captain to a junket aboard ship. Smith calls his host "Merham," which may represent the French name Mairan, or the like, influenced by the place-name Mareham, not far from John Smith's Willoughby.

As the evening wore on, a storm blew up, Smith writes, and before midnight the man-of-war was forced "to let slip cable and anchor, and put to sea." In such a roadstead, this was not surprising. But the continuance of the wind from the wrong direction, which forced them to spoon before it three hundred miles out into the Atlantic, combined with "Merham"'s invitation to try conclusions with him, seems to hint that the storm was added to the account to cover the bald fact that Merham sailed his man-of-war deliberately into waters where he had no business being, but where some lucrative prospect might lurk. (Such an escapade might have been called piratical.) These waters surged and splashed around the Spanish-held shores of those earthly bits of paradise known as the Canary Islands. And when they were becalmed in those waters, as developed, Merham, Smith, and the other guests (plus the sailors) "accommodated themselves, hoping this strange accident might yet produce some good event." The meaning shines brightly through the veil.

It was not long before the intruding Frenchman "took" a bark loaded with wine, Canary wine, from Tenerife. Then, having tasted blood, metaphorically speaking, he chased three or four more innocent traders, capturing two. The yield in goods, liquid and solid, was little, but the passengers of one bark let Merham know that five Dutch men-of-war were on the prowl not far away, thirsting for similar booty, or more. A lumbering Spanish merchant vessel might have aroused his curiosity; five nimble Dutch ships were something to avoid, quickly. The Dutch had little reason to love the French at the time, for many reasons which might be described as "of state." The high seas were no place for Merham to make a test of these particular Dutchmen.

Merham fled for Cape Bojador and the coast of Africa. Once there, he veered toward the cape called Cabo de Não, or Nun, or Noa, today of uncertain identity, from which he obviously hoped to regain Safi without risk. Before he reached that goal, however, his lookout spotted two sail of ships. Outrunning him, they were soon practically abreast. Merham, putting on a bold face, hailed them, asking who they were.* "Very civilly," Smith writes, "they danced their topsails, and desired the man-of-war to come aboard them and take what he would; for they were but two poor, distressed Bis-

* Since international "signals" were not yet known, this implies that they were close enough for messages to be bawled across the water.

cayners." The Frenchman, whom Smith calls an "old fox," was not
to be taken in by this. He realized that he was much too close to
danger — "in the lion's paws," in fact. He sprang his luff, as seamen
say, and headed into the wind as closely as he could, with all sails
set. But there was no escape. The battle was on.

John Smith's description of it, written years later, however ornamented by terms and turns of phrase he could hardly have known
in 1604, merits quoting:

> The other [the admiral, or larger ship] tacked after him,
> and came up close to his nether quarter, gave his broad-
> side, and so luffed up to windward; the Vice-Admiral did
> the like; and at the next bout, the Admiral with a noise of
> trumpets, and all his ordnance, murderers [small cannon],
> and muskets, boarded him on his broadside; the other in
> like manner on his lee quarter, that it was so dark, there
> was little light, but fire and smoke. Long he stayed not,
> before he fell off, leaving 4. or 5. of his men sprawling
> over the grating.*
>
> After they had battered Merham about an hour, they
> boarded him again as before; and threw four kedgers or
> grapnels in iron chains, then sheering off they thought so
> to have torn down the grating; but the Admiral's yard was
> so entangled in their shrouds, Merham had time to dis-
> charge two crossbar shot amongst them, and divers bolts
> of iron made for that purpose, against his bow, that made
> such a breach, he feared they both should have sunk for
> company. So that the Spaniard was as yare [nimble,
> quick] in slipping his chained grapnels, as Merham was in
> cutting the tackling [that] kept fast their yards in his
> shrouds. The Vice-Admiral presently cleared himself, but
> spared neither his ordnance nor muskets to keep Merham
> from getting away till the Admiral had repaired his leak.
>
> From twelve at noon, till six at night, they thus inter-
> changed one volly for another; then the Vice-Admiral fell
> a-stern, staying for the Admiral that came up again to him,
> and all that night stood after Merham, that shaped his

---

* The open woodwork cover for the hatchway.

course for Mamora [Mehdia, 200 miles north of Safi], but such small way they made, the next morning they were not three leagues off from Cape Noa.

By then the Frenchman knew that he had run across two Spanish warships which, if they could not take him, would sink him. The fact that they clung to him all night showed their intention. By daylight, they renewed their attack, and after an hour's bombardment called on Merham to surrender to the King of Spain, "upon fair quarter." The Frenchman "drank to them" in metaphor and sarcasm by discharging his quarter pieces, or ordnance placed toward the stern.

At this insult, the Spaniards boarded the Frenchman again, determined to take it by main force. The French fought back, tooth and nail, until an explosion set fire to the ship. The Spaniards then cleared themselves "with all speed," thinking the ship about to sink, but Merham's men succeeded in quenching the fire. Under a hail of shot from the Spaniards, they even covered the open places with old sails, and "prepared themselves to fight to the last man." Seeing this, the Spaniards hung out a flag of truce, the sincerity of which may well be questioned, but the Frenchman was not to be caught. He cut loose with all his ordnance, which he seemed to use with more advantage than did the Spaniards. "Thus," Smith concludes, "they spent the next afternoon, and half that night; when the Spaniards either lost them, or left them."

Merham had lost twenty-seven men killed, and sixteen wounded. His ship had taken one hundred forty great shot, yet still rode the waves. One wounded Spaniard, whom "they kept alive" (think of the implications of the phrase!), confessed that the admiral had lost a hundred men, and was so damaged that the crew feared it would sink before it reached a port, any port. Such were the results of Captain "Merham" 's cruise.

Laconically, after this petty paroxysm of human fury in three cockleshells upon the boundless ocean, Smith tells how they repaired their sails and uneventfully once more reached the roadstead of Safi. What day or month or year it was, he does not trouble to say. As if he wanted to turn the page of his earlier life quickly, he writes but six words to finish "the whole course of my passages," as he described his autobiography: "and then he returned into England." [4]

John Smith's apprenticeship under the hard master, Experience, ended off the coast of Africa. For simplicity's sake, we may say that it ended with his twenty-fourth year. No one knows. But certain it is that Destiny by then had shaped the future for John Smith. A new lodestar was faintly twinkling for him over England. Its name: VIRGINIA.

# PART II

# Colonist

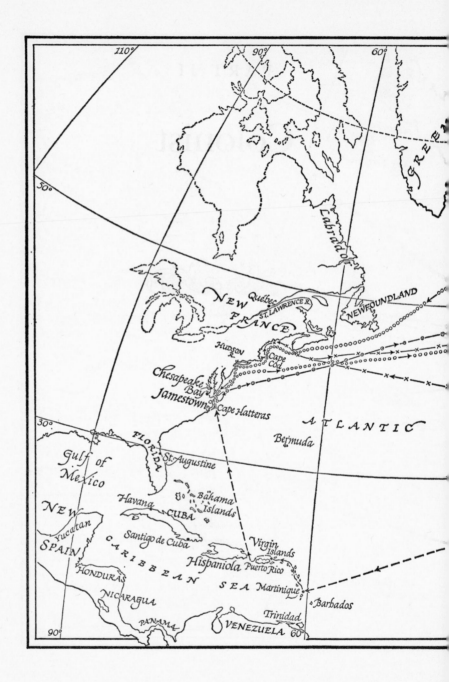

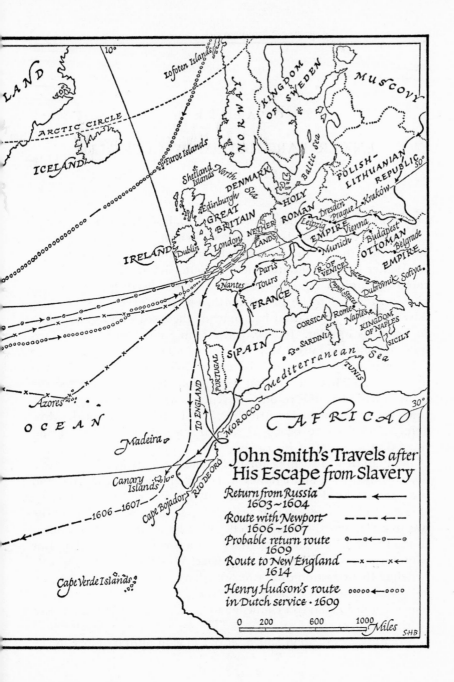

LAND

10°

Lofoten Islands

ARCTIC CIRCLE

ICELAND

Faroe Islands

NORWAY

KINGDOM OF SWEDEN

MUSCOVY

Baltic Sea

Shetland Islands

North Sea

DENMARK

POLISH-LITHUANIAN REPUBLIC

50°

Edinburgh

GREAT BRITAIN

NETHER-LANDS

HOLY ROMAN EMPIRE

Dresden

Prague

Kraków

IRELAND

Dublin

London

Leipzig

Vienna

Budapest

OTTOMAN

Belgrade

Paris

Munich

R. OF VENICE

Dubrovnik

Sofiya.

EMPIRE

Nantes

Tours

FRANCE

Papal States

Rome

Corsica

Naples

Azores

OCEAN

SPAIN

PORTUGAL

TO ENGLAND

Sardinia

KINGDOM OF NAPLES

SICILY

Mediterranean Sea

Madeira

Morocco

AFRICA

30°

TUNIS

Canary Islands

Cape Bojador

RIO DE ORO

## John Smith's Travels after His Escape from Slavery

1606—1607

Cape Verde Islands

*Return from Russia* 1603~1604   ——◄——

*Route with Newport* 1606~1607   – – –◄– –

*Probable return route* 1609   ◦—◄—◦—◦

*Route to New England* 1614   ×——×◄

*Henry Hudson's route in Dutch service · 1609*   ◦◦◦◦◦◄—◦◦◦◦

0   200   600   1000 Miles

S·H·B

CHAPTER 6

# ENTER BARTHOLOMEW GOSNOLD

VIRGINIA, when James I succeeded Elizabeth I, was a vast country, ill-defined and worse known, which stretched from Spanish Florida to the international fishing-waters of Newfoundland. Sir Walter Ralegh had attempted to found Roanoke Colony in the south of Virginia in 1584–1587, but that was dead; a great Indian city was reputed to lie in the north, but that never existed. Few adventurers of any nation had touched the coast of Virginia, none had seen its interior. Indeed, when John Smith went out of England to fight the Turks, Virginia seemed almost forgotten.

Yet within two years of his return, John Smith sailed for the almost forgotten land with an expedition that was to change the course of history: the colonizing venture which planted at Jamestown the first permanent British colony in the New World. How John Smith came to take part in that expedition is the next and most vital question of his career.

John Smith was turning (or had turned) twenty-five by the time his combined Iliad and Odyssey was over. In terms of life lived and life yet-to-be-lived as then conceived, he was practically on the threshold of middle age.[1] It was a matter of now or never, if he was to make something of himself. That he would not settle down to the life of a Lincolnshire farmer was a foregone conclusion. But why, among several choices, did he select Virginia?

Before that question can be answered, a broader one must be put. Why was there a "Virginia" to choose? What made all that that name signified embody a challenge to be taken up at enormous risk of life and treasure?

A century before John Smith set out to gain military glory in the

Low Countries, John and Sebastian Cabot crossed the North Atlantic to be the first Englishmen to sight the New World. Vikings had been there long before, but had left little or no trace of their stay. The Cabots left no trace, either, but it was not long before sailors from many European lands began to follow in their wake, to fish (mostly for cod) off the coast of the *New-found-land* which they had discovered. England was peculiarly slow to take advantage of the Cabot discovery, although it had been made under authority granted by Henry VII, and while Spain and Portugal built up empires in America, English merchants contented themselves, so to speak, with trading voyages in the Atlantic which, due to Iberian monopolistic claims, came to border on rank piracy. Any permanent English settlement in America was hardly foreseen, even in a dream.

At last in 1577, just eighty years after the Cabot voyage, a first English plan got under way to "occupy and enjoy" certain lands not held by any Christian prince — in other words, to start a colony. In the following year, Queen Elizabeth granted Sir Humphrey Gilbert of Devon, in the West Country, letters patent to this end. The project failed, for a variety of reasons, and Sir Humphrey died at sea, in 1583. Thereupon his younger half-brother, Sir Walter Ralegh, threw the weight of his influence and fortune behind another project, which planted an ephemeral English colony at Roanoke, in today's North Carolina, and gave the name *Virginia,* after (and with the permission of) the Virgin Queen, to the territories discovered.

War with Spain had broken out in 1585, with its climax in the Invincible Armada of 1588 but with its end long delayed. Under such circumstances, no really determined effort could be, or was, made to reinforce the "Lost Colony" in 1588 or after — or even to find out if it still existed. The Queen and her Council were by then too occupied with Irish rebellions, the Dutch War of Independence, the struggles of Henry IV in France, and finally the insane rebellion of the Earl of Essex that ended in his execution on Ash Wednesday, 1601.

In the meanwhile, however, privateering voyages to the West Indies kept the route to Virginia "open," not the least of which were those undertaken by privateer Captain Christopher Newport,

of Limehouse by London, who had helped Sir Francis Drake when
he "singed the Spanish King's beard." His was soon to be a decisive
role in Virginia history. At the same time, Ralegh, who was in
financial straits, transferred his Virginia patent to others, including
Richard Hakluyt, "consultant geographer" now as well as canon of
Bristol, and Thomas Smythe, outstanding London merchant. Hakluyt was to become the greatest propagandist of Virginia in all
England, and Smythe its sturdiest backer. For reasons which are not
even surmisable, this group took no action for a dozen years, but
it was ready to step in at the proper time.

In 1596 England turned from the defensive to the offensive, in the
famous raid on Cádiz. Philip of Spain attempted to retaliate, but
his fleet was destroyed by a storm. Undismayed, he wrote his
nephew (and son-in-law) the Archduke Albert, Governor of the
Netherlands, on the last day of the year to attack England *without*
any fleet. This may be called the pathetic end of Spanish efforts to
dominate the seas so far as England was concerned. The next year,
England attempted conquest of Puerto Rico, but failed; and the
year after that Philip II died. English privateering and raiding
continued.[2]

Then early in 1602, while Christopher Newport was again raiding the Spanish West Indies, a "small bark of Dartmouth," in
Devon, slipped all unannounced out of Falmouth harbor with
thirty-two persons aboard, and with sails set for a quick crossing,
God willing, to America. Its captain was a young Suffolk gentleman
named Bartholomew Gosnold — the herald of a fresh start at colonization.

That same year 1602 saw also a reconnaissance voyage sent out by
Ralegh to the site of the Roanoke Colony — a failure — and
another trial voyage to the northwest in search of a passage over the
top of North America to China — also a failure. Then the following spring Gosnold's co-captain of 1602, Bartholomew Gilbert (a
cousin), sailed for Virginia — to be killed by Indians there — while
his shipmaster of 1602 took off with Captain Martin Pring for what
is today New England. What Gosnold himself was doing at the
time is not known, but both his voyage of 1602 and Pring's of 1603
were successful, if not startlingly remunerative. All these scurryings
across the Atlantic were as swallows, harbingers of a new springtime

of colonial activity. But with the death of the Old Queen came a brief rest, while England waited to see what sort of a man King James I would be.

An outbreak of the plague delayed matters somewhat in 1603, so that it was Christmas before the new royal family was assembled near London. In the meantime, Sir Walter Ralegh was caught in a trap well set by his enemies at Court, and the King was occupied with such things as the Peace Conference he called with Spain, and the Hampton Court Conference which led to the new translation of the Bible. Nevertheless, a voyage for the plantation of Guiana set out under a mariner who had previously attempted a colony in Newfoundland — Captain Charles Leigh — and Thomas Smythe was knighted and sent off to Muscovy as James's ambassador. Peace came in August, and on October 24 James assumed the style "King of Great Britain, etc.," as Queen Elizabeth (unbeknown to James) had suggested three years before: "the King of Scotland," she said, "would become one day King of Great Britain." With that, the century-long process of uniting England and Scotland began.

Obviously, although there is no record of what went on, the promoters of colonization were at work all through 1604, for in March, 1605, the last private "trial-balloon" voyage was sent to Virginia by the Earl of Southampton (Shakespeare's patron) and his Roman Catholic brother-in-law, Lord Arundell of Wardour. Captain George Waymouth (or Weymouth) was in command — the same who had commanded the voyage in search of the northwest passage in 1602. On his safe return, four months later, Waymouth brought much valuable information, but above all landed five kidnapped Indians in England, whose significance became astoundingly vital. By then John Smith was already caught up in the idea that was to hold him for life, and by then the need for sound planning for a colony — along with solid financial backing and royal approval — was at last recognized. In short, it was time for *effective* settlement. John Smith dedicated the rest of his life to just that objective.

The change from exploration to settlement and from narrow, individualistic to corporate, joint-stock financing was due basically to the awakening interest of the merchants, to which a few specific points lent tone. Excuses for planting colonies became molded into reasons.

Legitimate trade had already begun on a small scale — furs and the like. Fishing was already a profitable industry. But the lure of valuable raw materials — even gold, hopefully — was more important. Economically, colonization was sound.

Politically, although the war with Spain was over in 1604, an English foothold or beachhead here and there along the fifteen-hundred miles of unoccupied coastline between Florida and Newfoundland was still an important strategic consideration. France, of course, had claimed "Canada," without permanent occupation.

Geographically, and commercially, it was important that the virtually unknown North American Atlantic coast be explored for possible westward routes to the Far East. An eastward route had been found in the 1560's as far as Persia, by the waterways of the White Sea, the Northern Dviná, and the Volga, with minor portages in central Muscovy. The same sort of river system might exist in North America, and in that case it would be possible to sail up a navigable river to a portage (presumably known to the savages living there), where goods could be carried briefly across land to the headwaters of a river that flowed down to "the other sea" — the Pacific. But a permanent settlement had to be established before these possibilities could be explored.

Lastly, there was a wonderful opportunity to convert many heathen peoples to the true faith of the Anglican Church. Though there was less stress in England than in Spain on the need for missionary work, at no time was the matter entirely overlooked or neglected. Papism particularly must be halted, kept from Virginia — native or white.[3]

Such matters as these stimulated interest once more in the colonization of the North American coast, in *Virginia*. The expansive flourishes of such individuals as Sir Humphrey Gilbert and Sir Walter Ralegh, the Earl of Southampton, and others, were ended. Careful businessmen took over, disposed to invest (or gamble) the vast sums needed, in the hope — the certainty, as they saw it — of reaping commensurate rewards, if not immediately, then in due time. John Smith stood ready to join forces, with his modest capital and his less modest determination to make something of himself.

That John Smith should have known much about Sir Walter Ralegh's Roanoke Colony before he returned to England is highly unlikely. The Spanish Armada came along at almost the same time, to overshadow every other memory of his youth. (Lincolnshire was not conspicuous for interest in colonization at the time, under any circumstances.) What boy in what country would remember anything else that happened when he was eight, if at that age his homeland was attacked by the greatest military power on earth? Would a farmer's son living several days' journey from the capital (on foot, with an occasional lift) hear of obscure privateering voyages or of plans to colonize? Would he read a huge volume, seven hundred thousand words in length, at the end of which were a few narratives telling of Virginia — Richard Hakluyt's *English Voyages,* of 1589?

Hardly. In fact, John Smith was twenty before he appears to have read much of anything outside of what was given him to read in school. His mind was almost literally virgin soil. For that reason, when the seed of the Virginia Venture was blown his way, it took root — mightily.

Nevertheless, John Smith did not merely chance upon that Venture. (It was still a rather nebulous plan when he returned to England.) To think this would be to ignore Smith's nature as blindly as the often-quoted "fit of absentmindedness" ignores the history of the British Empire. Smith's life is a continuous story of purpose in action — of something very close to that rare quality called vision. He did not run away from home to become a vagrant, nor did he abandon Sendall's countinghouse to drift. He had a purpose — that of self-advancement — which was slowly sublimated into the grander purpose of advancement of "Virginia" — of America, we should say today. In the end, that purpose became an obsession, but by then Virginia was established for all time.

A purpose, however, does not supply chronological data, and these are sorely lacking for John Smith between the unknown date of his arrival from Africa and the end of the year 1606. Nevertheless, there is considerable evidence of what he must have accomplished in that time. On that basis, with the aid of a little logic, the sequence of his activities can be fairly well established. Whether their order is entirely correct is unimportant.

One side issue can be disposed of briefly. An idle comment, recorded in scorn by an offended highborn gentleman, points to a trip by John Smith to Ireland, where "he begged like a rogue, without a license." Smith himself does not mention the event, although he refers to Irish mantles, as worn by the peasants of that country, as if he had seen them personally — but that could have been in London. In any case, if the statement was true, we must assign the Irish episode to this period, probably immediately after his return. Useless as it is to speculate on the motives for such a visit, Smith may have first thought of going to Ireland to become a colonist. A little time spent in Ireland with this in mind would have made him miss the Guiana expedition which came up next.

But the Irish had been in total and primitive turmoil for more than one generation before the arrival of Lord Deputy Mountjoy restored peace — the peace of the grave, with which John Smith was already familiar in Transylvania. Peace of this sort could not quickly wipe out the "ghastliness of famine and desolation" that reigned there, and English settlers began to move in on a small scale, here and there. John Smith may have thought of joining these — or he may have thought that sporadic warfare was still being fought. But whether it was the prospect of further military service or the idea of colonizing that attracted him, Ireland did not hold Smith long, if it held him at all. He must have been in England again very soon. In short, the Irish episode remains unproven and in a sense out of key with Smith's whole career. Nevertheless, it must be mentioned — for the record. The ground hereafter is more solid.

Everyone who has heard of Virginia has heard of Captain John Smith, usually in the company of an Indian maiden named Pocahontas. In popular history, Virginia is unthinkable without Captain Smith — although Sir Walter Ralegh was responsible for its name, and its settlement was determined on before the name reached Smith's ears. Yet John Smith came to merit the association. He himself called Virginia and New England "his children that never had a mother." (New England, named by Smith, has been noticeably reticent about acknowledging the parentage.) But he stopped there, and neither he nor anyone else has shown how John Smith came to join the Virginia Venture. The clue seems to lie in his later statement that Captain Bartholomew Gosnold, the "Pathfinder for New England," was also the prime mover of Virginia. How, then, did Smith meet Gosnold?

At twenty-five, John Smith was clearly uncertain of which way to turn. He had a little money and a farm or two of his own. Yet the excitement of four years abroad would not permit him to settle down, to be a nonentity with a Central European captain's title, shoved around by such neighboring nobles as the notorious Earl of Lincoln, or patronized by Robert Bertie, Lord Willoughby, his friend as well as neighbor. Casting about for something better to do, he heard about a relief ship being sent to Captain Charles Leigh in Guiana, where the plantation was by then a year old. Sir Oliph Leigh, the Captain's brother, was financing the expedition, and volunteers were undoubtedly accepted. But the relief ship sailed on April 12, 1605, and Smith was not on board. Laconically, he wrote, "I should have been a party to it." Nothing more.[4]

What had developed?

Accidents seem to have had little to do with John Smith's life. Only once or twice in fifty years can fate be said to have blown him off his course. Otherwise he appears to have thought out and carried out his ideas — so far as he could — with remarkable tenacity, taking advantage of propitious winds where he could, yielding to crosscurrents philosophically. The explanation of his not joining the Leigh expedition must lie in a choice of another course to pursue, and that choice was deliberately based on the opportunity offered for self-advancement. Once the choice was made, means to make it effective were provided by his friends.

In 1605 John Smith had three groups of influential friends or acquaintances in England whose names are still to be read in surviving documents. First and foremost of these were the brothers Bertie, the eldest, Robert, already seated in Parliament as the twelfth Lord Willoughby de Eresby, the next eldest later to be knighted as Sir Peregrine. Secondly, there was the Metham family, which included George, supervisor and executor of John Smith's father's will. The Methams were tied to the Berties by marriage, business, and friendship. And thirdly, there was Thomas Sendall, merchant of King's Lynn. Sendall's son married a Jenney who was a cousin of both the Bertie-Willoughby and Metham families, and there may well have been other ties.*

In other words, the three influential families known to John

* See the Commentaries for a condensed family tree.

Smith were in a sense all members of one larger clan. Evidently John Smith's father had put all his eggs in the Bertie basket. Thanks to the marriages plaited into it, that basket was ample enough to take care of John. There are only the faintest hints of outside friendships still surviving by 1605 — suspicions, not certainties.

The logical deduction from these bits of known fact would be that John Smith found his way into the Virginia Venture, or at least heard about it, through this group of families. We have John Smith's word for it that he visited Thomas Sendall, after eight years, when he got back to England. It is possible, obviously, that Sendall may have mentioned the development of colonial enterprises in London to Smith, but there is no evidence. The likelihood of unstilted conversation with the Methams on that or any other subject seems remote. Smith may well have seen George Metham or some other member of the family regarding the proper rendering of accounts to him — now that he was of age — and the formal assignment of the property owned at Great Carlton along with that held in grant from Lord Willoughby, and other such details. But any more personally friendly approach seems highly unlikely in view of Smith's known attitude toward the Methams. This leaves only the Berties as a possible source of contact between John Smith and the incipient Virginia Venture, working out, that is, from an assumption founded on logic.

As has already been mentioned, John Smith has left a clue in mentioning Bartholomew Gosnold as the primary organizer of the Venture. Gosnold, to be sure, first acquired a sort of fame by his 1602 voyage to what is now New England, but he had already had experience as a privateer in 1599. Before that (he was seven or eight years older than Smith) he seems to have been destined for the clergy, but soon took to the sea, where many a young man made fame and fortune. He was not a nobody, as John Smith was, but came of an ancient Suffolk family which had risen to local prominence through advantageous marriages — it was one way to get ahead, as it still is.

One of the most recent of these marriages was that of Bartholomew's uncle, Robert Gosnold (the third) to Ursula Naunton, whose maternal grandparents were Sir Anthony Wingfield and Elizabeth

Vere. Ursula's first cousin, Sir John Wingfield, married Robert Bertie's aunt Susan, while her fourth cousin, Mary Vere, was Robert Bertie's mother.* (If a fourth cousin sounds very remote today, Lord Macaulay has a pertinent comment: the Vere family was "the longest and most illustrious line of nobles that England has seen." This was not likely to be overlooked in 1600.) Thus, through his Aunt Ursula, Bartholomew Gosnold was twice related to John Smith's friend Robert Bertie. As if this were not enough, John Gosnold, a first cousin of Bartholomew's, married Winifred Windsor, sister-in-law to Robert Bertie's other aunt, Katherine Vere.

If Bartholomew Gosnold had been a failure, Robert Bertie might never have heard of him. But because he was anything but a failure, Robert could hardly ignore him. This need not mean that Robert saw John Smith and said, "Go talk to Gosnold!" It only means that a path to Gosnold through Bertie existed.

Assuming then that John Smith first paid a visit to Bertie, as a matter of duty, and in any case to renew a friendship interrupted only three years before, no overstretching of the imagination is needed to assume also that the matter came up of what John Smith was going to do next. Smith cannot have kept his Turkish and other adventures to himself; Robert Bertie cannot have failed to be interested.

Young Lord Willoughby was apparently a student by nature as well as by training, as is testified by his letters to his father — in Latin and in French — when he was sixteen to eighteen. He also seems to have been a careful manager of his estates. He had traveled at least in France and Italy, although his reputed military activities as a youth were later inventions to glorify his royalist service in the Civil War of the 1640's. His gentle, if determined, make-up may bear evidence that he had not forgotten in his youth that his grandfather was far from being a nobleman, or that his own position in society was due entirely to his illustrious mother and grandmother. (His father was looked down on by the Earl of Oxford, whose sister he married.) In addition, Willoughby must have had a friendly, sympathetic feeling for John Smith, whom he had seen in Europe on two occasions; in later life John Smith gives ample evidence that the feeling was mutual. The conclusion is

* See the Commentaries for family trees.

therefore unavoidable that Robert showed himself willing to help John Smith find a channel for his energy, and a way to advance himself in the world.

Although Robert Bertie's life is as full of blank spots as John Smith's, there are detailed records of his activities in the spring of 1605. His first appearance after his return from Italy and the Continent was on January 4, 1605, when he and a number of other young noblemen were made Knights of the Bath along with King James's infant son, Charles, Duke of Albany. A week later Lord Willoughby, now properly to be addressed as Sir Robert, was informed by the Lord Admiral, the Earl of Nottingham, that James had appointed him to take part in the special embassy which was to go to Spain to receive King Philip's signature on the new Peace Treaty. The last day of February, Willoughby married Elizabeth Montagu, of a distinguished family. (In later years, John Montagu, Earl of Sandwich, gave his name to a famous article of diet.) And by March 26, Willoughby and the balance of a magnificent retinue were gliding down the Medway en route to La Coruña. It was early July before they returned.

If it seems difficult to find time in which Robert Lord Willoughby could have helped John Smith personally, his brother Peregrine could have served equally well as a contact, and it is pointless to speculate on the details. It is enough that Willoughby was in England, and Smith was in England. Whether they met in London, where Robert had a mansion by the Barbican Tower, or in Lincolnshire, a meeting there must have been, and that meeting bears every evidence of having led to an acquaintance between John Smith and Bartholomew Gosnold.

Gosnold himself is unaccounted for between the end of 1602 and the spring of 1605, but by March of that year he is known to have been in Suffolk with his family. Thus, by the time Bertie is married and off on a mission to Spain, the mist of conjecture begins to lift, and Smith and Gosnold are working together.

By way of further confirmation of the approximate date when John Smith met Gosnold, there is the statement in Smith's autobiography to the effect that eight years elapsed between his farewell to Merchant Sendall (not later than 1597) and the next time he saw him. Then, the earliest account of Smith's participation in the Virginia Venture, edited by Smith (if not written by him, in part), adds the information that he and Gosnold waited a year before Gosnold's projects got royal approval. The royal approval bears the date April 10, 1606. In this way, both the autobiography and the surviving account point to the spring of 1605 as the time when Gosnold and Smith joined hands. This also fits in with the surmised date of John Smith's return to England.[5]

Gosnold's project was the effective settlement of Virginia. John Smith saw, or was persuaded to see, in this a greater, or more congenial, opportunity than in the Guiana relief expedition. This is apparently all that he meant when he wrote that he "should have" joined Captain Charles Leigh.

In Gosnold, the gradual emergence of the idea of planting a colony is apparent. What stimulus prompted this is part of Gosnold's story, not Smith's; but his gradual veering from the law to the sea, and from spoliation to exploration to colonization is clear. Possessed of youth, enthusiasm, and experience, Gosnold became the visible fulcrum for the final Virginia project.

John Smith was unaware, always, of the importance of the lever — the legal and financial backing — that got the voyage going. All he saw or cared about was the fulcrum. Therefore he, or some associate strongly influenced by him, wrote:

> Captain Bartholomew Gosnold, the first mover of this plantation, having many years solicited many of his friends, but found small assistants [assistance], at last prevailed with some Gentlemen, as Master Edward Maria Wingfield, Captain John Smith, and divers others, who depended a year upon his projects; but nothing could be effected, till by their great charge and industry it came to be apprehended by certain of the Nobility, Gentry, and Merchants, so that his Majesty, by his letters patent, gave commission for establishing Councils, to direct here, and to govern and to execute there.

There is no mention of the backers who made the "plantation" possible. Nevertheless, although Smith is wrong in historical emphasis, from his point of view he is basically right. The research of the past fifteen years has revealed the connection between the prime-movership of Gosnold and the guidance and support of the mercantile (and other) interests, without which nothing effective could have been accomplished.

Gosnold was not named in the original Virginia Charter, the "royal approval" of 1606. His historical obscurity makes him seem almost out of place, compared with the group which finally backed the undertaking. Yet it is quite conceivable that the idea as it was formulated was his, and so apparently irrelevant a source as the parish register of Latton, a village fifteen miles northeast of London, supplies the explanation of how this came about. The register records the marriage, in 1595, of Bartholomew Gosnold and Mary Golding.

Mary Golding's father was Robert Golding, a connection of Robert Bertie's grandmother, the Countess of Oxford. Mary's mother was Martha Judde, whose half sister, Alice, married the collector of customs of the Port of London, Thomas Smythe — "Mr. Customer Smythe," as he is known to history. Alice and Mr. Smythe had, among other children, a son also named Thomas who grew up to be one of London's greatest merchants.*

Knighted by King James in 1603, Sir Thomas quickly rose to political as well as financial importance. (As a result, his family changed the spelling from Smith to the more imposing *Smythe,* which is useful for the story of Captain John Smith.) Former Governor of the Muscovy Company, and a founder of both the Levant and the East India Company, and almost continuous Governor of the latter, Sir Thomas had many mariners at his beck and call, but none so familiar with the coast of Virginia (the New England end of it) as the young man who married his cousin Mary Golding. Excluding such independent privateers as Captain Christopher Newport, Bartholomew Gosnold was one of the few Englishmen who had so much as seen North America recently. Furthermore, Gosnold appears to have been liked and guided by the great "expansionists," Richard Hakluyt the geographer and Edward Hayes the explorer. (Hayes lived at the house of Sir Thomas's sister and her husband.) For a number of reasons it appears practically certain that Hayes would have backed, and did back, Gosnold's projects, as would Richard Hakluyt, especially

* See the Commentaries for a table of the relationship.

before Sir Thomas. This calls up a picture of Gosnold, returned from his 1602 expedition, setting to work to interest his wife's cousin in another, bigger, expedition to Virginia, with the support mentioned.

Before John Smith came along, however, Sir Thomas was sent to Muscovy as special Ambassador to treat with Tsar Boris Godunov on matters of trade privileges. The significance of Sir Thomas in the plan is underlined by the small progress Gosnold made during his absence, other than in the matter of assembling companions suitable to accompany him when the day came. John Smith was one of the first of these.

About the same time, perhaps even a little before, Gosnold interested an older cousin by the name of Edward Maria Wingfield in the idea. Smith credits him with being another of the first organizers of the Virginia Venture.

Meanwhile, the Earl of Southampton's reconnaissance ship, mentioned some pages back, had sailed to New England and returned. On July 18, 1605, Captain George Waymouth brought her safely into Dartmouth harbor with five kidnapped Indians aboard. On Waymouth's arrival, the Governor of Plymouth Fort (thirty miles to the west), for reasons which are anything but clear, relieved Waymouth of the Indians. This gentleman, whose protective authority extended far beyond Dartmouth, was Sir Ferdinando Gorges, an ex-soldier who had fought under Robert Bertie's father, Lord Willoughby, and by sheerest chance had been made prisoner with Edward Maria Wingfield in 1588. Although this sharing of prison life may have had some almost imponderable influence on later events, in July, 1605, Sir Ferdinando was interested only in the Indians.

Keeping three of them with him at Plymouth, Gorges sent the other two to London, to the Lord Chief Justice of England, Sir John Popham. The reasons are again obscure, but the matter of the legality of kidnapping Indians may have entered his mind. However it was, the Lord Chief Justice was immediately interested. (It is amusing to conjure up a picture of the huge, pompous old man, swathed in a mountainous scarlet robe, granting audience to two naked Algonkians in leather breechclouts and moccasins.) The presence of these aborigines seemed suddenly to remind

Popham of the existence of vast lands beyond the seas, and of plans regarding them already being formulated, so he had heard, by certain "undertakers, gentlemen merchants, etc." He foresaw, he said, "in the experience of his place the infinite numbers of cashiered captains and soldiers, of poor artisans that would and cannot work, and idle vagrants that may and will not work, whose increase threatens the State . . ." And, in brief, he announced in connection with the quoted rambling thoughts that he was "affectionately bent to the plantation of Virginia."

Up to the arrival of the Indians, then, the efforts of Gosnold, aided by Edward Maria Wingfield and Captain John Smith, and others not mentioned, *and* the conferences held in inconspicuousness if not in downright secrecy by the merchants, had led to little. Now, however, according to Sir Ferdinando Gorges, the Indians became an all-important factor in the success of the Virginia project. Waymouth, he specified,

> brought five of the Natives . . . whom I seized upon; they were all of one nation, but of several parts and several families; this accident must be acknowledged the means under God of putting on foot, and giving life to all our Plantations.

By that time, even outside of official circles, interest in Virginia was rapidly spreading. Ben Jonson, Shakespeare's great rival, had in those very days collaborated with George Chapman and John Marston in writing and producing *Eastward Ho!* — a satire on a penniless knight who married money and hoped to run away with the dowry to Virginia, "as pleasant a country as ever the sun shined on." The play was surely not intended as Virginia propaganda, but by reflecting public interest it suggests the state of enthusiasm for Virginia which prevailed in the late summer of 1605.

About the same time, Sir Thomas Smythe returned from Muscovy. Immediately, almost, he seems to have turned his attention to the matter of Virginia. Swayed by Smythe and his associates, and very likely by Hakluyt, Lord Chief Justice Popham abandoned his original vagrant-dumping-ground notions for America, and worked out a feasible, dignified basis for a charter of incorporation. Virginia was to be settled, at last, under the auspices of a joint-stock company. In that way, and under these auspices, Gosnold's long-delayed plan to return to America began to materialize. With that plan, John Smith's superabundant energies and limited capital found a lifelong objective.

Seldom has a man dedicated himself so unswervingly to, or so completely identified himself with, any single "glorious possibility" as John Smith did. Indeed, when that possibility came to him, Smith seized it without hesitation. His choice was sound, too. For a year later, the son of Lord Willoughby's "poor tenant" would be one of those to govern in Virginia.[6]

CHAPTER 7

# FORMING THE BAND

THE MERE FACT that the "Nobilitie, Gentrie and Marchants" began to interest themselves in the Virginia Venture before the end of 1605 does not mean that surviving records give a clear picture of what went on. Sir John Popham certainly got interested shortly after the return of Waymouth with his five Indians in July. Five or six months later, the Privy Council instructed Popham and Second Secretary Sir John Herbert to call together those they thought proper to discuss the proposed plantation. But beyond such indefinitely dated evidence, there is virtually no firm fact before the signing of the Charter. As to John Smith, there is no documented evidence at all. Nevertheless, there are certain guideposts which indicate remarkably well what he must have been doing. Smith began active work on the Virginia project, according to his own story, a year before April 10, 1606; but that is surely only a rough indication. Fairly certain it is that Smith and Gosnold began their collaboration by May, 1605, at the latest. Early in July, Lord Willoughby returned from Spain with the Lord Admiral and the rest of the special embassy, bearing King Philip's signature on the Peace Treaty. Less than a fortnight later, George Waymouth arrived from America with his Indians. About the same time *Eastward Ho!* was presented, and by mid-September its authors were in prison because of passages allegedly slandering the Scots. Sir Thomas Smythe got back from Muscovy by September 20, and before the end of that same month Captain Christopher Newport presented his homage along with two young crocodiles from Santo Domingo to His Majesty. What was more important, the Lord Chief Justice by then was presumably at work, drafting the Charter. All was going well, on the imperturbable surface.

Underneath, it was not. Right in the midst of the negotiations for the Charter, the most appalling might-have-been in English history all but destroyed the government of Great Britain. The Gunpowder Plot that promised to blow up King and Parliament alike was literally snuffed out a matter of hours before the fuse would have been lighted to send the House of Lords' Chamber flying high into the November air, in "a roaring, a thundering sin of fire and brimstone."

It was the unfortunate climax of the religious repression of Roman Catholics. Because of it the tolerance, so ardently wanted, could not be had for many and many a year. The Virginia adventurers were in no way involved — with minor exceptions — yet the plot had its harvest in the delay in getting the Charter signed.

The Gunpowder Plot eliminated one of the major groups interested in colonization — the Catholics who had brought the Indians to England and virtually started it all. But the Charter was at last signed ten weeks later, and preparations for the Virginia voyage could get under way "officially." These involved from the beginning the choice of a ship-captain to lead the expedition.

Although Bartholomew Gosnold was undoubtedly qualified for this position, he was too young. A man was needed who could command respect as well as maintain discipline, and who could be counted on to carry out orders from London unquestioningly. (The establishment of an American colony right on the heels of the new Peace Treaty with Spain involved international sensitivities.) Christopher Newport, he of the crocodiles, was chosen — for his experience in West Indian waters and his demonstrated knowledge of navigation, to which may be added his known courage in the face of attack. Bartholomew Gosnold apparently willingly took the post of second-in-command.[1]

As to John Smith's occupations during these months, later events supply a few details. These may be summed up as collaboration with Gosnold in the planning, and in the making of new acquaintances through whom he added materially to his education by acquiring some of the special skills needed for the Virginia Venture. In doing this, he laid the groundwork for the human contacts — the associations and friendships — that surrounded him in later life. That he did not specifically acknowledge his debt to those from whom he learned is not surprising. He was too busy promoting Virginia to write memoirs until he was too old to remember. One of Smith's important acquaintances dates from this period, without question. This was Henry Hudson, the immortal navigator of the river and bay that bear his name. In fact it was John Smith who later inspired Hudson with the idea of exploring the river. Here is how Emanuel van Meteren told the story in 1610:

> . . . the [Dutch] East India Company . . . [employed] a skilful English pilot named Henry Hudson . . .
> This Henry Hudson sailed from Texel on April 6, 1609, and doubled the Cape of Norway on May 5 . . . [but the cold was so great that the sailors rebelled, and Hudson then gave them the choice between two alternatives]. The first was to go to forty degrees [of latitude] on the coast of America, being mostly induced to this by letters and maps which one Captain Smit[h] had sent him from *Virginia,* by means of which he indicated to him a sea, [making it possible] to sail around their southern colony on the north, and from there to go into a western sea, which, if it were thus (for experience up to now shows the contrary), would have been a very profitable thing, and a short route for sailing to the Indies.

The implications of this passage are not only that John Smith had friends among the experienced mariners before he sailed for Virginia, but also that he knew how to draw maps, and was sufficiently informed on matters geographical to be familiar with the "received standard" conceptions and misconceptions of the day.

It is to be surmised that Smith met Henry Hudson somehow through Gosnold's "cousin," Sir Thomas Smythe, and the Muscovy Company. Hudson, a far mistier figure than Smith, first appears on the records of history as attending a Holy Communion Service at the Church of St. Ethelburga in London on April 19, 1607. He was about to go to sea, financed by the Muscovy Company, "for to discover a passage by the North Pole to Japan and China." (John Smith and the other colonists were nearing Chesapeake Bay by then, but to many sound Londoners Hudson's voyage was no more absurd than the Virginia Venture.)

Since Hudson was in command of this North Pole project, he

must already have been a mariner of proven capabilities. Such a person would hardly have been on the lookout for a talkative landlubber like John Smith, who was but little older than his son Oliver. But John Smith had good reasons for seeking out a friend among mariners from whom he could learn. What did he want to learn? Among other things, perhaps map-drawing.

No map drawn by Hudson survives, yet there are charts clearly based on sketches by him. These testify to the accuracy of his surveys of coastlines and so on. No map drawn by John Smith survives either, yet he supplied the detail for the map of Virginia that bears his name. It testifies to at least equally accurate surveying.

This makes it seem likely that John Smith studied surveying or charting under, or with the aid of, somebody in London before he left. It is logically probable that that somebody, as has been stated above, was Henry Hudson. If it was, then it becomes evident that Smith sent Hudson a copy of the results of his first surveys in acknowledgment of a debt — and probably to show off a little. (Only to Sir Thomas Smythe is he known to have sent another copy.)

These sketch-maps of 1608 were supplemented by a written report of importance to Hudson and to Sir Thomas alike, for a persistent geographical hypothesis of the times was that a navigable northwest passage existed over North America to China. Smith sent (mistaken) support for the hypothesis from Virginia, by reporting that the Virginia Indians said the head of Chesapeake Bay "seemed to be a mighty River issuing from mighty Mountains betwixt the two Seas." This misinformation guided Hudson to New York Bay, and the Hudson River.

More important to Smith than Hudson, however, was Richard Hakluyt, with whom Smith hints he was acquainted, and who was a friend and benefactor of Bartholomew Gosnold. Indeed, in the very days in which Gosnold was planning the Virginia Venture, Hakluyt was studying once more the known routes to and along the North American coast. Smith, evidently insatiable in his thirst for helpful knowledge, could understandably have wanted to meet the geographer, and there is no reason to suppose that he did not. At the same time, there is also no reason to suppose that John Smith sat long hours at the feet of Richard Hakluyt to learn all about geography and navigation, history and heroes of the sea. Hakluyt was a very busy man.

Less busy was an English wanderer who returned about then, like Smith, with news of Tartary and other distant places. This was a descendant of the ancient and prolific family of Berkeley, a merchant by the name of George. Somehow, George Berkeley (or Barkley, as he spelled it) ran across the Reverend Samuel Purchas, vicar of the village of Eastwood in Essex, near the mouth of the Thames and today almost engulfed by the resort town of South-end-on-Sea. How Berkeley met either Smith or Purchas is not known, but it has been suggested that Berkeley brought the other two together. That Berkeley knew Purchas in 1605 is certain. That Smith knew Purchas before 1612 is equally certain, and it is possible that the acquaintance may date back to 1605 or 1606. And, although Smith is nowhere specific about the matter, there are hints that Smith knew Berkeley.

Another uncertain, but logically to be postulated, acquaintance of this period was a man whom Smith calls "that learned Mathematician, Master Thomas Hariot." Hariot, formerly associated with Sir Walter Ralegh, had recently joined the staff (to use modern, if anachronistic, expressions for both relationships) of Henry Percy, Earl of Northumberland and one of the richest and most prominent noblemen in all England.

While he was in Ralegh's employ, Hariot had spent the year 1585–1586 in what is now North Carolina, had assembled an enormous amount of scientific information of all sorts, and — by no means least of all — had apparently learned a good deal about the language spoken by the Indians there. In fact, he compiled a list of words, a small dictionary, which has unfortunately been lost. John Smith showed such familiarity with Hariot's work, and so many of the Indian words occurring in Smith's writings are to be found also in surviving texts by Hariot, that it is arguable that Smith learned some Algonkian words from Hariot. Added to this is the plausible theory that Hariot interviewed the Indians brought back by Waymouth, who spoke an Algonkian language not too dissimilar to that of North Carolina and Virginia, and who were still in or near London at least until August, 1606. It would hardly be reasonable to rule out the likelihood of one or more meetings between Gosnold or Smith and these Indians. An interview or two with Hariot would provide a clue to the fact that Smith landed in Virginia possessed of more insight into what the Indians said and meant, and what their intentions were, than any of his associates during his whole stay in Virginia.[2]

While Smith was occupied with such matters as these — possibly even before — Bartholomew Gosnold's mentor (if that is not too strong a word), Edward Hayes, had approached Cecil as early as September, 1605, with a plan for the expedition: "a project of piety, charity, profit, opportunity, honour, concerning God, people distressed, King and commonwealth . . ." etc. This plan involved bringing Parliament into the picture. Though it was not adopted, it was significant because it probably broadened and strengthened the foundations for the plan that was adopted. Richard Hakluyt also had wanted public financing for any project of the sort, but had not suggested Parliamentary cooperation. In the end it was left for Lord Chief Justice Popham to reach the needed compromise, a joint-stock company.

There were other difficulties, however, before the project could be presented, with the blessing of the "lower level," for the King's approval. Three divergent groups were interested, after the Catholics had been forced to drop out of sight because of the Gunpowder Plot. The first and most important of these was composed of the London merchants, who still held certain rights as grantees of Ralegh (1589). Sir Thomas Smythe was the unquestioned leader of this group. Then there was the Plymouth group, represented in a sense by the Lord Chief Justice, whose aim was not Virginia but what is today New England. And lastly there were the merchants of Bristol, who were gathered about Hakluyt, the clergyman, and through him got associated with the Londoners.

After much compromising Popham and the Privy Council worked out a plan for two colonies, one in the north and one in the south — "for the better strengthening [of] each other against all occurrences," as John Smith later wrote. Smith has supplied the *excuse* for the arrangement. The *cause* lay in the London versus West Country jealousies. However, the plan was at last ready.

According to it, various connections of Popham and the late Sir Humphrey Gilbert, along with others, were to be responsible for exploration and colonization of the "northern part of Virginia" (New England), while Sir Thomas Smythe and the London merchants, and Hakluyt and his friends, took over the region around Ralegh's long-lost Roanoke Colony, which no one *knew* to be lost at that time.

The London group was specifically authorized to settle between the parallels of 34° and 41° north latitude (Cape Fear, North Carolina, to New York Bay), while the others were awarded the region between 38° and 45°, from the mouth of the then undiscovered Potomac River to the border between Maine and New Brunswick. Either group could plant colonies in the overlapping belt (virtually comprising Pennsylvania, New Jersey, Delaware, and Maryland), subject to certain restrictions. With agreement thus reached, it only remained to name a handful of "suitors" who could petition the King for a charter, in the name of all who were interested.

Too much has been made of the "puzzle" of the eight persons who were chosen to represent the others. It has existed only because not enough is known about them today; also, because not enough is known about the exact composition of the groups to which the charter was issued.

In actuality, the patentees all had connection with the enterprise; not one was a mere figurehead. That they formed a cover for the interests really involved in the project may have been simply a result of the delicacy of the situation, internationally. The new treaty with Spain did not say yes and did not say no, about trade, exploration, or colonization in America. No useful purpose would be served by naming such responsible individuals as the Lord Chief Justice of England, the Governor of the East India Company, or, say, the Governor of Plymouth Fort. If difficulties arose, why — no one knew too much about the whole thing. It was just the doing of a body of ex-soldiers (the Londoners) and merchants (the West Country people) . . .

Nevertheless, the project was entered into seriously and with forethought — not as some sort of bungling initiated by absent-minded shopkeepers. This was attested by the naming of Richard Hakluyt as one of the group representing the London, or "Southern," interests, along with Sir Thomas Gates, a Devonshire soldier who had been knighted for valor at Cádiz in 1596, and Sir George Somers, a member of Parliament who had made something of a name for himself in West Indies privateering. These were solid citizens and subjects, however odd their sudden appearance together as patentees may seem. As to the fourth "name," that of Edward Maria Wingfield, Esquire: here was another ex-soldier, and one who was planning to go in person — in fact, one of the original planners, if we may take John Smith literally.

That Hakluyt intended to go to Virginia is virtually nonsense, despite a deal of conjecture based on the peculiarities of wording in the dispensation to provide a living for a clergyman in Virginia. That Gates and Somers did eventually go to Virginia was possibly due only to the gods not watching their spinning too carefully. But that Edward Maria Wingfield took off with the first contingent was neither concealed nor accidental. He represented himself.

The four patentees for the Northern group concern Smith's story only tangentially, but they may be mentioned for later reference. They were: Sir Humphrey Gilbert's son, Ralegh Gilbert; Lord Chief Justice Popham's nephew, George Popham, and his son-in-law, Thomas Hanham; and a Plymouth merchant and ex-privateer by the name of William Parker. John Smith's lot was cast with the other four.

Eight months and a few days elapsed between the signing of the Charter and the departure of the colonists for Virginia, what with shipwreck, piracy, and governmental monopolies adding an element of muddling-through to the characteristic adagio tempo of the times. But whatever the great merchants were doing about ships, sailors, and supplies, John Smith himself went recruiting, as soon as he had invested his modicum of capital.

By the first anniversary of the Gunpowder Plot, some sort of order was emerging from the initial activities, and on November 20, 1606, King James set his hand and seal to a brief document setting up a "table of organization" for what we can loosely call the Virginia Company. This document is composed of "articles, instructions and orders" to the number of nearly forty, and includes the provision for the appointment of a King's Council to govern the Company in London. That Council in turn was authorized to appoint local councils to govern the colonists upon their arrival overseas. Nine knights, two esquires (who ranked below knights and above "gentlemen"), and three merchants were named to the King's Council — though it must be said that at least two of the knights were also merchant princes. Most important of these last mentioned was Sir Thomas Smythe.

The King's Council was about evenly divided between the West Countrymen and the Londoners. Popham's son, Sir Francis, and Sir Ferdinando Gorges were both members of the former group, which got two exploratory ships off to America in August, even before the Council was appointed. Their haste was rewarded with failure, but that does not directly concern John Smith's life. Sir Thomas Smythe and his associate, Sir William Romney (also of the East India and other companies), laid their plans more solidly, if more slowly. With them on the Council was also the Recorder of the City of London, Sir Henry Montagu, whose niece Elizabeth married Robert Bertie and had very recently been delivered of an heir to the House of Willoughby de Eresby. Although John Smith's interest in the Virginia Venture can hardly have been in any way due to Sir Henry, there can be little doubt that Sir Henry at least knew Smith's name.

The day after the promulgation of the *Articles* of November 20, a warrant was issued granting Richard Hakluyt and Robert Hunt, vicar of Heathfield, "full and free license" to go to Virginia, to "watch and perform the ministry and preaching of God's word in those parts." Then, for the next four weeks there is again no record of the doings of either the colonists or the councilors. Nevertheless, it is to that period that two acts should most reasonably be attributed. The first of these was the completion, with the assistance of Richard Hakluyt, and the approval of certain *Instructions by way of advice* "to be observed by those Captains and company which are sent at this present to plant there." The other was the appointment of a local council for Virginia, in accordance with King James's *Articles*.[3]

If the names of the "suitors" for the first Charter have struck some writers as amazing, appearing as they do out of the blue, the names of several of the first councilors appointed to govern the colony locally are hardly less so. Three of the seven (out of an authorized maximum of thirteen) seem logical: Gosnold, as "prime mover"; Wingfield, as "suitor" for the Charter; and Christopher Newport, as "Admiral" of the little fleet that was to transport the company. But the fourth councilor for Virginia was Captain John Smith.

To explain this nomination it must be assumed that someone had faith in Smith's ability in some direction, since his social status was too low to account for any sort of consideration on that basis, and his investment was as insignificant as his status. But the only witness to his ability was John Smith himself, supported by a document, signed by an almost unknown prince of an almost unknown land, merely giving license to "Iohanni Smith, natione Anglo Generoso, 250. militum Capitaneo," to wear three Turks' heads on his shield and to travel back to his own country. Two other, more weighty, factors undoubtedly secured Smith his position on the local Virginia Council. One was Robert, Lord Willoughby, who was available to testify to his earlier career and basic character. The other was Bartholomew Gosnold, whose friendship and confidence John Smith had won.

Although Smith's recorded subscription was minimal — nine pounds sterling — the total amount of his indirect investment in the Company was unquestionably many times that. He himself states that it was five hundred pounds, which corresponds with the amount of money Samuel Purchas says Smith brought back to England, and which comprised the money put out to "hire men to go" to Virginia — more than half of whom deserted as soon as they had time to think the matter over. (Whatever the real cash amount "invested" in the Virginia Venture, it is best to remember that accuracy in figures was in those days [as now] mostly limited to countinghouses, that John Smith seemed enchanted by the number 500, and that every account of what happened is tinctured by underlying purpose, prejudice, self-defense, or one or another of mankind's even less commendable infirmities.)

The three other appointees to the local council for Virginia, however obscure they seem today, appear to have had sounder claims to consideration than John Smith. Taking them in haphazard order, there was Captain John Martin, who had a small record of seamanship and privateering before his association with the Virginia Company. His father was Sir Richard Martin, gold-

smith and three times Lord Mayor of London, and his only
sister, lately deceased, had been the wife of Sir Julius Caesar, Chancellor of the Exchequer in 1606. Martin, who was fifteen or twenty
years older than John Smith, took with him his son, and a George
Martin who could have been his nephew tagged along. Young
John Martin did not survive the rigors of life in Virginia for long,
and George Martin returns to oblivion after a brief appearance,
but Captain John's name persistently recurs in various documents.

Captain George Kendall, the last-mentioned of the councilors
in all the lists, bears every evidence of having been a relative of the
Sandys and Manners families, and a political spy in the service of
Lord Salisbury. From his recorded behavior, we learn that Kendall
understood one side of the problem of planting a colony — self-
protection or defense — while hopelessly ignoring another — self-
discipline. He flashes across the first pages of American colonial
history like a St. Elmo's fire at the masthead, as the tempests of
jealousy threaten to swamp the ship of ordered government.

Seventh, and last, of the local councilors is the least clear figure
of all, the "Rear-Admiral" of the expedition, Captain John Ratcliffe (or Radcliffe). Ratcliffe's real name was Sicklemore and he
has successfully evaded identification up to the present time. He
is recorded as having subscribed fifty pounds to the Virginia Company, which was a relatively large sum. This lends some support
to the guess that he may have been a Sicklemore who married into
the distinguished Ratcliffe or Radcliffe family, one branch of which
had been raised to the peerage with the title of Earls of Sussex. Had
this been the case, however, it would be expected that Captain
John Ratcliffe-Sicklemore or one of his associates would have
dropped some sort of hint to that effect. In the absence of such
a hint, it is best to say that the background and reasons for the
appointment of Captain Ratcliffe to his two posts in the Virginia
Company are alike unknown.

In this list of the seven local councilors, only John Smith and
John Ratcliffe appear to have been of truly obscure parentage, although Smith has the advantage in that his paternity and date of
baptism are recorded. Since influences of one sort or another
patently operated in favor of all other members of the council, the
same influences must be assumed for Smith and Ratcliffe. The

Bertie family has been suggested for Smith. For Ratcliffe the question remains unanswered.[4]

The rest of the original colonists were divided, in such incomplete lists as have survived, into "gentlemen," "laborers," and an assortment of specialists — carpenters, bricklayers, a sailor, a blacksmith, a barber, a mason, a tailor, a drummer, a surgeon, and four boys. The total number is stated to have been one hundred and five, the names of ninety-three of whom are known.[*] Of the ninety-three, fifty-nine were listed as gentlemen. Since gentlemen hardly had any intention of doing any work, the proportion seems rather high, but may have been judged proper. Ralegh's Roanoke Colony in North Carolina offers no basis for comparison, since its lists do not indicate which were "gentlemen" and which were "others." Nevertheless, it is difficult to understand how the organizers planned to get the work done. Perhaps they thought that the gentlemen would contribute more muscular effort toward survival than they did.

A large proportion of the gentlemen colonists can be attributed with considerable plausibility to the influence and efforts of Bartholomew Gosnold. He and Wingfield were apparently responsible for almost 40 per cent of the colonists whose names are known, to which those attributable to Sir Thomas Smythe (Gosnold's wife's cousin, for sure) add another 15 per cent. This roughly accurate analysis corroborates the factual importance of Sir Thomas as the top-level leader of the project, and the grassroots importance of Gosnold and Wingfield (and perhaps Smith) which is vouched for by some documents and hinted at in others. (Smith's share cannot be determined.)

The remaining 45 or 46 per cent of the known colonists were about equally divided between those who are as yet unidentifiable with any certainty at all, and those — most probably connected through London contacts — who appear as isolated individuals, usually in pairs, with scattered ties: two almost unquestionably Cecil's men, and ex-spies of a sort; two in one way or another connected with such adventurers as Frobisher and Edward Fenton; two ostensibly friends with East India Company ties; and so on. Broadly,

---

[*] This is the outside figure. Four of these were mariners who may not have been considered colonists.

it may be said that the expedition seems to have been almost exclusively from Suffolk and London (including environs), with a handful of men from neighboring Essex, Hertfordshire, and Kent, and a *rara avis* or two from the West Country. Indeed, the fundamental basis for the entire group of colonists appears to have been a score or so of individuals who, like the later tobacco-merchandizing group, were "bound together by kinship, partnership and previous business experience" — the business experience in the Virginia Venture including privateering.

This basic group was decimated by disease within four months of the foundation of Jamestown, throwing the control of the remaining settlers into the hands of relative outsiders, with John Smith the only surviving councilor strong enough to rally the better elements and save the colony from extinction by famine and the Indians. Suffice it to add, for the moment, a brief reminder that Newport had lost a hand (or an arm) fighting Spaniards in the West Indies; Gosnold was an ex-privateer; Wingfield was an ex-soldier and ex-prisoner-of-war; Smith an ex-soldier; Martin had served under Drake; and Kendall was almost certainly an ex-spy. Ratcliffe, whoever he was, was a difficult man, as later events showed.

These seven, then, were to form the governing body of the colony: five far-from-outstanding men under Newport and Gosnold. Later, when they arrived in Virginia, they were to elect a president from among themselves — one who could serve for one year only. But since Newport was excluded from practical participation in the Council because he was a nonresident, an oligarchy of six men was left to govern.

It is remarkable that the hardheaded businessmen who formed the bulk of the King's Council in London could have thought that government by such a junta could produce the action needed to establish the colony, or should have disregarded the notoriously high mortality rate on such expeditions. Even ignoring the improbability of survival, councils are normally better suited to deliberation, planning, and review, at best; and the fact that the President was to have two votes, while the other councilors had but one, did not make a leader of him, necessarily. Yet a leader was precisely what the infant colony needed. Death reaped a frightful harvest before that leader manifested himself in the person of Captain John Smith.

Cautious in its delegation of authority, the King's Council was cautious also in its secrecy. It saw to it that the expedition would sail with a minimum of publicity. (Not even the sharp-eyed and keen-eared Spanish Ambassador, guardian of the sacred rights of Philip III in the foggy realm of Great Britain, learned of the voyage until the ships were well on their way.) Then, lastly, the Council's caution extended to its *Instructions* for the government of the colony. These were sealed, in three copies (one for each ship), so that not even the names of the appointed councilors would be known until after their arrival in Virginia. In the interim, military, or rather naval, discipline was to obtain, with Captain Newport in command, and Captain Gosnold associated with him. Captain Ratcliffe had control only as ship-captain of the pinnace *Discovery*.

As has been mentioned, there was perhaps some idle talk that Richard Hakluyt himself would accompany the expedition as chaplain. The royal warrant of November 21 authorized both him and Robert Hunt to hold benefices in "parts of Virginia or America" as well as in England. But Hakluyt, by then an "old man" of fifty-five or fifty-six, declined to go (or never had thought of going) and sent in his place Hunt, a man twenty years his junior, Edward Maria Wingfield claimed to have backed Hunt's appointment, and to have interceded with the Archbishop of Canterbury on Hunt's behalf. Little further is known about the matter, beyond John Smith's assertion that an income of £500 a year was assigned to the chaplain for Jamestown — a sum so large that it may be taken as a mistake. Perhaps it was a misprint for £50, perhaps it was a later monetary valuation for shares of company stock to be issued.

With the colonists' spiritual needs thus taken care of, there remained the question of their health. To that end, Thomas Wotton, "Gentleman," and Thomas Wilkinson, surgeon but not "Gentleman," were employed. Nothing is certainly known about either, beyond the fact that the surname Wilkinson appears once on the rolls of the Company of Barber Surgeons of London, and several Wottons are recorded both in the Company and in the Royal College of Physicians.

The plans, the supplies, the ships, the instructions, and the personnel all being at last ready, the tiny fleet "fell from London" on

Friday, December 19, 1606. Appropriately, their point of departure
was Blackwall, now in the London borough of Poplar, within sight
of the manor that had housed both Sebastian Cabot and Sir Walter
Ralegh. Only a stone's throw away were the East India Docks, where
Sir Thomas Smythe's chief interests lay.

Few epoch-making adventures have begun with less fanfare. Contemporaries heard nothing about it. Spain heard nothing about
it. Even that avid news-gatherer John Chamberlain was uninformed. For, two days after John Smith and his associates sailed,
Chamberlain wrote to his friend Dudley Carleton from only thirty
miles away:

> Sir, Though the waters be high, yet are we here at so lowe
> an ebbe for any matter of newes that were yt not for goode
> manners I shold leave your letter unaunswered till a fitter
> tide. Unles I shold tell you of paling, or ditching, plashing
> [interweaving] of hedges, stocking of trees, catching of
> moales or such other kind of husbandrie, that is all our
> countrie exercise . . . This weeke the King lay two or
> three dayes in an inne at Ware with his hawkes . . . The
> earl of Montgomery made a posting journy to visit his
> sister . . . I am setting forward to morrow towards Kneb-
> worth . . . I return hither soone after the holydayes . . .
> Commend me I pray you to our best friends at Cripplegate
> and so being passing wearie of this blotting pen I commit
> you all to Gods holy protection . . .

Indeed, *there was no news.* Only three little ships sailing into
the night and the North Sea, bearing the founders of English
America in their leaky hulls.[5]

CHAPTER 8

# A VOYAGE BOUND IN SHALLOWS
# AND IN MISERIES

I T IS difficult for us to conceive the hardships and contrarieties
that faced John Smith and his fellow colonists in December,
1606, and the early months of 1607. Even today, power-driven ships
sometimes wallow unhappily in the wind-swept North Sea, or crawl
apprehensively through chilling fogs, sounding or listening for
lugubrious horns. But when bad weather beset an Elizabethan or
Jacobean ship, it could only stop (if it could), cast anchor, furl
sails, and wait for wind and weather to change.

This was precisely what Newport had to do. Two weeks, and
only seventy-five miles out of London, the three ships anchored
in the Downs, off the east coast of Kent. There they lay at hull
through the month of January.

John Smith, there is every reason to believe, was a good sailor.
He had crisscrossed the Mediterranean, sat prisoner on a Turkish
Black Sea galley, weathered storms off Africa. But others of the
Virginia Venture were not so fortunate as he — notably the Rever-
end Robert Hunt, who wasted away, "making wild vomits into the
black night."

The crowded quarters, the uninhibited seasickness of nearly all
on board, the primitive sanitary arrangements, the hardening bis-
cuit and souring beer, and the timbers that groaned and the decks
that floundered ceaselessly — all made the stoutest heart (and
stomach) long for the shore, winter-gray yet beckoning, only a few
miles away. But the Reverend Robert Hunt's will was stronger
than any such lure. True, he

was so weak and sick that few expected his recovery. Yet
although he were but 10 or 12 miles from his habitation

[Reculver, Kent] . . . and notwithstanding the stormy weather, nor the scandalous imputations (of some few, little better than Atheists, of the greatest rank amongst us) suggestèd against him; all this could never force from him so much as a seeming desire to leave the business . . .

So runs the earliest account.

Even disregarding the ebullient language, in which it cannot be told whether "atheist" meant "nonconformist" or "Roman Catholic," it is clear that serious quarreling had already broken out among the colonists. Hunt evidently tried to put a stop to it, whereupon some of the malcontents wanted to set him ashore — perhaps even abandon the whole enterprise themselves. But Hunt persisted until "with the water of patience, and his godly exhortations (but chiefly by his true devoted example) [he] quenched those flames of envy and dissension."

All things have an end, however delayed. At length the ships were freed from the "unprosperous winds" and got away from their hateful anchorage. Yet it was certainly February before the cliffs of the English West Country were lost to sight behind them. Holding a generally southwest course, then more southerly, Newport led the way toward America. The majesty of the Atlantic and the knowledge that they were at last en route might have been expected to lessen the discord. So far as records show, it may have. Nevertheless, the charge of "atheism" lingered and festered. Its real portent must be considered.

There were only two persons among the colonists who combined the characteristics of rank and questionable theology. These were Edward Maria Wingfield, and a much younger, blue-blooded cousin-by-marriage of both Edward Maria and Bartholomew Gosnold by the name of Master George Percy. This member of the nobility, John Smith's junior by perhaps eight months, was the youngest brother of Henry Percy, ninth Earl of Northumberland, and a direct descendant of the immortal Harry Hotspur of King Henry IV's reign.

Master Percy had flitted over to Holland with his brother the Earl and the young Earl of Rutland in 1600, all of them bedight for a Court masque rather than a battlefield, and afterwards had been in Ireland — equally elegantly clothed, to judge by his tailors' bills. His interest in Virginia may be attributable in part to companions picked up in Dublin or near Kinsale. (There were several ex-soldiers from Ireland among the gentlemen bound for Virginia.) Or it may have stemmed from sheer idleness. But the chances are that all his reasons may be summed up in the words *Gunpowder Plot*. A second cousin of Henry and George Percy named Thomas Percy was a Catholic convert (or revert) who joined in that famous conspiracy. Killed resisting arrest, Thomas brought disgrace for a time on all the Percys. The Earl was tried and sentenced to the Tower of London with two other brothers. George escaped that ignominy, but it would have been logical for him to want to get away from it all.

Fortunately for the muse of history, George Percy — perhaps from sheer boredom — kept a diary which later got into the hands of Samuel Purchas and was published, in part, in that scholar's omnium-gatherum *Hakluytus Posthumus,* better known as *Purchas His Pilgrimes.* This diary is one of the few sources independent of John Smith which are available today for the story of the early days of the colony.

Percy, perhaps logically, makes no mention of the religious charges. (Purchas, of course, may have edited them out.) He merely writes that they were forced to stay some time in the Downs, "where we suffered great storms." John Smith likewise observes only that they had "many crosses in the Downs by tempests." But Edward Maria Wingfield, in his own account of the happenings, does not hesitate to admit that it was "noised" that he "combined with the Spaniards to the destruction of the Colony," adding other charges made against him, such as, "that I am an Atheist, because I carried not a Bible with me, and because I did forbid the preacher to preach." All of this he rebutted, somewhat elaborately. (Curiously, Wingfield claimed credit for Hunt — "whom I took with me" — yet admitted that he forbad his sermons on "two or three Sunday mornings," or afternoons.)

"Qui s'excuse, s'accuse." If Wingfield was not the butt of the charges mentioned, it is hard to imagine who could have caused so much turmoil — "garboils" was the sturdier word then used for such developments. Certainly not Newport or Gosnold, and they,

with Wingfield and Percy, were the only top-ranking colonists by
any standard.

Although at first this tempest did not get out of the teapot, it
was portentous in that it brought with it a few voices that clamored
for the abandonment of the expedition as early as January, 1607.
These voices whimpered and whispered, and occasionally cried
aloud, month after month, year after year, until long after John
Smith voyaged back to England.[1]

The route chosen for the Atlantic crossing was the "standard"
one followed by Newport before. It lay from Ile d'Ouessant, Finis-
tère, France, southwest to Finisterre in Spain, and then a compass
point or so more southerly to the Canaries.* Gosnold may have
wanted to follow his former short course directly west to New England, but the long delay in the Downs must have worked in favor
of the traditional route. They would need supplies before they
could hope to reach Newfoundland, but most of all, the southern
route was the route that Admiral Newport knew.

Nautically, the voyage proved uneventful. George Percy noted
only that "The twelfth day of February at night, we saw a blazing
star; and presently a storm [blew up]." Six weeks later, on March
24, they anchored off Dominica, in the West Indies. Judging by
Percy, the voyage was only tedious, and too long.

Percy concealed, or chose to ignore, as did John Smith in his
first account, the most ominous event of the crossing. Newport had
stopped at the Canaries for four or five days, no doubt for food
and water. (English merchants had been trafficking there for over
eighty years.) During the halt something happened which has never
been cleared up, and John Smith was arrested — "restrained," as it
was then called. The 1612 account reads:

> Now Captain Smith, who all this time from their depar-
> ture from the Canaries, was restrained as a prisoner, upon
> the scandalous suggestions of some of the chiefe [leaders]
> (envying his repute), who feigned he intended to usurp
> the government, murder the Council, and make himself
> king; that his confederates were dispersed in all the three

---

* Hierro (or Ferro), the westernmost of the Canaries, had been used since
Ptolemy's day to establish 0° longitude. An international congress established
the zero meridian at Greenwich in 1914.

ships, and that divers of his confederates that revealed it
[Smith's intentions] would affirm it; for this he was committed.

It is impossible to know whether anyone actually accused Smith
of such preposterous notions or plans, for the percentage of pure
rhetoric in Elizabethan verbal pageantry is not always simple to
calculate. Nevertheless it is obvious that John Smith, a mere
captain, stepped on somebody's silk-clad toes: since he had friends
on all three ships, he was a rabble-rousing commoner, and his suggestions for the good of the enterprise were cheeky. Evidently,
Smith forgot that he was doing business with English "gentlemen,"
not with Baron Khissl or Count zu Sultz. His opinions were not
wanted, and if he pressed them the one person who would take
serious umbrage at Smith's lack of subservience was without question Edward Maria Wingfield.

Whatever the details, even this was not a very grave matter, as
will soon appear. Its importance lies in the glimpse it provides
into the basic dissonances within the group of adventurers. More
trivially, it hints at the possible distribution of the more important
colonists among the three ships.

No passenger lists have survived, if any ever existed. There is
no roster of colonists as a whole. Not even the total number is
known, accurately — 104 and 105 are the figures mentioned. Samuel
Purchas, to be sure, states in a marginal note in his *Pilgrimes* that
there were 71 aboard Newport's *Susan Constant,* 52 with Captain
Gosnold on the *God Speed,* and 21 on Captain Ratcliffe's *Discovery*
— a total of 144, presumably exclusive of the crews. (George Percy
adds to the confusion by claiming that the company totaled "eight
score persons" when they stopped at the Virgin Islands — clearly
including sailors in this number — but Percy shows signs of fond-
ness for the number eight score.) All in all, at least one colonist
died on the way, others may have, and some may have returned
with Newport after casting an unhappy eye at the limitless forest,
the river wide as ten Thameses, and the red-bedaubed savages
dancing on the shore and lurking in the brakes. However the
total number is estimated, Newport, Gosnold, and Ratcliffe commanded the three ships, and Edward Maria Wingfield unquestion-

ably relaxed on the biggest, with the Admiral, and at least two personal servants.

Judging by the events which led to Smith's arrest, he must have been on the same ship, for it was Wingfield who without doubt demanded his restraint. That Gosnold would have carried out such an order from Wingfield is doubtful, in view of his friendship with Smith. Furthermore, Gosnold was commander on his own ship. Ratcliffe was not the type to take orders from Wingfield merely on the grounds of higher social rank, he too was in command on *his* ship, and he was friendly with Smith (at the time). Both were associate investors with Wingfield in the Virginia Venture. Newport, however, being employed by the Virginia Company, was in a different position. Edward Maria Wingfield was a patentee and investor, and therefore in a position to force the issue. And force it he would. In his eyes, Smith was insubordinate because he lacked "proper respect" for Wingfield. This was intolerable.

Before long, the most trivial pretext served Wingfield to rid himself of the nuisance. By arresting Smith, he achieved this for the moment. That Smith was not so easily to be subdued apparently did not occur to him. That, in brief, is the persuasive aspect of the argument. It seems to override whatever doubts may occur.

Nevertheless, a few additional points may be noted. George Percy, for example, treats John Smith with equity in his *Observations*. Then besides, Smith had not yet had any recorded differences with Martin or Kendall, or any of the other leaders, nor indeed with the chief of the expedition himself. Admiral Newport is not pictured anywhere as in any way antagonistic to Smith — at least for the first year. In short, everything leads to the conclusion that Wingfield, as the stubborn maintainer of social levels on an expedition where it was more important for blood to be red than blue, must bear the blame for Smith's arrest.

John Smith is reported as being "restrained" for thirteen weeks. The same report dates his arrest from the departure of the fleet from the Canary Islands. Although that date is nowhere stated, nor is the date of the "official" termination of the arrest, scraps of information supply clues.

George Percy's diary relates that they sighted Martinique on March 23, a Monday. Since they sailed from Blackwall the night of the preceding nineteenth of December, a Friday, it follows that the crossing took thirteen weeks and two or three days. Allowing for six weeks in the Downs, as implied in the 1612 account, and a stop of four or five days in the Canaries, as stated by John Smith in 1608, a rough balance can be reached of seven weeks' sailing time from the Strait of Dover to the West Indies. Assuming then that Newport sailed the most direct route (via the Canaries) which the winds would permit, his speed can be calculated at just under four knots. If that average is applied to the whole trip, it results that they would have employed about nineteen days from the Downs to the Canaries, and thirty from there to Martinique. (Although both Columbus and Sir Richard Grenville had made the latter lap in better time, still it was not a conspicuously slow voyage.)

Further, by figuring back from the date of landfall at Martinique, February 21 results as the date of sailing from the Canaries. This provides an earliest limit for the beginning of John Smith's arrest. Thirteen weeks from Saturday, February 21, would be Saturday, May 23. By that time the adventurers were landed in Virginia, and an official report of events is available: the *Relation of the Discovery of our River.* This was prepared for Captain Newport and taken back by him on his first return voyage. It tells that on Thursday, May 21, Captain Newport took five gentlemen with him on a trip. Among the five gentlemen was Captain John Smith — and there is nothing to indicate that Smith was under restraint. The thirteen weeks thus work out to within two days of absolute (and miraculous!) accuracy. We may now turn back to the arrival of the little fleet at Dominica.[2]

Admiral Newport, as has been said, was familiar with the West Indies. Since his first cruise there in 1590 (which was both his first command and the one that cost him his hand), he had raided and privateered right up to September, 1605, when he brought King James the present of crocodiles and a boar. For him it was a not very delayed homecoming to slip by Mattanenio, as Percy called Martinique (more faithful to the native name of Madinina than the French version), anchor at Dominica, and begin to trade with the "Cannibals, that will eat mans flesh."

John Smith, by nature obviously more interested in dangerous adventure than in natural beauty and undoubtedly impatient to be freed of his arrest, has little to say about the exotic tropical islands. But George Percy, far more impressionable, has left a glowing account of what he saw, including the naked savages "all painted red, to keepe away the biting of Muscetos," a fight between a whale and "a Thresher and a Sword-fish," and other strange things.

We learn next from Percy that the fleet passed Marigalante, following in the wake of Columbus's second voyage, to anchor off Guadeloupe, just as Columbus had, to let the men ashore. There, near the active volcano of Grande Soufrière, Percy wrote, they found "a Bath which was so hot that no man was able to stand long by it. Our Admiral, Captaine Newport, caused a piece of Porke to be put in it; which boiled it so, in the space of half an hour, as no fire could mend it." (*Mend* often meant "improve," in John Smith's day.)

It was a short sail from Guadeloupe past Montserrat and St. Kitts to Nevis, their next place of anchorage. Percy noted that the two islands they by-passed were uninhabited — information possibly obtained from Newport or some Spanish report — but stressed the treacherous nature of the aborigines of Guadeloupe and Nevis. In the latter case, at least, Percy's information proved wrong. Despite the colonists' fears, the Nevis Indians were harmless. The visiting colonists were not.

Newport ordered six days ashore to rest, and to cure his men, colonists and sailors alike, of scurvy and other ills such as were the inevitable concomitants of sea voyages in those days. Because of the Indians on the other side of the island, sentinels were stationed with "Courts *de gard* [pickets] at every Captaines quarter." John Smith, then still under arrest, was ashore with the others — presumably with the same protection as the other captains. Factions were thriving, as always. Another row broke out in which the odium of certain elements against Smith reached its climax. With or without benefit of encouragement from Wingfield, "a paire of gallowes was made," as Smith wrote many years later, "but Captaine Smith, for whom they were intended, could not be persuaded to use them."

A vivid picture is conjured up by this reminiscence. The short, sturdy veteran of Hungarian wars, Turkish slavery, Transylvanian duels, and a wild ride with a chain around his neck across the no-man's land of the Tatars, defying the "inventers" of this summary justice, all of them (including Smith) in English doublet and jerkin, sweltering under the heat of a tree-filtered tropical sun, scuffling among themselves while red-stained savages possibly peered in curiosity through the tangled undergrowth.

On Nevis the adventurers made the acquaintance of vines and shrubs that are poisonous to the touch. John Smith, describing some trees "like a wild fig tree," adds, "whether it was the dew of those trees, or of some others, I am not certain, but many of our men became so tormented with a burning swelling all over their bodies, they seemed like scalded men, and neere mad with pain."

Though Smith's description fits the red mangrove, that plant is not poisonous, and it could not have been poison ivy, for that does not exist in the West Indies. On the other hand, it could well have been the poisonous manchineel, or *Manchioneal*. Fortunately, Nevis has warm and cold mineral springs, and the men were able to be "well cured" in a few days.

After six days at Nevis, the fleet sailed past St. Eustatius northwest to Saba, then west to the Virgin Islands, where they anchored "in an excellent Bay able to harbour a hundred ships" — evidently Road Harbor, Tortola. Percy complains of the lack of fresh water there, and notes that there were no inhabitants.

Four days out from Nevis, on April 7, 1607, the fleet had passed San Juan, Puerto Rico, and reached the island of Mona, in the passage of that name between Puerto Rico and Santo Domingo, or Hispaniola. (This was precisely the route sailed by Newport as captain of the *John* of London, in May, 1590.) By that time the sulphurous water shipped at Nevis had begun to smell so vilely that no one was able to endure it, says Percy, and they were happy to refill their casks at Mona. While some of the sailors were thus engaged, Newport, accompanied by "the rest of the gentlemen, and other soldiers" (there might be Spaniards lurking about), marched inland for fresh meat. They killed two wild boars and some iguanas, and saw a huge wild bull which apparently escaped being added to their larder. At Mona, too, one Edward Brookes died, a gentleman "whose fat melted within him, by the great heate and drought of the Countrey." Others had possibly died before, but Brookes's death is the first recorded in the long inventory of the human cost of colonizing Virginia.*

Here George Percy noted down that on April 9 he and some others "went off with our boat, to the Isle of Moneta, some three leagues [nine miles] from Mona: where we had a terrible landing." When they had clambered up to high ground, however, they found huge flocks of fowl of all kinds, and eggs "which lay so thick in the grass." In three hours' time, they loaded two boats full of such supplies, to their "great refreshing."

The next day they left the West Indies behind, and on April 14 they calculated (or observed) that they passed the Tropic of Cancer. Soon the rumor began to spread that they should sight land in another week — hopefully Virginia. Whether this grew out of some careless remark of Newport's — for it is possible that he had sailed that same route not more than three years before — or whether it was sheer wishful thinking is not known. To reach the mouth of Chesapeake Bay from the Tropic of Cancer along a great-circle route from Moneta would have needed an accurate course and an increase of speed from an average of less than four knots to nearly five. Nevertheless, because they did not sight land at the end of a week, the congenital grumblers recommenced their grumbling.

Just what happened is again not clear. According to Percy there was a "vehement tempest" all night, April 21, which forced them to lie at hull, after which they cast the lead daily for four days, but found no ground at a hundred fathoms. (It is to be assumed that they were working their way north, the while. Judging by modern soundings, they need not have been more than twenty miles or so out of sight of land.) Smith's earliest account (1608) says that they were driven northward by a "cruel storm." And the 1612 account reads as follows:

> Gone from thence [Mona] in search of Virginia, the company was not a little discomforted, seeing the mariners had three days passed their reckoning, and found no land; so that Captain Ratcliffe (Captain of the pinnace) rather

* Ralegh's colony was in North Carolina. See Commentaries.

> desired to bear up helm to return for England, than make
> further search . . .

It is clear that there was a storm, as the 1612 account goes on to relate. And their impatience can be understood. But their "discomfort" — their fear, in other words — seems exaggerated. Any levelheaded member of the party must have known that the mariners' reckoning was only loosely approximative, that the exact location of their destination was unknown, and that their instruments were subject to many impediments that, as John Davis had written a dozen years before, "so disturbed the expected conclusion of [the mariner's] practice, as that they agreed not with the true positions of Art." These impediments — winds, leewardliness of the ship, magnetic variations, etc. — were taken into consideration by all experienced mariners; but the account says that "never any of them had seen that coast," and Ratcliffe wanted to run home. How characteristic of those unquiet Elizabethan souls!

> But [the 1612 account humbly continues], God, the
> guider of all good actions, forcing them by an extreme
> storm to hull all night, did drive them by His providence
> to their desired port, beyond all their expectations . . .

Percy continues the story: "The six and twentieth day of April, about four o'clock in the morning, we descried the Land of Virginia." And that same day they entered Chesapeake Bay.

The lack of enthusiasm in the accounts is telling. Neither Percy nor John Smith rejoices over their arrival, and theirs are the only surviving records of the landfall. Even Christopher Columbus's matter-of-fact *Journal* is more enthusiastic. Perhaps the four months of sickness, stench, and endless rolling and pitching, and human quarreling, left little spirit for jubilation, but rather a feeling of relief, coupled in many, certainly, with an ill-defined sense of anxiety.

John Smith was still under arrest. Now that they had reached their goal and the task of planting Virginia had begun in earnest, he may well have wondered if he was to play the vital role he surely sought to play. Or would the snobbery and chicanery and petty jealousy of "some of the chiefs" still keep him ostracized?

Most important of all, what would his position be, once the secret lists were drawn from the sealed boxes — the lists of those who made up the Council for Virginia?

John Smith can have had little doubt that his name was on those lists.[3]

## CHAPTER 9

# ACROSS A HUNDRED CENTURIES

THE VIRGINIA Company's three little ships were not the first European vessels to breast the unpredictable waters of Chesapeake Bay. In the 1520's at least three explorers had skirted that part of the Atlantic coastline, though they may not have entered the bay: Lucas Vázquez de Ayllón, Estevan Gómez, and Giovanni da Verrazzano. Half a century later, however, the *adelantado* of Florida, Don Pedro Menéndez de Avilés had supported a Jesuit missionary venture inside the bay, but that survived less than six months. The Indians wiped it out early in 1571. Menéndez got around to sending a punitive expedition up from St. Augustine in 1572, and then no further Spaniards were seen for a while.

In the 1580's, Sir Walter Ralegh had tried to establish a colony at Roanoke Island, behind the narrow barrier-beaches of northern North Carolina. During the winter of 1585–1586, which is less well known, the commander of that colony, Ralph Lane, appointed a group to reside on the south shore of Chesapeake Bay among the Indians, and a "multitude of bears." Although this assignment probably lasted only for about four months and little is known about it, it led in 1587 to the plan to establish a "City of Ralegh" on the Bay. That plan died young.

Then, in 1588, Captain Vicente González reconnoitered the bay at least as far as the Potomac. It was he who had brought the Jesuit mission in 1570 and had learned of its destruction in 1571. And fifteen years later, on July 29, 1603, Bartholomew Gilbert, Gosnold's ex-associate, was killed — also somewhere in the neighborhood. After Gilbert, Captain Newport may have been there, but that is uncertain.

Then came the fleet that bore John Smith, riding into the bay one spring morning at crack of dawn. Slowly, as if reluctant or frightened, they glided past the sand dunes of Cape Henry, while busy white-skinned men kept throwing something overboard and hauling it back up, with shouts. At last, three great weights splashed into the water, one from each ship, and the trio slowed to a halt. Down slid the billowing sails to rest. Up from nowhere men swarmed onto the decks, glittering like Spaniards as their armor caught the rays of the rising sun. Indians, ever alert, surely were not slow to spot the apparition. They had met and fought such humankind before.

Captain John Smith made no attempt to see their arrival as the Indians saw it. In his prosaic account, the story reads merely that the English first made land when they "fell with Cape Henry, the very mouth of the Bay of Chesapeake," an event which they just then "little expected," on account of the storm.

No one had any doubt that it was Chesapeake Bay, once they arrived there. Such navigators as Newport and Gosnold certainly knew its latitude, within the conception of accuracy then current. John White's maps of Virginia were reliable, with varying margins of error, and Ralph Lane had said that the Chesepians lived one hundred and thirty miles north of Roanoke, which White placed at 36° 35′ north latitude. (The distance is closer to one hundred miles, and the latitude is 35° 50′.) But until Newport and Gosnold actually entered the Bay, they were still literally "at sea" — as is attested by Ratcliffe's frightened call to return home. But for the storm, there is no telling how many days they would have wasted groping their way along the dangerous coast of North Carolina.

Six or eight miles west of Cape Henry the fleet anchored off shore, probably near the mouth of modern Lynnhaven Bay. Many land-eager colonists apparently wanted to stretch their legs on the beach, but Newport took only twenty or thirty ashore. John Smith remained on ship, in disgrace. Percy, ever ready with his writing pad, joined Newport, Wingfield, and Gosnold, as did that self-appointed recorder of the expedition, Gabriel Archer.

Archer had been with Gosnold at Cambridge University. A few years later, both of them studied law, Gosnold at the Middle Temple (where there is a record of him in 1592), Archer at Gray's Inn (record of March, 1593). In 1602 Archer accompanied Gosnold to New England, and wrote an account of the voyage. There can be no doubt that Gosnold was responsible for Archer's joining the Virginia Venture.

These five gentlemen, then, with perhaps some others, and a dozen or so soldiers and sailors, landed and explored a little. Finding little "worthy the speaking of," and no signs of human activity around, the shore party nevertheless dallied among brooks and meadows until after sunset. The moon was only four or five days before full, and there was plenty of light. But as they at last turned to go back to their boat, savages came creeping on all fours from the underbrush, their bows in their mouths. Suddenly they charged the unsuspecting English right in their faces, desperately oblivious to the superiority of European arms. The attack was brief, yet before they retreated noisily into the forest, they "hurt Captain Gabriel Archer and a sailor [Matthew Morton] in two places of the body, very dangerous" — Percy quaintly explains.

To Percy's description, John Smith added, from hearsay, that Captain Newport came up and fired at the Indians, which they "little respected, but having spent their arrows retired without harm." There seem to have been but five Indians who faced the platoon of Englishmen, and they did relatively little damage. Nevertheless, their act was a hint of hostility which John Smith seems to have taken to heart, although he was not one of the party. Newport and Wingfield, it developed, respected the hint less than their instructions "not to offend the naturals." They may have likened it to the bands of prowlers to be found in war-torn France or the Netherlands. What they did not, probably could not, gauge or understand was the gulf of a hundred centuries that separated Algonkian from European.

That night, with great solemnity no doubt, the sealed boxes with their identical contents were brought out and duly opened, and someone, possibly Newport as Admiral, read the names of those appointed by the Council in London to sit on the local Council in Virginia. They were: Bartholomew Gosnold, Edward Maria Wingfield, Christopher Newport, John Smith, John Ratcliffe, John Martin, and George Kendall — as already related. These seven men, as a body, were commanded by the royal document of November

20, 1606, to choose one of the same Council, "not being the minister of God's word," to be President, whose rights and duties were defined in some detail — as were those of the rest of the Council. Broadly, in the words of the 1612 account, the President ". . . with the Council should govern. Matters of moment were to be examined by a Jury, but determined by the major part of the Council, in which the President had 2 voices [votes]." [1]

For the next two weeks, during which John Smith continued in his state of ostracism, Percy's diary is the sole source of information. He writes, fully, of putting together their dismantled shallop — a sort of sloop with sails as well as oars — for preliminary exploration, and of sounding for a channel in the James River, of discovering what is now Old Point Comfort and the Indian village of Kecoughtan, of Indian entertainment, and finally of searching for a place suitable for their plantation. Indeed, so much is George Percy the center of activities that he almost seems to have been accepted into the Council in place of John Smith. (His social prestige and his relationship to Wingfield must never be forgotten.)

Meanwhile, they had named Cape Henry on April 29. The next five days Newport employed at Old Point Comfort and in making his way cautiously forty-odd miles upstream to the next village, named Paspahegh, where the werowance entertained them. (They had gotten the Indian title "werowance" from Ralph Lane's account of Roanoke, or from Hariot.) Percy took a party another forty miles farther, while the ships lay at anchor. Then, returning to the ships on May 12, and sailing downstream together, they discovered a point of land which, judging by Percy's enthusiastic description, appeared almost ideal — in natural protection, in good soil, in standing timber, and in wildlife. Since it had apparently been spotted by Captain Archer, it was quickly named Archer's Hope, not because they hoped to settle there, but because in those days "hope" was a fairly common word for a haven or inlet. But Archer's Hope, though approved by Gosnold, was not destined to harbor the colony. Edward Maria Wingfield roundly objected.

Two miles or so back up the river, someone — perhaps Wingfield — had noticed a site which seemed to fulfill the requirements of their *Instructions* better than Archer's Hope. (Wingfield, like Newport, tended to place the instructions above on-the-spot observation.) This site was an almost rectangular, low-lying peninsula, two miles long by one mile broad, attached to the mainland by a narrow sand bar which diverted Powhatan Creek through a figure-S into the James River just above Archer's Hope. At the extreme western end of this peninsula, near its tenuous link with the hinterland (since broken through), river erosion had carved a channel so close to the shore that the ships could tie up to trees in six fathoms of water. This for Wingfield (and possibly Newport), decided the issue, for it would enormously facilitate unloading.

Thus Wingfield, backed by a conciliating John Smith among others, overruled Gosnold, and the next day, May 13, 1607, the colonists moored their ships to Wingfield's trees and started to unload. John Smith's comments on the decision were three: that the place chosen was "a very fit place for the erecting of a great city," that "some contention passed betwixt Captain Wingfield and Captain Gosnold," and that "notwithstanding, all our provision was brought ashore, and with as much speed as might be we went about our fortification." After some discussion, the embryonic colony was named Jamestown.

It was time for Newport to relinquish his responsibility as commander. The *Instructions* had been complied with, and choice had been made of a site. The *Articles* of November 20 now required such procedures as the election of a president and the administration of an oath to all councilors. John Smith had been appointed to the Council before they left London. Since then he had been placed under restraint. Someone, perhaps Wingfield, possibly Archer, appears to have argued that this disqualified him from serving as councilor — there is no explanation in any account. On whatever grounds it was, only six of the seven councilors were sworn, and they elected Edward Maria Wingfield as their President. Then "an oration was made why Captain *Smith* was not admitted of the Council as the rest." (Since Wingfield as President had two votes, only two councilors had to side with him to make Smith's exclusion "legal.") This shabby proceeding being completed, the meeting broke up, leaving Captain John Smith in a mood readily to be imagined.[2]

There were others, too, whose mood should not be — and should not have been — ignored: the Indians. Recent archaeological work shows that Jamestown peninsula had been an Indian campsite within less than a century before the English arrived. The latter had no reason to suspect this, for a second growth of forest covered the former clearing. As John Smith wrote, "where now is Jamestown, [was] then a thick grove of trees; we cut them down." They therefore regarded the site as unoccupied. But how did the Indians regard it?

It is doubtful that the Algonkians had any conception similar to that of our private ownership of property, real estate. The idea of *state* or *nation* was certainly not developed either, although they were well aware of such things as clans, tribes, and totems. (*Totem* is an Algonkian word.) But if Jamestown peninsula was regarded as a *tribal hunting ground,* the English had no business there. That the Paspahegh tribe considered it *their* hunting ground is indicated in two ways: other tribes do not seem to have cared; but the Paspaheghs gave every evidence of considering the English intruders, and of resenting the intrusion. Unfortunately the English, whose unpracticed eyes saw nothing to indicate that this bit of forest had ever been occupied, made no move to ask permission to settle, or to "buy" it. They simply "squatted."

By dint of extraordinary effort the colonists were able to occupy the chosen site within two days. No one was conscious of any Indians around. The second night, however, "there came some Savages sailing close to our quarters," Percy noted, an alarm was sounded, and they vanished.

After this, the Werowance of Paspahegh, Wowinchopunk by name, sent messengers stating that he would visit the colony, and in fact arrived a day or two later, with a hundred armed Indians. The visit did not seem friendly from the start, and after a minor incident ended with Wowinchopunk leaving in a rage. But after another two days, he sent forty men to the colony — his entire fighting force — with a deer, and, it seemed, with instructions to spend the night in the "fort." The colonists were not that easily to be taken in, but passed a little time displaying the technological superiority of their arms. And again one of the Indians took off "in great anger," presumably followed by the others.

Wingfield meanwhile did not want to fortify the settlement (the *Instructions* said not to "offend the naturals"!), but George Kendall succeeded in surrounding it with protection of sorts, made of "boughs of trees cast together in the form of a half moon." Peaceful work went on, clapboard was split for shipment to England, and nets were mended, and even the Indians came again, bringing gifts and wanting to help. Only the werowance stayed away.[3]

A week later Newport remembered that the *Instructions* also mentioned exploring the river above the site of their settlement. He was authorized, which meant that he was supposed, to take Gosnold along with forty men and be gone up to two months. During this time, if any high lands or hills were seen, Gosnold was to test them for minerals, taking along twenty men with pickaxes, while Newport was to carry on the "discovery" with the other twenty.

The long delay in reaching Virginia made it late for a two-month excursion. The latent dissension in the settlement, combined with the Indians' maneuverings, told against taking forty men away and leaving Wingfield to muddle through without the support of his cousin, Gosnold. Then, too, it is evident from hints in the contemporary narratives that Smith's continued arrest and the Council's refusal to swear him in could not be kept up indefinitely. Gosnold decided to remain in Jamestown, with three other members of the Council — Martin, Ratcliffe, and Kendall — to bolster up Wingfield's authority. John Smith was chosen to go on the excursion with Newport.

Newport's party also included George Percy, Gabriel Archer, John Brookes, Surgeon Thomas Wotton, four capable mariners (including Prince Henry's gunner, Robert Tindall), and fourteen sailors. Archer was apparently chosen to record the events of the voyage, while Tindall drew a sketch map, thus providing Newport with documentation to take back to London. Percy continued his diary anyway, and John Smith made independent notes which he incorporated in the *Relation* he sent home a year later. Smith's account is fuller than the part of Percy's diary which survives, though by no means so detailed as Archer's, and it is especially important as the first reflection of his freedom from restraint since the colonists left the Canaries. There is no material disagreement among the three accounts.

The party left Jamestown about noon on Thursday, May 21. They by-passed the Paspahegh villages, without incident, rowing or sailing as far as a low-lying meadow that jutted sharply into the river from the north side, eighteen miles above Jamestown. There they anchored for the night. Archer writes that the Weanoc Indians welcomed them immediately with dancing and great festivities — the Weanocs were not on friendly terms with the Paspaheghs, and he implies that this may have made them cordial to the English. John Smith's account disagrees, for reasons which will soon appear, and it may be that Archer did not want to hint at such a widespread lack of friendly rapport so early. London had to be encouraged.

The next morning the explorers proceeded to a place they called Turkey Isle (possibly the same as that so known today), where they breakfasted on wildfowl "like blackbirds." Just then four or five savages came up in a canoe (Archer says they were eight), from whom the Englishmen attempted to learn something about the course of the river. According to John Smith, word of Newport's liberality in "tipping" the Indians for favors had already spread up the river. (Smith realistically saw that this would debase the currency, so to speak — little bells and trinkets would steadily buy less and less food and information.) Scarcely were Newport's desires understood, therefore, than one savage "offered with his foot to describe the river to us." Archer, who reports this, promptly gave him a pen and paper, showing him how to use such implements for drawing.

In a matter of minutes the savage sketched the waterway as far as it was navigable with boats, marking the detail of two islands — the one where they were, and another one farther upstream, where there was a great waterfall. Beyond the waterfall there were two great kingdoms, and a great distance beyond these were the Quirank, or Quirauk, Mountains, on the other side of which, Archer added, "is that which we expected" — presumably the Pacific Ocean.

Although "this fellow," as Archer terms him, promised to procure wheat (undoubtedly meaning corn) for them if they "would stay a little," the English were too eager, after they heard the good news. They pushed on with all possible speed, with the Indians following them overland and by canoe with offers of food (their sole wealth) in exchange for baubles. Indeed, their attentiveness and hospitality surely reflected little more than a desire for highly profitable trade. Venison stalked the forests and berries hung from bushes; little bells and glass beads from Venice did not.

By that time, Newport and his intrepid explorers were no longer frightened blusterers in a hostile jungle. Now that one object of their search seemed to be before them, they remembered that they were founders of empire. On they went, the Indians paddling now behind, now before — always friendly. Gradually the river narrowed, the land on either side grew higher, and all signs pointed to greater proximity to the mountains and the hoped-for sea that lay beyond.

On Saturday, May 23, two days upstream from Jamestown, they reached the domain of the Werowance of Arrohattoc, where another ceremonious reception awaited them, with a mat spread for Captain Newport as the werowance of the whiteskins. There the English first heard of the existence of a Great Chief over all the other chiefs around, whose name, as they then heard it, was Pawatah (or Powatah) — the famous Powhatan of American history and legend. There, too, they began to understand that a werowance was only a local head — though the English usually called him a king — whose power depended on favor from above as well as on personal resources.

As they sat banqueting merrily with the Arrohattoc werowance, Archer reports, "seeing their dances, and taking tobacco, News came that the great king Powatah was come." At this, all jumped to their feet except for the werowance and, of course, Messrs. Newport, Percy, Archer, Smith, Brookes, and Wotton. These seven "werowances" sat in silence until he who was called Powatah accommodated himself on a mat, too. Then the English gentlemen presented "gifts of divers sorts, as penny knives, shears, bells, beads, glass toys [trinkets], etc., more amply than before." And the newly arrived, supposed Higher Authority showed his complaisance by appointing five Indians to guide the imperturbable Englishmen on up the river. Had they known that Powatah was not the real Powhatan, the "emperor," they would have given less lavishly. Since they did not, Archer sought to perpetuate the English contentment there by naming the meeting ground Arrohattoc's Joy.

Farther up the river, with Indians "in clusters all along" cheering as they passed, Newport and his party at last reached the islet described by the map-drawer — "over against which on Popham side," Archer specified, meaning *north* because Popham was the "patron" of the North Colony, "is the habitation of the great king Pawatah, which I call *Pawatah's Tower.*" This habitation, or "royal residence," was situated, Archer continued, "upon a high hill by the water side, a plain between it and the water, 12 score [paces] over, whereon he sows his wheat, beans, peas, tobacco, pompions [pumpkins], gourds, hemp, flax, etc." There the Werowance of Arrohattoc awaited the English, seated in solemn barbaric majesty alongside the "great king Pawatah." Next to the latter sat a third dignitary, not a werowance, whose function remained a mystery.

Archer's account reports in some detail an interview between Newport and Pawatah which is a testimonial to Archer's intuitive imagination, aided by a number of gestures that were perhaps obvious. Pawatah, he wrote, indicated that all the neighborhood was allied to him, or under him, repeatedly saying, "Cheisk," which they took to mean "all," as it apparently did. He pointed out, however, that the Chesapeake Indians were not friendly, at which Archer showed his "hurts scarce whole," received the night of their landing from England, and vowed revenge.

Pawatah finally concluded the interview by moving "of his own accord a league of friendship." Thereupon Newport gave Pawatah his "gown," or cape, in token of ratification, putting it around the chieftain's shoulders himself, and saying "Wingapo chemuze" — a phrase, the English had understood, of greatest friendliness.

The next day being Whitsunday, the English prepared a small banquet for the Indian chiefs, but the Werowance of Arrohattoc left before it was served so that he could go back to his own bailiwick to prepare a return banquet for the Englishmen when they came downstream — rather complicated protocol, if it was not a ruse. Just as he was leaving, someone discovered a minor outbreak of endemic Indian thievery, but the chieftains caught the culprits and restored the loot. Newport took advantage of the occasion to warn the people in whose lands he was that in England the penalty for petty robbery was death. The Indians, with some degree of reason, seem to have ignored the foreign warning — if they understood it.

Arrohattoc, as Archer calls the man, then departed, and Pawatah joined the English, introducing himself copiously to beer, brandy, and Canary wine. Dinner done, the matter of further exploring was brought up insistently, and Pawatah grudgingly agreed to meet Newport at the falls, above the islet. Taking off overland, he left the map-drawer from Turkey Isle and Arrohattoc's brother-in-law, one Nauiraus, to sail upstream with the English as guides.

Newport and his men explored the region around the falls carefully, John Smith noting with interest that the rocks on the north side of the river were "of a gravelly nature, interlaced with many veins of glistering spangles" — a hint of valuable minerals. Percy lapsed into bucolic idylls over the trees, flowers, and fruits. And Archer snooped around to find out what was going on between Newport and Pawatah. The snooping proved more profitable than the poetry, or Smith's inexpert venture into mineralogy.

Newport, Archer learned, wanted to go on farther. Pawatah had a thousand excuses as to why he should not. It was a journey of a day and a half, he said, to Monanacanah, the land of the Monacans, who were his enemies. There would be no food on the way; the English would get tired; and so on and so on. In this clash of wills, Newport had to yield, despite the urging of some of the colonists to go anyway. It is idle to guess what might have happened if Newport had heeded the determined ones, but it is not idle to surmise that Pawatah was afraid of a possible alliance between Newport and the chief of the Monacans. The Monacans were Indians of other language, culture and background, and habits. They came down the river to raid the "Powhatan" country too often as it was. Contact with the English was to be avoided at all costs for just such reasons. For Pawatah it was a matter of divide to survive.

Having yielded to Pawatah in this matter, as was sensible, Newport seems to have thought that he ought to indicate that he had not given in entirely. Or he may have wanted to suggest to Pawatah that he was coming back to argue the matter further. Or he may have determined to "stake out a claim," as Californians put it centuries later, in the name of James I, King of Great Britain, etc. Whatever his reasons, Newport set up a cross on one of the islets at the foot of the falls. This act was witnessed by the Indians with conspicuous displeasure. Perhaps fortunately Pawatah had already stalked off in a huff over English insistence on exploring beyond his own domain. With no one else "in authority" around, Nauiraus seems to have calmed the remaining angry braves, by explaining the cross as applicable only to the islet (which did not tally with an unsubtle explanation by Newport that it was a symbol of Anglo-

Algonkian friendship), and that the islet in any case was "but a little waste ground, which doth you nor any of us any good."

Such was Percy's account. Archer's was more elaborate, and hints that it was written with an eye to what the Virginia Company might think, when Newport presented his story of happenings in Virginia. It is very difficult to believe that the extended discussions and explanations offered by Archer could have taken place between Newport, Pawatah, and Nauiraus without benefit of an interpreter, and there was none.

In the interim, however, the map maker from Turkey Isle believably was whispering to Archer that the metal they wore for ornament, their *caquassan* (possibly "red stone"), was "got in the bits of rocks and between cliffs in certain veins" in the mountains beyond. *Caquassan* was clearly understood to mean copper, and this information certainly did not serve to abate Archer's thirst for further exploration.

But Newport was satisfied for the moment. It was more important to lure Pawatah into a sense of being obeyed than to insist on further travels. He was apparently convinced, furthermore, that the tribes and mountains that separated Pawatah's realm from the rivers flowing into the "South Sea" (the Pacific) could be traversed in a matter of days. He would even volunteer to help Pawatah conquer his enemies on his way through to the mountains called Quirank. And thus, elated with what he considered news of real import to the colonists and perhaps of enormous significance to London, he determined to return to Jamestown.

Whitsun afternoon was almost spent when Newport sent Nauiraus on ahead to inform Pawatah of his return. Pawatah was not at the waterfront to meet him, however, when the shallop pulled up. Sensing that something was amiss, Newport commanded the company to stay on board while he alone went ashore.

A little later, as night was falling, Newport returned. Nauiraus had explained to Pawatah all about the cross and the help Newport would lend him against the Monacans. To show his sincerity Newport then gave Pawatah a hatchet, "which he took joyfully." Thus won over, Pawatah accompanied Newport to his boat, while Nauiraus led the English in appropriate cheers for the werowance.[4]

The moon, just past first quarter, was setting by the time they reached Arrohattoc's Joy again. The promised banquet was spread, but Arrohattoc only greeted them briefly and retired, indicating that he was indisposed. The next morning, however, he "came to the waterside," and the adventurers went ashore to meet him. He led them to understand that he had imbibed too many "hot drinks" the day before but was well again. His guests were more than welcome.

Banqueting began again and continued all morning. In his somewhat embroidered if matter-of-fact style, Archer relates the events as they transpired, with one brief interruption here to express his amazement at the physical energy of the chief. To Archer, as undoubtedly to the English in general (except, probably, for John Smith), a werowance was a king, a sacred ruler. That such a person should run after misbehaved subjects, and catch and punish them personally, was worthy of record. So Archer recorded for all posterity that the Werowance of Arrohattoc "might give any of our Company [a handicap of] 6. score paces in 12" and still win.

George Percy, always impressionable, noted other inconsequentialities, and John Smith registered "the manner of their diving for mussels, in which they find pearls." All in all, the expeditionary force dallied pleasantly at Arrohattoc most of the day.

Only a short distance downstream they were entertained again, at a place Archer called Mulberry Shade. There Newport had a piece of artillery fired "soldier-like" for the benefit of the Indians, whereat the werowance, for all his training in stolidity, had difficulty keeping his composure. Newport of course reassured him, professed amity and support against his enemies, and gave him a red waistcoat "which highly pleased him." With that, and with the two shouts required by Indian protocol, the shallop bore the English a few miles on toward Jamestown.

Nauiraus, who was still with them, soon pointed out the land of the Appomattocs, who were ruled by a weroansqua,* or queen. Archer promptly named the place Queen Appomattoc's Bower, as Nauiraus guided them through a cornfield up a hill to where the ruler herself awaited them "in selfsame fashion of state as Pawatah or Arrohattoc; yea, rather with more majesty." The weroansqua, a "fat, lusty, manly woman" in Archer's description, was very likely

* Composed of *werowance* and *squaw*, "woman."

the same Opossunoquonuske who was known to William Strachey three years later as a crafty, well-nigh Machiavellian defender of Indian supremacy in Virginia. She was the sister of the werowance of the tribe, and apparently exercised independent power over her own village. It took two hours of Newport's best diplomacy to win a grudging measure of cheer from her, aided by gifts and a display of terrifying war machinery — which Archer noted did not terrify her at all. Then Nauiraus directed them some five miles down the river to a temporary residence of the Werowance of Pamunkey.

The arrival of the English at this encampment was celebrated as usual by dancing, feasting, tobacco, and in this case by a demonstration of Indian boys diving for mussels. At the end of this ritual, the English were conducted before the werowance, who sat in stately majesty — so stately, Archer added, "as to our seeming he became [a] fool." It was clear from the manner of reception that this was no ordinary werowance, although the English paid it scant heed at the time. (If either Smith or Percy noticed it, the observation is lost.) Archer, however, duly noted that their host's name was Opechancanough ("He Whose Soul Is White"). Later it was learned that he was half brother to the Overlord of All Tidewater Virginia, the Great Powhatan.

The English were quite taken in by this "Werowance Pamunkey." They got the notion that his land was rich in copper and pearls, in testimony whereof Opechancanough was well decorated with both. Archer put an absurd valuation on his pearls, and tried to bargain with him and his warriors for some of their copper (undoubtedly to send to London), but "found them nice in parting with any" — reluctant, in other words. Enthusiastically, Archer named the spot Pamunkey's Palace, although Nauiraus said it belonged to the Werowance of Weanoc. Whoever owned it, it was good ground — a hundred acres, planted with wild peas, beans, "wheat" [corn], tobacco, gourds, pumpkins, and the like.

When it came time for the colonists to leave, Opechancanough wanted Newport to spend the night with him, an invitation which was accepted. But when the two walked off alone for perhaps a quarter mile, Smith, Percy, Archer, and others followed. They were not going to let their Admiral fall into any trap. Opechancanough, noticing that they intended to stay near Newport, "altered his purpose" and waved his hand for them all to return to their boat, including Newport.

Leaving the white-souled werowance "in kindness and friendship," the English sailed downstream past a sharp turn in the river to Point Weanoc, where they anchored for the night. The local braves, as John Smith wrote, "according to their former churlish condition," rebuffed all efforts to trade and showed no signs of friendliness, despite Archer's earlier optimistic report. Smith was already beginning to see, or to sense, that the Indians did not love them, and did not want them there — not, certainly, as colonists. A little more realism of the John Smith kind — a little less naïve trust of the Wingfield kind — might have saved both sides many a heartache.

In any case, on Wednesday morning, May 27, the voyagers went ashore at Point Weanoc, and Nauiraus persuaded a few natives to go fishing for them. Nevertheless, something was clearly in the air. Archer wrote that the fishermen "seemed" their good friends, perhaps meaning to stress the seeming, and Smith wrote that the English could perceive more signs of suspicion and nervousness among the Indians than before. Then Nauiraus all of a sudden discovered that he had to go to see the Werowance of Arrohattoc and, with many assurances that he would visit them at the fort, left.

Even after this strange action, Smith states that Newport wanted to call at Paspahegh and Quiyoughcohannock villages, although several colonists feared "some mischief at the Fort." (Archer omits Newport's intended stops in his account, possibly because of London.) But Lady Luck sent them an unexpected fair wind. Newport bowed to her, and they headed for Jamestown with all speed.[5]

Something had indeed been brewing. While the exploring party was away, the colonists at Jamestown had noticed that few Indians visited them, only "one or two single now and then, practising upon opportunity," observing what went on inside the palisade. After four days of this, on Tuesday, May 26, the day before Newport's return, they struck. More than two hundred warriors (Smith says four hundred) assaulted Jamestown, and might have overthrown the whole colony had not the ordnance on the ships routed them. As it was, at least eleven men were hurt (one of whom died) and a boy was killed. Edward Maria Wingfield had an arrow shot through his beard while valiantly leading the defenders, but suffered no injury. The other four members of the Council were hurt. Then, at very long last, the fort was properly palisaded.

For some time after the assault, little happened worthy of mention. Archer's account reports ambushes and Indians lurking in the woods nearby, a dog killed, and then a gentleman named Eustace Clovill (a connection of Gosnold's) shot with six arrows. He died eight days later. All the while, corn was being planted and tasks carried out. But the colony was dispirited. As Shakespeare had written not long before, "Danger, like an ague, subtly taints."

Factions twitched within the colony, Indians skulked without. There could not but be colonists who accused Wingfield of delaying proper safety measures until it was almost too late. With these were certainly associated some of John Smith's many friends. For Smith was back among them again, an "equal" member of the expedition to Pawatah, yet still not sworn a member of the Council.

Robert Hunt, the chaplain, undoubtedly backed by Gosnold and possibly also by Newport (of whose essential fairness there can be no doubt), preached "good Doctrine," and exhorted Smith's foes to bury the hatchet. At length, as Archer put it, "there being among the Gentlemen and all the Company a murmur and a grudge against certain preposterous proceedings, and inconvenient courses, [they] put up a petition to the Council for reformation."

This was on Saturday, June 6. Sunday passed without accident or incident. Monday was partly taken up with the death and burial of Clovill — secretly, in accordance with the *Instructions* not to "advertise the killing of any of your men, that the country people [the Indians] may know it." That same afternoon two Indians approached unarmed, calling "Wingapo! * [Friends!]" from a distance. Despite the friendly call, a trigger-happy gentleman took a pot shot at them, whereupon they dropped to the ground and then ran away, still crying "Wingapo!" Thirty-six hours after this, the Council at length met.

While it is not clear what the *Petition* was about, Archer's story points to one main issue: John Smith. Captain Newport made a speech, vehemently persuading the gentlemen to "uniformity of

* *Wingapo* — literally "Sweet people!" (Compare Cree *weh'ke*, "sweet, fond," and *-a'pāo*, "man.")

Consent" (the words are Archer's), so that at the end, out of love for him, they "confirmed a faithful love one to another, and in our hearts subscribed an obedience to our superiors this Day. Captain Smith was this Day sworn one of the Council, who was elected in England." The date, as recorded by Archer, was Wednesday, June 10, 1607. John Smith's work in Virginia was about to begin.

The rest of the week passed relatively quietly. The colonists organized defenses, cut down more oaks for clapboard, and labored clearing the fort. On one day two mariners were wounded by Indians hiding in the tall grass outside the palisade. On another, Newport's sailors caught a sturgeon seven feet long and gave it to the colonists. Trivial matters, these — even the wounds!

On Sunday, however, the map maker from Turkey Isle turned up again, accompanied by a friend. These two explained by word and gesture that Opechancanough and the Werowances of Arrohattoc, Youghtanund, and Mattaponi were friendly to the English — the latter two having their tribal territories forty miles or more to the northwest, as the wild goose flies. These four chieftains would either assist the English (in war), they promised, or make peace between them and the Paspaheghs, Quiyoughcohannocks, Weanocs, Appomattocs, and Kiskiacks, their professed enemies. The two visitors then recommended that the English cut down the "long weeds" around the fort before going on with their tree-chopping and sawing — advice the very need for which reveals the thoughtlessness, laziness, or ineptness of the would-be conquerors of new lands for King James.

Monday was spent on clapboard for England when they should have been making houses for themselves. Then, on Tuesday, two further visitors came, paddling over from the Quiyoughcohannock side of the river. Newport, thinking they were the two who had come on Sunday, went out to meet them in the barge. But when they cried "Wingapo!" and gestured that their werowance was on the other side of a point, Newport realized that they were unfriendly Quiyoughcohannocks and were plotting to run his boat onto the mud. He told them, in broken Algonkian, that they were bad people, and they laughed and went away.

By this time, Newport began to plan definitely to return to England. As John Smith repeatedly claims, Newport was employed only for the transportation of the colonists and their supplies. Though he was a member of the Council, that membership seems to have been honorary or ex officio — witness his continued absence as ferryman par excellence of the London Company, and witness the two votes given the President of the Council to break deadlocks. In view of his departure, and the continued discontent in the colony, Newport therefore had a meeting with President Wingfield to ask him "how he thought himself settled in the government."

Wingfield, by his own report, answered:

> that no disturbance could endanger him or the colony, but it must be wrought either by Captain Gosnold, or Master Archer; for the one was strong with friends and followers, and could if he would; and the other was troubled with an ambitious spirit, and would if he could.

It is clear from this, that Wingfield did not consider Smith a troublemaker, but that he did harbor some suspicion as to Archer's designs.

Newport appears then to have approached both Gosnold and Archer and informed them of Wingfield's statement. Not only that, he "moved them, with many entreaties, to be mindful of their duties to His Majesty and the Colony." This approach, however well-intentioned, seems remarkably artless. No better way to encourage Archer in his ambition could be found than to inform him officially that the President was afraid of him.

As for Gosnold, the exhortation to behave was gratuitous. Everything points to his sincere and self-sacrificing interest in the colony.

Understandably, Archer's account bears the comment for the four days, Wednesday to Saturday, "no accident" — nothing to report — after which comes the entry: "Sunday, we had a Communion: Captain Newport dined ashore with our diet [regular provisions], and invited many of us to supper as a farewell." With that, Archer's pen is silent.

George Percy picks up the story, however, stating that on "Monday, the two and twentieth of June, in the morning, Captain Newport in the admiral [the flagship] departed from James Port for England." The tie with the homeland slowly seemed to dissolve over the horizon with the two departing ships, leaving, as he put it, one hundred and four persons "very bare and scanty of vistuals; furthermore in wars and in danger of the savages." The "wars" were of course their own dissensions.

Archer's account went to England with Newport. In addition there went also two supplementary reports (one perhaps by Tindall, the other possibly by Gosnold) and a letter from the Council in Virginia to the Council in England, signed by the six councilors staying at Jamestown (with Smith's name appearing right under Wingfield's). In addition, there were various private communications from the colonists, of which only the opening paragraph of one from William Brewster to Cecil survives.[6]

In Virginia, George Percy continued to write, but much of his work is lost. John Smith quickly developed into the leading chronicler of events, although he is too taken up with angry exposure of the colonists' many shortcomings to be impartial as a historian. And Edward Maria Wingfield was soon forced, by the course of things, to draw up a vindication of his presidency. Thus, for the next few months the Percy-Smith-Wingfield memoirs supply details on life in the colony, generally agreeing on the facts but differing widely in their interpretation.

One signal event of the period up to Newport's departure coincided strangely with the intense activity occasioned by that event. An Indian emissary arrived from "the great Powhatan" — this time the true one — with words of peace. Whether it was a good or an ill omen, it is startling that just as Newport sailed away, the settlers had their first communication from the despot who lives in history as Powhatan.

## CHAPTER 10

# MISERIES MORE THAN MAY BE BORNE

A LMOST TWO months had passed since Newport's fleet had glided into Chesapeake Bay — eight weeks of majestic aloofness on the part of the Overlord of Tidewater Virginia. No doubt, he was quickly informed of the apparition from the sea. No doubt, every move of the unwelcome strangers on land and water was reported to him. Yet Powhatan sat and waited. Divinations, conjurations, invocations took time. And Powhatan must determine what to do.

Born in the 1540's, Powhatan had inherited six petty tribes, scattered north and east of modern Richmond perhaps for twenty-five miles. His real name was Wahunsonacock, and two other names had been given him from villages he conquered: Ottaniack (or Oraniock) and Mamanatowick. Then, when he came into his heritage he was given the name of Powhatan, from the village of that name which may have been the original seat of the group of tribes. (Sometimes the English called him "The Powhatan," hinting that the name was considered a title.)

Later, Powhatan set out to conquer the tribes to the east, until he ruled over no less than twenty-eight tribes (according to John Smith), numbering perhaps 8500 souls scattered over an area of about as many square miles. It was a petty "state," in size, but Powhatan was virtually its absolute lord. In his person, he combined the elements of king and priest, as he himself revealed to John Smith when they met. No "emperor," such as Motecuhzoma II of Mexico, Powhatan was the Despot of Virginia, and his realm was not a "confederacy," but an autocratically ruled despotate. No other term quite fits either the man or the domain.

Powhatan had been there when the Jesuits tried to bring the

faith of Christ to Chesapeake Bay in 1570. He had known of the landing of Ralegh's expeditions in the 1580's. Both of these essays at penetration had been repulsed in Indian fashion, largely by betrayal. Once more, in 1607 and the years following, "The Powhatan" like "The O'Neill," who was his contemporary in the fastnesses of Ireland, would resist the English invaders in every way known to a wily heart, and like The O'Neill would fail.

Powhatan's determination to resist was bolstered by prophesies not dissimilar to those current in Mexico when Cortés arrived. Not long before 1607, William Strachey later wrote, the priests had told Powhatan that a nation would arise from Chesapeake Bay that would put an end to his rule. The Despot insured himself from this by exterminating the Chesapeake Indians. But a second prophecy blistered up to the effect that, as Strachey wrote,

> twice they should give overthrow and dishearten the attempters, and such strangers as should invade their territories, or labor to settle a plantation amongst them, but the third time they themselves should fall into their subjection and under their conquest.

And behold, this was in truth the third attempt. What to do? It was a real-life "to be or not to be," and any answer Powhatan found would irrevocably compromise his future. Powhatan was not the Prince of Denmark, and the process of reasoning was distasteful and overtaxing to him. He could but invoke his helpless spirits, and dream uneasy dreams. The danger-ague gripped him, too.

But little did Powhatan imagine that no sooner had Newport's ship slid over the horizon than a suicidal struggle for power would begin in the colony. The colonists were used to social strata but not to discipline, and some thought that the former had gone back to England with Newport. As to the latter, those who had had a taste of it in the Continental wars took it that in Virginia discipline was for everybody but *them*. And although John Smith was a conspicuous exception to these ideas, even he showed that to his way of thinking Virginia called for new social strata that must depend, at least somewhat, on action as well as narcissistic contemplation of heredity.

Practical experience, which can mean hardship undergone,

warned John Smith that it was urgently necessary to go to work to prepare for the coming fall and winter. The supplies Newport left behind were theoretically sufficient for thirteen or fourteen weeks, but only the most chuckleheaded optimist could have expected Newport to make a round trip to England in that time — not when it was recalled that it had taken them thirteen and a half weeks to get only to Martinique.

Yet the bulk of the colonists appear to have gone about work listlessly, or worse, as if they hoped for the *Susan Constant* to swim over the horizon within a matter of days, bearing all manner of food and drink. Everything could wait, even housebuilding. The climate was warmer than any part of England in summer, and Newport would bring laborers on his return. Then, too, when he did, and while that new fleet was tied up to Jamestown's riparian trees, any man could cheat on his daily ration, by theft, friendship, or cash. Oh, happy days would return with Newport and the fleet. Meanwhile, token work (by somebody else) would keep hunger under control.

So it was that the story of John Smith and the Virginia Venture during the second half of the year 1607 was largely the story of silly quarrels inside the fort, while the redmen peeped hopefully from behind trees. They were always ready to step in and exterminate the victor in Jamestown's intramural "Battle of the Frogs and Mice."

John Smith had borne his "restraint" with dignity. When that was over, and he was freed to accompany Newport up the river, and finally admitted to the Council, he took his proper place in the colony quietly, with no hasty show of self-aggrandizing moves or even patent resentment. True, he never forgave Wingfield. But in the first days after Newport's farewell there is certainly no hint of trouble caused by Smith's freedom.

On the other hand, there is indication of disagreement between Wingfield and Gosnold, and of much chafing under Wingfield's pompous administration among such as Captains Kendall and Archer. Captain Martin, apparently a "neutral" in the strife, was sick and too weak to support either side. But Ratcliffe clearly stood opposed to the President. Among non-councilors, George Percy sided with Wingfield, as did John Waller, while John Robinson and Richard Crofts were antagonistic — to mention a few whose attitude is clear. Thus Council and colony festered within, destroying all unity of purpose.

Outside the palisade, the Indians saw the two big ships sail, leaving but the pinnace and a shallop with the colonists. The thundering ordnance of the *Susan Constant* no longer threatened, with lethal bolts and terrifying flashes of fire. Days passed without sign of the ships. Opechancanough decided to act.

On Friday, July 3, seven or eight Indians arrived at Jamestown, bringing a deer from the Werowance of Pamunkey — "desiring our friendship," wrote Wingfield. After the formal ceremony of presenting it, the Indians asked where the ships were. Wingfield told them they were gone to Croatoan, where Ralegh's colony was unrealistically hoped to have survived. "They fear much our ships," he added, and he did not want the Indians to think that they were far away. The Indians, seemingly contented with the answer, accepted a present (a hatchet) for their werowance and sundry trifles for themselves, and left.

Soon thereafter, great Powhatan himself sent a deer. Presumably he also wanted to know about the ships. Wingfield "contented" his emissaries with further trifles. Another day or two elapsed, and the Werowance of Quiyoughcohannock dispatched an ambassador of peace, without a deer, requesting an interview with the President. Wingfield sailed over the river in the shallop to learn that he, too, wanted information about the ships. "He received answer as before," Wingfield wrote, throwing in the comment that "his countenance was nothing cheerful." The werowance then said that he was all out of food, and that new supplies were not yet available, but he would trade when they were.[1]

That so much interest in the ships was more than idle curiosity ought to have been apparent to the whole colony by then. That the real military strength of the Indians was not known ought to have claimed attention. That the colony's food supply was running out ought to have prompted remedial measures. But, no! The petty quarreling increased in direct proportion to the diminution in their stocks. "Had we been as free from all sins as [we were from] gluttony and drunkenness," wrote John Smith in later years, "we might have been canonized for saints."

President Wingfield, Smith goes on, was by then suspected, perhaps not entirely without reason, of hoarding food, apparently for his own use, and that of his few cronies. For the hundred or so remaining colonists, the ration was one measuring-cup of wheat and the same amount of barley, boiled, for each man a day. But that was not all. These two cupfuls of nourishment had "fried" for twenty-six weeks in the ships' holds on the way over, and "contained as many worms as grains." To cap it all, with "castles in the air" for lodging, these Englishmen of 1607 who never touched water but to wash — they drank beer or wine for breakfast as well as the other meals — were reduced to nothing but water, except for emergencies.

It is astounding that the hundred-odd men could get so little work done in so many weeks. After two months, no houses, not even dogholes, had been finished. Little seed had been planted — they were not the kind to till the soil — and only some miserable clapboard had been loaded on the ships for England. Clearly, lack of leadership, even more than internal dissension, lay at the root of all this nonaccomplishment. John Smith unabashedly blamed Wingfield for no small measure of their troubles — certainly with an element of justice. But the cause of the moral as well as the physical distemper was more basic than mere individual failings. It was to be found in the transplanted English social scheme, in dietary ignorance, and in the giddy notion that communism produces agricultural benefits. The Virginia Company, operating in a curious sociological vacuum, evolved the theory that common stores, common responsibility, common seed-planting, common harvesting (and possibly common danger) would pull the erratic, essentially egotistic Elizabethan gentlemen into a common drive toward success.

On the contrary, the fact that no personal gain or private profit was to be derived from any personal activity (even though it was for the common good) was in itself enough to discourage any drive, common or individual. The more "aristocratic" adventurers retired into their hallowed isolationism, and the less or not at all aristocratic "surfeited" themselves on whatever food a capricious Nature supplied — to the extent that they developed intestinal complaints when somebody caught a sturgeon, and when no one did, allowed their intestinal emptiness to complain in another key.

In this way, the better part of six weeks passed. Nothing of any consequence occurred. Then, about the end of July (Wingfield claims it was much earlier), bad or insufficient food, subtropical heat, and inactivity, abetted by the typhoid bacillus, began to take their toll. As John Smith wrote, with his usual exaggeration, "thus we lived near three months: our lodgings under boughs of trees, the savages being our enemies, whom we neither knew nor understood; occasions I think sufficient to make men sick and die." The dreary necrology kept by George Percy was about to begin.

Bartholomew Gosnold was taken sick about August 1. Late in the next week, John Asbie (or Ashby) died, apparently of dysentery. Three days after Asbie, George Flower died, of beriberi it seems. Then William Brewster was killed by the Indians, as was Ensign Jerome Alicock. Two more died of disease that same day — probably typhoid fever. Then followed the deaths, on August 15, of Stephen Galthorpe and Edward Browne. Galthorpe had been the author of the "intended and confessed munity" in which John Smith had had some part, but which certainly was not mutiny in the modern sense. There is no evidence that Galthorpe was in any way punished, probably because his connections in England were too powerful — only Smith suffered.

About this time, Wingfield encountered John Smith in Gosnold's sick-tent (it may have been the other way around) and an argument ensued about the supplies for the colony. Smith said something about Wingfield's "feasting" himself, as he apparently had done. Wingfield admitted, in Gosnold's presence, that he had had half a pint of pease boiled with a piece of pork, of his private stock, for old Edward Short, a laborer, who was sick and later died. If Smith said that this was the colony's stock or that it was for himself, why, Smith was lying. Furthermore, Wingfield added contemptuously, "it was proved to his face that he [Smith] begged in Ireland like a rogue, without a license. To such," he concluded, he did not want his name "to be a companion." This is the only reference anywhere to Smith's possible voyage to Ireland. It was as irrelevant as it was insulting. Not even the presence of Gosnold on his sickbed was able to bend the pride of Edward Maria Wingfield.

It is useless to enumerate all the deaths. They were caused by food-deficiency diseases and bacilli, bad water, heat, and idiotically unsuited clothing. Though none were immune from the Indians, those who survived the sickness became immune from further attacks. John Martin was one — he was sick almost throughout the first year in Jamestown. Ratcliffe and Smith also fell ill, but soon got well. John Martin's son, on the other hand, died quite suddenly. Then came the real loss.

Gosnold's sickness steadily worsened, and at last, on August 22, he died, to the universal consternation of the colony. At his burial all the ordnance in the fort was fired, "with many volleys of small shot," Percy details. Characteristically, John Smith's praise for Gosnold was for the living man — his death Smith merely lists. But Percy goes on to show the effect of Gosnold's death on the colony: "After Captain Gosnold's death, the Council could hardly agree by the dissention of Captain Kendall." And Wingfield is even more eloquent, for his personal status suffered a body blow. On Gosnold's life, he wrote, "stood a great part of the good success and fortune of our government and colony."

News of all these tragedies was carefully kept from the Indians. The dead bodies, "many times three or four in a night," Percy writes, were "trailed out of their cabins like dogs, to be buried." Their enemies, the savages, must not know how feeble they were becoming — indeed, how feeble they already were.

Toward the end of August, Thomas Studley, the cape merchant, died, after which there was a slight letup in the toll. The stagnant summer air began to move a little, the oppressive heat to lift. And with September the weather broke suddenly, bringing rain. At that time, according to Wingfield (borne out by Smith), there were not six able-bodied men in the fort. A few had even run away to live with the Indians, apparently realizing that tribal custom would not permit guests to starve or to be murdered in cold blood. These now began to straggle back. Wingfield "rewarded" the strayed sheep with such severity that none strayed again. One of them, only, brought back some little news about how the Indians lived — a William White, listed as a laborer but evidently an exceptional one. George Percy mentions him, and half a dozen bits of detail from his pen are quoted by Samuel Purchas in his *Pilgrimage* of 1613. The one important fact learned from these men was that the Indians were not cannibals, as some had feared.[2]

By this time Captain George Kendall had made himself so

obnoxious that he was removed from the Council and sent to prison on the pinnace. Just about then, too, the Indians' "hungry" season, as they seem to have called it, was over. With their harvest begun, they began to think of trade once more. With corn they could buy beads and other invaluable commodities. They suddenly appeared at the fort.

As John Smith piously put it, "it pleased God (in our extremity) to move the Indians to bring us corn, ere it was half ripe, to refresh us, when we rather expected [wondered] when they would destroy us." John Smith did not know that "green" corn is much tastier than "ripe" corn, for neither he nor any of his companions had ever eaten corn on the cob.

Wingfield also wrote that the Indians "did daily relieve us with corn and flesh," so that he was able to get twenty men back on their feet. But what brought the Indians was surely no more Wingfield's popularity than it was the providence of a no-longer-angry God. It was trade.

Meanwhile another kind of harvest was reaped within Jamestown palisade — one of Wingfield's own sowing. On September 10, Captain Ratcliffe, Captain Smith, and Captain Martin went to President Wingfield's tent with a warrant, signed by all three, to depose the President — as was provided in the *Articles* of November 20, 1606. The warrant stated that Wingfield was "very unworthy to be either President or [a member] of the Council, and therefore discharged him of both."

While the idea seems to have been born in Archer's busy brain (and hawked about by Ratcliffe), Smith and Martin did not refuse their support. Ratcliffe's interest was of course in no small part stimulated by a proviso that he would succeed Wingfield as President. Martin, although unambitious for the presidency, blamed Wingfield for the death of his son, and so was somewhat spitefully ready to depose him. Smith seems to have been attracted by Archer's plot only because he was repulsed by Wingfield's unalterable mixture of pomposity and pride of ancestry.

What undoubtedly capped the climax for John Smith was not so much his arrest (or restraint), but the fact that he could not stomach Wingfield's insults after that incident. Not only had Wingfield called him a liar during the spat in Gosnold's tent, but he was now quoting Smith as saying that they might be equal in Virginia but that if they were in England Smith would not want to see his valet go around with Wingfield — implying a reverse snobbery quite foreign to his character. (Such, at least, seems to be the meaning of the confused account which has survived.) This points directly to the heart of the Wingfield-Smith quarrel. Smith felt that not only their association in the Virginia Venture, as investors and as members of the Council, but also the forest and the Indians that surrounded them made them all equal. Wingfield held to his certainty that nothing could make them equal, since God and English social structure had ordained it otherwise. In any event, Smith's disgust certainly smacked more of the Olympian than Ratcliffe's ambition and Martin's bereaved-father pique.

The uproar that ensued, and kept the colony in a white heat for a week, was the sillier and the more tragic in the light of their depleted manpower and the need for the remnants of the colony to band together to last out the winter. Hostile natural and human forces had reduced the company to forty or a few more, from over a hundred — a terrible price in human life for so inconspicuous a colony. Yet Wingfield was solemnly committed to a sergeant and sent to the pinnace. His parting shot, revealing the man's make-up, was: "I am at your pleasure, dispose of me as you will, without further garboil [hubbub]." To which the sergeant observed that, if they did him wrong, "they must answer [for] it."

With the arrest of Wingfield and the swearing in as President of Captain John Ratcliffe, alias Sicklemore, a state of confusion and disorder set in such as the Christmas-season Lord of Misrule in England never saw, for all his pranks. On September 11 the ex-President was haled back before the remaining councilors and some other gentlemen for examination. Captain Gabriel Archer was appointed Recorder for Virginia, the first step upward of that ambitious man, and Ratcliffe made a speech to acquaint the gentlemen with the reasons for Wingfield's deposition.

The superlative pettiness of the charges voiced reveals that Wingfield, gentleman though he was in more senses than one, was more than anything else simply not equal to the situation. None of the accusations against him amounted to anything — not even Archer's assertion that he was in league with the Spaniards to destroy the colony. Wingfield's true sin was what is known in Greek as *hubris,* polished insolence — an offense common in court society in those days, and in Sir Walter Ralegh's case fatal. It is to this that Archer's relentless prosecution — if not persecution — must be attributed, in part if not wholly. His attitude during the second interrogatory indeed was so irritating that one of the councilors (Smith or Martin) saw fit to suggest that the former President should have a guard to protect him, which Wingfield indignantly refused. So, finally, after enough mountains had been made of molehills, Edward Maria was sent back to the pinnace, and George Kendall was released, to admit him to the prison, in the brig.

With Wingfield's demotion came John Smith's first promotion. For a fortnight the colony had had no cape merchant or supply officer, and Ratcliffe appointed John to that post and "committed the managing of all things abroad," or out of doors, also to him. Although they still had no houses and their "best commodity was iron which we made into little chisels" for trade with the Indians, the colonists still "would rather starve and rot with idleness, than be persuaded to do anything for their own relief without constraint." So wrote John Smith.

A few days later, on September 17, Wingfield was brought before the court once more to answer a complaint brought by Jehu Robinson, an investor in the Venture, that Wingfield had said that he and others had consented to run away with Wingfield and the shallop to Newfoundland. Soon after this, Wingfield was also called up to answer, at last, John Smith's charge that Wingfield had said "he did conceal an intended mutiny." This was of course the basis for Smith's arrest when they sailed from the Canaries, and the only other person known to have been involved was Stephen Galthorpe, recently deceased. Wingfield protested that one of these charges would bear no action, for it was outside of the scope of their patent, though he does not make it clear which of the charges he meant.

Ratcliffe ignored the protest and appointed a jury. (Wingfield commented that Ratcliffe "did wear no other eyes or ears than grew on Master Archer's head.") The jury in time awarded one hundred pounds damages to Robinson and two hundred to Smith. In this the extravagant accusation against John Smith was finally quashed, although his arrest was not entirely forgotten and is sometimes brought up against him even today by some who fail to read the evidence and the verdict.

By this time John Smith, in his capacity of supply officer, observed that they had food left for only eighteen days, and was sent down to Kecoughtan to trade for corn and "try the river for fish." There, however, the Indians, by then suspecting the English of starving, showed unexpected talents for driving a hard bargain. Smith shrewdly ignored the miserable bits of food offered in exchange for a valuable hatchet or a piece of copper, but gave lavish presents to the children of "such trifles as well contented them." Then he retired to his boat and anchored for the night, despite "stormy weather."

This gave the Indians time to change their minds. The following morning, when Smith "under color to fetch fresh water" sent a man to the town, the Kecoughtans invited Smith ashore. He took four soldiers along, and soon traded his trifles for fish, oysters, bread, and venison. In due time he also had sixteen bushels of corn. With that he started home, but came across two canoes from Warraskoyack, across the river, from which he eventually got fourteen more bushels — "the very name whereof gave great comfort to our despairing company."

The last hot-season deaths had been recorded by then, and with sickness abating the more sanguine of the adventurers were beginning to dream in earnest of Admiral Newport's return. John Smith knew otherwise. He was confident that Newport would come back, but he did not know when. Therefore he estimated again — not how many weeks they would have to wait for Newport (Percy suggested at least six), but how many days' food supply they had. And on some unknown date after his return from Kecoughtan Smith estimated that it would last but two more weeks.[3]

Some of the colonists then suggested that Ratcliffe and Archer should go to England (was it they themselves?), now that Ratcliffe, thanks to Smith's nursing, was well again. But Martin was also able to walk around a little again, and he, as well as Smith, most likely saw another threat of abandonment in the proposed voyage. So, "with much ado it was concluded, that the pinnace and barge should go towards Powhatan, to trade for corn" — presumably meaning the village. The Powhatan voyage would certainly bring quicker relief than the one to London, and ruled out any foul play.

Upon this decision, Smith states, lots were drawn as to who should go, but it may be suspected that this was to avoid, rather than take part in, the expedition. John Smith won.

While the pinnace was being equipped with gewgaws for bartering and weapons for defense in case of need, Smith took off in the barge for Quiyoughcohannock. When he got there, however, the village was deserted but for women and children who were afraid to trade. Smith had no authority to force the issue, and so retired across the river to Paspahegh.

There his hopes were soon dashed. Although he managed to get ten or twelve bushels out of the Paspaheghans, they wanted guns and swords in payment, and when these were refused tried to steal them. Smith resisted. The Indians prepared an assault then, and he had to retire. Nevertheless, along the way home Indians slipped out from the shore by canoe to trade. Warriors from the villages observing this chased the English downstream. As a result, unprepared as he was for all-out war Smith "took occasion to return with 10 bushels of corn." Captain Martin later followed suit and brought back eight or ten bushels on each of two trips. By that time, the pinnace was ready.

Smith's plan was to take this little ship far up the river, where the Indians had not yet been spoiled by the overgenerosity of the weak-willed colonists. (This shortsighted profligacy, the child of selfishness, was often to ruin the market for economical barter.) Inland from the James River, he knew of a large tribe called the Chickahominies, living along the river of the same name.* This secondary stream has its source northwest of modern Richmond, and empties into the James only some six miles above Jamestown (eight, according to John Smith). Its channel is shallow and tortuous. In 1607, no colonist had penetrated the dense woods and marshes that marked most of its course.

Leaving instructions for the pinnace to follow him by the next tide, Smith set out on November 19 and reached the bay on the far side of the mouth of the Chickahominy before the ebb tide halted him. Here the water is today but two or three feet deep, and it is not likely that it was much deeper in 1607. Since the barge had to stop for the afternoon in any case, it was apparently Smith's

---

* *Chickahominy*, possibly from something like *tshikĕhämĕn*, "a clearing." See Commentaries.

idea to join the pinnace when it came upstream with the flow tide.

Toward evening, however, a handful of Indians hailed the barge from shore, and Smith went to meet them. They were Chicka-hominies who wanted Smith to visit their village. The Paspaheghs living on or near the shore there objected to this, most probably because the powerful Chickahominies, although nominally subject to the great Powhatan, enjoyed home rule and lived in the happy, democratic, if anarchic, Algonkian style. (Despots were a new im-portation, not to their liking.) The Paspaheghs conceivably feared friendship between the Chickahominies and the English, which would catch them in between. John Smith, ignorant of such nice-ties, disregarded the Paspaheghs, who were unpleasant anyway, and accepted the invitation.

With the moon nearing its full, John could follow his guides through the forest until midnight, when they reached the village. There Smith left one of his men and returned to the barge to bring it up the next morning. The village, called Manosquosick or Menoscosick, appears to have stood near the right bank of the river on the high ground south of Lanexa, where the river twists and turns endlessly before straightening out for the final north–south reach as it nears its mouth.

Back at Manosquosick with the barge the next day, Smith loaded it to the gunwales, between there and some five other villages. In fact, at Mamanahunt in the heart of the Chickahominy country two hundred Indians were assembled with more corn than Smith knew what to do with. Returning to Paspahegh, where darkness overtook him, he found no trace of the pinnace. Consequently, "considering the want of corn at our Fort," he hastened back to Jamestown, reaching it with the ebb tide at midnight. The pinnace had gotten stuck in the mud.

The next morning, Smith took the barge up again, reaching Mamanahunt a day later. There, the people, having heard of his coming, "were ready with 300 or 400 baskets, little and great, of which having laded my barge, with many signs of great kindness, I returned." To Jamestown, of course.

As he started downstream, the Chickahominies asked to hear the English guns. Smith was glad to comply. Out in midstream, he wrote, they "seemed a peal of ordnance," thanks to the echo. Be-tween the impression of power and the rarity of the baubles exchanged for their corn, these Indians seemed won to English friendship.

Now that the colony had enough food for a while, at least, it could have been thought that the dissensions would slacken. On the contrary, conditions grew worse. The running aground of the pinnace was evidently not exactly an accident. Captain Kendall, perhaps with the connivance of Wingfield, began whispering ideas about abandoning the colony before it was too late. President Ratcliffe apparently was even weaker and more self-indulgent than Wingfield had been. Martin was perennially sick. And above all, the pinnace was now ready to sail. She was prepared for Smith's trading voyages, but she could sail out into the Atlantic as well as up into Indian territory. So, some sailors and hangers-on of the schemers had begun to listen.

Smith returned before anything happened, but he did not have time to take over the pinnace for the agreed-on journey to Powhatan before the whole piece of treachery blew wide open. President Ratcliffe, in a fit of petulance over no one knows what, had an altercation with James Read, the blacksmith. According to John Smith, it was merely a "chiding," or reproof for some misdemeanor. According to Wingfield, Ratcliffe beat the blacksmith, and the latter struck back; although Smith said that Read only "offered to strike." Whichever it was, it was a very serious matter, since Ratcliffe — as President of the Council — was the local embodiment of King James's authority. Read might almost as well have hit out at the king himself. After a summary trial, he was condemned by a jury to be hanged, and Ratcliffe ordered immediate execution of the verdict.

Read, somewhat surprisingly, seemed quite confident of himself while the soldiers brought rope and a ladder, and leaned the ladder against a handy tree. He was calm even when he was prodded up the ladder, all the time, as Smith wrote, "continuing very obstinate as hoping upon a rescue." When none came, however, he "became penitent," and blurted out the whole conspiracy. Kendall was at the root of it all, and Wingfield seemed implicated.

Read was brought down the ladder again, and Kendall brought to trial. He seems to have made few bones about running off with the pinnace — but it was to Spain, not to England. Evidently a crypto-Catholic, almost certainly a former Continental spy for Lord

Salisbury, Kendall planned to supply King Philip with full information on the colony — undoubtedly for a price. What part Wingfield may or may not have played in this will probably never be known. But a jury judged Kendall guilty of mutiny and condemned him to be shot. The rope prepared for Read would not do for a gentleman.

Smith's tale of the proceedings varies somewhat from that presented here, and bears the earmarks of somewhat melodramatic coloring. Yet it may contain its share of the truth. According to him, the plot was uncovered on his return from Chickahominy, as stated above. But he adds to this that the pinnace was about to sail, with Wingfield and Kendall aboard, and that he halted it with musket shot and balls from a light cannon.

While this reads like a mere dash of bravado for self-aggrandizement, Wingfield's account bears Smith out in general, with a changed cast of characters, and places it after Kendall's execution. According to Wingfield, he had indeed determined to go to England, "to acquaint our Council there with our weakness," but he would not go with Ratcliffe or Archer (a hint that they wanted to go, too). Then he added that he would contribute a hundred pounds sterling toward taking the whole colony home. "They," he added (presumably meaning the colony, including Smith), did not like any of his "proffers," and fired several shots at the determined ex-President. Another brief conference patched matters up.

Apart from the sequence (neither Smith nor Wingfield is infallible in that regard), the stories contain virtually the same elements. Nothing in Wingfield's narrative indicates that John Smith did not order the shots fired, and his own story fits in well with his character. Always a man of action, Smith would logically have moved vigorously to stop the departing pinnace when Ratcliffe, a malcontent rather than a doer, hesitated to use violence. However it was, and whether it was the Council or Smith alone that moved to stop the ship, the execution of Kendall and the overthrow of Wingfield's plan ended an era in Jamestown.

John Smith was evidently emerging as the central figure in the colony. As such, he was not long in attracting the spite of his former allies, Ratcliffe and Martin, and the hatred of the ambitious Archer. But Smith's greatest adversary kept secret court in the forest, not in the decimated fort. It was time to seek him out.[4]

CHAPTER 11

# POWHATAN [1]

Nearly two months had slipped by since the Council had decided that John Smith should go "towards Powhatan" for supplies. In that interim, trading had proved profitable up the Chickahominy, the colony was "indifferently" well provided with corn, and after another argument over sending the pinnace to England, the Council determined that John should finish his "discovery" — that is, find the source of the Chickahominy.

Setting out early in December, he took with him Jehu Robinson, a "gentleman," Thomas Emry, a carpenter, George Cassen, a laborer, and six others. Robinson may have gone along, as the only gentleman, because of his association with John Smith in the judgment of damages against Wingfield. Whatever their stated goal — beyond picking up food by the wayside — it is obvious that Smith, of his own free will or under strong suggestion from the Council, wanted to see if the Chickahominy had a lake for its source. The *Instructions* said that, if the river where the colonists planted sprang out of a lake, "the passage to the other sea [the Pacific Ocean] will be more easy." Such a discovery would put Smith somewhat ahead of Newport, who had found nothing but the falls on *his* trip.

Smith's natural eagerness to add a little to his fame was spurred on by a group the sincerity of whose motives may well be questioned. These colonists, perhaps hoping that the Indians would relieve them of Smith (thus removing the chief obstacle to their abandoning the project), had complained that he had not gone far enough in his exploring and had therefore neglected his duty. Smith defended himself on the ground that he had to collect all the food he could while he could. But the obdurate Council (meaning Ratcliffe and Martin, manipulated by Archer) taxed him with excessive dilatoriness, as well (possibly) as incompetence, cowardice, or other reprehensibilities. He consequently set out with more determination than ever. Spurning the pinnace, by then surely anchored off Jamestown for the winter, he chose the barge to convey him. Its draft was suitably shallow.

Not halting at any of the villages he had passed before, Smith coursed some sixteen miles up the Chickahominy to a peninsula he calls Moysonicke, which can be identified almost certainly as the neck of land between the Chickahominy and Diascund Creek. There, the high ground between the two streams caught his eye. A better seat for a town, he wrote, could not be desired.

Above Moysonicke, the already tortuous channel of the river began to be dotted with low-lying islands until, after a stretch of a mile or so of such hazards, they reached Apokant, "the highest town inhabited"; that is, the last of the Chickahominy towns upstream. Narrow as the river had become, the party went on gallantly for another ten miles. By then, the stream was but eight to ten feet wide, with indications of a low-water breadth of only six or seven. The current was swift, the bottom of the channel hard, and the surrounding terrain flat with sandy soil. These characteristics led Smith to believe that he was not far from the head of the river, which by then he suspected (or hoped) was either a lake or a "broad ford."

It was clear, however, that the barge was not safe in such waters. Smith determined to take it back to Apokant and hire a canoe, for explore he must. If he did not, he told his party, those at Jamestown would say he "durst not." Some of the company being as "desirous" as himself, the barge was rowed downstream, to be tied up to the shore while Smith and those who shared his idea returned to traverse the "vast and wild wilderness."

Less than halfway to Apokant the explorers ran across a canoe with two Indians who agreed, for a price, to take Smith "fowling" — the excuse he gave for his curiosity. He then went on to Apokant, secured the barge, and spent the night. The next morning he gave orders that no one was to go ashore until he returned, and started back up the river with two Englishmen who supported his plan (Robinson and Emry) and the two Indians of the day before.

That John Smith perhaps had some qualms about what he was doing is indicated by his repeated defenses of his act: the probability of the river having its source in a lake; the desolateness of the country, which would diminish the danger of a large-scale attack; the carping at Jamestown; and above all the possibility of some discovery "of worth to encourage our adventurers [financial backers] in England."

The party of five quickly made the trip back to the stopping point of the day before, and then a dozen miles farther on into the interior. The channel continued navigable but was mazy. Often it was almost lost in the bordering marshes. About lunchtime, however, Smith noticed some fairly solid ground where the canoe could pull up, and decided to go ashore. He detailed Robinson and Emry, with one Indian, to light a fire and start cooking while he took the other with him across country to see the nature of the soil, as suggested by the *Instructions*. For safety's sake, he cautioned the two Englishmen to keep their muskets ready, with matches to fire them lighted, and to discharge one the moment any stray Indian was sighted. Upon such a signal, Smith would return forthwith.

In the meantime, back at Apokant, Smith was hardly out of sight before at least one of the men decided to go ashore. This was George Cassen, who got separated from his companions and was taken captive by Indians. The latter apparently had noted the arrival of the barge with Smith, and his subsequent departure with two other Indians. They wanted to know where he had gone. Cassen, to reconstruct the story as well as possible without much firm fact, refused to tell — perhaps realizing by then that he should not have disobeyed orders. The Indians insisted. Cassen persisted.

Out of patience, the Indians bound Cassen to a tree and began to hack his fingers and toes off with mussel shells and dried, sword-sharp reeds. In agony, Cassen screamed out that Smith had gone up the river, but it was too late. The Indians had tasted blood, and would not stop now. They lighted a fire, threw the severed pieces of George Cassen into the flames, and began to flay him alive, starting with his scalp and continuing with his face and neck — then on down his body, ripping open his belly. With that, they set fire to the tree, and soon George Cassen, tree and all, formed a blazing torch around which the Indians danced and whooped. The six remaining Englishmen meanwhile had escaped in the barge.

Not all of Cassen's torturers danced around the fire. Some of them sped through the forest toward John Smith and his companions. As they ran, others joined them. Soon they spied the canoe tied up or beached near three men and a fire. Slipping noiselessly around them, they let fly their arrows. Jehu Robinson was hit with twenty or thirty, and fell with a cry where he was. The other Indian and Thomas Emry were not seen again.[2]

Smith had not been gone more than a quarter of an hour when he heard the cry, "and a hollowing of Indians, but no warning piece [shot]." Aware that something had happened, John seized his Indian, bound him tight to himself, put his pistol at the Indian's back, and told him that he would be shot if anything happened to Robinson and Emry. The Indian seemed not to know what was going on, and advised Smith to run for it. Smith argued.

An arrow, striking him harmlessly on the thigh, stopped the argument. Smith spotted two Indians drawing their bows and fired his pistol — a French wheel lock, the finest money could buy. But with all its technological perfection, this weapon could not be fired rapidly in succession. When Smith's shot missed, the two Indians slipped away, and by the time he was ready to fire again, three or four more Indians were visible, drawing a bead on him. They too dropped to the ground and fled when the pistol cracked.

All this while, Smith held his Indian close to him, a living shield. Some twenty or thirty arrows fell short of the pair, while Smith retaliated with three or four more pistol shots. Then they were surrounded. Two hundred Indians closed in from the woods, arrows notched to bowstrings. This done, they laid their weapons on the ground. In Smith's words:

> My hinde ["man," the Indian he hired] treated betwixt them and me of conditions of peace; he discovered [revealed] me to be the Captaine [werowances were not put to death arbitrarily]: my request was to retire to the boat: they demanded my arms; the rest they said were slain, only me they would reserve.

Although there was no threat in the word, Smith apparently hesitated. His guide urged him not to shoot. Still hesitating to give up his arms, Smith moved backwards, paying more attention to the Indians than to his footing, and stepped into a quagmire. The Indian tried to pull him out, and got stuck also. Then indeed there was nothing to do but "to try their mercies." He threw his weapons onto the dry ground.

Straightway, the Indians pulled the two out of the icy bog, diligently rubbed the circulation back into Smith's benumbed legs, and led him to their chief, Powhatan's half brother, the Werowance of Pamunkey, Opechancanough.

Smith and the werowance had not met since Newport's voyage up the James, seven months before. He had observed on that occasion that Opechancanough was not only a remarkably "stately" Indian, but also one who was not to be trifled with. He must have realized too that on their previous meeting there had been nothing to show Opechancanough that Smith was in any way important. Accordingly, if he could not pretend to be the equal of Newport, and Opechancanough knew that he was not, then he must be someone else of importance — perhaps his son, and a medicine man or shaman to boot. (Certainly not in those words, for they did not exist in English in 1607.)

What John Smith was thinking is eminently clear from what he did. Taking a page from Thomas Hariot's book (or perhaps from Hariot himself), Smith began to demonstrate his medicine-man qualifications. Producing from his doublet an ivory double compass, with elaborate card of the kind used by seamen, he held it before Opechancanough with dramatic mystery. Slowly he turned the case to show how the card and needle remained pointing in the same direction. Opechancanough poked his finger at it, to see how it worked, but naturally could not touch the card. It was his introduction to a magic substance: glass.

Taking full advantage of Opechancanough's perplexity at being able to see but not to touch the card with its cabalistic markings, Smith began an impressive lecture on the "roundness of the earth, the course of the sun, moon, stars and planets," and wound up with a peroration on the greatness of the land and sea, the diversity of nations and races, how far off England was, and other complex truths. For an hour they heard him before they bethought themselves of blood again. Then they tied him to a tree to celebrate another orgy.

Opechancanough, however, was fearful. The short, muscular Englishman who held such arcane paraphernalia in his hand and stood unafraid alone among two hundred braves must have some unknown power working for him. He had discoursed of the sun and moon as if they were brothers, and of a mighty monarch of bearded white people across the boundless ocean. Everything pointed to the supernatural.

Opechancanough took the compass and held it hieratically above the prisoner's head. Awed, the Indians dropped their bows and arrows again. Once more Opechancanough gestured. There was a colossal shout, and the Indians untied Smith, to lead him with military mummery to a hidden hunting lodge half a dozen miles away.

At the head of the parade was the werowance, with twenty bowmen flank and rear, in fives, and with other warriors interspersed, armed with shields and wooden swords set with sharp stones or animal teeth. Behind came Captain John Smith, with a bowman before and one on either side, and all the rest of the braves in file behind.

When this procession reached the lodge, the women and children flocked around to watch, while the Indians put on a show of marching and countermarching in what Smith calls a *bishion*.* And the demonstration ended in a savage dance, thrice repeated, around Opechancanough and Smith. In this, as Smith described it, the Indians

> cast themselves in a ring, dancing in such several postures, and singing and yelling out such hellish notes and screeches; being strangely painted, every one his quiver of arrows, and at his back a club; on his arm a fox or an otter's skin, or some such matter for his vambrace [guard]; their heads and shoulders painted red, with oil and pocones [bloodroot] mingled together, which scarlet-like color made an exceeding handsome show; his bow in his hand, and the skin of a bird with her wings abroad dried, tied on his head, a piece of copper, a white shell, a long feather, with a small rattle growing at the tails of their snakes tied to it, or some such like toy.

Once this performance was concluded, a "Captain" conducted John Smith to a long house where thirty or forty tall "fellows" guarded him, while a quarter of venison was brought, along with

* Italian *biscione,* "a large snake." A snake-like troop maneuver.

some ten pounds of bread, for his supper — more than enough for twenty men, wrote Smith. The guard was soon reduced to eight, and for a few days three women came every morning with as many platters of fine bread and more than enough venison for ten men. Although Smith began to suspect that they were fattening him for some cannibal feast he could not but add that his acquaintance with them increased their "better affection," mutually.

By then, one friendly Indian to whom he had given beads and toys in the days when Jamestown was first being founded brought him his "gown," or cloak, the weather being bitter cold, and eventually he got back his "points and garters" (for holding up his breeches and stockings), his compass, and his writing tablet. Opechancanough visited him at least once, to learn more about the earth, the sky, and the seas, and especially the great English ships — possibly in a veiled attempt to find out if Newport would be back, and what retaliation might be expected if Smith were not there to greet him. (William Strachey noted that the Indians made wars "principally for revenge." They may have thought that the English would do the same thing.) And the Werowance of Paspahegh also came to see him, urging the Pamunkeys in Smith's own presence to attack Jamestown, after which he trotted down to Jamestown to express his sorrow at the capture of Smith by "his enemies" the Pamunkeys.

Smith meanwhile acquired such knowledge as he could of the course of the Chickahominy and James rivers, and of the Indians farther south, where Sir Walter Ralegh's colony had died. He learned that certain men clothed like himself lived at a place called Ocanahonan (North Carolina?), and that in the other direction there was a "great turning of salt water" within four or five days' march above the falls.

Taking advantage of these exchanges of information, Smith hit upon the idea of sending a message to the fort, "by which they should understand," he explained to the Indians, how kindly they treated him and that he was well, "lest they should revenge my death." Opechancanough was agreeable, for then he could send spies inside Jamestown to learn more about it (and possibly about the return of Newport, about whom Smith had purposely supplied terrifying information).

Three runners were sent with a letter from Smith, "in such weather as in reason were unpossible by any naked [savage] to be endured." In the letter was word that the Indians were plotting an attack, that the colonists should frighten the messengers with a show of force, and that they should send him without fail certain articles which might facilitate his escape.

The men at the fort rather amazingly carried out Smith's instructions in detail, frightening the Indians out of their skins with ordnance, and then giving them a letter for Smith. When the runners got back and Smith read the message aloud, the whole village was stricken with terror. Either the paper could speak or Smith could divine, said the Indians. Therefore when an Indian whose son Smith had wounded when he was captured attempted to take revenge (as was his traditional right), the guards interfered. They asked Smith to cure the hurt (as such miracle workers could), but when Smith slyly said that he would have to go to the fort for a curative "water" for it, they refused. They were sly, too. The boy died.[3]

Soon after, but probably not because of this, Opechancanough ordered Smith removed to another place. He was first led on a cross-country march to the headwaters of the Pamunkey River and the Mattaponi, where he was feasted and put up in one of the houses of the great Powhatan himself. When he heard this, Smith, still thinking that the Powhatan in question was the one who had met them at the falls, decided to insist on being taken to see that chieftain — and in that way maybe get back to Paspahegh and Jamestown. After several days, the Indians appeared to comply, but got only as far as the first village of his captivity, Rassawek. There they packed up their temporary houses in bundles of mats and set off eastwards for the great Powhatan. Since they were going in what was the wrong direction for Smith, this must have been as puzzling for him as his insistence on seeing the wrong man must have been for the Indians.

Although the chronology of Smith's captivity is impossible to establish accurately, it must have been about December 22 when Opechancanough marched Smith through the forest, canoed him across the Youghtanund River (now the Pamunkey) "as broad as Thames," and conducted him to Menapacant, the residence of Opechancanough and Powhatan's half brother Kekataugh. Kekataugh apparently received Smith with genuine hospitality, because of earlier fair treatment at Smith's hands in Jamestown. Yet his subsequent actions are quite inscrutable. John Smith was led off on another march which, combined with the previous one, was tantamount to walking this way and that over the whole state of Delaware or three quarters of his native Lincolnshire — all in the bitter cold of that exceptional winter.

From Kekataugh's residence near today's West Point, where the Pamunkey River flows into the York, John Smith was led north to a village near the modern town of Tappahannock on the Rappahannock River. There he was exhibited to the people. The cause of this, Smith learned, was that a year (or perhaps two or three years) before, "a ship had been in the River Pamunkey, [whose captain] having been kindly entertained by Powhatan their Emperor, they returned thence, and discovered [explored] the River of Toppahannock: where being received with like kindness, yet he slew the King, and took off his people." John Smith was supposed to be the same captain. But the people at Tappahannock reported that the captain had been a tall man, and Smith being conspicuously untall was treated kindly. The next day they left.

Smith was then brought back past the source of the Piankatank River to the Pamunkey-York, probably to Uttamussak, a village on the high ground near the northward loop in the Pamunkey four miles or so above West Point. One of the principal temples in all Powhatan's despotate stood in that village, and near it was a house-temple, or residence, of the Despot. Here John Smith was brought for interrogation and possibly conjuration. The priests wanted to know, presumably for Powhatan's information, if any more of his countrymen were expected to arrive, and what it was Smith intended when he went "fowling."

In order to get at the truth (there had to be magic), the Indians made a great fire in one long-house early in the morning, and placed two mats nearby, one on each side. Smith was then seated on one of the mats, and the guards went out. Immediately, to quote John himself,

came skipping in a great grim fellow, all painted over with coal mingled with oil; and many snakes' and weasels' skins stuffed with moss, and all their tails tied together, so as they met on the crown of his head in a tassel; and round about the tassel was a coronet of feathers, the skins hanging round about his head, back and shoulders, and in a manner covered his face; with a hellish voice and a rattle in his hand.

This weird figure proceeded to dance around the fire, beginning an invocation in broken sentences, "by starts and strange passions," and making a circle of corn meal around the fire. This done, three more "such devils" rushed in in like manner, painted half black, half red, with white eyes and red strokes like mustaches on their cheeks. These danced around the first conjurer "a pretty while," until three more "as ugly as the rest," but with red eyes and white mustaches, came in. At last all seven sat down, with the first conjurer in the middle. There they howled and sang and shook their rattles until the "great grim fellow" laid down five grains of corn, after which he stretched out his hands and arms with such violence that he broke into a sweat, and his veins stood out. A short oration followed, and then a brief groan from the other six, and the chief "priest" laid down three grains more.

The ceremony continued with the priests circling the fire twice, and then placing little sticks between the grains of corn, after sundry short orations. And on and on the singing and howling went until nightfall, without interruption. But when at last it came to an end, the seven priests feasted with John Smith "merrily, with the best provisions they could make."

While they ate they explained that the ceremony symbolized their country in the first circle of corn meal, while the grains stood for the bounds of the sea, and the little sticks were England — for the world was flat and they were in the middle of it. Then they showed him a bag of gunpowder which they were keeping to plant the following spring — they wanted to know what kind of seed it was.

On three days this ceremony was repeated, with unknown incantational efficacy, at the end of which Opitchapam, another half brother of Powhatan's, invited Smith to his house, where he was well treated and given a solemn banquet of bread, wildfowl, and game animals. At this banquet only John Smith was permitted to eat. His hosts sat and watched. Another kind of incantation, but one whose meaning it would be risky to conjecture! Then the guards led their revered prisoner back to Menapacant and Werowance Opechancanough, bearing all the remainder of the feast in baskets. There, all the werowance's women and children collected around John Smith for their share of the food.

Christian Christmas had meanwhile come and gone. At last Opechancanough escorted his prisoner down the river to Werowocómoco ("Rich [or Royal] Court"), where the Supreme Chief, Powhatan, resided. On Smith's arrival a great assembly of warriors, more than two hundred, stood watching as if "he had been a monster" — wrote Smith. There was a brief delay until Powhatan and his suite got themselves ready for the audience. And John Smith, diminutive warrior from the battlefields of Turk and Tatar, was admitted to the august presence of the autocrat of Tidewater Virginia. He was, like Cortés nearly a century before, the first of his nation to cast eyes upon the native overlord of an American "empire." But where Cortés had marched in at the head of victorious troops, John Smith was led in, defeated, solitary, and unarmed.[4]

Powhatan received his captive reclining on a dais of mats, his neck hung with chains of pearls, a mantle of raccoon skin drawn about him. A fire blazed before him. A young woman sat at his head, another at his feet. On either side, squatting on mats on the ground, his chief men were ranged ten in a row, with as many young women behind them, each ornamented with chains of white beads, and their heads painted red with bloodroot. Through the smoke and dark air, John Smith saw a tall, well-proportioned man, sour of countenance, gray of hair, with little beard, whose age might have been sixty years or more. (His evident hardiness did much to cut the years away.)

Captain Smith was received with a great shout, according to Indian protocol. Then the Werowansqua of Appomattoc — the "fat, lusty, manly woman" he had seen in May, but who did not trouble to greet him — brought him water to wash his hands, while another supplied a towel of turkey feathers. Only after this ceremony, similar in spirit to the bread and salt Smith had been offered in Muscovy years before (an escaped prisoner then), did Powhatan welcome him "with good words," and further platters of food. He assured Smith of friendship, and his freedom within four days. He acknowledged an "academic" interest in Opechancanough's report on Smith and the sun, moon, and stars, and such matters, but he really wanted to know more about the reason for the coming of the Englishmen to his realm.

John Smith answered evasively. The English, he said, had been in a fight with the Spaniards, their enemies. They had been over-powered and driven by adverse weather to Chesapeake Bay. There they had been shot at by the natives, but at Kecoughtan they had been well treated. They had asked for fresh water, and had been sent up the river, where the Paspaheghs had "kindly" used them. They had been forced to stay there to mend a leak in their pin-nace, and were waiting for his father, Admiral Newport, to come and conduct them away. That was all.

Powhatan gave no sign of being impressed by the relation be-tween Smith and the Commander — a trump card Smith had been reserving. He demanded why the Englishmen had sailed up the James River some months before. Smith answered that he would have occasion later to talk to him about the salt sea that lay on the other side of the mountains. It was more important to bring up the matter of another child of Admiral Newport's who had been slain in that region, a matter of days before. He assumed that Powhatan's enemies, the Monacans, had done this. The English, Smith concluded, intended to revenge the death of this man.

In the face of Smith's inspired counterattack and veiled reference to English touchiness, Powhatan paused to deliberate. At length he went on to say that it was the Anchanachucks who had slain his brother, and that he himself, not the English, would avenge his death. Then he digressed, much as Smith had. There were other savage tribes thereabouts, he volunteered, such as the Pocough-taonack ("People of the Place of Fire"), who were cannibals and warred continuously with his protected tribes, the people of Moyaons and Pataromerke (Potomac). The cannibals, he said, had shaven heads with long hair behind, and carried battle-axes for swords. Rambling farther afield, he described other nations and other visi-tors. Indeed, he assured Smith (clearly in answer to a question) that he knew of the tribes where Ralegh's men had landed — a day and a half, two days, even six days, south from where Smith's companions were. The Roanoke mentioned by Smith was in their territory. Lastly he described a country called Anone, where the people had much brass, and their houses were walled, as Smith had said of the houses in England.

John Smith presented planned comments on all this. Recognizing Powhatan's pride in his dominions, he offered a glowing picture of the territories of Europe and of the mighty monarch whose name was James, King of many realms, who had many ships, and whose trumpets led men to war. (He had noticed that the Indians were startled by their brass instruments.) To this he added vivid words about the terrible manner of fighting of all who were under Admiral Newport, his father, whom he called the Werowance of All the Waters.

Powhatan, Smith wrote, marveled at Newport's greatness and "not a little" feared it. This may or may not be true, but by then it was time to reach a decision about the prisoner before him. The petty werowances, priests, and warriors were getting impatient.

John Smith had been captured by one of Powhatan's most redoubtable commanders, his half brother Opechancanough. He seemed to possess powerful magic — witness the compass. He was demonstrably unaffected, unafraid, even in the face of the most poisonous conjurations of the priests at Uttamussak. He must therefore be charmed or forced into submission, or he must be destroyed. The former seemed difficult; the latter might be fatal. For it is a strange fact that Powhatan seems to have sensed, if not actually known of, Newport's impending return ("within four days"!). Verily, out of the East, a soothsayer had foretold, would come the force that would destroy Powhatan and his people. What to do? Kill him, or adopt him?

Just which solution Powhatan chose cannot be known; there is only John Smith's account of what he thought happened. Nevertheless, whether it was an adaptation of an annual puberty rite which Powhatan, as high priest, chose to inflict on Smith before adopting him, or whether he really decided to risk executing him for violations of some tribal law, or as a tribal menace, the scene was the same.

A fire had already been lighted. Now the abracadabra of ritual began to go up, along with the smoke. The priests howled the supplications and deprecations of their barbaric litany. Two sacrificial stones were brought in. Dozens of hands seized John Smith, dragged him over the beaten-earth floor, and placed his head on the improvised altar. The initiators or executors stood ready with uplifted clubs.

All this while Powhatan's "most dear and well beloved daughter," eleven-year-old Pocahontas, watched. She had certainly stared at unconquerable Indian muteness under torture, and learned not to suffer with the sufferer. But this was something new. The bearded little man was proud, like an Indian, but he was not one of them. His eyes were not dull with endurance; defiance danced in them. Yet he was alone, more alone than any Indian had been alone within her little experience. Loudly the priests renewed their invocations.

Spontaneously a cry burst from Pocahontas, startling the assembly, and even Powhatan himself. He remonstrated that this was a holy rite. But Pocahontas refused to be quieted. If she could not be heard, she would be obeyed. She ran forward, put her head by John Smith's, and defied the priests and the ministerial executioners. She was only a little girl, but she was the favorite daughter of the absolute Lord of Tidewater Virginia.

Clearly this was the will of the gods. Powhatan saw in Pocahontas's act the expression of that will. John Smith should live. Yet, how? What were they to do with him? He was a stranger, not an Indian. And he was a potentially dangerous foe.

Pocahontas, happy with her victory, apparently suggested that John Smith could play with her, and make her bells and beads and copper things — an English Hercules at the feet of an Indian Omphale. Powhatan solemnly nodded. John Smith could work for him as well, and make him hatchets.

Nevertheless, Powhatan was not entirely happy. Something was needed to ensure John Smith's benevolence. The unawed Englishman could not forever sit at Werowocómoco, making beads and hatchets. Newport was returning and would come for his son, and then all would be lost. Patently, further conjurations were needed, to bind John Smith to Powhatan.

Two days passed during which John was apparently left to his own devices, providing these did not include escape. Then Powhatan sent for him. Guards led him through the woods to a great house, took him in, and sat him on a mat again in front of a fire. And once more he was alone.

As he sat there, looking at another mat hanging across the middle of the room, the "most dolefullest noise he ever heard" slowly arose from behind it. Soon it was lifted, and Powhatan entered, disguised "in the most fearfullest manner he could," painted black and looking more "like a devil than a man." With him came two hundred warriors, as black as himself.

Approaching the imperturbable Captain, Powhatan told him that they were now friends, that he was free, and that in the future he would be to him as his beloved son, Nantaquaus. Furthermore, he gave him the neighboring tribal territory of Capahowasick and, although Smith does not mention it as occurring on that occasion, he also indicated that John Smith was now a werowance, and an adopted member of the Despot's personal circle. In return for all this, Smith was only to give him two "great guns" and a grindstone.

Whether or not Smith considered the gift of land at all seriously is not known. (It was seven or eight miles below Werowocómoco.) But the return gift of guns and a grindstone he was willing to give — the grindstone could be spared, and the guns were useless without "know-how." It was little enough to pay for his life.

That same day, Friday, January 1, 1608, John Smith set out across the mile-and-a-half-wide river to the deserted woods north of what is now Williamsburg. (Even today fifteen thousand acres of woodland in this region are pathless and uninhabited.) For company he had twelve warriors under the command of Powhatan's trusted lieutenant, Rawhunt — to take a present of food to the colony and bring back the ordnance and the grindstone. They had but fifteen miles or a little more to go, depending on their route, but the guides insisted on stopping for the night and feasting again, in "certain old hunting houses" belonging to the Paspaheghs. Smith's "persuasions" were so much wasted breath.

The next morning they started off again before daybreak and reached Jamestown within an hour. The day was the fourth day after Smith had been brought before great Powhatan. He had been assured freedom by that date. And precisely as great Powhatan had promised, so had it been.[5]

## CHAPTER 12

# A PORTENT OF BROACHED MISCHIEF

THE MORNING was still young when the guard at the fort spotted their long-lost Captain Smith emerging from the woods accompanied by a squad of half-naked savages. Even if he had not been given up entirely for dead, his return produced vast excitement. "Each man," as Smith wrote later, "with the truest signs of joy they could express welcomed me." Only Captain Gabriel Archer and two or three of his cronies hung back. To them, Smith was unwelcome, for obvious reasons. Archer had procured his own appointment to the Council during Smith's absence — in violation of the King's *Instructions,* in despite of the agreement made at the time Wingfield was deposed, and contrary to the voice and wishes of Captain John Martin. John Smith would certainly prove a more stubborn dam to the onrushing waters of Archer's ambition.

For the moment, Smith took no notice of Archer's ill-concealed churlishness. He had to live up to his promise to Powhatan. So, as he put it, he "used the Savages with what kindness he could," and "showed Rawhunt, Powhatan's trusty servant, two demi-culverins* and a millstone to carry [to] Powhatan." The Indians found all of this "somewhat too heavy," which is certainly not one of Smith's overstatements. Smith then offered to show how they worked, possibly to discourage them from sending for help.

Loading one of the clumsy cannon with stones, the gunners fired it at a big tree whose sagging branches glittered with icicles. The roar and flash, and the shower of falling ice and branches, produced the effect Smith desired: "The poor savages ran away half dead with fear."

* Small cannon weighing 3000 to 4500 pounds each.

Laughing pleasantly, Smith and his gunners coaxed them back and regained their confidence. And then, in place of the cannon they had come for, they "gave them such toys [for themselves], and sent to Powhatan, his women and children, such presents as gave them in general full content." But in plainer language, the Indians went away somewhat disappointed.

If the Indians dissembled their discontent, Archer and his clique did not. For two or three weeks the extreme cold had kept them from making another attempt to abandon the colony. Now, just as it was a little warmer, Smith arrived, and halted the move once more ("with the hazard of his life"). Evidently Archer would have to do something drastic to stop Smith from stopping him. He resorted to the law.

As has been mentioned, Archer had had some sort of legal training at Gray's Inn, in 1593 and perhaps later. In Virginia, he had used legal quibbles to drive Wingfield out of the presidency. Now he came up with "the Levitical law." Smith, he said, had been responsible for the lives of the men who went with him on the Chickahominy expedition. Robinson and Emry had been killed. (He made no mention of George Cassen, who started it all.) Smith was therefore guilty of leading them to their death. And the Book of Leviticus incontrovertibly had things to say about "breach for breach, eye for eye, tooth for tooth." It was all there, in Chapter 24.

In brief order, John Smith, providentially saved from Despot Powhatan, was sentenced to death by President Ratcliffe, alias Sicklemore — the mouthpiece of Archer the lawyer. The execution was set for the next morning; after that, the colony could be abandoned.

"But it pleased God," as Edward Maria Wingfield piously wrote, "to send Captain Newport unto us the same evening, to our unspeakable comforts; whose arrival saved Master Smith's life and mine, because he took me out of the pinnace, and gave me leave to lie in the town."

This extraordinary coincidence, which did indeed save John Smith's life, can hardly be credited merely as such. Although Smith himself was convinced that it was pure chance, and even wrote that the Indians "esteemed him an oracle" because Newport returned "near as directly as he foretold," the facts remain that Powhatan promised freedom to Smith within four days, that Smith was returned safe and sound on the fourth day, and that Powhatan saw to it that exactly four days should elapse before Smith was free. Thanks to the night in the forest, Smith's life was saved, for it permitted Newport to arrive in time to stay his execution.

While it is possible to interpret Powhatan's "four" as a magic number (or a round number for "a few"), there is the greater likelihood of Powhatan's keeping lookouts along the coast to see if Newport actually was coming back as Smith has said. Newport, as a matter of fact, seems to have hung around the entrance to Chesapeake Bay for a day or two, for reasons which will appear below. While he delayed, word would have been sent by the lookouts, and Powhatan, once the "tall ship" was recognized, permitted Smith to go free, but delayed his arrival at Jamestown until Newport began to move up the James. This hypothesis at least rationalizes the airy double intervention of Providence in John Smith's life — twice in one week.

However the matter is to be explained, the important fact is that Smith's life was safe again. And not only was Newport's authority recognized in the matter of John Smith; it served also to return Archer to his proper role of Recorder. "Now was Master Scrivener [a new colonist], Captain Martin, and myself, called Councillors," wrote Smith, implying Archer's exclusion from the Council.[1]

Newport had promised to be back within twenty weeks of his departure — that is, about November 9. Such speed under any circumstances would have been notable, but neither he nor the colonists seem to have taken into consideration the facts of political life in London. (The mutinies in Virginia were merely an aggravated case of the normal contention-disease of English nobles and gentlemen in the 1600's.) Because of Spanish intrigue at the Court, any sort of action on the colony had to depend on high authority. Robert Cecil, Earl of Salisbury, was that authority, but, although he was only one step from the King, he was also only one step from the Spanish Ambassador, and no step at all from Court intrigue. Such things could, and did, delay Newport's return.

Still, right after Newport's arrival in London, about August 8, and his report to the London Council, it appeared as if he might get away again quickly. Acting on information brought by Newport, one of the most active members of the Council, Sir Walter Cope, wrote Salisbury posthaste about *gold* in the colony. And *there* was a word that caught the eye. Captain John Martin, he said, son of a goldsmith who was then Master of the Mint, had sent back with Newport some "minerals" which he claimed were rich in gold.

But Salisbury bided his time, until an assayer analyzed the "ore" — and found no gold at all. Newport was then up to his ears in a sea of inquiry as to what sort of fraud this was. Sir Walter Cope's hopeful letter was followed on August 12 by a second one, written this time in a rage of disappointment. In it he accused Martin of deliberately cozening, or cheating, his own father, not to mention "the King and State."

Newport, always fair-minded if at times "unrealistic," promptly took some of the blame, claiming that he had possibly not brought back the same ore as that which Martin had "assayed." If the Council would but fit out a ship for him, he would bring the right ore back immediately. At that, Sir Thomas Smythe wrote to Salisbury, urging speed in dispatching the Virginia supply ship. Smythe was backed up by Sir Thomas Roe (another member of the King's Council) in terms that combined realization of the Spanish influence at Court, and the resultant delays, with sympathy for the colonists and their urgent needs. He added, pointedly, that there was nothing for the colony "but apparent ruin, except your lordship [Salisbury] would give some personal and prompt attention to the action."

Salisbury at last moved, quickly and decisively, and Newport was soon able to sail. With him went "a nimble pinnace" under the command of Captain Francis Nelson, the mariner who had gone with Newport, Percy, Smith, and others to explore the falls, near Powhatan's village. Nelson was to rush the *right* samples of ore back to the London assayer, while Newport stayed a little longer in the colony to carry out certain Company policies. That, briefly, was what had happened in England.

How much of this story Newport told the colonists is not known. But it is obvious from surviving accounts that he must have told them about Nelson's pinnace and what had happened to it, since it did not arrive with him. The two had sailed together from

Gravesend and had kept together for nearly two months — all the way across the Atlantic. Then a fog separated them on Christmas eve, four days after they sighted the coast of North America. Newport sailed on slowly, groping his way into the bay (perhaps delaying, as has been suggested), to arrive at Jamestown on January 2, 1608. Nelson was not heard from for many a month.

Newport brought eighty new colonists with him, and forty more were with Nelson. Housing was consequently desperately needed, and Newport took advantage of a warm spell to put his men to work with saw and hammer as soon as the new contingent of settlers was landed, bag and baggage, on Monday, January 4. But, as has long been known, whatever man intends, Dame Fortune oft forfends. Newport's haste came to nothing three days later in a fire. The tinderbox that was Jamestown went up in smoke, but for three small buildings. The colonists, new and ancient, not only lost their lodgings, clothing, and what few books made up the Reverend Mr. Hunt's library, but — far worse — much of their provision too, both private and public.

On the heels of the fire, winter returned with ferocity. Hunger, sickness, and cold brought death once more to Jamestown. The ill-fated newcomers suffered the blind castigation of Fate in the atmosphere of a Greek tragedy.

Nevertheless, the able-bodied quickly raised some sort of shelter for themselves and for their stores, and Newport put his men to work rebuilding the church. And while the mariners toiled, Newport himself had opportunity to learn about John Smith's captivity and deliverance, along with such geographical details as Smith had been able to note on his wanderings. These, however, certainly paled, in Smith's narrative, by comparison with his description (surely magnified) of the person of great Powhatan, the Algonkian Despot of Tidewater Virginia, whose wealth and magnificence (in terms of Virginian values) rivaled those of Motecuhzoma and Atahualpa.

Newport was less interested in generalities than he was in the specific bearing which Smith's "friendship" with Powhatan might have on the discovery of ore. Had he not sworn never to see Lord Salisbury again "before he bring that with him which he confidently believed he had brought before"?

Whatever his personal feelings toward Captain Smith may have been — the last six months had noticeably added to Smith's self-assurance — Newport must have realized that the ever-sick Martin was not going to produce any more gold than he had before. Not, at least, before winter had loosened its grip. But in Smith there might be a way to save face for Martin and the colony's credit. There was ample evidence that he was held in high regard by Powhatan, and Powhatan must know where gold was to be found.

By way of unintentional confirmation of Smith's status among the Indians, Powhatan sent presents to him at least once a week, of deer, raccoons, bread, and such things, half of which he specified was for Smith's "father," Newport. Then, too, Powhatan's favorite daughter, Pocahontas, Smith's benefactress, accompanied the gift-bringers on occasion, and it is clear from later evidence that Smith enjoyed playing with her, as a grizzled veteran of wars (nearing thirty!) will play with a vivacious little girl of eleven or twelve.

Newport observed also that beyond the gifts, which came from neighboring werowances as well, came products offered in trade. With a ship loaded with "beads and cloth," and pins and bells and other priceless gewgaws, standing offshore at Jamestown, the Paspaheghs and the Chickahominies, the Warraskoyacks and the Nansemonds, and many other tribes, came trotting or paddling up with food to barter. There was no "trading-with-the-enemy act" then (there was, in 1631–1632), and the Indians could not yet foresee that the fruit of their labors, exchanged for trash, would "warm the starved snake" that, curled up in their midst, would sting them fatally. Appropriately they called their Indian enemies "adders," but the English they apparently called "traders." How were they to know that the little band of silly men in sugar-loaf hats and cloaks would be their undoing?

While John Smith was endeavoring to maintain a "fair" price for Indian food, in terms of English barter-goods, Newport apparently had his mind set on the problem of finding gold. Therefore, until weather would permit him to go with Smith to visit Powhatan, Newport paid little attention to the vital matter of John Smith's application of theories of sound currency to barter trade. He did not even attempt to restrain the mariners in their squandering of valuable English bits of copper and metal tools for corn and what not. In vain Smith then protested that Indian produce "could not be had for a pound of copper, which before was sold for an ounce." Indeed, the momentarily surfeited colonists all only egged the mariners on, so happy were they to have them there.[2]

Thus the weeks of January passed, and the first two or three of February. Those were weeks of rebuilding Jamestown, settling the new colonists into the routine of life, trading, and burying the dead. Then at last there were signs that winter was breaking up. Newport felt that he could begin to plan a voyage which would bring him face to face with Powhatan. Somehow that encounter might provide some of the ore he so desperately needed to take to London as evidence of good faith.

Before that, however, an agreement was reached with the Werowance of Paspahegh to lead two of the colonists south to the village of Panawaioc (or Panawick), beyond Roanoke, in the hope of finding survivors of Ralegh's colony. Panawaioc appeared on de Bry's map of 1590, but no one knew if de Bry's map was accurate, and Werowance Wowinchopunk in any case played the villain. Although Panawaioc was not even a hundred and fifty miles away, the two colonists, Wowinchopunk, and the guides merely went twenty miles downstream to Warraskoyack, where they landed and stayed for three or four days. Then they returned — "deluding us for rewards," as Smith put it. And that was what was done about the Roanoke Colony at that time.

When this fruitless expedition was back, before the end of February, Newport at length set out for Werowocómoco and Powhatan. Moving with exaggerated caution, he took Smith as his lieutenant and guide, and young Matthew Scrivener along with thirty or forty chosen colonists as bodyguard — about one third of the entire population of Jamestown, discounting the sailors.

Down the James they sailed the pinnace to Kecoughtan, and around the tip of the peninsula up the lower Pamunkey, now called the York River. It was Smith's first arrival at the Despot's seat from downstream, and he studied the shoreline, compass in hand. He observed that the mouth of the Pamunkey was twenty-five to thirty miles northward of Cape Henry, which is reasonably accurate as to distance, but four points of the compass off as to direction. (The error, magnetic north for magnetic northwest, is perhaps excusable since Smith had not been back to the cape since the day of their arrival.) Meanwhile, Newport ventured the pinnace warily up the unexplored and narrow-channeled Pamunkey.

Werowocómoco was located on what is now called Purtan Bay, a little over twenty miles up from the point which Robert Tindall, Prince Henry's gunner, named after Newport (Tue Point today). As they approached, either Smith or Newport, or both, got the notion that all was not well. Although Powhatan had repeatedly insisted on their coming to visit him, something led somebody to distrust his motives at the last minute. Smith then characteristically volunteered to take twenty men, armed, and protected by quilted leather jackets called "jacks," to see what was really in store for them.

Smith describes the location of Werowocómoco as near three creeks, emptying into the river within less than a mile all told, and protected by a mile and a half of soft, oozy bank. (The width of the oozy strip may have been exaggerated, but the location is fairly conclusively identifiable.) There Smith and his half-platoon clambered into a boat to go ashore, the pinnace remaining anchored in the channel. Seven of the twenty were newly arrived "gentlemen," three were original gentlemen-colonists, and the balance was made up of Anas Todkill, soldier, and nine anonymous companions. Matthew Scrivener stayed on the pinnace with Newport, but Anthony Gosnold went with Smith. (It was probably Bartholomew's brother rather than his young cousin.)

Upon arrival off Werowocómoco Smith went ashore via the wrong creek, apparently due to a mistake, or a misunderstanding of directions from the Werowance of Kiskiack and Namontack, their guides. Soon he found the path intercepted "by a great creek over which they had made a bridge of grained [forked] stakes and rails." Here Powhatan's son Naukaquawis appeared, accompanied by the "Captain" who had taken him prisoner two months before in the Chickahominy marsh, possibly for the purpose of conducting Smith to the village. But Smith, not unreasonably suspecting "some mischief," directed the boat to the right landing, and then marched a handful of the Indians over the frail bridge first. Smith himself soon followed, with his men intermingled with Naukaquawis, Namontack, the Werowance of Kiskiack, the captain, and other "chief men." At that juncture, some Indians came up in a canoe and ferried him and four or five others across the creek. Once he was on the other side, Smith waited for his remaining men to pass the danger spot. This incident is of importance only as showing that John Smith was not to be caught off guard again.[3]

From there the party marched, two in a rank, to Powhatan's house. Before it, symbolic of wealth, stood forty or fifty great platters of bread. Passing these, and welcomed by a *basso ostinato* of "loud tunes and shouts of joy," Smith found Powhatan inside, surrounded by his "divan" (and forty wives), clothed in such majesty as Smith could not "express." "With a kind countenance," Smith wrote, "he bad me welcome, and caused a place to be made by himself" for Smith to sit. Thereupon, Smith presented the Despot with a suit of red woolen cloth, a white greyhound, and a sugar-loaf hat such as King James himself wore. It took orations by three Indian magnificoes properly to express Powhatan's acceptance of these gifts, along with "a public confirmation of a perpetual league and friendship."

Smith was then regaled with food as required by Indian protocol: a turkey cock, bread, and water, brought by the Werowansqua of Appomattoc. This he ate, in protocolary measure, and Powhatan was then at last able to address him. Ceremony is ceremony throughout the world.

Powhatan first reminded his guest "with a merry countenance" of the cannon he had been promised. Smith replied that he had offered Rawhunt four demiculverins (they were only two), but Rawhunt had refused them. Powhatan burst into laughter, saying for Smith to give him smaller pieces, since those were too heavy for anybody to carry. But, he added, looking around, where were Smith's companions?

Smith had already instructed his twenty men to leave an adequate guard outside at all times, since they could easily be overpowered once they gathered together in any building. Therefore when they were told to present their respects to Powhatan, they came in two at a time, each pair going back out before the next pair entered. As the men bowed to Powhatan, that supereminence thanked Smith (their chief) for the gesture, and commanded that four or five pounds of bread be given each man.

When this formality was ended, Smith reminded Powhatan of his promise of corn and a "manor" called Capahowasick. Powhatan renewed this, but said that Smith's men should lay their arms at his feet, in token of respect. Quickly Smith protested that "that was a ceremony our enemies desired, never our friends." He assured Powhatan, however, that he should not doubt their friendship, in token of which, he added, the next day his "father" (Newport) would give Powhatan a child of his "in token of our loves." Furthermore, he and his "father" were ready to go out and conquer his enemies, the Monacans and the Pocoughtaonacks, who roamed ill-defined regions above modern Richmond and Fredericksburg respectively.

Whether this "contented" Powhatan, as Smith thought, or not, no one knows. But Powhatan then officially proclaimed Smith a werowance, subordinate to himself, and emitted an ex cathedra decree, declaring that Smith's companions should no longer be considered strangers, or even Paspaheghans, but Powhatans, and that "the corn, women and country should be to us as to his own people," Smith explained.

Although it appears probable that John Smith had already been made a werowance at the end of December, Powhatan may have intended this edict to impress the privileges on a larger circle of Indians, and in addition to include the rest of the English under his protective mantle. In any case, Smith "for many reasons" did not despise Powhatan's kindness, but expressed his thanks "with the best languages and signs" he could. Then he took his leave.

Powhatan rose to accompany Smith to the door, ordered bread given to the men to the limit of their ability to carry it, and loaded Smith himself with baskets of bread for both his "father" and himself. "Victuals," Smith later found it necessary to explain, "you must know is all their wealth, and the greatest kindness they could show us." For the Englishmen barely recovered from starvation, it undoubtedly was.

By the time John Smith arrived at the river, the boat had drifted far downstream with the ebb tide, despite his orders to prevent just this. "The messengers deceived me," he ambiguously explained. But Powhatan quickly noticed what was wrong, and sent his son and Namontack to take Smith and his men to a large house for the night. It threatened rain.

Fires were lighted in the house, a quarter of venison was brought for food, and the Despot's heralds commanded the Indians one and all not to steal, not to take the English bows and arrows, and not to "offer any injury." The order did not necessarily mean that the English had any bows and arrows — but Smith noticed that the house where they were to sleep was "hung around" with Indian arms.

Later that same evening Powhatan sent for Smith to attend him in his "Residence," but to bring only "two shot" (armed men) with him. Smith complied, after issuing strict orders to his men to be on their guard, and to keep two sentries at the doors all night. After his experience on the banks of the Chickahominy, he had grown circumspect indeed. As Sir Walter Ralegh's friend, Edmund Spenser, put it, "The fish that once was caught, new bait will hardly bite."

Powhatan and Smith spent two or three hours in their "ancient discourses," after food for twenty men had been set before Smith and then passed on to his companions, as was Indian custom. And in the end, when the Despot had once again failed to master the farmer's boy from Lincolnshire, he courteously supplied him with "servants" to light him back to his lodging with a "fire stick."

In the morning Powhatan sent for Smith again, this time to conduct him personally to the river, where he showed him his canoes, and described "how he sent them over the Bay for tribute beads; and also what countries paid him beads, copper, or skins." (This was evidence that Powhatan knew what transpired in and around his domain.) The "royally" guided tour was interrupted, however, by a commotion aboard the pinnace. Captain Newport was being helped into a boat, followed by Scrivener and a guard. Powhatan hastily retired to his residence to prepare a proper reception for the Chief Werowance of the Whites, while Smith went to receive him on the bank.[4]

Some minutes later, in a minuscule procession with a trumpeter in the lead, Captain Christopher Newport made his state visit to "the Emperor." Powhatan, arrayed in barbaric finery, welcomed Newport "after his old manner kindly," speeches were undoubtedly made (although unrecorded), and Newport presented his "son," thirteen-year-old Thomas Savage, to Powhatan as a "gift," for whom

in exchange His Supereminence gave Newport baskets of beans —
one basket for each of his retinue.

By the time these amenities were concluded, it was nightfall. The
English retired to their pinnace, to rest with less need for constant
vigilance, and to return to the business end of their voyage the next
morning. Regrettably, this was the beginning of the estrangement
that developed between John Smith and Captain Newport. Newport, judging by his acts, was determined to obey instructions from
London — to the letter. Smith knew that local experience was a
sounder guide.

Powhatan, having failed in his wiles with John Smith, either
sensed the greater naïveté of Captain Newport or instinctively put
him to the test. No sooner had Newport arrived with his bargaining party than Powhatan, entertaining them at breakfast, asked him
why they came armed, seeing that he was their friend, and was
unarmed. What did they fear?

Smith promptly spoke up, answering that it was their custom.
Powhatan had heard this already, but before he had a chance to
press the matter with Newport, that trusting agent of London policies ordered the guard to retire to the river's edge, over half a mile
away. John Smith, who believed in Powhatan's friendship only so
far as it was convenient for Powhatan to be friendly, countered by
arranging with Scrivener to alternate with himself in being either
with Newport or at the barge. Powhatan, relentless in his efforts
to disarm the English, noticed Smith's absence a little later and
sent for him — with the result that Smith called for Scrivener to
replace him. Apparently Powhatan caught on. He sent for Scrivener. Smith straightway returned to the barge. And all the while
Powhatan was refusing to trade in the customary fashion, but demanding that Newport lay out his hatchets and copper for Powhatan to pick from, after which he said he would stack up for Newport as much corn as he thought the articles were worth.

Smith had experienced this trick along the Chickahominy, and
quickly suggested that Powhatan bring out his corn and they would
see how much he offered for one item. Powhatan then declared that
it was not for "kings" to haggle, and insisted that they give him
what they would, and he would freely give them in return. Newport, typically, decided to try him out. He got as much corn for

twelve great copper vessels as Smith had gotten along the Chickahominy for one, and that one of smaller size. Hatchets, too, the
Despot "bought" at his own rate, with demonstrations of affection
for Newport.

Smith saw that inflation had set in, and that their usual "currency" was on the verge of worthlessness. Cannily, he introduced a
new basis of exchange. He had with him a few strings of blue glass
beads, which apparently had come over on Newport's ship. (This is
the first mention of such an article.) As cape merchant, Smith recognized the trading value of any novelty, and already knew the fasci-
nation of glass for the Indians. More, he knew the importance of
reticence in barter.

As soon as he had an opportunity, Smith let Powhatan's eye fall
on a handful of blue beads. Powhatan immediately wanted some.
Smith said he had very few. Powhatan insisted, offering two pecks
of corn for the handful. Smith held out for three pecks and got
them.

The next day, John Smith returned to the attack with more blue
beads. With these, he bargained for two bushels of corn, with
equal success. Determined then to put his "currency" on the gold
standard, so to speak, Smith now established blue beads as worthy
only of Powhatan and his greatest werowances. Thus, by making
them status symbols Smith ended by realizing two to three hundred
bushels of corn for a pound or two of cheap Venetian glass beads,
of quite negligible value compared with copper pots.

During the next few days of the state visit, Smith had ample
opportunity to observe, appreciate, and also to see through, the
more obvious aspects of Indian character. The weather was abomi-
nable, the channel of the river forced the pinnace to stay some distance from shore, and the barge had problems with the tides, which
can reach an extreme of nearly six feet at Purtan Bay. More than
once Smith was "pestered in the ooze" and had to be rescued. The
last time, under threat of having to be carried out on the heads of
Indians willing to do this (in early March!), he refused their "im-
portunacy," and asked merely for some firewood and mats to cover
him. This, and other favors, were granted him with "pains a
horse would scarce have endured."

Powhatan's own chief seaman (Lord Admiral, the English would have called him) came on one occasion with bread and other food for Smith and his men under such conditions as proved that he, the same as the rest, "seemed to take pride in showing how little he regarded that miserable cold and dirty passage, though a dog would scarce have endured it." (Smith had no qualms about repeating a phrase he liked.) Yet, Smith adds, a couple of little bells contented them all, and he was amazed at such kindness when he "little expected less than a mischief." These were perhaps the common traits of the common Indians — kindly and cruel, by turns, and trained to a degree of stoicism such as proud Rome exhibited only in legends. The Indian leaders, on the other hand — their chiefs and werowances, cockarouses, priests, quiyoughcosucks — all these had a general reputation (regrettably extended to all Indians) for deceit, trickery, vengefulness, unpredictability, and thievishness, which recalls the Greek heroes of the Trojan War as described by Homer.

Newport, with his mercantile propriety (despite his privateering background), was no match for Indian cunning, even if he had thought that his instructions permitted parallel or reciprocal artfulness. But Smith was unrestrained by any thought other than providing for the necessities of life, regardless of any possible "injustice" to the Indians. He could not agree with Newport's generosity and trust.

Ample evidence was not long in coming to support Smith. The day after the beginning of the bartering, Powhatan brought up the matter of Smith's (and Newport's) offer to help him conquer his enemies. Suddenly reversing everything he had said before, he averred that the Monacans were not his professed enemies, but that he would help the English attack them if they wanted to. He and Newport would stay at home, in Werowocómoco, while Smith, Scrivener, Opechancanough, two of his sons, and a hundred braves set out for the west. A hundred or a hundred and fifty Englishmen would be enough for the expedition (there could not have been many more than a hundred in the entire colony at the time), and all precautions would be taken to provide surprise. To this interesting picture, Powhatan added the appealing detail that there was a "Great Water" beyond the falls; which led Newport almost to "undertake by this means to discover the South Sea." Smith was unconvinced, suspecting treachery if they grounded their plans on any "constancy" in Powhatan.

Opechancanough by this time decided to invite Newport to visit him too, but Powhatan (for his own reasons) placed subtle difficulties in the way until Newport almost gave up the idea. By then, Opechancanough sent his daughter to tell Newport that he could not come to escort him personally, since he had hurt his leg. Newport now (for *his* own reasons) decided to accept the invitation, and sailed the pinnace a dozen miles farther upstream to Cinquoateck (modern West Point, or thereabouts), where the Mattaponi River flows into the York.

So far as Smith was concerned, bygones appeared to be bygones, mutually. Opechancanough and his half brothers, Opitchapam and Kekataugh, all received him "kindly," along with his fellow emissary, Scrivener. Presents were then offered to Captain Newport on the pinnace — *he* was maintaining his station, while the two subordinates dirtied their hands with preliminary barter.

The next day Newport went ashore, to be received with all the honor due the Chief White Werowance. Then he returned aboard and sailed up to the next village, Menapacant, "twenty miles by water, and not one by land." There the English were gratified with a dinner of the Virginia equivalent of succotash, called *pausarowmena,* followed by dancing, games, and trading, that day and the day after. Later on the second day, Newport sailed off, loaded with food, in the pinnace, leaving Smith and a few others to "dig a rock" near Cinquoateck, where they supposed (or hoped) some sort of mine to be. By midnight Smith arrived at Werowocómoco with his samples of rock, and anchored his barge next to the pinnace.

One more day and the state visit to Powhatan was over. Apparently impressed (or merely puzzled) by the English, Powhatan reciprocated Newport's gift of Thomas Savage. He gave Newport his trusty servant Namontack, to go to England with Newport in place of his "son." So much for the surface. Smith was undoubtedly correct in his surmise that underneath there lay the will "to know our strength and Country's condition." For Namontack was, wrote Smith, "of a shrewd subtle capacity." Yet in the long run, he proved more friendly toward the English than his master had perhaps intended.

The day after their departure, the colonists stopped to trade at Kiskiack, some eleven miles downstream, and on the south shore. There they were so "scornfully entertained" that they sailed away shortly, "with what signs of scorn and discontent" they could show. On this occasion, well they might, for their ship was loaded with two hundred and fifty bushels of corn. Smith's blue beads had halted the plunging barter value of the company's goods.[5]

But the ultimate price of this plenty was a wall of misunderstanding between the two unquestioned leaders of the colony — unquestioned, except by Archer and one or two others. It was a clash between the initiative needed in Virginia, personified in Smith, and the obedience needed by London, personified in Newport.

Newport brought his ship back to Jamestown on March 9, according to Edward Maria Wingfield, "well laden with corn, wheat, beans and peas, to our great comfort and his worthy commendations." But Newport was not satisfied. Food for the colony appears to have been a secondary consideration for him — perhaps a matter that the colonists should take care of in his absence, so that he could look into more important matters. Gold, for instance.

Newport knew that the backers of the Virginia Venture were not overpleased with the results so far. (The Spanish Ambassador commented that the colonists were not happy either.) He knew also that the first group of adventurer-settlers had sailed to "North Virginia" (New England) the end of May, 1607, two months before he returned from his first trip. If this colony were to fare better than that at Jamestown, it would be most discouraging for the London investors. Some sort of profit must come out of "South Virginia" — the Chesapeake Bay colony.

But to have a profitable colony almost of necessity meant having an orderly colony. And Jamestown was anything but orderly. Worse, gold and profits were not subjects to produce orderliness. If Wingfield's bugbear was the lack of gentlemanly discipline, Smith's was the passion for gold. Both were one-sided, but both were right. Although the bits of information that survive are sketchy, they somehow fit together to form a fairly clear picture.

Captain John Ratcliffe, the President of the Council, appears by all accounts to have been vain and lazy, succumbing quickly to delusions of grandeur born of his emergence from virtual anonymity to the chief post in Virginia: personal representative of the Majesty of James Stuart, King of England, Scotland, France, and Ireland — and Virginia, some added. Captain Gabriel Archer supported Ratcliffe in his folly, apparently because Ratcliffe was sickly or weak or both, which permitted Archer to rule. (Ratcliffe split his hand "off" about this time, when his musket misfired.) Captain John Martin joined the other two as a tawdry Lepidus in a tawdry triumvirate — for personal reasons, largely financial.

Martin was the individual responsible for the gold scandal in London, and either voluntarily or under pressure from Newport, was determined to find gold to clear his reputation (and Newport's), not to mention clearing four fifths of the profits on any that might be found, as provided in the Charter. Thus the search for gold, to which Ratcliffe as President must assign men, brought about a clique in the Council made up of Newport, Ratcliffe, and Martin (with Archer behind the scenes) against John Smith, who had only Matthew Scrivener on his side at the time. It was four votes against two. Scrivener and Smith's "horns were too short," as the author of the 1612 account put it.

All the while, Archer (mistakenly called a councilor by Wingfield) kept the colony in continuous ferment. Newport and the Council, Wingfield wrote, "removed some officers out of the store; and Captain Archer, a Councillor, whose insolency did look upon that little himself with great sighted spectacles, derogating from others merits by spewing out his venemous libels . . . had not escaped the halter, but that Captain Newport interposed his advice to the contrary."

Meanwhile, John Smith frothed at the mouth at the sight of the assaying of the "ore." A witness, who appears to have been Todkill, writes that he heard Smith tell Captain Martin that he did not see any "sound" testing, and that he was "not enamored with their dirty skill" — a pun worthy of John Smith. "Breathing out these and many other passions," the witness continues, nothing tormented Smith more "than to see all necessary business neglected, to fraught such a drunken ship with so much gilded dirt." In later years, Smith apostrophized the events with a quotation from the Bishop of Salisbury: "Oh, cursèd gold!"

At last, on April 10, all was ready. The ship was loaded with "gilded dirt," and now a handful of "fed-up" colonists went aboard, the lines to the trees were cast off, and sail was hoisted. Tragically (and thoughtlessly) the ship's company, during its fourteen-week stay, had consumed all the pork, beef, olive oil, aqua vitae, fish, butter, cheese, beer, and so on that had been shipped from London for the colonists, leaving these once more on the threshold of starvation — to live off the land. But as partial compensation, two of the chief sources of contention sailed that same day: Edward Maria Wingfield and Gabriel Archer.

There were besides two other passengers of some note: Powhatan's "intelligence agent," Namontack, and a puzzling character named Francis Maguel (or Magner), who seems to have been a friend of Kendall's. Maguel was to try to betray the colony to the King of Spain in a couple of years, but by then it was too late. Virginia was to survive.[6]

CHAPTER 13

# BRIEF FREEDOM FROM MALICE

WITH NEWPORT'S departure, the Council was reduced to President Ratcliffe and Councilors Martin, Smith, and Scrivener. Martin, having gotten his "gold" off to England, apparently rested on his oars and waited for felicitous news of a bonanza. Ratcliffe, sick and with a wounded hand, did little but build a glittering castle in the air, the earthly counterpart of which was to cost him much trouble, and make some real or fancied profit out of distributing a portion of the colony's stores. (Both he and Martin were suspected of regarding such commodities as inheritable "revenues.") Of the Council, only Smith and Scrivener seem to have viewed both present and future through untinted glasses. At last, however, the hundred or so colonists began the year's work. It was already advanced spring.

Smith and Scrivener accompanied Newport to Cape Henry in the shallop, as a mark of appreciation and respect, and Powhatan sent a farewell gift of enough turkeys to strain the powers of five or six stalwart porters. In the case of Powhatan, it was Indian protocol — Newport had sent him a present of some swords when he got back from Werowocómoco. As for Smith's motives, he may have wanted to sweeten the air after his many disagreements with Newport, and at the same time convey last-minute messages or suggestions unimpeded by the presence of Ratcliffe and Martin. But, considering John Smith's innate pragmatism (which was not without its facets of politics and cajolery), it seems more likely that he used this courtesy-escorting as an excuse to explore a little. He was aware that the London Council wanted to know as much as possible about the "territories and countries" which it was their privilege to colonize. Scrivener would hardly have disagreed with such an idea, for his twenty-one years or so would not have stood in the way of a first adventure into the wilderness.

Once the last farewells were shouted over the gray-green surge of the Atlantic, Smith and Scrivener tacked about and sailed the shallop along the south shore of Chesapeake Bay and the mouth of the James as far as the tribal grounds of the Nansemond Indians. These were immediate neighbors of the Chesapeakes, and were considered by the colonists as the authors of the very first attack on them — the night of their arrival, in April the year before. They were a powerful tribe, with a great werowance and three subordinate ones, and their fighting strength was estimated at no less than two hundred men. This, combined with their situation across the James from the main body of Powhatan's domains, gave them a certain degree of independence from him, although they seem to have paid tribute.

Smith knew that Newport had "revenged" the 1607 attack on his return in 1608, and approached the Nansemond River warily. Therefore, when the werowance sent a messenger inviting him to come ashore, he replied that he came in peace, to trade. If they had corn to offer in exchange for the articles he had, he would be glad to discuss the matter.

After some jockeying for advantage on both sides, Smith and Scrivener finally agreed to land. They were entertained and spent the night in a village about two thirds of the way up to modern Suffolk, at a point where the river was a musket shot broad,* with a narrow three-fathom channel and bays of shoal water on either side. Here were the first Nansemond habitations, while farther upstream were a thousand acres, Smith wrote, "of most excellent fertile ground," high above the river and already planted with an "abundance of houses and people." He was within a day's journey, he thought, of Chawanoac, visited by Ralph Lane in 1586.

While there is a hint in what Smith wrote that he and Scrivener would have liked to make that journey, uncertainty as to the distance and the strength and attitude of the Indians, and as to where really to look for Ralegh's lost colony, persuaded them to return to Jamestown. They were, in their own judgment and probably in all

* 600–800 feet. See Commentaries.

truth, the only two sane and sound members of the Council. So, after trading for supplies, they sailed back to the fort on April 11.

There, Smith and Scrivener again took up the task of rebuilding the town (the church the mariners built had been "washed near to nothing in 14 days"), repairing the palisade, planting corn, reroofing the storehouse, and above all facing the problem of Indian thievishness.

Nothing was safe from the Indians that was not nailed down, as Smith and Scrivener saw it. If the Pamunkeys, for example, could be trusted within limits, their werowance, Opechancanough, was not above receiving stolen goods from other Indians, and these in turn appropriated what they could for his (and their own) benefit. It reached such a point that they tried to steal things out of the Englishmen's hands, and took a threatening attitude when resisted.

This was too much for John Smith, even if the indulgence of the bulk of the colonists was to blame for it. He obtained the Council's consent to put one Indian in the stocks for stealing two swords. Others, caught in *flagrante delicto,* tried to defend themselves, and one of them threatened to strike Smith with his tomahawk. Smith was not the kind to strike second.

When the wounded Indian's companions ran to his rescue, Smith charged the whole group, and even pursued them when they fled. Stopping short, then, Smith hurled such imprecations after them that within an hour a group came back to make peace by offering to help with the fishweirs. Three days later the Paspaheghs, the worst behaved, also wanted peace. And a stolen hatchet was returned even from Nansemond, thirty miles away. Such was the respect Smith gained by meeting what he considered deceit and insolence with prompt correction.

Members of the Council and other gentlemen of the colony, obedient to their *Instructions,* found fault with Smith's attitude. (We sense this, "between the lines.") But it is clear that Smith realized that strength and firmness were the only way to keep the upper hand, and if the English were to remain in Powhatan's "country," they had to keep the upper hand. Laxness, as the history of the colony was to prove, only brought disaster to the English, followed by catastrophe to the Indians. Yet the London Council persisted in its orders to treat the natives with all possible kindness.[1]

On Wednesday, April 20, while the colonists were at work felling trees and setting corn (under the instruction of friendly Indians), a sudden call to arms was sounded. Those at work dashed for their weapons, expecting some attack, but soon learned that it was a ship that had been sighted. This had its own implications of danger, for the sails now plainly visible down the river might bring Spaniards. Great was the relief, therefore, when the flag of St. George was spotted flying from the mast.

It was the *Phoenix,* at last bearing Master Francis Nelson, Newport's companion from London, to his destination. He had fled the winter's wrath to some island in the West Indies, where he had kept passengers and crew alike well and properly nourished. In fact, in addition to his quota of colonists, he brought a good stock of supplies which, somewhat surprisingly, he promptly added to the general store. The picture is a much pleasanter one than that of Newport's arrival.

Nevertheless, Nelson was no angel. He stuck to the letter of his contract, as undoubtedly he should, to the disappointment of Smith and Scrivener, who had immediately thought up an expedition beyond the falls. These two, impatient with the fort routine, took quick stock of the new colonists, the auspicious weather, and Nelson's mariners, and came up with a plan. By adding the mariners to the available colonists, they could dispose of seventy men to scour the country for mines, and study the terrain for hints as to the distance of the South Sea — that ever elusive Pacific Ocean which they thought to be just beyond their ken. Seventy men constituted a formidable force, considering their European arms and the scanty Indian population, but Smith and Scrivener still spent a week training the men in guerrilla warfare (an Indian tactic whose European counterpart lay disused from Ferdinand and Isabella's day to Napoleon's), to make them able "to fight with Powhatan's whole force," as Smith boasted. But Nelson said no, not without pay for his men, and the cost of the hire of the ship and himself for as many days as they were gone.

This produced misgivings among some of the colonists, especially those who already were murmuring that discoveries were Newport's sole prerogative. So, Smith and Scrivener, who were ready to go even without Nelson's men, were forced to give up the project. Nevertheless, further ill-feeling resulted — that ever-present plague

— leading some of those who at first did not want the expedition to go, to change strategy and back it. Their hope seems to have been that the two leaders would come to grief while away, and thus rid the colony of the only two councilors who prevented them from sitting on their hands all day.

Fifty volunteers for the expedition had to turn husbandmen again, felling trees and setting corn. The balance, about eighty men, "kept the Fort," according to Smith, "to do the command of the president [Ratcliffe] and Captain Martin." By then, it was after the first of May.

For the next thirty days or so, Nelson's ship lay at anchor, or tied to the trees at Jamestown. The long delay seems to have been due to disagreement on what freight to send to England this time. Smith was for a shipment of "red-cedar" logs, actually a kind of tall juniper, but Martin brought up his gold again. Smith, however, won out. Possibly backed by Scrivener, he argued that even wood, of immediate if small value, was preferable to "fantastical gold" or "uncertain" geographical discoveries.[2]

While the arguing and finally the lading of the ship went on, still more vehement troubles arose with the Indians. There are two somewhat differing accounts of these, but by blending them something near the truth can probably be reached. When Powhatan sent twenty or more turkeys to Newport on his departure, in exchange for a like number of swords, he was undoubtedly trying to build up his "modern" fighting equipment. Successful in his first try, he followed it up by a present of twenty turkeys to John Smith and (if the account is correct) Matthew Scrivener, undoubtedly expecting the same sort of barter-goods in exchange. Smith saw no reason for strengthening the Indians against the colonists and refused to comply. Powhatan thereupon decided to acquire by foul means what he could not get by fair.

It started early in May, when an Indian stole an axe, and upon being pursued by Scrivener threw it down and took a stand with his bow and arrows. Scrivener recovered the axe and retired. Four or five days later, two Indians in war paint appeared not far from the fort where Smith and Scrivener were working in the cornfields. Armed with cudgels, they came circling around Smith "as though they would have clubbed me," he wrote, "like a hare." Calling to

Scrivener to follow, Smith beat a retreat to the palisade. The Indians came right behind them, protesting that it was not the English they wanted to beat, but some Indians in the fort. To test them, Smith let them in, and they found one Indian they accused of being a spy. But when they began, or wanted to begin, to bastinado him, Smith objected. Thereupon the Indians "offered to begin" on him. Smith quickly shouted for the gates to be shut, and took the two Indians prisoners, along with two others who had come up. The Council, hastily summoned, remembered the first assault on the fort, the year before, and jailed these Indians, along with eight more, seized on suspicion.

An hour later, three or four more Indians came, armed with unusual elaborateness. When the colonists refused to admit them, they retired, but were followed the next day by two successive "ambassadors" who wanted to parley with Smith. Smith forestalled any complaints by announcing that the jailed Indians were held for theft, and that if all stolen spades, shovels, swords, and tools were not returned, the prisoners would hang — the very next day. The Indians replied that they had taken two Englishmen ranging the woods, and that they would exchange these for the sixteen or eighteen Indians in the jail.

All of this, following with persistence on the heels of Powhatan's attempt to get swords in exchange for turkeys, points to deliberate harassment, not improbably a "cover" for theft. Swords could be snatched in the confusion in the fort, or taken from Englishmen caught or killed in the woods.

In the face of so much provocation, and with two colonists in the Indians' toils, Smith and some others (probably including Scrivener) asked the President and Captain Martin to make a sortie against the Indians to show that they meant business. Whether this was done or not is unknown, but that same night Smith manned the barge for a brief cruise to throw firebrands into their highly combustible villages. The Indians hastened to return the two Englishmen unharmed.

By way of reward, and as a hint that submission was desirable, Ratcliffe released one Indian, but kept the rest in confinement. These were brought daily, under a strong guard, to morning and evening prayers, which were attended by the English in full armor.

The religious service in such style frightened the Indians out of their wits, smacking as it did of propitiatory offerings to the God who invented sailing ships, steel arms, cannon, and other monstrosities. The priest in his surplice (if Robert Hunt was still alive then) and the men in glinting steel armor, the psalm-singing and prayers on bended knee — all must have convinced the Indians that an appalling divine manifestation might materialize if they did not behave.

Not content with this bit of psychological treatment, the Council asked Smith to frighten the Indians with a threat of "civilized" torture, which was considerably more horrible as well as more subtle than that of the so-called savages. The purpose of this would be to attempt to find out what was behind all the anti-English activity. It did not occur to anyone that they were merely not wanted.

In compliance, Smith got everything ready, and a day later had one of the Indians taken below decks and bound to the mast of the *Phoenix,* after which six men with muskets, their matches lighted, were lined up before him in the obscurity. Smith stood there impassively, then calmly told the Indian that if he wanted to live he must speak. The Indian did not wait for any sort of pressure. He said that he knew nothing, but that one of his comrades was a Paspahegan "councilor" named Macanoe, and *he* could tell Smith all. Smith changed prisoners at the mast and enquired of the second.

Indians were known to be stoical in the face of danger. They were not inclined to yield to torture. Yet the combination of the darkness, with the rack looming in the background, and the six gleaming muskets proved too much for Macanoe. He volunteered to confess. Smith then sent for Scrivener to be present at the confession, which (assuming that it is reported correctly) is worth the quoting. The Indian admitted,

> That Paspahegh, the Chickahominy, Youghtanund, Pamunkey, Mattapanient, and Kiskiack: these Nations were all together a-hunting, that took me [Smith, near Apokant]. [Now] Paspahegh and Chickahominy had intended to surprise us at work, to have had our tools [swords]. Powhatan and all his would seem friends, till Captain Newport's

return, that he had again his man, which he called Namontack: where, with a great feast, he would so enamor Captain Newport and his men, as they should seize on him.
And the like traps would be laid for the rest.

In other words, Powhatan had been "laying traps" to get English
"tools" ever since he sent the turkeys to Smith and Scrivener. All
through this passage in Smith's 1608 account there runs a thread
of fear that Powhatan, by hook or crook, will succeed in disarming
the English.

Now, Powhatan had sent young Thomas Savage back to Jamestown with the "gift" of turkeys. Smith therefore, as soon as he had
the information he wanted from Macanoe, countered Powhatan's
moves by sending Savage to Powhatan again, with an involved
message. The English only wanted peace, Savage was to say, and
they proposed a trip to Werowocómoco to look for suitable stones
to make hatchets like the Indian tomahawks. If anyone said that
the English planned an attack, it was a lie. But, if the Indians began trouble by shooting one lone arrow at an Englishman, he,
Smith, "would destroy them." Then, less belligerently, he concluded his message with a request that Powhatan send him one of
his subjects named Weanock to act as a guide.

Despite the basically conciliatory tone of Smith's communication,
Powhatan returned Savage once again, this time bag and baggage,
and asked Smith to send him another boy. Smith took this to mean
that Savage understood what was going on, and Powhatan wanted
a "gift" from Smith who might be a little less perspicacious than
Newport's "son." (Perspicacity in that sense is an idea which could
easily be framed in Powhatan's language.)

Smith's retort was to send many "gifts" in the form of messengers,
but no one to replace Savage. Powhatan then tried to win confidence by sending Weanock, the guide Smith wanted, and begging
that they meet his gesture by returning one English boy to stay
with him. He even gave in to the extent of saying that he would
accept Savage again if need be. But Savage stayed in Jamestown.

There can be no doubt that Smith was sincerely seeking peaceful
coexistence, as it is expressed today, with the Indians. Nor did he
expect the concessions to be entirely one-sided — his efforts at rea-

sonably fair trade pointed to that. But the Indians he vainly expected to follow, or at least to learn to follow, a code of conduct, a way of life, which had been uniquely developed in England, and which took no cognizance of the hundred centuries of cultural growth that separated the realm of James Stuart from the despotate of Wahunsonacock Powhatan. This was patently impossible. Powhatan could not, even had he wanted to, become an Englishman overnight. Therefore, against the never-ending wile and boundless resources in guile that graced the Indian chief-of-chiefs, John Smith could summon only English dogged determination.

All the same, Smith's aggressiveness in fact left Powhatan in a continuing state of anxiety — was it bluff, or was it serious defiance? If the former, Powhatan would take advantage where he could; if the latter, discretion was imperative. In any case, Powhatan had one solace, if he considered it as such. His real opponent was one man, not the disunited Council. For the surviving records show that Smith, officially in charge of supplies and consequently of relations with the Indians, was *de facto* leader of those who took any stand at all. The slow drift toward John Smith's pre-eminence in the colony was gaining speed.[3]

Powhatan unwittingly contributed to this, as did at least two of his werowances. First, Weanock took French leave. Then a delegation of Paspaheghans arrived, asking to beat up one Amocis, long known to be a spy. Between Weanock and Amocis, Smith was convinced that the Indians were trying to pull more wool over his eyes. This time he acted without consulting the Council, and in spite of Captain Martin's pleas regarding Powhatan's "true meaning."

In another dizzy attempt to get at the real truth, Smith and Scrivener divided the captive Indians into two groups, and shortly afterwards had volleys of shot fired so that each group would "think that their fellows had been slain." Then, separately, they put all of them to a test to learn whether Macanoe told the truth. Despite Captain Martin's defense of Powhatan, the evidence obtained by these devious means pointed to him as at least the chief recipient of stolen weapons.

Word of this further detention of "certain Savages" soon reached Powhatan, who (possibly divining why they were detained) sent his daughter, "the only Nonpareil of his Country," to cast a spell over John Smith's heart. This of course was Pocahontas, whose intervention or intercession had saved Smith's life four months before. She came accompanied by Rawhunt, misshapen of body but "of a subtle wit and crafty understanding." Rawhunt had apparently not visited the fort since the episode of the demiculverins that were too heavy to carry.

Pocahontas and Rawhunt had for their mission to assure John Smith, in their quite divergent ways, that Powhatan truly "loved and respected him" — the latter verb possibly corresponding more closely to Powhatan's feelings than the former. They brought a deer and a presumably outsized pannier of bread by way of offering, to induce a thaw in Smith's obviously unwarm stand. Powhatan, they averred, was ready and happy to receive Thomas Savage once more at his side. He loved Thomas exceedingly. (That much wormwood pudding Powhatan was ready to eat.) But he carefully instructed Pocahontas, as Smith observed, not to take any notice of any Indian prisoners until their fathers and mothers, or friends, taking their cue from Rawhunt, came to plead for their release. The Despot of Tidewater Virginia would not belittle himself personally or through his daughter to sue for pardon for his serfs.

Opechancanough, however, took pains to solicit the release of two friends who were held captive. He went so far as to throw his shooting glove and wrist guard (a sign of submission) onto the scales of justice in their favor. The appeals were, indeed, so strong that the Council decided to yield. Marching the prisoners to the church, the colony subjected them — if that is not too strong a word — to further attendance at the divine mysteries of Christian worship, after which they entertained them at midday dinner, returned their bows, arrows, and other belongings, and released them to Pocahontas, that extraordinary little girl of a dozen winters. Pocahontas herself the colony "requited with such trifles as contented her," asking her to let it be known that they had acted most kindly in releasing the Paspaheghans. Then, except for a flurry of suspicion the very next day, it seemed that past contention had given way to peace and at least skin-deep mutual trust.

But this was not for long. Two days after the flurry a seemingly friendly Paspaheghan brought a glittering bit of stone to the fort, gesticulating to the effect that much more of the same "mineral" was to be found in a rocky formation he knew of. The Council dispatched John Smith with a dozen helpers to investigate, and with bits of copper to reward the Indian if anything materialized. Smith got suspicious only two miles from the fort, and decided to return. But before, he showed the Indian the copper he had, and said that he would have had it if he had led them to anything.

At that, the Indian got very angry, which was a mistake. Smith, never one to tolerate disrespectful behavior, gave him twenty lashes with a rope "for his scoffing and abusing us," and let him go, "bidding him shoot if he durst." At a dozen to one, the one could hardly have been expected to let fly an arrow. Yet this behavior, outrageous to our twentieth-century way of thinking, kept mutual murder between the Indians and the English down to its lowest point by far in the early history of the colony.

By then the month of May had all but passed into history. Nelson was ready to sail. Smith was eager to explore farther afield. The colony was well. And the crops were growing. All that remained was to load the *Phoenix* with her red cedar.

While the ship was being loaded, "in very good time" be it said, Smith set to work to finish a long letter to a friend. This letter, better known as Smith's *True Relation* or *Newes from Virginia,* was a voluminous epistle of a kind far from unknown in those days which recounted the events of the first year and a half of the Virginia Venture — from the end of December, 1606, to the end of May, 1608. Luckily it was circulated, as such letters often were, among interested parties, with the result that it was published (somewhat edited and cut) in the amazingly short time of only ten weeks after Smith handed it to Nelson at Cape Henry, the day he sailed for England.

Along with the letter, Smith prepared a "clean copy" of a sketch map of the region north of the James River so far as his personal knowledge went, but extended far beyond this on the basis of what he had learned (or thought he had learned) from the Indians. Smith may have known of the sketch map drawn by Robert Tindall and sent by Newport's return voyage in April, and wanted to improve on it. (It was both limited in scope and inaccurate, to judge by Tindall's own revision of it.) Whatever the details, it is certain that Smith wanted to get word to his friend Henry Hudson that the Indians reported there was a passage to some sort of a great body of water to the north of Chesapeake Bay. All of this he apparently described in a letter (now lost) and portrayed in a sketch preserved by the not disinterested zeal of the Spanish Ambassador to the Court of St. James's.

Smith finished his maps and letters — the long one was at least forty pages of folio writing-paper — while surrounded by the excitement and hubbub of Indian affairs, loading ship, and recurrent gold palsy. Then came a propitious breeze and on Thursday, June 2, Nelson unfurled sails and loosed the *Phoenix* from her moorings. John Smith gathered fourteen men onto the barge, and side by side the two vessels sailed down the James into the broad bay and finally the immense Atlantic. Smith delivered his letters to Nelson off Cape Henry, not before.

The sole passenger of note to go with Nelson was Captain John Martin, the sickly. Martin's motives in returning to England were undoubtedly bound up with the matter of gold, but it may also be that he wanted personally to counteract some of the contrary rumors he felt might be in circulation, or might be put into circulation by Smith's packet of documents. His almost uninterrupted sickliness may have been an added factor, but whatever his real reason, the bald fact is that he went.

This released his man, Anas Todkill, for other service, which he seems to have performed faithfully and with unusual selflessness. Little as is known of Todkill, it is evident that he admired men of action, and enjoyed an eventful life. By that token, it is not surprising that he should have attached himself to John Smith after Martin's departure — to be one of Smith's most loyal supporters during the rest of his stay in Virginia.

With the parting of Smith and Nelson at Cape Henry, we enter a new phase of Jamestown's history. Troubles lay ahead, as always, but the future was bright on the surface. Smith took advantage of that to see what lay beyond the core of Powhatan's "empire." No member of the colony had yet cast an inquiring eye along the eastern and northern shores of Chesapeake Bay.[4]

## CHAPTER 14

# THE FIRST VOYAGE UP CHESAPEAKE BAY

COUNCILOR JOHN MARTIN left behind him but three members of the local government. Therefore, as much as John Smith would have liked to take Scrivener with him to explore the great bay, it was obviously impossible to leave President Ratcliffe sole ruler. Scrivener might be able to restrain the President's ever-growing prodigality with the general stores, even though technically Ratcliffe had two votes to Scrivener's one. Furthermore, Scrivener and Smith together could only have bogged everything down by a tie vote. Scrivener was consequently left behind, with the hope that he, perhaps helped by George Percy's unofficial prestige, could hold back some of Ratcliffe's giddier projects. Smith considered it important to carry out the Company's *Instructions,* and explore the bay.

Instead of Scrivener, Smith chose a Dr. Walter Russell to be his chief assistant on the trip. (Russell was a newcomer about whom nothing is specifically known.) Six other gentlemen and seven "other ranks," four of whom were veterans, made up the balance of the party. Their "strong ribb'd bark" was but a humdrum barge of two or three tons burden, open to wind and rain.

The fifteen explorers steered straight across the mouth of Chesapeake Bay, coasting the swampy, low-lying islands off Cape Charles. These they christened Smiths Isles — collectively called Smith Island today. Then, rounding the cape back into the bay, they saw two "grim and stout Savages upon Cape-Charles, with long poles like javelins, headed with bone." These challenged Smith and his men, demanding to know who they were and what they wanted, and only after much ado were they set at ease. In the end, however, they took the English to their village of Accomac, a few miles up modern Cherrystone Inlet, and more than thirty miles south of the modern town of that name.

The werowance of the village, Kiptopeke by name, entertained the Englishmen with stories of a strange epidemic which had visited his Indians not long before, when two dead children were found miraculously preserved. The Indians flocked to see such a phenomenon, but all who did soon died. Not one escaped.

After this tale, which may have had some hidden motive, Kiptopeke cheerfully described the coastline of his domain for Smith. He was the brother of Werowance Debedeavon, "the laughing king of the Accomacs" to later Englishmen, and he and all his people seem to have been comely and hospitable. They lived in a state of semi-independence of Powhatan, thanks to the breadth of Chesapeake Bay.

Above Accomac the party explored the numerous inlets, bays, and creeks, looking for harbors, and sites for settlements, until they reached the archipelago which Smith named for Dr. Russell. These must have been the low-lying flecks of land that serve to mark off modern Pocomoke and Tangier sounds from the bay. There the barge was caught in a sudden storm while the colonists were hunting for fresh water. Finding none after the storm, they followed the nearest channel to the east, Smith's "Wighcocómoco River," today's Pocomoke. The Indians seemed much less friendly there, but finally welcomed the English "with songs, dances, and much mirth," but so far as supplies were concerned, they could give them only such "puddle-water" that Smith dedicated two days to a vain attempt to find something more drinkable.[1]

In the end, they had to sail on, so short of water that Russell and Todkill later wrote "we would have refused two barricoes [kegs] of gold for one of that puddle water of Wighcocómoco." The most notable fact of this spot, however, was that there the colonists were already outside Powhatan's realm. These Indians were conspicuously small, spoke another Algonkian language, and were "rude" — more primitive.

Once this river and the low-lying islands were left behind, the explorers reached "a high land upon the main" where they found a great pond of fresh water. This was so hot that they supposed it to be some mineral bath or spa, but apparently they made use of it as drinking water. John Smith called the place Point Ployer, in honor of the Comte de Plouër, Baron de la Moussaye, who had befriended him in Brittany eight years before. It is impossible to be sure which point this was, but the location of Deal Island and Haines Point would correspond roughly with Smith's map.

Leaving Point Ployer, they steered for "other Isles," probably Bloodsworth and neighboring islands, but another summer storm struck them. This time so furious was the combination of thunder and lightning and rain that they lost their foremast, and kept the barge afloat only by dint of continuous bailing. They finally tied up at one of the islands, then as now not permanently inhabited, where they lay for two days. Someone, possibly Smith, named the place Limbo, or hell itself.

When good weather returned, Smith explored the east shore farther, entering "a fair river on the east called *Kuskarawaock*," undoubtedly the river known as the Nanticoke today, which is still half a mile wide ten miles up from its mouth. There the party was welcomed by diminutive warriors and their families, who ran about in wild confusion and showered them with arrows. Some of the nimbler Indians even scrambled up trees, the better to see and to shoot; nor were they sparing of "the greatest passion they could espress of their anger," as Russell and Todkill later wrote. Smith endeavored to make peace with them, unsuccessfully, and for the moment there was nothing to do but anchor offshore, out of reach of their arrows.

The next day the Indians came down to the riverbank, carrying baskets and dancing in a ring. Although the gesture was peaceful enough and seemed to mean "Come join us!" the explorers saw that "there was nothing in them but villany," and fired a volley of pistol shot with their muskets, to frighten or at most to wound rather than to kill. The Indians tumbled to the ground and slithered off into the thick tangle of reeds and underbrush.

Toward evening, when no further Indians were in evidence, the party approached the shore gingerly, firing five or six shots into the reeds to start any hiding there. All was still. They landed then, near some baskets dropped in flight, and saw blood on the ground, but not a single savage. Spotting smoke on the other side of the river, however, they rowed across and found two or three little houses (wigwams), each with a fire in it, but still no Indians. There was nothing to do but leave some pieces of copper, bells, and little looking glasses around, and return to the barge.

The next morning four Indians paddled up in a canoe. They had been fishing, they somehow informed Smith, and knew nothing of the fracas of the day before. The colonists treated them with "courtesy." That is, they gave them a few baubles and showed vast interest in them. In return, the Indians asked the Englishmen to wait a bit, that they would be back; which they were, "and some twenty more with them."

Before the day was over, "two or three thousand men, women and children" (undoubtedly an exaggeration) came clustering around the explorers, giving them presents, which were requited with a bead or two, and trying in every possible way to be friendly. From these Indians Smith learned that there were at least five villages along the river, the chief of which was called Kuskarawaock, like the river. (It was possibly near modern Laurel, Delaware.) Another town they named, Nantaquake, is significant because it is obviously the same as Nanticoke, the name by which the Indians of that region came to be known in later history. (Nanticoke or -quake was possibly opposite Sharpetown, Maryland.)

Although these Indians spoke a language differing from that of Powhatan perhaps as Italian from Spanish, it is clear from what little survives of their tongue that Smith could have understood isolated words or phrases, while needing an interpreter to catch the whole sense. He himself, judging by the phrases in his vocabulary, spoke a kind of "pidgin" Powhatan in which the involved structure was reduced to unadorned fundamentals. Nevertheless, possibly because the Nanticokes were "the best merchants of all other Savages," and had interpreters to carry on business, Smith could directly or indirectly learn a good bit about both them and their neighbors. These latter included "a great nation called *Massawomekes*," who lived beyond the Nanticokes (or Kuskarawaocks).

While the "greatness" of the Massawomekes was merely the terrified esteem in which they were held, with Smith it was a matter of mention the devil and he would be off looking for him. And this could not but please the Nanticokes, for it gave them three delight-

ful prospects. Smith's "exploding gadgets" might wipe out that
horrid tribe. Or, if the tribe was less dangerous than Smith, perhaps
the encounter would turn out the other way around. Or, best of
all, there might be a blood bath that would drown English and
Indian enemies alike. However it was, they painted such a picture
that John Smith took off at once.[2]

Returning by Limbo and always in search of fresh water in the
low-lying spit of land called today the Delmarva Peninsula, Smith
apparently skirted modern Hooper Islands, the tip of which he
named Momford Point after one of the gentlemen of the expedition.
Chesapeake Bay is eleven miles wide there, so broad, wrote Smith,
"that we could scarce perceive the great high cliffs on the other
side." (These were obviously the cliffs above Cove Point.) The
fact that Smith did not notice the mouth of the Patuxent River on
the western shore hints that he was hugging the east shore until he
sighted the cliffs, where the bay is only five miles wide, and where
Rocky Point rises nearly a hundred and forty feet. The only important detail here, however, is the fact that John Smith named
the cliffs Rickards Cliffs, apparently as a unique memorial of his
mother and her family.

From Rickards Cliffs the party sailed on some seventy miles to
the north. (Although Smith estimated the distance as thirty leagues,
or ninety miles, it is easy to tell how far he actually went.) His sailing was of course indirect, but his description of their route implies
that they skirted the western shore all along, perhaps because the
eastern was made up of a succession of low islands, or fingers of
land, overgrown with woods even today. Indeed, wherever they
went the woods were "extreme thick, full of wolves, bears, deer,
and other wild beasts," with no visible sign of mankind. Shallow
creeks there were, and rolling hills and valleys, green with countless
trees. But the hand of the Almighty seemed to have halted in the
middle of the last day of creation there. Not even an inimical arrow
betrayed the presence of a fellow human being. The barge was ven-
turing into an Unknown more hostile, perhaps, than the unsailed
seas that tried the hearts of Columbus's shipmates — for land where
no man lives is terrifying by its silence.

In all this long journey, the first inlet the expedition found was
the Patapsco River, which Smith named the Bolus, "for that the

clay (in many places) was like (if not) Bole-Armoniack." Bole armeniac, as it is properly called, was a kind of clay, reddish, brown, or yellow in color, imported from Armenia, and famous for its medicinal properties. Since it is highly doubtful if any of the party had ever seen bole armeniac in its native beds, the yellow clay and loam of tidewater Maryland was hopefully, but not too confidently, taken for a kindred substance. It is not even certain that the party brought any samples back to Jamestown, for none seem to have been sent to England for analysis. Perhaps John Smith wanted to make more certain of the value of his discovery, if such it was, and avoid a parallel scandal to John Martin's "gilded dirt."

In any event, after an excursion up the Patapsco River, the party did not venture much farther. As Smith wrote, his gallant company started out with such enthusiasm that they were afraid at first that he would return too soon. Life on a barge, the prospect of encounters with Indians or of finding great Indian cities, the ever-unfolding expanse of water and wilderness — all combined to excite and interest the men. But after twelve days, out of contact with natives who made fresh bread, straining at the oars when they could not sail, the barge had become a cramped prison, and their moldy bread an abomination. Murmurs to return grew into noisy demands.

John Smith was not a man to be deterred by human contrariness. Seeking inspiration from Hakluyt's pertinent *Voyages* once more, he delivered a speech in which he reminded gentlemen and soldiers alike that Sir Ralph Lane's companions had seen fit to carry on, twenty-odd years before, even though they might be reduced to the extremity of eating their watchdogs, boiled with sassafras leaves. Smith's party still had bread, albeit rotten, for a month more. Smith himself would share their diet, their hardships, their storm-tossed and often drenched lodging — indeed, he would take the worst part of everything. But return he would not, before with God's assistance he had "seen the Massawomekes, [and] found Patawomeck, or the head of this great water," which the others conceived to be endless. No doubt his speech was brief, to the point, and simple. The version which has survived in print he undoubtedly wrote later, in the comfort of London, and in Elizabethan rhetoric.

But it appeared that God was not ready to assist. Near the island today known as Pooles Island, a dozen miles above the Patapsco, the explorers waited for wind and weather to change. But wind and weather would not let them go on. And Smith would not return. Then enforced idleness and the rough seas collaborated with the maggoty bread at last to make three or four of the men seriously sick. There was then nothing to do but retreat. Reconciled to the inevitable, Smith noted for his map that at that point the bay was still "some 10 miles broad at 9 or 10 fathom water."

On Thursday, June 16, the valiant gentlemen and crew were back at the mouth of the Potomac, nearly a hundred miles toward home. Pertinently, John Smith noted: "Fear being gone, and our men recovered, we were all contented to take some pains to know the name of this nine mile broad river." It was clearly not only the moldy bread and bad weather that made the men sick. It was fear of silence and emptiness.[3]

But even along the shores of the Potomac inhabitants seemed scarce. The party sailed thirty miles before they sighted a brace of savages, who conducted them "up a little bayed creek toward Onawmanient," a name which endures in abbreviated form as Nomini Bay. The lack of evidence of human beings indicates that Smith followed the north shore of the Potomac, since he later visited or learned of at least two important Indian villages on the south shore below Onawmanient which were obviously, this time, passed unseen.

It is not entirely clear whether Smith took the barge up Nomini Creek — there is a bar at its entrance today — or went with the Indians in their boat. In any case, the party had not gone far when they found themselves all but surrounded by three or four hundred Indians (again, probably exaggerated), "so strangely painted, grimed and disguised," the account reads, "shouting, yelling, and crying, as we rather supposed them so many divvels." Smith of course was not to be frightened. He opened fire with such "seeming willingness" that the Indians dropped bows and arrows and gesticulated for peace. Smith accepted, also "of course" since that was actually what he wanted, and exchanged hostages, sending James Watkins (a laborer turned soldier) six miles inland to the habitation of the local werowance. At the same time he learned from the frightened Indians, seeking to excuse themselves, that they had orders from Powhatan to "betray" Smith and his men, and that Powhatan in turn had been thus directed by the malcontents at Jamestown. No one can be sure of the truth of any or all of this information, but there is little doubt that Smith's expedition received most unfriendly greetings in several spots along the Potomac.

One of the more hospitable places, however, was Wighcocómoco, a village of the same name as the one on the east shore of the bay but at the mouth of the Potomac, where the expedition picked up a "lusty Savage named Mosco" with a thick black, bushy beard. Mosco was attracted to the Englishmen, as he put it, because they were bearded too, and must be his "countrymen." The English in turn thought that Mosco must be a Frenchman's son, since the Indians seldom had any beard at all. By mutual consent, therefore, Mosco joined the exploring party, guided them up the river, helped fetch wood and water, and drafted Indian help when wind or tide made navigation difficult.

With such unexpected help, Smith determined to pursue his course upstream, having by then undoubtedly learned that the river he had found was the same Patawomeck he had wanted to find. The reason here, however, was more specific than had been the case with his wanting to sail farther up Chesapeake Bay. Some Indians they had talked to long before had mentioned a "glistering metal" which they got from the Potomac Indians, and Newport had apparently come to the conclusion, or had been told, that it was half silver. (The text is not clear.) Obviously John Smith was not going to turn back after advancing only thirty miles toward such a find. Neither were his companions.

The decision to go on was to take them up the Potomac beyond the site of Washington, which was not then honored by even a hunting lodge. Still, it is an interesting coincidence that John Smith sailed past the flats where the Washington Monument now stands almost on the same day that Samuel de Champlain drove the first stakes in the ground to establish a permanent French settlement in Canada — a fort called Quebec.*

Newport had wanted to explore Chesapeake Bay to its head. John Smith had also, but was thwarted in that direction by his sick men. He then tried the Potomac, where he had to turn back when the

* Champlain landed at Quebec on July 3, 1608, corresponding to June 23 in the English calendar.

channel became unnavigable. The route to the "big sea water" that lay somewhere to the northwest still eluded him. But if he could get no farther just then, at least he could look for "furs, metals, rivers, rocks, nations, woods, fishings, fruits, victuals, and other commodities" — especially metals.

Near what is today the David Taylor Model Basin, five or six miles above the District of Columbia boundary, Smith and his party met "divers Savages in canoes" who were coming downstream with bear meat and venison, part of which they purchased with baubles. This took them ashore, where (after trading) they found rocky cliffs below which the rushing waters of the Potomac had left a "tinctured spangled scurf [deposit] that made many places seem as gilded" (Yellow Falls?). By digging in the ground above, they discovered a kind of loam liberally sprinkled with "yellow spangles as if it had been pin-dust." This had to be some sort of mineral, although John Smith did not jump at the conclusion that it was gold. Nevertheless when he returned downstream and visited the werowance of Potomac village, on modern Marlboro Point, he mentioned it. (Odd, Smith had probably found gold, and did not quite believe it!)

The werowance, calling the "pin-dust" *matchqueon,* which probably meant something pretty or "eye-catching," suggested that his guests might find what they wanted closer at hand by going up the Quiyough River just to the north (today's Aquia Creek). He even, at Mosco's insistence, gave them guides to help them find the place. But Mosco "rested" with the werowance. He may have suspected treachery. Mosco, it seems, was intensely loyal.

Smith took six well-armed men and his guides in the barge as far as he could go. Disembarking then, he chained the guides to himself and his companions so that they could not easily run away, and overcame their objection to this strange procedure by promising to give them the chains when they got back to the boat. That made the Indians "proud so richly to be adorned"!

Some eight or ten miles inland, the party found the "mine," which the Indians had dug with shells and tomahawks. Smith and his men picked up as much of the "ore" as they could carry conveniently, and took it back to the barge. Nothing further is said or known about the matchqueon mine.

More potentially profitable than the armloads of questionable minerals were the otters, beavers, martens, lynx or wildcats, and "sables" (minks) which they saw or heard about, alive or as skins. News of such animals would be of interest in London. Less glamorous, but of immediate interest along the Potomac, was the vast quantity of fish, "lying so thick with their heads above the water, as for want of nets (our boat driving amongst them) we attempted to catch them with a frying pan."

Under such circumstances, it is hard to say which should be marveled at the more, the lack of foresight that permitted exploration without so elementary a food-provider as a fish net, or the solemn statement that the explorers found a frying pan "a bad instrument to catch fish with." In fact, the writer of the account (perhaps Russell or Todkill) rubs it in by adding that none of them had ever seen better or plentier fish anywhere than in Chesapeake Bay, "but they're not to be caught with frying pans." This in a body of explorers which listed as two of its members "Richard Keale, fishmonger," and "Jonas Profit, fisher"! Had the ever-prepared John Smith left it up to these two to bring lines and net?[4]

It was time to return to Jamestown. Their food supplies were about spent. Nevertheless, John Smith wanted to visit the Tappahannock River, just to the south, where he had been brought during his captivity to see if he was the tall white-man of unpleasant memory. The barge was consequently sailed down the Potomac, around low, creek-laced Smith Point, and southward in the bay for twenty-five miles to the mouth of the Tappahannock, now called the Rappahannock. (The two are the same word, in different dialects.) There the barge was caught by the ebb tide and grounded in the shallow water off the south shore. While waiting for the returning high water to float them again, Smith amused himself spearing fish with his sword. The others copied him, and within an hour they had more than they could eat. But Smith the spearer was himself speared while taking a stingray off the blade. The dying fish's poison tail stuck in his wrist, penetrating an inch and a half into his arm.

Before the tide returned, four hours later, his hand, arm, shoulder, and part of his body became so swollen that all hope was given up of saving his life, and Smith personally chose a place to bury his tormented body. Doctor Russell, however, had not been idle, and the oil he had applied to the wound at last proved an antidote for the poison. Before nightfall, Smith was out of danger, and was able to eat his would-be assassin for supper. Solemnly they named Smith's proposed burial place Stingray Isle, today known as Stringray Point.

Lacking any further means of treating Smith, the company decided to return immediately to Jamestown. By sailing most of the night, they reached Kecoughtan, ninety miles away at the mouth of the James, the next morning, where they were welcomed by the natives. Some of the "simple savages" there paddled out to meet the barge, and quickly spotted not only the wounded Captain Smith and a fellow explorer with a bloody shin from some carelessness, but also the "bows, arrows, swords, targets [shields], mantles and furs" they had brought down from the Potomac. These articles along with the wounded men were understood immediately as signs of a war. The truth did not prevail, and the Kecoughtans persisted in asking which enemies the colonists had conquered. (Clearly, if they had lost they would not have returned.) Smith and his companions, deciding that an appropriate lie might prove very white for their future relations with the Indians, resolved "to tell them anything that might affright them." And they confided the "secret" of what spoil they "had got and made of the Massawomekes."

This secret naturally went up the James faster than the barge. In fact, when they stopped at Warraskoyack they heard it, already in more elaborate detail. So they took full advantage, trimming the boat gaily with painted streamers and other bunting. Then they soon covered the remaining twenty-odd miles to the fort, dismaying the jumpy colonists, who thought they were a Spanish frigate! *

Safely on shore again on July 21, Smith found "all" the January arrivals sick, while some of the original settlers were lame or bruised. Submitting his wound to surgery at the hands of Anthony Bagnall (Russell was a physician, not a surgeon), Smith quickly took stock of the situation. The colonists were in rebellion against President Ratcliffe, who had evidently fallen victim to delusions

* Then a light, fast [war-]ship, invented or introduced by the Spaniards not long before the Invincible Armada.

of grandeur. Abusing his privileges as President more than Wingfield, whose deposition he had promoted for just such misdemeanors, Ratcliffe had not only wasted their store of supplies, but had ordered the construction of "an unnecessary palace in the woods." For this, the incensed colonists, when they heard the tales of the expeditionaries and the (misunderstood) Indian tidings of a route to the South Sea by way of Chesapeake Bay, demanded that Ratcliffe be deposed, and that Captain John Smith, the successful commander of the Chesapeake expedition, be elected in his stead.

Smith agreed to the deposition of Ratcliffe, and was apparently sustained in this by Matthew Scrivener. Unless Ratcliffe agreed to resign, however, it is not clear how the deposition could be legally effected, since Ratcliffe had two votes in the Council, and Smith and Scrivener one each. It is quite uncertain what was done, but one possible interpretation of the murky reports is that Scrivener became the acting President at this time. But Scrivener had unfortunately fallen sick "of a calenture" (perhaps a mild sunstroke), and was unable to serve in full capacity. Somehow a working agreement was then reached by virtue of which Ratcliffe (whether deposed or not) ceased to govern (at least, to rule), and a junta was formed to carry out such provisions as Scrivener might suggest. At all events, Scrivener's term would last less than two months, when Ratcliffe's presidency would expire by law. (This would explain Smith's refusal to take over, and seems to be the key to understanding a highly confused account.)

Meanwhile, or because of this solution, John Smith felt obliged to return to his explorations. He must find out if indeed there was a route to the Pacific Ocean through the rivers emptying into the northern stretches of the bay. This route, next after the discovery of valuable minerals, was the most pressing of the *Instructions* not yet implemented.

Amazingly, Smith was cured (almost) of his wound, the colony calmed down (almost), sensible government was restored (perhaps), and the barge readied for another voyage (after a fashion) — all between a Thursday morning and the following Sunday. Then, with two less men but an otherwise only slightly altered company, John Smith set out once more into the Unknown.[5]

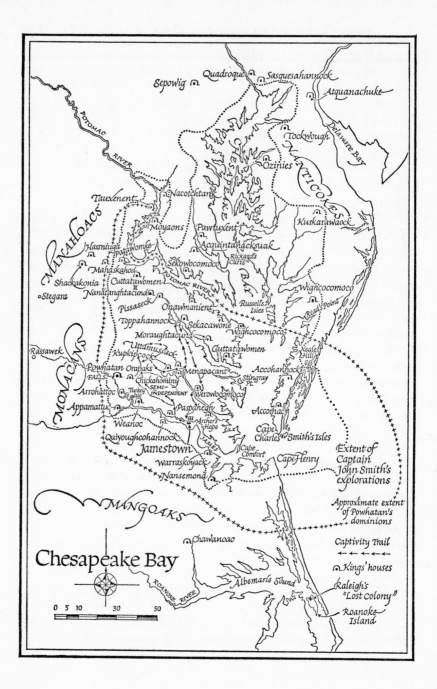

Sepowig

Quadroque  Sasquesahannock

Atquanachuke

Tockwough

Ozinies

Nacotchtank

Tauxenent

MANAHOACS

Moyaons  Pawtuxent

Kuskarawaock

Hassniuga
Pamunkwomke

Acquintanacksuak

Rickard's
Cliffs

Sekowocomoco

Mahaskahod

Shackakonia  Cuttatawomen II

Stegara  Nandtanghtacund

Wighcocomoco

Pissaseck

Onawmanient

Russell's
Isles

Bead's Point

Rassawek

Toppahannock

Moraughtacund

Sekacawone

Wighcocomoco

MONACANS

Uttamussack
Kupkipcock

Cuttatawomen
I

Keale's
Hill

Powhatan Orapaks
FALLS

Menapacant

Accohannock

Arrohattoc

Chickahominy
Turkey
Isle  SEMI-
INDEPENDENT

Stingray

Werowocomoco

Appamattuc

Paspahegh

Accomac

Weanoc

Archer's
Hope

Cape
Charles  Smith's Isles

Quiyoughcohannock

Jamestown

JAMES

Cape
Comfort

Cape Henry

Extent of
Captain
John Smith's
explorations

Warraskoyack

Nansemond

Approximate extent
of Powhatan's
dominions

MANGOAKS

Chawanoac

Captivity Trail

Kings' houses

Chesapeake Bay

Raleigh's
"Lost Colony"

Albemarle Sound

Roanoke
Island

ROANOKE RIVER

0  5  10      30      50

## CHAPTER 15

# THE SECOND CHESAPEAKE VOYAGE

THE SECOND exploring party sailed from Jamestown on July 24, 1608. From the outset, it was clear that this expedition would be timed so as to return before September 10, when the legal term of President Ratcliffe would terminate — hence the haste in getting started. At best, the arrangement for governing the colony until then was makeshift, and there can be little doubt that John Smith's mind was made up to be back in time for the elections.

Since Ratcliffe was barred by the *Articles* of November 20, 1606, from succeeding himself, and Scrivener was both very young and very recently arrived, there could have been no doubt in the colony that Smith would be the next President. Still, from his point of view it was better for him to be there. In the meantime, the seven weeks could be spent profitably looking for the fabled passage across the top of North America.

It seems strange today that otherwise intelligent men and women could believe that at worst a portage was all that separated Chesapeake Bay (or later, the Hudson River) from lakes or rivers with outlets into the Pacific Ocean, yet it was an all too popular article of geographical faith during John Smith's life and for some years after. Richard Hakluyt, an eminent (though armchair) geographer, reasoned that some sort of passage ought to exist, just as gold ought to exist, and Sir Walter Ralegh's colonists ought still to exist. It did not matter that Hakluyt was already gracefully retiring, in a sense loaded with honors, from active colonial promotion. Others took up his ideas with more conviction and less knowledge, and Christopher Newport was soon to return to Virginia "with a private commission" to find the short passage to the Pacific, or gold, or one of Ralegh's colonists.

John Smith fortunately could not know of the "private commission" and other grotesque objectives to be unfolded before him for compliance and implementation when Newport reached Jamestown again. He was merely determined to test the Indians' statements, so far as he could, regarding the passage to the Pacific Ocean. (The gold was dismissed for the time being, and the Roanoke search postponed.) He does not seem to have taken too much stock in the idea by then, despite his letter to Henry Hudson. But that did not dim his enthusiasm for the completion of his "discovery."

Contrary winds delayed the barge at Kecoughtan for two or three days, which gave the werowance a chance to entertain Smith and his party "with much mirth." This young brave had apparently not made his appearance before, since he is first mentioned here. According to Strachey (writing in 1611), he was a son of Powhatan's named Pochins, and this may be the reason why he was not in evidence on Smith's previous visits. Smith naturally recognized the importance of making a show of strength before the chief of so strategically located a tribe, and gave him and his people reason to believe that this second expedition was purely for the sake of revenging themselves on the Massawomekes. Then he gave Kecoughtan an example of how they would do this. They fired two or three rockets of the kind that bedazzle holiday resorts today. The wildfire trailing through the sky so terrified the "poor Savages" that "they supposed nothing impossible" which the English might attempt. They even offered to help — with all the twenty warriors that made up their fighting force.

In this regard, Smith was a master strategist with the Indians. Between his psychological warfare and his immovable firmness he was able to maintain a position of extraordinary strength, without having to resort to the petty murders or exaggerated reprisals that had only brought trouble before, and would bring trouble later.

The first night out of Kecoughtan they spent at Stingray Isle, and on July 27 or 28 hastened past the Potomac to the Bolus (Patapsco) River. It can be surmised that they spent the night there, in what was, so to speak, familiar territory, after which they sailed the remaining dozen miles to their previous turning-around place. After passing that point, they observed what appeared to be two "heads" to the bay, which later turned out to be four. (While the account is not entirely clear, these rivers have been identified as the Susquehanna, the Northeast, the Elk, and the Sassafras.)

By this time the eight newcomers of Smith's twelve men were sick. Only the seasoned colonists (Nathaniel Powell, gentleman, soldiers Anas Todkill and Edward Pising, and Jonas Profit, sailor and fisher) were able to help Smith with the barge. Small wonder it therefore is that they explored two of the rivers only superficially — without running across any Indians — and that they proceeded carefully, as anyone without a chart must do even today.

Crossing the bay somewhere above Bush River, the expedition unexpectedly "encountered 7 or 8 canoes-full of Massawomekes," the redoubtable savages they had pretended to conquer before, who were prepared to assault the intruding barge.

Retreat being impossible, on account of the sick, Smith took the offensive and sailed right at them. Covering the deck with a tarpaulin to hide as well as to protect the incapacitated, Smith had the men's hats stuck up on sticks by the side of the barge, and stationed one man with two muskets between each pair of hats. The glint of the musket barrels, the mystery of the dark barge with perhaps no one but Smith himself (undoubtedly in full, shiny armor) visible aboveboard, and the inexorable advance of the strange white-sailed apparition unattended by human figures, was too much for the Massawomekes, brave as they were. They paddled for the shore. But Smith pursued them until he anchored in shallow water "right against them." Then he beckoned for them to come aboard.

This seems to the modern reader little short of senseless, unless (as is possible) the text is garbled. There were but five able-bodied Englishmen, who would have been outnumbered, in a hand-to-hand fight, by at least three to one. Furthermore, Smith seems to have wanted to hide his weakness from the Indians. Yet he persuaded them so urgently that two of the bravest braves paddled over, unarmed, to investigate. All the rest hovered in the background, waiting to see what would happen.

Somewhere on the barge, Smith received the daring emissaries (apparently without uncovering his sick bay), and presented them with a bell each. The gift being as unexpected as it was unusual, the rest of the Indians flocked up in a body. Trade ensued, and soon the English had acquired bear meat, venison, bearskins, fish, bows, arrows, clubs, and shields — the last-mentioned apparently of basketwork. Their canoes, Smith noted, were not dugouts, but birch bark, well "luted" (cemented) with gum or rosin. Since the Powhatans had neither canoes nor shields of similar construction, Smith knew that he had run across a quite different tribe, and this was promptly confirmed by their language. The Powhatan language was of no more use than English or Latin.

By means of signs, however, these Indians conveyed the information that they were returning from a raid against their traditional enemies on the east shore of the bay, by pointing first in the direction of the said enemies and then at their "green" wounds. Smith took it for granted that these raiders were the famous Massawomekes.

By that time it was night, and the Massawomekes were off, leaving the English anchored there expecting them to return to trade again the next day. But no canoe whatsoever was seen in the morning. Smith does not say, however, that they waited long, and the next thing we know, the barge was entering the Tockwough River (now the Sassafras), to find the savages there all armed, in a fleet of dugouts "after their barbarous manner." Nothing daunted, John Smith called out friendly greetings in Powhatan, and was fortunate enough to find that one of the Tockwoughs could speak that language. This individual volunteered to act as interpreter, and persuaded the rest to enter into a friendly parley.[1]

Since Smith had discovered that these parleys effected his purposes better when accompanied by a show of strength, he displayed the assortment of Massawomeke weapons and supplies he had bought by trade, and asserted that he had won them by armed might. Promptly the Tockwoughs, a branch of the people later known as the Nanticokes, conducted the triumphant Englishmen to their palisaded village, where "their men, women and children, with dances, songs, fruits, furs, and what they had, kindly welcomed us, spreading mats for us to sit on, and stretching their best abilities to express their loves." They sensibly did not want to cast the gauntlet at the leader of so valiant a band.

As the entertainment led to the inevitable exchange of gifts,

Smith and his companions caught sight of hatchets and knives and other bits of iron and brass such as were unknown to the tribes subject to Powhatan. Astonished at finding this sort of metal objects among the Indians, Smith asked the interpreter where they had acquired them. The Tockwoughs replied that the source was a nation called the Susquehannocks, a "mighty people and mortal enemies with the Massawomekes." They lived at the "chief spring" of the four branches of the head of Chesapeake Bay, a couple of days' journey upstream. But Smith could not reach them in his barge, on account of "rocks." (Modern maps show many obstructions just above the railroad and highway bridges at the mouth of the Susquehanna.) Smith of course wanted to see the "chief spring," as well as the Susquehannocks, and asked for an interpreter who could speak Susquehannock, an Iroquoian language, and interpret his own interpreter. Equipped with this essential, the party set out in the barge from the Tockwough village (near Georgetown, Maryland) for the neighborhood of what is now Havre de Grace, twenty-five miles away.

There they waited three or four days while the interpreter went up alone to the first Susquehannock village to persuade some of the tribe to come down to trade with the Englishmen. (The village was probably near Safe Harbor, Pennsylvania — a trip of well over thirty miles each way.) Meanwhile, John Smith did a little exploring, but he was stopped by a waterfall a mile or two above modern Conowingo Dam. This he named after himself. And it remained Smith's Falls as long as the falls remained in their natural state.

In due time, sixty Susquehannocks turned up, under the command of five "werowances." (The number was probably exaggerated, and the Iroquoian name for "chief" was not recorded.) They were very tall, "giant-like" Smith calls them, and they brought three-foot-long ceremonial tobacco pipes. They also bore gifts for the white werowance: venison, wicker baskets, wicker shields, bows and arrows. And they agreed to accompany Smith across the bay. The wind being too strong for their birch-bark canoes at the moment, the five werowances mounted into the barge, and left their men and canoes to follow when they could.

Back in the Tockwoughs' village, it seems that the interpreter did a superb job of storytelling. With gestures, and talking two languages, he magnified Smith's exploits until Captain Smith of Transylvanian fame emerged as John the Massawomeke Slayer. Not only that, but John's own actions soon revealed the source from which he drew his mighty magic.

Every morning, he and his white-skinned confederates knelt before a mystic symbol, muttering through their beards in harsh, unpronounceable syllables, after which they solemnly rose and burst into song. No Indian had ever heard of, not to say seen, morning prayer according to the Anglican rite, but they all knew what conjurations were. If the Massawomeke Slayer got the power to overcome such ruthless foes by these conjurations, they, the Susquehannocks (and presumably the Tockwoughs, too) had better look to it. He might be propitiating the white Great Spirit against them next. And they consulted among themselves.

> Then [as the account vividly describes it] they began in a most passionate manner to hold up their hands to the sun, with a most fearful song; then, embracing our Captain, they began to adore him in like manner. Though he rebuked them, yet they proceeded till their song was finished, which done, [one of them] with a most strange furious action, and a hellish voice, began an oration on their loves.

At least, so the interpreter explained.

As if this were not enough, the Susquehannocks next covered John Smith with a "great painted bear's skin," after which one of them hung a chain of white beads weighing six pounds or more around his neck, while others laid eighteen mantles made of skins sewn together at his feet, along with many other gifts, "stroking their ceremonious hands about his neck" to signify that they created him their Governor and Protector whom they would support and serve if he would but stay with them, to defend them and take vengeance on the Massawomekes.

Regrettably, John Smith had other things to attend to, but he promised he would return the next year. For the time being, however, he wanted some information from them. This they gladly supplied, giving him a description of the Atquanachukes, who dwelt on the Ocean Sea (actually on the Delaware River, a few miles below New Castle), and the famous Massawomekes and other peoples inhabiting "upon a great water beyond the mountains."

From this, John Smith understood that it was a matter of a great lake or the St. Lawrence River in Canada, not the Pacific Ocean. He also guessed that the Susquehannocks got their hatchets and other "civilized" articles from the French by trade. (Smith would have read about Canada in Hakluyt's *Voyages*.)

With that valuable information, and with the conviction that he would get to Canada, not to the Pacific, by going up these rivers, John Smith took leave of the Susquehannocks and the Tockwoughs alike. The annihilation of the Massawomekes would have to wait another year.

On the way back to Jamestown, John Smith paid tribute to his friends the Berties, in far-off Lincolnshire, by naming the most conspicuous hill at the head of the bay Peregrine's Mount (probably Gray's Hill, just east of Elkton), and the "rocky river, where the Massawomekes went up," Willoughby's River. This, he wrote, was in "honor of the town our Captain was born in, and that honorable house [of] the Lord Willoughby, his most honored good friend." At the same time, he flattered several of his companions with points, bays, rivers, and so forth named after them, although some of these names may not have been bestowed until his sketch maps were consolidated in the chart engraved for him by William Hole in 1612.

Everywhere they went the English cut crosses in trees, to show how far they had gone, or left notes in holes in them, or set up small brass crosses, "to signify to any, Englishmen had been there." Only the brass markers could have survived, but none of them have yet been found. Nevertheless, the engraved map, on which the limit of each exploration is indicated by a cross pattée, shows that Smith and his party went inland nearly as far as the modern state border of Maryland, both to the northeast (with Delaware) and the north (with Pennsylvania). Furthermore, having explored the Potomac previously beyond the District of Columbia, they had also gone up the Patapsco beyond the junction of the North and the South Branch to the west, and the Sassafras about as far as the Delaware line to the east. In other words, John Smith now had a good notion of the river geography of practically all the northern half of eastern Maryland. He next set out to explore what remained to the south.[2]

The first important river below the site of Baltimore is the

Patuxent. This John Smith ascended, apparently to the narrow reach above Nottingham, before the river divides, five miles or so higher. (He would surely have indicated the Western Branch on his map had he seen it.) Yet he has little to say about the Indians he met. He found them "very tractable, and more civil than any," and they inhabited "together, and not so dispersed as the rest," as the seventeen villages shown on his map along a little more than thirty miles of river would indicate. That was about all.

For some reason, John Smith avoided the east shore. From the Sassafras River south to Taylor's Island, at the mouth of the Choptank, he charted that coast of the Bay only very roughly, tossing in the name *Ozinies* toward the north (they had sixty fighting men, he noted), but generally blanketing the area with extensive woodland on his map — which he baptized Brookes Forest.

Below the Patuxent, Smith sailed past the mouth of the Potomac to explore the Tappahannock, a task from which the poisonous fishtail had diverted him two or three weeks before. Missing at least one important Indian settlement hidden in the woods, the party went nearly thirty miles upstream before halting at Moraughtacund (today's Morattico, village or creek), where they encountered Mosco, last seen at Potomac village. Delighted, they enlisted his services once more.

At that point the river divided the Moraughtacund tribe, with eighty fighting men, from the Rappahannocks, with a hundred. According to Mosco, the Moraughtacunds had recently stolen three of the women of the Werowance of Rappahannock, and warned Smith against crossing over. The Rappahannocks would kill the English for being friends of the thieves. (Apparently Mosco had promoted this friendship remarkably quickly.) Smith was not to be frightened away by such stories, and suspected that Mosco might perhaps merely be trying to keep all the valuable English trade (bells, beads, and bits of copper) for his friends; so Smith and his party "crossed the river to the Rappahannocks."

The river bulges out to a width of three miles opposite Morattico, and the south shore forms a shallow bay. A dozen or more Rappahannocks were waiting as the barge drew near, gesticulating for Smith to sail to a little creek (probably Parrott's Creek, a mile or two downstream), where there was a good landing place. Soon the explorers saw three or four canoes lined up in the designated creek, piled with commodities for trade. Smith demanded an exchange of hostages, as was his custom before starting any barter, "in sign of love" — by which he meant security and good faith. After an inaudible consultation, four or five Rappahannocks came part of the way to the barge, showing that they were unarmed, and offering to exchange a man with the Englishmen.

This done, the English hostage (old-timer Anas Todkill) insisted on reconnoitering before the barge would come in closer. The Rappahannocks tried to prevent him, but Todkill, looking for an ambush, succeeded in getting "two stones-throws" up into the clearing. There he caught a glimpse of two or three hundred men, "as he thought," hiding behind the trees. (Another exaggeration, undoubtedly, although there is no reason to question the ambush.)

Todkill edged away then, and started to return to the barge. At this, the Indians tried to carry him away by force. Todkill shouted that they were betrayed. The Indian hostage leaped overboard to try to escape. Soldier James Watkins, detailed to keep an eye on him, shot him dead in the water. And the battle started. Anas Todkill dropped to the ground just in time, as a shower of arrows flew at the boat, while English muskets spat indiscriminately into the mob of Indians.

John Smith had already set the Massawomeke shields in the guise of a forecastle on the barge, and his men were able to fire between them without danger. In this way a thousand arrows or more were spent in vain before the Rappahannocks took to their heels into the forest. Todkill crawled toward the shore, covered with Indian blood, but himself unwounded, as the barge crept gingerly through the shallow water to meet him. A brief reconnaissance revealed a few victims, dead, and pools of blood, but no wounded. The Rappahannocks had shot their last arrow and decamped.

Mosco had been proven right (perhaps to nobody's surprise), and he was duly rewarded with arrows and Rappahannock canoes. But the unprovoked attack had a constructive effect on the colonists and their future strategy. Having learned that the Massawomeke shields were all but impervious to arrows, John Smith set about converting the barge into an armored frigate. The tholes against which the rowers pressed their oars were replaced by long sticks, sturdy as bedstaves (wrote Smith), to which the Massawomeke shields were firmly fixed with an overlap that girdled the barge like decorative waist-cloths, hiding and guarding all on board. Thus accoutered, the barge ventured on into the wilderness.

That night the colonists anchored offshore, to start upstream again the next morning. Mosco, for some reason, chose to trot along the shore for a while, but later called to be taken aboard. Twenty-five or more miles up the river, they passed three towns on the north bank, perched on "high white clay cliffs; the other side all a low plain, marsh, and the river there but narrow."

In that vicinity, probably on what is today Payne's Island, thirty or forty Indians had "accommodated" themselves with branches in such fashion that Smith and his companions mistook them for little bushes, growing among the sedge, until a flight of arrows struck the boat's armor. Mosco dropped flat, crying "Rappahan-nocks!" while Smith's men fired into the "bushes," which promptly and mysteriously collapsed into the reeds. But when the barge was half a mile farther on, the "bushes" became men, "dancing and singing very merrily." It is doubtful if the chronicler of the event interpreted their spirit correctly.

Beyond this narrow stretch of river, the colonists came to Pis-saseck, Nantaughtacund, and Cuttatawomen (the upper town of that name), where they were entertained. Not far beyond, they came to a broader span of river, where there were two islands (apparently no longer there). At that point Richard Fetherstone, one of the most promising gentlemen of the new supply, gave up his struggle against heat and discomfort. By a little bay he was buried, as a volley of shot rang out. The rest, despite bad diet and sickness, had by then all recovered.[3]

The next day the party went on as far as they could in the barge, possibly within two or three miles of the modern railway bridge at Fredericksburg. All seemed quiet, and Smith left a sentinel on guard while he took the bulk of the party upstream to search for rare herbs, signs of mineral wealth, fresh water, and so on. When they had been gone an hour, more or less, an arrow fell unheralded at the sentinel's feet. The alarm was given, but by the time the advance party got back to the boat and seized their arms, a hundred "nimble Indians" came "skipping from tree to tree, letting fly their

arrows as fast as they could." The clumsy European weapons were
none too useful in the woods, and Mosco came close to being the
one who saved the day. Having shot all his arrows, he darted back
to the barge for more, making such a to-do about it that the attackers apparently thought that the Englishmen had a body of
savages with them. Within half an hour they had disappeared as
unexpectedly as they had shown up.

Mosco pursued the fugitives as far as he could without losing
sight of the Englishmen, while the latter returned to the boat. On
the way they found an Indian "as dead," shot in the knee. Mosco
came running up just then, and seeing the wounded enemy, "never
was dog more furious against a bear." He wanted to beat out the
man's brains then and there. But the English, more curious as
well as more compassionate, picked up their prisoner and carried
him onto the barge, where Bagnall, the surgeon, dressed the wound
— just, says the account, as he was dressing Smith's wound from
the stingray. (This is an interesting sidelight on the persistence of
the stingray poison, John Smith's determination, and the slow ef-
fectiveness of early-seventeenth-century medicine.)

While Bagnall was treating the Indian, Smith "contented" Mosco
by permitting him to gather up an armful of enemy arrows. Then,
when the apprehensive prisoner regained the use of his tongue,
Smith interviewed him, using Mosco as an interpreter. While the
account is not entirely clear (which is not surprising, considering
the difficulties), the Indian said in substance that he and his companions were all from Hassinunga (or Hassniuga), that his name
was Amoroleck, that the "Kings" of Stegara, Tanxsnitania, and
Shackaconia had joined the "King" of Hassinunga to come to a
nearby village named Mahaskahod, and that they were all members
of the Manahoac (or Mannahoack) tribe. Mahaskahod, he explained, was a hunting village, the last outpost between the Manahoacs and the Nantaughtacunds.

When Smith asked why they had attacked him, Amoroleck answered that they had heard that the English "were a people come
from under the world, to take their world from them." To Smith's
question as to how many worlds he knew, he answered that he
knew only that which was under the sky that covered him, which
included also the Powhatans, the Monacans, and the Massawomekes,

who were higher up in the mountains. Smith, still interested in the "southern sea," then pointedly inquired what was beyond the mountains. Amoroleck answered, the sun. Anything else? Nothing — the woods were not burnt. (That is, travel was virtually impossible.)

By way of ethnological information, Smith learned from Amoroleck that the Monacans were very backward in agriculture, "living upon roots and fruits, but chiefly by hunting," while the Massawomekes were apparently not only more numerous, but also more advanced "politically" and economically. More pertinent to the matters at hand, Amoroleck said that the Manahoac Kings were gone hunting, "every one a several way with their men." Those Manahoacs who had been with him when they spotted the white men were fishing, as he was, but they would all be together that night at Mahaskahod.

Smith gave his prisoner a handful of gewgaws for his pains, at the same time inviting him to accompany him on his further travels. Amoroleck reciprocated by inviting Smith to stay around until the "Kings" turned up — especially because "he was brother to Hassinunga." Mosco added to his translation of this the suggestion that they make off, but Smith insisted on staying until nightfall, meanwhile preparing for the best and the worst alike. Mosco indicated his own guess as to the way the wind would blow by trimming his arrows diligently.

Since the river was narrow at the point where they had anchored, with high ground on the north bank making them uncomfortably vulnerable, the colonists embarked and moved downstream. An Indian attack followed so swiftly that it seemed that their departure had acted as a preconcerted signal. Arrows showered on the boat, while Smith got his Indians to shout to the Manahoacs for peace and a parley. But such was the hullabaloo that Mosco and Amoroleck could not be heard. Meanwhile, the boat made slow headway into the night.

At daybreak, some twelve miles downstream, Smith found himself in a broad bay, which is now overgrown with cattails and marsh grass, where he was safely out of range. There they anchored again and breakfasted, waiting for sunrise before making any further moves. The hidden enemy's presence was felt rather than seen or heard.

Soon after sunup Smith had the Massawomeke shields untied from the waist board, or gunwale, and ordered all his men to show themselves, armed with shield and sword, along with the wounded Amoroleck. Then a long harangue began between that worthy and his "countrymen," who had apparently made themselves visible on the shore. This talk was reported to Smith as having to do with the good treatment Amoroleck had had at the hands of the white men, with mention of Mosco's urge to kill him, and the intervention of his "friends." He would be freed, he said, if his people would be friendly, and to do Smith and his companions any hurt was impossible — they were protected by magic. (Bagnall's surgical expertise and the guns and steel swords were, of course, evidence of that.)

In the end, Amoroleck's brother ordered his men to lay down their arms; that is to say, to hang them up on trees. Then one Indian came swimming out to the barge, a bow tied to his scalp lock, followed by another with a quiver of arrows. These presents they offered to John Smith. Smith in turn welcomed them aboard, gave them trinkets, and suggested that the other three kings should send similar tokens of friendship, whereupon James, the great King of the English, would be their friend too.

Whether it was Amoroleck's persuasiveness or Smith's manner, the gifts they received or the guns they saw, the first two emissaries soon induced the rest of the Indians to offer friendship. Smith and a party of men went ashore then, and delivered Amoroleck to the four kings. These proffered bows and arrows, and tobacco bags and pipes, and in return Smith distributed "commodities" which contented the Indians. The kings thought that the pistols were some kind of pipes, and wanted some, but Smith apparently explained that they were dangerous pipes, not for innocent Indians. And at last the explorers and Mosco sailed away, leaving "four or five hundred of our merry Manahoacs, singing, dancing, and making merry." [4]

It was only a few miles to the Rappahannock territory, and members of that tribe were not long in coming to see how the barge had fared that had so boldly sailed into the Manahoac domain. Everything points to a childish volatility of temperament among the Indians, along with unbounded curiosity. Innocent of any wrongdoing the day before, the Rappahannocks "rejoiced" at the English "victory" over their ferocious enemies, and now wanted Smith for a friend. (That the Manahoac bows and arrows could have been obtained peaceably or by trade was evidently inconceivable.) Smith, again bargaining from a position of strength, replied that the Rappahannocks had assaulted him twice without provocation, when he had only wished them well, and that he was now going to burn their houses, ravage their fields, and hold them for enemies. With that, he made some show of his military might.

The Rappahannocks were dismayed. What could they do to placate him? Very simple, said Smith, "present him the King's bow and arrows, and not offer [presume] to come armed where he was." But this was not all. He added that they must be friends with the Moraughtacunds, who were his friends, and give him their own King's son as a pledge to carry this out. Then would all King James's men be their friends as well.

But since the Moraughtacunds had started the trouble by stealing the Rappahannocks' women, Smith then brought the Werowances of Nantaughtacund and Pissaseck into the picture; and all the chieftains involved at last met in peace at the spot where the first fight had been. There, Smith played Solomon.

When the Werowance of Rappahannock said that he had but one son, whom he needed, but would give Smith the three women belonging to him whom the Moraughtacunds had stolen, Smith seized the opportunity to get the women back from their abductors. That done, he told the Rappahannock werowance to choose the one he loved the best, after which he divided the other two between the Werowance of Moraughtacund and, as a reward, Mosco. Peace being thus reached, the Indians spread in all directions to kill deer for a feast, and night once more fell.

The next day there was a Lucullan banquet (washed down with nothing but water), with much dancing and singing, and no weapons in sight. Overcome with pride and emotion Mosco celebrated the event by changing his name to *Uttasantasough,* which was an Indian name for the English. Then with promises of supplies on the one side and artifacts on the other, the colonists sailed off in a bedlam of salvos and Indian peace-whoops.

The voyage was now uneventful for many miles. An exploratory sail up the Piankatank River revealed only a few old men, women, and children tending corn — their fighting strength being but forty all told — who promised to trade when the grain was ripe. Nearer home, the barge was driven by a storm into Gosnold's Bay (north of Back River), but reached Old Point Comfort, ten miles or so to the south, the morning after. There the explorers rested and fed well on the provisions available from the Kecoughtans. (Smith never used what he had when he could live off the land.

Jamestown being so near, John Smith felt that he had time for further exploration. He had learned a good deal about the geography and ethnology of distant shores; it was therefore "fit to know all our neighbors near home." Setting sail for the southeast, he crossed the mouth of the James and soon was sounding his way over the shallows toward the creek-and-swamp-entangled forest where the Chesapeake Indians lived. But finding no inhabitants, and few signs of human occupation, the explorers turned back, after going half a dozen miles up some creek, and steered west, "coasting the shore towards *Nandsamund,* which is mostly oyster-banks."

Once arrived at the mouth of the river, still called the Nansemond, they caught sight of a handful of Indians mending their weirs, who fled at their approach. Smith sent (or led) a party ashore to leave "divers toys" where the Indians had been working. As soon as the party returned to the boat, the Indians bit at the bait. Coming back, they began to sing and dance, calling to the white men to join them. A parley ensued, and one of the Indians invited Smith to come to his house up the river, eagerly clambering into the barge to show him the way. Nothing loath, Smith headed upstream, while the other Indians ran along the shore, "with all show of love that could be."

Seven or eight miles they sailed, until they came to some large cornfields on the western shore of the Nansemond, and a little island (which may have been Dumpling Island). There was much show of friendliness, and a brief stop there brought on further invitations to visit houses, or wigwams, until the barge reached an extremely narrow stretch of river. Smith tried to get more Indians to join him aboard, probably as a sort of guaranty of good behavior, but they were most coy about accepting. Finally, after long hesitation, some agreed to go get their bows and arrows and come along. But no sooner had they gone ashore in their canoes and gotten their arms than no amount of persuasion could get them into the barge, or even in their canoes.

Smith then realized that he was being let into a trap, with usual Indian cunning. He did not get far "ere seven or eight canoes full of men armed appeared," following them and apparently waiting to see what would happen. Almost immediately arrows began to fly, as fast as two or three hundred Indians could shoot them. Smith tacked about and sailed into the cluster behind him, firing with like speed. Surprised, the Indians jumped overboard or paddled away, clearing the return route and permitting concentrated fire from the English flanks. At this point the river, though narrow, meandered through flat marsh, meadow, and cornfields, with no cover for the Indians. There, scarcely twenty shots were fired before they all disappeared.

Once the colonists were out of the trap, they seized the Indians' canoes and moored them nearby. Fortunately, the Massawomeke shields had prevented any injury to the English, though Bagnall was shot through his sugar-loaf hat — worn in obedience to style rather than common sense. But Smith knew that he faced a large force, perhaps a joint one of Nansemonds and Chesapeakes. He asked for the opinions of his associates: Should they retaliate right away by setting fire to the whole island, or should they declare a truce until they were provided with all available corn and other edibles? It was sensibly decided to try the latter first, and then consider punitive arson.

With that the explorers laid hand to axe, and went to work on the canoes with a vim. These were dugouts, not birchbarks that are relatively easily built, and in proportion as it cost the explorers more work to destroy them, so too had it cost the Indians infinitely more work to make them, burning and scraping great logs with sharp stones and shells. In a trice the Indians laid down their weapons and ran up to make peace.

Smith's terms were hard, as they always were. The Indians must bring him the werowance's bow and arrows, in token of submission, and a chain of pearls as damages. Then they must solemnly agree to furnish him with four hundred baskets full of corn when he returned in harvest-time. Otherwise, he said, he would break up their canoes and burn their corn, their houses, and all they had. The

Indians agreed to comply, but said they had to have a canoe to fetch what was wanted. Smith disdainfully set one adrift, and told them to swim after it. Meanwhile, he called, he would merely chop up the dugouts that were left.

The Indians implored him to leave them their only means of transportation, which would take them weeks to replace, promising to obey Smith's orders to the letter. Whereupon he halted the work of destruction until he saw the weapons thrown aside, and until the submissive warriors, "tag and rag" (every man Jack), came with baskets of corn. Loading the ship with all it could carry, the party finally sailed away, "departing good friends" — a somewhat ironic way of putting it.

That same evening Smith and his men were back in Jamestown. It was September 7, and they had been gone six and a half weeks. Matthew Scrivener, the acting President, was well again and had seen to the gathering of the colony's little harvest. President Ratcliffe, apparently having attempted to regain or reassert control, had been arrested for mutiny. Some of the colonists were still sick, many were dead, and unfortunately rain had spoiled part of their supplies from England.

All in all, the hot months of 1608 had taken far less of a toll than those of the year before. Still, the balance sheet was not encouraging. John Smith's voyage of discovery was a constructive step, but good government and the building up of the colony were perhaps far more to have been desired.

John Smith possibly undertook the voyage to keep out of the way in the wrangling over Ratcliffe's mismanagement, as well as to find the extent and general lie of the bay. He had previously gotten along with Ratcliffe. But it had become apparent that it was impossible to do so any longer. His power-born madcappery proved too much for the whole colony.

Another reason for the voyage was that Smith was certain of being elected to succeed Ratcliffe as President. Seen in that light, the expedition from which he returned three days before the expiration of Ratcliffe's term was one of double convenience. But beyond these petty and selfish aims, it was of great importance for Smith's conception and knowledge of the Indians, as well as for its geographical significance. Much was to come of this, which Smith could not foresee. Yet within a few months, reports of mismanagement in the colony combined with the news of Smith's discoveries and Indian contacts brought about radical changes in what military men call the "thinking," in London.[5]

## CHAPTER 16

# PRESIDENT SMITH: I. NEWPORT'S RETURN

The 10 of September, 1608, by the election of the Council, and request of the company, Captain Smith received the letters patent, and took upon him the place of President; which till then by no means he would accept, though he was often importuned thereunto.

So the 1612 account of John Smith's presidency opens. Bluntly it adds that the building of Ratcliffe's presidential palace was halted, and the men went to work on more utilitarian projects: the repair of the church, and reroofing the old storehouse and building a new one for the supplies they soon expected from London. The fort was strengthened — perhaps reshaped — and the watch reorganized and more efficiently trained. Besides, the entire colony was drilled on Saturdays.

In short, President John Smith intended to have an orderly, strong, and energetic colony, so far as his presidential powers could inspire or impel his "subjects." Meanwhile, in London, Destiny's Wool Spinners busily twisted new thread into the web of colonial planning.

During the first week in July, John Smith's first sketch-map of Powhatan's realm had arrived, courtesy of Captain Nelson, along with his "letter to a worshipful friend," and other documents, not of Smith's authorship. There is no way of knowing who the friend was (it could have been Robert or Peregrine Bertie), but the letter reached the hands of a printer, William Welby by name, with remarkable speed, and on August 13 was entered for publication, somewhat "edited," by the Company of Stationers. John Tapp, the nautical publisher, brought it out, as has been said, and with it Welby began a career of printing small books for the Virginia company — an association which lasted half a dozen years.

Originally published without the author's name, the little book, briefly called the "True Relation" or "News from Virginia," was first attributed to one Thomas Watson, probably the Watson who was agent to Sir George Carey, the King's Treasurer for Wars in Ireland. If this is the case, it is possible that Watson got the letter through Sir George and passed it on to Tapp and Welby, directly or through someone in the Virginia Company. When Watson's name appeared on a reset title page, however, he apparently denied responsibility. Smith was the author, somebody said. And so a note "To the Courteous Reader" was prefixed to the book, written by one I.H., in which the mistake was explained, and the book was finally credited to "Captain Smith, colonel of the said Colony" of Virginia.

The Spanish Ambassador, who enjoyed a liberal expense account for bribery, quickly got a copy of either the letter or the book, and sent a summary of it to King Philip in much reduced and certainly garbled form. More important, he also got and sent along a copy of Smith's sketch-map. In this way, Philip's insatiable desire to know what the English were up to in *his* America preserved for posterity what is apparently the only surviving copy, or presumed copy, of that sketch.

Newport had already brought word that the Indians told John Smith, during his captivity, of a route to the South Sea through Chesapeake Bay. This could not but arouse enthusiastic interest among the members of the Virginia Company. Newport must return at once, the Council said. And when Nelson arrived a month later with a map showing Chesapeake Bay rounding off northwestward in an exaggerated "Potomac River," and with Captain John Martin and his gold-rush fever in person, it is small wonder that preparations for a second supply reached the impetuous stage.

The leaders of the Company held consultations. Policies, largely based on rumors and misunderstandings, were formulated. Expansive Elizabethan mentalities went to work on the proper psychological approach to the Indian "Emperor," Powhatan. And before Smith's book was off the press, Newport set out for Virginia. Carrying rich presents for the "Emperor" and newly formulated policies for the government of the colony, he little suspected that Smith's explorations were dissipating the dream of the South Sea route through the bay, or that Martin's "gold belt" up the James River was at best a gross misrepresentation, and at worst sheer hallucination.[1]

Newport was well on his way across the Atlantic when John Smith was elected President. His return was possibly expected even then, although no one could know that he had had a quick voyage back to England, or that his turn-around time there would be so short. Still, when George Percy, graced with the new courtesy title of Lieutenant, sailed down the James River to barter for corn toward the end of September, it may have surprised him to encounter Newport in the Mary and Margaret, with seventy new colonists — including two women and eight "Dutchmen and Poles" sent over to start one or another industry. Far more surprised was President Smith when Newport handed him a letter addressed "To the President" (although the Company must have been fairly certain of his identity) containing new instructions. To these, Newport seems to have added a few more, verbally.

In later years Smith published a copy of a letter which he sent "to the Treasurer and Council of Virginia" in answer to the letter brought by Newport. (Newport took it with him on his return.) While it may be doubted that the letter Smith sent was exactly in the form in which he finally published it, there can be little question that the substance was the same. Since the Council's letter is not in existence, Smith's reply is the only clue to its contents.

It appears that the Council in London sent word that Captain Newport's verbal instructions must be obeyed. Also, every effort must be made to freight the returning Mary and Margaret with commodities to the value of two thousand pounds sterling to defray expenses. And furthermore, the President of the Virginia Council was caustically admonished to put an end to "faction and idle conceits."

Smith took personal umbrage from the start, although the letter was addressed impersonally, and when Newport's instructions were laid before him his rage hardly knew bounds. As Smith understood it, Newport had orders not to return to England unless or until at least one of three basic projects was carried out, viz.: find gold, or establish the certainty of a route to the South Sea, or find one or more survivors of Ralegh's long-since abandoned Roanoke Colony. In addition to these virtual infeasibilities, Newport was to crown Powhatan according to English rites (very considerably modified), and tender him gifts of a royal washbasin and pitcher, a royal bed, and "civilized" clothes. And finally, to cap the impractical "thinking," a five-piece barge was sent over dismounted, so that the colonists could carry the pieces around the falls, reassemble them, and merrily sail up to the "Mountains Quirank," with results soon to be seen.

All these matters were somehow or other attended to, in spite of John Smith's ardent disapproval — though he in no way refused to comply with the instructions. He merely protested, after complying. First, however, and without comment or objection, President Smith accepted and swore in as new councilors Captain Richard Waldo and Captain Peter Winne, about whom nothing seems to be known beyond the fact, recorded by Smith, that they were "ancient soldiers and valiant Gentlemen." He also accepted Ratcliffe back into the Council, although that threw a vote directly against him. This, compounded with Scrivener's youthful itch to travel and see the sights, not to mention his sense of obedience with regard to the Company's instructions, meant that Smith's two votes could easily be offset by the three of Newport, Ratcliffe, and Scrivener, with Waldo and Winne probably inclined to obey instructions also.

This accomplished, and while the five-piece barge was being unloaded and plans made for an expedition up the James to look for mines, Newport insisted on the formal coronation of Powhatan, as commanded by the King's Council. Smith, in a last attempt to keep control over that wily despot, suggested "as a time-saver" that he take Waldo, two other gentlemen, and a boy, across country to Werowocómoco and attempt to persuade Powhatan to come to Jamestown to be crowned. (He possibly thought that this might show Powhatan that the English considered themselves "above" his sway.) With him, when the Council agreed to this, he took Powhatan's trusty, Namontack, freshly returned from England with Newport.

When they got to Werowocómoco Powhatan was reported to be

away — thirty miles away — perhaps hunting. Smith asked the Indians to send for him, he would wait. Pocahontas, delighted to see her "protégé" again, offered to entertain the guests after Powhatan fashion, the while. Their curiosity piqued, the five Englishmen followed her to a clearing, where the Indians made a fire and sat their guests down on mats. Moments later, such a "hideous noise and shrieking" came from the woods that Smith and his companions took to their arms and seized two or three old men as hostages (or shields), thinking that Powhatan had come in a surprise attack. Pocahontas quickly ran up, however, crying that no harm was intended, and that they could kill her if it were. This, added to the fact that the other onlookers included women and children as well as men, convinced Smith, and the guests put their pistols away and watched.

Very shortly, thirty young women ran out of the woods, stark naked but for a few green leaves, before and behind. Their bodies were painted a variety of colors and designs. Their heads were adorned with bucks' horns. Otter skins and the like were draped over their arms, and some had quivers full of arrows, while others had bows and arrows, swords, clubs, and even potsticks (for stirring soup) and the like. With "most hellish shouts and cries" these maidens rushed to form a ring around the fire, dancing and singing "with most excellent ill variety," only to fall into "their infernal passions," and then solemnly to sing and dance again. After an hour of this, they retired to the woods to take off their costumes. On their return, they invited the Englishmen to their wigwams and their beds.

After this salutation, as Smith calls it, a banquet was prepared, and the guests ate to the accompaniment of more singing and dancing, until at last they were conducted to their lodgings, with firebrands to light their way — punctuating the primitiveness of life in the forest.[2]

Powhatan arrived the next day. It was the first time John Smith had seen him since March, and as President saluted him, as Despot, with proper dignity. He then turned Namontack over to him, and conveyed Newport's invitation to Jamestown to receive the presents he had brought. In addition, he informed Powhatan of Newport's planned expedition into the Monacan country, urging that he join forces with the English and "conclude their revenge." Powhatan himself had blamed the Indians beyond the falls for the murder of "his brother," Jehu Robinson.

Powhatan considered this presumptuous. He told Smith that if their King sent him presents, he too was a king, and in his own country. They would therefore bring the presents to him, there. As for the Monacans, he was quite prepared to revenge his injuries himself. Finally, it was ridiculous to look for a salt-water sea across the mountains. If any Indian had told him about such a thing, it was a lie, he said — illustrating the true shape of the land by drawing a plan on the ground before him.

After some persistence, Smith gave up the idea of getting Powhatan to go to Jamestown. The five took their leave, and a few hours later reported to Newport. The presents from the Virginia Company were then loaded on a boat, including three shillings' worth of finger rings sent with some bits of copper by the Earl of Northumberland to his brother George Percy for "the Indian Prince." And the boat went around the peninsula, of necessity, a trip of better than eighty miles (Smith says "near a hundred"), while "the Captains" went by land, with "fifty good shot" — musketeers.

Once the colonists and their presents were all together again at Werowocómoco, the solemn ceremony of crowning Powhatan was set for the next day. That evening and part of the night, it may be imagined, was spent in arranging the details, for it is certain that no one present had ever crowned a king before, or probably ever witnessed a coronation.

In the morning, Christopher Newport, Admiral of the Virginia Fleet, donned his full regalia of ship-captain, marched in stately procession to Powhatan's long-house, presented himself, and ordered brought in the basin and pitcher, the bed and other furniture, and at last a scarlet cloak and other apparel. But Powhatan was suspicious, and when they tried to robe him, it cost Namontack some little trouble to convince the "Emperor" that they were not going to hurt him.

Then came the matter of the crown. "Neither knowing the majesty nor meaning of a Crown," the account of the event relates, "nor bending of the knee," Powhatan endured every variety of persuasion, instruction, and illustration without yielding one hair-breadth toward bowing or kneeling. At last, however, somebody leaned so hard on his shoulders that Powhatan stooped just a little. Immediately three of them clapped the copper crown on his head; and a pistol shot informed the world that Powhatan was crowned.

At that signal the boats anchored offshore let loose such a salvo that Powhatan jumped to his feet "in horrible fear." But in a flash he saw that all was well, recovered his composure, and with great courtesy and dignity gave his old shoes (his moccasins) and his deerskin mantle to Newport.

If Newport or the King's Council thought (as they undoubtedly did) that this gesture would make Powhatan an obedient sub-king to the Majesty of James I, they were, as Smith knew, lamentably wrong. No sooner was he invested with scarlet cloak and copper crown than he began to act more autocratically than before. He personally and definitively dismissed Newport's suggestion that the two head a joint expedition against the Monacans. All the coopera-tion he would give was a miserly offer of the services of Namontack as a guide — but no further support. Not only that, but his largesse as newly crowned monarch was meager in the extreme: only some seven or eight bushels of corn.

By purchase, in the village, the coronation excursion obtained as many more bushels, and therewith they returned to Jamestown. Smith referred grimly to these "but fourteen bushels" obtained by Newport, in his letter to the Company in London.[3]

Once he was back in Jamestown, Newport decided to go ahead with his plan to explore the river above the falls regardless of Indian help, other than Namontack. (It is reported that he even accused Smith of hindering his plans, both directly, and by antagonizing the Indians by his "cruelty.") Selecting a hundred and twenty men under himself, with Captain Waldo, Lieutenant Percy, Captain Winne, young Francis West, and Matthew Scrivener as his staff, he left Smith and eighty or ninety less fit colonists to lade the *Mary and Margaret* for the return voyage. The freight, unless there were fortunate finds beyond the falls that could be valued at the two thousand pounds the Company wanted, was to consist largely of as much clapboard and wainscoting as they could hew, split, and saw. Clearly, it is no cause for marvel that Smith, the only councilor with experience in exploring, was incensed over the charge given him by Newport (was not Smith President?), and that relations between the two altered radically for the worse.

The Newport expedition sailed as far as the falls without incident, anchored or beached their boats, and went to work, presumably, to transport the five-piece barge around the impassable stretch of river. What precisely was the trouble with the barge is not known, but in Smith's letter there is a statement that "Newport had 120 of the best men he could choose," with the implication that they could not carry the five pieces. It read: "If he had burned her to ashes, one might have carried her in a bag; but as she is, five hundred cannot, to a navigable place above the falls." The barge was then left, apparently still in five pieces, and the party marched overland into the Monacan domain.

According to the account written by someone on the expedition, which is too brief to give much information, they visited two Indian towns, Massinacack and Mowhemcho, which have been fairly certainly located at points in Powhatan County opposite Goochland and Manakin Town respectively. Since they followed the north shore of the James, as is shown on John Smith's map, the distance covered can easily be estimated by comparison with modern State Route 6. Goochland is thirty-one miles from the center of Richmond, Manakin Town about half that distance. The contemporary account estimates, however, that they marched forty miles — which they covered in two and a half days. The Indians, of uncertain tribal affiliations, but not "Powhatans" and possibly not related to the Manahoacs, treated them "neither well nor ill." Nevertheless, Newport seized one of their chiefs as a precaution, and had him led with them, bound, wherever they went.

Newport's search for gold and silver was all but fruitless. Although the Virginia Company had sent five jewelers, goldsmiths, and refiners over with the first supply (which arrived January 2), and one with the second (William Callicut, a refiner), no employment had been found for any of them before this expedition. (Surely a goldsmith would not have analyzed Martin's "gilded dirt" as gold.) Therefore when they found many places they "supposed mines," Callicut wanted to stop long enough to assay the ore they found in one of them. When he was allowed to spend some time working on this, he came up with the belief that he had extracted a small quantity of silver, and that "better stuff might be had for the digging." With that, Newport was content. He named the mine after Namontack, who found it, and having marched his men up the land he marched them down again.

Back at the falls, the expedition encountered direct evidence of Powhatan's disapproval. No corn was to be had at any price, empty excuses were offered for not supplying it, and nowhere could any trace of it be found. So the exploring party returned to Jamestown footsore, hungry, and disillusioned.

Disgusted perhaps but probably not surprised, Smith immediately dispersed the able-bodied expeditionaries to help those already busy establishing Virginia's first industrial works — as he quaintly put it, "some for glass, others for needed tar, pitch and soap-ashes." And before the Council awoke to what he was doing, he himself had disappeared with thirty able-bodies five miles down the James to camp in the woods and chop trees for clapboard.

Apparently these thirty were socially what were called gentlemen. Two of them, in fact, were singled out for special praise by President Smith — Gabriel Beadle (a neighbor of Edward Maria Wingfield's) and John Russell. (Both were investors in the Virginia Company, to the extent of twelve pounds ten shillings each.) But strange as life in the wilderness was to all thirty, the example set by Smith soon converted them from clumsy lubbers into expert lumbermen. Still, the unaccustomed labor blistered their hands so that every third blow elicited a loud oath. The President, who took the pious Lord Willoughby for his model, discountenanced swearing, and promptly began punishing offenders by counting their oaths during the day, and pouring as many cans of water down their sleeves as he heard oaths. It was not long, says the contemporary account, before "every offender was so washed (himself and all) that a man should scarce hear an oath in a week."

By the time their task was finished, these thirty gentlemen had indeed grown so used to honest labor that it became a pleasure to them to hear the great pines and cypresses and oaks come crashing down. Later John Smith reflectively wrote that thirty or forty such men could voluntarily do more than a hundred forced laborers. But, he added, twenty good workmen "had been better than them all."

Meanwhile, Scrivener, Waldo, and Winne carried out their tasks at the fort, but no one bethought himself of provisions, although the ship *Mary and Margaret* lay idle all the while in the port. Newport apparently did not think that provisioning was part of his duty. (Strictly speaking it possibly was not.) Smith, returning and seeing the vanishing supplies, sized up the situation, seized the discovery barge and one other boat, left orders for Percy to bring a third as soon as it was available, and raced up the Chickahominy to trade for corn.

But the Chickahominies refused to trade. For once they were obedient to Powhatan's wishes, if not actually in league with him. Smith, who could not and would not brook any refusal (particularly regarding food), changed tactics and informed the Chickahominies that he did not come to trade so much as to take revenge for their attack on him the winter before, and for the death of his men, whom they had murdered. Then, suiting action to words, he landed his eighteen men and ordered them to charge. As the Chickahominies fled, Smith advanced, to ravage their land.

The threat was enough, as Smith knew from experience it would be. Emissaries ran up, bearing corn, fish, fowl, and whatever other foodstuffs they had. Complaining loudly that the year had been bad, and that they were in want themselves, the Chickahominies nonetheless loaded the barge and boat with a hundred bushels of corn, and in addition filled Percy's boat, which came up shortly thereafter. Smith in turn evidently repaid them in such commodities as they most appreciated.

For ill-defined reasons, men such as Ratcliffe (and perhaps Newport) resented Smith's success with the Indians. It may be that latent jealousy and a tinge of vague animosity were among them. But the only manifestation of resentment that was allowed to appear on the surface took the form of a complaint that Smith's means of getting provisions were contrary to their *Instructions*. He should not threaten the Indians.

This zany imputation boiled up headlong into a move to depose Smith for leaving his post without the consent of the Council — the only thing he had done which they could put a finger on. Because he had gone to chop wood to load the ship, he should be banished from Jamestown. Whoever instigated this nonsense (Smith blamed it on Newport and Ratcliffe) did not get far, but it shows how captious some of the colonists were.

These internal troubles were overshadowed, however, by external misbehavior. Mariners and colonists alike, rolling in marketable goods brought by Newport, were trading with one another and with the Indians for furs of all sorts; or baskets, or little animals such as *mussaneeks* (chipmunks or squirrels?); or butter, cheese, beef, pork, brandy, and beer; or axes, chisels, and hoes; or even pike heads, shot, and powder — to the detriment of the colony's supplies. The general store did not have a fur in it, for example, yet one ship-master alone admitted later that he had traded for furs in Virginia that sold in London for thirty pounds sterling.

Smith did everything in his power to correct all this, not without success. Even Newport is reported to have admitted errors and failings in discipline when threatened with exposure by Smith. If this report is correct, it offers further evidence of Newport's basic obedience to authority, even when that authority was merely the President of the Council in Jamestown.

One more voyage was made for provisions at the time. Scrivener was sent to Werowocómoco with the pinnace and barges to "buy" as much corn as he could get. But the Indians there were far more ready to fight than to sell, and it required all of Scrivener's vigilance combined with Namontack's artfulness to prevent a war and obtain supplies without one. Thus three or four hogsheads of corn and as many of puccoon root (for dye) were finally loaded before the party returned to Jamestown.

By then Newport, who had long overstayed his welcome (at least, so far as Smith was concerned), ran out of pretexts for delaying longer, and hoisted anchor. At Old Point Comfort he encountered the returning Scrivener, the last colonist to see him that year. Then he put out to sea. The date of his departure is unknown, though it has been guessed that it was in December, 1608. Whenever it was, Newport took with him not only Captain John Ratcliffe in person and President Smith's letter to the King's Council for Virginia, but also the far more important Smith "Map of Chesapeake Bay and the Rivers," with *A Relation of the Countries and Nations* there. This *Relation,* later expanded into a small volume and published in 1612, is even more valuable as a source of ethnological informa-tion than the map is of geographical. The geography is still there. The Indians are not.

With Newport and Ratcliffe gone, President Smith had a breathing spell to consider the situation and take stock of what had to be done to live through the winter. The Council as then composed included Scrivener, Waldo, and Winne, besides the President. If one of the three would vote with him, Smith had a majority. But so set were the three on carrying out orders invented in London that they seldom seem to have seen the situation as it actually was in Virginia. Their obedience to the *Instructions,* when it carried the majority vote, usually constituted rebellion against practicality. Smith's rebellion against London dogma was in obedience to the need for survival. The emergence of a clear-cut conflict here signalized the beginning of the colony's second winter.[4]

CHAPTER 17

PRESIDENT SMITH: II. THE INDIANS

THE JAMESTOWN COLONY numbered about two hundred souls
as John Smith began the fourth month of his presidency. Only
about thirty of these were original settlers. Seventy had come in
the second supply. The balance were from the first supply, which
had arrived in two installments, on January 2 and April 20. Obviously, the mortality rate had dropped — from over 60 per cent
to 20 per cent or less. But to keep it low, food was necessary — a
need to which the King's Council in London seemed to pay little
attention, and which their good servant Christopher Newport appeared to consider none of his business. Far from bringing food
with him from England, he took three hogsheads of provisions away
to England, to feed his mariners on the return voyage.

President Smith considered a pint of corn a day essential for
each man (and woman, now). This amounted to two hundred pints,
or three and one-eighth bushels, per day for the entire colony. The
four hundred baskets of corn demanded of the Nansemonds would
go a long way toward staving off hunger. But the Nansemonds did
not just refuse to deliver; they refused to trade at all. Powhatan's
orders, they said. John Smith then began to realize that Powhatan
had truly made up his mind to starve them out — crown and all
notwithstanding.

There were no two ways about it. The President's duty was to
feed his colony, and if that had to be done by taking supplies by
main force, then force was necessary. Smith consequently prepared
an expedition, waited for Winne and Scrivener to return from
Werowocómoco, and immediately set off for the Nansemond River
in three boats.

The Indians saw them coming, and were ready. Protesting that Powhatan had commanded them strictly not to let the English "come into their river," they tried to keep Smith out. Smith scattered them with musket shot and landed his men. Not a bowstring twanged. Then he coolly set fire to the first wigwam he saw.

The Nansemonds, realizing the implications of this move, sent messengers to plead with Smith not to destroy their shelter. Winter was already setting in. If he needed corn, they would bring half of their own supply. And before night, Smith's boats were loaded with food.

But the determined President had not yet finished with the Nansemonds. He took his companions to spend the night in the open woods, in the snow, four miles downstream. The next day, returning to the village, he made the Indians promise to plant corn "purposely" for the white men in the spring. Only then did he sail away to Jamestown.

Staying there long enough to unload the corn and to attend, and possibly solemnize, the marriage of John Laydon, an original settler, and Anne Burras, John Smith fitted out two barges for Captain Waldo and himself to go trading up the James. Passing by the Chickahominy and the Paspahegh settlements, they stopped among the Weanocs on both sides of the river, but that "churlish nation" fled into the forest. They knew only too well what Smith wanted. Seven miles or so farther on, however, the Appomattocs gave them what little they could, in exchange for copper. Thus almost empty-handed, Smith returned to Jamestown to find that efforts in the same line by Scrivener and Percy had been even less productive.

To Smith's way of thinking, it was clear that Powhatan was the chief source both of their trouble and of their potential relief. Therefore, after discussing the matter with Waldo, who had a level head, Smith resolved to make a surprise raid on the Despot right in the midst of his imperial hoard.

Yet when he communicated this (in all truth, sound) plan to the Council, as was his duty, he found to his disappointment that a great change had come over Matthew Scrivener. He would not agree with Smith's proposal, and neither would Peter Winne.

Smith attributed the change in Scrivener to letters from England instructing him to see that orders of the King's Council were obeyed, President or no President — as Smith put it, "to make himself either Caesar or nothing." From Scrivener's point of view, on the other hand, it may merely have been that he saw *lèse majesté* in such behavior toward the Indian Chief-of-Chiefs, who had just been crowned by order of the Council, and thought that that body might not approve. Whatever the real reason for Scrivener's "decline in his affection" for the President, the result was the same. The President capitulated.

Fortunately for the colony, however, Powhatan chose just then to send a message to Werowance Smith. (He had undoubtedly heard of the colony's panicky search for food.) If Werowance Smith, he made known, would send men to him to build him a house (European style), give him a grindstone, and send him fifty swords, some muskets, a pair of those strange birds called chickens, and a quantity of copper and glass beads, then his newly crowned Majesty would load the Werowance's ship with corn.

Smith, whom (as he put it) no persuasions could persuade to starve, yet well aware of Powhatan's "subtlety," jumped at the chance, and promptly dispatched three Dutchmen and two Englishmen ahead to Werowocómoco. Then, with Waldo and forty-six volunteers backing him, he equipped the pinnace and a barge or two to collect the corn. And he appointed Scrivener as his deputy, to govern during his absence. Scrivener's earlier failure to obtain provisions had not weakened Smith's trust, even though it had indirectly brought some criticism of the project. It is useless, some murmured dispiritedly. (Between petty carping and the do-nothing laziness that came of scanty diet and chronic depression, three fourths of the colony would rather sit and warm their hands and starve than search for food.)[1]

Despite all, the expedition set sail, with Lieutenant Percy and his cousin-in-law West in the pinnace, under the naval command of William Fettiplace (they needed a mariner to run the ship), along with seven other gentlemen, Bagnall the surgeon, and twelve soldiers. Smith himself took the barge, with six gentlemen and six soldiers. Richard Savage went with the Dutchmen to build Powhatan's house. That the detailed figures do not add up to forty-six must be blamed on the carelessness, forgetfulness, and printers' errors which always stand in the way of accurate statistics on the early Jamestown Colony.

Wanting to save the fort's meager supplies, Smith loaded only

enough food for three or four days on the pinnace and barge, and
stopped at Warraskoyack on the way downstream for more. The
old werowance there, Tackonekintaco, who seems to have been
generally friendly to the English, urged Smith not to go to Werowocómoco. Powhatan, he said, had sent for Smith only to cut his
throat. Therefore he would be kind and affable until he had a
chance to seize their arms. Then — well, do not trust him, he
insisted.

The advice, unnecessary as it was, was received with proper
gratitude. Then, because he did not completely trust Tackonekintaco either, Smith asked for guides to take Michael Sicklemore
(apparently no relation of John Sicklemore, alias Ratcliffe) to
Chawanoac. He wanted to send a present to the werowance there,
he said, and bind him to him as a friend. (The real purpose was
naturally to look for Roanoke survivors.) Tackonekintaco quickly
supplied two guides, while Smith added a suggestion to Sicklemore
that he look for silk grass there at the same time. Silk grass was
a valuable commodity (as already mentioned) about which much
had been talked and written since Ralegh's men first reported on
it in 1585. (Winter would seem an odd season to look for it.)

Smith then left his page, Samuel Collier, at Warraskoyack to
learn the language, the first youth deliberately trained in such a
manner. And with that the little fleet sailed on, only to run into
adverse weather that forced them to drop anchor at Kecoughtan.
Wind, rain, and snow compelled a stay over the Christmas holidays,
until Twelfth Night, or Epiphany. But it was a fortunate bit of
adversity, for the men were "never more merry, nor fed on more
plenty of good oysters, fish, flesh, wild-fowl, and good bread."
Even the dry, if smoky, Indian houses had fires almost as good as
those in England. Nevertheless, thanks to Smith's training, the
company was ready to lie under the trees by a fire whenever shelter
was not to be found — regardless of the weather. Parenthetically,
Smith noted down that he, Bagnall, and Sergeant Pising killed one
hundred and forty-eight fowl "at three shots."

The ships had hardly gotten away from Kecoughtan when they
had to put in again at Kiskiack, on account of frost and contrary
winds. This time, Smith quartered only the men from the barge
among the Indians. (The pinnace was of course weatherproof.)

The Indians resented the intrusion, but Smith was not one to put up with what he called insolence. For three or four days they fed and sheltered his men whether they wanted to or not. Meanwhile a wary eye was kept on the barge lest it disappear into some convenient creek.

It was January 12 before the expedition arrived at Werowocó-moco, to find the river frozen nearly half a mile from shore. Smith characteristically pushed on, breaking the ice as he went, until the ebb tide left the barge stranded. Sooner than sit there, freezing, he clambered out and waded through the deep icy mud to the pinnace, making his dozen companions follow. (John Russell, who was both ill and overweight, so strained his energies on this tramp that they had a hard time bringing him around again.) Then, when the tide freed the barge, Smith had it hauled aboard the pinnace.

Being reduced to melted snow for drinking water, Smith took a few men with him to the nearest wigwam, where he rested while word was sent to Powhatan that his guests had arrived. Powhatan promptly sent bread, turkeys, and venison, and the next day received them in audience. After the protocolary offering of food, however, he inquired with great insistence when they would be gone. He said he had not sent for them, and that if he himself had little corn, his people had less. Yet, he added, he would give them forty baskets for forty swords. John Smith looked around him, and spotted among those present the messengers who had come to Jamestown, and, repeating in their presence the invitation and Powhatan's conditions, asked him how he could be so forgetful.

Powhatan, caught lying, laughed the matter off by agreeing to trade, though he added that he wanted weapons, not bits of metal — he could eat his corn, not the copper. Smith, seeing what he was up to, told Powhatan that he had sacrificed his men to comply with his wishes, and that out of love he sent Dutchmen to build him a house, men whom he could better use at home. Then, indicating that he was gravely disappointed, he added that he still would not steal, or use force, or break their friendship, except — and here was a veiled threat — in the event Powhatan forced this by his bad treatment.

Powhatan retorted that he did not trust Smith's stated purposes, and believed that he came not to trade but to invade. Nevertheless, if Smith would leave his weapons on the pinnace, then they would all be friends, all Powhatan tribesmen. Since Smith, however, was understandably not ready to comply with this, the rest of the day was spent arguing — until such an hour, indeed, that quarters were provided for the Englishmen for the night.

At this point begins one of the most obscure affairs in the early history of the colony. As is known, eight "Dutchmen and Poles" had arrived with the second supply. According to the accounts, four of these were "Dutchmen" and one was Swiss — though the Swiss may have been a "Dutchman," and one of the four. As for the Poles, the only other reference to them mentions "two *of* the Poles," which implies at least three. However it was, the puzzling part of the story is what the Dutchmen really did, and what their real motives may have been, if the accounts are to be trusted.[2]

It all began with John Smith finding the Swiss to be of such great "spirit, judgment and resolution" that he "knew not whom better to trust." When the plans were made to get corn from Powhatan, Smith therefore sent this individual, name not mentioned, as a spy "to discover Powhatan's intent." The spy, however, joined forces with objects of his spying, and while all three, four, or five of "the Dutchmen" (the accounts vary, as usual) went to work building Powhatan's house they apparently also discussed the perils facing the colony.

Here was the situation as the Dutchmen seem to have sized it up. Powhatan had plenty of food. Powhatan also had men (several hundred of them), and apparently a strong determination to rid himself of unwanted English squatters. The Dutchmen applied logic and arrived at the conclusion that the Englishmen could not escape famine without Powhatan's help, while with Powhatan around they could not escape destruction. They began dropping hints (this is factual) that would show Powhatan that they were with *him,* not with President Smith. Kindred minds need no interpreters, so language proved no bar. Powhatan divined the meaning of the hints, and slowed down work on the building. In that way he could keep the Dutchmen with him while he set about deleting Jamestown from the map.

Possessed thus of John Smith's spy as a spy of his own, Powhatan was ready, on the second day of his meeting with Smith, to unleash his cold war in earnest. Using a long haggle over the corn-value of a copper kettle as a pretext, Powhatan soared into the philosophy of war and peace, and how much better it was to co-exist in trade than to fight — especially since he had already lived through three murderous wars, and now hoped with all his heart for peace with Smith, for himself and for his heirs: his brothers Opitchapam, Opechancanough, and Kekataugh, and his sisters and their descendants. Therefore, he rambled on, Smith should lay down his arms (which frightened the people), for indeed if it came to war, he would have to flee into the woods. And then — then, the English would starve for lack of corn.

Smith countered by limiting himself to agreeing that mutual trust and promises were desirable qualities, but pointed out that carrying arms was the custom of his country. He would be happy to see the Indians follow the same custom, for he had no objection to the Indians bringing their bows and arrows to Jamestown. And as for Powhatan's thinking to hide himself and his provisions, Smith had a "rule to find" beyond Powhatan's knowledge. Once again he was playing on fears born of ignorance and superstition.

The trading, and the argument, continued, and Powhatan soon returned to the attack. He treated Smith better, he said, than any werowance in all his realm, yet Smith refused to recognize or carry out his wishes. Even Newport, Smith's "father," laid down his arms when so requested.

Smith quickly caught the implication that he was subject to Powhatan. That point he intended for all time to make clear. Yet for a moment he evaded it. He sent Indians to break the ice that held the barge, and with them one of his own men to call his troops ashore. Then he turned to Powhatan.

One God he recognized, he said, and one King. To Powhatan he was not a subject but a friend. No one could buy that friend-ship. If Powhatan would visit him as he visited Powhatan that would become clear. He could come guarded by his entire people, and Smith would not take it amiss. But meantime, to show how he trusted Powhatan, the next day he would come unarmed. Al-though he had to admit to Powhatan that his men saw how little care Powhatan showed for Smith, and told him to look to his safety, still he would show him that he really loved him as a father.

But even while Smith was talking and his men were coming up from the boat, Powhatan got word that his Indians were ready, and on some trivial excuse slipped away from Werowocómoco with all his luggage, his women, and his children, leaving only two or three talking to the unsuspecting Smith. Outside, warriors silently began to circle the house.

Smith's soldiers quickly saw this move, and sent John Russell with word of the treachery. Smith jumped to his feet, and "with pistol, sword and target" he and Russell cut a passage through the "naked devils," firing at any who tried to stop them.

When the Indians saw that Smith had reached his bodyguard, they changed tactics, pretending that it was all a misunderstanding. Smith, however, lined up his eighteen men in threatening array, determined not to lose the corn which all along had been the real object of the trip. At this, Powhatan (obviously not yet very far off) sent Smith a "great bracelet and a chain of pearl, by an ancient Orator" who delivered a harangue.

Powhatan had fled, he intoned, because he feared the guns, and the men who surrounded his house were merely protecting the corn. Smith had misunderstood, and because of that some men were hurt. But no matter. The ice was broken in the river, and Powhatan's men would help Smith load his corn and send it away. But please put by the guns; the Indians dared not come to help.

This was the epilogue to John Smith's last interview with the Despot. Never again did they meet. Yet the trial of strength, the battle of wits, went on. From his hideaway Powhatan proved an even greater threat to English safety than before.[3]

Not realizing that Powhatan had truly fled for good, Smith supervised the loading of the corn. The Indians, many of them "goodly well-proportioned fellows, as grim as devils," saw the soldiers with their guns ready for action, and worked quickly. Nevertheless the tide had ebbed again before the boat was freighted, and Smith was forced to make the best of it another night in the same long-house.

Powhatan got word of this, and once more tried to rid himself of Smith. But Pocahontas, ever loyal to Smith and the English, slipped through the night to tell him of the plot. When she stole away, refusing any sort of reward (for Powhatan would kill her if he knew), Smith did not see her again until many years later, when they met in London.

The night passed on the *qui vive,* but without incident. In the morning, Smith left Edward Brinton, a soldier stationed on the pinnace, to kill wildfowl for Powhatan as a peace gesture, and put the Dutchmen back to work on the new house. Smith expected Powhatan to return to Werowocómoco, and decided to employ the time until he did so by sailing up the Pamunkey to get what additional corn he could. When he got back to the seat he would land, if the frost permitted. A further talk with Powhatan might prove profitable after he had had time to think things over.

Scarcely in fact had the pinnace passed the marshes of Purtan Bay and Island when the Despot re-entered his "capital." Calling two sturdy Dutchmen to him (Adam and Franz by name), he dispatched them to Jamestown on a treacherous mission. They were to tell Captain Winne, commandant of the fort, that the expedition was progressing well, but that Captain Smith had commandeered their arms, and would Captain Winne issue replacements? Furthermore, would he also issue additional tools and apparel, which they needed?

Since the story was plausible, Winne complied. But while the additional supplies were being assembled for the Indians with Adam and Franz to carry away, these began to smell out half a dozen colonists who were discontented and might want to go along to Werowocómoco, too. At least, they would not starve there, and if Powhatan carried out his threat to destroy the colony, their lives would be safe. In token of their sincerity in this treachery, the malcontents stole a few swords, pike heads, and muskets, and some shot and gunpowder, turned it all over to the Dutchmen, and promised to follow in person with more.

Meanwhile, Powhatan, who did not trust Adam and Franz, kept a third one, named Samuel, as a hostage for their good behavior. Samuel had already obtained his diploma as a thief by providing the Indians with three hundred tomahawks, fifty swords, eight muskets, and eight pikes. The two Englishmen, however, Edward Brinton and Richard Savage, could not but observe that Adam, Franz, and Samuel were arming the Indians, and attempted to dash to Jamestown to warn the colony — that being a shorter race than trying to reach Smith, up the river. They were almost inevitably caught, but rather surprisingly Powhatan did not put them to death. (Was he still mortally afraid of Captain Smith?)

In ignorance of all this, and much delayed by bad weather, Smith, Percy, West and company reached Opechancanough's headquarters two or three days after leaving Werowocómoco. There they feasted for another two or three days, as was proper, and at last John Smith was able to get down to trading. But by then word of developments at Werowocómoco, twenty-five miles away, could have been brought by Aesop's tortoise. The result was that Opechancanough's men came laden more with bows and arrows than with food for barter.

Smith did not wait to be hopelessly outnumbered. He opened negotiations with a fiery speech, telling Opechancanough that he had not forgotten his promise to supply him with corn, that Opechancanough was going back on his word, and that such behavior ill befitted a werowance. Besides, he knew that Opechancanough's people had plenty of provisions, and he intended to have part of them. However, to show his good intentions, he began by offering the werowance certain commodities for his acceptance, without strings; after that, President Smith would exchange goods for corn in proper proportion — according to Smith's lights, of course.

Opechancanough appeared contented with this, and the exchange began on Smith's terms. Then, when the immediately available supplies were exhausted, the werowance pleasantly suggested that Smith wait another day, when more would be brought. Nothing loath, Smith stayed over. The next morning he put Master Fettiplace in charge of both the pinnace and the barge, and marched up to Opechancanough's long-house with a guard of fifteen tried soldiers to go on trading. Four or five well-loaded Indians were waiting, and Opechancanough himself soon came up, making speeches about how hard he had tried to accommodate the Englishman.

In the midst of this verbose monologue, John Russell came running up, despite his weight. They were betrayed, he shouted to Smith. Six or seven hundred well-armed savages (undoubtedly an exaggeration) had surrounded the house and were scattered through the fields. The news frightened the Englishmen, who were immediately for shooting their way out. But Smith, observing that Opechancanough had apparently guessed the import of Russell's message and was himself nervous over the outcome, stopped them.

Rash action, he said, would scare the Indians away; they might have some dead bodies, then, but they would not have any victuals for Jamestown. He proposed that he talk their way out, and at the same time get hold of the provisions they needed.

There was no time to argue, so all promised to obey any orders Smith might give. Smith then turned to Opechancanough. He now saw, he said, how Opechancanough wanted to murder him, but happily no one had yet been harmed on either side. He therefore proposed that he and Opechancanough go to a nearby island, and fight it out between them there. He for his part would agree to equal arms, and the victor would take all. (In just such a combat, of course, Smith had won the Three Turks' Heads for his shield.)

Opechancanough, unfamiliar with single combat of that sort, pretended that no ill was meant. In fact, he had a great present for Smith, which he would give him at the door. Smith, noting that forty or fifty of Opechancanough's chief warriors were with him, decided that this was a ruse to get him at a disadvantage. He ordered a soldier to see what the present was. The soldier refused, he was too frightened.

All the rest volunteered to go, but Smith was infuriated over such cowardly behavior. He would go himself, he said. Percy, West, and ten others he commanded to cover the house and its occupants, and Powell and Beheathland to guard the entrance. Then, still fuming with rage, he snatched Werowance Opechancanough by his scalp lock, right in the midst of his Indian bodyguard, put a pistol between his ribs, and pushed him, trembling, out before the entire assembled throng.

Petrified with fear and astonishment, Opechancanough, brother of the great Powhatan himself, ordered his vambrace (forearm guard), bow and arrows given to Smith, in token of submission. At this, all the Indians laid down their arms — none of them dreaming that anyone would dare thus assault so great a chieftain.

Smith then relinquished his grip on Opechancanough. Peremptorily summoning the leaders of the tribe before him, Smith began the most irate speech he was possibly ever called on to give. He was amazed, he thundered, that they dared presume to threaten him. He was amazed that they had failed to give him the corn they had promised — though he had not hurt a single one of them in any way. Now, by the God of his faith, if one lone arrow was shot, or one drop of English blood spilled, his revenge would not cease so long as a sole Pamunkey Indian lived who was still so rash as to say he was of that tribe. He spurned them with his foot, one and all.

> Here I stand [he fulminated], shoot he that dare. You promised to freight my ship ere I departed, and so you shall; or I mean to load her with dead carcasses. Yet if as friends you will come and trade, I once more promise not to trouble you, except you give me the first occasion. And your King shall be free and be my friend, for I am not come to hurt him or any of you.

Allowing for Elizabethan eloquence added in the later setting down of this speech, and Smith's limitations in the Powhatan language, this is undoubtedly the gist of what he said. Down went any weapons that might still have been held, and men, women, and children hurried to obey the terrifying Captain. (This did not prevent another attempt on his life from being made while he was resting several hours later.) The loading began, and the Pamunkeys flocked with basket after basket of all sorts of provisions, as well as special gifts to mollify President Smith.[4]

As the day wore on and the tension slowly subsided, Opechancanough pulled himself together to entertain his guests. The atmosphere was strained, although outwardly peaceful. Then, as night fell, an unexpected courier slipped in from Jamestown. Richard Wiffin, a loyal veteran of the first supply, had come with urgent messages for the President.

Smith drew him aside, only to hear how willful disobedience had hurt the colony. Young Scrivener, for reasons still unknown, had taken Captain Waldo, Anthony Gosnold (Bartholomew's brother), and eight others with him on a boat ride across the James to Hog Island, a little more than a week after Smith left, leaving Winne in command. A wind blew up, and the boat sank. How or why, no one could tell. Indians came to the fort the next day to tell of finding an overturned skiff and English bodies, which were later identified.

At first, nobody dared undertake the journey to inform the President of the accident, for fear of the Indians. After some discussion, Wiffin volunteered to go alone. But the journey had taken him nearly two weeks, through snowbound woods, and only Pocahontas had made it possible for him to get there at all. She had hidden him at Werowocómoco, and had sent her father's men in the wrong direction.

Smith swore him to silence for the moment, in view of where they were. Then as soon as he properly could, he excused himself and his party and went aboard ship. Opechancanough he left in liberty behind, as he had promised, although (as he probably knew) good faith of this sort was wasted consideration. Powhatan had decided that Smith and "his" colony must be destroyed. Opechancanough, for personal reasons, was more than ready to help.

The next morning, the fields along the winding lazy river were covered by sunup with people and baskets of produce, despite the January cold. They beckoned the colonists ashore, but refused to trade unless John Smith was present. They refused to trade, also, if anyone brought a gun.

Nothing Smith said could make them change their stand, and Smith did not want to trade unprotected. But when they began to leave, sooner than lose the opportunity to barter, he devised a stratagem whereby he sent unarmed men ashore, while he himself disembarked with only Percy, West, and Russell for companions. Choosing a site then where he could be seen, but retreat if need be, he hid the other three with their arms, and showed himself.

This move drew the crowd quite openly around the colonists. The tribal werowance sent word for Smith to come and join him, but when Smith refused, himself went to Smith. It was hardly a cordial gesture. With him, the chief had two or three hundred men (again, exaggerated, no doubt), armed, and spread out in a clawlike pincers movement, but concealed. As a decoy, twenty men and many more women brought painted baskets on, preceding the chief. Once these had come up to Smith, the women fled, leaving Smith (as they thought) alone, while the Indian force rose out of the sedge.

In a flash, Smith ducked down the bank, and Percy, West, and Russell jumped up in his place, armed to the teeth. The startled

Indians, always a little afraid of Smith, took to their heels. Smith, again in a fury, hurled a verbal Parthian shot as he reached the pinnace: a promise to demolish everything they had, houses, boats, fishweirs and all, if further treachery prevented trade.

That night Smith told his companions of the tragic mischance at Jamestown, and ordered Raleigh Crashaw and Robert Ford, both reliable gentlemen, to take the barge there with supplies and messages that all was well.

The Indians, spotting the departure of the boat, assumed right off that Smith had sent for reinforcements — at least, that is Smith's interpretation of their actions. Greater fear than before seized them, with double-headed results. While one group spent days in the wintry wilds gathering up all the reserves of food they could spare without starving themselves, others went to work with still more determination to destroy the English parasite. Opechancanough, or his fellow Werowance of Potauncack, the next village, thought to buy off President Smith with another chain of pearls, while sending runners to Chesapeake Bay and the eastern shore to barter with the Nanticokes or Tockwoughs for the deadly poison that only they knew how to brew.

As the month of February came, then, both the food gatherers and pearl bearers, and the poison runners, arrived where Smith and his white-man braves were ever trading. Ceremonially feasted, as often before, an unexpected violent nausea attacked Smith, West, and several others while they were loading the almost unhoped-for extra supplies. Their European stomachs fortunately rebelled before the Indian poison could set to work.

So involved had the situation become by then that suspicions and accusations materialized out of nothing to confront the colonists. Collective guilt sense took hold of the Indians (if that was possible), while collective fear and hatred possessed the English. One young Indian accused of bringing the poison thought to beard the English lion on his passage through Potauncack, and faced him (John Smith, in person) with some forty armed redskins. But Smith, disgusted more than frightened, only "spurned him like a dog" — a dog too worthless to do him harm. The forty companions took to the woods. And once more the pathetic villagers came, bearing food and other gifts to buy off the white Werowance's ire.

The young culprit, they said, was Wecuttanow, their chief's son. It is worth noting that, however exaggerated these accounts may be, there is evidence of little bloodshed — only violent words, threats that smack of the melodramatic, and what seems like empty posturing. Yet that manner of action undoubtedly made up President John Smith's peculiar gift, or better his instinctive understanding of the Indians. They, too, did business, fought wars, and built their modest culture with little fighting, little bloodshed, even little courage — but a vast amount of hit-and-run, bluff, and wile. Smith once wrote, apparently without bravado, that Powhatan, seeing that his will was not admitted as law, *sighed* as he said, "Captain Smith, you insist on having whatsoever you demand." That sigh tells volumes, not only about Smith, but about why Jamestown, under Smith, was the first English colony to survive in America.

To conclude the story of the first part of John Smith's administration of the colony with suitable dispatch, it only remains to note that the expeditionary force probed the nearby Youghtanund and Mattaponi valleys for provisions, without great profit. Not even Smith, with starving Englishmen before his eyes, could rob the necessitous tribes of what little they had. So he sailed back to Werowocómoco, satisfied that he had gotten all that the ordinary folk could spare. Once more he planned, God willing, to surprise Powhatan, for surely the Despot had by then returned to his great long-house. But so that Powhatan's provisions should not slip through his fingers he sent Richard Wiffin and Thomas Coe ahead, to spy.

The incomprehensible Dutchmen voided all this. With persistent self-seeking, they maligned the English, worked on Powhatan to abandon Werowocómoco (as in fact he did), and so stirred up the remaining villagers that Wiffin and Coe were in danger of their lives when they arrived. In this way, Smith found his plans frustrated, but he took no revenge on the hapless Indians. He laid the guilt where it belonged, sent Michael Fettiplace overland to Jamestown to announce his imminent return, and sailed with all the speed he could around the peninsula and up the James.

The balance sheet on the expedition's return, at the end of John Smith's first five months as President, showed that they had "spent" twenty-five pounds of copper and fifty pounds of iron and glass beads. In return, the forty-six men had been fed during the voyage, and each of them received a month's provision extra. For the colony, President Smith brought home a pound of deer suet for each colonist, and over two bushels of corn apiece. It was not much, but winter at last was almost gone.[5]

## CHAPTER 18

# PRESIDENT SMITH: III. THE ENGLISH

EVEN BEFORE he left for Werowocómoco, President Smith had set about putting the Dutchmen and Poles to work, in accordance with their contract. While the details of this are not known, it seems that the Dutchmen were hired primarily for construction work, with the Poles for pitch and tar. Between them, a glasshouse was to be built about a mile from Jamestown, to establish a glass industry. Enough construction had been finished on this for Newport to be able to take trials, or samples, of Virginia-made glass with him when he sailed. Enough had been finished in another sense for the glasshouse to be a winter rendezvous of Poles and Dutchmen alike.

By the time President Smith got back to Jamestown, the Dutchmen who were still "building a house for Powhatan" began to wonder what had happened to the handful of malcontents who had promised to join them. There was no sign of them, and the trickle of arms and tools from the fort had ceased. They sent Franz to investigate.

Smith heard of Franz's arrival and dispatched a soldier to pick him up. Franz, however, had already vanished. Smith then sent twenty men to fan out in the woods and cut him off, accompanying them himself past the blockhouse as far as the glasshouse, some three furlongs beyond. Starting back alone, he came across Wowinchopunk, "a most strong, stout savage." Though Wowinchopunk radiated friendliness, he was not able to draw Smith into any potential trap. Moments later, having made sure he had the President really alone, he suddenly whirled into position and nocked an arrow to his bowstring. In no time, Smith went at him with his falchion (a short sword built along the lines of a sickle). Wowinchopunk grappled. In the tussle, both of them fell into the river, where the savage's nakedness was a distinct advantage. Before long, however, "perceiving two of the Poles upon the sands," the werowance changed tactics, and tried to shake Smith off and escape. Smith, anything but vanquished, only held on the tighter, tangling his fingers through the Indian's scalp lock and around his throat. The Poles, wading in, quickly had the werowance pleading for his life. Smith ordered him off to the Jamestown jail.

About that same time the posse had rounded up Franz. Haled before Smith, he pleaded that he did not know enough English to understand or be understood. The truth of the matter, he said, was that his compatriots had been forced to stay with Powhatan against their will, and as for himself, he was merely out walking, gathering nuts, when he was arrested. He really had no intention of going back to Powhatan. Yet, the account dryly comments, "for all this fair tale, there was so small appearance of truth, [that] he went by the heels," which was to say that his heels went into irons.

With both the Indian and the Dutchman in the stocks, Smith thought he would manage to entice the other Dutchmen away from Powhatan. He got Franz and Wowinchopunk to send messages to them to come back. But Adam and Samuel knew where they were best off. No message could argue them into returning, nor could Wowinchopunk's pleas move Powhatan to send them back. Nor, the account adds, were Smith's envoys able to bring them fifty miles on their backs.

By that time, Wowinchopunk had managed to slip past his nap-prone warders and escape into the forest, shackled as he was. Captain Winne tried to catch him, but was stopped by bands of Paspaheghans. Smith, who had been away, heard of the escape and scooped up a brace of Indians who were known to him to be "the most exact [consummate] villains in the country, Kemps and Tassore." These two, who would have betrayed anybody for a piece of copper, he turned over to Winne to help him catch Wowinchopunk. Winne embarked with them, and fifty picked men, and would possibly have captured their prisoner had he taken the advice of both Smith and the Indians. Instead of setting off immediately, although it was night, he dillydallied until sunup, and by that time the Paspaheghans were shouting at him to come and fight.

The outcome was merely that shots were exchanged, the Indians fled, and Winne burned Wowinchopunk's house and took two canoes. Smith, certain that this ineffective raid would only encourage the Paspaheghans, stormed off after them himself. In short order he had killed or wounded half a dozen, taken another half-dozen prisoners, burned a village, and sent such of their fishing boats (with weirs and all) as were handy down to Jamestown for the colony's use.

As he followed in his boat, Indians unwisely taunted him from the shore, with the inevitable result that Smith lost his temper again, and directed his boat at them. No sooner was his figure recognized than the Paspaheghans threw down their arms, and a sturdy young warrior named Okanindge stepped out. Wowinchopunk was there with the warriors, he said, and had attacked because he thought it was Captain Winne, whom he had never offended, and whose wanton destruction was therefore unjustified. But since it was Captain Smith, said Okanindge, the werowance begged him to remember that fishes swim and birds fly, and that the lowliest animal tries to escape a trap. So he fled when he could. If Smith took this amiss, he should remember that Wowinchopunk helped save Smith's life long months ago, when he was taken prisoner. He asked that bygones be bygones, and that they live in peace. Otherwise, he and his people would leave the country, and Smith would have no one to harvest corn for him.

Smith's policy always was to seek trade, although he stood for no threats or signs of resistance. The wholesale massacres of later years formed no part of it. He punished only specific wrongs. He therefore agreed to renew peace with Wowinchopunk, since no injury was done him or the colony. But trade was to be the guaranty of peace.

Leaving an apparently gratified Wowinchopunk to rebuild his village, Smith returned to the problems of the fort. Michael Sicklemore had long since gotten back from Chawanoac with the report that he found "little hope and less certainty" of any survivors of Sir Walter Ralegh's colony, but said nothing about silk grass. Nevertheless, to make one last attempt to follow instructions, Smith sent

Nathaniel Powell with that ubiquitous soldier Anas Todkill to Quiyoughcohannock for guides to help them find the Mangoaks, and possible traces of the Roanoke colonists there. Nothing was learned but that "they were all dead," in spite of the apparently sincere efforts of the friendly werowance (Pipsco?) to be helpful.

All too soon another Indian crisis materialized. The Chickahominies, generally well behaved, were suspected of thievish habits — more than could be tolerated. At last a pistol was stolen. The culprit escaped, but two confederates, brothers, were apprehended. One of these the President sent to get the pistol, while he put the other in jail. If the pistol was not returned within twelve hours, the brother would be hanged. In the meantime, however, he was given a charcoal fire to warm his nakedness.

The other brother returned before midnight with the pistol, only to find that the one in prison had somehow managed not only to burn himself severely, but to seal the jail room so tightly against the cold that he was overcome by carbon gas. To all appearances he was dead. The living brother then set up such a wailing that Smith promised to bring the "dead" one back to life, if they would quit stealing — although Smith was not certain how far gone the "dead" one was. Brandy being considered a panacea for all ills, Smith administered large doses of it along with vinegar. No one knows which of the two brought the Indian around, but the brandy exacted its tribute. Reared in total innocence of alcohol, he revived "so drunk and affrighted, that he seemed lunatic."

This upset the healthy brother as much as seeing him dead — as he thought — but President Smith, now confident of success, promised to restore his mind, upon further vows of good behavior. Thereupon the drunken Indian was put to rest where he could be comfortable. By morning he had slept off the effects of the brandy and was again well, though still badly burned. Smith had the burns dressed and sent the pair away. Obviously it was not long before the Indians for miles around had heard that Werowance Smith, renowned for bravery, could also work miracles and raise the dead. But the real miracle was that from then on, so long as the memory of the event was fresh, stolen goods were returned, even from as far away as Orapaks, and those who were caught stealing were brought to President Smith for judgment, even when the stolen goods did not belong to the English.[1]

It was a bitter sequel to this period of tension with the Indians that Captain Peter Winne, whose honest but artless make-up had indirectly fostered a small part of it, did not live to see peace concluded. Both he and a gentleman named Henry Ley (or Leigh) went to their graves about then, with none so kind as to record why, where, or just when. Winne especially, a friend of Gates and trusted by Smith, seems to deserve better at the hands of the chroniclers.

The colony's internal affairs meanwhile continued in bedlamite disharmony because of the psychotic aversion of the great majority to work. John Smith called it "untowardness" — disinclination to productive action. Ralph Hamor, a later colonist, was more specific. He wrote in 1614 that the English "would rather starve in idleness . . . than feast in labor." Therefore, although President Smith somehow got them to work, he evidently did not cure the endemic sloth.

As soon as external relations permitted, Smith called a general assembly and left little unsaid. Neither he, he fulminated, nor the adventurers of the Virginia Company would continue to maintain the colonists "in idleness and sloth." Some few deserved honor and reward greater than they could be accorded, but the balance of them, by far the majority, "must be more industrious, or starve." Due to misfortunes and accidents, he was now left the sole surviving member of the Council. No longer could anyone appeal his commands to other councilors. Therefore, he bluntly went on, quoting from St. Paul, "he that will not work, shall not eat," except for the sick. Because "the labors of thirty or forty honest and industrious men shall not be consumed to maintain a hundred fifty idle varlets."

Finally, to anticipate and prevent any "sit-down strikes" in defiance of his authority, he concluded:

> Though you presume the authority here is but a shadow, and that I dare not touch the lives of any, but my own must answer for it, the letters patent each week shall be read to you. Their contents will tell you the contrary.

In brief, there was no longer any Council to plead for or excuse loafers, and the President intended that his orders should be obeyed.

Whoever offended (by disobedience), "let him assuredly expect his due punishment."

For the first time, the colony had a strong governor. Some complied willingly, others had to be forced. But between the encouragement offered by the posting of merits and demerits on a public bulletin board, and the refusal to accept any excuses, the colony got down to work. Within three months, three or four lasts of pitch, and tar, and soap-ashes were made — roughly six or eight tons. The glasshouse produced some samples. A sweet-water well was dug inside the fort. The church was once more reroofed. Nets and weirs were made for fishing. A blockhouse (already mentioned) was erected on the eighty-foot-wide strip of land that then connected Jamestown peninsula with the mainland, probably with a curtain-palisade extending to Powhatan Creek on one side and the James River on the other. And a garrison was kept there night and day to control trade with the Indians, and to permit no one to pass, English or Indian, without proper orders from the President.

In addition to these measures for safety and comfort, Smith began to provide for the future. Thirty or forty acres of ground were dug up and planted. The three sows brought over in 1608 had increased to sixty-odd pigs, so they were all transported across the river to Hog Island, where another blockhouse was built to keep an eye on them and to watch out for approaching ships. Finally, toward their future food supply, despite food shortages the chickens had been allowed to multiply to nearly five hundred.

In anticipation of Newport's return with further supplies and colonists, trees were cut down, and clapboard and wainscoting stacked up for shipment back to England. At the same time, work was started on a "New Fort" across the river. The purpose of this was to have a safe retreat in case of an attack from the sea (presumably by Spain), but it was never finished. A grim discovery put an end to all such work.

One day someone who was looking for something in the storehouse found that the corn that had been casked for future use had gone bad, and that what was not rotten had mostly been devoured by the "thousands" of rats sprung from those brought over on the ships. (Rats are not native to America.)

The immediate concern over what to do to keep what little corn

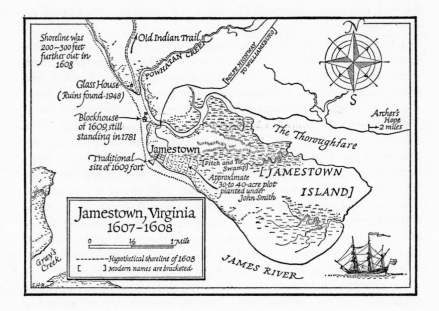

Shoreline was
200–300 feet
further out in
1608

Old Indian Trail

POWHATAN CREEK

ROLFE HIGHWAY TO WILLIAMSBURG

N

S

Glass House
(Ruins found · 1948)

Blockhouse
of 1609, still
standing in 1781

Archer's
Hope
2 miles

The Thoroughfare

Traditional
site of 1609 fort

Jamestown

[Pitch and Tar
Swamp]

[JAMESTOWN

ISLAND]

Approximate
30-to 40-acre plot
planted under
John Smith

Gray's
Creek

JAMES RIVER

Jamestown, Virginia
1607–1608

0            ½            1 Mile

-------- Hypothetical shoreline of 1608
[      ] Modern names are bracketed

S.H.B.

he had troubled Smith far less than the problem of what to do until the first corn crop. Certainly, no more was to be had from the Indians.

Smith declared the equivalent of martial law or national emergency forthwith. About one third of the colony he sent down the river under Ensign Laxon — a carpenter who had come over with Pising among the original planters and had also "made good." Twenty were put under Lieutenant Percy, to settle on Old Point Comfort, and live by fishing. (Such was the laziness and dissension there that in six weeks they could not agree once to cast their nets!) Similarly, twenty were turned over to Francis West to go upstream to the falls to find what they could. But pickings at the falls were slim — only berries and acorns. And as for the rest, many were billeted among the Indians, to learn to gather and use Nature's fruits as the Indians did. Kemps and Tassore, who had stayed around the fort working, were of course told to fend for themselves.

Anomalously (or was it?), Kemps and Tassore repaid any consideration they might ever have had from the English a thousandfold. For more than two weeks they brought in daily at least a hundred wild animals, mostly squirrels, but some turkeys and deer. Then, the thirty or forty energetic colonists caught sturgeon in plentiful quantity, which they prepared in a number of ways, and dug up tuckahoe roots for bread, so that they were not actually starving. They were living out the season like, and as improvidently as, the improvident Indians. Only the unvarying dead-weight body of a hundred and fifty avoided work with a tenacity that bordered on, or was already, a depressive mania.

These "distracted lubberly gluttons," as Smith furiously named them, were ready to bargain kettles, tools, iron, swords, muskets, and even their houses for those forest and river products that the Indians gathered for themselves. Smith was hardly exaggerating when he wrote that if he had allowed it, they would have eaten one another sooner than gather and prepare what was theirs for the picking or catching.

In spite of this, the President refused to budge on the matter of who would not work would not eat. So a handful of the most determined nonworkers set off to find Kemps. He, they reasoned, would feed them in return for the gifts they brought. But Kemps, who had his own sense of what was right, showed his fellow Indians how the English rule worked, and told the runaways that where *he* was, they would have to work or starve. In fact, he even prevented their going back to the fort until he could take them personally — to get a just reward for himself and an equally just one for the drones.

Inevitably, the situation grew worse as Smith refused to permit these colonists to throw away everything they had for little in exchange. At last an incident over the price of half a basket of corn which Smith agreed to buy at Orapaks, fifty miles away, culminated in cries to abandon the colony, to mutiny, to do anything but work for food. Through this, Smith uncovered the identity of the chief instigator, one William Dyer, a gentleman who had previously shown dislike for Smith. And another dressing down followed.

Smith decried as malicious lies any rumors that he wanted to starve the colonists. No one had enough food, not even Powhatan, but such as could be got, he would distribute fairly, even among his slanderers. As for running away, if anyone tried to sail the pinnace to Newfoundland, his destination would be the gallows instead. The colony would work, the colony would feed the sick; and any man who failed to gather as much food daily as he, the President, would forthwith be sent down the river, banished, to starve or mend his ways. What the savages ate was edible. If they wanted better food, they should have brought it with them from England.[2]

Despite the grumbling at this "cruel" order, no one had to be sent down the river to starve. In fact, during this trying time only seven or eight died, except for those drowned. Even the Indians suffered, not only because of corn perforce bartered away to Smith and others, but because of unusual weather. Pipsco, the Werowance of Quiyoughcohannock, for instance, sent presents to Smith, begging him to pray to *his* God for rain, for Pipsco's gods were angry all this time.

At this juncture President Smith decided to send William Henry Volda (the Swiss) to Orapaks to bring the "other Dutchmen" back, with a promise of pardon; he would need them for work as soon as food was plentiful again. He trusted Volda, as he appears to have trusted everybody until they showed reason why he should not. But Volda, as suggested before, was secretly in league with

Adam, Franz, and Samuel, and harbored treacherous designs. He developed the idea, or all four of them did, that while the colony was dispersed on account of the food shortage it would be easy for them, with Powhatan's help, to destroy Smith's faction, and bring such colonists as survived their plot to Powhatan to serve him and teach him the benefits of steel swords, guns, and other civilized contrivances.

A number of the most discontented sluggards of course shared this idea with Volda and company. Smith suspected nothing. And soon Volda, by pretending not to like the Dutchmen or the sluggards, gained Smith's confidence to the point that he was able to take with him on the proposed journey the very weapons and tools he needed to carry out the long-planned treachery.

But where there are traitors there are countertraitors. Two laborers from the second supply, Thomas Dowse and Thomas Mallard, who had at first joined Volda, got cold feet. They took Smith aside and whispered the story in his ear. Smith, never nonplused, asked the two to go on as if they were with the plotters, and bring the Dutchmen along with a body of Indians to a place where he could surround them with an ambuscade. To form the ambuscade, however, Smith had to bring others into the picture, and some of these insisted that Smith punish nobody but the Dutchmen who originated the plot. And to show that they really meant what they said, they volunteered to go and cut the Dutchmen's throats right in the face of Powhatan himself.

The upshot of it all was that the Dutchmen were condemned to death for treason, and Richard Wiffin and Jeffrey Abbot were sent to execute them. When these informed the Dutchmen of their fate, however, the latter pleaded so eloquently that Abbot refused to carry out his orders, even though Wiffin was ready and willing. Powhatan got word of the plot by then and, fearing that Smith might involve him in it, sent messengers posthaste to tell him that he had nothing to do with it, that he had no intention of preventing the execution or of protecting the Dutchmen or helping them escape, or indeed of doing anything whatsoever that was contrary to Smith's wishes.

At this moment one of those frequent Jamestown unforeseeables halted the execution of the Dutchmen and temporarily dulled the

ZSIGMOND BÁTHORY, PRINCE OF TRANSYLVANIA

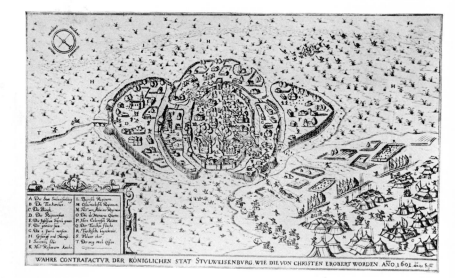

WAHRE CONTRAFACTVR DER KÖNIGLICHEN STAT STVLWEISENBVRG WIE DIE VON CHRISTEN EROBERT WORDEN AÑO 1601

The Liberation of Alba Regalis (Stuhlweissenburg),
September 20, 1601

The Duke of Mercoeur's camp is at bottom right. The horsemen, bottom center, shooting Turkish fugitives, were under the command of Kollnitz (Smith's "Culnits"). Russworm and his men are shown wading through the swamp, upper right.

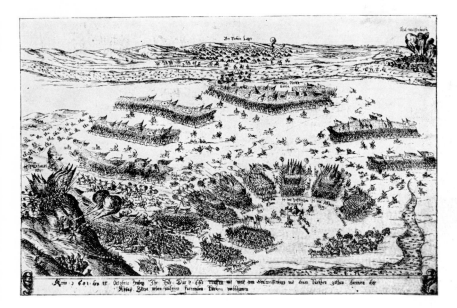

THE BATTLE OF TSCHARKA PASS, OCTOBER 15, 1601—
JOHN SMITH'S "PLAINES OF GIRKE"

Six Imperial regiments, in the foreground, fan out against "those halfe
circuler Regiments of *Turkes*." Smith fought under "Culnits," whose compact group, to the right and marked *H[err] Kollonicz*, attacks a Turkish
regiment (extreme right center). The Turkish camp is in the center background, and Alba Regalis at the upper right, in flames.

WAHRE CONTRAFACTVR DER BELEGERVNG DER VOESTVNG CA

IN NIDER VNGERN. ANNO CHR. 1601.

THE SIEGE OF NAGYKANIZSA LATE IN 1601

This view shows the pentagonal fortress in the middle of swamps. The
Mur River, top left, is actually 15 miles to the west, with Smith's
"Olumpagh" another 15 miles beyond. The outer town is in flames.

Within the engraving:

ANN. 1604. IACOBVS D.G.ANGLIAE, FRANCIAE, SCOTIAE ET HIBERNIAE REX. AET. 38.

*Ut tribus eximijs ornatus dotibus est Rex;*
*Ut pote Fortunæ, Corporis, atque Animi:*
*Singula quæ tantis exis tunt prædita donis,*
*Non sine mente Deûm, sic tria Regna tenet.*
*Uiuite felices tanto sub Rege Britanni,*
*Ipsius et laudes sæcula quæque canant.*

Crispin de Pass
excudit Coloniæ.

Quad Iudeb.

KING JAMES I OF ENGLAND, FRANCE,
SCOTLAND, AND IRELAND

SIR FRANCIS BACON, LORD KEEPER
OF THE PRIVY SEAL

SIR THOMAS SMYTHE, AGED ABOUT FIFTY-EIGHT

The title shows the vast interests of Sir Thomas
at the time John Smith virtually abandoned all hope
of returning to Jamestown.

The portraiture of the illustrious PRINCESSE
FRANCES DVCHESS of RICHMOND and LENOX
daughter of THOMAS L.ᵈ HOWARD of BINDON
second sonne of THOMAS DVKE of NORFO.ᵏ
whose mother was ELISABETH daughter
of EDWARD DVK—E of BVCKINGHAM

FRANCES HOWARD, DUCHESS OF RICHMOND
AND LENNOX, AGED FORTY-FIVE

CAPTAIN SAMUEL ARGALL HARANGUES THE CHICKAHOMINIES,
TO PERSUADE THEM TO ACCEPT JAMES I AS THEIR KING

Argall is backed by 40 men; Sir Thomas Dale is aboard the ship in the background with 10 more men. This visit took place in the spring of 1614. Note that the Indians here and in the drawings which follow are very European in appearance. The artist De Bry never came to these shores, but even the artists who visited America were bound by the influence of preconceived notions and by artistic routine. Nevertheless, these drawings convey some of the atmosphere of the times and are quite accurate in regard to ships and European costume.

POWHATAN RECEIVES RALPH HAMOR

Accompanied by Thomas Savage, Hamor came asking for Powhatan's
favorite daughter to marry Sir Thomas Dale "for surer pledge of peace."
Powhatan refused. The story is in Hamor's *A True Discourse of the
Present Estate of Virginia* (1615).

IAPAZAWS, AN "OLD FRIEND OF CAPTAIN SMITH'S," AND
HIS WIFE PERSUADE POCAHONTAS TO VISIT CAPTAIN ARGALL'S
SHIP, EARLY APRIL, 1613

Thus they betrayed her into the hands of the English. The burning of the village in the background did not take place until March, 1614.

POCAHONTAS IN HER TWENTY-FIRST YEAR

CAPTAIN JOHN SMITH ESCAPES FROM HIS FRENCH CAPTORS
IN OCTOBER, 1615

In the foreground, the caravel and other ships are breaking up in the
storm. In the background, Smith meets "certain fowlers," who help him
get to La Rochelle.

Effigies eximij viri Dñi Didaci Salmicütü de Acuña Comitis de Gondomare. Equitis nobii ordinis Calatrava

*Potentißimi & Catholici PHILIPPI IIII Hispaniarum, Indiarum, Neapolis, Siciliæ &c. Regis; Ad Serenißimum JACOBUM Magnæ Britanniæ Regem &c LEGATI.*

A°.1622.    insculptum a Simone Paßeo eidemq, Comiti DD.

DON DIEGO SARMIENTO DE ACUÑA,
CONDE DE GONDOMAR

Called Machiavellian by the English, Gondomar was
undoubtedly the most able diplomat in the service of Spain
during the latter half of King James's reign.

THE PERILS FACED BY THE DOUGHTY CAPTAIN

This illustration was added to the Dutch version of John Smith's *Description of New England,* published nearly a century after the event (1707).

sting of Volda's treachery. During the week beginning July 9, a ship flying English colors came sailing up the James, bearing food — English luxuries, ship's biscuits, and even wine. Samuel Argall, a young mariner, was her captain. His mission was to explore shorter routes across the Atlantic (and to fish profitably for sturgeon). Argall sailed with the blessing of the Virginia Company, as will appear later. He may or may not have been actually employed by a merchant — accounts are not in agreement.

Whatever the details of the voyage, Argall brought a letter from the King's Council to President Smith (probably from Sir Thomas Smythe and based on something Newport or Ratcliffe had said) in which Smith was reprimanded for "his hard dealing with the savages, and not returning the ships freighted [loaded with profitable goods]." Smith apparently took this in his stride, for the communication was of comparatively little consequence as a whole. (The annoyance caused by the letter may well have been lightened by word-of-mouth information that the Council still placed implicit trust in him, as will shortly be seen.) What *was* of vital concern for the colony was the news that another supply fleet, the third, was being organized in England. Whatever particulars Argall could or did bring were not recorded — the news of imminent relief overshadowed all else.

Unknown to the colonists in Virginia, the combined effect of various and often conflicting reports brought from Jamestown to London by Newport, Wingfield, Archer, Martin, Nelson, and Ratcliffe, as well as in letters from Percy, Brewster, Smith, Perkins, and others, had been a realization of basic error in planning, in conception. Meetings were held, a partial report of one of which, for example, survives to inform posterity that it was held at the house of the Earl of Exeter, the half brother of Salisbury, and that Richard Hakluyt and Thomas Hariot were among those summoned for consultation. The outcome was a decision that the "inconveniences" which had arisen in Jamestown were due to two primary causes: the form of government, and the needlessly long supply-line (through the Spanish-held West Indies). Trivial though the latter detail may appear, the former led to the drawing up of a new charter.

To the end of securing royal approval, Sir Thomas Smythe

headed the group which approached King James's ministers of state. What was imperative, they said, was to set up a large colony all at once, instead of sending driblets of men and supplies that almost evaporated as they landed. To do this, far greater financial backing was needed, which could only be obtained by subscriptions to a joint-stock fund. (This oversimplified statement conveys the main point.) Interim approval was obtained while His Majesty's thoughts were consulted.

Such popular enthusiasm was there, however, for this aggrandized threat to Spain's "monolithic" position in America that the Spanish Ambassador reported, in extreme distress, that fourteen earls and barons had already subscribed forty thousand ducats before the end of February, 1609. Three months later there were over six hundred and fifty individual subscribers, in addition to fifty-six city companies — not to mention some six hundred who volunteered to go to Virginia in person.

Obscure though some of the reasons may have been for King James's consent to a new kind of organization for the Virginia Company, Spain must be recognized as one. The King was unquestionably weary of being importuned by Ambassador Zúñiga about the colony. Consequently when a charter appears, and is approved, by virtue of which the government of the colony is relinquished by the Crown to a private body, no one need be surprised. James had reasons to be very happy to have nothing further to do with Virginia and its bothersome planters.

Within a little more than two months after Newport was back in England, the principles according to which the Virginia Company would be run in the future were clear enough for Captain Argall to be sent ahead as a harbinger of good things to come, and he took final leave of England from Portsmouth on May 5, 1609. Meanwhile between five and six hundred new colonists were effectively enrolled for transportation to Jamestown. Seven ships and two pinnaces were readied, and with surprising celerity on May 15, a week and a day before King James set his hand and seal to the Second Charter authorizing all this, the bulk of the fleet left Woolwich. The Charter signed, the expedition "fell from England" on June 8.

The following Tuesday, June 13, the harbinger arrived in Virginia. Argall could not know, of course, that the big expedition was already under sail, but he could assure President Smith that it probably was. By the same token, he could not specify what the new Charter provided, since it had not been signed when he left Portsmouth. But he could help the colony out with "good provision." Such were the colony's "necessities," says the account, "as enforced us to take it." Thus in a few days the company was all recovered, "grown hearty, able and ready to undertake every action," but for their "bestial sloth."

Argall had tried a new route on the way over, as he had been instructed, and was satisfied that the voyage could be made in seven weeks from England. This accomplished, and the colony relieved, he could dedicate himself to his other chief objective, sturgeon-fishing.

Four uneventful weeks passed. It was by then just about harvest-time for the first corn crop, and time to begin thinking of trading voyages among the Indians, when suddenly, on August 11, scouts brought word of sighting ships at the mouth of the James.[3]

Smith, not expecting the third supply so soon, first thought of Spaniards, whose possible interference in the colony had been vaguely feared for many a moon. He therefore issued prompt orders to stand to the defense of the fort, and put messengers on the alert to run to the neighboring Indian tribes for aid if need be. Such Indians as were working there with the English of course volunteered to help to the best of their ability.

It was not long, however, before it was known that the four ships advancing on Jamestown were English, and all too soon President Smith descried a familiar and most unwelcome figure on the deck of one of them: Captain Gabriel Archer. Of him, Smith had written to the Company in London that if he and Ratcliffe "return again, they are sufficient to keep us always in factions." Less unwelcome was Captain John Martin, and Smith was possibly glad to see Master Francis Nelson, in command (under Martin) of the *Falcon*. The other captains, or masters — Webb, Wood, and Pett — were apparently as unknown to John Smith then as they have remained virtually unknown to history.

With undoubtedly pompous solemnity, President John Smith was informed (by Archer?) that there was a new government for the

colony, and that he was no longer in command. Smith demanded
to see the documents stating this. There were none. How, then?
was probably Smith's retort.

Quickly the story was told him, "neutrals" apparently keeping
relative calm between Smith and the obnoxious Archer and the distasteful Martin. This is possibly the story as John Smith heard it:

Lord Chief Justice Popham's North Virginia colony had been
abandoned after surviving one winter in New England (then called
North Virginia). Its backers merged with the South Virginia group,
on which Jamestown depended, late in February, 1609. Lord De
La Warr, Francis West's oldest brother, was then named Lord
Governor and Captain General for South Virginia. At first, he was
to have sailed for the colony, but it was decided to send Sir Thomas
Gates instead. Sir Thomas would act as deputy until De La Warr
arrived.

Gates, the first patentee mentioned in the Charter of April 10,
1606, was to have for his deputy, in turn, Sir George Somers, second
patentee mentioned, who was made Admiral of the Fleet for the
voyage. Newport was demoted to Vice-Admiral, since Somers was
a knight, although he may have been considered chief navigator.
With this trio went the soon-to-be-nominated Secretary of the
Colony, William Strachey, who had served in that capacity under
King James's Ambassador to the Sublime Porte in Istanbul.

Gates, Somers, and Newport promptly, and characteristically of
the age, got into a quarrel over precedence, with the result that
all three of them embarked on the same ship. This vitiated the
Company's safety plans, since between them they had the only
three copies of the document which established the authority of
the new Governor. (The copies were intended to be distributed
among three ships, just in case of mishap; but when the Company's
first mishap occurred they were all on one ship!)

Between experimenting with a new route and Newport's habit of
sailing the time-honored southern route, Gates found himself by
mid-July almost directly under the torrid rays of a tropical sun. At
least thirty-two of the colonists died of "the calenture" (sunstroke)
on one ship. Then, just as the company was beginning to look
forward to ending their long crowded discomfort, a hurricane struck

them near the Bahamas, driving the admiral, or flagship, far to the north, and to temporary oblivion.

A little over two weeks later, the four ships which brought the news limped into Chesapeake Bay. The fate of Gates's ship, of the "rear-admiral" with Ratcliffe aboard, and of a ship with a relative of Somers (not to mention a little ketch), was unknown.

President Smith still refused to yield the presidency without written orders. A few days passed, in a deadlock, presumably to the delight of all nonworkers. Then to Smith's further displeasure, Captain Ratcliffe brought his ship in, with a Captain King as master; and by about August 20 Captain Moone and Master Matthew Somers made it, in a badly leaking, demasted ship. Now only the most important ship, and the least, were missing. Ratcliffe delayed no longer in joining his voice to that of Martin and Archer for moving Smith out of his post.

The President, refusing to give way, bolstered up his authority by an appeal to the mariners. (Percy later insinuated that he bribed them.) Right, in that he had the word of untrusted or unknown men against him — right, in that he knew what would happen to the colony if it was left to Ratcliffe, Archer, and Martin — Smith was adamant. And there appear to have been many to support him.

Ratcliffe and Martin and some others, backed if not prompted by Archer, then "chose" Francis West to be Governor, with a proviso: "not to disturb the old President during his time, but as [when] his authority expired." It was a move typical of Archer's legalistic mind.

This government outside the government then "ratified" the new Charter, or patent, and apparently went about its business practically as if Smith's term had already expired. Fortunately, enough of the ship-captains and other colonists sided with Smith to keep order for the time being. After all, Smith was President by virtue of the 1606 Charter, which had been executed by the King himself.

The state of confusion by that time must have been remarkable, even for Jamestown, what with the arrival of some three hundred new colonists, the uncertainty of authority after September 10, the immediate need for housing (for there were many women and children in the new supply), and the season for harvesting and "buying" corn already arrived. Under such circumstances it was peculiarly unfortunate that the new minister of the Gospel, the first since the death of Robert Hunt, drove a further wedge between the already antagonistic factions. He was a strict Puritan, and therefore hardly any more welcome among the Anglicans than he would have been among so many Catholics. Small wonder it is that Smith said he was ready to leave the moment Governor Gates arrived, or that Percy applied for (and received) his passport, effective immediately. (The *Instructions* permitted no man to leave without a passport.)

But the days passed with no signs of life or message from the flagship of the fleet. The colony had to be organized for the winter. And Smith was still President. Realizing that the survival of the colony during the recently experienced "starving time" was due to his inspiration (borrowed from the Indians) to break it up into self-sustaining groups, Smith sent one body under Captain John Martin to the mouth of the Nansemond River, which had been the site of a very short-lived occupation before. This daughter colony was made up of sixty men, and Percy was originally sent along with Martin to help establish it. The second group he then put under Francis West, to go up to the falls again, this time to establish a permanent settlement — at least, permanent for the coming winter.

At Nansemond there were troubles with the Indians from the start. Percy and Martin were less patient with them than Smith, or their patience was more severely tried, as the case may be, but the result was that an island had to be occupied by force, and woeful destruction visited on the Indians. That made trade impossible, so that the colony soon had to be abandoned (though not before Smith himself had left Virginia). The colony at the falls, initiated right after Percy and Martin took off for Nansemond, was larger and apparently better planned from the start. One hundred and twenty accompanied West (one hundred and forty according to George Percy), with a six-month food supply.

This left nearly three hundred at Jamestown, to grumble and get in the way of making urgent preparations for the coming months. Smith had gotten so disgusted on one occasion that he appointed John Martin President in his stead — before the Nansemond expedition — but Martin refused the responsibility. Now, as his term neared its end, he decided to make sure that all was in order at the falls. Taking a young newcomer by the name of Henry Spelman along, he started up the James. Along the way he met Francis West on his way down.[4]

Although he was undoubtedly surprised at West's sudden return, Smith said nothing, and went on. At the falls he found the settlement in his opinion too near the river, and in danger of flooding. He suggested moving it up on the hill, where Powhatan village stood. As President, and a man of action besides, he did not wait for an opinion from the settlers. He paid a call on Tanx-Powhatan, the Despot's son. Dusting off the old story of the Monacan threat, Smith persuaded (or forced) young Powhatan to sell him the village for protection against the Monacans, plus a quantity of copper. There were minor additional considerations also, involving "tribute" of puccoon to King James, provisions for barter, and an agreement about handling thieves. Finally, Henry Spelman was to be left with young Powhatan, possibly to learn the language, possibly as a pledge of good faith on Smith's part, possibly both. (Spelman thought he had been sold to Powhatan as the price of the village, but he could not understand a word of the language.)

When everything was in order, the settlers objected to Smith's interference, and took up arms against him. An affray followed in which it appears that Smith had the worst of it — the settlers were not going to yield to anybody. (Perhaps they thought that at the falls they would have control of the route to the gold country.) Smith says that their treatment of the Indians from Powhatan village was outrageous, which hints that Smith called on some of Powhatan's men to help him. However it was, Smith left for Jamestown. For the first time, there are signs that he is giving up the battle against headstrong, selfish "lubbers."

No sooner had Smith left, however, than the Indians attacked the infant settlement, killed many of the colonists, freed some Indians apparently held prisoners there, and retired up their hill, little harmed and bearing the swords and cloaks of such white men as they had slain.

But it so happened that Smith's boat had run aground only a mile or two below the settlement, and the noise attracted the President's attention. He returned. At the falls he learned that a band of only twelve Indians had had their will of ten times as many colonists. Furious over such weakness and cowardice, Smith browbeat the colonists into submission with his tongue, clapped half a dozen of the ringleaders in irons, and reasserted his authority. Whether they would or not, he settled them on the hilltop and named the place Nonsuch (probably for Queen Elizabeth's favorite palace, in Surrey). The account does not say what he did to the Indians.

Smith was ready to leave when West returned. Either West did not like the hilltop, resented Smith's intrusion, thought he was already President, or gave in to the will of his colonists. Whatever it was, he moved the settlement back down again, and named it West's Fort. Once more John Smith gave up.

Returning to his boat, Smith set sail for Jamestown, seventy-five miles downstream. Weary of wrangling and bickering with the English (the Indians tired him much less), he stretched out to rest while his mariners stood guard. Somehow a spark from the matches for their muskets or from a tobacco pipe lighted on Smith's powder bag, which burst into flame right on his lap. Dazed with pain, Smith jumped overboard. With difficulty the mariners got him back into the boat, where they discovered a frightful burn, with the flesh seared between his body and his thighs, nine or ten inches square. No Anthony Bagnall or Walter Russell was there with a soothing oil. The sailors madly plied their oars in what might be a race with death.[5]

## CHAPTER 19

# PRESIDENT SMITH: IV. FINALE

JOHN SMITH's days as President were over. He was incapacitated morally as well as physically, and his term of office was about to expire as a matter of course. If the new Governor had arrived, it was quite possible that Smith would have gone to work eventually with a will (he was named to an important post in the Governor's instructions), to help the colony survive another winter. But as it was, not only was he a wounded man, incapable of leading the colonists in search of food, but he was powerless. He had heard that young West had been chosen as his successor. Martin was a more logical choice. But neither of them had the determination or the knowledge to rule the colony, and who but Smith had ever won out against the Indians? Certainly neither Martin nor West, nor Percy — the latter killing them and driving them away just when their corn was needed. Unhappy colony!

The days of the authority of the Council were over as well. Under the Second Charter, no copy of which was yet in Jamestown, there was still a royal Council in England (of fifty-two members), which was to guide the "Company of Adventurers and Planters in Virginia," but the real executive power was vested in the Treasurer, Sir Thomas Smythe, whose representative in Virginia was the Governor. With neither the Governor, nor a copy of the Charter there, certainly there were almost as many ideas as to what ought to be done as there were colonists — gentlemen-colonists.

As a result, John Smith for the first time did not know which way to turn. And added to his uncertainty as to what was best for the colony was the nagging pain of his wound. He could not even rise from his bed.

There a report reached his ears that Ratcliffe, Archer, and some confederates planned to put him out of his misery, and that William Dyer (or was it Thomas Coe?) would have shot him had he not had a change of heart, or suddenly become afraid. Instead, the would-be assassin joined Ratcliffe in a move to take over the government before September 10 — so it was said. Smith's friends urged him to resist, and volunteered to "take off their heads, who would resist his command," probably meaning this literally. But Smith would have none of it. Rather, he sent for the masters of the ships that were ready to sail back to England, and arranged for his own passage. John Smith had capitulated.

This was the signal for the rebels to act. Before the President could appoint a new Council or a successor, as lay completely within his still-existent authority, Ratcliffe, Archer, and Martin moved to suppress Smith's commission, and within the space of one hour, while Smith was being carried aboard, the day before the ships were to sail, the three had it out between them as to who was to rule. Being unable to agree on West in the end, they finally compromised on George Percy (also on the verge of leaving), and persuaded him to stay and be their President. Smith, from his bunk on the ship, only commented that he could never have consented to deliver the government to those who now had it, but that "he was not unwilling that they should steal it." With that, he appointed a guard for himself, and lay back, awaiting the departure of the fleet. The date was roughly that of the end of his term as President, September 10, 1609.

But the unholy triumvirate had not finished with John Smith. They summoned all those who had any grudge whatsoever against him — all those he "had either whipped, punished, or in any way disgraced" — and prepared an indictment. The idea was conceivably Archer's, for to him a mere letter of complaint would not have been legal enough. In any case, whoever drew it up, these were some of the charges:

1. The mutineers at the falls complained that Smith caused the savages to assault them, and would not avenge their losses. (Witness: A colonist who had been whipped for perjury and theft.)

2. The Dutchmen swore that he had sent ratpoison to poison them. (The facts: Smith had ordered their execution for treason.)

3. The "Council" stated that he would not submit himself to their authority. (The facts: The Council had been dissolved with the presidency.)

4. Coe and Dyer swore that they had heard a colonist say that he had heard Powhatan say that he heard someone else say that if he, Powhatan, would not send all the corn he had, Smith would take away his crown and robes; also that Powhatan was ready to exchange corn for certain specified tools, but Smith would not agree. (The facts: Powhatan had no corn to spare, and Smith did not have the tools demanded. As for the other charge, it could hardly have been upheld in any court.)

5. Others complained that Smith would not let them lie in the fort, but forced them to go to the oyster banks to live or starve. (The facts: True; it was the only way the colony could survive. Even the Indians dispersed in the "starving season.")

6. One colonist "calculated" that Smith had the savages in such subjection that he was going to make himself King, by marrying Pocahontas, Powhatan's daughter. (The facts: Marriage with Pocahontas would not have brought with it any claim on the chieftainship [witness John Rolfe who married her], nor did the friendship between Smith and Pocahontas amount to anything more than that. Smith was almost thirty; Pocahontas, "at most not past 13 or 14 years of age." But that was beside the point. Smith could have done what he wanted, and he did not marry her. He did not regard her ever as anything but a child. "Tell Pocahontas," he wrote in his Algonkian phrase-book, "to bring me two little baskets, and I will give her some white beads for a chain.")

There were other complaints, although Smith says that only eight or nine witnesses "could say much," and there were also a few who got travel passes from the new government by promising to testify against Smith in London. All in all, it was a characteristically selfish, venomous attack. Even Ratcliffe seemed to know this, for he preferred innuendo to direct charge when he wrote to the Earl of Salisbury that Smith was "sent home to answer some misdemeanors, whereof I persuade me he can scarcely clear himself from great imputation of blame."

By then it was October 4, and the last of Gates's fleet (except for the flagship) arrived in Jamestown. The little pinnace *Virginia,* built by Popham's colonists in Maine, had brought sixteen more settlers the day before. With the fate of Gates, Somers, Newport, and their contingent apparently sealed by this last arrival, George Percy took up the reins till then so firmly held by President John Smith. Five hundred refractory settlers now depended on *him* for leadership, provision, and defense.

It was undoubtedly a puzzled and bitter, as well as physically wounded, man who left the shaky colony. Fate had dealt him a hard blow by sending back such unreliable leaders as Ratcliffe, Martin, and Archer. That much he realized. But there had been a harder blow, of which he was ignorant. Fate had sent Governor Gates with the Company's orders to be wrecked on the Bermuda Islands without permitting those orders to be known to Smith. John Smith was not to learn until he was once again in London of the high esteem in which the Company held him.

# PART III

# Promoter

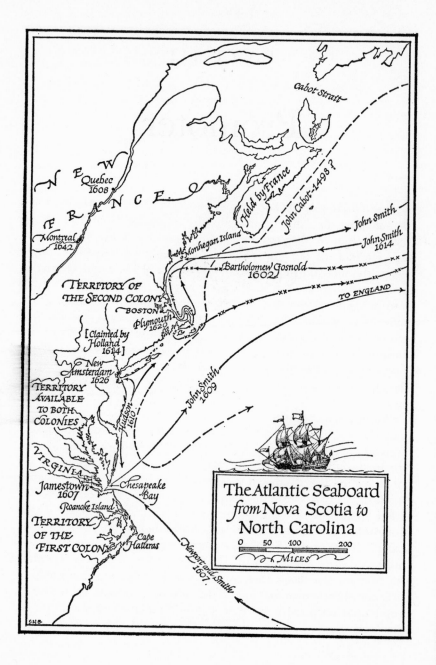

The Atlantic Seaboard from Nova Scotia to North Carolina

Cabot Strait

Quebec
1608

Montreal
1642

Held by France

John Cabot–1498?

John Smith

John Smith
1614

Monhegan Island

Bartholomew Gosnold
1602

TO ENGLAND

TERRITORY OF
THE SECOND COLONY
BOSTON

Plymouth
1620

[Claimed by
Holland
1614]

New
Amsterdam
1626

TERRITORY
AVAILABLE
TO BOTH
COLONIES

Hudson
1610

John Smith
1609

VIRGINIA

Jamestown
1607

Chesapeake
Bay

Roanoke Island

TERRITORY
OF THE
FIRST COLONY

Cape
Hatteras

Newport and Smith
1607

0   50   100   200
MILES

CHAPTER 20

## " 'TIS ALL IN PIECES . . ."

JOHN SMITH was halfway across the Atlantic when Henry Hudson hove in sight of Dartmouth, returning from the voyage that took him to Virginia and to the river that bears his name today. He had all but encountered the Virginia Company's supply fleet at the mouth of Chesapeake Bay. Indeed, the night of August 11, according to Robert Juet's account, the ship's cat "ran crying from one side of the ship to the other, looking overboard, which made us to wonder; but we saw nothing." Perhaps the cat had seen or heard Ratcliffe's *Diamond*, trailing the others to port. But Hudson did not venture up the river to Jamestown. He was flying Dutch colors. (Neither did a Spanish ship that had slipped up to Chesapeake Bay a month before, and ran away without reconnoitering.)

Hudson stayed a while in Dartmouth before going to London, since the English authorities refused to allow him to sail back to Holland. Meanwhile, a week or ten days behind him, came Samuel Argall, straight (if somewhat delayed) from Virginia. Hudson did not know of the disappearance of Gates, Somers, and Newport. Argall did. His was the first ship to report their supposed loss.

The details of the misfortune were contained in a letter Argall brought back from Gabriel Archer. Not only had the colony's three leaders disappeared, but orderly government in Jamestown was threatened with an upheaval. Archer and his associates, Ratcliffe and Martin, the letter said, were going to impose a president or governor of their own making on the colony, as soon as John Smith's presidential term expired. It was to be Francis West, Lord De La Warr's brother.

This forewarned the Council of a kind of anarchy, which could not but be disturbing. Already in their *Instructions,* given to Gates before he sailed, the Council had ordered:

> We require you to call before you Captain John Radcliffe and one Webbe [Thomas, an original settler?] who hath complained by petition delivered unto you of divers injuries and insolences done unto him in the government of the said Captain Radcliffe, and accordingly to hear the cause and do justice in it . . .

Besides, Edward Maria Wingfield had testified lengthily against Ratcliffe in 1608, that "he did wear no other eyes or ears than grew on Master Archer's head." Furthermore, Wingfield said, Archer was "always hatching of some mutiny."

By the same post, so to speak, with this ill-boding letter there seems to have arrived a message from John Smith, who was still President when Argall sailed. This may have gone by word of mouth, since there is no trace of it anywhere, and if it did it is witness to basically friendly feelings between Smith and Argall. In any case, the 1624 account states:

> . . . we revictualled him [Argall], and sent him for England with a true relation of the causes of our defailments [failures], and how impossible it was to return that wealth they expected, or observe their instructions to endure the Savages' insolences, or do anything to any purpose, except they would send us men and means that could produce that they so much desired; otherwise all they did was lost, and could not but come to confusion.

Whatever the exact facts of the case, the London Council quickly prepared a *True and sincere declaration of the purpose and ends of the Plantation begun in Virginia,* which was in shape to be entered for publication on December 14, 1609. It was a twenty-four-page apologia for the colony, explaining so far as possible the loss of the flagship with the Governor on board, and the determination of the Virginia Company to carry on. In evidence of that determination, the apologia was followed by a two-page summary of what sort of people were needed for Virginia. The pamphlet was writ-

ten in a lofty vein, ornamented with pious expressions and trust
in Divine Providence, and might have allayed concern over the
Company's colonial plans had not the ships bearing John Smith
(and a number of malcontents, flying squirrels, and other Virginia
products) arrived before it could reach the public.

About two weeks after Argall's return, three ships straggled and
limped up the Thames from across the Atlantic — the last remnant,
but one, of the proud fleet of nine that had sailed from Plymouth
nearly six months before. On one of these, perhaps limping more
literally, came Captain John Smith, ex-President of the Council in
Virginia.

Five ships in all had left Virginia, and all had suffered in storms.
Their voyage was slow. If they sailed just after October 4, as seems
likely, it had taken seven weeks or so. Then, when they were almost
home, two ships were lost in a storm off Ile d'Ouessant: the *Diamond,* with Captain King, and another ship — probably the *Unity,*
with John Smith's friend, Captain Wood. Smith himself had possibly sailed with Captain Francis Nelson in the *Falcon,* since they
appear to have been friends, although he could have been with
Captain Webb in the *Lion.* (That he was with Captain Adams in
the *Blessing* seems highly unlikely.) Wherever he was, the arrival
of these three ships, bearing news of the double tragedy — their
own, and that of Jamestown — aroused something akin to consternation in the London Council.

As has already been mentioned, that body had issued a lengthy
and detailed set of *Instructions* to Sir Thomas Gates. In this document the Council stated that they had provided a sealed "black
box, marked with the figure of one," containing their choice for a
second governor in case of the death of Sir Thomas Gates, and
two additional black boxes in which were their "commissions in
cases of death or other vacation [absence from duty] of the Governor." And there were further precautions.

Despite all this, the three chiefs of the expedition and all the
boxes and other instructions, letters, etc., left England on board
the same ship. It was a strange risking of all their eggs in one
basket, which can hardly have been intentional on the Council's
part. Indeed, that the Company was embarrassed by it is attested
by the Council's explanation, published in 1610, after it was learned

that Gates, Somers, and Newport were all alive. That communication reeks of musty cloth hastily thrown over a mistake: "No other Commissioners were in [Gates's] ship but such as (for especial reasons) were . . . appointed." In other words, no important people were in one boat except all of them!

This offense against common sense and prudence must bear the blame for the trouble which followed in Jamestown. John Smith could not know, with certainty, that the Virginia Company had been reorganized, that it had a new charter, and that Sir Thomas Gates had been appointed royal Governor. He had no document, no proof — only the word of a handful of men, some of whom had all but wrecked the colony before. Worse, he could not know that the Governor's *Instructions* of May, 1609, named him, John Smith, second member of the newly appointed Governor's Council, preceded in rank only by Sir George Somers. (A knight would inevitably precede a captain.) Nor could he know that the *Instructions* required of Governor Gates that he appoint Captain John Smith to the specific post of defense of the colony: "To this command we desire Captain Smith may be allotted [appointed] as well for his earnest desire as the great confidence and trust we have in his care and diligence."

Under such an arrangement, with Sir Thomas as Governor, Sir George Somers as his presumed Deputy, and Captain John Smith next ranking member of the Council, and Chief of Colonial Defense, Smith would have occupied the post of most vital practical importance in the colony, and would *ceteris paribus* have been in a position consonant with both his ability and his deserts. In time, considering the relatively advanced years of both Gates and Somers, John Smith could have looked forward to promotion to Deputy and perhaps to Governor — with an eventual knighthood. Gates and Somers were not Newport (Newport was not scheduled to stay in the colony anyway), and there is no reason to doubt that Smith would have fallen in line with the new *Instructions* without qualm. The post provided for him in them may have made a smaller frog of him than had the presidency of the Council, but the puddle was incomparably bigger. It would have been another step up the ladder.

It is idle, however, to expatiate on the ifs and would-have-beens.

They have been mentioned only because it is important to know that John Smith's letter of late 1608, which was highly critical of certain measures of the London Council, had been received by that body before the *Instructions* were written, and that those same *Instructions* are evidence that the letter was neither resented nor disregarded.

All this, then, hints that John Smith, contrary to Ratcliffe's persuasions (and hopes), may well have been received in London with friendliness on the part of the London Council, including Sir Thomas Smythe, and with some move by one or another of the Company to help him get on his feet again — perhaps working for or consulting with the Company. It is true that Edward Maria Wingfield had been welcomed with something less than cordiality on his return, a year and a half before, but there is no reason to believe that Ratcliffe's note to Salisbury about Smith ("This man is sent home to answer some misdemeanors") need be taken too seriously. Word that Wingfield was "accused of some treachery" got around. Not even a hint that Smith was similarly accused is to be found in surviving documents and correspondence.[1]

As a matter of fact, the Virginia Company was too occupied with grave problems to concern itself deeply over John Smith's alleged misdeeds. It still had to complete plans as quickly as possible to get a relief expedition off to Jamestown — plans begun as long before as June, while Sir Thomas Gates was still in England. Sir Thomas West, Lord De La Warr, the older brother of Francis West, was appointed to take charge. Weekly meetings had been held and De La Warr's departure was all but scheduled even before Samuel Argall returned. The discouraging news he brought speeded up the scheduling.

Then, along with the somber reports brought by John Smith, came a mass of uncontrollable gossip damaging to the good name of the Virginia Company. A sample of this is contained in a newsy letter from Jean Beaulieu to his friend the English chargé d'affaires at Brussels, William Trumbull, which reports on the Virginia troubles as of November 30:

> . . . dissension is reported amongst them [the colonists] by reason of their Minister, being somewhat a Puritan, the most part refused to go [to] his Service and to hear his

sermons, though by the other part he was favored. He will not stay amongst them.

Although this seems relatively inconsequential today, religion was a highly sensitive subject in 1609 (and before and after). The letter shows dissension in any case. Greater dissension was reflected, undoubtedly, in other letters which have not survived, and in talk.

The preceding February, Sir Thomas Smythe's assistant, Robert Johnson, Deputy Treasurer of the Virginia Company, had put out a rather large booklet called *Nova Britannia*. Johnson had been moved by "the wise and prudent speech of a worthy Gentleman," he wrote, to yield his "money and endeavors as others did to advance" the plantation. Many were influenced by his words and his example. But now the great effort had literally foundered, or so it seemed.

In doubt and confusion, the Company issued a broadside, more or less simultaneously with the *True and sincere declaration*. It was designed to counteract, by its wide distribution, not only the mischief wrought by correspondence but also (and more especially) the damage done by

> . . . some few of those unruly youths sent thither (being of a most lewd [base] and bad condition), and such as no ground can hold for want of good directions there, were suffered by stealth to get aboard the ships returning thence, and are come for England again, giving out . . . most vile and scandalous reports, both of the country itself, and of the carriage of the business there.

None of this vindication of the Company, however, was as defensive as might have been expected, largely because the Council did not know what had really happened and without a doubt still hoped that Gates, Somers, and Newport would eventually turn up — as indeed they did. In addition, however, by the time this broadside was distributed further support for the Company was thundered from the pulpit by the Reverend William Crashaw, Puritan, father of the aberrant Roman Catholic poet, Richard. Nevertheless, a week before Crashaw's sermon, Parliament on February 14, 1610, declared Sir George Somers deceased, and entered the

name of his successor after great debate. (Somers was M.P. for
Lyme Regis, Dorset.)[2]

During this time, John Smith was presumably being interviewed
by the Company, possibly getting medical treatment, and certainly
arguing with the Council about returning to Virginia. In between,
he was almost certainly looking up old friends — his noble patron
Lord Willoughby, Henry Hudson, the Gosnold family, and many
others. Lord Willoughby and the rest of the Berties were very
likely the first to be sought out.

Details of Robert Bertie's life are scant for this period, but later
biographers have assumed that he was mostly occupied with attending Parliament in London and running his estates in Lincolnshire.
His house in Barbican, London, would probably have been his
residence on visits there, while Grimsthorpe was his home in the
country. Wherever he was at the time, and as undocumented as
any meeting between him and John Smith remains, various happenings point to a renewal of old ties, begun soon after Smith's
return.

Henry Hudson, on the other hand, was surely not back in London when Smith got there. Then, when he did reach the capital
(possibly in January, 1610), he was accused of having gone on a
voyage "to the detriment of his own country," and was forbidden to
leave England. Nevertheless, Hudson got around the interdiction
by going to sea for a group headed by two great London merchants
and a young man of vision: Sir Thomas Smythe and John (later,
Sir John) Wolstenholme, merchant adventurers, and Sir Dudley
Digges. Prince Henry gave his support to the voyage, and on
April 17, 1610, it sailed. John Smith's meetings with Hudson must
therefore have been between January and April.

There was another matter of priority for John Smith, however, a
call of duty which there is every evidence did not go unheeded.
The prime mover of the Virginia Venture, Bartholomew Gosnold,
had died, almost in John Smith's arms. The Gosnold family knew
of this. But did they know of the death of Bartholomew's brother,
drowned on an expedition undertaken against President Smith's
orders?

Samuel Argall might have brought back word, but it is likely that
he did not. He does not seem to have known the Gosnolds, al-

though there were tenuous ties between the two families, and Anthony had died more than six months before Argall arrived (for the first time) in Virginia. Furthermore, the colony was in such a state when he got there, and in such confusion twice confounded when he left, that the dispatch of word of Anthony's death by him, or by his ship, can hardly have been thought of. John Smith almost perforce was therefore the bearer of the unhappy tidings. Thus it may not be a mere coincidence that Anthony Gosnold, Sr., died about the end of the year 1609, when the news of the loss of his other son reached his ears.

By then, John Smith had certainly learned of the appearance in print of his long, personal letter, under the title of *A true relation of such occurrences and accidents of noate as hath hapned in Virginia since the first planting of that Collony, which is now resident in the South part thereof, till the last returne from thence.* Reference has already been made to this matter at the start of Smith's presidency. It is proper now to give the details.

John Tapp was a specialist in the publication of navigational aids who put out a number of important works of the type of his *Seamans Kalender.* He also published a number of religious treatises, as did practically all publishers of the period. John Smith's letter from Virginia, his *True Relation,* did not fall into either category. William Welby, on the other hand, was a younger man who had published his first book as recently as October 1, 1604. For Welby, John Smith's communication was the first in a series of works on Virginia which rolled from his press until the end of the year 1614. All of the subsequent books and pamphlets were more or less sponsored by the Virginia Company. Welby is noted primarily as the *seller* of Smith's *True Relation,* while Tapp was the *publisher,* in the modern sense. This hints that some individual or individuals in the Virginia Company, rather than the Company as such, backed the Smith book.

Another curious point in connection with the *True Relation* is that the title page at first stated only that it was written "by a Gentleman of the said Colony"; then, that "Thomas Watson, Gent., one of the said Colony," wrote it; and only at long last that it was the work of "Captain Smith, Colonel of the said Colony." Even that "final" form was corrected, however, and the first three letters along

with the final *l* of "Colonel" were erased (none too thoroughly)
so as to leave only the letters *one*.

A three-page address "To the Courteous Reader," signed "I. H."
and placed right after the title page, attempted to explain the confusion about the author, and in so doing has left a valuable bit of
information for historians. While making it clear that he, I. H., did
not write the work, he states that he took the liberty of editing it:
". . . somewhat more was by him [Smith] written, which being as
I thought 'fit to be private' I would not adventure to make it public." The identity of I. H. unfortunately remains undetermined,
but Thomas Watson is known, and his association with the printing
of the *True Relation* throws a little light on the happenings of
mid-1608 in London, while Smith was away.

Although Thomas Watson, as a name, was and is relatively common, and no surviving document connects any specific Thomas
Watson with John Smith's book, an accident has preserved a single
printed slip of paper connecting *one* Thomas Watson, along with
a John Bingley, both "esquires," with John Smith, as will appear
below. This Thomas Watson was one of the tellers of the Exchequer* at the time, and many references to him still exist in
various state and other papers. One of these shows that he was in
communication with George Calvert and Sir Thomas Smythe in
April, 1604. Given such a contact, it is possible that Thomas
Watson of the Exchequer was one of those who saw John Smith's
letter, and even that he may have been the one who finally passed
it on to Tapp and Welby — thereby getting the credit for having
written it. Since Bingley was also employed in the Exchequer, the
identification seems fairly certain. (It is only necessary to add that
Watson was honest, or sharp, enough not to want his name attached
to a work which was not his.)

What John Smith thought of the publication of his letter is not
shown in anything he wrote. He may have been disappointed at
the omission of some of the information he sent from Virginia. The
fact, for instance, that I. H. considered some of the information
"fit to be private" may explain the absence of a detailed account of
what really happened when John Smith was taken prisoner in

* The four officers "formerly charged with the receipt and payment of moneys."
(*OED*)

December, 1607. This may hint that I. H. was connected with the Virginia Company, for they would not want a horror story of that sort printed (to the detriment of enthusiasm for the Venture), or would not want Smith to appear as even more of a hero than was already manifest in his letter. Whatever the facts, Smith had made his appearance in print. Whether he liked it or not, his future career was already virtually determined.

During the winter of 1609–1610, however, John Smith was undoubtedly seeking further active service, with zeal. When he was not pestering someone close to Sir Thomas Smythe, he was unquestionably soliciting support among more readily accessible people, such as the Berties. Still, so many things were happening, Smith could make progress only slowly.

Sir Thomas Smythe himself, for example, was occupied with the building of England's greatest merchant ship of the day, which was christened on December 30, 1609, by the King in person, bearing presents to Sir Thomas with his own sacred hands. Then there was the return of Robert Harcourt from Guiana to Bristol not long before, of interest to Sir Thomas. And most of all, Sir Thomas was busy with the preparations for Lord De La Warr's relief voyage to Virginia. The excitement over this culminated in a two-hour sermon preached by William Crashaw, as already mentioned, and seven days later, on February 28, 1610, Lord De La Warr received his commission from the Virginia Company — the first such document ever issued to the Lord Governor of an English colony in America.

That John Smith does not seem to have turned to Lord De La Warr is probably explained by the manner of man he was, and his relations with the Company. Sir Thomas West by family name, the new Lord Governor had succeeded to the barony of De La Warr (or Delaware) a few years before. His mother, Anne Knollys, was a granddaughter of Mary Boleyn, the sister of Anne Boleyn, Queen Elizabeth's mother, and he was also connected with the Earls of Essex and Northumberland. These connections, along with his personal qualifications, presumably justified the placing of vice-regal power in De La Warr's hands, and granting to him untrammeled choice of his assistants. The Virginia Company's "interference" in the naming of any individuals for posts or responsibilities in Virginia was gone forever.

This made it useless for John Smith to apply for a position in the new government; he would have had to apply to a "sole governor" just such as he himself had been denounced as trying to be. Even when it came to the Berties, both Robert and Peregrine seem to have been well occupied with their own affairs at the time. Still, there were connections of the Berties who could be of help, and it appears that John Smith did not hesitate to try his luck with them.

One of these, if it is possible to read correctly between the lines, was old Sir John Peyton, who had been a supervisor of Robert Bertie's father's will. Sir John had several connections involving Virginia, not the least of which was his cousin Sir Henry Peyton, an investor in the Virginia Company. Sir Henry had married Mary Seymour, sister of Edward Seymour, Earl of Hertford. In this way, through the Peytons, Smith seems to have gained the Earl's ear, and before long he had found the "best friend" he had.

In the harbor of Seymour's favor, as John Smith put it, he hoped he would ever "rest secure, notwithstanding all weathers; lamenting others, that they fall into such miseries, as I foreseeing have foretold, but could not prevent . . ." The way was clear for John Smith to dedicate himself to activity once again.

Although the date when John Smith found this new rock in the midst of howling waves, to paraphrase Virgil, is far from certain, it must have been within a matter of months after his return from Jamestown, for by the end of the year (1610) Smith is evidently in the midst of new friends, and new work. It is apparently the Earl of Hertford who must be credited with backing John Smith at this juncture.

It does not seem to have been one of Smith's aptitudes, as an actor on the stage of the drama "Virginia," to observe what was going on beyond his immediate range of vision. Therefore, when the accidents of his wound and the presumed loss of Gates's ship removed him effectively from Virginia, he was helpless — precisely because performance had so far been his forte. He did not know how to compromise with ideas that seemed to him silly or arbitrary. Consequently, even though his wound may have influenced his remaining in England at the time, it was far more likely his mental attitude which kept him there.[3]

After the last flurried appeal for "sufficient, honest and good artificers" for Virginia, Lord De La Warr sailed from the Isle of

Wight on April 1, 1610, with a fleet of three ships. Two weeks later, the smallest of these got separated from the others at the Azores and encountered De La Warr's brother, Francis West, scurrying home. West, the youth who had braved John Smith's scorn in Virginia, arrived in England uninvited. He had taken one of the colony's three ships to sea, during the "starving time," to procure food for Jamestown. Having collected what he could, he took off with the food and a bevy of malcontents, and baldly deserted. Had he not had Queen Anne Boleyn's sister for a great-grandmother and the Lord Governor of Virginia for a brother, he would undoubtedly have been clamped in irons. Instead, he was put in command of another vessel to return to Virginia in some state.

News of incidents such as this must have reached John Smith's ears. "Everybody" knew about it. Yet not a damning word escaped from the pens and lips of the Virginia Council or its paid publicists. Even Smith referred to Lord De La Warr's insubordinate brother as "gentle" of nature — presumably out of respect for his family.

By then, the chief propagandists for the Virginia Company were Sir Thomas Smythe, Sir Dudley Digges, and Robert Johnson, later Alderman. Deprived of indirect as well as direct participation in the Virginia enterprise, Smith seems to have floundered about in an unsympathetic mercantile sea through the summer of 1610. The publishers of his book were not interested in further works by him (Welby gave over his rights to the *True Relation* in October), and there were few ears that seem to have welcomed his plaints. It is idle to guess whether he had already approached Samuel Purchas or any other uncertain acquaintances of the period before his departure for Virginia. With Henry Hudson gone since April, there is no compelling probability. But with September came two ships from Virginia, Lord De La Warr's *Blessing* and *Hercules,* bearing Sir Thomas Gates and Captain Christopher Newport, and presumably at least one friend of Captain John Smith, Richard Potts. (There were probably two or three more, Richard and David Wiffin, and Post Ginnat, the surgeon.)

Potts had been Clerk of the Council in Virginia. Of obscure origin, he had joined the first supply, and had attached himself to John Smith from the day of his arrival, January 2, 1608. On returning to England, he would have had his own records with him

(at least a copy of them), and he probably brought others. Smith
and he met, as was to be expected, probably along with the two
Wiffins. And new, fresh blood began to course through John Smith's
veins. The old gunpowder wound was forgotten.

Another close associate of Smith's in Virginia, Raleigh Crashaw,
although he stayed behind, nevertheless seems in all likelihood to
have played an important part in Smith's activities. This Crashaw
must have been a relative of the Reverend William Crashaw,
probably even a younger brother. Whatever the tie, he apparently
sent a letter or other message to the preacher, with some account
of what was going on in Virginia, and undoubtedly with a good
word for Captain John Smith. As a result, the Reverend Mr.
Crashaw interested himself seriously in the happenings in Virginia
as related by Potts, and vouched for by Smith and others. The
outcome was a project for a new, *truly* truthful book on the con-
troversial colony.

Here the group apparently ran into snags. The ships that probably brought Potts certainly brought still further horrible rumors
from Jamestown. The whole of London can be expected to have
known details which the Virginia Company would have given much
to have kept secret — or at least labeled "unconfirmed." But what
the new Spanish Ambassador soon learned may be assumed to have
been known far beyond diplomatic and governmental circles.
Among other tales, Don Alonso de Velasco relayed home that:

> . . . those who [just] arrived . . . report that the Indians
> hold the English surrounded in the fortress which they had
> erected there, having killed the larger part of them . . .
> the survivors eat the dead, and when one of the natives
> died fighting, they dug him up again, two days after, to
> be eaten . . . and almost all who came in this vessel died
> from having eaten dogs, cat skins, and other vile stuff.

In the face of this, Smith and his associates, including the Reverend
Mr. Crashaw, apparently bowed to the need of the Virginia Company, and held off with their project.

The Company, needless to say, put someone quickly to work on
a revised version of their *True and sincere declaration of the purpose of the Plantation begun in Virginia*, to be called *A true*

*declaration of the estate of the Colony in Virginia.* Only a greater mass of public complaint than has usually been visualized by modern writers could have accounted for the remarkable revision. The Company's excuses were guiltily evasive in many cases, the history was occasionally falsified, and downright untruths were here and there laid before the public for acceptance. And the sixty-eight-page book was entered for publication on November 8, 1610, "under the hands of Sir Thomas Smythe, Sir Maurice Barkley, Sir George Coppin, and Master Richard Martin [all of the Virginia Company] and the Wardens," of the Stationers' Company.

With William Barret publishing this, and with William Welby by then dedicated to publishing the Company's story and other publishers working for Sir Thomas Smythe, it would not be simple for three or four returned colonists to put out a book which vitiated much of what the Company had said. At this point, however, William Crashaw seems to have decided to intervene — the year 1611 having by then undoubtedly rolled in. He was a friend of the Reverend William Symonds, some fifteen years his senior, who had a curacy at Halton Holegate, Lincolnshire, bestowed on him by Robert Bertie, Lord Willoughby. Symonds (or Simmonds, as it is sometimes spelled) was then in the process of moving toward London, to become preacher at St. Saviour's in Southwark. Between his friendship with Crashaw and the common debt he and John Smith had with regard to Robert Bertie, Symonds was persuaded to undertake the task of pulling together a book written, or to be written, by Captain John Smith, Richard Potts, Richard Wiffin, and other colonists.

Somewhat before this, in fact before John Smith returned from Virginia, the great Richard Hakluyt made his final significant contribution to the Virginia Venture. In April, 1609, he dedicated his translation of de Soto's narrative of adventures to the Virginia Company, under the title *Virginia richly valued.* Two months later, suggested only by Hakluyt, a translation of part of Lescarbot's *Nova Francia* was entered at the Stationers' Company. Smith may have called on the old geographer when he got to London, and certainly he knew the books, as will be seen in the next chapter. But after that, Hakluyt's direct interest in Virginia began to subside. Another took it up.

Rival or successor to Hakluyt only as the moon is the rival of the sun, the Reverend Samuel Purchas slipped into a place ready for his occupation principally because there was no other to occupy it. Yet when Hakluyt had spent himself in his incomparable work, it was fortunate that a successor, however pale by comparison, stood there, eager to take up the challenge. More, it was fortunate that John Smith and Richard Potts and countless others, however reckless some of them were as historians, were available to Purchas to throw what light they could. Whether Purchas and Smith met before 1611 is therefore unimportant. That they knew one another by then is unquestioned.

Samuel Purchas, although educated at Cambridge, was a self-made man who had risen from obscurity much as had John Smith. He was not a man of action, but of contemplation, being, as he wrote, "addicted to the study of history" — in an academic way, be it said. But he was persistent.

While Purchas borrowed some of John Smith's material for the *Pilgrimage* which he had begun to compile in the year mentioned, William Symonds seems to have gone over the whole as a sort of general editor, as we should say today. As a result, the projected joint effort of Smith and his fellow ex-colonists was divided in two parts, the first to be descriptive of Virginia and its inhabitants, the second to recount what happened there, from the colonists' point of view, up to the date of Potts's departure. John Smith was (evidently) the sole author of what was later called *The Description of Virginia,* and Potts assembled all available accounts (including Smith's, of course) into *The Proceedings of the English Colony in Virginia.* The book was to be entitled *A Map of Virginia,* as many such circumstantial accounts were then called.[4]

Smith's *Description* is an outstanding work of its kind. It still constitutes well-nigh the only source of ethnological information on the Indians of Tidewater Virginia before 1700. (William Strachey, as will be seen immediately, added somewhat to Smith's work.) Indeed, only Thomas Hariot's *A briefe and true report,* prepared twenty years before, competes in any sense with Smith's broad, careful survey. The Indians described by Hariot are North Carolina Algonkians, however, so it is a parallel rather than a rival study, and it must be added that the illustrations drawn by John White increase its value immeasurably. Yet, even though Hariot was a scientist, and in that sense left perhaps a more "scholarly" essay, John Smith does not suffer by comparison.

It is obvious that an analysis of John Smith's *Description* would belong rather to the domain of ethnology and anthropology than to a biography. Nevertheless it is well to note that thorough investigation, comparison with the occasional independent sources (Henry Spelman, George Percy, Gabriel Archer, and others), retrospective scrutiny of later works, and comparative examination of related or neighboring Indian tribes — all have equally confirmed Smith's fundamental understanding and accurate perceptive powers. In a few instances he characteristically took the superficial for the basic, as for example his interpretation of what was going on in Powhatan's great-house in the last days of December, 1607 — he was hardly in a position to regard the performance with cool scientific detachment. Yet his mistakes, and mistaken judgments, are wonderfully few, where we can be sure that they were mistakes at all. Even his exposition of eight or nine dozen Indian words, some of them included in examples of sentences, is to all purposes verifiable through comparison with related Indian languages still spoken today. All in all, it is a remarkable performance for a rough-and-ready soldier with a grammar school education.

At the same time that John Smith was working on his *Description*, Richard Potts apparently began gathering surviving bits of information and, with Smith's undoubted help or supervision, writing connecting paragraphs and entire sections for the second part, the "historical" *Proceedings*. In this he was helped by Richard Wiffin and Anas Todkill (that ex-servant extraordinary of Captain Martin who became so valuable an aide to Captain Smith), who were certainly by now back in England. Two or three other colonists named on the title page may have been in England too, but that is uncertain — one was surely dead — and they may not have helped personally. This, however, did not prevent Potts from using their notes and jottings.

When both the *Description* and the *Proceedings* were ready, they were submitted to another returned colonist, Thomas Abbay, for comment, and two prefaces were the result, one for each part. Then Symonds summed up what he did in these words, printed at the end of the volume: "The pains I took was great." Meanwhile another colonist had returned, William Strachey of Saffron Walden, Essex.

Strachey had gone over to Virginia with Gates, Somers, and Newport. He had been wrecked with them on the shoals of Bermuda, and with them he had made it to Jamestown in May, 1610, where he served as secretary of the colony. From Jamestown, he sent a letter, probably to the wife of Sir Thomas Smythe, describing their experiences in Bermuda — a letter which is said to have gotten into the hands of William Shakespeare and supplied him with much of the background for *The Tempest*. The letter also reached Samuel Purchas's acquisitive talons, to be published by him in 1625. If it had not, no one would know the details of that tragedy today. Parenthetically, it is worth noting that Gates himself brought the letter to England in late summer, 1610, and while the Virginia Company refused to allow publication of Strachey's letter, the Company's Secretary, Richard Martin, wrote Strachey in Virginia, begging him to send *the truth,* even if only in private.

Strachey, as stated, returned to London early in the fall of 1611. Still in the employ of the Virginia Company, his first task was the preparation of a set of the laws proclaimed by the Governor in Jamestown. This was ready for the press and licensed on December 13, 1611. At the same time, he was already at work on a history of the plantation. The implications of this are that he was in touch with John Smith, for one third of Strachey's work, titled *The historie of travell into Virginia Britania,* was lifted bodily or condensed from John Smith's work. In all fairness, however, it should be added that there is much in Strachey which is not in Smith, and that the large Strachey vocabulary of Powhatan Indian words — with six times as many as are to be found in Smith's writings — is invaluable for modern students of Algonkian languages.

But with publication of all "outside" works on Virginia, such as Smith and Potts's apparently halted by the Company, the three clergymen who were interested had already put their heads together to get Smith and Potts's work printed elsewhere. (Strachey's was never completed.)[5]

At that time, there were but two legal presses in England, outside London: those of the Universities of Oxford and Cambridge. Symonds was an Oxford man, the other two came from Cambridge. Joseph Barnes, the Oxford printer, had a son, John, who was a member of the Stationers' Company in London. John Barnes published Sir Dudley Digges's book on the Northwest Passage in June, 1612. Sir Dudley was an Oxford man, like Symonds. Still, the details of what happened in 1612 are not known.

Meanwhile, a complete stranger had appeared on the scene. An obscure merchant named Philip Fote (or Foote) had a presentation slip printed for a book, which reads in part as follows:

> To the Right Worshipfull Thomas Watson and John Bingley, Esquiers . . .
> . . . constrained by duty and affection, I hope you will pardon me for presenting your Worships with this little Book [John Smith's!]; howbeit, it is not mine by Birth, yet it is by Gift, and purchase from the Press . . . I have occasioned the Impression, which if it give you content, my charge and pains is highly recompensed.

No other notice of Fote and his contribution to the printing of Smith's book seems to have survived. Indeed, of Fote himself there is only a brief note that six years later he got a license to sell clay for making tobacco pipes. Obviously, he was somehow interested in Virginia.

As for Thomas Watson and John Bingley, they had just been appointed members of the Council for Virginia, under the new, liberalized Third Charter, of March 12, 1612. The next surviving bit of information is supplied by the title pages of the two parts of the now famous "little Book": Part One, *A Map of Virginia, With a Description of the Country . . . by Captain Smith . . .* and so forth; Part Two, *The proceedings of the English Colony . . .* and so forth, with a list of those whose writings were drawn on. The whole work acknowledges W[illiam] S[ymonds] as the "editor," and below an ornament is the statement: At Oxford, Printed by Joseph Barnes. Somewhere in the tangle of Fote and Watson and Bingley, Crashaw and Purchas, Symonds and Sir Dudley Digges (perhaps), the secret of the Oxford publication of John Smith and Richard Potts's book lies well hidden.

John Smith put heart and soul into his share of the work of

producing this book — a small quarto totaling one hundred and forty-nine pages of text. Under his guidance, William Hole, perhaps England's most refined engraver, prepared a map of Virginia and decorated it with two pictorial illustrations — Powhatan seated in state, and a Susquehanna brave — inspired in part by John White's earlier drawings. So accurate were John Smith's observations and so detailed his sketch-maps that Hole's engraving was copied or adapted in every major geographical work on Virginia during the seventeenth century, and was used as late as 1873 with reference to boundary discussions between Maryland and Virginia.

The rest of Smith's true share in the *Map of Virginia,* that is, the book, will never be known. Beyond the *Description* and the geographical map which are definitely his, there is frequent evidence of his personality in the *Proceedings,* and some of the details must have been supplied by him, especially in the part signed by Thomas Studley. Studley was dead long before the events related in the last third of the section attributed to him took place. At the same time, Smith quite properly used the observations of others in rounding out his own part of the book, and it may be that sketches by Robert Tindall, and perhaps Nathaniel Powell, were incorporated in Hole's engraving. None of this denies to Smith the basic authorship, which is also accorded him by William Strachey: ". . . their [the Indians'] several habitations are more plainly described by the annexed Map, set forth by Captain Smith. Of whose pains taken herein, I leave to the censure of the Reader to judge."

When the 1612 book came out, John Smith was clearly under criticism still. His unyielding defense of what he saw to be right could not endear him to merchants of the type of Sir Thomas Smythe. (Sir Thomas was by then raised so high that he forgot where his grandfather lived because the house "was rather insignificant for a man of his wealth and position.") Yet Smith unfortunately was usually right, despite the Company, and they eventually put into effect many of the basic principles which Smith had advocated. Where the Company was right and Smith was wrong, however, was in their knowledge that the government by one man in Virginia, which Smith had instituted with astounding success despite desperate odds, could not be carried on by a nobody. A peer of England was needed, to command obedience — or a ruthless military tyrant. Jamestown was to have first one and then the other before the Company and its Council would wake up to facts. Even then, the London management would be overthrown before an effective government could be initiated.

John Smith apparently sensed much of this, and attempted in his *Description,* and in the *Proceedings* which were only partly his, to present both what there was in Virginia, and what needed to be done. The history of mistakes made, as well as progress achieved, had to be known and recognized so that the colony could march ahead. With unfaltering enthusiasm John Smith set out to do this, as his first important work joined that of Samuel Purchas in seeing the light of day toward the end of 1612.

In the interim, George Percy had returned from Virginia sometime in July, and William Strachey conceived the idea of getting him to present a copy of his unfinished *Historie* to Percy's brother, the Earl of Northumberland. Although the Earl was still in the Tower of London, he was influential, he was a friend of Sir Walter Ralegh's, and he was interested in colonization. Strachey had no more been allowed to return to Virginia than had John Smith, and everything points to his wanting or needing someone to back his work financially. Therefore, about the time Smith's book appeared in Oxford, Strachey got George Percy to take a copy of his own, in manuscript, with suitable dedication, to the Earl. In it he summed up John Smith's status at that time in words far more informed than any modern writer can string together. Pleading his own cause, he also pleaded that of Captain John Smith:

> Sure I am, there will not return from thence in haste, anyone who hath been more industrious, or who hath had (Captain George Percy excepted) greater experience amongst them, however misconstruction may traduce him here at home, where is not easily seen the mixed sufferances both of body and mind, which is there daily, and with no few hazards, and hearty griefs undergone.[6]

CHAPTER 21

# NEW ENGLAND

Two MAJOR BLOWS struck King James's Court before 1612 was out. On May 24, one week before his fiftieth birthday, Robert Cecil, Earl of Salisbury, succumbed to a lingering illness. On November 6, Henry Frederick, Prince of Wales, died of typhoid fever. He was not yet nineteen.

The death of the heir to the throne threw England into anguish, where Cecil's disappearance seemed (falsely) to liberate England from too long a political tyranny. On the contrary, the chief result of both deaths was to permit the accession to power of King James's handsome young favorite, Robert Carr, twenty-five years old. Scandal soon came knocking at the royal gates.

This has little to do with John Smith, to be sure. Nevertheless it is necessary to note that firmness in government and at least superficial propriety in the royal ménage encouraged honesty and Christian morality among the rank and file of subjects. With the laxness in court circles that attended on what has been called "the Jacobean Pageant" came the enthronement of Gold and Power, to the detriment of national solidity and coherence. Gold and Power were one joint cause of John Smith's troubles in the next few years, especially Gold, which sometimes meant Power. They became not the means, but the ends themselves of the *greater* men on whose whims John Smith's future hung.

What Smith heard from Virginia was disconcerting in the extreme, in those very days when he was preparing his picture of the colony for publication. Lord De La Warr had stuck it out for a year only, to be succeeded by Sir Thomas Dale, whose sternness in the name of discipline became little short of proverbial. George

Percy, as has been said, left the colony, under conditions which offer a strange parallel to Francis West's discreditable flight of the year before. So conspicuous was the rottenness that no Danish Marcellus was needed to suggest that something was amiss. John Chamberlain, the man noted for writing letters, spelled it all out on July 9. If the Spanish Ambassador was going to protest to James I about the colony, Chamberlain wrote, he might as well save his breath,

> seeing it is to be feared that that action will fall to the ground of itself, by the extreme beastly idleness of our na-tion, which (notwithstanding any cost or diligence used to support them) will rather die and starve than be brought to any labor or industry to maintain themselves. Two or three of the last ships that came thence bring nothing but discomfort, and that Sir Thomas Gates and Sir Thomas Dale are quite out of heart, and to mend the matter [make it worse], not past five days since, here arrived a ship with ten men [including George Percy], who (being sent forth to fish for their relief, and having taken great store), have given them the slip and run away, and fill the town [Lon-don] with ill reports, which will hinder that business more than the Lottery or any other art they can use for the present will further it: and yet they have taken good order [measures] to have these runaways apprehended and pun-ished or at least sent back again.

Naturally, when Francis West, as the brother of a baron, was not molested, George Percy, the brother of an earl, was if possible less so. Perhaps he was praised!

Whatever John Chamberlain knew about what was going on in Virginia and in the Virginia Company, John Smith surely knew more. It is accordingly small wonder that he soon began to turn to other objectives. Bermuda had recently been included in the Virginia Charter, for instance, and on November 25, 1612, it was sold to a group of London merchants. Since only one of these seems to have been at all intimately acquainted with John Smith (George Barkley, who had traveled in Tartary), and since Smith can hardly have had any money to invest in a developmental scheme at the time, it is not surprising that he was not associated with the group. At the same time, it is apparent that he was broadening his circle of friends in London. Perhaps his book served as an introduction.

Meanwhile, one of those unnoticed weddings that alter history had taken place in mid-March, 1611. A young member of the Clothworkers' Company named Marmaduke Rawdon, or Roydon, married Elizabeth Thorowgood, a nineteen-year-old heiress. (She brought an enormous dowry, for the times, of ten thousand pounds sterling.) The marriage was blessed with a son in March, 1612, and by March, 1613, Marmaduke, an incipient merchant prince of thirty, was casting about for means to augment his fortune.

John Smith was also casting about, without the financial backing of a wealthy wife. A small book, published with the aid of one or more clergymen and possibly a merchant, in an edition of a thousand copies or so, would neither supply him with an income nor improve his social standing. At about that same time, Sir Ferdinando Gorges, chief promoter of the "North Virginia" colony since the death of Lord Chief Justice Popham, was again interesting himself seriously in that project. Once more, it was the arrival of an Indian at Plymouth, in 1611, which prompted this, but it was three years before Sir Ferdinando got around to doing anything about it.

John Smith could have heard about Gorges's Indian as well as his rumored renewed colonial activities through Samuel Purchas, the success of whose *Pilgrimage* soon opened the road to London for him, and to advancement in the ministry. Certainly, Purchas had the complete story of the voyage not long after Gorges had the Indian. It is therefore possible that John Smith went to Plymouth, as is hinted in a document of uncertain authorship. But if he did go, nothing came of it at the time.

On the other hand, Smith must have run across Marmaduke Rawdon at this point, though just how is not known. Rawdon took in three associates, Captain George Langham (apparently of St. Edmund's Bury, Suffolk — perhaps the contact for John Smith), Master John Buley (of uncertain connections), and Master William Skelton (a merchant adventurer of London). Since Rawdon was a clothworker with side interests in wines and sugar, and Skelton was an adventurer interested in cloth, it is notable that the chief object

of the voyage proposed for John Smith's consideration was whaling!
(Rawdon's nephew later wrote that his uncle's transactions "extended to almost all parts of the world.")

Whatever the main objective, John Smith entered Rawdon's employ, took charge of the voyage, and on March 3, 1614, was again
able to stand on the prow of a ship westward bound. There were
two ships in the "fleet" under Smith, the second one having for
captain a Master Thomas Hunt, whose behavior seems to have
been regrettably similar to that of many other Europeans "out for
gain." The crew totaled forty-five men and boys, and the final plan
was to "make trials of a mine of gold and copper," as well as "to
take whales." If the whales and the trials both failed, then Smith
and his company were to save the cost of the voyage, as it was then
expressed, any way they could — with fish or furs, for instance.
"One Samuel Cramton" was the whaling expert, along with "divers
others." [1]

It was late in April when the two ships arrived off Monhegan Island, a few miles out to sea from West Penobscot Bay, Maine.
Cramton and the other "experts" promptly went to work whaling,
while Smith bethought himself of one or two matters which were
hardly contemplated in the original agreement with Rawdon and
his associates.

Unluckily, the expertise of Cramton and the other whalers hardly
seems to have been adequate. The whales which thronged Maine
waters were of the species called *jubartes* by the French (was
Cramton a Frenchman?), which comprise the largest and fastest
whales known. (Rorqual or finback whale are other names for
them.) They are also the fiercest of all whales, with a rush and a
vitality which make an attack with an old-fashioned harpoon, such
as Cramton probably had, practically useless. Small wonder it was
that Smith wrote that "they could not kill any; they being a kind
of Jubartes, and not the whale that yields fins and oil as we expected."

Whales were not, however, all they had come to seek. There was
also gold. Gold was surely the best of all catchwords for snaring
investors, and Master Thomas Hunt had apparently used it with
Rawdon. As Smith candidly (as usual) wrote, "it was rather the
Master's device to get a voyage that projected it, than any knowl-

NEW ENGLAND 307

edge he had at all of any such matter." This hints that Hunt may have been the one who stirred up interest in the voyage, and perhaps used the magic word "gold" to clinch the matter, although John Smith taxes him with deluding the backers. Yet without it, Smith might not have gotten away at all. Furthermore, it should be said on Hunt's behalf that sounder minds than his went on for years believing tales of "gold and bounty" in all Virginia as in Guiana.

Patience John Smith had, but not to excess. He had rowed or sailed past real gold on the shores of the Potomac; he had not recognized it as such, partly because he had been deceived by fool's gold before. He had halfway believed the Indian reports of Big Sea Waters to the west, not far away. He had tested other hints and rumors. But in the end his pragmatism and skepticism won out. Better it is to make a decent profit out of what you have, than everlastingly to dream of alchemy. Fish and furs, he came to realize before long, were their "guard," the only thing that could save them from failure, financially. While engaged in "saving" the trip with fish and furs, he could explore. Perhaps there might be a site for a colony. Of exploring and colonies there had been no talk with Rawdon and the other merchants.

From John Smith's behavior subsequent to the failure of the whaling it is obvious that he had not only talked with others who had sailed the northeastern coast of North America, but had read whatever was available. Marc Lescarbot's *Histoire de la Nouvelle-France*, for example, published in Paris in 1609, had appeared in part, in that same year, in English, translated at Richard Hakluyt's instigation. Lescarbot vouched for the existence of copper mines in Newfoundland, and suggested that there might be "a golden mine, which is very probable." But, he added, "the first mining and working is to have bread, wine and cattle . . . Our felicity consisteth not in mines, specially of gold and silver, the which serve for nothing in the tillage of the ground . . . and the more [man] hath thereof, the less rest enjoyeth he . . ." John Smith was clearly of the same mind, whether he got the notion from Lescarbot or not.

Monhegan Island, where the ships stood at anchor, was already familiar to sailors, but this did not mean that it was either permanently settled, or even very frequently visited. Sir John Popham's group, which had established a short-lived colony at Sagadahoc in 1607, still continued to send a ship more or less every year, however, and one (under a Captain Williams) was anchored off Pemaquid peninsula when Smith hove to at Monhegan. Since it was only ten or twelve miles away, the Popham ship pre-empted the local market of furs and skins, and the French rumored to be at Mount Desert Island to the east did likewise. Furthermore, the best part of the local fishing season was by then past. Despite hauls of "cor-fish" (salted) and dry fish, called Poor John because it was such poor fare, whaling and fishing had not produced enough to pay expenses. It was necessary to remedy this defect.

Taking advantage of the ideas he had assimilated before he left England, and despite hearsay that two French ships were trading forty leagues to the west, Smith left about thirty-five men with half a dozen locally built fishing boats to keep on fishing, while he took off with eight or nine men in one small boat to range the coast. There is some evidence that he had with him an Indian who had been brought to England the year before.

While the strict order in which he visited (and surveyed) the bays, rivers, and Indian villages is not certain, Smith wrote that "the principal habitation northward we were at was Penobscot." This was unquestionably the Indian settlement marked on Champlain's map of 1607, now called Castine, across the Bay from Belfast, Maine. (Until Samuel Argall wiped out the French toe hold on Mount Desert Island, Maine, there had been French sailors and Jesuits around. In 1614, Smith saw none.)

From Castine John Smith worked southward, surveying. Although he traded for furs, it becomes steadily more apparent that mapping and thinking about a colony were actually uppermost in his thoughts. He has left little about the furs, but a great deal about maps. The six or seven which he had already seen, for instance, he describes as so different between themselves and so erroneous in their depiction of the coast that they did him "no more good than so much waste paper," although, he adds with wry humor, "they cost me more." However, he confesses that "it may be it was not my chance to see the best."

In any event, Smith decided to sketch out the region for himself:

. . . lest others may be deceived as I was, or through dangerous ignorance hazard themselves as I did, I have drawn a map from point to point, isle to isle, and harbor to harbor, with the soundings, sands, rocks, and landmarks, as I passed close aboard the shore in a little boat.

What is most remarkable about Smith's map, which will be discussed in the next chapter, is what a wealth of detail it shows, despite his further statement:

although there be many things to be observed, which the haste of other affairs did cause me to omit; for being sent more to get present commodities, than knowledge of any discoveries for any future good, I had not power to search as I would. Yet it will serve to direct any who shall go that way to safe harbors and savages' habitations.

Few men of those days would have taken the time to go exploring as Smith did. Still fewer would have produced such a map.

It is unnecessary to follow Smith's voyage in detail. His record is brief, and because of haste does not contain that amount of ethnological information which characterizes his similar narrations regarding Virginia. Yet his description of the coastline is so applicable even today that it is possible to follow his route without difficulty.

Noting first that the region to the east of Penobscot Bay was inhabited by the Micmacs, Indian invaders from Nova Scotia, Smith crossed the Bay to Mecaddacut, now Camden, nestling at the foot of Mount Battie, just as described in his account. Here he was in the territory of the Bashabes of Penobscot, a local overlord, less despotical than Powhatan, who was recognized as the chief of the sachems (possibly pronounced *sawkem*), or sagamores, of the Abnakis who then populated the region. (A third tribe of Indians, the Maliseets or Etchemins, lived farther to the west, on into modern New Hampshire.)

Bartholomew Gosnold, who died in Virginia, had first sighted land somewhere near here a dozen years before, but John Smith obviously did not know just where. He therefore merely sailed or rowed his boat out to sea, hugging the coast for better views and perhaps to stop and exchange a few difficult remarks with the Indians, and to trade. (Abnaki and Maliseet were both related, and basically similar, to the Powhatan language of Virginia.) One by one Smith listed the Indians' village-names, many of them still in use, and an occasional river-name. Soon he was at Pemaquid, known to George Waymouth in 1605 and to the Popham expedition of 1607. It is a prominent rocky point, jutting far out into the ocean, a landing place for Englishmen and Americans now for more than three and a half centuries. Farther on he came to the mouth of a great river — the greatest in Maine that empties directly into the sea. This was the Kennebec, which Smith amusingly christened the River Forth, in honor of the Scottish firth near whose shores James I was born.

In this region the aptness of Indian place-names can be particularly noted. Smith's map, for example, shows a village at the mouth of a river with the name Sagadahoc; in the local Indian language it means "mouth of a river." Kennebec, the modern name for the whole river, was entered by Smith as the name of a village up the river, at a point where there is a long "reach," or straight, level stretch. This is precisely what the name means — "Long Level Water" — and Long Reach is the local name for the Kennebec at Bath. It has been at least since 1662. Finally, Smith posted the name *Anmoughcawgin* for a village halfway between Sagadahoc and Kennebec. This is a slight distortion of the Indian *-nahmays -coggin*, which means "a place for curing fish." The name survives in the Androscoggin River, a tributary entering the Kennebec about at the point where Smith placed the village, and where the river widens out.

A little beyond, Smith reached what he described as the "Country of Aucocisco, in the bottom of a large deep Bay, full of many great Isles." This is now the Back Bay of Portland, and the name Smith put down is "perfect" Micmac Indian. It means "Head of the Bay, [with] Mud." As has been written, "No name could better fit the place than this when the ebb-tide has drained it."

A few miles westward, Smith came to a cape which can hardly be other than that named Savage Rock by Bartholomew Gosnold. Smith gives no Indian name for the place — perhaps it had none — but calls it Cape Davies, probably after a poet in England who was a friend of his. But the location on his map suggests Cape

Neddick, and Cape Neddick agrees in description also with Gosnold's Savage Rock: a rock or nubble stands in the midst of a
narrow peninsula, such as is found along the Maine coast only at
this specific point. The name *Neddick*, first recorded twenty-four
years after Smith was there, is distorted from an Indian word for
a solitary, isolated object just such as this. Through that name it
seems possible to tie Gosnold's Rock with John Smith's Point.
Smith himself certainly had no suspicion that he had reached the
point named by his friend back in 1602.

This whole region, Smith learned ("for anything I could perceive"), differed little in language, customs or tribal government —
all being subject to the Bashabes, even as far south as what is today
the Commonwealth of Massachusetts. On he went, surveying,
sketching and naming places, and, it is to be hoped, trading. Soon
he passed Agawam (Ipswich, Massachusetts). Just beyond he came
to a great cape, which he named Cape Tragabigzanda, for the
Greek girl whose slave he had been in Istanbul the year when
Gosnold was exploring from Cape Neddick to Cape Cod. (It is
perhaps just as well the name did not stick.) And soon he entered
Massachusetts Bay.

John Smith's explorations here had a significance not then —
and seldom since — realized. In spite of all the busyness of previous
sailors and explorers, no one had yet ransacked the coast for information with an eye to planting a colony there. But with Smith,
as he poked about with the prow of his capering boat, his enthusiasm waxed, as poets say, mightily.

Massachusetts (Natick Indian for "At the Great Hill") was the
country, "of another language, humor and condition," which John
Smith called "the Paradise of all those parts." Pertinently, he
added:

> . . . here are many isles all planted with corn; groves
> [small woods], mulberries, savage gardens, and good har-
> bors: . . . We found the people in those parts very kind;
> but in their fury no less valiant. For, upon a quarrel we
> had with one of them, he only with three others, crossed
> the harbor of Quonahasset [Cohasset] to certain rocks
> whereby we must pass; and there let fly their arrows for
> our shot, till we were out of danger.

It was many years before the English took over Quonahasset.

Twenty-odd miles beyond, John Smith came to another Indian village. In his own words:

> Then you come to Accomack, an excellent good harbor, good land; and no want of anything but industrious people. After much kindness, upon a small occasion [over nothing] we fought — also with forty or fifty of those. Though some were hurt, and some slain, yet within an hour after, they became friends.

True Englishman of his time, John Smith was always ready to make friends "when the hurly-burly's done, when the battle's lost and won." Especially when the others lost.

Accomac ("Across the Water") and neighboring Patuxet ("Little Falls") together equal the most famous place in America, north of Mexico. In English the site is called Plymouth. And John Smith gave the Rock its name. Or, if we want to believe Smith literally, Prince Charles, the later "Martyr King," so baptized it.

Beyond Accomac (or Plymouth), John Smith followed Bartholomew Gosnold's invisible traces south. His route was closer to the shore, but it was substantially the same as Gosnold's as far as the bottom of Cape Cod Bay, where he found the Indian village of Chawum — a village which apparently escaped the eye of Gosnold completely. From there he cut across the bay to the Cape, where he noted the Indian village of Pawmet, seven miles more or less southeast of modern Provincetown.

Rounding Cape Cod in the vanished wake of Gosnold's ship the *Concord* — it "is only a headland of high hills of sand overgrown with shrubby pines, hurts [cranberries], and such trash," he wrote — Smith observed the excellent harbor "for all weathers" which he called Milford Haven (Provincetown Harbor). Beyond, on the ocean side of the Cape, he took his boat as far south as the "Isle of Nauset," the swampy region southeast of modern Eastham. That was the limit of his exploring. John Smith turned north again, for Monhegan.

As soon as he reached his ship, Smith loaded the furs he had gotten by trading (eleven hundred beaver skins, a hundred martens and nearly as many otter), and the whale oil and cor-fish his men had prepared, and sailed for England. It was July 18, 1614.[2]

Unhappily, because John Smith trusted his fellow captain, Master Thomas Hunt, he left him behind to dry fish, and sail with it directly to Spain, where there was a market for Poor John. Hunt not only did what he was supposed to do, but added the detail of following Smith's route down into Cape Cod Bay, where he raided the coast and kidnapped twenty-four Indians. These he took to Spain, to sell as slaves. Hunt's treachery lived on in Indian memory until the Pilgrims landed on Cape Cod six years later.

In retrospect, when he heard of this, Smith wrote that Hunt had seconded Smith's idea of starting a colony in the region called Massachusetts, but that he tried to steal his maps and logbook,

> and so to leave me alone in a desolate isle, to the fury of famine, and all other extremities, lest I should have acquainted Sir Thomas Smythe, my honorable good friend, and the Council of Virginia, to the end [that] he and his associates might secretly engross it [i.e., make the plan theirs], ere it was known to the State.

Although this seems rather exaggerated, Sir Ferdinando Gorges independently hints that something of the sort must have been in Hunt's mind. Hunt, according to Sir Ferdinando, was "a worthless fellow of our nation, set out by certain merchants for love of gain," who violated the Indians' trust in the manner described. That the man was capable of attempting to ruin Indian-English relations after failing to get Smith out of his way seems evident. That is the main point, regardless of the Elizabethan flamboyance of the accounts.

Meanwhile, Gorges himself, inspired by the lone Indian brought back from the Cape Cod area in 1611 by Captain Edward Harlow (of the Popham Colony of 1607) and Nicholas Hobson, persuaded some associates to finance an expedition in 1614. Harlow and Hobson would take the Indian back to Cape Cod, and all three would hunt for gold — with the Indian pointing the way. (Gold was the Indian's lure, to get his captors to take him home.) They left England in June, with high hopes. But despite all precautions, the slippery Indian escaped almost as soon as they reached America, and the expedition returned, frustrated, to England.

About the same time, John Smith arrived in Plymouth. It was August 5, 1614. Two things seem to have been on his mind: first, his cargo was inadequate to cover expenses; second, and far more important to him, he had developed a plan for a colony. The former would explain his delay in returning to London; the latter would account for his seeking out Sir Ferdinando, Governor of Plymouth Fort to be sure, but also a leader in the Plymouth Company, which had the "colonial rights" for that part of America. By no means least, Smith was by then at bitter odds with the Virginia Company, and in a very human way he wanted to start a rival colony in the north.

Details of the Harlow-Hobson voyage are virtually limited to the loss of the Indian, and the failure to find gold. They do not tell us the date of the return of the expedition. Nevertheless, it appears that Smith was still in Plymouth when the ship rounded Fishers Nose back into the harbor, for it was the failure of Harlow and Hobson which threw Gorges into the arms of Captain John Smith. That disappointed ex-Virginian brought Sir Ferdinando the very idea which he had been wanting.

Smith, inspired by the name *Nouvelle-France,* came up with *New England,* and laid his plans before Gorges. It may be said that on that day New England was conceived. Six years passed before the Pilgrims gave her birth, but to his dying day, John Smith considered the land that he had named as much his child as the land that he had saved — Virginia.

John Smith was greatly encouraged by his talks with Sir Ferdinando and others of the Plymouth Company. The Company, in turn, got a new grip on life from Smith's evidence of the value of New England. With enthusiasm, it seems, Smith was given assurance "to have the managing their authority in those parts, during my [Smith's] life," and he engaged himself "to undertake it for them." In token of this, he was granted the title of Admiral of New England.

By then it was clear that he must return to London with the goods for which he had bartered trifles in America. The master of his ship, Michael Cooper, soon brought her up the Thames to London, yet there, if Smith's later account of what happened is true in all its details, there were those who "suggested there was no such matter [as furs] to be had in that so bad abandoned country." If there had been anything worth while in it, others would have found it, these people said; therefore they suspected that Smith had gotten the furs by robbing the French in New France or Canada. More important, the merchants who sent him to New England were obviously displeased with Smith's stay in Plymouth, and his conversations with Gorges. They can hardly be blamed.

Cooper and Smith then parted company. Shortly thereafter, Cooper accepted a proffer of a group of London merchants which included Messrs. Rawdon, Langham, et al., and sailed for Monhegan in January, 1615. Fishing was apparently the sole objective of this voyage, although a fleet of four ships was supplied. Virginia Company interests were involved, too, as is shown by the fact that one of the ships took her catch directly from New England to Virginia. But even that rather massive invasion of the Plymouth Company's domain did not stir Gorges and his associates into action on Smith's scheme. Gorges personally sent a ship out to fish, but that returned without profit because of Indian hostility caused by Hunt's razzia down the coast (or, less likely, by Indian tribal wars). The guess can be hazarded that Gorges's ship was possibly the one under the command of Sir Richard Hawkins which carried some fish to Virginia, but the accounts are vague and confused.

In the very days in which Cooper sailed, John Smith was back in Plymouth, bearing two hundred pounds cash for the adventure, obtained from friendly investors in London, and with six gentlemen fully equipped for the voyage and eager to sail with him. Despite the refusal of London merchants to join hands with Plymouth in Smith's New England Venture, some support he had thus found. But then Plymouth itself disappointed him. Not even Gorges was able to raise the rest of the necessary money. Potential investors were ready to send out ships to fish or to trade, or even to hunt for elusive gold mines, but not for colonies.

John Smith's enthusiasm and persistence in the end, "with a labyrinth of trouble," produced results. Gorges pressed the wealthy Dean of Exeter, Dr. Matthew Sutcliffe, to invest, along with a number of Plymouth merchants, and Smith's industry in canvassing the market made up the balance. By summer two ships were ready, one of two hundred, the other of fifty, tons.

The final plan was simple. While the bulk of the crew and passengers were to secure fish, oil (from whales), and whatever other valuable cargo they might, John Smith himself was to settle in some convenient spot, with four gentlemen, eight soldiers, and four others who "were to learn to be sailors." With supplies sufficient to last them the winter, these seventeen men were to form the nucleus of a colony. A relief ship (or more) would follow in 1616 — especially if some vendible cargo was brought back in the large ship.

The names of Smith's associates on this voyage are for the most part of little evident significance, with one or two exceptions. Thomas Dermer (or Dirmer), who was second in command, was new to the scene (so far as is known) but seems to have been a good mariner and a loyal man. Edward Rowcroft (variously spelled), alias Stallings (also variously spelled), had been with John Smith in Virginia, although no mention of him exists in any work by Smith on the Jamestown plantation. A few years later he was killed in Virginia.

Of the remaining gentlemen, Daniel Cage was almost certainly one of the Cages of Suffolk, related to the Gosnolds and long interested in overseas exploration and settlement. Francis Abbot may have been a relative of Jeffrey Abbot, who was with Smith in Virginia and who had been executed for some sort of infraction of Sir Thomas Dale's iron laws about two years after Smith left Jamestown. As for the soldiers and sailors, they are little more than names today, beyond the possibility that a Thomas Watson, listed by Smith, may have been a son or other relative of the Thomas Watson who was a teller of the Exchequer.

Smith states that he had not the means to provide for a larger colonial nucleus — probably including funds to buy supplies. Yet he felt confident that he could survive the winter, with the aid of a sachem, or chief, whose name has been preserved in a remarkable disarray of forms, ranging from Tahanedo through Dehanida to Nahanada. (Smith even calls him Dohoday!) Tahanedo had been kidnapped by George Waymouth in 1605, was one of the five Indians whose part in the final colonization of America is unquestioned, and had been returned to his native shores by the Popham colony in 1606. He had last been seen or heard of in 1607, but the absence of news did not deter John Smith. Unless the man was dead, Smith would use him. Not only that, Smith would live with Tahanedo's tribe. (In another account, Smith mentions another Indian called Tantum, whom he "set on shore at Cape Cod." This statement, parenthetically added in 1624, seems unsupported by any other reference.)

Thus making up in plans and hopes for shortages in factual assets, John Smith set out once more, bravely, for America. Dermer, in the smaller ship, rapidly vanished into the limitless Atlantic. Smith, lumbering behind, would meet him at "the landfall for Pemaquid" — Monhegan, which means *"The* Island" in Micmac.[3]

But Fate had not so decreed. John Smith's "big ship" was far from soundly built. The surge of the Atlantic proved too much for her timbers, and before she had plowed a hundred and twenty leagues from Plymouth, her masts snapped, her sails and gear went overboard, and "only her sprit sail remained to spoon before the wind." In such conditions, John Smith had no choice but to rig up a jury mast to take them back to Plymouth, "or founder in the seas."

Although Sir Ferdinando Gorges can hardly have been pleased over this turn of events, his faith in Smith and his idea does not seem to have weakened. Another ship was put in order, the remainder of the provisions for the colonizing effort stowed on board, and John Smith set sail once more in what he calls a "small bark of sixty tons," with thirty men, "which were the 16 before named, and 14 other sailors for the ship." The date was June 24, 1615.

The prospective colonists did not get far. Somewhere out on the broad Atlantic, an English pirate named Fry sighted the lonely little ship and gave chase. According to a later account, when the case was investigated officially, the pirate pursued them for two days, while Smith's shipmaster, the master's mate, and the pilot importuned Smith to yield. Smith was obdurate. And despite the fact that the pirate ship was more than twice the size of Smith's bark, had thirty-six pieces of ordnance against Smith's four "guns," and enjoyed a crew of eighty (Smith had fourteen) of whom forty or fifty were "master" gunners, the heavy seas made it impossible for the pirates to board Smith.

But gold did the trick — or so it was rumored. Smith's officers agreed to yield, over Smith's protests, and an agreement was reached which not even the official examination makes clear. Whatever it was, this made it possible for some of the pirates to board Smith's ship — Smith refusing the while to come out of his cabin to meet them — and having found nothing of value, to inquire about the ship's destination, purpose, and the like. This inquiry revealed the fact that Smith was the captain, if that was not known already. Thereupon the boarding party admitted that many of them had been Smith's own sailors (it is not stated where), that the pirates were "in combustion among themselves" (a picturesque way of saying they were wrangling), that they had stolen the ship in Tunis, and that if Smith would take charge they would add their ship to his and make a fleet to sail wherever he wanted to go. Smith remained in his cabin.

Apparently the pirates then returned to their ship and sailed away, for nothing further is reported about them. Soon thereafter, however, as Smith approached the Bay of Horta, Fayal, in the Azores, two French pirates caught up with him and commanded him to surrender. His officers, as before, begged Smith to strike his topsail, courageously

> alleging they [the pirates] were Turks, and would make them all slaves; or Frenchmen, and would throw them all overboard if they shot but a piece [a gun]; and that they were entertained [hired] to fish, and not to fight.

Smith's (typical) answer was that he would blow up the ship sooner than yield. Shots were exchanged, but Smith got away.

They had sailed but a day according to the official examination, however, when four French "men-of-war" closed in on them near the Island of Flores. Once more the officers begged Smith to surrender. Otherwise, they said, "there was nothing but ruin by fighting." A parley evidently followed, during which Smith, thanks to his knowledge of French, was able to find out that the captain, a Monsieur Poyrune according to Smith, would give them fair quarter, since the "men-of-war" were Protestant vessels of La Rochelle (a Huguenot stronghold). Smith also learned that they had the French King's commission only to take Spaniards, Portuguese, and pirates. Under these circumstances, he chose to be discreet, and the next day the Frenchmen boarded his ship.

Great confusion followed, if the surviving account is to be trusted.

(It was clearly altered when it was reprinted eight years after its first appearance.) Smith seems to have been called aboard the French flagship to show his credentials, while French sailors took what they wanted from the English ship, including virtually its entire crew. These were dispersed among the French ships, where they remained five or six days. During that time, the number of French ships was increased to eight or nine — if this is not mere exaggeration in the account — and the entire flotilla amused itself chasing all the ships they saw — which is quite believable.

In the end, regardless of the accuracy (or lack thereof) of these details, the Frenchmen restored the Englishmen to their ship, along with their possessions, victuals, and provisions for the colony. Only their weapons they kept. Even so, Smith was determined to sail on to New England, or at least to Newfoundland, where he hoped to pick up what he needed. His pusillanimous officers, however, declared that they had had enough. They were going to sail to England, not to America. But "those that were soldiers [i.e., the "brave men and true"] concluded with their Captain's resolution," and agreed to carry on. They wanted only the rest of their equipment, which the Frenchmen had promised to restore.

Smith apparently then got a boat from the French and went back to the French ships to try to collect everything. Meanwhile, bad weather blew up, resulting in a minor accident, which gave the by now mutinous English shipmaster his opportunity. He called on Smith to return on board at once, or he would sail off without him. Smith shouted back for them to send him a boat. The master lied, calling out that their boat was split, and that Smith would have to get a French boat to take him over. Smith answered that he could not command the French to do his bidding. With that, Smith's master allowed his bark to drift astern. During the night, then, he slipped away. England was his goal.

Smith was left on the French ship, alone, "in his cap, breeches, and waistcoat." New England must wait again, for no colony was destined to be founded that year, nor the next, nor the next. John Smith was a captive on a French "man-of-war." [4]

## CHAPTER 22

## "A MAN NOTED OF NOT GOOD HAP BY SEA"

JOHN SMITH was as free in naming ships "men-of-war" as Shakespeare was chary. Any vessel that carried armament sufficient for self-protection deserved a title, Smith seems to have thought, and the more belligerent the better. In this case, the "man-of-war" was the good ship *Don de Dieu,* whose captain was François Perret, Sieur du Poiron (Smith's "Poyrune"). Its burden was one hundred and fifty tons, ten more than Smith guessed, and it carried eighty "sailors and mariners," a complement which may or may not have been expanded to ninety by the time John Smith was caught on board.

Du Poiron had sailed on June 29, 1615, new style, on what pretended to be a commercial voyage, with iron, steel, linen, and hardware for his freight. Where he was going, or said he was going, is not indicated in the three surviving documents which mention him. His real objective, however, seems to have been piracy, masked under letters of marque. John Smith was one of the first potential victims he spotted.

The French corsair obviously thought Smith's bark was a privateer. In a report later made to the French Admiralty office in Luçon (whose bishop, Richelieu, would one day be named Cardinal), it was described as armed with four heavy guns, several muskets, and other arms. The surviving abstracts mention no names, but merely add that du Poiron "is said to have attacked and taken, and later released" the ship. That John Smith was kept on board the corsair is not even hinted.

Smith did not sail from Plymouth until June 24, which corresponded to July 4 in the French calendar. Du Poiron passed São

Miguel about July 20. He hung around between there and Pico for two weeks, but by August 5 he was "at the Islands of Flores and Corvo," where on that date he entered into a partnership with at least two other ships to remain at sea together for six months. "Being together" there, for fifteen days, the corsair fleet encountered John Smith's ship. That Smith says that there were then eight or nine ships in the fleet is unimportant, for du Poiron may have had other ships with him which were not in the partnership.

After Smith was deserted by his men, du Poiron kept hoping to intercept some ships from the Spanish West Indies fleet. Meanwhile, some of the nonpartner ships took off, Smith says, but du Poiron continued in the neighborhood of Fayal. Unable to get ashore, Smith employed his time writing a book about his experiences in New England. This work, soon to be published under the title of *A description of New England,* has been drawn on for the preceding chapter as well as this one.

The weather was not good, and the *Don de Dieu* was eventually separated from all the other ships. Some time thereafter, an English pirate named Barra caught up with the Frenchman. Whatever Barra's motives were, he fell into a trap. Du Poiron put one of his own crew aboard and forced him to sail to Brouage, the most famous salt mart in France, just south of La Rochelle. This was but the beginning, but of the several piratical attacks mentioned by Smith or in the French records only one has direct bearing on Captain John.

This was the capture of what Smith calls "a poor carvel of Brazil." Du Poiron specifies that it was a caravel of seventy tons, under the command of a Portuguese captain, and that he encountered it thirty leagues* from the Azores. The Portuguese captain made the mistake of firing two shots at du Poiron, which brought on a "small fight," as Smith puts it. Several were wounded on both sides, but in the end the Frenchman took her, Smith writes, "with three hundred and seventy chests of sugar, one hundred hides, and thirty thousand reales of eight."

Du Poiron put his lieutenant, André Prevost, Sieur du Pons, on this ship, and sent him off to the roads of l'Aiguillon, just north of

* The French league of the time was just under three and a half miles (5.555 modern kilometers).

La Rochelle, where he unloaded ship on October 23. Smith writes that they took a West Indiaman next, which is confirmed in French documents, and that du Poiron often broke his promise to put Smith ashore at the Azores, or to let him board and sail off in the next ship he took and released. But in the end the Frenchman at last was persuaded that Smith "should go for France in the carvel of sugar; himself resolved still to keep the seas."

Once on board the smaller ship, John Smith notes only one further encounter (with two more West Indiamen) before "with much ado, we arrived at the Gulion [l'Aiguillon], not far from Rochelle." The French account gives the date, as mentioned above.

Smith's trials were not over yet, however, for the lieutenant kept him prisoner for five or six days in the caravel. Perhaps with some reason. He was probably afraid that if he released Smith, Smith would tell what had really happened on the voyage, the description of which in French Admiralty records is patently subdued with intent to deceive.

To justify himself, Lieutenant du Pons accused Smith of responsibility for Samuel Argall's raid on the French settlement in Maine, in 1613, but he agreed to make no further complaint if Smith would subscribe to a document absolving him and du Poiron of any culpable acts — in Smith's words, to "give them a discharge before the Judge of the Admiralty." The alternative, it was hinted, was prison, "or a worse mischief."

To prevent both these undesirables, Smith took advantage of a stormy night, when all hands were below, to creep into the ship's boat. This he set adrift, with his manuscript safe from the weather but with no other oar than a half-pike that was handy, and attempted to make "Rat Isle" (Ile de Ré, Ratis Insula in Latin), across the Breton Strait from l'Aiguillon, but only a stone's throw from La Pallice and the port of La Rochelle.

The current swept him out to sea. The wind and tide swept him back. In the darkness and rain, sculling and bailing until he was exhausted, John Smith shot through the narrow passage between La Pallice and Sablanceaux and fifteen miles beyond, where he was driven aground on "an oozy isle by Charowne [the Charente river]." * There, when morning came, some men out fowling found

* Possibly this was the Ile d'Aix, where Napoleon said farewell to France two centuries later (July 15, 1815).

him, "near drowned, and half dead, with water, cold and hunger."
With their help, and after selling the ship's boat, Smith got to La
Rochelle, where excited voices told him that the Sieur du Poiron's
ship had been split by the storm, and the captain drowned — as is
confirmed by the records. Smith wasted little time with this, but
went to the Admiralty office in La Rochelle, to complain.

He heard many "good words and fair promises," but little else,
until he ran across some of his companions on the voyage from the
Azores. They had thought him dead, but a very lively John Smith
had them arrested, to force testimony from them that he was telling
the truth. This accomplished, Smith received a document, "from
under the judge's hand," the tenor or meaning of which is not clear.
Nevertheless, it is patent that Smith expected to get some share
of the Brazilian booty in recompense for his unlawful detention.

Clearly, Smith had legal advice from some French lawyer, yet he
characteristically conceals this detail. He only mentions the "boun-
tiful" assistance of a "Madam Chanoyes at Rochelle," who is otherwise unidentified. The likelihood — there is no plausible alternative — that this is a misprint for *Chaurroy,* the name of a family of
lawyers in La Rochelle at the time, points to what sort of help he
may have received. And he even seems to have been prompted by
the same family to present his "order of justice" to Sir Thomas
Edmondes, the English Ambassador, to get action. The only problem was to locate that dedicated diplomatist.

In October, however, word was already around that the Spanish
Infanta, Anne of Austria, future Queen to Louis XIII, would come
to Bordeaux to be married. John Smith made inquiries, and by
November learned that Sir Thomas Edmondes was there, to take
part in the festivities. This happy accident facilitated Smith's meeting the Ambassador, and thus at Bordeaux, on November 21, 1615,
John Smith was among the thousands who cheered the entry into
France of the mother-to-be of Louis XIV. Four days later the King,
aged fourteen, married the Infanta, five days his senior.

While he was in Bordeaux, Smith not only presented his legal
papers to the Ambassador, but also sensibly had them gone over
by French lawyers for validity. There, too, he ran across the whaling expert who had gone to New England with him in 1614, Master
Samuel Cramton. And Cramton did what he could to help Smith
out. Indeed, Smith later went out of his way to state that he was

more beholden to Cramton, Mme. "Chanoyes," the lawyers, and the survivors of the storm at La Rochelle "than all the rest of my countrymen I met in France." Perhaps the Ambassador helped with promises only.

In any event, Smith apparently succeeded in laying legal claim to some share of the moneys realized from the sale of three thousand six hundred crowns' worth of merchandise salvaged from the Brazilian ship — nine hundred pounds sterling, in terms of English coin at the time. Nevertheless, Smith had his doubts about getting his hands on any of it. Booty from a pirate ship or a West Indiaman was legitimate French prize money. What an Englishman could get out of it was questionable. So the best Smith could do was to leave the matter in the hands of the lawyers, and return to England. There is no evidence that he ever got a penny.[1]

The economic aspects of John Smith's career, in fact, are baffling. If great nobles at times kept accurate account of income and outgo, men of the impecuniousness of John Smith seem to have paid no attention either to money or to where they got it. Smith's real estate in Lincolnshire could not possibly have fed and clothed him except while he was on that property, and the "royalties" from the pirated book made out of his letter of 1608, or even the slim volume of 1612, if anything at all, could not have exceeded a mere pittance. Consequently, when he returned to England by way of Plymouth early in December, 1615, he must have dedicated himself immediately to finding means to live.

Sir Ferdinando Gorges may by then have presumed that Smith was dead. Certainly the officers who had left him at the mercy of the French did. Taking his clothes, books, instruments, arms, and everything he had, they split the loot between them. This was an injury to be borne, or to be remedied by law; but when the insult was added of justifying by lies their action in running away, Smith raged. Some he had thrown in prison, while the others testified before the Vice-Admiral of Devonshire, Sir Lewis Stucley — turned state's evidence, so to speak. How much of his property Smith retrieved is not known. Gorges and friendly Plymouth merchants conceivably made up the difference, at least in part.

John Smith had not by any means given up, however. Hardly had he set foot on the Barbican, or on Plymouth's famous Hoe, than he began laying plans for another New England voyage. His second ship had "come home well fraught in August, and all her men well." Yet Gorges and the Plymouth merchants were not happy. Smith was put off—"all their great promises nothing but air." Disappointed but not disillusioned, he went to London.

As we know, John Smith had whiled away the hours of his captivity on du Poiron's ship writing down what he remembered about his 1614 voyage as well as the voyage which was just ending. Part of the lack of sequence in the product may be due to the circumstances surrounding its composition, and part may be due to sheets of paper damaged in carrying and rewritten later. But whatever its condition, Smith still had the manuscript with him, and six weeks to two months or so after his escape, presented it to someone in London as a propaganda pamphlet for New England. Curiously, only then had John Smith found his true métier.

Who Smith's friends and backers were in London is not known in detail. Nevertheless, he calls Sir Thomas Smythe an "honorable good friend." There was also Samuel Purchas, by then a man of certain importance and unquestionably close to Smith. The Berties were still there, and a great new circle of friends and admirers soon gathered around. His unfaltering, indeed expanding, enthusiasm for New England gave vitality to his words, as he came to recognize his own worth in the colonial enterprise. His pen is dipped in self-confidence and races on with mounting ease and flamboyance. From apologist for his past career, John Smith begins to emerge in 1616 as an unblushing promoter. He begins to pour words into the printing presses as Sir Thomas Smythe and other adventurers poured money into the bottomless needs of colonial beginnings.

The new John Smith appears in the dedication of his *Description of New England* to King James's Privy Council—the "Cabinet" that advised His Majesty on affairs of state. This dedication was written while he was on board the *Don de Dieu*. When he got to London, he went one step higher. Prince Henry, who had died four years before, had been an enthusiastic supporter of the Virginia Venture. Prince Charles, his surviving brother, turned fifteen years of age in January, 1616, when Smith was surely back in London. He, Smith seems to have thought, might be persuaded to regard New England as Henry had Virginia. So Smith ventured to dedicate his new book to Charles, with the additional touch of assuring some response by asking him to accept a newly drawn map, and "please to change their barbarous [place-]names for such English, as posterity may say, Prince Charles was their godfather." This favor Prince Charles deigned to grant. Other favors, hinted at by John Smith, remained favors hinted at.

Since the *Description* was entered for publication at Stationers' Hall on June 3, 1616, it is obvious that the map to accompany it was at least being drawn by then. Somewhere between January and June, 1616, therefore, John Smith was going over his sketches with the engraver, guiding the expert's hand in delineating the coast of New England. And while the final result of this collaboration shows far less detail than appears in Smith's map of Virginia, it is nevertheless remarkably accurate, considering the short surveying-time at Smith's disposal in 1614. The distances generally correspond with those known to be true today, and the magnetic declination reflected in the "true north" as drawn (about 14° 30′ West) is close to that deduced for 1615 from available scientific data (11° 36′ West). One thing appears clear: Smith had more mental tranquillity while sketching and surveying the New England coast than he had in the Chesapeake Bay area. His compass readings are consistent, all owing for local magnetic disturbances.

In addition to the map of the coast, a "portraiture" of Smith himself was thought fit to embellish the "illustration" of the book. The engraving of map and portrait alike was entrusted to Simon van de Passe, the youngest son of the renowned Crispin van de Passe of Utrecht, who had settled in England about the time John Smith was struggling to get back to New England in 1615. Simon van de Passe's technique was perhaps finer than that of the Englishman, William Hole, who had done such a notable job with Smith's *Map of Virginia*. Partly for this reason, the map of New England, for all its deficiency in detail, is at least as illustrative. Its importance is usually overlooked because of Smith's portrait which, with its "frame" and John Davies' bit of verse, takes up a striking eighth of the engraving.

Careful examination of the earliest impressions of van de Passe's map seems to hint that he may have been the contact who found the publisher for John Smith's book. In the lower left-hand corner, beneath a clear "Simon Pasaeus sculpsit," the name of Robert Clerke is uncomfortably squeezed. If this obvious afterthought means that van de Passe suggested Clerke as publisher, it is the engraver's truly greatest gift to Smith. Robert Clerke was the son of one John Clerke of St. Giles in the Fields and had been admitted free of the Stationers' Company in January, 1605. John Smith's *Description* is the only book he is known to have published. Whether van de Passe had anything to do with it or not, Clerke's publishing of the book in London apparently broke the ice. John Smith had no need to resort to Oxford again.

The actual printer — the one who had the type — was Humphrey Lownes, a master printer and on occasion Warden of the Stationers' Company. It was in this capacity that Lownes not only printed the book, but also authorized its appearance. And finally George Low acted as printer of the map, and was presumably in some way responsible for its availability to the trade and to the public. (Both Lownes and Low were investors in the Virginia Company in 1609.) While there is nothing to indicate that more than the usual number of copies of the book were printed — 1000 to 1250 — Smith hints that eventually several times that number of copies of the map were struck off.

It is evident that Lownes and Low were as interested as Smith himself in putting out the most eloquent possible propaganda for New England. Not only was the accompanying map done by one of the best engravers, but a prominent poet wrote verses for Smith's portrait, and for the first time a book of Smith's was dignified by "commendatory verses" — more doggerel than poetry, perhaps — such as were commonly prefixed to prose treatises. Seven such appear at the beginning of the book (one by the author of the octet beneath the portrait), and two more are appended at the end, probably to fill up a blank sheet or two. All these authors are new names in John Smith's life.

How John Smith met these people, and how they were persuaded to write poems in praise of him (or his work), is not known. Verses of this sort were so common that the details are unimportant. At the same time, some indication of the identity of the writers may be illuminating.

One of these was R. Gunnell, who must have been Robert Gunnel, an M.A. from Cambridge in 1587. Robert was evidently related to James Gonneld, or Gunnel, Master of the Stationers' Company when Smith's printer, Humphrey Lownes, was an apprentice. Such a tie would be sufficient to persuade him to write his ten lines of rhyming couplets, urging Smith on to New England, to "Return as Jason with a fleece of gold."

Then, perhaps through Gunnel, perhaps through Lownes, George Wither of Lincoln's Inn was inspired to commend Smith and New England. Wither was of independent mind — which won him stretches in prison from time to time — and praise and encouragement from his satirical pen was worth while.

An associate of Wither's, John Davies of Hereford, sometimes called the "most famous penman of his day," was even more taken by John Smith and his experiences and plans. Not only did he write eight lines to put under Smith's portrait, but he also opened the group of commendatory verses with a stanza that called attention to the troubles Smith was having with past associates and potential investors. The line in the portrait-verses, "thou art Brasse without, but Golde within," is worth quoting for its sincerity and aptness.

These were the outsiders who wrote on Smith's behalf. In addition, Nicholas Smith, a teacher who appears to have been John Smith's cousin, worked out an acrostic on John Smith's name, while various soldiers who had served under him rounded out the poetic endorsements. None of it was great poetry, but occasional lines were much to the point. All in all, the book widened Smith's group of friends, at the same time that it gave him tangible sales arguments to present to men who might invest in his project. The *Description* was thus entered for publication on June 3, 1616 and printing was completed on June 18. A small quarto volume of sixty-odd pages, it was easy to handle and to carry around.[2]

In the meantime, Sir Thomas Dale, Governor of Virginia in fact if not in name, returned to England. His reign, terroristic for all it had established some sort of discipline in the colony, was over. It was followed by a reign of systematic robbery — by Samuel Argall — but that was over the horizon so far as John Smith was concerned. Smith's business when Dale's ship finally came up the Thames in mid-June was with the unexpected arrival of Pocahontas, his guardian angel and benefactress.

Pocahontas had been kidnapped by Argall, held as a hostage by despot Dale (Powhatan could have learned a few things from him), and then courted by John Rolfe, a widower ten or twelve years older than herself. Rolfe, regardless of otherwise sterling qualities, suffered as only a righteous Puritan could over his love for a girl whose skin was not white and whose morality was heathen. His first wife had died four years before. The lack of a mate and the physical appeal of Pocahontas tortured him. At last Rolfe sat himself down to address a remarkable letter to Sir Thomas Dale. He wanted the Governor to consent to his marrying the Indian "Princess."

Rolfe's letter was a long one, far too long for full quotation, yet some of the thoughts it voices are pertinent to any study of Englishman and Indian in 1616, and the years before and after. God disapproves, Rolfe wrote, of marrying "strange" wives. He has therefore looked about "warily and with circumspection, into the grounds and principal agitations which thus should provoke me to be in love with one, whose education hath been rude, her manners barbarous, her generation cursed, and so discrepant in all nutriture" from himself that he had decided that his love for Pocahontas was a wicked instigation "hatched" by the devil. But in the end he came to the conclusion that everything was all right and pure, and he humbly submitted himself to love's call — for God's glory, Sir Thomas Dale's honor, "our Country's good, the benefit of this Plantation, and for the converting [of] an irregenerate to regeneration, which I beseech God to grant for his dear son Christ Jesus' sake." Perhaps this explains why men have always romanticized about the love of Pocahontas for John Smith, not the love of John Rolfe for Pocahontas.

Smith's first step when he heard of Pocahontas's arrival in London was to address a "little book," a formal epistle or memorial, to Queen Anne, through which he "made her qualities known to the Queen's most excellent Majesty and her Court." Whether or not the surviving abstract of this is even in part verbatim is unimportant. Its spirit shows that John Smith cherished a sincere brotherly, if not fatherly, affection for the daughter of Powhatan, and wished to tell the Queen to how great an extent Jamestown was in her debt. One passage deserves quotation because it contains the earliest account we have of how Pocahontas directly saved Smith's life, and indirectly that of the colony:

> After some six weeks [actually, more than four] fatting amongst those Savage Courtiers, at the minute of my execution she hazarded the beating out of her own brains to save mine; and not only that, but so prevailed with her father, that I was safely conducted to Jamestown; where I found about eight and thirty miserable, poor and sick creatures, to keep possession of all those large territories of Virginia. Such was the weakness of this poor Commonwealth, as had the Savages not fed us, we directly had starved. And this relief, most gracious Queen, was commonly brought us by this Lady Pocahontas.

After further details of how, and how often, Pocahontas interceded for the colony and helped preserve it, Smith goes on to suggest that through Pocahontas the kingdom of Great Britain may "rightly have a Kingdom" in Virginia, but that, spurned, she might forget her love for England and Christianity. With the Queen's aid, he added, Pocahontas could well be able to bring about what "Your Majesty and all the King's honest subjects most earnestly desire."

The contrast between Smith's realistic and honest approach to the matter of relations between the Despot of Tidewater Virginia and the English thorn in his side, and the specious arguments with which the Virginia Company sought to show that Powhatan had voluntarily subjected himself to British rule, is striking. Indeed, the Company's *True Declaration* stated that Powhatan had accepted subordination by accepting a copper crown from Newport — a crown which he did not want. John Smith showed the way to peace, understanding, so far as that was possible, and cooperation. The mentality of the lords and magnates, and Sir Thomas Smythe, was the way to domination, resistance, and the pathetic war to the death that inevitably followed.

John Smith was painfully preoccupied with securing backing for another voyage to New England when John Rolfe and Pocahontas turned up in London. Even if he had not been, there was little he could have done for them. He had neither money nor influence. The Virginia Company itself seems to have contributed to the

proper maintenance of the couple and their child — Great Powhatan's grandchild! — but meagerly. As a result, it is doubtful that
they remained in London for any length of time. Certainly they
were lodged in Brentford, just across the Thames from modern Kew
Gardens, before too long, and there John Smith went to visit them,
accompanied by some friends.

Pocahontas was visibly disturbed when Smith arrived, turned
aside from her guests, and remained silent for so long that Smith,
as he puts it, repented "to himself to have writ [that] she could
speak English." Rolfe and Smith and the others then left her for
a while, "as not seeming well contented," but an hour or two or
three later returned, to find her in a more talkative mood.

Turning to Smith, with tones of reproach, Pocahontas reminded
him of her "courtesies" to him — her help in time of need — and
added:

> You did promise Powhatan what was yours should be
> his, and he the like to you; you called him father, being in
> his land a stranger, and by the same reason so must I do
> you.

The artificial stratification of English society seized Smith's
tongue. Although he well knew what "kingship" meant in Virginia,
he dared not allow Pocahontas to call him father because "she was
a King's daughter."

Pocahontas cut him short. He was not afraid, she said, to come
into Powhatan's country, and cause fear

> in him and all his people (but me), and [yet] fear you here
> I should call you father. I tell you, then, I will; and you
> shall call me child, and so I will be for ever and ever your
> countryman. They did tell us always you were dead, and I
> knew no other till I came to Plymouth. Yet Powhatan did
> command Uttamatomakkin to seek you, and know the
> truth, because your countrymen will lie much.

Part of the success of John Smith's Indian policy shines through
Pocahontas's words. She believed in Smith, as the Indians believed
in him. For Smith did not lie, nor evade issues. Others for fear
or disdain had no regard for what the Indians might think.

Therefore, perhaps in the vain hope that if Smith was alive he might indeed return to Virginia, Powhatan sent his "councilor," Uttamatomakkin, to London to try to find him, and to learn if he were really dead. At the same time, the wily Despot wanted a report on the strength of the enemy — the English. Uttamatomakkin was instructed to take a long stick with him, and cut a notch in it for each person he saw in England. The findings of this census-taking were to be reported back to Powhatan. "He was quickly weary of that task," wrote John Smith.

Uttamatomakkin was instructed also to get Smith (if he found him) to show him God, King James, Queen Anne, and Prince Henry — of whom Smith had said so much. Smith did what he could to explain God, and then added that he had heard that Uttamatomakkin had already seen King James, and would surely see the Queen and Prince in time. The Indian roundly denied having seen James, but when Smith described the circumstances under which the meeting had taken place, he shook his head sadly. "You gave Powhatan a white dog," he said, "which Powhatan fed as himself; but your King gave me nothing, and I am better than your white dog."

Lord De La Warr had Pocahontas and her train, including her humble husband, John Rolfe, under his wing, and John Smith was not only free to pursue his plans for New England — he was undoubtedly expected to. Pocahontas was being presented to the Queen and the Court. She was having her portrait painted. (Simon van de Passe made an engraving from the portrait — another association of the names of Smith and Pocahontas.) There was clearly no need for the rough little Captain to come along, even though graced with the title Admiral of New England.[3]

Smith's hope to bring the Londoners and the West Countrymen together in one glorious campaign to settle a plantation in Maine was lightheaded, to say the least. Merely because a few personal connections of his were willing to risk a few pounds with Gorges's group, Smith had no real grounds for belief that the merchant princes would join in. As he himself put it, a little later, "that had been more than a work for Hercules." The groups were too jealous of each other.

Still, this did not prevent both from sending out a total of eight ships, according to John Smith, between 1615 and 1616. The aim of these ships (these *ventures* would be more accurate) was trading and fishing, not colonization. Although this did not need to interfere with Smith's plans, it did constitute a drain on available capital. As a result, Smith decided to set out for Plymouth again, apparently shortly after seeing Pocahontas.

Smith had dedicated his *Description of New England* not only to Prince Charles but also to the Privy Council, undoubtedly in the hope of official backing, and to "the right worshipful Adventurers for the Country of New England," undoubtedly in the hope of financial backing. Since he got neither kind from this tactful approach, he decided to visit the cities personally. London he had already explored with that objective. Now he added the other cities named in his dedication: Bristol, Exeter, Plymouth, Dartmouth, Barnstaple, Totnes, and so on. (The "and so on" included at least Bodmin, the county town of Cornwall, Penryn, Fowey, Saltash, and Abson.)

The upshot of Smith's trip was that he got a wild promise of a fleet of twenty ships to go with him to New England in 1617. The organization under which these would sail was presumably the "Council for the Second Colony," or "North Virginia Company," dating back to 1606, the legal existence of which might be subject to doubt. But this quibble remained academic since Smith, when he finally arrived in Plymouth in 1617, found a repetition of the delays and evasiveness of 1615. The twenty ships dwindled to three, and the potential colonists from an unnamed number to a "task force" of fifteen. It would have taken a remarkably philosophic head to face such disillusionments with equanimity — a head which would have been quite unsuited for promoting overseas colonies.

About this time, with the chronology again uncertain, Sir Ferdinando Gorges personally sent out a "servant" or acquaintance, a physician by the name of Dr. Richard Vines, "for trade and discovery," or exploration. Furthermore, Vines was to spend the winter there, to determine empirically whether or not the English constitution would survive a season that far north in America. This experiment stamps Gorges as a practical man, despite Smith's apparent conviction, also as a practical man, that Gorges was a visionary.

John Smith fortunately did not hear about this seeming double-dealing on Gorges's part. He would hardly have understood that Gorges, for reasons of character and experience, was less sanguine of temperament than he was. He would undoubtedly have regarded the move as underhanded, where it was mere caution. Clearly, the loss of a small ship with a few men would only have been one of the costs of experiment; the loss of twenty ships, with many men, would have been a catastrophe.

In March, 1617, Samuel Argall had sailed for Virginia to take over the reins of government in so self-centered a fashion that it took great influence at Court, later, to prevent his ruination. (Instead, he was knighted!) Among his associates in financing prospective settlers in Virginia was one John Tradescant, afterwards a friend of Smith's. Smith heard of this in the midst of his preparations, but so far as he was concerned the dispatch of another Governor for Jamestown could have been only an additional prod to move ahead with his own plans for New England. The skein of maneuverings in the southern colony was past the disentangling stage. It was best to hope, and close one's eyes. Perhaps that was what Sir Thomas Smythe was doing . . .

By about that time, however, John Smith's three ships were ready, riding at anchor in Plymouth harbor. A southwester was blowing that pinned Smith and a hundred other mariners in the Sound. It was like the wind that had caught Drake in that same place nearly thirty years before, and threatened to blow the Spanish Armada up the Channel to victory over England. But the contrary wind had died down in time, and Drake could get most of his fleet clear of the land. Not so John Smith. Day after day the tireless blast sang through the trees at Cawsand and Kingsand and on Mount Edgcumbe. Day after day, the ships and barks danced in the Sound. Day after day, John Smith's anxiety rose.

Three months, unbelievably, passed, while no ship moved. Rowboats and skiffs could defy the gale, if they wanted, but no man could sail a ship in the teeth of it. And so the season passed when Smith could get away to New England. When calm breezes once more livened Plymouth harbor, the expedition had already been called off. Against such adversity, Smith was powerless.

A generation before, when Sir Humphrey Gilbert had first projected a settlement in the unnamed domain now called New England, "Southwest winds of God's making and sending" had delayed him, as had other accidents which were not his "fault or negligence." Queen Elizabeth had then, as Gilbert wrote, wished his "stay at home from the personal execution of my intended discovery as a man noted of not good hap by sea." She yielded, nevertheless, upon the persuasion of Sir Francis Walsingham. Sir Ferdinando Gorges was firmer with Captain John Smith. Sir Humphrey Gilbert had died on the voyage which Queen Elizabeth had wanted to forestall. John Smith was kept in England, to fulfill his task of forwarding the fortune of New England.[4]

CHAPTER 23

# CROSSES, CARES, AND GRIEFS

POCAHONTAS died toward the end of March, 1617, before the ship that was taking her back to Virginia passed Gravesend. She had attended the Twelfth Night Masque at Court, and had been unwillingly waiting for more than two months for a favorable wind to waft her home. The penny-pinching Virginia Company that scantily provided for her, yet sought to bolster up its own finances by her presence, had no further need of her.

Despite romantic stories, Pocahontas was not a great beauty, nor did her insignificant size lend that majesty which some have wanted to bestow on her. Yet she undoubtedly radiated the sincerity of her personality, the innate self-possession of her people, and the loyalty of a heart that had not had to learn deceit. With her died any hope that Indian and Englishman could coexist in Powhatan's domain. With her, too, died for that age the fairytale of the Indian Princess. The very place of her burial, traditionally the parish church of St. George, Gravesend, is uncertain. Even John Smith's valedictory to her, sincere though it was, reflects merely the somewhat absurd piety of the age: it was a source of "joy to the beholders to hear and see her make so religious and godly an end."

In those same days, Sir Walter Ralegh, released from the Tower a year before, slipped down the Thames on his way to Guiana — in haste, lest the King countermand his permission. It might have been better had he delayed, but there are many might-have-beens in Ralegh's life. In any event, Ralegh was delayed in Plymouth and did not get away until June 12. Meanwhile John Rolfe stopped there and left his little son, Thomas, with Sir Lewis Stucley, the Vice-Admiral of Devon. Little Thomas was sick too, but he would survive so that many people living today can say they have the blood of Pocahontas in their veins.

Smith's oldest Virginia tie, Captain John Martin, left England then also. Although Smith completely ignored Martin's visit home at that time, he can hardly have failed to hear about it, since Martin succeeded in getting a patent for lands in Virginia such as no other planter ever got, before or after. Martin had done far less than John Smith to promote or to preserve the colony, but such was his stubbornness that he succeeded in purely selfish aims. Smith, laboring for the colony, failed.

Failure had also been his reward from Sir Ferdinando Gorges. A mutual distaste seems to have arisen between the knight and the belligerent Captain. Smith had learned not to trust Gorges's promises. Gorges had learned to question Smith's luck, if not his ability. The deciding factor may have been extraneous — pirate raids on English shipping, for instance — but whatever the immediate cause, "the cord breaketh at the last by the weakest pull," as Sir Francis Bacon had written not long before.

What John Smith did for the next few months is not recorded. Indeed, it is not known just when the break between him and Gorges finally occurred. It is only clear that, despairing of getting another voyage to New England started at the time, Smith took up his pen once more. He had apparently found inspiration in a reference in Hakluyt's *Voyages* to a work by that great mathematician and wizard, Dr. John Dee, which Smith called the *British Monarchy,* and it contained his own slogan for colonization of New England: fish, furs, and trade. Smith set to work in earnest to attract investors and settlers through profits (or at least "saving voyages" — that is, ones with no loss) from fishing and trading, and letting the Indians do the trapping. Gorges, in contrast, seems to have decided that proof that the country could be lived in was more important. The actual settlement which was just below the horizon showed that neither was entirely right.

While John Smith was pulling into some sort of shape a pamphlet designed to promote — in the broadest sense of the word — the factual birth of New England, portentous news began to arrive from America regarding Sir Walter Ralegh's Guiana Venture. Spanish intrigue had seized on Ralegh, and peace-loving James I was ready to sacrifice honor or even freedom for that illusory phantom. By mid-May Ralegh's fate had been sealed by the royal love for peace. Sir Lewis Stucley, whose sense of what was right was too feeble to stand on its own legs, hastened to comply with James's desire. On July 25 he set out for London with Ralegh, his prisoner, and on October 29, 1618, the headsman's axe fulfilled King James's promise to Don Diego Sarmiento de Acuña, Conde de Gondomar.

John Smith, for the moment truly insignificant in the midst of the commotion raised by the decapitation of the last Elizabethan, finished the draft of his pamphlet, and sent it, nicely penned in clear secretarial hand, to Sir Francis Bacon, Lord Chancellor, and newly created Baron Verulam. Politely, if not (for it was impossible for him) subserviently, he discoursed:

> Right Honorable,
> Having no better means to acquaint Your Lordship with my meaning than this paper, the zeal, love and duty [I owe] to God, my country, and your honor, I humbly crave may be my apology . . .

Then, mentioning briefly the nineteen years he has spent learning "what here I write in these few leaves," he suggests that five thousand pounds would be enough to effect settlement in New England, which in turn would greatly facilitate fishing, fur trading, exploration for raw materials, and eventually the building up of a royal navy. England's forests were depleted, America's, untouched. He admits that such a sum has twice been obtained and spent on his project, but the urge for immediate profit bred such "particular humors" that the investors had their way, while he suffered loss and the colonial project suffered wrong. He intimates that Basque, French, and Dutch traders would gladly finance him (a suggestion not without factual support), but he would prefer to serve England — although it was in fighting abroad that he got his captain's title. Therefore he appeals to Bacon, as "a chief Patron" of the state, and as "the greatest favorer of all good designs and their authors."

Smith then presents the case for New England, with a number of statistics incorporated in a sketchy historical background. The statistics may seem odd to modern readers, and the history is suspiciously slanted, but the whole can have been no more misleading in 1618 than is much American promotional "literature" today.

Toward the end of his appeal, his manifesto for the benefit of the State, Smith's personal problems slip in. He begs Bacon not to let his poverty "cause the action [project] to be less respected," for he is not interested in money, beyond what is necessary for the settlement. He will make his living there. But in the interim he must live. He therefore concludes:

> . . . I humbly desire your Honor would be pleased to grace me with the title of your Lordship's servant. Not that I desire to shut up the rest of my days in the chamber of ease and idleness, but that thereby I may be the better countenanced for the prosecution of this my most desired voyage . . .

In short, with Bacon's patronage Smith's book would be read more carefully, and investors would be more ready to loose their purse strings.

Bacon was not interested, if he even troubled to look over the document. In his position, he was the recipient of unnumbered appeals. With another Lord Chancellor, equally busy, John Smith might possibly have gotten somewhere. But Bacon's intellectual make-up, for all its brilliance, had an amoral twist. He did not hesitate to line his pockets with bribes. Smith, having no wherewithal, was unheard.[1]

While he was thus crying in the wilderness, some of Smith's former companions were off fishing and exploring in New England, under the aegis of Sir Ferdinando Gorges. As Captain Edward Brawnde had written from there two years before, so Edward Rowcroft, alias Stallings, wrote now. The letter held nothing of importance, but he promised Smith to meet him "the next spring [1619] in New England." The meeting could not take place, for one reason because Stallings was killed in Virginia in a private quarrel.

Indeed, during the two and a half years between October 29, 1618, when the anonymous voice in the crowd cried, "We have not such another head to be cut off," and May 1, 1621, when the Great Seal of England was taken back from Sir Francis Bacon, "guilty of corruption," John Smith's activities were lost in a court-centered wilderness of mischief. National and international affairs at that time merged into one great problem for King James I.

The Thirty Years' war broke out, involving his daughter Elizabeth and her husband Prince Frederick of the Palatinate; Queen Anne died, and James himself almost succumbed to gallstones, gout, and arthritis; then came the ruin of Frederick at the hands of the Spaniards. James became more and more entangled in direct government due to his personal concept of kingship. Yet he disliked the task so fervidly that he once cried out, "I am not God Almighty!" Undoubtedly the French Ambassador was right when he wrote that old age was carrying James into apprehensions, while vices diminished his intelligence.

The Ambassador from Spain, however, did not waste time describing James. He acted. Having seen to it that Ralegh was executed, he stepped in to run things pertinent to Spanish relations as he saw fit. Buckingham, virtual ruler under James, was no match for him. And thus the sands of governmental things-not-done slipped through the higher fingers toward the outstretched lower hands of Parliament. Commons, unyieldingly anti-Spanish, watched King and Court drift away.

Meanwhile, in Virginia the abuse of power by Captain Samuel Argall was at least one of the causes for new instructions from the Virginia Company, given to Sir George Yeardley in November, 1618. The following April, Sir Thomas Smythe resigned, after twelve years as Treasurer. Sir Edwin Sandys, long a fighting figure in Parliament, stepped into Sir Thomas's shoes. But Argall had slithered away from Jamestown before Yeardley's arrival and was not prosecuted — quite the contrary. Three years later he was rewarded by being knighted, unless he bought the honor. With Argall gone, the first general assembly, or "Parliament," was soon held in Jamestown, from July 30 to August 4, 1619. It was the first democratic assembly held on the continent of America. Significantly, the records of what went on in the Virginia Company survive, at least in large part, beginning with that same year.

Captain John Smith was still an adventurer, or investor, in the Company at that time. Nevertheless, his interest in New England had grown so great that there is no mention of any Virginia Company activity on his part. Following his new bent, he polished the text of his memorial to Bacon, and on December 11, 1620, it was entered for publication under the title *New Englands Trials,* approved by Doctor Thomas Goad, rector of Hadleigh (Suffolk), for the clergy, and Master Humphrey Lownes for the Stationers. It was not dedicated in the usual sense of the word, but was accompanied by a "presentation address" of slightly varying text, with printed headings for various individuals and organizations. Smith himself says that two or three times the usual number of copies were printed, one thousand of which were accompanied by maps of both New England and Virginia. Thirty of the chief London city companies received copies specially imprinted, one of which has survived. Other, uncounted, copies had endorsements dedicating them to the adventurers who had invested their money overseas, "especially to New England," one of which survives, and to individuals (one copy each exist, to Sir Edward Coke and the Earl of Bridgewater, son of Bacon's predecessor as Lord Chancellor). Since there are only these four copies of the book, it is impossible to know what other influential persons or bodies were similarly honored. It is equally impossible to know who paid for the printing.[2]

While dotage in two senses of the word seemed to be seizing on His Britannic Majesty, and a great gulf began to yawn between King and country, a small English community of voluntary religious exiles in Holland was growing restive. Called by various names, they formed the extreme fringe of Protestantism which rejected not only certain aspects of the Anglican Church, but the Church itself. This attitude earned for them the name Separatists, which lingered with other epithets such as "Brownists" until years later they became known as the Pilgrims. Their birthplace was in the country round about Scrooby, in northwestern Lincolnshire, south of Doncaster. Their Dutch asylum was the great and free city of Leiden, then a third as large as London.

Leiden was a tolerant city, and the Separatists were too stanchly Puritan to suffer tolerance. Furthermore, the Dutch had another language and a quite different set of prejudices. The Separatists were aggressive, but so were the Dutch, and these were in the enormous majority. By 1617 it was clear that the community was threatened with absorption into Dutch life, which was a worse fate in their eyes than destruction at the hands of such instruments of

Satan as the Anglican bishops. The only alternative between the Dutch and the Devil was to form a new state, where they might worship their God according to pure Scripture, undefiled by "human inventions."

The catalyzing force which made the year 1617 a climacteric for the Pilgrims is not specifically known. Nevertheless there is a hint in the fact of Elder Brewster's possession of *Good News from Virginia,* by the Puritan minister in Jamestown Colony, Alexander Whitaker, and of two books on silkworms. Silk was a hoped-for commodity in Virginia, and one of the leading Pilgrims was a silk weaver in Leiden. Sir Thomas Dale, bringing enthusiastic reports from Virginia in 1616, and the person of Pocahontas, may have stirred hopeful thoughts in the minds of the unhappy Leiden group. Some logic, at least, seems to attach to this reasoning.

Also in 1617 there was open for settlement, at least on paper, "all the land between the Amazon and the Essequibo," in Guiana, South America. A Robert Harcourt, of County Oxford, had held a patent since 1613 pursuant to his voyage to that territory a few years before. Then, too, 1617 saw Sir Walter Ralegh set out for Guiana. If not Virginia, Guiana was a place where a Puritan state might be set up, to the greater glory of God and the preservation of a sinless life.

Since March, 1607, Sir Edwin Sandys, parliamentary leader and fearless democrat, had been a member of the King's Council for Virginia and its successors. Son of the late Archbishop of York, Sir Edwin was vigorously Protestant, and a Puritan. (His elder brother, incidentally, was landlord of Scrooby manor.) He, if anyone in England, would extend a helping hand to the Pilgrims. He knew, as they did, that the impending end to the truce between Holland and Spain might make Leiden alarmingly dangerous for Protestants in general, not to mention Puritans as extreme as the Separatists.

In 1618, therefore, John Robinson, sole clergyman, and William Brewster, ruling elder, drew up seven *Articles* which summarized the attitude of the Pilgrims toward King James, his Government, and his Church, in the hope that they might be a foundation for negotiations toward transplanting the Leiden group to Virginia. (Guiana had already been dropped.) Since the general tenor of these articles was not overoffensive, Sandys apparently passed them on to a merchant prince, Sir John Wolstenholme, who might be a more acceptable spokesman to King James than himself, and that wealthy knight volunteered to intercede with George Abbot, Archbishop of Canterbury. Abbot, if he was not a Puritan, at least leaned in that direction. In the end, the reaction was favorable enough for it to be proper for Elder Brewster to go to London.

In April of the following year, Sir Edwin Sandys was elected Treasurer of the Virginia Company, with John Ferrar as his deputy. This was anything but pleasing to James I, since Sandys was the leader of the opposition in Parliament. Nevertheless, six weeks later, the Virginia Company acted favorably on a motion of young Theophilus Clinton, Earl of Lincoln, to grant to the Pilgrims a patent of land in the extreme north of the Company's territory. The patent was issued to John Wincob, a servant of the Earl, not to the Separatists. The following February, this patent was superseded by a new one, issued to a Pilgrim adventurer named John Pierce. In this patent, a tract of land near the mouth of the Hudson River was specifically mentioned.

Such was the confused state of the Virginia Company by that time, however, that it was suggested that the Pilgrims wait until a proposed New England Company be formed, and sail under their auspices. King James had refused to permit the Virginia Company to re-elect Sandys as Treasurer, and Sir Thomas Smythe's faction was fighting hard (even literally in the King's bedchamber!) for re-acquisition of control. To add further confusion, the Pilgrims themselves were briefly torn in strife over their new agent, Robert Cushman.

It was at this juncture that Captain John Smith got wind of the Pilgrims and their plan to colonize northern "Virginia." Although there is some possibility that he met one or another of them as early as 1619, it seems more probable that the meeting was in 1620, since there is no mention of the matter in his *New Englands Trials,* of 1620. Whenever it was, no sooner did Smith hear about the project than he wanted to lead the Pilgrims to their Canaan.

There can be no question that this would have been a fortunate arrangement had it not been for total incompatibility of temperament. Smith was so fully persuaded of his own superior ability in colonial enterprise by then that it is not far from certain that he would have brooked no interference from anyone. Such an attitude would not have been tolerated one minute by the Pilgrims, who were moved by religious aims and principles, and who had suffered too much already to compromise with a hard fate. They were a determined people. And since their plans were already laid, they would carry through with them, regardless.

Therefore, instead of hiring Captain John Smith, they bought his books and his maps, and hired Miles Standish, a captain four years younger than Smith. He, like Smith, had seen service on the Continent, and had undoubtedly won his military title in the Netherlands. Captain Standish was a willing servant of the Pilgrims. Captain Smith could not have been. The result was to the initial detriment of the Pilgrims, and the immediate disappointment of John Smith. Yet in the long run the Pilgrims learned — the hard way — and Smith was saved for the major work which still lay ahead.[3]

While these developments were unfolding, John Smith's former friend Sir Ferdinando Gorges was determinedly pursuing his objective of founding a colony within the territory granted the "North Virginia" Company in 1606. This colony was to be based on fishing, as the Jamestown Colony had by then found economic roots in tobacco. In this, however, Gorges ran head on into Sir Edwin Sandys, who was convinced that the Jamestown Colony would have to keep fishing rights in the north (never before under discussion) regardless of Sir Ferdinando's plans. The Pilgrims sailed before a compromise was reached, the details of which are foreign to John Smith and his career, but on November 3, 1620, a "Council for New England" was chartered. One week later a battered and storm-tossed *Mayflower* made land off Cape Cod.

Whether with Gorges's permission or connivance or without it, or despite Gorges and all his works, John Smith took up his trumpet the moment his book appeared on the market, and began to sound his colonial theme. Long idleness, or effort exerted in vain, was beginning to tell upon him.

Smith had fruitlessly dedicated copy after copy of his book to the City Companies which might finance a settlement. Fruitlessly, he had appealed, through similar dedications, to overseas adventurers for both north and south Virginia. At length, in the body of the book he wrote:

> I never had power and means to do anything . . . but in such penurious and miserable manner, as if I had gone a-begging to build a University; where[as], had men been

as forward to adventure their purses as to crop the fruits of my labors, thousands ere this had been bettered by these designs. Thus betwixt the spur of Desire and the bridle of Reason I am near ridden to death in a ring of despair. The reins are in your hands, therefore I entreat you to ease me.

He then went in person to follow through.

His first approach was, logically, to the Viginia Company. On Wednesday, May 2, 1621, a "Great and General Quarter Court" was held for Virginia, under the presidency of the Earl of Southampton, who was named Treasurer of the Company when the King refused to have Sir Edwin Sandys serve in that capacity. To that court John Smith sent a formal petition, of which he himself makes no mention, but which is recorded in the Company's Court Minutes:

> Captain John Smith in his petition showeth that for so much as he hath not only adventured money for the good of the Plantation, and twice built Jamestown and four other particular Plantations, as he allegeth, but for that he discovered [explored] the Country and relieved the Colony willingly three years with that which he got from the Savages with great peril and hazard of his life: that therefore in consideration hereof the Company would please to reward him either out of the Treasury here, or out of the profits of the generality in Virginia: Touching which request, the Court hath referred him to the Committees appointed for rewarding of men upon merits.

In the incomplete records of the Company, there is only one other mention of such a petition, and in neither case is there any evidence of payment of a reward.

Although this petition may have been so much wasted time and effort, Smith's renewed contact with the Company was almost certainly useful in another way. At a meeting held three weeks before, another John Smith (spelled Smyth) rose to make a motion of vital importance to Captain John's life. This John Smyth was a gentleman a dozen years older than the Captain, born in Nibley, Gloucestershire, and for more than twenty years steward of the household of Lord Berkeley. Undoubtedly influenced by the Berke-

leys, he not only invested in the Virginia Company, but eventually
— certainly by 1620 — became a regular attender of "courts," or
meetings. Seeing the continuous difficulties in which the Company
found itself with regard to financial backing, Sandys had relied (as
had Sir Thomas Smythe before him) on a lottery to finance their
colony, but this had been terminated by order of the Privy Council,
confirmed by the King's Proclamation of March 8. Five weeks
later, on April 12, 1621, John Smyth of Nibley came up with an
idea. He moved:

> That for so much as the lotteries were now suspended,
> which hitherto had continued the real and substantial food
> by which Virginia had been nourished; that instead
> thereof, she might be now preserved by divulging fame and
> good report, as she and her worthy Undertakers did well
> deserve, declaring that it could not but much advance the
> Plantation in the popular opinion of the common subjects,
> to have a fair and perspicuous history compiled of that
> Country, from her first discovery to this day.

Mentioning the deceased "worthies" who had contributed to the
effective settlement of Virginia as proper subjects to be commended,
though the living "worthies" should be omitted for decorum's
sake, Mr. Smyth pointed out that Virginia, now twelve years old,
afforded at least as good "matter of relation" as the Spanish
(colonial) annals, and continued to afford the same,

> which, what effect such a general history (deduced to the
> life to this year) would work throughout the Kingdom with
> the general and common subject [citizen], may be gathered
> by the little Pamphlets or declarations lately printed: And
> besides, [a] few succeeding years would soon consume the
> lives of many whose living memories yet retained much,
> and devour those letters and intelligences which yet remain
> in loose and neglected papers.

The whole court applauded this "worthy speech" greatly, as
spoken freely "to a special purpose," and considered it fit to be
considered of, and put in practice in due time. Mr. Smyth was

thereupon "exceedingly commended, as preferring always motions of special consequence." [4]

For the time being, nothing happened. John Smith soon paid a call on the Fishmongers' Company, one of the earliest of the city gilds. Since the sale of fish would presumably reimburse any backers for his colony, Fishmongers' Hall may have been the first company hall he visited. In any event, this Company was one of the few who preserved any record of his visit.

Smith arrived with one or more copies of his book, outlining "a project for fishing beyond the seas by a country termed by him New England." A great part of the book was "read unto them," apparently with additional explanation of the benefits to be derived for the entire kingdom if the Company would undertake to invest in it. Cautiously, the members present agreed to take the matter under advisement, as the old-fashioned phrase goes.

Smith did not stop with the Fishmongers. At least one other company has some scant mention of him, and there must have been others. But the Fishmongers eventually came to the not illogical conclusion that a single company could do little, and that they would cooperate only if others did. That seems to have put an effective stop to Smith's efforts in that direction. It was then past mid-November.

Word had of course already reached London, six months before, that the Pilgrim colony was located at John Smith's Plymouth, in Massachusetts Indian territory, not at the mouth of the Hudson, and had survived the winter. John Pierce took out a new patent for the Pilgrims, under Sir Ferdinando Gorges, to remedy any trouble that might result from their unauthorized settlement in New England. And preparations were quickly made to send supplies. The fate of the Pilgrims had not been so painful as that of the first colony, Jamestown.

Gorges meanwhile had won out in a long argument with Sandys and the Virginia Company, mostly over fishing rights. With the dissolution of Parliament, at the close of 1621, he was ready, other things being equal, to begin afresh his own attempt to colonize New England. But other things were most unequal.

The peace for which James I had struggled so hard was not only broken by the Thirty Years' War in Europe, but England herself threatened to get involved. Spain, as already mentioned, had invaded James's son-in-law's Palatinate, and Parliament wanted war, in spite of James. France also contributed her share of the trouble by breaking out with religious distemper again, which indirectly drove some French ships right into Plymouth harbor. Gorges had to spend time fortifying his Fort.

By then John Smith's plan to base a colony on the fishing industry did not seem vast enough to Gorges. If he was to colonize in the face of threats from the French settlements in Canada, and the ever-increasing interest of the Dutch in New York harbor, he had to get a considerable amount of capital. Instead of trying to do this according to recognized business principles, he hit upon the unhappy scheme of proposing taxes on fishing in New England. This idea, despite certain merits, naturally ran into obstacles among the fisherfolk who did not see why the matter of sailing a ship to New England to get fish should be made so complicated — and costly.

In the end, through a combination of circumstances, Gorges won out, at least temporarily. He could carry on with his plans. Yet grave doubts arose among potential backers. The western fishing interests were opposed to the taxes, and although they had suffered a setback in Parliament, there was no doubt that they would renew their opposition as soon as there was a chance. This did anything but promote enthusiastic financial support. Still, on July 15, 1622, *A Briefe Relation of the Discovery and Planting of New England* was entered for publication in London. Its purpose was to offset criticism and encourage backers. Its author is generally supposed to have been Sir Ferdinando, since the ideas voiced in it are known to have been his.

The details of these ideas are not immediately pertinent to John Smith. The publication of the book, on the other hand, is. For at almost the same time, John Smith had set his own pen to work on a revised edition of his *New Englands Trials,* the bulk if not all of which task was certainly completed before October 16 of that same year. Sir Ferdinando had dedicated his *Relation* to Prince Charles, turned twenty-one the previous November. John Smith could do no less. His *Trials* enjoyed a similar dedication. Both little books referred to John Smith's name *New England* and Prince

Charles's "gift" of the name to the country. In purpose and in essence they differed widely. But both breathed hopes of colonization — and indeed urged action.

The chief addition to the new edition of Smith's *Trials* consisted in a few paragraphs on the Pilgrim establishment at Plymouth, a copy of a private letter from there to England, and a few other items, the most important of which is the mention of the massacre that decimated Virginia on March 22, 1622. This tragedy sparked John Smith's next enterprise, even as it lighted a slow match leading to the powder keg known as the Virginia Company. For some reason, this edition of the *Trials* has survived in a fair number of copies. For some reason, it was also kept standing in type for some little time before it was printed.

Six years of wasted effort and confusion had slipped by. John Smith was over forty. If he still had any hopes of going to Virginia, or to New England to inaugurate a colony, it was only because of the devotion he had come to feel for "his colonies," as he called them. *He* was convinced that a great future lay ahead, and that only selfishness, wrong people, and wrong government stood in the way. Why, in those "queasy" days when England's peaceful increase of trade and shipping was endangered, these colonies could easily provide lumber for ships — ships "of any proportion and numbers you please." A new and great Royal Navy for England!

But faith was needed, and enterprise, and will. And this recalled to John Smith's mind verses he had heard quoted by Richard Hakluyt, the Father of English Colonial Expansion:

> Oh Incredulity! The wit of fools,
> That slovenly do spit at all things fair;
> A sluggard's cradle; [and] a coward's castle.
> How easy 'tis to be an infidel.[5]

## CHAPTER 24

# THE GENERAL HISTORY

THE GREAT POWHATAN had died in the spring of 1618. He was perhaps the only man who openly respected John Smith; as he was the only man, perhaps, whom John Smith respected. Wits and guile subsisted between them, but for the most part it was respect. At least, that is what the little that is known seems to say. With Smith gone, Powhatan withdrew into a shell of dislike and suspicion. The white strangers kidnapped his favorite daughter, and one of them married her. A reticent peace followed. But she died, perhaps as a passion vine dies in the cold north. And Powhatan died, too. Okee so willed it.

Powhatan's half brother Itoyatin, or Opitchapam, succeeded to the overlordship — briefly, for he was not young. Then came the savage who years before had striven to be so "stately, as to our seeming he became a fool" — Opechancanough, whose soul was white. Samuel Argall, the greedy, acted then as governor, and renewed the peace between Indian and Englishman.

Argall did not care about a naked savage or the problems one or more of them might present. He toured Tidewater Virginia for provision and plunder, and when he got back, a vessel was there that took him aboard and he sailed off for England. Yeardley took his place, to rule the little group of English outcasts clinging to the edge of a subtropical forest. He was impressive, fit to be governor, with a clear-cut understanding that he was to obey orders, and with an exceptionally expensive wardrobe, worthy of George Percy. Yeardley came to face the waiting wiles of old, cunning, and fearless Opechancanough. That same year, in August, "a Dutch Man of War landed twenty Negroes for sale," as Robert Beverley wrote — the first slaves in Anglo-America. Then two years and more of conqueror-over-conquered peace followed. Opechancanough bowed to what he could not remedy, and held himself aloof. The time had not yet come.

Nothing survives to tell the Indian side of the tale. Even the English accounts are far from clear. Nevertheless the suspicion cannot but protrude through the mist of uncertainty that twelve years of bad to worse mismanagement had dire effect on relations between Indians and Englishmen. Dale and Argall particularly, execrated by the colonists, must have stirred deep resentment, which easily lay hidden under imperturbable Indian faces. Yeardley, for all his silly show, was not a bad governor, still he sensed no latent threat — not even when he heard that Opechancanough approached the "Laughing King" on the eastern shore with a request for a quantity of poison such as those Indians were noted for. The Laughing King was friendly to the English, particularly to young Thomas Savage, known to John Smith as a boy, but now a man. The Laughing King reported all this, and the fact that Opechancanough had employed an Indian to murder Savage. Was it because Savage employed some of John Smith's tactics? Savage did not command the respect Smith did.

In any event, in November, 1621, a new governor, Sir Francis Wyatt, took over — beginning what proved to be the best leadership the colony had yet had. With Wyatt came his wife's uncle, George Sandys, brother of the Treasurer of the Virginia Company, Sir Edwin. George was an adventurer, built a bit like John Smith, and a poet. On the way over from England he had translated parts of Ovid's *Metamorphoses,* to which he had been dedicating himself for some time. In addition, George Sandys had published *A Relation of a Journey begun Anno Domini 1610,* and this had been issued in a second edition just before he left for Virginia. For all this, he was less than two years older than Captain John Smith.

The winter passed calmly and even profitably, and on March 3, 1622, George Sandys sent home a glowing account of the state of the colony. All was peace, progress, and prosperity — in a very minor way. About ten or twelve days later, the Governor sent a messenger to Opechancanough, apparently purposely to learn whether his longstanding "friendship" with the colony was still warm. The answer came back that "the sky should sooner fall than it dissolve."

On March 20, a handful of settlers were guided through the woods by friendly Indians. No microscopic shadow, even, lurked over the land. Two days later, in the morning, Opechancanough's men fell upon the English — at the breakfast table, in the fields, building, sawing, planting, whatever they were doing. Before noon that bitter Friday, March 22, between a third and a fourth of the entire Virginia Colony was clubbed or tomahawked to death. Some were forewarned by truly friendly Indians, many were protected by enclosures, others were able to fight back. But the devastation was none the less appalling.

Word of the disaster reached London by July 3 — it had taken the Council in Virginia two months to collect their thoughts, survey the damage, and get a ship off to England. Sir Edward Sackville was commissioned on that date "to acquaint the Lords of His Majesty's Council" with the news. Then business proceeded astoundingly as usual. In time, Edward Waterhouse, a secretary of the Virginia Company, published what may be called the official statement regarding the matter, *A Declaration of the State of the Colony and Affaires in Virginia: With a Relation of the Barbarous Massacre in the time of peace and League* . . . Even with all its forced optimism, the effect of this, on the heels of the publication of the Reverend Patrick Copland's "pre-massacre" sermon of thanksgiving for the prosperity of the colony, was disheartening. "The Infamy," the Council wrote to Jamestown, "hath spread itself to all that have but heard the name of Virginia, to the detestation of all good minds, the scorn of others, and our extreme grief and shame."

John Smith was naturally not quiet under such circumstances. Ever dedicated to the cause of defense and sound handling of the Indian-English problem, he addressed himself promptly to the London Council:

> If you please I may be transported with a hundred soldiers and thirty sailors by the next Michaelmas [September 29, 1622], with victual, munition, and such necessary provision; by God's assistance, we would endeavor to en-

force the Savages to leave their Country, or bring them in that fear and subjection that every man should follow their business securely . . .

These I would employ only in ranging the Countries [inhabited districts] and tormenting [harrying, plaguing] the Savages, and that they should be as a running army till this were effected; and then settle themselves [the English] in some such convenient place that should ever remain a garrison of that strength, ready upon any occasion against the Savages, or any other[s] for the defence of the Country, and to see all the English well armed, and instruct them [in] their use.

It is particularly to be noted that nowhere does Smith mention *exterminating* the Indians. The punishment he suggests is driving them back from the settlements and scattering them. The remedy for the conditions that permitted the massacre, he continues to insist, is preparedness and military efficiency.

Although there is no record of John Smith's proposals in the surviving books of the Virginia Company, his statement that Sir John Brooke favored them seems sound. Such mention of Sir John as is still to be found in the Company's papers points to a levelheaded, fair-minded man. David Wiffin, also mentioned by Smith, was a far less conspicuous figure. In any event, the Company answered that "the charge would be too great, their stock was decayed [they were short of money], and they did think the Planters should do that of themselves." Smith could go help them, but the Company would limit itself to not standing in his way.

The credibility of these statements by Smith is considerably enhanced by what is known of the condition of the Company. Despite the lack of confirmation in the Company's papers, where there is practically no mention of the massacre either, the Company's "stock was decayed" indeed — it was on the verge of bankruptcy. Sir Edwin Sandys, for all his vision and his integrity, was a promoter, not a financier. Therefore, when the sudden call for help came from Jamestown, the Company had no funds for relief supplies. The planters must take care of themselves. How well they did this is shown in a letter from George Sandys, dated March

30, 1623 — the mortality in one year had doubled the toll of the massacre.[1]

By this time word of the martyrdom of the colony had spread over London. Samuel Purchas was certainly quickly alert to the news, and searching for details. Conceivably it was John Smith who supplied the first information, for Smith had renewed reason for seeing Purchas, as Purchas always seems to have wanted to see Smith.

Purchas had begun work, not long since, on his magnum opus, *Purchas His Pilgrimes,* and was feeding it bit by bit to Henry Fetherstone, the publisher. A good part of the enormous work was in print in June, 1622, but the dedicated parson continued to assemble material, particularly from America. In fact, Purchas had already determined on his own role as the successor to Richard Hakluyt. HAKLUYTUS POSTHUMUS was to be superscribed to the title on the engraved title page, for Samuel Purchas "would not be misconstrued to ungratitude."

Smith, who had helped Purchas greatly in his earlier *Pilgrimage,* had surely called on him more than once while endeavoring to promote his colonial ideas. Therefore when the thought came to John Smith that he was the man to write the *General History* which John Smyth of Nibley had recommended in April, 1621, it would not be surprising if he went to Purchas with the idea and laid it before him as the noblest and best thing he could do for Virginia. In fact, it may be surmised without too much implausibility that Smith prepared a trial section to show to Purchas in 1622. Purchas was the heir to Hakluyt's vast collection of manuscripts and maps. Granted his friendship with Smith, it seems logical that Smith should have wanted to show him how he had handled the material he had already extracted from Hakluyt's published works. Even the date for this consultation can be construed from Book One of Smith's history — September 23, 1622.

Another factor which may have influenced John Smith in setting to work on a major literary effort was William Strachey. He had begun just that sort of a history about ten years before, but had left it a draft, composed only of so much of his diary and notebooks as he had "had time to digest into form and method." Strachey had presented a copy of this to Sir Francis Bacon in 1618, about the time John Smith had made his appeal, but was disappointed if he hoped for any help. And Strachey was dead within two months after John Smyth of Nibley made his motion. There may have been some slight Strachey influence in Smith's decision to do the history himself. There may also have been influence from one or another member of the Virginia Council, for Smith had by then shown himself to be a capable author. It is only certain, however, that within a few months of putting together a draft of the first twenty pages, John Smith had dedicated himself entirely to the completion of his historical work.

Such a designation for Smith's *General History*, it must be quickly explained, is not to be understood in the modern sense. Smith himself, in later years, gave his meaning to the word "history" when he wrote, "History is the memory of time, the life of the dead, and the happiness of the living." This sort of definition, indeed, was "in the air" in those days, for Ben Jonson had penned a similar thought to face the frontispiece of Sir Walter Ralegh's immensely popular *History of the World*. To Ben Jonson, history was

> Time's witness, herald of antiquity,
> The light of truth, and life of memory.

There were of course no professional "standards" for histories in the 1620's, although many books called such existed. Tales and tall tales, and unverified "facts," abounded in practically all. Furthermore, the proper religious or political slant had to be maintained if the author wanted to keep his head and right hand attached to his body. Accuracy was desirable, but variations and digressions did not mar a work provided it was good reading. Much more important was, as the historian John Selden wrote in 1618, "to give other light to the Practice and doubts of the present."

In short, John Smith's work did not purport to be professional history in our sense — indeed, could not. It was merely a thorough, somewhat egocentric compendium of facts as John Smith saw them, elaborated by extensive quotation from other, and usually unacknowledged, sources. Primarily, it was the first attempt to circumscribe historical writing within the geographical limits of the English New World.

Of first importance to Smith undoubtedly was the matter of

finding a publisher. He neither could afford, nor was he willing, to perform the task of assembling what he considered pertinent at his own expense, with the profits going to the printer or publisher. At one time, he apparently talked with a printer named James Boler, or Bowler, but nothing came of it. Then someone, perhaps Boler, found a publisher for him in the person of Michael Sparkes, or Sparke, of Eynsham near Oxford, a Puritan who was made free of the Stationers' Company in June, 1610.

Even before he met Michael Sparkes, however, Smith was undoubtedly casting about for a patron to finance the publication. It was not likely that Smith, presumably ever guided by Samuel Purchas, would trust his fortunes to a "mere stationer," with implications of dishonesty, for the "honest stationers" were in a decided minority according to Smith's friend, the scorpion-tongued poet George Wither. There was the case, for instance, of Ben Jonson himself, who not long before had entrusted his First Folio of plays and verses to stationer William Stansby (busy in 1622 printing Purchas's work for Henry Fetherstone). Even with that reliable agent Ben Jonson knew that he needed a patron. In fact, he eventually assembled not one but several: King James, the City of London, the Earl of Pembroke, and the enormously wealthy Sir William Cavendish, Viscount Mansfield, later Earl and Duke of Newcastle. John Smith was far from being another Ben Jonson, and had more difficulty finding someone who would back him.

But there was an alternative. A few years before, a now-forgotten scholar named John Minsheu had run into grave difficulties getting his polyglot dictionary, *Guide into Tongues,* printed. In despair, he hit upon the scheme of financing it by subscription, the first author in England to do so. That this venture seems not to have been too successful apparently did not deter John Smith, who set out to do the same thing.

Obviously, before subscriptions could be solicited, Smith would have to have his work sufficiently planned to interest subscribers. This fact threw him back on his own resources and at the same time into a maelstrom of activity. He had to collect material. He had to frame a sequence. He even had to fashion an underlying philosophy. (Whether he had to, or not, he did.)[2]

In what order Smith approached these matters no one knows. There may not have been an order at all, and he may have plunged into a literary and historical chaos. Nevertheless, although Smith seems to have been working with several matters at once, careful reading of the product would seem to justify the thought that with Smith first things were first.

Technically, the first of several first things was Smith's basic accord with Purchas, that "History without that so much neglected study of Geography is sick of a half dead palsy." He had the copper plates for two maps already, Virginia and New England. He wanted one more. These, with the remarkably adequate measure of geographical description he had included in his first letter home (the 1608 *True Relation*) and in his *Description of New England*, would provide the complete picture of English colonization which was his aim.

Once this was fixed in his mind, Smith seems to have proceeded rapidly with quill pen and paste and shears to produce his chef-d'oeuvre. Much of the information was ready at hand, written by somebody else, and it is only just to state that patience rather than a peculiarly keen mind was needed, at least at the beginning. Helping himself freely to Hakluyt's *Voyages*, as mentioned, Smith finished the bulk of Book One in 1622. The balance, less than five folio pages in print, he summarized from a printed account by John Brereton and from manuscripts being used at the same time by Samuel Purchas for his *Pilgrimes*. There is nothing new in this book, yet it supplies a handy sketch of English preliminary voyages to America — before the voyage in which Smith himself took part. It is amusing, though of no great moment, to note that Smith went out of his way to use the account of Bartholomew Gosnold's 1602 voyage to New England which was written by John Brereton, rather than that done by Gabriel Archer the manuscript of which was in Purchas's hands. Archer's life of involved motives had already long since been cut short by the Indians, or the climate or diet of Virginia, but John Smith apparently never forgave him for his persistent personal animosity.

Before Book One was finished, however, Smith seems to have decided that a collection of quotations and abstracts cemented and amplified by his own words but without further adornment would follow too closely in the path of the great Hakluyt and the lesser Purchas. By then he had surely seen George Sandys's *Relation*, with its apt citations from ancient authors, almost exclusively

Latin. Sandys had borrowed freely from contemporary guidebooks (themselves vast borrowers), and from ancient geographers and historians, and philosophers both sacred and secular. That he availed himself liberally of already existing anthologies may or may not have been recognized (few would have known), but the general impression given by the book is one of vast erudition. Nothing quite like it in the field of travel books had appeared in English before. It did not matter if much of his translating was hackneyed, stiff, and unpoetic. John Smith, like thousands of others, was plainly impressed.

But George Sandys was a Latin scholar, the son of an Archbishop of York and the brother of a Parliamentary leader. He had been educated at Cambridge and the Middle Temple. And he had traveled like a gentleman — living with ambassadors and other officials — through the Turkish Empire, Egypt, the Holy Land, and "the remote parts of Italy and Islands adjoining." John Smith was neither scholar nor lawyer, was without significant family connections, and had traveled in Europe mostly as a soldier or a slave — only very briefly as a gentleman. Yet he seems almost necessarily to have set out to write a book of similar construction to Sandys. Due to Smith's personality, his is eminently a more readable book, although Sandys's *Relation* went through more editions than Smith's *History* in the seventeenth century, probably because of the learning it displayed, and its pages on the Holy Land.

Without much command of Latin, however, John Smith would have been hard put to follow the trail blazed by Sandys, or whoever his model was, had not a theological treatise appeared in that same year of 1622 which suddenly solved his problem for him. Martin Fotherby, the learned Bishop of Salisbury, had finished a massive work "against Atheists and Infidels" with the barbarous title *Atheomastix, The Scourge of Atheists,* not long before he died in 1619, but publication had been delayed for unremembered reasons. A glance at the book seems to have satisfied Smith of its usefulness to him.

There is ample evidence that John Smith was deeply pious, in a Protestant — perhaps even a Puritan — way. He knew at least three ministers in London (Crashaw, Symonds, and Purchas), possibly one occasional visitor there (Thomas Adams), and was evidently friendly with Robert Hunt, the minister in Jamestown who died so soon. He was a friend of William Strachey, of extreme piety, and Smith himself is described by a soldier who fought under him in Transylvania thus:

> I never knew a warrior yet, but thee,
> From wine, tobacco, debts, dice, oaths, so free.

Bishop Fotherby's piety, sympathetic as it was to Smith's ears, was curiously supported in all his published works by learned references to the wisdom of the ancient Greeks and Romans. In brief, Fotherby tended to be philological as well as scriptural in his writings and sermons, and it was surely his encyclopedic reading of the Greeks and Romans rather than his theology that interested Captain John Smith.

Smith did not have the keen sense of aptness possessed by George Sandys. Neither did he trouble always to use the sources provided him by Fotherby in precisely the sense in which they were originally intended. (Nor did Fotherby, for that matter.) He seems at first to have found a few bits of poetry, conveniently translated from Latin by the Bishop, which had enough connection with the text he was summarizing or quoting both for illustrative value and as some indication that the author, John Smith, was well read, and perhaps pious. It was in line with his self-advancement. From there he went on, systematically.

Beginning with the "Preface to the Reader," Smith spotted a quotation from an author he had probably had to read in school, Marcellus Palingenius, whose *Zodiacus Vitae* or "Zodiac of Life" was prescribed as a Latin textbook in a number of schools. At the end of the passage from Thomas Hariot's *Report* which he was abridging for his *History,* Smith saw an opportunity to decorate and emphasize the final phrase by means of Palingenius, as quoted (and translated) by Bishop Fotherby. The result was unquestionably effective.

In referring to the proper way to deal with the Indians, Hariot had written:

> The best nevertheless in this, as in all actions besides, is to be endeavored and hoped; and of the worst that may happen, notice to be taken with consideration; and as much as may be eschewed.

To which John Smith added:

the better to allure them hereafter to Civility and Christianity. Thus you may see how

Nature herself delights herself in sundry Instruments
That sundry things be done to deck the earth with Ornaments;
Nor suffers she her servants all should run one race,
But wills the walk of every one frame in a divers pace;
That divers ways and divers works, the world might better grace.

The verses are from Fotherby, verbatim but for the accidental omission of the word "single" in the third line, which should end "one
single race."

The details of the rest of Smith's borrowings from Bishop
Fotherby are beside the point. After finding one or two passages
which seemed suited to his purpose, he evidently studied the
*Atheomastix* to the saturation point. As his work of compiling and
commenting continued, Smith's freedom with Fotherby increased,
until he did not hesitate to recast the original to suit his purposes.
Fotherby, however, had not hesitated to turn savagely indignant
Juvenal into a pietistic Christian, and so John Smith, when faced
with the need of altering Fotherby's Juvenal, without realizing
it returned the verses almost back to the way Juvenal had written
them. Smith had his quota of righteous indignation, too.

Armed then with a philosophy, source material, personal feelings
based on experience, and a serviceable anthology of potentially
pertinent quotations, Smith was ready to solicit financial help.[3]

Which way he turned first is impossible to determine today. The
only indication which survives is a single printed copy of a prospectus which he sent to nobles, merchants, and gentlemen in general, appealing for contributions. This contains a detailed table
of contents which corresponds so closely with the printed *General
History* that it is evident that his manuscript was virtually in final
form before he wrote the prospectus. He even mentions the number
of printed sheets his work will run to ("less than eighty sheets"),
with only reasonable excess in the estimate.

The prospectus concludes thus:

Therefore I humbly entreat your Honour, either to adventure [invest], or give me what you please towards the im-

pression, and I will be both accountable and thankful; not doubting but that the Story will give you satisfaction, and stir up a double new life in the Adventurers, when they shall see plainly the causes of all those defailments and how they may be amended.

And so I humbly rest.

[Space for personal signature]

Evidently John Smith had something more than "impartial history" in mind.

This prospectus was published, and presumably circulated, during the legal year 1623, which ended on March 24, 1624. What success Smith had in raising money by these means is again one of the many unknowns about his life. But with or without widespread support, he did succeed in finding a patron, thanks to whose generosity publication was ensured, and on Smith's terms.

John Smith, it will be recalled, had somehow found help in the person of the Earl of Hertford on his return from Virginia in 1609. Although there is no record of how long the Earl continued to bolster up Smith's morale as well as his finances, he may have continued to be interested in the man, if not in his projects, up to 1621 when he died, a very old man. Sometime during those twelve years he could hardly have failed to present Smith to his wife, who was about of an age with Smith. She was Frances Howard, daughter of Thomas Howard, Viscount Bindon.

Frances Howard's character has been summed up, pointedly, by a historical writer of the mid-nineteenth century in these words: "Beauty, folly, vanity, and eccentricity, appear to have constituted the character of this remarkable woman." Beauty, folly, and vanity scarcely need explaining, but it may be worth while suggesting that Frances's eccentricity may have been due to family environment: Her uncle Henry and his son Thomas were both beheaded, and her father's first cousins, Queen Anne Boleyn and Queen Catherine Howard, met a like fate. This was all before Frances was born, but either the beheadings or the character which brought them about could be interpreted as having produced some effect on Frances's mental make-up. Turning from pure guesswork to facts, however, Frances evidently sought safety (and money) in the arms of an anything but noble wine merchant. The vintner conveniently died in 1599, when Frances was at most twenty-one, and left her a considerable fortune. Pursued for her beauty (and money?) by an earl and a knight, she accepted the earl, leaving the knight to commit suicide, after penning some farewell verses to Frances in his own blood. The earl, needless to say, was the Earl of Hertford.

When Hertford died in 1621, he also left Frances a sizable fortune, which added to her inheritance from the vintner made her one of the richest women in England. By that time a still more noble nobleman was waiting for the Earl to join his ancestors, and when that "happy event" occurred delayed little in offering to console Frances by a third marriage. This nobleman was Ludovic Stuart, second cousin to the King — a close relationship, since James was an only child and had but one first cousin, the famous Arbella. Frances, Countess of Hertford by her second marriage, accepted the hand that led her to the side of royalty, and by early May, 1621, she was Frances, Duchess of Lennox. Two years later, Ludovic was created Duke of Richmond, the second man to hold that title. Frances Howard thus acquired the title held before by her aunt Mary, who had married Henry VIII's natural son, the first Duke of Richmond.

All this raised the double Duchess, as she was called, to heights of most uncommon pride. One of the richest women in England, she was now the ranking noblewoman. What an opportunity for John Smith!

Perhaps because of old times, perhaps merely as a tribute to the honor she had had (through her third husband) at the hands of the King, John Smith approached the double Duchess with his prospectus. Would her Grace deign to cast an eye upon his work and vouchsafe him her protection? And would she also pay for the publication of the *General History*? It would cost only a hundred pounds, even with three maps . . .

John Smith, if he was admitted to her august (and frivolous) presence as seems highly probable, without a doubt somehow captivated the lady. She was ready to finance his book, to what extent no one has left a record, and in addition would permit him to include an engraving of her as an illustration. And the number of maps was raised from three to four, with an engraved title page to boot. So willing was the Duchess to help that she had two engravings made of herself, one by Simon van de Passe's brother William, who did the entire royal family not long after, and the other by Francis Delaram. It is easier to find some trace of her vaunted beauty in the latter than in the former.

John Smith in gratitude penned a dedication which is as remarkable for its restraint as for its sweeping acknowledgment of his indebtedness to other ladies:

> The beauteous Lady Tragabigzanda, when I was a slave to the Turks, did all she could to secure me [from harm]. When I overcame the Bashaw of Nalbrits in Tartaria, the charitable Lady Callamata supplied my necessities. In the utmost of many extremities, that blessed Pocahontas, the great King's daughter of Virginia, oft saved my life. When I escaped the cruelty of pirates and most furious storms, a long time alone in a small boat at sea, and driven ashore in France, the good lady Madame Chanoyes bountifully assisted me.
>
> And so verily these my adventures have tasted the same influence from your gracious hand, which hath given birth to the publication of this Narration.

In conclusion, Smith begs the Duchess to see that the King get a copy, as well as Prince Charles and Princess Elizabeth.[4]

With this solid encouragement, John Smith was able to go ahead with his plans. He employed a hack engraver by the name of Robert Vaughan, a Welshman living in London, to make a copy of Theodore de Bry's engraving based on John White's old map of the region around Roanoke, and this he studded with the names of the Duchess's relatives and of his own friends, while preserving the bulk of the names shown by de Bry. Around this are eight engraved illustrations, inspired by or copied from John White's drawings of Indians (made nearly forty years before), but with the figure of Captain John Smith added. Vaughan was not John White, and the illustrations should not be taken seriously. They were undoubtedly intended only to excite the interest of seventeenth-century readers.

The map, however, which John Smith calls "Ould Virginia," offers some interesting information regarding his activities at the time. Obviously Vaughan and Smith got along famously, for in a playful mood Vaughan translated the "Rat Isle" (Ile de Ré) of Smith's salvation off La Rochelle into his native Welsh as *Ynys Llygod,* and placed it next to Savage Isle, where de Bry had *Wokokon.* In addition, Vaughan seems almost certainly to have been the person who suggested to John Smith a name for the region in Tartary where he had been a slave. Smith did not know its name, especially because he did not know exactly where he had been.

Purchas had probably already helped out with the classical names of Nalbrits, Lastillo, and so on (for he had a vast collection of maps), but it took a Welshman to suggest that Smith call the country Cambria, a Latin name for Wales which was growing very popular in that generation. Vaughan also may have suggested the name for the river (almost certainly the Don) up which John Smith had sailed to Nalbrits. Smith, telling the story of Rat Isle, either mentioned the estuary of the Charente where he landed on an "oozy isle" or pointed to it on a map. Just below were the famous saltpans, harbor, and town of Brouage. This may soundly be surmised to be the origin of Smith's mystery-name of Bruago for the river in Tartary up which he had sailed to Nalbrits.

Smith himself certainly worked with Vaughan on the sketch for the engraving, supplying names of persons whom he wanted to honor. His earlier map of Virginia was so full of Indian villages that there was little room to add anything in 1623 or 1624. But de Bry's map was nearly empty. Vaughan saw to it that it was "peopled" with the Stuarts, the Howards, the titles Lennox and Richmond, the late-lamented Earl of Hertford, and his son Baron Beauchamp. Then there were two other Howards, grandchildren of the Duchess's much older first cousin, Lord Howard de Walden and Thomas Howard, Earl of Arundel. Only a step more distant was Sir Robert Gordon, a gentleman of the Privy Chamber and close to Ludovic Stuart. (Gordon was interested in Nova Scotia, to which an expedition or two were sent in 1622–1623. Smith may have had further motives than the mere friendly tie between Gordon and the Duke.)

In addition there were many more marks of recognition, such as Point Bacon, Cecil's Harbor, and the like. An Alice Smith-Field raises the unanswerable question, was this rehabilitation of his mother's side of the family a memorial to his sister, or a gesture to

Sir Thomas Smythe, who had a sister named Alice? Then, below this a grove honored Sir William Segar, whose services to Smith will be mentioned shortly, and nearer to the ocean is the first indication of a lasting friendship with the Mildmay family, and (perhaps) a last remembrance of a Towneraw whom Smith had known in Lincolnshire. To conclude, there is also a token of Smith's hope for some backing from a Scotsman who came to England with King James. This was John Murray, a gentleman of the King's Bedchamber who was created Viscount Annandale in 1623. Murray had already appeared under his family name on Smith's map of New England, but his name was erased there about the time it appeared on the map of "Ould Virginia." If the toponymical flattery produced any favors, there is no evidence today.

There are other place-names commemorating the deceased, and propitiating actual and potential backers, but it would be tedious to list each one. The over-all picture tells the story. Smith got Vaughan to refurbish and deck out de Bry's old map with place-names primarily to acknowledge thanks — for help already received, or hoped for. Secondarily, it supplied a geographical setting for the primitive illustrations he and Vaughan, perhaps with Purchas's help, concocted from John White's drawings.

The fourth map was of the "Summer Isles" (named for Sir George Somers), now known as Bermuda. The surveyor of the islands was Richard Norwood, but John Smith, who had never visited the place, was responsible at least for the arrangement of the drawings around the map. The plate was printed by James Reeve.

By the time these things were well under way, the Duke of Richmond and Lennox suddenly died of apoplexy, on February 16, 1624. The Duchess, as John Chamberlain wrote, took it

> extreme passionately, cut off her hair that day, with divers other demonstrations of extraordinary grief, as she had good cause, as well in respect of the loss of such a lord, as for that she foresees the end of her reign.

It is fortunate that John Smith's book was safely on its way toward publication before this disaster occurred. Frances Howard was never the same woman again.

Meanwhile, the Virginia Company was frankly bankrupt. In

addition, it was torn by internal factions. As early as May 9, 1623, a justice of the Court of Common Pleas headed a commission to examine the "whole state" of the Company. When the Privy Council demanded that the Company surrender its charter some months later, the Company resisted. At an extraordinary meeting held on October 20, 1623, only nine of about seventy members present voted to comply, among which were Sir Samuel Argall (knighted in spite of his depredations) and Captain John Martin, the perdurable colonist. The Company's books were nevertheless sequestered early in November, and by May 24, 1624, after months of legal battle, the Virginia Company ceased to exist.

Sometime during the winter, John Smith had been called before the Commissioners, "for the reformation of Virginia" as Smith calls them, to answer questions regarding the Plantation. For this he prepared a brief "relation" in which he summed up his personal experience in the colony, and added a pointed complaint that he had not been given "one foot of land" either in Virginia or New England, despite his efforts and his sacrifices. Then, with rather startling frankness he answered their inquiries. Without going into detail, it may be said that he put his finger on sloth as standing in the way of the colony's prosperity, tobacco-based economy as discouraging to crop-raising, and lack of discipline as leaving the door open for the Indian massacre. For the future, he repeatedly stressed the importance of a permanent garrison, willing and capable workmen, abolition of the selling of servants, central and consistent management in England, and above all the return of the Virginia Venture to royal authority. It is evident that these opinions were delivered before the dissolution of the Company.

That dissolution, of course, did not mean that the colonial project, or the colonies themselves, came to an end. The Company's affairs floundered around for a month or more and the colonists were not even aware of what had happened. Then, on July 15, King James gave to Sir Henry Montagu, Viscount Mandeville, Lord President of the Privy Council, and a special commission authority to govern the colony of the Virginia Company, and to work out a solution to the problems that had been pestering it. Three days before, John Smith's book had been entered for publication.

Sir Henry Montagu had been a member of the King's Council for Virginia since 1606. It has been assumed that because his niece married Robert Bertie, Lord Willoughby, Sir Henry may have had something to do with John Smith's being a member of the local council for Virginia. If that was the case, it may not have been sheer accident that John Smith's book was patently rushed through the press just as the government of the colony reverted to the direct control of the King—to the status, more or less, of the original colony for which Smith had fought so hard. (There were others on the commission, however, who were known to be friendly to Smith: Gorges and Dr. Sutcliffe, and perhaps Sir Thomas Smythe, who may have forgiven Smith his brashness.)[5]

Whatever the details, Smith's *General History* was delivered to two printers, who were to work on it simultaneously. Books One, Two, and Three, and the preliminary matter, were given to John Dawson; the remaining three books, to John Haviland. A guess was hazarded that the first three would take up signatures A to O, so Haviland was instructed to begin with signature P, and page 105. In the meantime, John Smith went out collecting, or was offered, a handful of the customary commendatory verses. Samuel Purchas labored out four doggerel stanzas, bursting with pedantry, while John Donne contributed passable verses—for that sort of thing. Donne himself had been "made free and of the Council" for Virginia on July 3, 1622, which may have influenced his appreciation of John Smith. The other "poets" were associates of Smith, or travelers, with no poetical skill, while two signed with initials only, and one with *Anonymos,* in Greek characters. The anonymous poem hints that it was Smith who did the soliciting, at least in this case.

When the printing was done, it came out that Dawson did not have enough material to fill signature N, and none for O. Smith stepped into the breach and provided him with the verses prefacing the *Description of New England,* omitting those by Gunnell and Wither, to fill out signature N. Signature O was not printed at all, which gave rise to all sorts of guesses in modern times as to what had happened, as profound as they were silly. Last of all, so great was the rush that there was no printed title page at all. The book—Smith's book—was needed. With all its faults, it could quiet doubting, puzzled Englishmen.

It is beside the point to go into particulars regarding the proof that the book was hurried through the press. There are many incontrovertible technical aspects to the case, and there is self-evident hurry in the writing. Books Five and Six have almost no poetical "illustrations," from Fotherby or anybody else. Book Five, particularly, is largely a condensation of a single work, which points to haste again, although it might have been disinterest from lack of personal knowledge. Book Six, dealing with New England, is very largely made up of Smith's own previous works on the subject, but is brought down to the date of publication with the latest information available. But the last paragraphs once again testify to pressure. John Smith, never afraid of writing fully what he thought, obviously had little time to round those final thoughts into effective prose.

Throughout the *General History* there are passages purporting to be verbatim transcripts of speeches or of letters. No one who has read much so-called history of contemporaneous authorship will be misled by this. Smith's history was written with a purpose, as were Bacon's *Henry VII* and Sir Robert Cotton's *Henry III*, for instance. It was also written to be readable, by Jacobeans, as were the others of the type. Therefore, although the general subject matter of a speech or a conversation is undoubtedly correctly reported, the language is polished, elaborated, tricked out, for readers used to the volcanic vigor of Shakespeare, Ben Jonson, and a dozen lesser lights. Even the astounding letter to Sir Thomas Smythe which John Smith, with a straight face, states he has copied from the original sent to London, can hardly be the sort of copy we should expect of a "serious" historian. For all his frankness, Smith would hardly have written quite such a letter. At the same time, it cannot be doubted that he did write a letter in which the true state of the colony — as he saw it — was reflected without mincing words. He has merely polished the letter for greater effect.

Another side of Smith's *General History* which has been considered, in modern times, to detract from its historical value is his almost total lack of modesty. Again, it is a matter of meaning. The *General History* is not a history; it is not even a journalistic narrative. It is John Smith's Memoirs, his Apologia, and his Defense, rounded out with information from others bearing on what he considered *his* colonies. He knew, or thought he knew, what was right for the colony, how it should behave, how it should be governed, how it could survive — whether the colony was in Virginia or in New England. That characteristic of his mind is spread over the pages of his book. He was not attempting to lie to readers, nor even in a mean way to prejudice them. He had a story to tell, his story. He had a plan to expound, his plan. That was the basis for his book.

Whatever others might think of his purposes, Smith knew that his aim was morally pure — for the tortured ostracism he had suffered from the Company that he had helped form had scourged but not embittered his soul. To rise above these past — and even future — contrarieties became with him a glorified set purpose. He could not but heap scorn on what he considered wrong. But that scorn became as sublimated as his blind loyalty to his ideal. Facts and figures, and even consistency and abstract truth, swam crazily in the tide of his enthusiasm. It was not that he thought foul was fair for being in a good cause. It was that the cause was so fair that there was no foul.

As John Smith wrote on, however, his angered regrets often got the better of him — regrets not for what he had or had not done, but for what others had or had not done. The recollections of his advice ignored or denied, or of his warnings unheeded, surged up far too self-evidently in his story. At times it is impossible to avoid the impression that Smith thought that only *he* could organize, manage, and make a success of a colony in America.

But in part he was right — in the part born of experience. Until he left Virginia, no other Englishman had faced the problem of life there among hostile elements squarely, and, within the bounds of possibility, won out. He knew that pettily squabbling factions would be the literal death of the colony unless somehow a stop was put to them. He knew that scarlet robes belonged in London, not in Jamestown, and that neither Indian nor untamed wilderness knew what bearing gentlemanly rank might have on such things as survival. And yet John Smith was far from "going native," as we say today, in the way Henry Spelman thought he could and should. A true Englishman, Smith sought a compromise. He sought the preservation of what was basically sound in English habits, and a proper "composition" with the needs of a new environment. That fluid principle forms the undercurrent of the *General History*.[6]

CHAPTER 25

## "FREED FROM SERVILE BANDS . . ."

THE *General History* suddenly brought John Smith back into the colonial limelight. If he was not yet a made man as a promoter, he was certainly no longer a broken, forgotten one, if indeed he had ever really been broken. His book was taken in some circles as further support for the return of the Virginia Venture to royal administration, as had already been determined. In others, it was not welcome. George Percy, for example, loftily resented the book as denigrating his own ability as temporary Governor in 1609–1610 and falsifying the story of the events prior thereto. Taking up an aristocratic goose-quill, he addressed a *Relation* to his brother, the Earl of Northumberland:

> . . . in regard that many untruths concerning these pro-
> ceedings have been formerly published wherein the author
> hath not spared to appropriate many deserts to himself
> which he never performed and stuffed his relations with so
> many falsities and malicious detractions, not only of this
> present and time which I have selected to treat of, but of
> former occurrences also, so that I could not contain myself,
> but express the truth unto your Lordship concerning these
> affairs.

Having made this accusation, Percy went on to "deliver the truth briefly and plainly," but instead of correcting the author and his many untruths, he chose essentially to limit himself to the details of what happened while he was Governor, after John Smith had left. Percy was in a position to point out Smith's reputed untruths, and the only conclusion to be reached from his silence is that he was unable to put his finger on any.

The one passage in Percy's *Relation* which bears on the time prior to Smith's departure, about one tenth of the whole, describes the events immediately following the arrival of the 1609 "Gates" fleet. In it Percy accuses Smith of having feared that "the seamen and that [Ratcliffe-Archer] faction might grow too strong," and of "juggling" with the seamen by entertaining them. This, Percy says, was done for Smith's own vainglory, adding that

> that which was intolerable [he] did give leave unto the seamen to carry away what victuals and other necessaries they would, doing the same more safely in regard the contents thereof was in the Admiral [the flagship] which was cast away.

While the meaning of this statement is vague, it is obvious that Percy aligned himself with Ratcliffe, Archer, and company, either at the time or in retrospect. But that this alignment was only in retrospect becomes fairly evident when Percy writes on, without a trace of resentment, that Smith sent him and John Martin to do things, which they accomplished with a vengeance. In fact, on entirely hearsay evidence of some sort of Indian treachery, Percy initiated a campaign of terrorism which could not have had Smith's approval.

Following this, Percy told his brother how Captain West and his men at the falls had refused to obey Smith (who was still President, by the way), and that therefore later he (Percy) and Ratcliffe, Archer, and Martin had deposed Smith, "being an ambitious unworthy and vainglorious fellow," although he admitted that there was "no other certain appointed government" than that of Smith.

While it is beside the point to go into further details — the balance of Percy's account having to do with justification of his own misdeeds — it is pertinent to note that this *Relation* remained in manuscript among the Northumberland archives until modern times. By 1624, when it was written, there were much more serious matters afoot than the petty quarrels of fifteen years before. Yet Percy's account, which under its surface whispers that Smith had no right to pretend to govern such gentlemen as Percy and Francis West, is valuable today as throwing further light on one of the basic shortcomings of John Smith's character. This feature, rather than defect, of his make-up enabled him to keep the colony alive in its infancy, but prevented his serving the Virginia Company on his return to London. It made him one of the fathers of New England, but kept him from planting a durable colony there. For all his devotion to the cause of colonizing America, John Smith could not rise above the details. Immediate cost, in human lives or in money, was always before him.

Sir Edwin Sandys, on the other hand, lost the enterprise back to the Crown for almost exactly the opposite reason (with political undertones). He envisioned a new English state, more popularly governed than was England herself. Unfortunately, his planning fell short in detail, and the Company collapsed from lack of capital.

John Smith did not see Sir Edwin's underlying democratic idea. He only saw the death rate (70 per cent or so for the period 1619–1624 inclusive), and the "disappointment and disgust" of the colonists who returned home. He therefore attacked the Sandys administration wholeheartedly when the Commissioners gave him the opportunity in 1623–1624. It was not the theory — the far-seeing aim of Sir Edwin Sandys — but the practice which he deplored. King James without a doubt deplored the aim even more than he did the practice.

When the Virginia Company surrendered the colony to the King, the Council and Assembly in Virginia had already taken measures to prevent a break in continuity of government as early as March 5, 1624, by promulgating thirty-five laws and orders, including one:

> That no person within this Colony upon the rumor of supposed change and alterations presume to be disobedient to the present Government, nor servants to their private officers, masters or overseers, at their uttermost peril.

Such an edict, could it have been issued by John Smith in 1609, when Ratcliffe and Archer arrived, would have at least put the troublemakers on their guard. In 1624, it at least kept the colony quiet until official word arrived from England.

All this while, nationwide events at home distracted the attention of the populace from such minor matters as the struggling colonies in Virginia and New England. The amazing George Villiers, Duke of Buckingham, at thirty the premier peer of England (and the second richest), had virtually declared that he was the ruler of England — not James I.

Buckingham had been with Prince Charles during the flamboyant fiasco of Charles's courting of the Spanish Infanta. He had ingratiated himself with Parliament later, and Charles had made a more popular marriage treaty with France, which resulted in his engagement to the sister of Louis XIII. During an unhealthy winter, however, several old actors on the stage of government died, and James I was taken sick in March, 1625. In three weeks he was dead. Buckingham was then really supreme.[1]

Sometime before this (it is impossible to say just when), John Smith had given to Samuel Purchas an eight-thousand-word story of his life, from "about the year 1596" to his return to England in 1604. Somewhat more than a third of this purported to consist of "Extracts of Captain Smith's Transylvanian Acts, out of Fr[ancisco] Fer[neza] his Story." This source was explained by Purchas to be "a Book entitled *The Wars of Transylvania, Walachia and Moldavia,* written by Francisco Ferneza, a learned Italian, Secretary to Sigismund Bathor, the Prince." Smith's account, including the *Extracts,* is sandwiched in between other extracts and summaries of accounts and letters by George Sandys, William Biddulph, and Sir Thomas Glover, and a portion of the supplement to Richard Knolles's *History of the Turks* (including 1623).

While there is nothing to hint that the book attributed to Ferneza (Farnese?) was not in Purchas's hands and was not translated by him (as John Smith later stated), it is strange indeed that no other mention of this book (or manuscript) has yet been found. It is known that members of the Farnese family were in Hungary fighting the Turks at the time, and it is known that Zsigmond Báthory had many Italians on his staff. That such a history could have existed is therefore far from unlikely. Nevertheless, it must be mentioned that there is some doubt about the genuineness of Purchas's source — which is mitigated by the fact that this would be the only example of such dishonesty in all the serious, honest parson's vast work.

Purchas's *Hakluytus Posthumus,* better known as *Purchas his Pilgrimes,* was in print before he signed his will, on May 31, 1625. In fact, parts of it were at least in the proof stage by the time Smith's *General History* was in the press, as is indicated by Smith's correct reference to volume and page for a letter used in Purchas. This seems to show that Smith and Purchas were in some measure close together in those days. There is evidence even of a real affection between the two.

Because of this, Purchas apparently urged Smith to produce "official" evidence of his experiences in central Europe. The mere commendatory verses by Sergeant Edward Robinson, who said he had fought under Smith in Transylvania, were not enough. Smith had said that Zsigmond Báthory gave him a pass, "intimating the service he had done, and the honors he had received, with fifteen hundred ducats of gold to repair his losses." Did John Smith still have that pass?

Smith had, understandably, preserved this old document through all the vicissitudes of more than twenty years. He apparently took it to Purchas. Purchas in turn told him to take it to the Heralds' Office, then as now on Paul's Wharf hill, between St. Paul's and the Thames, and have it recorded by Sir William Segar, Garter King of Arms of England. When Smith finally did this is not certain, for the sequence of events cannot always be made to fit together chronologically, but it can hardly have been before 1624, nor later than August 19, 1625. On that date, Sir William officially recorded Báthory's patent, dated December 9, 1603, and inscribed in the records not only a copy of the text (which seems to have been damaged by then), but also his statement: "I . . . do witness and approve, that this aforesaid Patent, I have seen, signed and sealed under the proper hand and seal manual [i.e., his own] of the said Duke of Transylvania."

Certain reservations have been voiced about the genuineness of Segar's record that the document he saw was genuine. Under the circumstances at the time, these reservations seem entirely unjustified. Segar had quite recently been reproved by the King himself for gullibility, but had since received rewards for exceptional service. Furthermore, the patent has not been seriously attacked by anyone in the College of Heralds. That it was perhaps not a "conventional" patent does not mean that it was not a genuine one, and the tenor of it is certainly strongly similar to documents of Báthory's whose authenticity has never been questioned. The "impossible" names given as titles (perhaps four out of nine) could easily be due to wear and tear, as could the incorrect family name given to Graf Modrusch. The burden of proof, in short, still lies on those who would like to negate the patent.[2]

About this time, and surely during the first year of King Charles's reign, John Smith saw the second issue of his *General History* appear, with the addition of a printed title page, and a few minor changes in text. He added a name or two to his maps, to show appreciation, not the least interesting of which are two on his map of Virginia: *Democrites Tree* and *Burtons Mount.* The latter was most likely in honor of George Burton, who had accompanied him to Werowocómoco in late December, 1608. The former must refer to George's brother, Robert, author (under the pseudonym "Democritus Junior") of the immortal *Anatomy of Melancholy,* which had been revised and reprinted in 1624. John Smith seems to have read it in spare moments.

King Charles by then was about to marry Henrietta Maria of France, and he and Buckingham were ready to begin a war with Philip IV over Spanish interference in central Europe which had made Charles's sister and her husband exiles from the Palatinate. A fleet was made ready, and Charles went down to Blackwall to inspect some of the new royal navy; it was his first public appearance as King.

On May 1, the Privy Council disseminated an order to press into service ten thousand landsmen, to augment the "fighting force." That they would be somewhat worse than merely untrained soldiers was a foregone conclusion. Then, trained sailors were needed as well. In recent months the coast of England had been threatened by a rash of pirates, from near and far. Peaceful residents of Channel towns and villages were clamoring for protection, as defense had been let slide while James firmly held to his policy of peace. Now preparations for war with Spain required also the training of patrols for England herself.

Charles I then issued his first proclamation, "for the well manning and arming the ships of war belonging to this realm upon their setting forth to sea." The proclamation of itself did not teach anyone how to accomplish this, however, and Gervase Markham, a hack writer, stepped into the breach with *The Soldiers' Accidence, or An Introduction into Military Discipline.* (For fifty years and more, an elementary "grammar" of any subject had been called an *accidence.*)

John Smith had been on shipboard enough to know a few rudiments of sailing. Markham, though ready to try his hand at almost anything, was no great writer, and Smith — with his *General History* behind him — surely did not feel inferior to him. Picking up his idle pen, he set to work to do for sailors what Markham had done for soldiers.

It is remarkable that the farmer's boy from Lincolnshire who won a captaincy fighting the Turks in Hungary and who by then was not noted for his good hap by sea should have set himself to write the first manual for seamen in the history of England. It is even more remarkable how he went about it. Aware of the depth of his own ignorance, Smith studied the most useful books he could find, worked over the latest aids to navigation, and tempered these sources with what he had learned in the Mediterranean, along the African coast, and on the Atlantic. He carefully shunned the theory of navigation, saying "practice is the best," and on October 23, 1626, his work was entered for publication by Jonas Man and Benjamin Fisher. Its title:

> *An Accidence, or The Pathway to Experience. Necessary for all Young Seamen, or those that are desirous to go to Sea, briefly showing the Phrases, Offices, and Words of Command, Belonging to the Building, Rigging, and Sailing a Man-of-War; And how to manage a Fight at Sea. Together with the Charge and Duty of every Officer, and their Shares: Also the Names, Weight, Charge, Shot, and Powder, of all sorts of great Ordnance. With the use of the Petty Tally* [account of provisions]. Written by Captain John Smith, sometime Governor of Virginia, and Admiral of New England.

The occasion which prompted this book is explicitly stated in Smith's address "To all the Right Honorable and most Generous Lords in England, and Others: Especially of His Majesty's Privy Council, and Council of War." He wrote:

> In regard of the present occasion, for the art of navigation (and many [of] you gentlemen and valiant spirits of all sorts do desire to try their fortunes at sea), I have been persuaded to print this discourse, being a subject I never see writ before. Not as an instruction to mariners nor sailors — whom I entreat rather amend it than condemn it, con-

fessing it might be a task for a most excellent seaman —
but as an introduction for such as want experience, and are
desirous to learn what belongs to a seaman.

The "present occasion" was the recognized national danger, with
the specific detail that Smith's friend Lord Willoughby was even
then, in August, 1626, and after, attempting to get away from
Portsmouth with a fleet of thirty-nine ships. His objective was the
coast of Spain and possibly the Spanish ships coming from Mexico.

One copy of Smith's book is known to have been offered to Sir
Robert Heath, then Attorney-General and much involved in investi-
gating the attempt of Parliament to impeach the Duke of Buckingham. Smith, for his own peace of mind fortunately, had nothing
to do with the political upheaval which was already beginning to
rumble far beneath the surface.

The immediate success of his new work led him to plan an
augmented edition. His dedication to the general reader had stated,
"for this small pamphlet, if I find you kindly and friendly accept
it, I mean ere long more largely to explain the particulars." Pointedly he included in this dedication all adventurers by sea, and well-
wishers to navigation, and especially the masters, wardens, and body
of helpers of Trinity House, that brotherhood which had charge of
all sea marks (beacons, buoys, and the like) and acted in an advisory
capacity to the navy. When they and the public showed interest,
Smith was ready. On August 13, 1627, the book was entered for
publication.

Once again John Smith took his idea for a title from Gervase
Markham. Markham had followed up his *Soldiers' Accidence* with
*The Soldiers' Grammar* (1626) and a *Second Part of the Soldiers'
Grammar* (1627). John Smith's new work was called: *A Sea Gram-
mar, With the plain Exposition of Smith's Accidence for young
Seamen, enlarged.* It ran to seventy-six pages, as against thirty-eight
in the *Accidence*.

What is immediately striking about the *Sea Grammar* is that the
cost of printing was borne by a newcomer among John Smith's
friends and benefactors, Sir Samuel Saltonstall. The appearance
of Saltonstall is sudden, unexplained, and of far-reaching effects.

Although Sir Samuel was the son of a wealthy Lord Mayor of
London who died in 1601, he led a remarkably retired life. Even

the precise nature of his ties with Smith is obscure. It is only clear that, in addition to financing Smith's book, he opened his house to Smith, for in 1631 Smith mentions a "trunk standing in my chamber at Sir Samuel Saltonstall's house in St. Sepulchre's Parish." Beyond this, there is less certainty.

Sir Samuel had a son named Wye, who was a poet and translator of some note. This fact, and the presence of commendatory verses for the *Sea Grammar* signed S.S. and W.S., leads to the assumption that the versifiers were Sir Samuel and Wye. This is in a sense confirmed by a third commendatory poem by John Hagthorpe, who apparently married a sister of Sir Samuel's wife. Then, by way of further relations with Smith, a younger son of Sir Samuel, Captain Charles Saltonstall, was known to Smith, while Sir Samuel's first cousin, Sir Richard, headed the list of adventurers to Massachusetts in 1628, thereby founding the Massachusetts branch of the family. And finally there remain to be mentioned two facts which may or may not be connected. Sir Samuel had an illegitimate half sister by the name of Abigail Baker, alias Saltonstall, and Smith honored an otherwise unidentified Abigail on his map of "Ould Virginia," along with the Duchess of Richmond and his own mother. This completes the inventory of factual and potential links between Smith and the Saltonstall family.

One other author associated with Hagthorpe and the Saltonstalls in the *Sea Grammar* should be mentioned. This is Edward Jorden, apparently the noted physician and chemist, who became a friend of Smith's. Jorden, if it is the man, was a graduate of Padua as well as Oxford, was ten or eleven years older than John Smith, and was endowed with enough common sense — in that age! — to attribute a case of supposed demoniacal possession to natural causes. His appreciation of John Smith contains humor, which is rare in such verses:

> Much travelled Captain, I have heard thy worth
> By Indians, in America set forth:
> Me, silence best seems to keep; and then,
> Thy better praise be sung by better men,
> Who feel thy virtue's worthiness. Who can
> Derive thy words is more Grammarian
> Than Camden, Clenart, Ramus, Lyly, were;
> Here's language would have non-plussed Scaliger . . .

Anyone who takes up the *Sea Grammar* will quickly agree with Jorden: "A [dry] dock is a great pit or pond . . . made convenient to work in . . . A wet dock is any place where you may hale [draw] in a ship . . . A cradle is a frame of timber . . ." and so on. But as a modern authority on things nautical has written, Smith's book "did for ships and seamanship" what had been done by others in allied fields; it is an invaluable *Grammar* of "ordinary workaday knowledge." Curiously, the *Accidence* was reprinted the year the *Grammar* appeared, although there is no comparison between the finished work of 1627 and the earlier hurried sketch.[3]

In the meanwhile, the Reverend Samuel Purchas had died, in September, 1626. He was not yet forty-nine, if the day of his baptism (November 20, 1577) followed close on the heels of his birth. To John Smith it was the loss of an old and loyal friend, and perhaps the first hint that his own death was not far off. (Normal life expectancy in those days is said to have been but forty-eight years.) Yet there is no sign of this in his activities.

Summer, 1627, was past when Smith got fresh word from Virginia, through an old friend there. Nathaniel Causey, who had landed at Jamestown on January 2, 1608, returned unexpectedly to England, accompanied by other colonists. Smith had continued to be in touch with one or another of the King's Commissioners for a while after the death of James I, which was followed six months later by that of Sir Thomas Smythe. But King Charles held all the reins in his own hands by the end of that year, and connection between John Smith and the Virginia Colony virtually ceased. Whatever word Causey would bring him would be all the more welcome.

The news Causey supplied, however, was both humdrum and mildly incorrect. Through him, Smith was misinformed about the development of "democracy" in the plantations — Charles was rigorously opposed to the popular meetings begun in 1619 under Sir Edwin Sandys's policies. Smith of course may have misunderstood Causey, but whatever the source of the error, it was not true that in 1627 the colonists had a general meeting "to consider of their public affairs." Among the more reliable details, on the other hand, were such bits of information as the beginning of making drinks by malting Indian corn and barley — "good ale," says Smith, "both strong and small [weak]." (Corn whiskey would not be thought of for many a year.) Then, too, with Causey's return to England, the modern English word "hominy" appears for the first time, in place of the cumbersome Powhatan word *ustatahamen* or *usketehamun* reported by Smith and Strachey nearly twenty years before.

These and other items John Smith jotted down for incorporation in still another book, as yet only vaguely planned. There was the information that Yeardley was Governor (he died on November 13, 1627) and that Captain Francis West (another old "friend") was still active in Virginia. Other members of the local elite may not have been known to Smith at all, other than by hearsay. But Smith was disappointed that these new leaders of the colony made no further discoveries, and that tobacco had become the sole commodity in which any interest whatsoever was shown.

Of New England, Smith admits in the published results of his inquiries which appeared later, he knew little. In fact, he had had no special news since the publication of Edward Winslow's *Good News from New England,* which had appeared before his own *General History* was finished. Yet he cannot forget that he had wanted to go himself with those determined Pilgrims for whom, he writes, "my books and maps were much better cheap to teach them than myself." But the isolated, disassociated way these explorers and founders of New England had of "going in small handfuls . . . to be several Lords and Kings themselves" irritated his conception of how it ought to be done. Virginia had failed, he knew, by that very independence and fragmentation and lack of help from England which these New Englanders were enduring "with an infinite patience." Neither he nor, probably, the Pilgrims themselves realized how great a gulf there was between the self-willed gentlemen of Jamestown and the nonconformists at Plymouth with their obdurate will-to-be-free.

Of Bermuda, Guiana, and the beginnings of the British West Indies, John Smith knew even less. Yet he kept in touch with news, as well as he could. Needless to say, the departure of Captain Charles Saltonstall, Sir Samuel's son, for St. Kitts, did not escape him. But other plans that were afoot he heard about with apparent disinterest. Only Virginia and New England really captivated his fantasy. They, he repeated to himself, were his children.

Quite possibly John Smith would have continued to busy himself seeking news in the Royal Exchange or around St. Paul's indefinitely and somewhat aimlessly, had not his pittance of fame reached the ears of an eccentric, romantic scholar, Sir Robert Bruce Cotton, who claimed collateral descent from Robert the Bruce, author of Scottish independence and royal forebear of King James.

This truly extraordinary personage, a lingering spirit of the days of Elizabeth living in the troubled days of Charles I, sided with Puritans and democrats in the burgeoning struggle between the Crown and the people, delved into antiquities with the energy of a Camden or an Antonio Bosio, and kept his eyes open to whatever was worth while in the living womb of English history. Possessed of curiosity as boundless as his interests were catholic, Sir Robert somehow — probably through Robert Bertie, Lord Willoughby — heard of John Smith and his exploits.

From word of mouth to personal investigation was but a step. Sir Robert "perused" the *General History,* as Smith puts it, and where the Virginia Company itself meant little to him, despite the shares he held in it, the book and its author caught Sir Robert's attention. That he then should have interested himself in a man, to him a nonentity, who belabored so unrelentingly the sluggishness and pusillanimity that thwarted colonial growth is not surprising. Cotton was an active, energetic man, and a courageous fighter for what he thought was right. Once Smith came under his eye, therefore, Sir Robert insisted that Smith prepare for him an autobiography which would explain Smith's somewhat incredible past.

Smith was ever ready with a pen to defend himself, as well as to relate, with unrestrained verbal coloring, the hazards Fate had woven into his career, thick as pearls in one of Queen Elizabeth's state gowns. And he was all the more ready to satisfy Sir Robert's desire, he said, "because they have acted my fatal tragedies upon the stage, and racked my relations at their pleasure."

The "they" who did not greet Smith's life history with wholesale belief were probably many. The "they" who acted, or took off, Smith's tragedies, however, are not easily discovered, unless Smith's skin was peculiarly thin when it came to theatrical ridicule. Ben Jonson, for instance, found Smith's mention of the "blessed Pocahontas" in the dedication of his *General History* fit subject for a little fun, particularly since she stayed at an inn called the *Bell*

*Savage* for a while — a name which was a century old before the Rolfe family arrived there. Jonson therefore wrote in his *Staple of News,* in 1625:

> *Pennyboy Canter:* I have known a princess, and a great
> one,
> Come forth of a tavern.
> *Picklock:* Not go in, sir, though.
> *P. Canter:* She must go in, if she came forth: the blessed
> Pocahontas, as the historian calls her,
> And great King's daughter of Virginia,
> Hath been in womb of tavern . . .

Here is the first mention of John Smith as a historian. That he should have been offended by the passage seems incredible, and there may have been unkinder remarks in other plays which have not survived. But the reference in Jonson's satire has significance for Smith's life because it shows that Smith, for all the lack of mention of him in contemporary sources, cannot have been a forgotten man.

Yet Smith apparently approached Sir Robert Cotton's request with something less than alacrity. Turning to his old account, printed in Purchas's *Pilgrimes* he seems to have been satisfied with what was there. He only added two printed pages of confused account of his childhood at the beginning, interspersed a brief chapter on a fight in the Straits of Otranto before his account of going to Graz, and added the details of the story of his African adventures with Captain Merham, and virtually let it go at that. Here and there, the text is amplified and odd bits are inserted, but by and large the "book by itself" he penned for Sir Robert Cotton was little more than a reprint of his earlier work.[4]

By then, Smith apparently felt that some token of his appreciation of Robert Bertie was due, and he decided to dedicate his new book to him. But for unknown reasons he wanted to add the name of the wealthiest peer in England — William Herbert, Earl of Pembroke. Since Pembroke ranked above Bertie, his name was placed first. Then, also for unknown reasons, Smith included the newly created Earl of Dover, Henry Carey.

With these three sponsors, and the mention of Sir Robert Bruce

Cotton and Sir Samuel Saltonstall in the dedication, Smith's book had illustrious patronage. To this, for sales appeal, he added a page of nine amusing drawings of his early life in Europe, done by Martin Droeshout. And incongruously, but inevitably, he rounded out the volume with random bits of information from all the English colonies, as a second part. At last, John Smith's *True Travels, Adventures, and Observations*, ready for the press, was entered for publication on August 29, 1629.

Again a collection of "complimentary verses" was provided, rather more than would seem necessary for a small folio of only sixty pages. Nevertheless, any biographer of Smith must be grateful for them. They tell the story of his last associates and friends, and an interesting group they are, so far as they can be identified.

In the first place, there are two old friends, Edward Ingham (or Engham) and Edward Jorden. To these are now added two poets, famous in their day: Richard Brathwait, a friend of Robert Vaughan, whose latest work was even then in the process of publishing by the same printer as had Smith's *True Travels;* and William Hawkins, master at the Grammar School at Hadleigh. Hawkins was a friend of Doctor Thomas Goad, who had "allowed" the publication of the *General History.**

Then there was Richard James, more scholar than poet, who was librarian to Sir Robert Cotton at the time. (It is easy to see how John Smith's circle of acquaintances grew, but that these men were ready to write poems in his favor is in itself a testimonial to his character.) Four others are not identifiable with certainty, and two are signed with initials only. One remains, the most curious of all, Brian O'Rourke.

O'Rourke was the grandson of Brian Ballach, who built Leitrim Castle in 1540, and the son of Brian-na-Mota — all three noted for their pride and inextinguishable hostility to the English. After the conquest of Ireland, Brian (the grandson) was taken to England "to be brought up in religion, and to have that education as is meet for a gentleman of his fashion and means." This proceeded properly until St. Patrick's Day, 1619, when he "fell into a brabble," several people got hurt, and Brian landed in the Gatehouse Prison, Westminster, where he was to stay until he could pay £300 damages. A

* At that time, all books had an "allowance" of some kind.

poem of five rhyming jingle-couplets sent to King James seems to have gotten him out, but in less than two years he was committed to Marshalsea, then to Fleet, and between these and the Gatehouse he languished for several years, reasons unknown. In some unexplained way his debts mounted higher and higher until in 1627 a warrant was issued to pay £6342 12s. 7d. for him, which was the unpaid balance of £7602 4s. 7d. granted him sometime before by King James. This apparently procured O'Rourke's release. His next and last appearance is as a poet extolling the virtues of Captain John Smith.

It is easy to see that the caged Irish Prince would have felt great sympathy for the unappreciated John Smith, but how Smith ran across him, or he Smith, is an unclarified mystery. In any case, O'Rourke's concluding couplet is worth quoting:

> Thy actions crown themselves, and thy own pen
> Gives them the best and truest Epiphonem.

It was precisely John Smith's acclamation of his own deeds which troubled many who were not his uncritical friends.

The last third of Smith's *True Travels*, as has been said above, sketches what had been happening to English colonization from the conclusion of his *General History* to August, 1629. Appended to this is a final chapter which provides a synopsis of the history of piracy in England since the days of Captain Callice, half a century before. It ends with an appeal to seamen and soldiers, once esteemed but now regarded as "the scum of the world." To them Smith says:

> Regain, therefore, your wonted reputations, and endeavor rather to adventure to those fair plantations of our English Nation; which, however in the beginning were scorned and contemned, yet now you see how many rich and gallant people come from thence, who went thither as poor as any soldier or sailor, and gets more in one year than you by piracy in seven. I intreat you therefore to consider how many thousands yearly go thither, also how many ships and sailors are employed to transport them, and what custom they yearly pay to our most Royal King Charles; whose

prosperity and his Kingdom's good, I humbly beseech the immortal God ever to preserve and increase.

Even in calling the blessings of God on King Charles and the kingdom, John Smith could not forget the oriflamme of his adult life: *Colonization*.[5]

CHAPTER 26

# THE SEA MARK

FOR REASONS not yet discovered, John Smith's *True Travels* did not appear until at least seven months after it had been entered for publication. The publisher, one Slaughter or Slater, was a minor and rather inactive member of the Stationers' Company, and the "secret" of the long delay may lie in that bald fact. Haviland's press, which printed it, was on the other hand one of the busiest in London. And it is possible that a recent colonial venture may have held up the appearance of the book deliberately.

As far back as 1620 a Council for New England had been formed under the aegis of Sir Ferdinando Gorges. Contrarieties even greater than those which afflicted Smith had assailed Gorges without in any way diluting his zeal for colonies, or for serving his country loyally, but before his troubles began in earnest he had hopefully granted a temporary license to fish in New England to a group in neighboring Dorset, through the Council. The group, bankrupt within three years, maintained a settlement of sorts at what is now Cape Ann, Massachusetts. Master John White of Dorchester, Puritan pastor, was one of those who took over the business. Before long, a typical convulsion flared up over the pilfering of a hundred and seventy-one hogsheads of salt stored on Cape Ann. The incident was trivial, but the resultant litigation throws the first clear light on a band of Dorchester merchants and others, predominantly if not entirely Puritans, who proposed to establish a colony on and in the neighborhood of Cape Ann.

In June, 1628, the first shipload of Puritan planters sailed from Weymouth, without any special authority, and in March, 1629, the Massachusetts Bay Colony came into existence by royal letters-patent. Within two or three months, the forerunners of the "Great Puritan Migration" were bobbing their way over to John Smith's *Naumkeag*, in Massachusetts. Unwittingly, King Charles had sealed the eventual repudiation of the British King for all that land.

John Smith knew of the departure of the ships, and wrote of it in his *True Travels:*

> Now this year 1629, a great company of people of good rank, zeal, means, and quality, have made a great stock, and with six good ships in the months of April and May they set sail from Thames for the Bay of Massachusetts, otherwise called Charles River.

Word of the safe arrival of the company was back in England by October 9. Any delay in the publication of Smith's book beyond the end of October must therefore remain unexplained. John Smith was certainly not waiting for further news from any venture. On the contrary, he was already at work on another little volume.

From an unrelenting fighter, Smith turned at the age of fifty into an incurable reader. Indeed, his belligerence was necessarily tamed by then, for it could no longer be a question of his leading Englishmen against the primitive threats of the North American wilderness. Twenty-three years had slipped by since he sat on the stormbound *Susan Constant* in the Downs, eager to face the Unknown called Virginia. It was time to take stock.

Still close to Sir Samuel Saltonstall, Smith had acquired other new friends with whom he stayed from time to time. Probably foremost of these was the relatively young Sir Humphrey Mildmay, a grandson of the great Puritan who founded Emmanuel College, Cambridge. Sir Humphrey had traveled in Europe, owned a fine estate called Danbury Place in Essex, and married one of the daughters of Sir John Crofts of County Suffolk. Since Sir John was almost beyond doubt related to the Richard Crofts who had argued bitterly over a copper kettle with Edward Maria Wingfield in Jamestown, it is possible that this is the way John Smith met Sir Humphrey. Also Sir Humphrey was a first cousin, by marriage, of Theodosia Montagu, the aunt of Robert Bertie's wife. However it was, John Smith went to spend at least part of 1630 at Danbury Place.[1]

There he wrote his last colonial appeal. Once more he was determined to place before the reading public what he considered the right idea and the right plan for *any* English colony — even for those already maintaining a more or less precarious existence. He called his book *Advertisements for the unexperienced Planters of New England, or anywhere.* And to show that in the long run the *best* way is the best, he dedicated it to the aged Archbishops of Canterbury and York, the one a devout (and royally unpopular) Puritan, the other a high-church (and royally most welcome) Anglican. Since it is unbelievable that John Smith should have tried to curry favor with both sides of the religious argument then threatening to split England, the only sound conclusion is that he had become more convinced than ever that successful colonization must in some way be dependent on proper respect for the Almighty.

There is a premonition of the end in Smith's dedication, as he opens it, "My most gracious good Lords, I desire to leave testimony to the world, how highly I honor as well the mitre as the lance." Yet this premonition is not so much a lament that he had not accomplished what he had known should be accomplished, as a plea for right aims and right deeds in the planting of colonies. New England is on his mind, rather than Virginia, and one may pause to wonder why. Compared with Virginia, the Pilgrim and Puritan colonies had taken root far less painfully and far more firmly. Still, John Smith felt it vital to put before the Primate of All England and the Primate of England the triple care: God's Church, the Indians, and the King's Dominions. It is an interesting solicitude, for a man so little informed, as we think, on things behind the scenes.

To the "Reader," Smith addresses an equally significant solicitation. Finding, heaven knows where, a legend that "Apelles by the proportion of a foot, could make the whole proportion of a man," John Smith bitingly begs of his friends not to judge Britain's colonies by what they hear in the gossip forums of London, but by sound knowledge. People who believe all they hear of Virginia and New England could "tell as well what all England is by seeing but Milford Haven," or "what Apelles was by the picture of his great toe." John Smith will give them a true and proportioned picture.

For those who expected in this a reduplication of Smith's righteous indignation and often irritating apologetics, the new volume must have come as a surprise. For all the verbal elaboration of his day, Smith plainly indicates his unsolicited commendation of the Founders of New England. Of their religious quirks, he had no inkling. He only saw what was good in them, and what was good in what they did. And his heart swelled merry in his breast.

"Pardon me," he wrote, "if I offend in loving what I have cherished truly," and, he added, "if it over-glad me to see industry herself adventure now to make use of my aged endeavors." But he deeply hoped, despite all rumors, that that industry was not exercised by "a many of discontented Brownists, Anabaptists, Papists, Puritans, Separatists, and such factious humorists" — such seditious faddists. He admires the Pilgrims for their "wonderful patience," not for their religion; but he trusts that the colonizers of Massachusetts Bay are "good Catholic Protestants according to the Reformed Church of England." Not that he expects them all "to be so good as they should be" — no. "Christ had but twelve apostles, and one was a traitor, and if there be no dissemblers among them [the Puritans], it is more than a wonder." Yet, however they were, Smith seems to foresee that they would be better material than the first colonists in Virginia.

In this he was right. Although he was incapable of understanding the religious principles that motivated the Massachusetts group, he sensed their determination and efficiency. As he puts it: "If they do ill, the loss is but their own; if well, a great glory and exceeding good to this Kingdom, to make good at last what all our former conclusions [experiments] have disgraced."

From there, for thirty pages Smith glows with vicarious pride over the accomplishments of the new settlers of Massachusetts. What they have done, especially in so short a time, is more than praiseworthy. And yet, and yet. Faction in religion can have miserable effects. Smith is no divine, yet he pleads to be heard. He pleads on the side of peace and tolerance. He pleads for at least as much Christian unity as there is unity amongst the Turks. For him, that is strong speech.

The last chapter in this work is John Smith's true testament. He left a will, to be sure, bequeathing paltry things — much of his earlier writings are paltry, too. But his last pages are not only lofty in thought and intention; they are exceptional prose, in an age of exceptional writing. They lead a reader to wonder how the genuine and far greater genius of William Shakespeare ever could be doubted as his, when so truly ill-educated a man as Captain John Smith could write the peroration to his *Advertisements for the unexperienced.*

Nearly ten years before, Smith had said of New England and Virginia:

> By that acquaintance I have with them, I may call them my children; for they have been my wife, my hawks, my hounds, my cards, my dice, and in total my best content, as indifferent to my heart as my left hand to my right: and notwithstanding all those miracles of disasters [which] have crossed both them and me, yet were there not one Englishman remaining (as God be thanked there is some thousands) I would yet begin again with as small means as I did at first.

Now, in the *Advertisements,* he points out the many errors made in Virginia: that the purses and lives of the planters "were subject to some few here in London who were never there, that consumed all in arguments, projects, and their own conceits, every year trying new conclusions [experiments]," and so on; that material profit was expected in much too short a time; and that London blamed the planters "for not converting the Savages, when those they sent us were little better, if not worse." So, in the end the Company went bankrupt, as we know, and the colony reverted virtually to its status when John Smith first went there.

With New England, it was a different story. They had made, and were still making, great mistakes. But the Puritans (he does not call them such) have voluntarily undertaken a greater plantation, and Smith sees here the opportunity to offer his counsel. Each attempt at settling in America has been made as if no one had done such a thing before. Smith knows that colonists should profit by experience, and so, taking his cue from Ben Jonson's verse opposite the frontispiece of Ralegh's *History of the World,* he writes:

> . . . seeing history is the memory of time, the life of the dead, and the happiness of the living; because I have more plainly discovered, and described, and discoursed of those

countries than any as yet I know, I am the bolder to continue the story, and do all men right so near as I can in these new beginnings, which hereafter perhaps may be in better request than a forest of nine-day pamphlets.

A store of sage and practical advice follows, with not a few asides that throw bright light on the weaknesses of the Englishmen of his day as settlers and colonists. It is strange to Smith "that Englishmen should not do as much as any [people]." But no; "upon every slight affront, instead to amend it, we make it worse." Religion is needed in the colonies, and with it law and authority: "the maintainers of good orders and laws is the best preservation next [to] God of a Kingdom." But when these maintainers are "stuffed with hypocrisy and corruption," the results will be "not doubtful but lamentable," especially in a colony which is just begun. "As the laws corrupt, the state consumes," he moralizes.

Perceiving then that he has perhaps written too much, Smith goes on to say that he knows that people do not like advice, but he hopes that intelligent men will excuse him for making his opinion clear. In fact, he has so often been asked for suggestions by honest men that as for the ones who do not want advice, "the more they mislike it, the better I like it myself."

Four or five pages of further exhortation to good government, self-protection, and resolute action follow, after which Smith summarizes his attitude in a few words:

> Lastly, remember as faction, pride and security [over-confidence] produces nothing but confusion, misery, and dissolution; so the contraries well practised will in short time make you happy, and the most admired people of all our plantations for your time in the world.

"John Smith writ this with his owne hand," is proudly appended to the book. It was the last public comment that hand ever penned.[2]

Smith brought his "discourse" back from Danbury to London, apparently before the end of October, 1630. The only remark in it which had a touch of bitterness was that regarding the "paper" division of the New England Council's territory, made in 1624. The twenty patentees split the land between them, a tract from the

Atlantic to the Pacific east and west ("at least more than two thousand miles"), and from New York Bay to Newfoundland. All this, Smith writes,

> They divided into twenty parts, for which they cast lots; but no lot for me but Smith's Isles [today's Isles of Shoals, off Portsmouth, New Hampshire], which are a many of barren rocks, the most overgrown with such shrubs and sharp whins [thorny bushes] you can hardly pass them; without either grass or wood but three or four shrubby old cedars.

But despite such sordid treatment, John Smith had friends who cared for him. Saltonstall's house was open to him, and there he seems to have gone. John Haviland set to work to print the new book — none too hastily, it appears — and Smith visited acquaintances. In Lambeth an old friend, Richard Hinde (or Hynde), son of a salter, had a trunkload of Smith's books in his house, and the Captain may have stayed there on occasion.

More of a companion in tastes was John Tradescant, an associate of Samuel Argall's back in 1615, in a project to transport twenty-four persons to Virginia. Tradescant, of Flemish extraction, had two shares of stock in the Virginia Company, perhaps more. He had traveled far and wide, including voyages to Muscovy and what is today Algeria. As Sir Robert Cotton collected books and manuscripts, Tradescant collected curiosities and books. It was he, apparently, who came into possession of the robe Powhatan had given Christopher Newport in October, 1608, in exchange for the copper crown and Newport's old shoes and cloak given him as tokens of his "royal" status (and subjection to James I as overlord). This deerskin mantle was one of Tradescant's "items" which later went to the Ashmolean Museum at Oxford.

Sometime after March 25, 1631, John Haviland completed the printing of Smith's *Advertisements*. The map of New England, engraved in 1616, was furbished up freshly for inclusion in it, and the inscription stating that Prince Charles had named "the most remarkable parts" was altered to read *Prince Charles, now King*. Oddly, the book seems not to have been entered for publication in Stationers' Hall — perhaps merely a slip of some clerk in posting entries. The book was intended, obviously, to be sold.

Perhaps most significant of all in the book, for the biographer, is the brief poem on the back of the dedication. It is not a "commendatory verse," and it stands alone. Everything in it points to Smith himself as the author, but whether he was or not, the underlying thought reflects the weary spirit and ailing flesh of John Smith as his fifty-first birthday approached.

### The Sea Mark

Aloof, aloof; and come no near,
    the dangers do appear;
Which if my ruin had not been
    you had not seen:
I only lie upon the shelf
    to be a marke to all
    which on the same might fall,
That none may perish but myself.

If in or outward you be bound,
    do not forget to sound;
Neglect of that was cause of this
    to steer amiss.
The seas were calm, the wind was fair,
    that made me so secure,
    that now I must endure
All weathers be they foul or fair.

The Winter's cold, the Summer's heat
    alternatively beat
Upon my bruised sides, that rue
    because too true
That no relief can ever come.
    But why should I despair
    being promised so fair
That there shall be a day of Doom.

A few months later, John Smith lay on his deathbed. There was no known epidemic, or "plague," at the time, and there is no mention of his sickness anywhere. Perhaps it was that he was merely no longer young, at fifty-one. Whatever the malady, on June 21, 1631, he dictated his last will and testament. In it we find for the first time the names of a handful of people who must have been close to him, and yet, with one exception, had no apparent significance in his life. The exception is Sir Samuel Saltonstall, in whose house he probably died.

To Thomas Packer, one of the King's Privy Seal clerks, Smith left his Lincolnshire property and his treasured grant of arms from Zsigmond Báthory. To other members of the Packer family there were specific bequests, as there were to an old friend, John Reynolds of the Goldsmiths' Company, to a "Mistris Tredway" who is otherwise unidentified, to his sister-in-law, and to his cousin. His library Smith divided among the son of Thomas Packer, Richard Hinde, and John Tradescant. Through the last mentioned, some of his books should eventually have reached the Bodleian Library at Oxford, but none have yet been identified. And finally for his funeral he left a respectable twenty pounds. In modern times it might sound out of proportion to his estate, but funerals in Elizabethan and Jacobean days were costly. Custom decreed that there be a "sad burial feast."

Ten days after John Smith had scrawled his ✠ at the foot of his will, it was probated. Although there was a flurry of contest by his sister-in-law, Thomas Packer seems to have won out. Not only John Smith's houses, lands and tenements, but also his "Coate of Armes" became Packer's. The Sea Mark's life was over.

Captain John Smith has lived on in legend far more thrillingly than even he could have foreseen. Much has been made — largely by ill-informed people — of trivial inconsequences in his narratives, and controversy has at times raged rather absurdly. Today, passions have died down, except here and there, as more and more evidence of John Smith's basic honesty has been dug out of obscure and widely scattered records. To be sure, much of what John Smith wrote was exaggerated. That was only proper. Rare indeed was the man who wrote in Stuart times without ornament, without exuberance. Let it only be said that nothing John Smith wrote has yet been found to be a lie.[3]

# COMMENTARIES

# COMMENTARIES

To AVOID disfiguring the text with galaxies of asterisks, the author has divided each chapter into sections, numbered only at the close. Sources, authorities and general references for each section will be found grouped together. No attempt has been made to indicate *all* sources, but those are indicated which have been most useful in piecing John Smith's life story together, along with those which can supply the curious reader with further pertinent information.

The references are strictly to works personally consulted by the author (usually in the original language). In the case of sources in some languages, notably Hungarian and Turkish, the author has had to rely on translations; in such cases, the language in which the work was consulted is indicated. In a few instances, works were consulted in translation merely because the original text was either unavailable in the original, or less convenient to use. In a few other instances, a work in a foreign language was used when equally pertinent or reliable works are available in English. These vagaries have been a matter of convenience only, and the author craves the reader's indulgence.

John Smith's life has presented peculiar problems for two reasons. In the first place, ill-informed and virulent "criticisms" have been leveled at him to such an extent that almost every statement a biographer makes must be substantiated by independent sources available in one or another library or archives. Secondly, John Smith's field of action was divided between three widely separated regions. The "English" field is so rich in material that much surely was overlooked. The central and east European field, on the other hand, suffers from paucity of available material, aggravated by the inaccessibility of that portion of it still (presumably) archived in Hungary, Rumania, and Yugoslavia. Finally, much still remains to be done in the field of the Indian tribes whom John Smith met, and attempted to understand. Here again controversy rages, though mildly. (It should be stressed that the author found no complete scientific analysis yet made of such elementary sources as the contemporary Algonkian vocabularies assembled by John Smith, William Strachey, and George Waymouth. He has had to make his own attempts at analysis.)

The author can only say that he has tapped every source available to him, and that the commentaries which follow are the "cream" that has risen to the top. The quantity of unreferred-to skim-milk beneath may be conjectured.

### EPIGRAPH

Ben Jonson's *Works*, eds. C. H. Herford, Percy and Evelyn Simpson (11 vols., Oxford, 1925–52), VIII, 27.

### PREFACE

On Thomas Fuller: William Nicolson, *History of Libraries* (London, 1696), 14.

On Henry Adams: Edward Arber, Introduction to John Smith's *Works* (Birmingham, 1884), p. cxviii.

On the English: A. L. Rowse, *The England of Elizabeth* (New York, 1951), 173.

On "attractive personalities": Neal W. Gilbert, in *Renaissance News*, XII (1959), 269.

## PART I

### CHAPTER 1

1. See Dr. Heinrich Schäfer, *Geschichte von Portugal*, Band III (Hamburg, 1850), 416; Julián María Rubio, *Felipe II y Portugal* (Madrid, 1927), 200; and Queiroz Velloso, *A Perda da Independência*, Tomo I, "O Reinado do Cardeal D. Henrique" (Lisbon, 1946), 129.

2. John Smith finished his *True Travels* for publication in 1629. The first two pages of this work, dealing with his birth and youth, are confused and difficult to follow. I have therefore altered the sequence of the paragraphs to give what seems to be a more logical order to the story, and trust that in so doing I have not falsified it. Details have been added from independent sources.

On Smith's parents, see *Works*, 821–22. His father's home, "Crudley," properly Cuerdley, is a parish on the Mersey near Liverpool. His mother's family, Rickard or Riccard, was well known in Great Heck, Yorkshire (see *The Visitation of Yorkshire*, by Robert Glover, with

1612 supplement by Richard St. George [London, 1875]; Joseph Hunter, *South Yorkshire: The History and Topography of the Deanery of Doncaster* [London, 1828], I, 176; and *Lincolnshire Pedigrees*, Harleian Society, LII, 820).

The record of John Smith's baptism is copied from the parish register in *Works*, p. xxi, along with the record of his brothers and sister. The size of George Smith's land holdings is in his will (*Works*, pp. xix–xx), and the value of his goods and chattels is found in the Lincolnshire Archives, INV/87/250, transcribed and printed in Bradford Smith, *Captain John Smith: His Life and Legend* (Philadelphia, 1953), 343–45. I am deeply indebted, as all students of John Smith's life must be, to Bradford Smith for this first serious attack on the secrets that lie hidden in Smith's life and works, and take this opportunity of expressing that debt.

The definition of a yeoman is taken from Sir Thomas Smith, *The Common-wealth of England* . . . (London, 1589), I, xxiii, 32. (Cf. Mildred Campbell, *The English Yeoman* [New Haven, 1942], 22–26.)

3. On Philip II, see Sir Charles Petrie's *Philip II of Spain* (London, 1963). Alba's march on Lisbon is summarized on pp. 176–77. See also the article on Alba in *Esp. Cal.*, IV, 1046–49.

On this period in England, see J. E. Neale, *Queen Elizabeth I* (London, 1934, and Garden City, New York, 1957), and the same author's *Elizabeth I and her Parliaments* (2 vols., London, 1952 and 1957).

On Queen Elizabeth's payment of her foreign debt, see L. C. Knights, *Drama and Society in the Age of Jonson* (London, 1937, and Penguin Books, 1962), 40, quoting J. M. Keynes, *A Treatise on Money*.

4. On Mendoza's dismissal, see the details in James Anthony Froude, *History of England from the Fall of Wolsey to the Defeat of the Spanish Armada* (London, new ed., 1870–75), XI, 622–26.

For John Smith's schooling, the account of that of William Shakespeare in Thomas Marc Parrott's introduction to his *Shakespeare: Twenty-Three Plays and the Sonnets* (New York, 1938), 4–6, will do as well as any guesswork story.

On Henry IV's life, in addition to any history of France, see the *Journal* of Pierre de l'Estoile (new edition in 3 vols., with notes by André Martin, Paris, 1948–60).

On Lord Willoughby and his sally into Normandy, see S. C. Lomas's excellent introduction to the Hist. MSS. Comm. *Report on the Manuscripts of the Earl of Ancaster* (Dublin, 1907), especially pp. xxv–xxvi. There are three works on the Lords Willoughby, none of which can be relied on too fully: Elizabeth Heathcote Drummond Willoughby, *Chronicles of the House of Willoughby de Eresby* (London, 1896), perhaps the most reliable; Lady Georgina Bertie, *Five Generations of a Loyal House* (London, 1845), never completed; and Lady Cecilia Goff, *Three Generations of a Loyal House* (privately printed, 1957) which attempts to complete the former work, but suffers from slips from accuracy. Studies of John Smith's friend Robert Bertie, later Lord Willoughby, have suffered seriously from the *fantaisiste* biography by David Lloyd, in his *Memoires of the Lives, Actions, Sufferings and Deaths of those Reverend and Excellent Personages that suffered . . . for . . . Allegiance to their Soveraigne* (London, 1668), where there are "almost as many errors as lines."

On the situation in Brittany, see Jacques Levron, *La Bretagne* (Paris-Grenoble, n.d., but post-1949), 19–20.

On Burghley, Sir Walter Ralegh *et al.*, and the royal navy, see Neale, *Parliaments*, II, 301–4. On the same subject, and the Drake rumor, see E. F. Benson, *Sir Francis Drake* (London, 1927), 288.

The Duke of Mercoeur, under whom John Smith later served, has apparently not had a biographer since J.-C. Bruslé de Montpleinchamp published his *L'histoire de Filipe Emanuel de Lorraine, Duc de Mercoeur* (Cologne, 1689 — not consulted).

5. On the value of the loot from the *Madre de Dios,* see Hakluyt, *Voyages*, VII, 117. As to the corresponding sum in terms of today's purchasing power, it is "common practice" to multiply by 25 for pounds sterling and by 75 for U.S. dollars. Even taken with due allowances, however, this conversion rate can be very misleading.

On the *business* of becoming a merchant, see J[ohn] B[rowne], *The Marchants Avizo,* edited by Patrick McGrath (Baker Library, Harvard University, Boston, 1957).

On Thomas Sendall, see Bradford Smith, *Captain John Smith,* 30–31, although I regret that I cannot agree with Bradford Smith in his interpretation of this phase of John Smith's life.

The Captain Duxbury who fought under Sir Francis was killed at Nieuport, Flanders, on June 22 (July 2, new style), 1600. See several references in *Battle of Nieuport, 1600* (see Bibliography). Apropos of the Veres, they combined strict discipline with great piety, a characteristic of John Smith throughout his life.

Attention should be called here to the fact that England still adhered to the Julian calendar until 1752, and in addition began the legal year on March 25. The "legal year" has been ignored throughout this work, but I have preserved the Julian dates to avoid confusion. Where there is any doubt, I have either indicated "old (Julian) style" or "new (Gregorian) style," or given both dates.

On the obscure years 1596 or 1597 to 1599 in John Smith's life, there were English contingents in the Netherlands throughout that period.

6. Robert Bertie was born on December 16, 1582, and therefore lacked two to three weeks of being three years younger than John Smith, if John Smith was baptized shortly after his birth. The details of his activities in France are contained in his Latin and French letters to his father (*Ancaster MSS,* 341–48). The license for Peregrine Bertie is taken from Edward D. Neill, *Virginia Vetusta* (Albany, New York, 1885),

10, copying the original document in the London Public Record Office. On the need for a license to travel, there are some obscure reflections in Sir Thomas Palmer's *An Essay of the Meanes how to make our Travailes, into forraine Countries, the more profitable and honourable* (London, 1606), 26–29 (on soldiers) and 45 (apparently for gentlemen).

On the application of the word "servant" at the time, see Gerald Brenan, *A History of the House of Percy* (2 vols., London, 1902), II, 176–77: Servants were gentlemen of the household and secretaries, as well as ordinary domestics.

On Willoughby's lack of funds, see (for example) Lady Cecilie Goff, *Three Generations*, 70–73.

As for the Humes, David Hume, the poet, was quite certainly the man who dipped into John Smith's pocket. Robert Bertie's friend Lord Hume was most likely the distant cousin I have mentioned. A letter from Sir Henry Nevill to Secretary Cecil, dated Paris, January 14/24, 1600, seems to identify the Lord Hume in Paris with the one who was later created Earl Home (or Hume), who was the one I have suggested. (See Winwood, *Memorials*, I, 146.) Dr. C. T. McInnes, former Curator of Historical Records, and his successor, Mr. John Imrie, Scottish Record Office, Edinburgh, have been most helpful by correspondence and in person in solving these problems.

For a description of the Holy Isle of Lindisfarne, I can recommend no more readily available or interesting sketch than that contained in J. H. Ingram, *The Islands of England* (London, 1952), 32–46.

7. John Smith would have been an anomaly if he had not been somewhat of a romantic in that age. But the knight-errantry often attributed to him — the real-life Don Quixote, with various Dulcineas del Toboso, which some have attempted to make of him — these are patently dream figures of their proponents. John Smith's whole career is marked by practicality and realistic rationale of behavior. The man must be considered in the light of his surroundings, and these surroundings included not only Elizabeth and Shakespeare and James I, but fops such as Nicholas Hilliard's "Young Man," romantics such as Sir Philip Sidney — and the unabashed dishonesty of the greatest thinker of the time, Sir Francis Bacon. (There is a reproduction of Hilliard's miniature in G. M. Trevelyan's *Illustrated English Social History*, II [London/New York, 1950], opposite p. 20.) The road to knowledge is always study and practical application. This is precisely the significance of John Smith's "romantic" seclusion. We must not be misled by the trappings of the times.

Unfortunately, there appears to be no surviving catalogue of Lord Willoughby's library, although evidence does survive that he had one — bills paid for books and for binding books. As for the "Marcus Aurelius," Willoughby may well have had both.

As for Theodore Paleologue, John Smith's "Theadora Polaloga," his fascinating story has been investigated and written up in typescript by Canon J. H. Adams, Landulph Rectory, Saltash, Cornwall, inspired by the monumental brass commemorating him in the parish church. According to Canon Adams, Paleologue was born about 1560. His early history is dark, but it is known that he went to England and was employed by the Republic of Lucca as a hired assassin, to rid the Republic of a fugitive traitor. Paleologue failed to accomplish this patriotic mission, but his lack of principles seems to have endeared him to the equally unprincipled Earl of Lincoln, and Paleologue resided at Tattershall for a number of years. (I am indebted to Canon Adams for the loan of his typescript, and only regret that it has not yet been completed for publication.)

As for any favor or encouragement from Lord Willoughby, it sprang, I believe, only from the paternal and affectionate interest of a great man in a young, capable, and aspiring tenant. England, no one knew better than Lord Willoughby, always had need of young men such as Smith.

## CHAPTER 2

1. The connection between the Battle of Nieuport and John Smith's actions is, of course, unattested. Nevertheless, it is inconceivable to me that Smith should not have been influenced or even prompted by it.
2. Smith's adventures in France can be called typical of the period. Lithgow, Coryate, and even the scholarly Moryson had adventures, at times even more wondrous. As for the names, the great bulk of them are derived from place-names, and are easily recognizable (see my "Fact and Fiction in Captain John Smith's *True Travels*," *Bulletin of the New York Public Library*, LXVII [1963], 517–28, for further details on this period of Smith's life, including several points which I have restudied since the present work went to press.)

Smith's Lord Depreau should be mentioned here, however. In the mid-1580's the French ambassador to Scotland was a Sieur de Courcelles who used the name of DePreau. He had been expelled from England, and Queen Elizabeth insisted that he receive like treatment from James VI, which he eventually did. But at the same time the almoner of Mary Queen of Scots during her last days (in England) was Camille DePréau — said to have been an old man. The coincidence of this combination of names in Scottish history and in John Smith's travels leads one to wonder. It cannot be pure accident. (See *Extract from the Despatches of M. de Courcelles . . .* , ed. Robert Bell, Bannatyne Club, XXII [Edinburgh, 1828]; *CSP Scotland*, IX (1586–88), see Index; and *Letters of Mary, Queen of Scots*, ed. Agnes Strickland [2 vols., London, 1843], see Index.)

As for the Duke and Duchess of Mercoeur, *he* was at the court of

Rudolph II or in the field, and *she* was probably not in Brittany at the time but at Anet, only 50 miles west of Paris. (Information obtained personally from Mr. Buffet, Director of the Departmental Archives in Rennes.) On Mercoeur's departure from Brittany in 1598, see, *inter alia,* Auguste Dupouy, *Histoire de Bretagne* (Paris, 1941), 210–38.

I have corrected Smith's spelling of names throughout (viz., Mercoeur, where Smith has Duke Mercury), according to identifications which range from the certain to the highly probable. Where I could find no convincing prototype, I have used Smith's spelling, in quotation marks. It is in line with this policy that I have written *Mortain* for Smith's *Mortaigne, Courcelles* for *Cursell,* and so on, to *Plouër* for *Ployer* and beyond.

It was Bradford Smith, in his note "Captain Smith's Earl of Ployer," *VMBH* 62 (1954), 348–49, who first called attention to the Comte de Plouër. The data he obtained told part, but not all, of the story, and in 1960 I was able to obtain further information from a descendant of the same family, M. Henri de la Villehuchet, in the Château at Plouër itself. (See, on the same subject, the *Mémoires de Charles Gouyon, baron de la Moussaye,* eds. G. Vallée and P. Parfouru [Paris, 1901], pp. xx, xxvii–xxviii, 76–77, and 168–69, for pertinent historical data.)

On General Norris and the Earl of Lincoln, see Norreys Jephson O'Conor, *Godes Peace and the Queenes* (London, 1934).

3. On traveling in 1600, see Bates, *Touring,* generally; on taking ships "even from Genoa to Rome," see pp. 70–71. (Travel by land was very slow, and dangerous; 25 mi. a day.) To summarize pp. 71–76, in the Mediterranean a large proportion of sailors were Greeks, with vivid superstitions, and courage only on St. Catherine's Day (November 25), when nobody ever got drowned. Very few *dis*believed in the influence of sorcerers on weather.

On John Smith's "little isle of S. Mary," it should be remembered that the coast of Provence was far from peaceful at the time, and it is difficult to know what islands were inhabited in 1600. None of the books on the Lérins which I have consulted have provided any clue.

With regard to the English trade in the Mediterranean, see Sir William Foster's *England's Quest of Eastern Trade* (London, 1933), 68–78; *Histoire des Relations Internationales,* II, "Les Temps Modernes," by Gaston Zeller (Paris, 1953), 1ère partie, 68–73; and Clarence Dana Rouillard, *The Turk in French History, Thought and Literature* (in English, Paris, [1941]), especially pp. 128–45.

On Cape Ras-et-Tin, the text requires this rather than the famous port on the Nile known as Rosetta. It shows clearly in the much later map of Africa in John Harris, *Navigantium atque Itinerantium Bibliotheca: or, a Compleat Collection of Voyages and Travels . . .* (2 vols., London, 1744–48), I, 288ff.

On the "argosy," John Smith estimates her tonnage at 400 to 500, which was relatively small for such vessels. Technically, they were a kind of *carrack*. Ragusa, also called Aragouse in English, was an independent republic at the time (paying tribute to the Sultan) and was a center of culture and good living.

On the behavior of La Roche, we must remember that piracy still flourished, even among "civilized" nations, partly as a result of the religious wars. In fact, Protestant captains assaulted Catholic ships for loot with the clear conscience of men performing a pious deed — the Pope being in league with Satan himself. (See Ch.-A. Julien, *Les voyages de découverte et les premiers établissements* . . . [Paris, 1948], 278.)

For the value of the loot La Roche and Smith acquired: *piaster* was the Italian name for Spanish *peso duro* (famous in story as pieces-of-eight), and applied to Turkish coins of a value of about 5 shillings at the time; the Venetian *zecchini* were gold coins, worth from 7s. to 9s. 6d.; *sultanies* (*sultanons* or *sultanins*) were gold also, and worth 8s. (Arber says 9s.), but Fynes Moryson says that the Turks valued Venetian zecchini higher than their own coins. The whole picture of currency values at the time is chaotic.

The phrase "between wind and water" means "that part of a ship's side which is sometimes above water and sometimes submerged, in which part a shot is peculiarly dangerous." (*OED, wind*[sb], 8b.)

4. Although Smith's account is void of dates, it is clear that his wanderings began at St.-Valery by November and that he could not have returned to Antibes before the end of March or early April, 1601.

As to the affray in which the Berties were involved in or near Siena, no record seems to have survived in the local archives.

On Clement VIII, any good history of the Popes will supply basic facts. For the city of Rome during his pontificate, I have availed myself largely of Dr. J. A. F. Orbaan's *Rome onder Clemens VIII (Aldobrandini), 1592–1605* (in Dutch, The Hague, 1920).

On Father Parsons (also spelled Persons), A. L. Rowse has given a very fair picture in his *The England of Elizabeth* (New York, 1951), 461–64.

On the *uskoks*, see Minucio Minuci, *Historia degli Uscochi* . . . *Fino all'anno 1602* (Venice, 1683).

For John Smith's possible contacts in Graz, see Dr. Laura Polanyi Striker's "Captain John Smith's Hungary and Transylvania," in Bradford Smith, *Life*, 316.

With Smith's arrival in Austria, in both the account presented in Purchas, *Pilgrimes,* and in Smith, *True Travels,* it is claimed that the source is "a book entitled 'The Wars of Transylvania [or Hungary], Walachia, and Moldavia,' written by Francisco Ferneza, a learned Italian, Secretary to Prince Sigismund Bathor," or words to that effect (*Pilgrimes,* VIII, 325, and Smith, *Works,* 852). There is further reference to Ferneza (or Farnese?) in Smith, *Works,* 788, and Purchas, *Pilgrimes,* VIII, 334. Arber has some substantiating evidence in his Introduction (*Works,* p. xxiii), but Dr. Striker is inclined to believe that Ferneza was fictitious, and represented Captain Smith himself. Her conclusion is based, however, on Henry Wharton's juvenile "Life" of Smith (*The Life of John Smith, English Soldier*, by Henry Wharton, trans. with an essay by Laura Polanyi Striker [Chapel Hill, 1957], 16–18), and on Anthony Szerb's deductions (*Hungarian Quarterly*, VI [1940], 734), which can hardly be considered authoritative. Despite the fact that my own investigations in the principal European libraries have failed to produce results, I still feel that I must state: Case not closed.

5. On Smith's "exotic" personal and place names in the *True Travels*, see Part III, Chapter 25, Commentary 5. The problem of Smith's nomenclature in general will be discussed in the footnotes to the forthcoming complete edition of John Smith's *Works* now in preparation by Dr. Lawrence W. Towner and myself.

For present purposes it may be stated that two factors are involved: some degree of phonetic similarity, and some logical association. In the case of Smith's "Ebersbaught," for example, there is reasonable similarity between *Eibiswald* and what Smith wrote if we remember that *w* could be (and often still is) pronounced like *b*, and "ald" like "awlt" — i.e., Eibiswald was then pronounced roughly as (English) ee-bis-bawlt, which is very close to Ebersbaught. But this is not enough. It is necessary to show that a family of that name had contacts with other families also mentioned by John Smith.

Here is the deciding factor. The Eibiswald family was associated with other families mentioned by Smith, more often than not related (at least by marriage), living in the same region (now called Slovenia) and fighting in the same struggle (in Hungary). Finally, the group was important in local affairs, but quite insignificant outside of their own province. Their very obscurity, which was the chief cause of 19th-century disbelief in John Smith's story, circumstantially proves his presence among them.

On the basis of genealogical tables I prepared in Graz and Klagenfurt (summarized below), it is possible therefore for me to suggest that John Smith, having found an entry into the circle through one member, was soon in contact with others. Their names will be found scattered through the following pages.

*Condensed Genealogical Table*

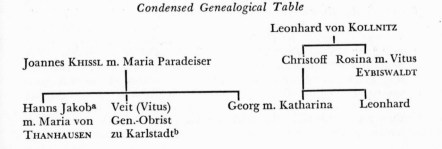

Leonhard von KOLLNITZ

Joannes KHISSL m. Maria Paradeiser     Christoff   Rosina m. Vitus EYBISWALDT

Hanns Jakob[a]   Veit (Vitus)     Georg m. Katharina     Leonhard
m. Maria von   Gen.-Obrist
THANHAUSEN   zu Karlstadt[b]

. . .

Caecilia Karshanerin (1) m. Sigismundus m. (2) Margarete Grässlin
EYBISWALDT

Vitus m. Rosina von KOLLNITZ    Christoff    Joannes    Katharina<sup>c</sup> Oswald

Anna, m.                          Sigismund
Daniel zu KOLLONITSCH<sup>e</sup>
                                  Sigismund <sup>d</sup>

                                  Karl Ludwig
                                  (killed in 1602)

*Notes:*

a. Hanns Jakob von Khissl, Graf von Kaltenbrunn und Gonowitz, was John Smith's *Baron Kisell.*

b. Karlstadt was the fortress of the Frankopan family, Grafen von Modrusch, one of whom was Smith's *Meldritch.*

c. Katharina Eibiswald was related, by her third marriage, to the Wagen von Wagensberg family. Felician Wagen v. W. was stationed for a time at Olsnitz (now Murska Sobota), between Radkersburg and (Lower) Limbach. He may well have been Smith's *Vahan.*

d. Sigismund Eibiswald was active all through these campaigns until he died in 1607. He may have been Smith's *Ebersbaught.*

e. This Kollonitsch family was granted the Kollnitz arms when that family died out in 1587. Smith's *Culnits* was undoubtedly a Kollonitsch, often spelled Kollnitz after the old family.

The printed sources for the foregoing include such works as Dr. Hans Kloepfer, *Eibiswald* (Graz/Wien/Leipzig, 1933); Johann Weichard, *Die Ehre des Herzogtums Krain* (2nd ed., Rudolfswerth, 1877–79); Gabr. Bucelini, *Germaniae Topo-Chrono-Stemmatograficae Sacrae et Profanae, Pars Tertia* (Frankfurt-am-Main, 1672), with many references; and so on, many of them difficult to find outside of Graz.<sup>j</sup> The personal help I received is acknowledged in the Introduction.

6. On Olumpagh, see Dr. Franz Pichler's "Captain John Smith in the Light of Styrian Sources," *VMHB,* LXV (1957), 341–48, and Laura Polanyi Striker's "The Hungarian Historian, Lewis L. Kropf, on Captain John Smith's *True Travels," VMHB,* LXVI (1958), 32–33. These explanations of Limbach-Olumpagh are, however, needlessly involved. The Révai (Hungarian) *Lexikon,* under *Alsólendva* (Lower Limbach), quite clearly points out that the town in the plains was a strategic fort, and was known from early times. Upper Limbach was nothing more than an "inhabitable turretted fortress," whose church was built in

1660. Not only is there a recorded Turkish attack on the "lower" town in 1601, but the contemporary writer, Wolfgangus Lazius, states that Limbach is "Olimacum with the 'o' cut off by barbarians" (*Reipublicae Romanae in Exteris Provinciis . . . Libri duodecim* [Frankfurt-am-Main, 1958], 968–69), thus explaining the "descent" of Purchas's Olimpach and Smith's Olumpagh.

On John Smith's "devices," see Peter Whitehorne, *Certain waies for the ordering of souldiers in battelray . . .* and more over, how to make saltpeter . . . (London, 1560 and 1588); and William Bourne, *A Booke called the Treasure for traveilers, with Inventions or Devises . . .* (London, 1578).

The detailed history of this campaign is largely hidden in uncommon sources. Readily available, but with little detail, is Joseph von Hammer-Purgstall's *Geschichte des Osmanischen Reiches* (Pest, 1827–35), particularly Book XLII. More specialized histories, to be found in a number of libraries, are: Richard Knolles, *Generall Historie of the Turkes* (London, 1603, which I have used in the edition of 1700, by Sir Paul Rycaut); Michel Baudier, *Inventaire de l'histoire generale des Turcs* (Paris, 1628); *Ortelius Redivivus et Continuatus,* by Hieronymus Ortelius (Frankfurt-am-Main, 1665), with valuable excerpts from earlier sources); Franz Ilwof, *Die Einfälle der Osmanen in die Steiermark,* IV (Graz, 1867); Friedrich Schuler von Libloy, *Aus der Türken- und Jesuiten-zeit vor und nach dem Jahre 1600* (Berlin, 1879); and Franz Salamon, *Ungarn im Zeitalter der Türkenherrschaft* (Leipzig, 1887). These are largely secondary sources, however, and I have relied rather on the primary sources printed in the *Monumenta Hungariae Historica: Scriptores* (Budapest, various dates), especially for details.

On the developments along the Krain border, see Gunther Erich Rothenberg, *The Austrian Military Border in Croatia* (Urbana, Illinois, 1960), 52–63.

On the viciousness of the fighting in these frontier skirmishes, see Naima, *Annals of the Turkish Empire from 1591 to 1659,* trans. by Charles Fraser (London, 1832), I, 141–42.

With regard to Smith's captaincy, Dr. Sokoll has pointed out to me (his letter of March 10, 1961) that later-known practice indicates that volunteers often were rewarded with the title "Captain" after an expedition. This did not necessarily imply a regular command.

## CHAPTER 3

1. This chapter and part of Chapter 4 (up to the battle of Red Tower Pass) comprise Chapters V–X of Smith's *True Travels,* which were based to some extent on Knolles's *Generall History of the Turkes.* There are at least two long passages quoted almost verbatim from

Knolles, which, with minor borrowings, add up to a total of about 21 to 22 per cent of the whole. In retelling the story, I have availed myself of sources unknown to Smith (including modern studies), despite the fact that contemporary Turkish and Hungarian writers often disagreed in detail. I hope that I have not erred too far in my correlation of such conflicting accounts, and regret that the period is so confused that any briefer account would be virtually unintelligible.

*Ortelius Redivivus* has a full account of the reconquest of Alba Regalis, with a contemporary engraving (opposite p. 294) on which my description has been based. This account is derived largely from an anonymous MS in the Haus-, Hof- und Staatsarchiv, Vienna, which contains a few details missing in the printed work.

Russworm (variously spelled) was one of the Empire's most courageous and capable generals. (Wilhelm Kohlhaas's historical novel, *Mars und Skorpion* [Stuttgart, (1942?)], is basically authentic and pertinent.) On Russworm's leading a thousand men personally through a swamp, it was more characteristic of the man than of the age. Nevertheless, even kings got killed in battle — three in the battle of Alcazarquivir in 1578, when Sebastian of Portugal fell, leaving the Portuguese crown to Cardinal-King Henry.

"Bemers" — a survival of Middle English *Beamer,* from *Beme* (French *Bohème,* Bohemia).

Smith's "fiery dragons" were straight out of Biringuccio, via Whitehorne. (There is a modern translation of Biringuccio by Cyril Stanley Smith and Martha Teach Gnudi [New York, 1942].) The anonymous MS does not mention these, but Baudier describes French troops attacking through a hail of missiles which included "pots à feu" — fire pots.

Smith alone is responsible for the statement that Modrusch was the commander who brought the Pasha to Mercoeur. Is this merely a touch of flattery? (His estimates of numbers of men are probably exaggerated.)

2. Here Smith got his figures from Knolles, who in turn got them from the same source as Baudier. Ortelius estimates only 30,000 Turks.

As to the commanders mentioned by Smith, Ortelius's list of troops under arms in March, 1602, shows Karl Ludwig von Sultz (mentioned by Smith) with Seyfrid Collonitsch and Otto Wild und Rheingraf — probably Smith's "Culnits" (or "Kollnitz") and "Rhinegrave." The absence of Wagen's name from this list is not significant.

On the skirmish in the "Plains of Girke," two sources have enabled me to identify the location, beyond, I believe, any reasonable doubt. A contemporary drawing of an engagement of October 15 which I found in the Viennese Archives shows "Kihchai Bassa" (Kâhya Mehmed Pasha) attacking two regiments of Christians from the East, while "Kollonicz" is charging toward the west in an apparent attempt to get around to the rear of help coming from "General Fisier Bassa." The scene is "nit weit" (not far) from Alba Regalis. This sketch illustrates the skirmish described in Hammer-Purgstall's *Geschichte* (Book XLII, Vol.

viii in the French translation which I used for convenience). This is stated to have taken place near Velencze Lake, two German miles (10 miles, plus or minus 1/2 mile) from Alba Regalis, at Tscharkaboghazi (Charka Gorge), on the date mentioned. Between Charka and Smith's "Girke" there is certainly little difference.

It is worth underlining here that Smith mentions "Vahan" and "Culnits" as friends of "Meldritch" — both the Wagen and Kollonitsch families had marital ties with the Eibiswalds, and an Eibiswald was responsible for Smith's meeting Modrusch. (See the genealogical table above.)

For a vivid description of the failure of Russworm's expedition to Nagykanizsa, see Maria Bellonci, *A Prince of Mantua* (New York, 1956), 187–95.

3. On Transylvania, the amount of pertinent literature is enormous, mostly in Latin, Hungarian, and Rumanian, with secondary sources also in German. The most convenient modern history is in French: Ladislaw Makkai, *Histoire de Transylvanie* (Paris, 1946). Older are the works by Schuler von Libloy and Salamon, mentioned above. Contemporary accounts are assembled in the *Monumenta Hungariae Historica*, mentioned in the last Commentary to the preceding chapter: István Szamosközy, *Rerum Transylvanarum*; Wolfgangus Lazius, *Reipublicae Romanae* . . . ; Grof Illésházy István nádor, *Följegyzése;* and others mentioned by Dr. Striker (Bradford Smith, *Life,* 333–35). Much of Dr. Striker's work was wasted, unfortunately, on an attempt to track down a Henry Volda ("Earl of Meldritch"), a name which appears but twice in Smith's *True Travels* (never, in the Purchas version), and then *ad hoc,* as will appear in Part III, Chapter 25, Commentary 2.

As to individuals, Zsigmond Báthory is fully described in Alfonso Carrillo, S.J., *Levelezése és Iratai (Epistolae et Acta),* ed. Dr. Endre Veress (Budapest, 1906). A genealogical table of the family is in S. Orgelbrand, *Encyklopedja Powszechna,* II (1898), 199. — Giorgio Basta's *Correspondence* has been edited also by Veress in the *Monumenta,* while there is an ample general biography in *Meyers Konversations-Lexikon* (19 vols., Leipzig/Vienna, 1894–99), with further detail in Eugenio Barbarich, "Un Generale di Cavalleria italo-albanese, Giorgio Basta," *Nuova Antologia* (Rome, 1928), 459ff. Szamosközy, who most likely knew him, spared no words damning him for his atrocities and his inability to control the "free hajdúk." — The best life of the Emperor seems still to be Anton Gindely, *Rudolph II und seine Zeit* (2 vols., Prague, 1868). — On Michael the Brave, there are studies by Nicolae Balcescu and Nicolae Iorga, but I have relied on the brief (but more balanced) biography in Demetrius Alexander Sturdza, "Uebersicht der Münzen und Medaillen des Fürstentums Romanien," *Numismatische Zeitschrift,* IV (1875), 104–11.

The details of the negotiations between Basta and Zsigmond are largely in *Oesterreichische Staatsvorträge, Fürstentum Siebenbürgen*

(*1526-1690*), ed. Roderich Gooss (Vienna, 1911), 268–78.
The date of Mercoeur's death is taken from *Ortelius Redivivus* (p.
310). The news probably took seven or eight days to reach Transylvania, although special messengers *could* have made it in about five.
4. Basta's correspondence indicates contact with Archduke Matthias of
which the Emperor was uninformed. Matthias was Mercoeur's commander, as Mercoeur was Basta's. Basta probably took off when he
heard of Mercoeur's death because he was concerned about who would
succeed him.

As for Modrusch's shift in allegiance from Basta to Zsigmond, it was
quite possibly with Basta's blessing, for the purpose of rounding up
the "free hajdúk." The scenes *they* enacted were beyond the power
of Dante to describe or Brueghel the Younger to depict.

The image from Revelation is not in Smith, but was "popular" among
Protestants of the time. The burning hatred toward Rome of that
vivid work must have had a strong appeal for such as Modrusch.

Alba Iulia is the Gyulafehérvár of the Hungarians and the Weissenburg of the Germans. Although I have found no instance of *Urbs
Regalis* being applied to it, there are sources which lend presumptive
support to such a title: Szamosközy, *Történeti* (I, 205), has "Alba Iulia,
Transylvaniae urbs," which implies that is was the capital, if not royal;
and Schwandner, quoting Georgius a Reichersdorf (a witness of the
events), says, "Alba Iulia . . . fuit enim regia Daciae Regum." Alba
Iulia had also been the capital-seat of John Zapolya as King of Hungary.
Such matters would have justified unbalanced Zsigmond in referring to
it as "royal."

On the Turkish history, see Naima, *Annals of the Turkish Empire*
(see Bibliography), I, 141, 163 and 203ff. The date of Zsigmond's
presence in Alba Iulia is from *Oesterreichische Staatsvorträge*, 273.

As to the incursion into the "Land of Zarkam" ("Zarkain" in Purchas), we may guess, on geographic as well as phonetic grounds, that
this was the neighborhood of the villages then called Schelken, of which
modern Seica Mare (in Rumanian) is the largest, grouped near the
river now called Târnava Mare (Hungarian, Nagy Küküllö), less than
50 miles east of Alba Iulia.
5. On the general behavior at "Regal," compare the description of similar
doings in Bellonci, *Prince of Mantua,* 189. As for Smith's duels, the
description might almost have been taken from István Szamosközy,
*Történeti,* I, 237 — which he could not possibly have read. Though
the story is dressed up, I have no doubt that it is basically true, since
Smith named a group of islands off the coast of Massachusetts "the
Three Turks' Heads" as early as 1614.

Zsigmond was in Alba Iulia on April 1, 1602. When Smith states
that Székely "came to Esenberg, not far from the Prince's Palace, where
he encamped," it is clear, therefore, that this refers to Weissenburg,
which was merely the German name for Alba Iulia itself.

CHAPTER 4

1. It is worth noting that Smith added considerably to his original version, printed in Purchas.

The quotation on the "couch of war" is from Shakespeare, *Othello*, I, iii, 230–32: "The tyrant custom . . . /Hath made the flinty and steel couch of war/My thrice-driven bed of down." Zsigmond Báthory by then had obviously lost all interest in beds of that sort of down. Nevertheless, he gave in slowly. His first move toward a truce was on February 8, 1602. It was March 2 before Rudolph came through with a firm offer of fiefs, a 50,000-gulden annual pension (an Englishman of the time could consider himself wealthy with a third of that); and a general amnesty for himself and his followers. As Dr. Striker states, "Fierce fighting continued from March into June" (Bradford Smith, *Life*, 328). Further details are in *Oesterreichische Staatsvorträge*, 272–75, and in Makkai's *Transylvanie*, 202–3. Makkai also has a work on *Kolozsvár-Klausenburg* (Budapest, 1944?), with some discussion of these events on pp. 28–30.

It is interesting to note that Smith's associates now begin to have Transylvanian names — previously they were from the Krain. His distortions are not enough to obscure their undoubted origin. (In one or two instances, Smith apparently helped his memory by consulting De Bry's map, as in *Veltuz* for Wöltz.)

As regards Radul Şerban, as he is spelled in Rumanian, when the death of Michael the Brave left the voivodeship of Walachia vacant, the Turks seized the opportunity to set up the Moldavian Simeon Mogila, or Movila, as Michael's successor. Basta appointed Radul as voivode of the same region, and Radul chased Simeon out. Simeon's brother Jeremy then appeared on the scene and returned the compliment.

As to the size of Jeremy's army, Smith's figure of 40,000 may, of course, refer to his *eventual* army — after the arrival of detachments of Ghazi Geray's hordes. In that case, the figure may well be fairly accurate.

On Ghazi Geray, see Joseph von Hammer-Purgstall, *Geschichte der Chane der Krim* (Vienna, 1856), 21–57, 90. For those who read Turkish, there is a life of this many-sided descendant of Genghiz Khan (properly, *Chingiz Han*) by Professor Ismail Hikmet Ertaylan, *Gazi Geray Han — Hayati ve eseleri* ("Life and Works," Istanbul, 1958, in Turkish).

The Romans had attempted to colonize the region beyond the Danube, but Transylvania was about the extent of what they managed to hold — and that not for very long.

As to "Raza," Arber identifies this with *Retch*, but that seems of little help. On geographical grounds, and some phonetic probability,

I believe the place to have been at or near modern Brezoiu, a cross-roads village of some importance for transport (recorded on maps, and mentioned in D. L. Armand, *Rumynia* ["Rumania," Moscow/Leningrad, 1946, in Russian], 89–90.

On the atrocities practised by Radul and Jeremy alike, John Smith's later attitude toward the North American Indians must have been tinged with memories of butchery that indeed made Indian torture clumsy and ineffectual by comparison.

As to the "25,000" slain in the battle against Jeremy, it is sheer exaggeration. The account Smith first gave Purchas, two lines long, reads "two thousand on both sides," in plain English. When the two lines were expanded to fifty, and vivid color was added, 2000 seemed too paltry a figure. It would have been an artistic letdown. Smith's writings, after all, are memoirs, not history; impressions, not photographs.

2. With general reference to Smith's last battle in Hungary, I must stress the fact that it was, historically, only a skirmish, any record of which would exist only in another detailed account, such as Smith's. No other such account has yet been found, so far as I know.

3. The date of John Smith's capture is given in the printed copy of the document given him by Zsigmond Báthory in Leipzig in 1603 as November 18.

The surmise that slave markets were not held in Axiopolis during the month of Ramadan is purely that. I know of no records from that vanished city of any sort.

The statement that Smith *marched* from the Olt to Axiopolis is based on the fact that the winter is generally reported as having been unusually cold. Navigation on the Danube was undoubtedly at a standstill.

Axiopolis was a Roman fort on the Danube which appears on maps as late as 1781 (Grenet's *Atlas Portatif* [Paris, n.d.], "Hongrie" plate), but that does not necessarily mean that it still existed. It was located two miles upstream from Cernavoda, Rumania, which is 588 miles from Istanbul by modern roads.

Smith's account of the slave market parallels Fynes Moryson's (*Shakespeare's Europe*, ed. Charles Hughes [London, 1903], 14–15), which adds considerably more detail:

> The merchants or bawds buying these captives, lead them bound one to another in chains, forcing the sick and weak with whips to march as fast as the rest, or else cut their throats if they be not able to go, and at night when they are brought into a stable, and might hope for rest, then they suffer hunger, the men are scourged with whips, the women and boys so prostituted to lust, as their miserable outcries yield a woeful sound to all that are near them.

(See also William Lithgow's *Totall Discourse* [Glasgow, 1906], 122–23, and George Sandys's *Relation of a Journey begun An. Dom. 1610* [London, ed. of 1673], 54–55.)

The presumed original form of Charatza's name in mid-twentieth century Greek (not much different from that of John Smith's day) would be: τὸ κορίτσι τῆς Τραπεζοῦντος, or ἀπό τὴν Τραπεζοῦντα, according to a native Greek university-graduate. (I have transcribed the last syllable of Trebizond with a *d* to accord better with Greek pronunciation.) The fact that the name Smith recorded is Greek seems to indicate that the lady may have been Greek also. William Strachey, later Secretary of the Virginia Company, and a friend of Smith's, records the same word in his *Historie*, p. 73: "I have seen the *Carazzaies* of Scio [Chios] and Pera [probably the "suburb" of Istanbul now usually called Beyoğlu]." Bashaw Bogall may also have been a Greek, but Professor Franz Babinger has suggested that it might be "Baqqāl," modern Turkish *bakkal*, a dealer in spices (personal communication of October 3, 1960).

4. On the details of John Smith's route from Istanbul to Charatza's brother's timar, the curious reader can consult my studies, "Captain John Smith's Route through Turkey and Russia," and "Fact and Fiction in Captain John Smith's *True Travels*" (see Bibliography for details).

Suffice it to say here that some of Smith's names seem to have been picked up in London, on his return, from the Reverend Samuel Purchas, who had many maps at his disposal.

From Varna, Smith mentions crossing the Black Sea to the Capes of Taur and Pergilos, between which he passed into the Sea "Dissabacca," from Italian "delle Sabacche" (see my study "Smith's Route," p. 363, for full discussion).

Smith includes a lengthy description of life among the Turks in his Chapter XIII, which I have not troubled to quote. This is followed by a considerable account of the Crimean Tatars, in Chapters XIV–XVI. For an analysis of these chapters, see my study, "Captain John Smith's Observations on Life in Tartary," *VMHB*, LXVIII (1960), 271–82. I need only add here that the great bulk of the narrative is made up of passages from Friar William of Rubruck's *Peregrinations* (as published in Purchas, *Pilgrimes*, XI, 10–15), followed by extracts from Martin Broniovius's "Descriptions" (as quoted by Purchas, in his *Pilgrimes*, XIII, 461–91). Scattered through these ten pages of borrowings there are morsels which are uniquely John Smith's.

It is worth adding, with regard to Nalbrits, etc., that although the *name* was picked up from a map studied long after Smith had left Tartary, basic support for Smith's *description* came to light relatively recently. A stone fortress, two storeys in height (at least in part) and measuring some 700 feet in length by half that in width, was found by Soviet archaeologists not far from the presumed site of Ptolemy's Nalbrits (or Nalbars), and excavated between 1949 and 1951. This was

Sarkel, "White Tower," a fortress of the Khazar Turks that dated back
to the 10th century at least. A building half the size of the Tower of
London would certainly have impressed Smith as being "vast"! (NOTE:
Information on Sarkel seems to be confined to works in Russian. See
Professor M. A. Miller, *Don i Priazov'ye v drevnosti; Chast' III. Ran-
neye srednevekov'ye* ["The Don and the Azov Region in Early Times;
Part III. The early Middle-ages," Institute for the Study of the USSR,
Munich, 1961].)

For a full discussion of the timar system, see M. Fuad Köprülü,
*Alcune osservazioni intorno all'influenza delle istituzioni bizantine sulle
istituzioni ottomane,* translated from Turkish (Rome, 1953), 64–89. A
briefer study is to be found in Leopold Ranke's *Die Osmanen* (Berlin,
1857).

5. The caravan route Smith chanced on was undoubtedly the caravan
route to Astrakhan, called the *Chorny Shlyakh* in Russian.

Aecopolis is again a name taken from a map, based on Ptolemy.
Smith had probably run across Valuiki or Izyum, the nearest Muscovite
outposts to his "route." Throughout, Smith's description of the villages
and fortifications he saw is borne out by contemporary drawings. But
for the fact that he *did* not, John Smith *could* have introduced log
cabins into Virginia or Massachusetts — he described such buildings per-
fectly (*Works,* 868). (See Harold R. Shurtleff, *The Log Cabin Myth*
[Cambridge, Mass., 1939], especially pp. 186–208.) Smith's description
of the roads he found, however, merits quoting:

> You shall find pavements over bogs, only of young fir trees laid
> cross one over another, for two or three hours journey, or as the
> passage required: and yet in two days travel you shall scarce see
> six habitations.

Those words, but for the 17th-century flavor of language, could have
been the very ones used by a German soldier (released by Russia in
1947) in describing the roads in the Ukraine to me, in Berlin, a few
months after his release.

CHAPTER 5

1. The so-called "Long War" (1593–1606) in which Smith took part consisted largely of a series of attacks and counterattacks on various strong-
points. To avoid the Turks in 1603, Smith had to travel north of Eger
(Erlau), which had surrendered to them in 1596. He writes that he
went first to Fülek (Fil'akovo), then to Tokaj and to Kaschau (Košice).
This region was subject to Turkish raids then, and it is possible that
Smith's zigzag route was due to some such cause.

Beyond Košice, however, his route to the Castle of Orava, on the Kraków–Budapest road, to Olomouc, and to Prague, was direct.

Prague was more agreeable to Rudolph II than Vienna, possibly because it was farther from war's alarms. But for the ordinary citizen, be it said for the record of John Smith's travels, it was unimpressive at the time, "and so filthy that the saying ran that the Turks would never take it despite the feebleness of its fortifications, because it was so well-guarded by its stenches" (E. S. Bates, *Touring in 1600* [London, 1911], 121).

With regard to the possible troubles on the Polish side of the frontier late in 1603, I have followed the detail supplied in the *Istoriya Pol'shi*, edited by V. D. Korolyuk, I. S. Miller, and P. N. Tret'yakov ("History of Poland," in 3 vols., Moscow, 1956, in Russian), I, 260–61.

On *some* of Zsigmond's wanderings at the time, see Carrillo, *Epistolae*, 669. Although this passage has to do with the latter part of 1602, I believe the restlessness there depicted was typical.

With regard to John Smith's passport, this has been blown up into a major issue by historian and polemicist alike. The matter is discussed in Part III, Chapter 25, Commentary 2. For the moment, suffice it to say that the significance of this document lay in the fact that people were anything but sticklers about the *source* of the arms, so long as there was some visible authority.

John Smith's narrative also states that Modrusch was in Leipzig with Zsigmond. According to Dr. von Mettnitz, that Smith should have found Modrusch there he "considers completely possible," since the member of the family who, in his opinion, may have been Smith's friend "was a convinced Protestant, and Leipzig (Saxony) was then a bulwark of Lutheranism" (letter to me, dated January 16, 1961).

2. With regard to John Smith's itinerary through Germany: The order in which Smith writes he visited the various cities seems confused and my conclusion is that the typesetter got two lines mixed. The account evidently should read: "Dresden in Saxony, Wittenberg and her university, Magdeburg and Brunswick; Kassel in Hessen; Ulm and Munich in Bavaria; Augsburg, Hanau, Frankfurt . . ."

On the book fairs in Frankfurt, see for example Svend Dahl, *Histoire du Livre* (French translation, Paris, 1933), 137–38.

It should be underlined in passing that John Smith took the long way around from Frankfurt-am-Main to Paris, apparently only to visit such Protestant sanctums as Worms and Speyer.

On travel down the Loire, see Bates, *Touring*, 79.

3. Don Juan Fernández de Velasco, Constable of Castile, passed through Paris in mid-December, 1603, on his way to the Netherlands (*Journal* of Pierre de l'Estoile, II [Paris, 1958], 120). This was the first hint of the Anglo-Spanish Peace Treaty. Four months later, Salisbury informed Ambassador Ralph Winwood in the Netherlands that the Constable

was ready to come to England to sign the Treaty (Winwood, *Memorials*, II, 18, letter dated March 29, 1604; April 8 in France). Hence my guess that John Smith may have heard about the negotiations as early as April.

On travel to and in Spain, see the full list of known accounts in R. Foulché-Delbosc, "Bibliographie des Voyages en Espagne et en Portugal," *Revue Hispanique*, III (1896). There is no account by any English *casual traveler* who had to fend for himself before that of Captain John Smith.

4. Smith loads his narrative from here on, with detriment to the story of his life, with bits of history taken largely from John Pory's translation of *A Geographical historie of Africa by John Leo* (reprinted in Purchas, *Pilgrimes*, V, 307ff.), Abraham Hartwell's translation from Filippo Pigafetta (*ibid.*, VI, 407ff.), and Robert Cottington's *A true Historicall discourse . . . (ibid.*, VI, 54ff.). Smith curiously acknowledged his debt to Hartwell only, although he must have known Pory personally, and could have known Cottington.

To these borrowings, Smith added tales which he apparently picked up later in London, for examples of which see my "Fact and Fiction in Captain John Smith's *True Travels*" (see Bibliography).

As for Safi, recent harbor work has converted the open road into a safe haven (information courtesy of the Moroccan Consulate General, New York, April 1963).

As to the adventure with "Captain Merham," despite the lack of clarity, and of stated motive for the trip, the final story of the battle rings true through all the luxuriant verbiage. It may be that the very vividness of his memory of the final scenes obscured Smith's recollection of what had happened before.

In any event, that Smith later saw a prelude to, or preparation for, Virginia in these experiences is evident in the conclusion of the account he gave to Purchas. In that, from Africa to the West Indies and to his capture by the Indians is a matter of only a few lines. But there is an important detail: When he returned to England he still had a thousand ducats in his purse to remind him that farmer John Smith was no more. He was Captain-of-Horse John Smith, with *Three Turks' Heads* on his shield.


# PART II

## CHAPTER 6

1. I have prepared a guesswork chronology for John Smith's travels from Leipzig to London which allows 25 miles a day and is adjusted for

his various stops and for his adventures with "Captain Merham." According to this, Smith was home by about December 9, 1604.

As to what the age of twenty-five meant in those days, Bacon said in 1592, "I wax now somewhat ancient; one and thirty years is a great deal of sand in the hour glass" (James Spedding, *Letters and Life of Francis Bacon* [7 vols., London, 1861–74], I, 108). And Leibnitz was elected to the Royal Society "scarce yet middle-aged" when he was twenty-six (Stephen P. Rigaud, *Correspondence of Scientific Men of the Seventeenth Century* [London, 1841], II, 453).

2. On the early history of English exploration of the American coast, see the Bibliography, *Publications of the Hakluyt Society, The Cambridge History of the British Empire*, I (Cambridge, England, 1929), 1–206; and E. G. R. Taylor, *Tudor Geography, 1458–1583* (London, 1930) and *Late Tudor and Early Stuart Geography, 1583–1650* (London, 1934).

The historical background of the period is covered in detail by: James Anthony Froude, *History of England* (12 vols., London, 1870–75); Edward Potts Cheney, *History of England from the Defeat of the Armada to the Death of Elizabeth* (London, 1914); and Samuel R. Gardiner, *History of England, 1603–1642* (new impression, London, 1904–5). John Lothrop Motley's *History of the United Netherlands* (several editions) gives the Dutch background. Henry IV of France is treated in many histories, as is also the picturesque Earl of Essex. On the latter, see G. B. Harrison, *The Life and Death of Robert Devereux, Earl of Essex* (London, 1937).

On the privateers, see Kenneth R. Andrews, *English Privateering Voyages* . . . , and Irene A. Wright, *Further English Voyages* . . . , both listed in the Bibliography in detail, under The Hakluyt Society.

On Christopher Newport, in addition to Andrews's *Privateering Voyages*, see Kenneth R. Andrews, "Christopher Newport of Limehouse, Mariner," *WMQ*, 3rd ser. XI (1954), 28–41. The raid on Cádiz is described in Hakluyt, *Voyages*, IV, 236–68.

3. The story of Bartholomew Gosnold's voyage is told in detail in *Bartholomew Gosnold, Discoverer and Planter* . . . , by Warner F. Gookin and myself (Hamden, Connecticut, and London, 1963).

The basic documents for these voyages, not yet gathered into one study, are to be found in Purchas, *Pilgrimes*, XVIII, 298–360, and in Charles Herbert Levermore, *Forerunners and Competitors of the Pilgrims and Puritans* (Brooklyn, N.Y., 1912, 2 vols.). See also D. B. Quinn, "Edward Hayes, Liverpool Colonial Pioneer," *Transactions of the Historic Society of Lancashire and Cheshire*, CXI (1959), 41.

My statement that "England waited to see what sort of man King James I would be" is, of course, an oversimplification. For a full discussion, see Astrid Friis, *Alderman Cockayne's Project and the Cloth*

*Trade* (Copenhagen/London, 1927), 131–60, modernizing and adding to the story as told in the first two volumes of Gardiner's *History*. On James's reign, there are innumerable works, not the least of which, by any means, is the latest: G. P. V. Akrigg, *Jacobean Pageant* (London, 1962).

On Queen Elizabeth and the title "King of Great Britain," see *Mémoires de Maximilien de Béthune, Duc de Sully,* ed. by M.L.D.L.D.L. (3 vols., London, 1745), II, 80.

On colonization in general, see, in addition to *The Cambridge History of the British Empire,* Howard Mumford Jones, "Origins of the Colonial Idea in England," *Proceedings of the American Philosophical Society,* LXXXV (1942), 448–65, and its historical forerunner, David Beers Quinn, "Sir Thomas Smith (1513–1577) and the Beginnings of English Colonial Theory," *Proceedings of the American Philosophical Society,* LXXXIX (1945), 543–60. The phrase "effective settlement" is taken from Quinn's *Edward Hayes,* 41.

The notion that North America might enjoy a river system similar to that of Russia is implied in the *Instructions by way of advice, for the intended Voyage to Virginia,* drawn up (in consultation with Richard Hakluyt, most probably) for the "Captains and company" who took part in it, and printed in Smith, *Works,* xxxiii–xxxvii. For Hakluyt's part in it, see *The Original Writings & Correspondence of the Two Richard Hakluyts,* edited by E. G. R. Taylor (2 vols., Hakluyt Society, 2nd. ser., LXXVI–VII [1935]), II, 492–96, and the *Cambridge History of the British Empire,* I, 79.

On the religious issue, see Louis B. Wright, *Religion and Empire* (Chapel Hill, North Carolina, 1943), p. 91 and elsewhere.

4. On Smith's "purpose in action," the following is pertinent: ". . . it is customary to think of life as being like a grand lottery . . . But connections between early fantasy and later developments in experience and in personality make it seem that events may be unconsciously sought and chosen" (Percival M. Symonds with Arthur R. Jensen, *From Adolescent to Adult* [New York, 1961], 200). It is in this sense that I mean "purpose" — not a planned purpose, but a subconscious or unconscious one, the reality of which came to Smith himself only late in life.

On the Irish episode, see Chapter 10, p. 145 and the Commentary thereon.

On conditions in Ireland, see for instance Thomas Leland, *The History of Ireland* . . . (Dublin, 1814), II, 410, and Gardiner, *History of England, I,* 373 ff.

On Captain Charles Leigh, see the *Cambridge History of the British Empire,* I, 74, 86–87; J. A. Williamson, *English Colonies in Guiana, 1604–1688* (London, 1923), 30–41; and *Colonising Expeditions to the West Indies and Guiana, 1623–1667* (see Bibliography, under The

Hakluyt Society), pp. lxviii–lxix. Leigh was a separatist, or "Brownist," which could have been the cause of Smith's not joining the expedition. Although he may have been a Puritan in leaning, John Smith was a loyal subject to the grave, and not an extremist in such matters. (I am indebted to Professor D. B. Quinn for calling my attention to Leigh's religious convictions, as stated in George Johnson, *A Discourse of some troubles in the exiled Church at Amsterdam* [Amsterdam, 1603].)

5. With regard to the Bertie family, I have prepared for use in connection with this work a family tree, based on the various "peerages" by Arthur Collins and John Burke, the Harleian Society's *Visitations* and *Pedigrees*, and the *Baronagium Genealogicum*, by Sir William Segar, continued by Jos. Edmondson (London, 1764). (In a few instances, George Edward Cokayne's *Complete Peerage* and *Baronetage* [London, 1887–98, and 1900–6] have been consulted.) From this I have extracted four condensed genealogical tables which I hope will help clarify the Bertie connections, whose influence on John Smith's life was all but paramount.

Table A below shows the tie with the Methams, and a possible connection with Merchant Sendall — the period of Smith's earliest youth. Tables B, C, and D show the connections which by all evidence appear basically responsible for Smith's joining the Virginia Venture. Only essential names have been entered, and in some instances further connections will appear later in the book.

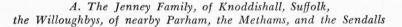

*A. The Jenney Family, of Knoddishall, Suffolk,*
*the Willoughbys, of nearby Parham, the Methams, and the Sendalls*

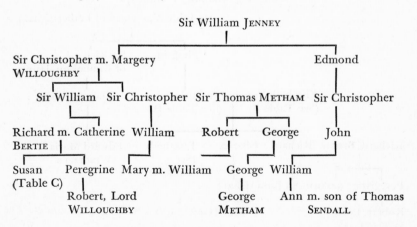

*B. The Vere Family, of Castle Hedingham, Essex,*
*the Berties, the Wingfields, and the Percys*

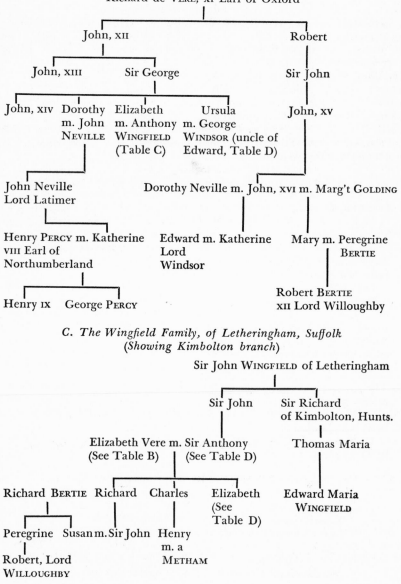

Richard de VERE, XI Earl of Oxford

John, XII                                                    Robert

John, XIII              Sir George                          Sir John

John, XIV   Dorothy   Elizabeth        Ursula              John, XV
            m. John   m. Anthony   m. George
            NEVILLE   WINGFIELD    WINDSOR (uncle of
                      (Table C)    Edward, Table D)

John Neville                Dorothy Neville m. John, XVI m. Marg't GOLDING
Lord Latimer

Henry PERCY m. Katherine    Edward m. Katherine     Mary m. Peregrine
VIII Earl of                Lord                              BERTIE
Northumberland              Windsor

                                                    Robert BERTIE
Henry IX   George PERCY                             XII Lord Willoughby

*C. The Wingfield Family, of Letheringham, Suffolk*
*(Showing Kimbolton branch)*

Sir John WINGFIELD of Letheringham

Sir John          Sir Richard
                  of Kimbolton, Hunts.

Elizabeth Vere m. Sir Anthony     Thomas Maria
(See Table B)  |  (See Table D)

Richard BERTIE  Richard   Charles    Elizabeth     Edward Maria
                                     (See          WINGFIELD
                                     Table D)

Peregrine   Susan m. Sir John  Henry
                               m. a
Robert, Lord                   METHAM
WILLOUGHBY

### D. The Wingfields, the Berties, and the Gosnolds

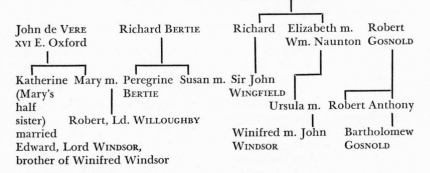

Sir Anthony WINGFIELD m. Elizabeth VERE

John de VERE     Richard BERTIE     Richard   Elizabeth m.   Robert
XVI E. Oxford                             Wm. Naunton GOSNOLD

Katherine Mary m. Peregrine   Susan m. Sir John
(Mary's        BERTIE            WINGFIELD
half                                 Ursula m. Robert Anthony
sister)    Robert, Ld. WILLOUGHBY
married                       Winifred m. John   Bartholomew
Edward, Lord WINDSOR,           WINDSOR        GOSNOLD
brother of Winifred Windsor

Next to Thomas Sendall, the most significant name in Table A is that of George Metham, who "flourished" from 1590 to 1646. His father apparently died before George Smith.

In Table B it should be noted that George Percy was one of John Smith's companions in the Virginia Venture. In Table C, Edward Maria Wingfield was one of the patentees of the Virginia Venture. In Table D, the principal character is Bartholomew Gosnold, to whom John Smith attributed the very creation of the idea.

The background of the knighting of Robert Bertie may be found in G. B. Harrison, *A Jacobean Journal . . . 1603–1606* (London, 1946), pp. 179–82, 191–92, and 213–16. The letter from Nottingham to Sir Robert, dated January 14, 1605, is in Hist. MSS. Comm., *Ancaster MSS* (Dublin, 1907), p. 353. The date of Sir Robert's marriage is given in a letter from Rowland White, dated March 4, 1605, in Edmund Lodge, *Illustrations of British History . . .* (2nd ed., London, 1838), II, 140.

6. The story of Gosnold and the development of the idea of planting a colony in "southern" (i.e., modern) Virginia is outlined in my concluding part to *Bartholomew Gosnold, Discoverer and Planter*, by Warner F. Gookin.

The tie between Gosnold's wife and Sir Thomas Smythe is shown in this condensed genealogical table:

Mary Mathew m. (3) Sir Andrew JUDDE (1) m. Mary Mirfyn

Martha m.                  Alice m.
Robert Golding (a relation     Thomas Smythe
of the Countess of Oxford)     "Mr. Customer"

Mary m.                                         
Bartholomew GOSNOLD     Sir Thomas SMYTHE

There is apparently no biography of Sir Thomas Smythe, beyond the sketch in *DNB*. All works dealing with English merchants of the period, with the East India Company, the Virginia Company, and other such enterprises, and with the beginnings of English colonization, necessarily refer to him. Some of the sources I have used are listed in the Bibliography.

Edward Maria Wingfield also lacks a biographer. See, however, the articles in *DNB* and *DAB*, Brown's *Genesis*, and Neill's *Virginia Vetusta*. There are a few references in the Calendar of State Papers, Ireland.

That Bartholomew Gosnold was at home in the spring of 1605 is presupposed by the record of the baptism of his son Paul on December 11, 1605. (See Fulmer Mood, "Notes," in *The New England Historical and Genealogical Register*, LXXXIII [1929], 374.)

Details regarding Gorges are to be found in James Phinney Baxter, *Sir Ferdinando Gorges and his Province of Maine* (Boston, 1890), and in the much more up-to-date study by Professor Richard Arthur Preston, *Gorges of Plymouth Fort* (Toronto, 1953). For Gorges and the Indians, see the latter work, pp. 137–39.

For Popham and the Indians, see Hist. MSS. Comm., *Cecil MSS*, Part XVIII (1940), p. 84, letter of Sir Walter Cope to the Earl of Salisbury, endorsed 1605.

With regard to the Indians, it should be remembered that Thomas Hariot had studied North Carolina Algonkian at the same time that he was teaching two Indians to speak and understand English. It is quite possible that he was again summoned to try his hand at Algonkian in 1605.

On *Eastward Ho!*, see especially Act III, Scene iii, the speech by Seagull. Anyone who read Brereton's *Relation*, however, would have gotten a still more glowing account of Virginia. (See numerous references to Brereton in Gookin's and my life of Gosnold.)

### CHAPTER 7

1. Generally speaking, the documents assembled in Alexander Brown's *Genesis* begin at this point. Brown's entire work has immediate bearing on the life of John Smith, and can be studied as a running commentary. It is only necessary to remember that his personal antagonism to John Smith was so great as to warp his judgment, and at times to vitiate his honesty. But with a word of caution taken verbatim from William Wirt Henry (*Virginia Historical Magazine*, VI [1898], 209–22), I cannot recommend the study of Brown's *Genesis* too highly: "As a collector of historical matter, [Brown] proved to be a great success, as a historian he is a lamentable failure."

On the Privy Council, Popham, and Sir John Herbert, see Charlotte Carmichael Stopes, *The Life of Henry, Third Earl of Southampton, Shakespeare's Patron* (Cambridge, England, 1922), 322.

On the period between the return of Waymouth and the signing of the Charter, see Alexander Brown, *The First Republic in America* (Boston, 1898), 3–6, with "new style" dates throughout. A more modern account of the happenings, unfortunately only broadly sketched, is that in David B. Quinn's *Raleigh and the British Empire* (revised ed., New York, 1962), 177ff.

The most accessible outline of the events of 1603–1606 is contained (with valuable references) in G. B. Harrison's *A Jacobean Journal* (London, 1946).

2. My account of those whom John Smith most probably first met sometime between his return from Africa in 1604 and his departure in December, 1606, is largely inferential, although in the case of Henry Hudson, there is proof.

The passage from Emanuel van Meteren's *Historie der Nederlandsche ende haerder Na-buren Oorlogen en geschiedenissen, tot den Iare M.VIᶜ.XII* (The Hague, 1614), I have translated from fol. 629 *recto*. More of the whole Dutch angle on the Virginia colony is to be found in John Parker's *Van Meteren's Virginia, 1607–1612* (Minneapolis, Minn., 1961), which is basically valuable, despite a number of trivial slips with regard to petty detail.

I have adopted the linguistic term "received standard" from Henry Cecil Wyld's *A History of Modern Colloquial English* (Oxford, 1936), p. 2, because the conceptions and misconceptions to which I refer existed "among the same kind of people . . . everywhere, allowing for individual idiosyncracies, in precisely the same way." It is important that the *acceptance* of these standard conceptions be emphasized.

For a highly readable account of the life of Henry Hudson, see Llewelyn Powys, *Henry Hudson* (London, 1927). As to Hudson's sketchmaps, the information is based on conversations with R. A. Skelton, Superintendent of the Map Room, British Museum, London, to whom I am grateful for much casual but important information.

There are three important sources of information on John Smith's maps: Wilberforce Eames's bibliography of Smith's works in Joseph Sabin, *A Dictionary of Books Relating to America* (New York, 1868–1936), XX, 227–31; Coolie Verner, "The First Maps of Virginia," *VMHB*, LVIII (1950), 8–12; and Ben C. McCary, *John Smith's Map of Virginia* (Jamestown Booklet, 1957). On Hakluyt and Gosnold, see Gookin and Barbour, *Gosnold*, 28–32, and elsewhere.

The relationship of George Berkeley to the rest of that huge family is shown in *The Berkeley Manuscripts, The Lives of the Berkeleys . . . From 1066 to 1618*, by John Smyth of Nibley (Gloucester, England, 1883–85, 3 vols.), I, 347ff. For the suggestion that Berkeley (spelled

Barkley) may have been contact man for Purchas and some of his "useful friends," see E. G. R. Taylor, *Late Tudor and Early Stuart Geography, 1583–1650.* (London, 1934), 53–54. For his travels (again spelled Barkley), see Purchas, *Pilgrimes,* XIII, 451–61. As to the hint that John Smith may have known George Berkeley (Barkley), there is a *Point Barkley* named on Smith's map of *Ould Virginia,* but this can hardly be dated before 1624, and is therefore inconclusive. (See the discussion of Smith's maps in Part III.)

On Thomas Hariot, the basic material is to be found in Quinn, *Roanoke,* I, 35–40, 47, 49–60, and 63, with further references indicated in the Index. Further brief, but pertinent, information is to be found in Edward Edwards, *The Life of Sir Walter Ralegh* (London, 1868); Gerald Brenan, *A History of the House of Percy* (London, 1902); and G. R. Batho, *The household papers of Henry Percy, ninth earl of Northumberland (1564–1632)* (Camden Society, 3rd ser., vol. XCIII, 1962) — see the Index in all instances.

With regard to the language question, it is to be suspected that John Smith (and his associates) had access to the vocabulary prepared by Hariot in 1585 (on which, see Quinn, *Roanoke,* I, 389, footnote 4 and reference therein mentioned). Smith incorporated about half of Hariot's Indian words surviving in Hakluyt's *Voyages* in his own works, but his *proficiency* in Virginia Algonkian, compared with the abysmal ignorance of his fellow colonists, points to something more than mere acquaintance with a vocabulary, or a "gift of languages." Until Hariot's vocabulary is found, however, it will be impossible to know just what Smith's debt to him was.

Waymouth's Algonkian Indians could only have been of general value to Smith linguistically.

3. The fact, well known to historians and other specialists, is that the official records of the Virginia Company from January 28, 1606, to July 28, 1619, have been lost — perhaps deliberately destroyed. The task of reconstructing the Company's early history was taken up, however, nearly a century ago, and a number of sources can supply the interested reader with considerable detail. The chief of these are: *The Records of The Virginia Company of London,* ed. Susan Myra Kingsbury (4 vols., Washington, 1906–35), I, 11–38; Wesley Frank Craven, *The Virginia Company of London* (Jamestown Booklet, 1957), and *The Southern Colonies in the Seventeenth Century* (A History of the South," Vol. 1, Louisiana State University, 1949), 60–66; and *The Cambridge History of the British Empire* (Cambridge, England, 1929), especially I, 74–82 — to mention only a few of those which have appeared since 1900.

On Hayes's plan, see D. B. Quinn, "Edward Hayes, Liverpool Colonial Pioneer," *Transactions of the Historic Society of Lancashire and Cheshire,* CXI (1959), 25–45. On Hakluyt's suggestion, which was in line with Ralegh's old ideas, see Quinn's *Raleigh and the British Empire,* 229. On Popham, see Alexander Brown's *First Republic,* 5–8, which is generally sound, although his identification of one document ("the Hayes plan," p. 5) has not been proven (Quinn's article on Hayes, just mentioned, p. 42, note 40).

As to the general sponsorship of the colonies, the "patron" of the northern colony was Popham, while Robert Cecil, Earl of Salisbury, was the southern patron. This is reflected in William Strachey's writing (1611) "Quiyoughcohanock on the south-shore or Salisbury side" (*Historie,* 64).

The basic documents, letters patent, etc., are in Brown, *Genesis,* I, 46–75, and (more recently) in Samuel M. Bemiss, *The Three Charters of the Virginia Company of London* (Jamestown Booklet, 1957), 1–22. The suggestion regarding the "names" listed as patentees is purely mine, and is intended only to de-stress the importance of these names.

What I have briefly termed, in modern military jargon, "table of organization" is explained in full in the *Articles* of November 20, 1606 (Bemiss, *Charters,* 13ff.). The membership of the King's Council is detailed in the same place, and brief biographical sketches of all of them are in Brown's *Genesis.*

On Hakluyt and the chaplaincy, as well as the *Instructions,* see Parks, *Richard Hakluyt,* 205–6, 256; and Taylor, *Writings of the Hakluyts,* II, 492.

4. The most biographized member of the local council for Virginia is Captain John Smith. (See the special Smith Bibliography.) On the other councilors there are the following historical studies (mostly quite new): NEWPORT, see K. R. Andrews, "Christopher Newport of Limehouse, Mariner," *WMQ,* 3rd ser., XI (1954), 28–41, and references in *English Privateering Voyages;* GOSNOLD, the study by Gookin and myself, already mentioned; WINGFIELD, see Chapter 6, Commentary 6; MARTIN, see James P. C. Southall, "Captain John Martin of Brandon on the James," *VMHB,* LIV (1946), 21–67, and Samuel M. Bemiss, "John Martin, Ancient Adventurer," *VMHB,* LXV (1957), 209–21; KENDALL, see my "Captain George Kendall: Mutineer or Intelligencer?" *VMHB,* LXX (1962), 297–313. RATCLIFFE remains a mystery. Brown's biography of him in the *Genesis* is virtually worthless beyond the final note suggesting that one Dorothy, widow of John Ratcliffe of St. Andrew, Holborn [London], may have been the widow of Captain John. This clue has so far led nowhere, but should be followed further if possible. (Brown's interpretation of Hamor's characterization of Ratcliffe cannot be sustained.)

On the Berties and their possible influence on John Smith's career, there is no firm evidence. I can only say that almost all of Smith's contacts were in one way or another connected with the Berties.

Smith mentions "having spent . . . more than five hundred pounds" on the Virginia Venture (*Works*, 613). This could be the value of the 1500 ducats given him by Zsigmond Báthory in Leipzig (*Works*, 869), but Purchas states that he came home with only 1000 ducats (Purchas, *Pilgrimes*, VIII, 342). The value of the ducat varied, however, and 1000 ducats could be £466 13s. 4d. down to £375. We need not insist on absolute accuracy. As mentioned in the text, Smith seemed fascinated by the sum *500 pounds*. (See *Works*, 617: "though he [anybody] have adventured five hundred pound," he can lose it all . . .)

5. It is dangerous to indulge in statistics regarding the early colonists of Virginia. Careful investigation has barely started. Yet, as a general guide — always to be taken as subject to correction in the light of future study — I have felt it worth while to attempt to localize the origin or ties of as many of them as possible. (Ten of fifteen of them are nameless.)

Since the bulk of these people may be dismissed as irrelevant to John Smith's story (died early, or did nothing), I have not troubled to list them here. Occasional reference to one or another will explain who they were (when possible) as they enter the scene in Virginia. (One *rara avis* from the West Country, by way of illustration, can be identified in the form of Robert Beheathland. See note in *WMQ*, 2nd ser., IX [1929], 60, with reference to *VMHB*, XI [1903–4], 363.)

As to government by a council, compare Claude-Joseph Gignoux, "The [Dutch] States General governed alone, and it is rare that an assembly be very suited to conduct a war" (*Histoire du Commerce*, ed. Jacques Lacour-Gayet [Paris, 1950–55], IV, 193). Or a colony, be it added!

On the appointment of Robert Hunt to go as chaplain in place of Hakluyt, and his identity, see: Walter Herbert Stowe, "The Reverend Richard Hakluyt and the First Charter of Virginia," *Historical Magazine of the Protestant Episcopal Church*, XXVI (1957), 10–14; and Charles W. F. Smith, "Chaplain Robert Hunt and His Parish in Kent," *ibid.*, 15–33. See also: Louis B. Wright, *Religion and Empire* (Chapel Hill, 1943), Chapters II, IV and V; and George MacLaren Brydon, *Virginia's Mother Church* (Richmond, 1947), 1–29.

On the surgeons, see Wyndham B. Blanton, *Medicine in Virginia in the Seventeenth Century* (Richmond, 1930), fully indexed. I have inquired further in the Royal College of Physicians and in the Guildhall, London, without finding anything beyond what is in the text.

On the date of sailing, George Percy gives "Saturday the twentieth of December" (Smith, *Works*, lvii). The discrepancy may be due to the fact that the ships sailed shortly after midnight. Percy was more of a stickler for dates than some of the others.

John Chamberlain's letter is to be found in *The Letters of John Chamberlain*, ed. Norman Egbert McClure (2 vols., Philadelphia, 1939), I, 239–40.

CHAPTER 8

1. The chapter title is borrowed from Shakespeare's *Julius Caesar*, IV, iii, 218–24.

The phrase "lie at hull" is somewhat antiquated, but I have preserved it for its flavor of the times. It is more common today to say "lie to," or lie ahull.

The vivid picture of seasickness is quoted from Richard Henry Dana, *Two Years Before the Mast*, Ch. II (Modern Library edition [1936], p. 8).

For the quotations regarding Robert Hunt, see Smith, *Works*, 90. On my suggestion that the term "atheist" referred rather sweepingly to any sort of extremist, there is no tangible evidence. That the name "atheist" (or "atheism") was very loosely broadcast in the early 1600's, however, there can be no question. (See George T. Buckley, *Atheism in the English Renaissance* [Chicago, 1932], and more pertinently Ernest A. Strathmann, "The *History of the World* and Ralegh's Skepticism," *The Huntington Library Quarterly*, III (1940), 265–87.) As to Hunt's illness, see Chapter 10, Commentary 2, below. As to Wingfield's attitude toward him, Professor Quinn has suggested that preaching had a Puritan taint to some rigid Anglicans (*e.g.*, the Queen), and Wingfield was merely evincing a good Anglican defense against a pro-Puritan element. How strong this element may have been is difficult to determine, but it is known that Gosnold came of a stanchly Puritan family.

Wingfield's unpopularity, however, was due largely to his snobbery, impracticality, and "gentlemanly" self-indulgence. George Percy, at least equally snobbish, was less in the limelight, though his known expenses for fripperies would have been enough to irritate any man of the type of John Smith. See references below.

Percy was born on September 4, 1580 (*DNB*). It is believed that he saw some service in the Netherlands in 1600 (Gerald Brenan, *A History of the House of Percy* [2 vols., London, 1902], II, 208). On Percy's expensive wardrobe, see the *6th Report of the Hist. MSS. Comm.* (London, 1877), Part I, 228–29, and John W. Shirley, "George Percy at Jamestown, 1607–1616," *VMHB*, LVII (1949); the latter loses perspective when he states that £58 14s. 8d. for clothes seems "well in keeping with George's new position as President of Virginia." Peregrine Bertie set out for *three years* in Europe with £60, including a small retinue.

Percy was in Ireland sometime between February 12, 1599, and March 27, 1602, and again sometime between March 27, 1603 and the same date 1604. (See Hist. MSS. Report mentioned above.) Among the colonists who may be identifiable with Irish veterans were (Captain) Richard Crofts, and (Captain) Edward Morris (see Moryson's *Itinerary*, II, 345, and III, 13 and 250). These were in Ireland during

Percy's first stay. So, presumably but unprovably, was Edward Maria Wingfield. On the Percys and the Gunpowder Plot, see, in addition to Brenan's *History* (above, II, 99–143), Edward Barrington De Fonblanque, *Annals of the House of Percy* (2 vols., London, 1887), especially II, 275ff.

Wingfield's whole *Discourse* is in Smith, *Works,* lxxiv–xci. The passage quoted is on p. lxxxviii f., and appears to be a later addition.

Percy's "diary," on the other hand, has not survived complete. The first part of it was printed by Purchas in his *Pilgrimes* (XVIII, 403–19; Smith, *Works,* lvii–lxxiii), but was cut short after one paragraph on the Indians, with a side note by Purchas: "The rest is omitted, being more fully set downe in Cap. Smiths Relations."

2. On the route followed by Newport, the *Tiger* Journal of the 1585 Grenville voyage (for Ralegh) hints that it was already the "standard" by then (Quinn, *Roanoke,* 180, 403, and pertinent footnotes.) Gosnold's 1602 route is discussed in Gookin's and my *Gosnold.*

On Englishmen in the Canaries at the time, see *English Merchants and the Spanish Inquisition in the Canaries,* eds. L. de Alberti and A. B. Wallis Chapman, Camden Soc., XXIII (London, 1912), v–ix.

The account of Smith's arrest is in *Works,* 92. On the vagaries of the Elizabethan *gentleman,* see Professor Walter Raleigh's essay *The English Voyages of the Sixteenth Century* (Hakluyt, *Voyages,* XII, 55): "The Elizabethan gentleman adventurer was the ruin of many an expedition on which he embarked; he was full of courage and initiative, but headstrong, giddy, and insubordinate."

As to the numbers and names of the original planters, accuracy is impossible. I have "cut the Gordian knot" by assuming that the total number was between 100 and 105, the names of 89 of whom are known.

As for Wingfield's servants, they are mentioned in the plural in p. lxxxix of his *Discourse.* John Martin also had "a man," Anas Todkill — later an invaluable assistant to John Smith. One of the "four boys" was later page to Captain Smith (Samuel Collier), and another became a sailor (Nathaniel Peacock).

With regard to the voyage, the following chronology may help fix the picture:

> December 19–20, 1606. Sailed down the Thames.
> January 5, 1607. Anchored in the Downs.
> [January 29. Left the Downs. Estimated date.]
> February 12. Percy saw a "blazing star."
> [February 17. Arrived "upon the southwest part of the
> great Canaries." Estimated date.]
> March 23. "Fell with" (arrived at) Martinique.

In calculating the over-all average speed of the fleet, I have determined great-circle distances roughly as 1750 nautical miles from the Downs to Hierro, and 2600 from there to Martinique. (Since the route actually followed is not known, these rough distances are accurate enough.) Reducing the 47 days of sailing time to the round figure of 1130 hours, we get 3.85 as the average speed in knots. This basic average has been applied to the various sections of the voyage, merely as a crude guide.

The account of Newport's trip of May 21 with the five gentlemen is in the *Relation* printed in Smith, *Works*, xl–lv. This account is usually ascribed to Gabriel Archer, later Recorder. (See Arber's arguments on p. xl, and Maurice A. Mook's concurrence in the latter's "Virginia Ethnology from an Early Relation," *WMQ*, 2nd ser., XXIII [1943], 104 and footnote 8.) The fact that Archer had previously written an account of Gosnold's 1602 voyage and was to become official Recorder of Virginia in September, 1607, supports the surmise.

3. Here in general I follow George Percy's diary (Smith, *Works*, lvii–lxxiii). Purchas seems to have snipped away at the body of the text as well as at the conclusion, but the account is still valuable. For Percy's first impressions of the New World, see p. lviii.

The account of the attempted hanging of Smith at Nevis was not printed by anybody until Smith put it in his last work but one, the second part of his *True Travels* (*Works*, 910). The recollection of the event seems to have been stirred up by the beginnings of the English colonization of Nevis, in 1628. Page 909 of the same work contains the earliest description of the poisonous plants.

As to these poisonous plants, I am indebted to Professor A. D. Skelding, Department of Botany, University College of the West Indies, and to Mr. George R. Proctor, Botanist, Science Museum, The Institute of Jamaica, both of Kingston, for this information. (Mr. Proctor suggested manchioneal in a letter to me dated March 8, 1957.)

As for the "death-roll" beginning with Edward Brookes, I have started afresh since Ralegh's entire colony in North Carolina was wiped out, and before that Sir Humphrey Gilbert was lost at sea, with all his men. These losses were in Virginia in the old sense, but modern usage restricts the name to the Chesapeake Bay colony.

As to the distance from Mona to the Islote del Monito, it is about three *miles* to the nearest point. The error may be Purchas's.

John Davis's remark is taken from D. W. Waters, *The Art of Navigation in England in Elizabethan and Early Stuart Times* (New Haven, 1958), 202–3. On the possibility that Newport may have known the Virginia coast, see p. 40, footnote 36 of K. R. Andrews's article mentioned in Chapter 7, Commentary 4.

On Columbus, see *The Journal of Christopher Columbus*, trans. by Cecil Jane (Hakluyt Society, extra ser., No. 38 [London, 1960]), 22–23.

## CHAPTER 9

1. Various meanings have been given to the name Chesapeake, which was first reported by Ralegh's explorers. (The Spaniards had previously

called it *Bahia de Santa María*.) I am inclined as a matter of principle to prefer the simplest possible explanation in all such cases, and therefore suggest that Chesapeake merely meant "at or by the big river," or "Big-River People." (Compare "Chisapeake Bay," Maine, analyzed by Fannie Hardy Eckstorm in *Indian Place-Names* [see Bibliography], 138.)

For the story of early exploration of the region, see Clifford M. Lewis and Albert J. Loomie, *The Spanish Jesuit Mission in Virginia, 1570–1572* (Chapel Hill, N. Car., 1953), especially the "Historical Synthesis," pp. 3–64 and 193–97. Although some of the points made in this work are open to question, it adds further details to what is available in the Quinn work.

As for Bartholomew Gilbert, I was fortunate in locating his grandfather's will in the Archives, Suffolk, at Ipswich, which establishes him as a second cousin of Bartholomew Gosnold. (Ipswich Probate Office, Bk. 27, fol. 337. Galfridi Gilbte de Giperico.)

For the latitudes, see Quinn, *Roanoke*, II, 848.

On Archer's activities at this time, he may have been appointed recorder by Newport, who almost certainly availed himself of Archer for his report to London. Archer was officially made recorder (by Ratcliffe?) on September 10 or 11, 1607 (see Smith, *Works*, lxxx).

For the astronomical information, I am indebted to K. Aa. Strand, Director, Astronomy & Astrophysics Division, U.S. Naval Observatory, Washington (personal letter of February 16, 1961).

The four early accounts on which this chapter and the next are based are: *A relation of the Discovery of our River*, generally attributed to Archer and briefly referred to under his name hereafter (Smith, *Works*, xl–lv); Percy's *Observations*, or "diary," (*ibid.*, lvii–lxxiii); Smith's *True Relation*, or "account," (*ibid.*, 5–8); and *The Proceedings of the English Colony in Virginia*, the "1612 account," edited by William Symonds (*ibid.*, 89–174). Further detailed reference to sources seems unnecessary.

My "hundred centuries" need not be taken as statistical. It is merely a way of hinting at the gulf between the "savages" and the Jacobean colonists. (The application of the name "savage" to the North American Indians seems to be directly traceable "in descent of usage" to the earliest French accounts of Canada. The word then clearly meant "wild" [living in a forest] as opposed to "civilized" [living in a community], and probably had little connotation of fierceness. See Hakluyt's *Voyages*, VIII, 195–396 *passim*.)

The Virginia Algonkians had reached only a low level of cultural development by 1607, some of the civilizing factors possibly borrowed not long before (*i.e.*, within four to five generations) from more "advanced" neighbors to the south and west. (See the specialized study of Nancy Oestreich Lurie, "Indian Cultural Adjustment to European Civilization" [see Bibliography], 33–60. This work assumes a sort of political sophistication or maturity among the Powhatan Indians, however, which seems to me unevidenced. The work should, I believe, be read with just as much care as one which dubs the Indians "savages.")

2. On the use of the name "werowance," Percy here shows that he has read Hakluyt's *Voyages,* since in that work Ralph Lane states that the Chesepians have "sundry Kings, whom they call Weroances" (Quinn, *Roanoke,* 257), although at Kecoughtan he had referred only to the "chiefest" of the Indians. There may well have been a copy or two of Hakluyt's compilation in Jamestown.

For the unusual meaning of the word "hope," see *OED.* The site of Archer's Hope has been established beyond reasonable doubt by Charles E. Hatch, Jr., in "Archer's Hope and the Glebe," *VMHB,* LXV (1957), 467-84.

John Smith's predicament may be compared, in a remote way, with the imprisonment of George Percy's brother, the Earl of Northumberland, in the Tower of London — on charges as trumped-up as those against John Smith. It has been written that "there was a stoicism underlying the Earl's impetuous nature which enabled him to bear misfortune with admirable equanimity" (Fonblanque, *Annals,* II, 330). The same thing could be said of John Smith.

3. On the previous occupation of Jamestown peninsula, see John L. Cotter, "Archeological Excavations at Jamestown Colonial National Historical Park and Jamestown National Historic Site, Virginia," *Archeological Research Series Number 4, National Park Service* (Washington, 1958), 6.

As to the threat of trouble at Jamestown in the very beginning, there can be little doubt that the Paspaheghs regarded the English as interlopers, in one sense or another. See Dr. Flannery's *Analysis,* 16, 76-77; Speck's *Powhatan Tribes,* 320-21; and Lurie's "Cultural Adjustment," 46 — as well as Smith, *Works,* 81.

To describe the action of the colonists in planting themselves at Jamestown I have borrowed the "Western" verb "to squat," in the sense of "occupy without legal right." ("Western" is unnecessary; it was used by James Madison in Virginia in 1788!)

The name of the werowance (Wowinchopunk) was not recorded until Smith had left, but it must have been the same man (see Strachey, *Historie,* 66-67).

*Clapboard* was "a smaller size of split oak, imported from north Germany [or the Baltic], and used by coopers for making barrel staves" *(OED).* One of the economic reasons for planting a colony in America was to relieve England of dependence on foreign countries for certain raw materials.

4. The exploring trip was required by the *Instructions* (Smith, *Works,* xxxvii). For a thorough study of how these *Instructions* were carried out, see Maurice A. Mook, "Virginia Ethnology from an Early Relation,"

*WMQ,* 2nd ser., XXIII (1943), 101–29. A good deal of work on the subject has been done since.

Tindall's original sketch-map has apparently not survived, but one made in 1608 is to be found among the Cotton MSS in the British Museum. This one was redrawn and reproduced in Strachey, *Historie,* opposite p. 31. It offers some evidence that Tindall remained in Jamestown at least until 1608.

The name of the Weanock Indians is apparently taken from that of the sassafras tree, *winauk* (Quinn, *Roanoke,* I, 329, and II, 899), although the word seems incomplete as a place- or tribe-name (see Hamill Kenny, *The Origin and Meaning of the Indian Place Names of Maryland* [Baltimore, 1961], 145–46). As regards the sassafras tree itself, see Wyndham B. Blanton, *Medicine,* 100–109. It was valued for many uses.

The wildfowl "like blackbirds" were probably a kind of ouzel (see Smith, *Works,* 60, and Quinn, *Roanoke,* I, 451).

On the Indian map-maker, both Samuel de Champlain (*Les Voyages de la Nouvelle France* . . . [1632], trans. by Annie Nettleton Bourne [New York, 1922], 106) and John Lawson (*History of North Carolina* [Richmond, Va., 1951], 217) refer to the map-making abilities of the Algonkians generally.

The mountains called Quirank (or Quirauk) were obviously the Blue Ridge. It is possible that the name may correspond to the Indian tribe called *Queyonks* (*r* sometimes representing *y, l, n* or *t* of other dialects), described in 1671 by John Lederer as a nation of "the South West Indians" (*The Discoveries of John Lederer,* ed. William P. Cumming [Charlottesville, Virginia, 1958], 99).

Pawatah, or Powatah, later came to be called Tanx ("little") Powhatan. He was the son of the overlord, and his position as werowance of the village which gave Powhatan and his tribe that name is testimony that Powhatan was feeling his way toward establishing an inheritance of the succession in the male line, in defiance of the tradition of descent through brothers and the female line. (He did not succeed.)

The title *werowance* literally meant "he who has a rich manner of life, he who lives 'royally,' " and probably should be translated as "Magnate," although "Chief" will do, with "Great Chief" for Powhatan (see Quinn, *Roanoke,* II, 899). I prefer the descriptive title "Despot," however, as will be seen below.

As to Archer's detailed account of what transpired between Newport and the presumed emperor, it is obvious that he relied pretty much on his imagination.

As for the location of the village of Powhatan (Archer's "Pawatah's Tower"), it appears to have been on the high ground, a mile and a half to two miles below the falls, on the left bank of the James (Mr. Howard A. MacCord, President of the Archeological Society of Virginia, verbally to me late in March, 1963). As to Archer's "12 score," the reference must be to geometric paces (see William Bourne's *A Regiment for the Sea*, ed. E. G. R. Taylor [Hakluyt Society, 2nd ser., CXXI (1963)], 90).

As to the Algonkian words, both Archer and Strachey record *cheisk* or *chesk* as meaning "all." (Compare Cree *kuh'keyow*, "all, every.") The meaning of *chemuze* is uncertain. (Compare Smith's *chammay*, "friend," and Cree *chēmāo*, "he accompanies him [in a canoe].")

As to the local name for copper, the usual local Algonkian word seems to have been something like *matassin*, recorded by John Smith. Archer's word *caquassan* could be a contraction of a cognate of Cree *mihkwaw'*, "it is red," plus the element *-assen (usinne)*, "stone."

On Newport's last visit to Pawatah, only Percy has recorded it (Smith, *Works*, lxix). On John Smith's activities, here we have the first hint that he was planning to survey the country and sketch out maps for England — and for Henry Hudson.

5. For a brief description of the Appomattocs and other Indian tribes of the region, see Ben C. McCary, *Indians in Seventeenth Century Virginia* (Jamestown Booklet, 1957), 3-10. For the redoubtable "Queen" Opossunoquonuske, see Strachey, *Historie*, 64.

For the analysis of *Opechancanough*, I am indebted to William R. Gerard's "The Tapahanek Dialect of Virginia," *American Anthropologist*, new ser., VI (1904), 314; "from *O'pĭchankwēnú*."

On Quiyoughcohannock (also Coiacohhanauke), Strachey's *Historie* (p. 64) says: "Coiacohhanauke, which we commonly (though corruptly) call Tapahanock, and is the same . . ." I have changed Tapahanock to Quiyoughcohannock wherever it appears, to avoid confusion.

6. The accounts of the casualties varied considerably. Without going into unnecessary detail, it may be pointed out that Smith by degrees raised this figure to "one and twenty," all slain! (*Works*, 610.) Inconsistencies and slow expansion of factual accounts were not uncommon in those days.

Eustace Clovill was undoubtedly a close relative (if not a son) of the Eustace Clovill of Clovill Hall, West Hanningfield, Essex, who died in 1589 (Philip Morant, *The History and Antiquities of the County of Essex* [2 vols., Chelmsford, 1816], II, 37). The Shakespearean line is from *Troilus and Cressida*, III, iii, 232.

With regard to the date of Smith's admission to the Council, June 10, it is clear from this that the 13 weeks of restraint to which Smith refers ended when he went up the river with Newport, not when he was admitted to the Council.

Archer's account says that Newport told the two visitors from across the river that "Tapahanauk [Quiyoughcohannock] was 'matah' and 'chirah,' whereat laughing they went away" (Smith, *Works*, lv). Strachey's *Historie* (p. 182) has *marapow* for "enemy," which would be *matapo* in another dialect. This is parallel to Cree *mache-*, "evil, bad," plus *-apāo*, "man," as mentioned before. *Chirah* almost certainly is Strachey's *kear* (p. 207) or *quire* (p. 190), "you." It is small wonder that the Indians laughed.

As for Newport being hired by the Company to transport the colonists, Smith was quite right; but it was tactless to insist so much on the point. See *Works*, 386 and 442–45.

The account of the extraordinary meeting between Newport and Wingfield, and the explanations to Gosnold and Archer, is in Wingfield's *Discourse* (Smith, *Works*, lxxv), which I have referred to as his *Apologia*.

As to Smith's reliability "as a historian," his writings should not be considered as history. His first published work was "edited out of" a letter to a friend. His next works were accounts of what he himself did. If his *Generall Historie* merits that title, it is only in so far as it contains the raw material of history, and is a sincere (if at times highly biased) effort to compile the available accounts into a coherent story. It still falls short of *history*, however, in that it remains only a collection of personal narratives, by no means all of them Smith's. (Dorothil Desmond Patterson's *Captain John Smith: An Analysis of his Ability as a Historian* [thesis presented at Columbia University, New York, May, 1942, toward an M.A. degree], though fair, misses the point. See rather R. G. Collingwood, *The Idea of History* [Oxford, 1946], 304, and *L'Histoire et ses méthodes* [Encyclopédie de la Pléiade, Paris, 1961], 1524–26, for rationale.)

On the first communications sent from Virginia to England by Newport's ship, the so-called Archer *Relation* is in Smith, *Works*, xl–lv. The other two "official" reports are in The American Antiquarian Society's Transactions, *Archaeologia Americana* IV (Boston, 1860), 59–65.

The letter from the Council in Virginia is in Brown's *Genesis*, I, 106–8. Tindall's brief note to Prince Henry is also in Brown, I, 108–9 and Smith, *Works*, xxxviii–xxxix. George Percy's letter and that from the uncertain Dutchman are both mentioned in a letter from Dudley Carleton to John Chamberlain, dated August 18, 1607, and printed in Smith, *Works*, lvi. And the letter from Brewster to Cecil is in Brown's *First Republic*, 33–34.

CHAPTER 10

1. On Powhatan, Strachey's *Historie* supplies details not to be found in John Smith's works. Much of my account is therefore illuminated by Strachey. Whatever the source, however, there is evidence that Powhatan was kept informed of what went on in his domain, that he practiced divination and allied arts, and that he was as uninclined to take

drastic action as his earlier fellow despot of Mexico, Motecuhzoma II. (Motecuhzoma is the correct form for Montezuma, a name given popularity by Prescott and others. See León Portilla, *Visión de los Vencidos* [see Bibliography], and *Esp.-Cal.*, XXXV, 1182.)

My guess as to Powhatan's age is based on Smith (*Works*, 80) and on the reputed age of his younger brother, Opechancanough, who died in 1644 "about a hundred." He took his name from the homonymous village already mentioned, which has long mistakenly been interpreted as meaning "waterfall," because of a misreading of the Archer text. (See William W. Tooker in *American Anthropologist*, new ser., VI [1904], 467, and William Alexander Read, *Louisiana Place-Names of Indian Origin* [Baton Rouge, 1927], 55.)

Having said what in my opinion the name Powhatan does *not* mean, I regret that I cannot at the moment offer a sound substitute, although there are several possibilities. Consequently, for the purposes of this work, it may be stated that the meaning of *Powhatan,* as well as of Powhatan's original given name, has not been established, and I see no reason for blind guessing. The other names were probably acquired by the conquest of the villages mentioned, as was local custom (see John R. Swanton, "Aboriginal Culture of the Southeast," *BAE 42nd Annual Report* [Washington, 1928], 698). (The lack of correspondence in spelling need not disturb anyone — Powhatan was spelled Pawatah, Poetan, Pewhakan, Poughwaton, and so on.)

As to calling Powhatan the *Despot* of Tidewater Virginia, the word was applied by the Greeks "to the absolute ruler of a non-free people" (*OED*). The dominion of such a ruler is properly called a despotate. See Speck, *Ethnology*, 291, for concurrence in opinion as to the true character of Powhatan's rule. The usual description "Powhatan Confederacy" is misleading.

For the prophecies which gave Powhatan food for thought, see Strachey, *Historie*, 104–5.

On the comparison with Hamlet, the famous monologue magnificently presents the irrevocability of a decision which must be made (see Jean Paris, *Hamlet* [Paris, 1953], 157). As to Powhatan's distaste for what we should call reasoning, there is evidence that *dreaming* in the sense of divination (implicit in the word *powah*) was more the mental activity of primitive man than reasoning (see, *inter alia,* Raoul Allier, *Le non-civilisé et nous* [Paris, 1927], 36).

On the quarrels between the colonists, see particularly Wingfield's story, in Smith, *Works*, lxxiv–xci.

The word *thundering* is peculiarly applicable here. Roger Williams (of Rhode Island fame) mentioned that the Indians saw a "similitude" between the English guns and thunder (Roger Williams, *A Key into the Language of America* [London, 1643, reprinted as Vol. I, Collections of the Rhode Island Historical Society, Providence, 1827], 82).

On the behavior of the Indians at the time, Wingfield reports that

Powhatan's peace-messenger brought word that Powhatan had ordained "that the werowances Paspahegh and Tapahanagh [Quiyoughcohannock] should be our friends; that we should sow and reap in peace, or else he would make wars upon them with us."

The great curiosity of all the Indians about the departure of the ships shows that Powhatan was not necessarily too sincere in his attentions. A little trade was all right, settlers were not. He very correctly divined that the permanence of the English would presage a highly transitory empire for himself.

2. As to the mistaken basis for operating the colony, Edward Eggleston has still harsher words in his *The Beginners of a Nation* (London, 1897), 26.

On the Jamestown epidemic, see Wyndham B. Blanton, *Medicine,* 47-55 and elsewhere, and Gordon W. Jones, "The First Epidemic in English America," *VMHB,* LXXI (1963), 3-10. The latter brings forward reasons for suspecting that the Reverend Robert Hunt was the carrier.

The whole period is well described by Percy, Wingfield, and John Smith (Smith, *Works,* lxxi-lxxiii, lxxvi, 9, 94-95). The precautions regarding burials were in line with the *Instructions (ibid.,* xxxvi).

As to Wingfield's charge that Smith had "begged in Ireland, like a rogue," it is possible that the mysterious Francis Maguel, or Magner, who may have been Irish, told Wingfield that he saw Smith in Ireland, "like a rogue," to discredit him. (See the end of Chapter 12.) In any event, careful investigation with the help of Professor David Greene, Trinity College, and Mr. Gerard Slevin, Genealogical Office, Dublin, failed to produce any evidence of Captain John Smith in Ireland.

With regard to William White, he was still in Virginia in 1621 (Kingsbury, *Records,* I, 534). He seems to have been an exceptional "laborer," and is quoted in Samuel Purchas (*Purchas His Pilgrimage* [London, 1613], 952, as well as in Purchas, *Pilgrimes,* XVIII, 419).

3. The name John Smith gives for the season is *cattapeuk.* Unless I am greatly mistaken, this word represents a Powhatan Algonkian form related to Delaware (*Walam Olum*) *kahtúuppu,* Natick *kodtuppoo,* meaning "be hungry, famish."

My account of Wingfield's troubles is based on his own work (Smith, *Works,* as above), with what little Smith and Percy have to offer. The confusing passages in Wingfield's account, dealing with his troubles with Smith, I have interpreted to the best of my ability. The passage regarding Smith's begging in Ireland is fairly easy to untangle (Smith, *Works,* lxxxix), but the other one is far from simple. It reads verbatim as follows: "Then start up Master *Smyth,* and said that I had told him playnly how he lied; and that I said, though wee were equall heere, yet, if he were in *England,* he would think scorne his man should be my companyon" (Smith, *Works,* lxxx). It is perhaps significant that this passage is in the first part of Wingfield's *Discourse,* while the clearer passage (about Ireland) seems to have been added after some discussion or inquiry.

On the number who remained alive after Percy's last entry (September 19), I have taken the figure of 38 who were reported alive on January 2, 1608, and added the two who were killed by the Indians in December. I have not run across any further mention of deaths in the colony during the last hundred days of 1607.

Regarding *hubris*, regardless of the oddity of the word in American English, it seems to fit better than any other. I am indebted to Morris Marples's *University Slang* (London, 1950), 100, for the appropriate and pointed definition of its meaning.

4. On the amount of corn necessary for, and consumed by, the Jamestown colony, it is worth noting that William Bradford considered two gallons of meal a week proper for each person. A bushel was (and is) eight gallons.

As to the date of Smith's departure, the account in Smith, *Works*, 11–12, says that he started on November 9, adding a few lines below that they "went along by moonlight; at midnight he [the guide] brought us before his town . . ." It was new moon on or about November 9, and I have corrected the date to November 19, considering it a simple misprint. "In 1607, the moon was exactly at the Full phase on November 23, Julian [English] calendar, at about noon, Greenwich time [7 A.M. in Virginia]" (personal letter from K. Aa. Strand, Director, Astrometry & Astrophysics Division, U.S. Naval Observatory, Washington, February 16, 1961).

With regard to Manosquosick, recent archaeological excavations at a point not too far removed from its presumed location revealed a large, undisturbed village-site which has proven of great archaeological interest. For the details, see Ben C. McCary, "The Potts Site, Chickahominy River, New Kent County, Virginia," *Archeological Society of Virginia, Quarterly Bulletin,* VIII (1953), No. 4.

With regard to Read and the plot to run away with the pinnace, Read had visited Wingfield in prison (on board) only two or three days before, bearing greetings from George Percy, John Waller (apparently another connection of Gosnold's), George Kendall and others. They said "they would be glad to see him on shore" to which Wingfield made the curious reply that he "prayed God that they did not think of any ill thing unworthy of themselves" (Wingfield, in Smith, *Works*, lxxxiv). He added, to Read, that he might attend the sermon the next Sunday, if the weather was good. Since this apparently occurred after Smith's return from the Chickahominy (not before November 23), the Sunday must have been November 29, and Read's execution must have been ordered for Tuesday, December 1, at the latest.

With regard to Kendall, see my article on him, already mentioned. As to his being shot rather than hanged, this was a customary commutation of sentence accorded to gentlemen.

## CHAPTER 11

1. In my presentation of the story of John Smith and his first meeting with Powhatan, I have sought to combine all available pertinent material from Smith's writings and other contemporary accounts into a logical whole. A great deal has been written about the "truth" of John Smith's rescue by Pocahontas, and the fact that no mention of the occurrence is made in his first account. But since that account is known to have been subjected to editing "to make it suitable," the absence of the rescue story means nothing. Just what did happen, however, is neither clear nor certain. Pocahontas was a little girl of eleven or so, and she saved Smith's life — of that there can be no sound doubt. Why? How?

I believe that Smith did not correctly interpret what he saw and thought was going to happen to him (see Robert Beverley, *History and Present State of Virginia,* ed. Louis B. Wright [Chapel Hill, 1947], 201–9). It might be that Smith was merely being initiated into the tribe. On the other hand, executions were carried out, as suggested in the text. I have only chosen the latter hypothesis, after considerable thought, as the one which best explains the known facts.

Here, I would like to call the reader's attention to Section A of my Indian Bibliography, for I have relied on the works there listed for general guidance. My basic principle has consistently been that some cause or purpose prompted each Indian move.

2. Jehu Robinson is also listed as John, but the latter appears to have been another person. The name can easily be read as John in the handwriting of the period.

The site of Apokant has not been identified, to the best of my knowledge, but it was possibly not far from the present Providence Forge.

Although there may be a large pinch of hindsight in John Smith's explanations, such a trip in the dead of winter could well have been undertaken with misgivings, particularly in view of the turmoil that seldom died down in Jamestown, and the possibility of stirring up a hornet's nest by prying into unknown Indian domains.

As for Smith's looking into the quality of the soil in accordance with the *Instructions,* these read: "Captain Gosnold may take twenty of the company to cross over the lands, and carrying a half dozen pickaxes to try if they can find any minerals" (Smith, *Works,* xxxv). Gosnold was dead and Smith was alone, but the idea was the same.

The account of Cassen's death is that of the Indians themselves, who told it to Smith later (Smith, *Works,* 82, 377). There is no record of what the remaining Englishmen did, but it is clear that they were not reported as missing in Jamestown on January 2, 1608. They must have gotten back.

The silent manner of attack was characteristic. Henry Spelman later reported: they take "their bows and arrows and having made ready to shoot they softly steal toward their enemies" (Smith, *Works,* cxiv). Opechancanough himself showed Smith Jehu Robinson's body, "with 20 or 30 arrows in him" (*ibid.,* 16).

3. The discussion of John Smith with his "hind," or servant, is of more than superficial interest. It shows, by the casual, unadorned way in which it is reported, that John Smith had undoubtedly acquired some command of the Powhatan variety of Algonkian.

With regard to the pistol, Smith himself says it was French (*Works,* 15). "The French proved not only to be leaders in technical development [of pistols] but also in design" (J. F. Hayward, *European Firearms* [London, 1955], 10).

On my bracketed explanation that Werowances were not put to death, this seems to me an important point which is often overlooked (see Smith, *Works,* 72). On the Indians rubbing Smith's legs, it is to be assumed that a white man would not have had to stand for long in December-cold mud for his legs to get numb.

On the march to the temporary hunting lodge, as Smith says, Opechancanough had been on a hunt when the Indians from Apokant began encircling him; campfires here and there in the woods bore witness to this (Smith, *Works,* 16, 37, 70). The lodge seems to have been near the permanent village of Orapaks, and its name was Russaweck.

Smith's use of his compass as "magic" seems based on Thomas Hariot's actions at Roanoke, described in his *A brief and true report* (Quinn, *Roanoke,* I, 375–76). Hariot made great use of Christian "magic" to influence the Indians, and John Smith shows many signs of copying him.

The account of the dance performed around Opechancanough and Smith is quoted from the *Works,* 395–401.

The passage in Strachey on vengeance reads in part: "They seldom make wars for lands or goods, but for women and children, and principally for revenge . . ." (Strachey, *Historie,* 104).

As for Ocanahonan, that was the name of the region where Ralegh's colonists settled. It undoubtedly corresponded to the Spanish name Ajacán, which was applied to the coast of North Carolina and Virginia, and to Chesapeake Bay (Lewis and Loomie, *Jesuit Missions,* 244–49, and Geary, in Quinn, *Roanoke,* II, 853).

As to the "great turning of salt water," which Smith took to refer to the Pacific Ocean, just what the Indians meant is unknown. Smith's own words are far from clear. My feeling is that wishful thinking made an ocean out of half-understood descriptions of the Kanawha Valley salt licks, the Ohio River, and the Great Lakes beyond.

The accounts of the incident of the wounded Indian vary in timing. In the 1608 account it occurred after the reply was received from Jamestown (*Works,* 17). In the 1624 account it was before Smith's letter (*ibid.,* 397). I have followed the 1608 version.

4. On the "tall man" who might have been Smith, Kenneth R. Andrews, in his article on Newport (*WMQ*, 3rd ser., XI, 40 n.), says, "It seems at least possible that in 1604 and 1605 Newport made some examination of the Virginia coast." This may tie in with a Spanish letter quoted by Alexander Brown which mentions an "otherwise unknown" English voyage of about 1604 (*Genesis*, I, 110–11, where Brown dreams that it might have been Bartholomew Gilbert). See also Lewis and Loomie, *Jesuit Mission*, 61–62 and footnote. All in all, it seems that the Indians were telling the truth, but the mysterious stranger has not yet been identified.

With reference to my statement "there had to be magic," see Lucien Lévy-Bruhl, *La mentalité primitive* (15th ed., Paris, 1960), 350 (and elsewhere): "According to an American observer, 'success is never obtained by natural means,'" with a reference to the *Jesuit Relations*, ed. Thwaites, XXVII, 52. Other general works will support this.

For the distribution of the leftover food to the women and children, see the summary given in Philip Alexander Bruce, *Economic History of Virginia in the Seventeenth Century* (repr. New York, 1935), I, 176–81.

5. John Smith's evasive answers to Powhatan's questions are the first real evidence of his innate knowledge of how to handle his opponents. His approach to the Indians was governed by the principle that, since the English were in Virginia and meant to stay there, they had to eat, they had to survive. He was consequently unblushingly Machiavellian. Yet his policy preserved the Indians' lives, their customs, and most of their traditional rights. His mixture of great white father and avenging god superbly achieved what he wanted — a food supply. Other questions were academic until the colony got on its feet.

As for his personal safety, it is particularly noteworthy, and indicative of his character, that even when he was a helpless prisoner Smith seems to have saved his own life by putting Powhatan in the wrong — with some help from Pocahontas, of course.

On Powhatan's presumed fear of "Newport's greatness," John Smith's 1608 account says that Powhatan at that time or before asked Smith to become one of his werowances — possibly with the idea of getting so stout a hero away from the colony he wanted to uproot (Smith, *Works*, 20).

As to Powhatan's being "high priest" (medicine man) as well as Despot, this is based on the fact that werowances seem to have been dressed like other Indians, but the priests (medicine men) wore distinctive dress. In a short while we shall encounter Powhatan garbed in all the savage canonicals of a high priest.

Henry Spelman's *Relation of Virginia* (Smith, *Works*, cv–cvi) has a long passage describing what appears to be a human sacrifice (of children) which is not without its points of similarity to the ordeal undergone by John Smith. Spelman's somewhat illiterate story of his own experiences among the Indians between September (?) 1609 and late 1610 was not written down until perhaps 1613, but is vivid in its quaint way. Its bearing is rather one of background than of direct parallel. I can only add that there does not seem to be any real reason for Powhatan to have ordered Smith's *execution* (for a description of executions, see Strachey, *Historie,* 60), while some sort of sacrifice, or initiation, seems to me implicit in the circumstances described by Smith — a *threat* of death, and salvation by Pocahontas.

As to Pocahontas's age, Smith stated in 1608 that she was "a child of ten years" (*Works,* 38), which was obviously only a guess. Her portrait, dated 1616, is of the "twenty-first year of her life" — probably only hearsay. She was possibly born in 1596, and not yet twelve when she "saved" Smith.

On Smith's making hatchets, Powhatan himself made his own robes, shoes, and bows and arrows. (See Smith, *Works,* 20, 400.)

On Smith's "appointment" as a werowance and the gift of real estate, see *Works,* 20, 25. I have attempted to correlate slightly differing versions.

On Smith's return to Jamestown, the number of warriors is first stated to have been four (*Works,* 20). This account is so defective, however, and bears so many marks of severe cutting by the editor, that I have relied on the later account (p. 401), even at the risk of including some spurious additions. It is unfortunate that the 1612 account (pp. 98–99) is not more detailed, although it does tend to confirm the elaborate story of 1624 (p. 401, already mentioned). Wingfield's account merely states the fact of Smith's return, and regrettably gives the wrong date for that. See the next chapter for the details.

On the curious delay of one night between Werowocómoco and Jamestown, this delay apparently brought Smith to Jamestown on the fourth day, as promised by Powhatan (Smith, *Works,* 19). It also brought it about that Smith arrived the morning of the day on which Newport returned. For reasons which will appear in the next chapter, I feel that Powhatan well knew what he was doing all along, and that the only intervention of "magic" was his daughter's intercession on Smith's behalf. Even that may have been planned (as a sop to those who wanted Smith's death), or it may have been Pocahontas's intuition that her father did not want Smith executed despite the council of his warriors.

CHAPTER 12

1. The chapter title is taken from Shakespeare's *First Part of King Henry IV,* V, i, 20–21.

The account of Smith's return is taken from his letter of 1608 (*Works*, 22–23) and from Wingfield's *Discourse* (*ibid.*, lxxxv–vii).

The weight of the demiculverins is taken from Smith for the maximum (*Works*, 801) and the *OED* for the minimum. Smith is mentioned in connection with gunnery by A. R. Hall, *Ballistics in the Seventeenth Century* (Cambridge, England, 1952), 29, 35 n., but in the latter reference Smith is hardly to be credited. In any case, there are indications elsewhere that Smith knew a thing or two about guns.

Shakespeare's *Titus Andronicus*, I, i, 443, contains the phrase: "Dissemble all your griefs and discontents."

On Archer's resorting to "the Levitical law" to get Smith out of his way, the Ten Commandments were considered binding in those days (as now), along with portions of the Mosaic law. Since the thirty-eight men then living in Jamestown included loyal friends of Smith's, Archer was not in a position to defy Smith in any other manner.

As for the date of Newport's return, it is incorrectly given in Wingfield's *Discourse* as the "viijth [8th] of January." The correct date was January 2, as is explained in Commentary 2, immediately below.

On the "lookout" theory versus the "magic-number," see Strachey, *Historie*, 58, which vouches for the existence of the lookouts.

As to Archer's status, he was made "Recorder of Virginia" in September (Smith, *Works*, lxxx), and Newport apparently returned him to that rank.

2. See Percy's *Relation* for the "due date" of Newport's return (Smith, *Works*, lxx). It is curious that Newport should have promised to be back in precisely the time mentioned for a round trip *to* Virginia by Sir Walter Ralegh, in a letter to Cecil dated August 21, 1602. It is highly improbable that Newport could have seen this. (See Edwards, *Ralegh*, II, 252.)

The various letters mentioned here are to be found in Brown's *First Republic*, 43–50.

The details of the Newport-Nelson expedition (on Nelson, see *Genesis*, II, 955) were first brought to light through the search conducted for Alexander Brown in the Simancas Archives, in Spain. Brown's representative found what purports to be a Spanish translation of a letter by Francis Perkins, dated at Jamestown March 28, 1608, which states that they sailed from London on October 8, 1607. On Sunday, December 20, they sighted the American coast, but on Christmas Eve Newport lost Nelson's ship in a fog. Newport's ship then arrived at Jamestown on January 2. Since it made only 100 to 125 miles in eight to nine days, a good deal of time was wasted somewhere, and this again fits in with the delay imposed by Powhatan on Smith's return.

Perkins also writes that the colonists disembarked on the Monday after their arrival, which would have been January 4, and that a fire broke out on the following Thursday, obviously January 7. Wingfield gives January 7 too as the date of the fire (*after* Newport's landing), thereby fixing the chronology firmly. (For Perkins's letter, see Brown, *Genesis*, I, 173–77; for Wingfield, Smith, *Works*, lxxxvi.) As for Nelson, he chose to winter in comfort in the West Indies, and did not arrive until April 20.

The adage paralleling "man proposes, God disposes" I have adapted from Publilius Syrus, *Sententia* 253, "Homo semper aliud, Fortuna aliud cogitat." There were many versions of the maxim in John Smith's day.

For Newport's promise to Salisbury, see Brown, *First Republic*, 47.

On the goods brought by Newport, a Court Minute of the East India Company, quoted by Brown (*Genesis*, I, 115), reads: "Beads and cloth very much moth eaten, sold to the Governor Sir Thomas Smythe for £3. 5s. for the Virginia Voyage," September 4, 1607. We see what Sir Thomas thought of the Indians!

The phrase "warm the starved snake" is from Shakespeare, *Second Part of Henry VI*, III, i, 343–44.

3. As to the weather in February, while such evidence of spring as swelling of buds would not have been in evidence yet, by February 15 the cold would almost certainly have begun to abate in Tidewater Virginia.

On Panawaioc, see Quinn, *Roanoke*, I, 113; II, 872; and the map in the pocket of Vol. II. The distances by modern roads would be 142 miles from the village of Scotland, opposite Jamestown. (Smith's report is in *Works*, 23.) The legend of the survivors from Roanoke persisted, and Strachey retold it, along with some mention of Panawaioc, in his *Historie* (p. 34). Nevertheless, no real effort to *look* for anybody was made for a long time.

On Werowocómoco, I should first explain that I have indicated the correct stress because the word is misleading in appearance, and because for once the meaning of the word is practically certain: from *werowo-*, as in *werowance* (perhaps "chief, royal") and the common Algonkian radical represented in Powhatan by *comoc-*, meaning "an enclosed place, a house, a walled village."

There have been various guesses as to the location of Werowocómoco, and the derivation of the name Purtan Bay. Careful consideration and personal discussion with Professor Ben C. McCary, of the College of William and Mary, had led me to settle on Purtan Bay as the site of Powhatan's residence. Werowocómoco was abandoned in 1609, and is not mentioned thereafter other than in retrospect.

On the bad landing and the rickety bridge, there are three accounts, none of them clear: Smith, *Works*, 24, 102 (very brief), 405.

4. On Powhatan's proclaiming Smith a werowance, and his companions no longer "strangers," the matter may possibly have more significance than appears on the surface. I therefore venture this hypothesis: John Smith was almost certainly adopted or initiated into Powhatan's tribe

the last day of December, 1607. The gift of Capahowasick then made to him presumably indicated that Powhatan considered him his representative there — a werowance, in short. The confirmation of this in March, coupled with Powhatan's comments about the English no longer being strangers, or even Paspaheghans, must have been for a purpose.

The English were certainly strangers, but in the eyes of the Werowance of Paspahegh the fact of their squatting on his territory may have made them *his* subjects. Powhatan now wanted to make them directly subject to himself, therefore he made them Powhatans. Whether this was an omen of trouble to come, we cannot know. Yet when Powhatan moved to get rid of the English by starvation less than two years later, it may have been convenient for him to have the English considered as his own people. The Werowance of Paspahegh might (at his peril, naturally) side with the English against the Supreme Overlord if they were Paspaheghan subjects, but if they were Powhatans, and he obeyed Powhatan, he would have nothing to say.

Though this may be rationalizing too much, I feel it wise to point out that Powhatan pretty surely had some plan or other in mind, whether I have hit on the right one or not.

On the "English bows and arrows," Dr. William C. Sturtevant, Smithsonian Institution, has supplied the information that archaeologists have found crossbow parts and boltheads at Jamestown (personal letter, dated June 5, 1963).

The quotation from Edmund Spenser is from *The Faerie Queene,* Book II, Canto i, 4, line 9.

As to the tribute Powhatan received, Strachey's *Historie* (p. 62), describes Powhatan's later treasure house at Orapaks, with its "skins, copper, pearls and beads, which he storeth up against the time of his death and burial." For the size of the store, see the pamphlet of the Council of Virginia, *A True declaration of the estate of the Colonie in Virginia* . . . (London, 1610), 29: "Our men have seen 4000 deerskins piled up in one wardrobe of Powhatan's." (The figure may of course be an exaggeration.)

5. With regard to Thomas Savage, according to *The Ancient and Noble Family of the Savages of the Ards,* ed. George Francis Savage-Armstrong (London, 1888), 113, young Thomas Savage was stated to have been one "of the Cheshire family [of Savages] and to have come from Chester." Sir John Savage of Rock Savage, Cheshire, would therefore have been some sort of a relative — perhaps an uncle or a first cousin.

On the behavior of the Indians, and my comparison with the Greek heroes, I believe the Indians could show a better record for decent behavior. (See R. B. Onians on "The Earliest Greeks," in *The Origins of European Thought* [Cambridge, England, 1951], 3–9.)

On the trip to Menapacant, ten miles would be closer to the truth. (Coast and Geodetic Survey maps.)

For the benefit of those unfamiliar with succotash, it is a dish of Indian corn and green beans, preferably lima beans, boiled together (and flavored today with butter, etc.).

With regard to Smith's return to Werowocómoco, Smith says that the distance from Menapacant was 20 miles. Actually it is about 12 miles to Purtan Bay. These errors, primarily in connection with the Pamunkey region, are all the more remarkable because of Smith's general accuracy. They may be misprints (which abound in all of Smith's works), or they may be due to carelessness or forgetfulness. Whatever the cause, they have brought about a great deal of unnecessary wrangling among modern scholars, who too often forget that John Smith did not survey the river with metal tape and theodolite. He used his naked eyes (one of which was always trained on the Indians), an uncertain compass, and a log.

As for Namontack, he was apparently little more than a boy, perhaps of the same age as Thomas Savage. When he got to England, the Virginia Company used him for "publicity." Ambassador Zúñiga's letter regarding him (June, 1608) reads: "This Newport brought a little boy, who they say is the son of an Emperor of those countries, and they have instructed him that when he saw the King [James], he should not take off his hat . . . it has amused me to see how much they esteem him, thinking it (as I do) much more certain that he must be a very ordinary person." (Brown, Genesis, I, 172.) This silly move to magnify the importance of Powhatan was to have serious consequences later. (See Chapter 16, below.)

6. On the basic troubles between Smith and Newport, the quarrel between the two apparently was a quarrel between the spirit of initiative and the spirit of obedience. Smith's bitterness over Newport's blind implementation of his orders increased as the years passed. Of this there is a record. There is, however, no record in comparable detail of what Newport did or thought.

The date of Newport's return must be considered approximate. Wingfield's Discourse shows signs of shaky chronology. The "wheat" was probably corn meal as opposed to the coarse grains used for hominy, and so on. The Indians had no wheat, but beans and wild peas were native American plants, and were raised (in Virginia) in the same fields as the corn — the beans climbing up the cornstalks, and the peas running luxuriantly over the ground in between (Wingfield, in Smith, Works, lxxxvii; see also Bruce, Economic History, I, 153–54, and elsewhere).

The letter of the Spanish Ambassador, Don Pedro de Zúñiga, dated August 22, 1607 (new style), is in Brown's Genesis, I, 110–11.

On James's title "King of Virginia," a letter from George Popham, President of the North Virginia Colony and nephew of the Lord Chief Justice, to King James, dated December 13, 1607, is superscribed: "To the most high and mighty my gracious Sovereign Lord James of Great Britain, France and Ireland, Virginia and Moasson, King" (Levermore, *Forerunners*, I, 383). Moasson was that part of Maine where Popham had settled.

As to Matthew Scrivener, although he was not much over twenty-one, he was the largest investor in the Council in Virginia. In that way, perhaps, he "bought" himself a seat in the local government. His sister married a Wingfield, which created for him a vague tie with Robert Bertie, Batholomew Gosnold, and Edward Maria Wingfield — a combination which would have thrown him against Archer and all that he stood for. (See Warner F. Gookin, "Notes on the Gosnold Family," *VMHB*, LVII [1949], 311–13.) On Ratcliffe's accident, see Smith, *Works*, 31. Wingfield's story of what happened is in Smith, *Works*, lxxxvi–vii. The story on hunger versus gold in the 1612 account (*ibid.*, 104) is signed by Anas Todkill (along with the deceased cape merchant, Studley).

On John Smith and the quotation on gold, see *Works*, 408. The quotation is from Martin Fotherby, *Atheomastix* (London, 1622), 204–5. See my "Captain John Smith and the Bishop of Sarum," *The Huntington Library Quarterly*, XXVI (1962), 11–29, for the story of Smith's acquaintance with Fotherby's book.

On Francis Maguel (or Magner), his offer of service to Philip III was witnessed in Spain by the Archbishop of Tuam (Ireland), on July 1, 1610 (new style), but he was apparently back in England by December of the same year. See Brown, *Genesis*, I, 393–99, and II, 940; also my "George Kendall, Mutineer or Intelligencer?" *VMHB*, LXX (1962), 297–313. On Archbishop Conry, see *Enciclopedia Universal Ilustrada* of Espasa-Calpe, XIV, 1361.

CHAPTER 13

1. The idea for the chapter title is taken from John Donne's "Witchcraft by a Picture," last line.

On Newport's pernicious gift of swords, Smith's original account says that he sent the swords as a present when they returned from Werowocómoco in March. Although the 1624 account seems to say that twenty turkeys were sent on condition that a like number of swords be sent in exchange, the earlier account is more logical. Newport was "courting" Powhatan, to John Smith's not inconsiderable disgust and misgiving.

As for Newport's revenge on the Indians near Chesapeake, it is impossible to tell just when it took place. Smith's often awkwardly cut letter only says that Newport "well revenged [the attack] . . . at his return. Where some of them enticing him to their ambuscados by a dance, he perceiving their intent, with a volley of musket shot slew one, and shot one or two more, as themselves confess" (Smith, *Works*, 31–32). The final phrase implies that the Indians, not Newport, told Smith about it.

As for the Nansemond village, it was probably within a mile or so of modern Reid's Ferry, Virginia, north of Suffolk on State Route 32.

On Chawanoac, Smith's guess was not far wrong. It could hardly have been more than forty miles from where he was to Lane's Chawanoac. (For the site of the village, see Quinn, *Roanoke*, II, 857, and Douglas L. Rights's *The American Indian in North Carolina* [Winston-Salem, 1957], 16–17.)

For a study of John Smith and the Indians, see Keith Glenn, "Captain John Smith and the Indians," *VMHB*, LII (1944), 228–48, which sums up previous articles on the subject. On the attitude of the Council, see Smith, *Works*, 410–11. For the change in attitude which only began to take place in London in 1609, see the Instructions given by the Virginia Council to Sir Thomas Gates in May of that year, in which Smith's policies are broadly approved (Bemiss, *Charters*, 57–58).

2. The number of volunteers for the expedition is given in Smith, *Works*, 35, while the total of 130 is taken from *Works*, 122. If the total is correct, some 30 colonists had died since January 2 (or would die by the end of summer). It is useless to attempt to be accurate regarding the number of colonists alive at any one time, since the number of those who arrived in the first place is no more known than the exact number of those who came with Newport and Nelson.

3. As for the troubles with the Indians, it is difficult to arrive at the truth. Smith's 1608 letter implicates Powhatan less directly (*Works*, 35–36) than the second and third accounts (*ibid.*, 106–7 and 409–10), but it should be remembered that the direct references to Powhatan may have been cut by the editor of the letter. After all, the Company had decided to send a "royal" copper crown to Powhatan at least a month before it was entered for publication as a book. (Newport had sailed in July bearing gifts for Powhatan, which turned out to be "Greek" in reverse, while Smith's book was not licensed until mid-August. For the story of the crown, see Chapter 16, below.)

On my surmise that the solemn services of the Anglican Church frightened the Indians, it is necessary to look a little into the religious beliefs of primitive men in general, and of the Powhatan tribes in particular — so far as they are known. These, judging by highly unsatisfactory contemporary documentation, appear to have believed in some sort of Great Spirit who freely donated *good* things with a lavish hand. But the Evil One (Okee, or whatever name he had) demanded, and was accorded, worship. It is therefore not hard to picture the fright that the formal prayers of the English might have instilled — for the Indians would surely have been certain that they were adoring and propitiating *their* Evil One. For a summary of the surviving accounts, including the Indians south of Virginia (who exercised some influence on the Powhatan tribes), see Swanton, *Indians*, 742–82.

The account of the threatened torture is from the 1608 account (*Works*, 37). It is curious that it was not reprinted in 1612 or 1624. Possibly the London Council criticized Smith for such "barbarous" conduct, and Smith preferred to forget the incident. It is by no means a unique case of conflicting accounts, however, and therefore need not be stressed.

On the meaning of the word "tools" in this passage as quoted, the plot was much too cumbersome for merely getting hold of some hatchets and saws.

4. Smith's famous description of Pocahontas as the "only Nonpareil" is in his *Works*, p. 38. This is the earliest mention of her by name. Later, in his letter to Queen Anne, Smith describes her as "the King's most dear and well-beloved daughter." Here, too, he says that she was twelve or thirteen when he first met her (*Works*, 530).

As to Smith's letter or letters and maps sent to Henry Hudson, see Chapter 7, above.

### CHAPTER 14

1. The status of the local Council may be summarized here. The Charter of April 10, 1606, provided for thirteen councilors. The first settlers sailed with seven, including Newport. On June 2, 1608:

> Newport was on his way back to England,
> Wingfield had sailed with Newport,
> Gosnold was dead,
> Smith was in Jamestown,
> Ratcliffe was President,
> Martin had just sailed,
> Kendall had been executed.

Matthew Scrivener was the only new councilor to be appointed.

As for Ratcliffe, once his sickness and his injured hand were cured, he seems to have conducted himself with really silly self-importance. Smith was not the only one to complain. The *Instructions* given to Gates, in May, 1609, for instance, read:

> 30. We require you to call before you Captain John Ratcliffe and one [blank] Webbe [original planter Thomas?] who hath complained by petition delivered [herewith] unto you of divers injuries and insolences done unto him in the government of the said Captain Ratcliffe, and accordingly to hear the cause and do justice in it as you shall find reason in it your own discretion. (Bemiss, *Charters*, 67.)

In addition, Ralph Hamor wrote in 1614 that Ratcliffe was "not worthy remembering, but to his dishonor" (Hamor, *True Discourse*, 7). On Smith's barge, cf. Shakespeare's *Troilus and Cressida*, I, iii, 38–44.

The account of the expedition in general follows that of 1612 (Smith, *Works*, 109–14) with some elaboration taken from the expanded version of 1624 (*ibid.*, 413–20). There does not seem to be any valid reason for discounting the later interpolations with their additional detail, and in some cases (see below) they are patently genuine. It is obvious that Smith, like Hakluyt and Purchas, had a great deal of material which he did not use, or used in one place and not in another.

The identification of Smith's sites is generally based on: (1) for Virginia, Ben C. McCary's *Indians*, 3–10, and personal discussion with him; (2) for Maryland, John Leeds Bozman, *The History of Maryland* (Baltimore, 1837), I, 107–45, and articles by William B. Marye in *American Antiquity*, Vols. II (1936–37), IV (1938–39), and V (1939–40); (3) for Delaware, A. R. Dunlap and C. A. Weslager, *Indian Place-Names in Delaware* (Wilmington, 1950). There are many other sources worth consulting by specialists.

On Debedeavon, see Jennings Cropper Wise, *Ye Kingdome of Accawmacke* (Richmond, 1911), various passages between pp. 29–81, and Charles E. Hatch, Jr., *First Seventeen Years*, 92.

2. On *Point Ployer*, it is interesting to note that the 1612 account (at this point probably by Smith) merely reads "That place we called Point Ployer," while the 1624 account adds "in honor of that most honourable house of *Mousay* in Brittany, that in an extreme extremity once relieved our Captain" (*Works*, 110, 414). Amaury II Goyon was created Marquis de la Moussaye in 1615. Does this hint that Smith saw, or heard from or about, him between 1615 and 1624? (My suggestion as to the location of Point Ployer is only a guess.)

On the Kuskarawaocks, see C. A. Weslager, *The Nanticoke Indians* (Harrisburg, Pennsylvania, 1948), 18–21. Smith estimated their fighting force at 200 (*Works*, 55), in 1612. The story of the two or three thousand first appeared in 1624 — another example of the multiplication-by-ten from which that work so often suffers.

On the language spoken by these Indians, see Weslager, *op. cit.*, 115–16, which points out that Nanticoke was "very similar" to Lenape (see Daniel G. Brinton's "Vocabulary of the Nanticoke Dialect," *Proceedings of the American Philosophical Society*, XXXI [1893], 325–33).

On the phrase "exploding gadgets," Smith's Powhatan word *pawcussaks*, "guns," seems to show relation to Cree *pa'skisikun*, which, as analyzed by Robert A. Logan in a personal letter means literally "a thing made for use, involving exploding, bursting, shooting."

3. As to *Rickards Cliffs*, the reference must almost inevitably be to John Smith's mother's family — apparently the only one by the name of Rickard in England. (Bradford Smith, in *Captain John Smith*, p. 17,

was the first to recognize that the name *Rickands* for Smith's mother was a misprint.)

As to the animals mentioned, cf. Bruce's *Economic History,* 125–26.

My supposition that silence and the absence of signs of human life had a marked effect on Smith's companions is based on my own impressions in both jungle and desert — not fear, but "creepiness." But add to this nameless feeling the real terror of Elizabethan superstition! (Cf. Shakespeare's *II Henry VI,* I, iv. 19–22. . . .) As for John Smith's attitude, it was not necessarily that he was more courageous. He had taken care of himself over an equal area in Transylvania, and in the face of the Turk.

As for the Patapsco River, if Smith included his voyage up that stream, his "thirty leagues" would be practically explained. — Bole armeniac was an astringent used for cuts and bruises, and later in toothpowder. Hariot had reported finding a kind of earth called *wapeih* in 1585, which he desribed as "very like terra Sigillata" (practically synonymous with bole armeniac), and this may have influenced Smith's opinion (see Quinn, *Roanoke,* I, 328, 898). If any clay with similar properties were found in Virginia, it would be *one* means of making a little profit for the Virginia Company.

With regard to Smith's oration, Sir Ralph Lane referred the matter of carrying on "to the greatest number of voices," and it was the majority which pointed out that they could, if need be, live on their two dogs for two days. They even volunteered to starve for two days after the dogs were eaten (Quinn, *Roanoke,* I, 267). Smith's companions were conspicuously less enthusiastic.

At Pooles Island the width of Chesapeake Bay is nine miles, from northwest to southeast, and thus corresponds well with Smith's estimate. (Bozman's *History,* I, 117, agrees with this site.)

On the breadth of the Potomac at its mouth, the maps of the U.S. Coast and Geodetic Survey show about seven miles.

4. On the Indians of the lower Potomac, Smith lists 100 fighting men for Onawmanient and a total of 160 for the two smaller villages downstream, or less than 900 total population for the neighborhood. (See *Works,* 52.)

Powhatan's desire to eliminate the English was probably common knowledge among the Indians. The report that Jamestown wanted Powhatan to help rid them of Smith is less obviously plausible. Talkative Englishmen, however, eager to win favor among the Indians by blaming their continued presence only on Smith (and prompted in this by the anti-Smith faction), could easily have said, "Without him, we'd be gone," and such welcome words would have reached Powhatan's ears with the results just related.

As to what John Smith was looking for, it is his expanded version (of 1624) which lists these specific commodities after mentioning the main objectives: the hunt for a silver mine, furs that were found at Kuskarawaock (along with white beads "that occasion as much dissension among the Savages, as gold and silver amongst Christians"), and "whether the bay were endless or how far it extended" (*Works*, 418).

As for the farthest point reached by Smith on this voyage up the Potomac, I am indebted to my friend Craig Wylie, of Virginia and Boston, for pointing out the existence of an old gold mine, never profitably operated, beyond the U.S. Naval Reservation mentioned in the text. This mine (or these mines) were being worked less than a century ago, but I have not learned just when they were "discovered" (see S. J. Martenet, H. F. Walling, and O. W. Gray, *New Topographical Atlas of the State of Maryland and the District of Columbia* [Baltimore, 1873], 9). Yellow Falls is the name of the rapids between Turkey Island and the Virginia shore a mile above the Reservation.

As for the meaning of *matchqueon*, Robert A. Logan suggests in a personal communication that it may be "something to put on the face to make it pretty," but the specific elements are hard to put a finger on. As for the mine, Smith stated baldly in his first account that it was of no value, but in 1624 changed this to a suggestion that it was antimony. This may have been *his* guess, or someone else's, but it was a "safe" one. It would not cause an antimony fever similar to the gold fever of Jamestown, for neither Smith nor his associates can have known much about antimony other than that it was prized by alchemists.

5. As to the problem of Ratcliffe, both the 1612 and 1624 accounts say that he was deposed and Smith made President, and that Smith then resigned in favor of Scrivener (Smith, *Works*, 115, 420). But both categorically state also that Smith would not accept the presidency until duly elected on September 10 (*ibid.*, 121, 433).

In view of these discrepancies, the most plausible theory is that Smith refused the honor in July, and suggested Scrivener as a sort of interim president, or head of a caretaker junta. The important fact, which is entirely clear, is that Smith did not begin to govern the colony until September.

## CHAPTER 15

1. A passage through or across the top of North America was so strongly hoped for that at least one map (Michael Lok's) showed a Panama-like isthmus somewhere near New York Bay (see reproduction in Quinn, *Gilbert,* II, opposite 313); while less visionary enthusiasts assumed the existence of navigable waterways almost across the unknown width of the continent, with the Russian Volga-Dvina hydrographic system as the model (see the *Instructions,* in Smith, *Works,* xxxiv-xxxv).

As to the "commission" Newport received in London to verify "the certainty of [a passage to] the south sea," see Smith, *Works,* 121. Although "commission" may be too strong a word, there can be no doubt of what was wanted (see Brown, *First Republic,* 63). For this, however, Smith himself was partly responsible. He had written in his letter of 1608 what Opechancanough told him about "a great turning of salt water," as related in Chapter 11. But while London was considering the significance of this, and giving instructions to Newport, Smith began the voyages of exploration described in these chapters, after which — it should be noted — he began to urge the London Council to put first things first, and establish the colony on a sound basis before wasting any more time on the South Sea, gold, and the Roanoke survivors (letter to the Council, in *Works,* p. 443).

On Pochins, see Strachey, *Historie,* 67.

The identifications of the four "heads" to the bay as listed are based on careful study of Smith's map in comparison with the U.S. Coast and Geodetic Survey map of "Chesapeake Bay, Sandy Point to Susquehanna River" (no. 1226), personal reconnaissance during July, 1961, and Bozman's *History.* (See also Chapter 14, Commentary 1.)

The Massawomekes are regarded by Donald A. Cadzow, of the Pennsylvania Historical Commission, as the group which later came to be known as the Five Nations — the Iroquoian Confederacy ("Safe Harbor Report No. 2," *Pennsylvania Historical Commission,* III [Harrisburg, 1936], 13, 17–18). Obviously, they were not only fierce warriors, but bold traders, and by John Smith's testimony considerably advanced in material culture beyond the tribes of Chesapeake Bay. (On the Susquehannocks, see Commentary 2, immediately below.)

2. On the linguistic affinities of Tockwough, see Weslager, *Nanticoke,* 115. As to the meaning of the name, John Smith gives *tockwough* as a kind of root, the source of the English form "tuckahoe," which is applied to a fungus as well (see Smith, *Works,* 68, 363 [misprinted as *tocknough*], and 155; and *OED*).

Specific information on the Susquehannocks is to be found in such works as: "Safe Harbor Report No. 2," by Donald A. Cadzow, and the *Susquehannock Miscellany,* edited by John Witthoft and W. Fred Kinsey, III (see Bibliography).

On the identification of places, I have also availed myself of a map published in Louise Welles Murray, ed., *Selected Manuscripts of General John S. Clark Relating to the Aboriginal History of the Susquehanna* (Athens, Pennsylvania, 1931), 50–51, with General Clark's notations. Everts and Stewart's *Combination Atlas Map of Lancaster County, Pennsylvania* (Philadelphia, 1875), pp. xv and 30, has been of great help in bringing Clark's map and text into accord with topographical maps. As for the persistence of the name *Smith's Falls,* it was mentioned by Bozman before he died in 1834 (*History,* I, 131).

On propitiating the Great Spirit, John Smith (*Works,* 423) wrote:

Our order was daily to have prayer, with a Psalm; at which solemnity the poor Savages much wondered. Our prayers being done, a while they were busied with a consultation till they had contrived their business [decided what to do].

I have taken the liberty of adding my surmise as to the subject of their consultation. As for the Great Spirit, I have used the term quite loosely, to apply both to the *Gitche Manito* of Longfellow's *Hiawatha* (apparently a specifically Algonkian concept) and to the Iroquoian *orenda,* or Magic Power.

Although the Susquehannocks were Iroquoians, they did not belong to the Five Nations. There were apparently about 5000 of them all told in Smith's day. Little is really known about them, but their "creation" of John Smith as their Protector does not sound improbable. See Raphael Semmes, *Captains and Mariners of Early Maryland* (Baltimore, 1937), 504–38, for a summary of their history, and William N. Fenton and John Gulick, *Symposium on Cherokee and Iroquois Culture, BAE* Bull. 180 (Washington, 1961), 30, 71, 257, and 268–71, for details on the Susquehannocks and the general chieftain-system of the Iroquoians.

Smith's observations on the mutual ignorance of one another between the Powhatans and the non-Powhatans held good at least until 1621, when William Claiborne went to Virginia as Surveyor General.

On William Hole and Smith's map, see Part III, Chapter 20.

3. On the Patuxent, Acquintanacksuak and Mattapanient Indians, all three were still friendly to the English when the next white visitor arrived in 1621.

On *Brookes Forest,* the name was added to the map between 1624 and 1626, apparently to honor Sir John Brooke (or Brookes), who backed Smith's proposals regarding Virginia in 1624.

On the Massawomeke shields (which Smith calls targets), they were round or oval and "made of little small [slender] sticks woven betwixt strings of their hemp and silk grass, as is our cloth." Just what silk grass was is still uncertain—perhaps milkweed, perhaps a kind of nettle.

4. On Smith's "never was dog more furious against a bear," the reference is to bear-baiting, "a legitimate sport" to Shakespeare's contemporaries (see *Shakespeare's England* [2 vols., Oxford, 1917], II, 428–29).

On the Manahoacs, it has been customary to consider them Siouans who spilled over the mountains from West Virginia and the Ohio Valley (see, *inter alia,* Swanton, *Indians of the Southeast,* 148–49). Carl F. Miller's *Revaluation of the Eastern Siouan Problem . . . (BAE* Anthropological Papers, no. 52 [1957]) questions this hypothesis, but (it seems to me) without offering a better substitute.

5. As for Mosco's new name, that was a common procedure, witness Powhatan, who took several names in the course of his life.

On the location of the Chesapeake Indians at the time, Lynnhaven Bay is the region usually given (see Quinn, *Roanoke*, II, 855). There is a possibility, however, that the Elizabeth River is actually the stream indicated on Smith's map, and that the Chesapeake village was consequently in the neighborhood of modern South Norfolk. In any case, the site was marked on Smith's map by hearsay only, and it is even uncertain just what tribe comprised the Chesapeakes in 1607 and 1608. Powhatan is said to have "destroyed and put to the sword" all the original inhabitants at some time before 1610 (see Strachey, *Historie*, 104–5). Was this also before the English arrived, in 1607?

On Dumpling Island, which today is a small oval, surrounded on three sides by marsh, there is of course no way of telling if it existed in 1608. (Newsletter No. 5, The Archeological Society of Virginia [October, 1963], states that the Nansemond Chapter has begun digging at Dumpling Island, in the hope of finding evidence bearing on Smith's trading voyage.

## CHAPTER 16

1. The text of the opening quotation from the account of 1612 is in Smith, *Works*, 121. When it was reprinted in 1624 the clause "and took upon him the place of President" was omitted (*ibid.*, 433) — an example of how arbitrary some of the 1624 changes were.

On the reshaping of the fort, the 1624 account says that it was "reduced to a five-square form," or one with five equal sides (see *Works*, pages as above). (The original fort, finished on June 15, 1607, had been triangular, and had enclosed about one acre of land.) Despite systematic archaeological excavating for the 1957 Jamestown Anniversary Celebration, no trace of any fort has been found. (Full details on the excavations are in the National Park Service, Archeological Research Series Number Four, *Archeological Excavations at Jamestown . . . Virginia*, by John L. Cotter [Washington, 1958], with pp. 11–17 dedicated to the fort. I am personally indebted to Dr. Cotter, J. Paul Hudson, and Charles E. Hatch, Jr., for their courtesies on visits to Jamestown, Yorktown, and Williamsburg.)

The "True Relation" appeared with a typical "long title" of the period: *A True Relation of such occurrences and accidents of note as hath happened in Virginia since the first planting of that Colony, which is now resident in the South part thereof, till the last return from thence* (spelling modernized).

As for the names on the title page, the surviving copies with Watson's name sometimes have the explanatory preface, as does at least one with "By a Gentleman." See below, Part III, Chapter 20. The identity of I.H. has not yet been established.

As for the copy of the sketch-map, it was sent to Philip III by Ambassador Zúñiga with his letter of September 10, 1608, which corresponded with the English date of August 31 — about eight weeks after Nelson's arrival in London.

As for the psychological approach of the King's Council to the problem of Powhatan, the phrase is undoubtedly an anachronism. Nevertheless, what the Council evolved was just that, by whatever name you want to call it — and it was generally sadly wrong.

As for the excitement in London, Brown's *First Republic* gives a good summary (pp. 62–63). For precious metals in Virginia, see Bruce, *Economic History*, I, 81–82. Gold and silver have been found, but not for two hundred and forty years after Smith's day in Virginia, and much farther from Jamestown than "his" colonists ever got.

2. On the eight Dutchmen and Poles, see Chapter 17, Commentary 2, below.

The wording "addressed to the President" is only approximative, since the letter has not survived in any form. My point is merely that it was not addressed to Smith personally, since the King's Council could not know that he was the President. At the same time, the tone of the letter may have pointed to Smith as the person addressed — in fact the body of the letter may have mentioned him.

On Winne and Waldo in Jamestown, the former was soon appointed Sergeant Major of the fort, and the latter Master of the Works. When Gates was shipwrecked in Bermuda, he appointed Winne Lieutenant Governor, but Winne never got word of the appointment. (See William Strachey's letter in Purchas, *Pilgrimes*, XIX, 27.)

3. On the discussion between Powhatan and Smith, I have omitted part of the account, since it appears that there was a misunderstanding (probably by Smith) regarding who the murderers of "his brother" were. The details are of little importance in any case.

With regard to Powhatan's mantle, the so-called *Powhatan Mantle* in the Ashmolean Museum at Oxford may be the same article. It is decorated with Indian beadwork, with a crude figure of a man, two animals, and a number of disks or spirals. There is an excellent modern photograph of it in Kaj Birket-Smith's *Primitive Man and His Ways* (London, 1960), facing p. 176.

It is not known who persuaded the Virginia Company to send a crown and other "regalia" to Powhatan, but within a year the Company was talking about his excesses, exactions, and tyranny! See Kingsbury, *Records,* III, 18–19.

4. Francis West, who turned 22 on October 28, 1608, was a younger brother of Thomas West, Lord De La Warr. Their great-grandmother was Anne Boleyn's sister, which gave them considerable status during the reign of cousin Elizabeth I. Francis West was not likely to strike up a buddyship with John Smith.

For the account of the expedition into the Monacan country, see Smith, *Works,* 438; for the matter of the barge, *ibid.,* 443. For a study of the trip in the light of modern knowledge, see David I. Bushnell's "The Five Monacan Towns in Virginia," *Smithsonian Miscellaneous Collections, LXXXII* (Washington, 1930), no. 12, 2–10.

As to the condition of the returning expeditionaries, John Smith specified in his letter to the Company in London that 89 came back "lame and sick" out of the 120 *(Works,* 444). How exaggerated this figure is — if at all — is a matter of speculation.

Clapboard, pitch and tar had been expensive imports for years. Glassmaking had been proposed as an industry the moment it was learned that boundless forests for the furnaces were available in Virginia. (See J. C. Harrington, *Glassmaking at Jamestown,* Richmond, 1952.)

Gabriel Beadle is one of the few lesser lights of the Virginia Venture whose identity can be determined "officially." According to the *Visitation of Northamptonshire* (Harleian Society), LXXXVII, 12, Gabriel Bedell, son of William Bedell of Great Catworth, Huntingdonshire, is stated to have "gone to Virginia," and to have died unmarried. Gabriel had a brother named John, who is most likely the "John Bedle" who arrived with Gabriel in the second supply. (His half brother's son, also Gabriel, has been confused with him.)

On the identification (tentative only) of *mussaneeks* with chipmunks, the first element probably represents some form of the Algonkian radical meaning "great," while the second corresponds to Narragansett *anéqus,* "the ground or striped squirrel, or chipmunk" (Trumbull, *Natick Dictionary,* 9). As for the troubles due to thoughtless trading, particularly by the mariners, see Strachey's long lament in Purchas, *Pilgrimes,* XIX, 50–51.

The date of Newport's departure is as uncertain as that of his arrival. Alexander Brown hazards a guess that he arrived in October and left in December *(First Republic,* 68, 70).

Smith's *Map* and *Relation* are both mentioned in his letter to the Company, but the originals have not been found. The *Relation* may very likely have been substantially the same as the *Description* which was published in 1612 *(Works,* 47–84), but there is no way of telling what the map looked like. It may of course have been incorporated in the map engraved in 1612, known as the *Smith Map,* or it may have merely formed the basis for that. We "just don't know."

CHAPTER 17

1. As to the number of colonists: 6 of the 38 surviving original settlers went home or died; 20 of the 120 1608-supply died; balance, 132, when the second 1608-supply of 70 arrived. This corresponds with Smith's note that there were about two hundred all told when Newport left

(*Works*, 442). Robert Hunt's will, incidentally, was probated in England on July 14, 1608. He must therefore have died before Nelson sailed, on June 2 (see Charles W. F. Smith, "Chaplain Robert Hunt . . ." [see Bibliography], 22).

Newport's taking food from the colonists is mentioned in Smith's letter to the Council (*Works*, 444). A similar depredation is reported from New England, where the *Fortune* had to be "revictualled from the scanty stores of the colonists" in 1623 (John A. Goodwin, *The Pilgrim Republic* [Boston, 1920], 196).

On the amount of corn needed, a bushel contained (and contains) eight gallons, or sixty-four pints.

The first marriage ever celebrated in Virginia was that of John Laydon and Anne Burras (or Burroughs). Smith, as commanding officer, may have officiated in the absence of any minister after Hunt's death.

Smith's use of the phrase "either Caesar or nothing" is interesting. It had no reference to Julius Caesar, as he thought, but to the famous *condottiere* Cesare Borgia. Apparently Smith picked up the phrase in Italy, for I have been unable to find any use of it in English works before his time, or for many years after. See Giuseppe Fumagalli, *Chi l'ha detto?* (Milan, 1946), 314–15. Any good Italian encyclopedia will supply details on Borgia.

2. On Richard Savage, Edward Brinton, and the Dutchmen, the accounts vary. On pp. 130 and 447 of the *Works* they are three Dutchmen and two English; on pp. 132 and 448, four Dutchmen and Richard Savage. Only three Dutchmen are mentioned by name.

On the Christmas holidays spent at Kecoughtan, Smith states that the weather caused them to "keep Christmas among the Savages," although the reference is to December 30.

Sergeant Edward Pising, a carpenter on his arrival, was appointed sergeant for the winter voyage for provisions. It is worth noting that Jeffrey Abbot, a "gentleman," served as sergeant on the same trip. The records of the Worshipful Company of Carpenters (Vol. III, *Court Book*, 1533–73, transcribed and edited by Bower Marsh [6 vols., Oxford and London, 1913–37]), show a Jefferie Abbott made a freeman of the Company on January 28, 1573. It is highly probable that the Jeffrey Abbot of the Smith expedition was either a son or a nephew of the member of the Carpenters' Company.

On the protocolary offering of food, examples of hospitality of this sort can be found today, far from America and the Algonkians.

The conversation, or exchange of speeches, between Smith and Powhatan, is reported by Smith in the style of Thomas Heywood's translation of Sallust (1608, reprinted in *The Tudor Classics*, 2nd ser. [London and New York, 1924]), including a "discourse" by Smith worthy of Cato or Memmius. (See Part III, Chapters 24 to 26, for other literary influences on Smith.)

With regard to the eight Dutchmen and Poles, the former could have been Hollanders, Germans, or Swiss, as the term was then applied in England. It is virtually certain, however, that in this case none of them were true "Dutch." As for the Poles, there has been a flurry of excitement during the past ten to fifteen years over their possible identity. Those interested may find the details in my report, "The Identity of the First Poles in America," *WMQ*, 3rd ser., XXI (1964), 77–92.

3. On the "three murderous wars" through which Powhatan had already lived, the accounts put the following words into Powhatan's mouth:

> Captain Smith, you may understand that I — having seen the death of all my people thrice, and not any one living of those three generations but myself — I know the difference of Peace and War better than any on my country . . . (Smith, *Works*, 135, 451).

It is useless to attempt to guess what wars or tribal calamities were in Powhatan's mind, or why he forgot about his brothers ("not any one living . . ."), at least one of whom was not much younger than himself (Opechancanough). While a number of intangibles point to an encounter between Powhatan as a young man and some Europeans (most likely Spaniards), we cannot pinpoint any as to place or time. On the other hand, Powhatan may have been referring to the struggles by means of which he became overlord. And there remains the possibility that John Smith may not have understood him, in detail.

On Smith's "rule to find, beyond your knowledge," while there was undoubtedly some deliberate mystification in Smith's words, we may imagine that in the back of his mind was the arithmetical *rule of three* (or Golden Rule), which was learned by all gunners (see A. R. Hall, *Ballistics in the Seventeenth Century* [Cambridge, England, 1952], 35 n., with mistaken reference to Captain John Smith), and all pilots (see E. G. R. Taylor, *The Haven-finding Art* [New York, 1957], 158, 190). Since they found their destinations by such rules, Smith could talk glibly about rules for finding Powhatan's supplies. It was of course nonsense, but Smith always brought up force or bluff, as needed, with uncanny aptness, to win out over Powhatan and the other chiefs. Indeed, until the London Company decided to overwhelm Powhatan by force of arms, no other Englishman was even remotely as successful with the Indians as Smith. (Cf. Waters, *Art of Navigation*, 346.)

4. The accounts of the other attempt on Smith's life seem to be badly cut, or worse edited. They begin:

> Two or three hours they [the Indians] so througed about the President and so overwearied him, as he retired himself to rest . . . But some Savages perceiving him fast asleep, and the guard somewhat carelessly dispersed, forty or fifty of their choice men, each with a club or an English sword in his hand, began to enter the house with two or three hundred others, that pressed to second them . . . [undoubtedly exaggerated].

This mob of Indians made such a racket that Smith woke up and grabbed his sword and shield, whereupon Raleigh Crashaw and others came running in and "cleansed" the house. Opechancanough and some of his "ancients" were then brought up, and "excused this intrusion." The two accounts are virtually identical (Smith, *Works*, 142-43, 459-60).

For the rest of the story, it appears that Smith started out from the river, walked a quarter-mile to Opechancanough's house, and found almost everything abandoned. Then the King arrived, and after that some people brought commodities. Smith made a speech, they traded, and so the first day ended. On the second day, the same walk, but the English found men with baskets. Not long after, Opechancanough arrived and "held [them] in discourse." Then came the flurry over the betrayal, a long oration by Smith to his soldiers, another to Opechancanough, the uproar at the door, Smith's seizing Opechancanough, and further speeches. Then, peace and trading, and two or three hours of Indians pestering Smith. Next, Smith takes a nap, an attempt is made to murder him, much confusion, more orations, the "rest of the day" spent trading, Wiffin's arrival with the sad news, and Smith "dissembling his sorrow" until "night approached," which in Virginia in February would have been between 5:30 and 6:00. Since this seems to me much too much for one day, I am inclined to believe that the story as told is not complete, though I am unable to reconstruct one which would make more sense. I have therefore dismissed the incident with brief mention in the body of the text. Its most significant feature anyway lies in its position in a continuous chain of attempts to get rid of Smith, and crush the colony during that winter and the ensuing year.

5. As to the date of the death of Gosnold, Scrivener, Waldo, and the others, the account says that they left Jamestown nine days after "the President's departure," which would have been on January 7, 1609 (Smith, *Works*, 143-44).

The passage on Powhatan's *sighing* is found in both accounts (*Works*, 136, 453).

On the amount of supplies brought back at the end of the trip, the two accounts do not agree. The 1612 account mentions only 279 bushels of corn and no deer suet, while that of 1624 states 479 bushels of corn, and adds the suet. (See *Works*, 147, 463.) I have quoted the larger figure since the 279 bushels would have provided essential food only, barely enough for 90 days.

## CHAPTER 18

1. On the glass industry, J. C. Harrington's *Glassmaking at Jamestown* (Richmond, 1952) contains a summary of its known history, along with an account of the excavations which uncovered the site, beginning in

1948. One of the facts revealed was that the blue beads which so appealed to the Indians apparently were not made in Jamestown in 1608–1609. The factory was abandoned then, and the industry not revived until 1621.

The casual note that the Dutchmen were *fifty miles* away, working for Powhatan, is the first word that Powhatan had moved finally — to Orapaks — as he had threatened (Smith, *Works,* 468, 472).

As for Kemps and Tassore, the latter flits but briefly across the scene. Kemps, however, turned Christian and stayed with the English. Strachey got a great deal of information from him later about Powhatan and the other chiefs, and their women. He died of scurvy in Jamestown, Strachey says, in 1610 (*Historie,* 61).

On Wowinchopunk, there is an obscure hint here that he was present when Smith was a prisoner at Rassawek, but there is nothing in the accounts of that incident to confirm it (see *Works,* p. 16, and compare p. 152 with p. 15).

2. The Biblical quotation is from II Thessalonians 3:10. John Smith must have been the first Englishman to apply St. Paul to government.

As for the blockhouse at Jamestown, see Henry Chandler Forman, "The Bygone 'Subberbs of James Cittie,' " *WMQ,* 2nd ser., XX (1940), 478 and map.

On the area cultivated at Jamestown, the whole peninsula contained about 2000 acres of "high land" suitable for cultivation (Beverley, *History,* 28).

The new fort was probably on a 100-foot hill a mile up Gray's Creek, opposite Jamestown (Hatch, *First Seventeen Years,* 79).

3. On the Indians "scattering" during the lean season, compare Chapter 10 (incl. Commentary 3). Ralph Lane had done the same thing at Roanoke in the spring of 1586, and Smith was canny enough to decide to scatter *his* colony. But if the Indians scattered voluntarily and regularly because of their primitive food-economy, the English, unaccustomed to living on what they could gather with their hands, had to be driven to care for themselves.

Volda-Faldo died "of a burning fever," apparently in 1610 (Strachey, *Historie,* 131). He had invested £12 10s. in the Virginia Company (Kingsbury, *Records,* III, 83, 324), and may have lived in England before sailing for Virginia.

As for Samuel Argall, see Part III, Chapter 20, and Commentary. Argall's arrival was a godsend in another sense too. On Saturday, July 15/25, Captain Francisco Fernández de Écija arrived at Chesapeake Bay, sent by the Spanish Captain General of Florida to spy. Spotting a ship riding there which seemed to be moving to catch him in a trap, Écija slipped away, unnoticed but also uninformed (see Irene A. Wright, "Spanish Policy toward Virginia, 1606–1612 . . . ," *American Historical Review,* XXV [1920], 460–61, and translation on pp. 463–64).

On the causes for the new Charter, see Alexander Brown's *First*

*Republic,* 73–74, with further references in his *Genesis,* I, 342. The facts as given are solid, but Brown's deductions unfortunately (and customarily) suffered from biased thinking. The Company was to be reorganized along mercantile (*i.e.,* big-business) lines, rather than cast in the mold of a democratic republic, as Brown seems to have (wishfully) thought. (See also Wesley Frank Craven, *The Virginia Company of London,* Jamestown Booklet, 15–20.)

As for the value of the total subscription of the nobles, 40,000 ducats probably meant (in the Ambassador's letter) £14,000 (usually the exchange would have made it £13,333 6s. 4d.), or £1000 per earl and baron. This seems high, for the time. There is no *record* of investments of that size, although some may have subscribed, but not paid in, such amounts. In any case, the information we have is only spotty, and Zúñiga's letter is cited principally to illustrate the interest aroused. Craven, *loc. cit.,* has further pertinent information on the potential profits for the subscribers (or investors).

On King James's being glad to have the burden of the Company lifted from him, and other details, see the Introduction to Kingsbury, *Records,* I, 11–25, and especially pp. 21–22 and 24 for the specific changes effected in 1609.

Smith presumably paid for the supplies acquired from Argall in some legal fashion, since there is no critical reference to his action (see *Works,* 476 for the account). As to the condition of the colony after Argall's arrival, see Brown, *Genesis,* I, 344.

On Argall's voyage over, see Brown, *Genesis,* I, 343, which gives nine weeks for the trip from Portsmouth to Jamestown. (It was closer to ten.) The account as given there adds that Argall was becalmed for fourteen days, on the basis of which the theoretical seven-week passage is calculated.

The very first crossing (December, 1606, to April, 1607) had taken eighteen weeks and two days. The first ships of the 1609 fleet made it in ten weeks and one day (little slower than Argall's "fast" crossing). Two years later Sir Thomas Dale crossed from Land's End to Old Point Comfort in exactly eight weeks.

4. The North Virginia Company's settlement survived one winter in Maine, after which all surviving colonists returned to England, except for Daniel Tucker, who went to Virginia instead. A pinnace which had been built in Maine and christened *Virginia* arrived at Jamestown, trailing the rest of the fleet, on or about October 4, 1609, a mute testimonial to the cessation of colonizing activities in the north. For a brief account of the Popham Colony, see Preston, *Gorges,* 144–48, and there is some mention of it in Part III, below.

On William Strachey's life, see Strachey, *Historie,* Introduction, xiii–xxxii, and a number of references in Part III.

For the account of the voyage from England, supplementary to Archer's letter (Smith, *Works,* xciv–xcvii), see William Strachey's "Letter to an unknown Lady" (Purchas, *Pilgrimes*, XIX, 5–72), and Silvester Jourdain, *A Discovery of the Barmudas* (London, 1610).

On the decision of Ratcliffe, Archer, and Martin "not to disturb the old President during his time," it is possible that Archer — almost certainly responsible for this — was attempting to conciliate Smith, but if so he went about it the wrong way. See his letter of August 31 (Smith, *Works*, xcvii, which is also the source for the quotations in the text).

George Percy's more angry account says that Smith staged a sort of "Triumph" for the newcomers *after* an agreement was reached about the peaceful completion of his term. But Percy, about whose activities there is much more in Part III, is unintentionally the person who puts his finger on the principal cause of all the trouble, when he refers to Ratcliffe, Archer, and Martin as "the three busy instruments in the plantation" (Percy, *Relation*, 262, 264). Francis West, incidentally, had apparently gotten along with Smith up to that time.

On the new minister of the Gospel at Jamestown, the Reverend William Mease, or Mays, the account is to be found in Hist. MSS Comm., *Report on the MSS of the Marquess of Downshire*, II, 195, in a letter dated November 30, 1609, from J. Beaulieu to William Trumbull.

Henry Spelman was the son of Erasmus Spelman and nephew of the famous historian and antiquarian Sir Henry Spelman. He was evidently under twenty-one years of age. Erasmus and Sir Henry had an uncle named Francis Saunder (or Sanders) who disinherited Henry (August, 1613; see "Virginia Gleanings in England," communicated by Lothrop Withington, *VMHB*, XV [1907–08], 304–5), which tallies with Henry's own statement to the effect that he left England "being in displeasure of my friends" (Smith, *Works*, ci). Spelman's report on Virginia, although somewhat illiterate, contains valuable information — if it is all true.

5. West's behavior at the falls, seen in the light of his being the "heir" to Smith chosen by men opposed to Smith, was tactless in the extreme — but we should not look for tact among these "gentlemen." Nevertheless, his behavior may have been the cause of the later choice of Percy as President. Neither Ratcliffe nor Archer could have tolerated West's independence. Percy was not only more malleable; he was also sick (Percy, *Relation*, 264).

It is worth mentioning here that Spelman accused Smith of having afterwards conspired with Powhatan (which? — the son?) to kill West. This is hardly to be credited, since Smith was burned immediately after leaving the falls, and could not have laid a plot with "the Powhatan." (See Smith, *Works*, cii, for the Spelman account.)

The seriousness of Smith's wound has never been factually determined. There is no doubt that it was painful, and that Smith at first despaired of his life. (See the Commentary on Chapter 19.) But as time went on, the burn must have begun to heal, so that his final departure from Virginia can probably be attributed to about equal amounts of need for treatment, desire to find out what was going on in London, and the impossibility of staying on in Jamestown under Ratcliffe, Archer, and Martin — and with young West around. Ratcliffe claims that Smith was sent home. It is possible. But basically I believe Smith left because he could not sit by, a wounded underling, and watch the colony lapse into do-nothingness and starvation.

## CHAPTER 19

IN connection with Smith's wound, there is a pertinent story having to do with the temporary settlement at Nansemond. Smith "cannot omit" mention, he says, of the heroic George Forest, "that had seventeen arrows sticking in him, and one shot through him, yet lived six or seven days as if he had small hurt; then for want of chirurgy [surgery] died." It may be that Wilkinson and Wotton, Bagnall and Walter Russell had either gone back to England or were dead. In that case (substantiated in a sense by the lack of mention of *any* medical care for Smith), Smith's return home may indeed have been occasioned by his burn.

As for Smith's hearing that West had been chosen as his successor, this is not documented. I have surmised it, in view of the boundless gossip we know existed in Jamestown. Archer's statement that "they generally" chose West would point to everybody's having heard about it. (See Smith, *Works,* xcvii.)

The charges brought against Smith are listed in the 1612 account (*Works,* 168–69) but do not appear in the *General History* of 1624. The latter contains in place of them a list of what Smith accomplished in Jamestown, along with generous criticism of the bulk of the colonists (*Works,* 486–87).

For the quotation from Smith's "phrase-book," see *Works,* 46.

Ratcliffe's letter was addressed to Salisbury, not because (as some have assumed) of anything like an acquaintance, but because (I believe) it was proper for the captain of Gates's "Vice-Admiral" to report in the absence of the "Admiral" directly to the Secretary, who was also the first person named in the new Charter. See Smith, *Works,* xcviii–xcix, for the letter.

# PART III

## CHAPTER 20

1. The chapter title is taken from John Donne's "anniversary poem," "An Anatomy of the World" (1611): a lament for the passing of the old

order of things. (*The Complete Poems of John Donne,* ed. Roger E. Bennett [New York, 1949], p. 206, line 213.)

What happened to John Smith on his return has been the subject of considerable dreaming among his biographers, and others. The bare fact seems to be that nothing is known. This in my opinion points more to an assumption that nothing happened than to a trial or even a serious investigation. In the case of Edward Maria Wingfield there is a hint that he may have been interrogated. Even that is absent in John Smith's case.

The reference to the strange behavior of Hudson's ship's cat is in Purchas, *Pilgrimes,* XIII, 357. The cat's behavior and the known proximity of one of Gates's ships suggest that the cat saw more than the seamen did. Hudson's troubles in Dartmouth are described in Powys's *Henry Hudson,* 117–19. The river which he had "discovered" was the original goal of the Pilgrim Fathers in 1620, and New York Bay eventually became a temporary dividing point between the Virginia colonists and the New Englanders (see references in Edward Arber, *The Story of the Pilgrim Fathers* [London, 1897]).

For Gabriel Archer's letter, see Smith, *Works,* xciv ff.; for the Council's Instructions, Bemiss's *Charters,* 55–69 (reference to Ratcliffe on p. 67). As for Wingfield, his entire *Discourse* (Smith, *Works,* lxxiv–xci) implies that he testified before some body — presumably the Virginia Company. A letter from Ralph, Lord Eure, to Sir Robert Harley, dated May 28, 1608, states that Wingfield was then "not yet tried" (*VMHB,* XXVI [1918], 315). There is no evidence, however, that he ever was.

Argall's voyage has been mentioned above (Chapter 18). The Virginia Company's *True and sincere declaration* (see Bibliography) states (p. 8) that "Captain Argoll received our Commission under our Seale," for the trip. (This need not conflict with Smith's statement that he sailed for Master [John] Cornelius, an investor in the Company.) Argall was probably chosen for the command, despite the fact that he was only in his mid-twenties, because of a family tie (by marriage) with Sir Thomas Smythe. His first cousin, Sir John Scott, had married Sir Thomas's sister, Katherine, ten years before (his second wife).

On the improbability of John Smith's having voyaged from Virginia with Captain Adams, it should be remembered that Gabriel Archer was with Adams on the way over, "brainwashing" him with regard to John Smith — in advance.

As to Smith's refusal to accept the news of the new Charter and the change in system of governing the colony, it must be remembered that no *document* could be presented which removed him from office. It is true that the ship-captains who brought the third supply must all have been able to testify that Sir Thomas Gates was the new Governor, but Gates was not there. Neither was Somers, his second-in-command.

Regardless of what he knew about the capabilities of the returning un-
hallowed trio (Ratcliffe, Martin, and Archer), Smith felt himself obliged to retain the presidency until the end of his term, or the arrival
of Gates with his commission. (The Company's *Instructions* placed
Smith next after Somers in rank, but he could not know that.) See the
*Instructions* to Gates (Bemiss, *Charters*, 55–75, and Kingsbury, *Records*,
III, 12–24), Archer's own account (Smith, *Works*, xcvii), and Smith's admittedly biased version (*Works*, 162–63), in which some reading between the lines is needed.

2. A running commentary on what was happening in London is to be
found in Alexander Brown's *First Republic*. A less detailed, but reliable, account is given in Wesley Frank Craven's *Dissolution of the
Virginia Company* (New York, 1932).

Jean Beaulieu's letter to William Trumbull is in the Hist. MSS
Comm. *Report on the Manuscripts of the Marquess of Downshire*, II
(London, 1936), 195. It is the same collection of manuscripts (p. 126)
which establishes the return of the ships bearing John Smith as prior
to November 9.

Robert Johnson's little book was entitled *Nova Britannia: Offering
most Excellent fruites by Planting in Virginia*, and was entered for
publication on February 18, 1609.

The quotation regarding the "lewd and bad" youths is taken from
a broadside published by Thomas Haviland for the Virginia Company,
through William Welby, early in 1610 (Alexander Brown, *Genesis*, I,
354). William Crashaw's sermon was preached on February 21, 1610,
and entered for publication the following March 19. The item regarding Sir George Somers, taken from the Commons Journal, is quoted
from Brown's *First Republic*, 122.

3. There is little or no direct evidence of John Smith's doings during the
period between his return from Virginia late in 1609 and the publication of his *Map of Virginia* in 1612. The account I have given is based
on such scraps of information as have survived and on what I hope
is sound deduction. The chronological sequence is as hypothetical as
are a few of the details. Yet in whatever order they took place, the
events described are required to explain subsequent known occurrences.

On Hudson, reference may be had again to Powys's eminently readable book, pp. 122–23.

Argall seems to have developed unpraiseworthy traits before long,
but was stanchly protected by Sir Thomas Smythe. Brown's brief
biography of him in his *Genesis* seems to skim rather too lightly over
what must have been glaring deviations from honesty (*Genesis*, 815–16;
cf. numerous references in Kingsbury, *Records*, consult Index).

The story of the publishing of John Smith's letter home (to Robert
Bertie, or to Sir Thomas Smythe?) is lost in a haze of uncertainty. The
main sources I have drawn upon are: Edward Arber, *A Transcript of*

*the Register of the Company of Stationers of London* (5 vols., London, 1875–94), consult index for scattered references; D. W. Waters, *The Art of Navigation in England in Elizabethan and Early Stuart Times* (New Haven, Conn., 1958), consult index on John Tapp and John Smith; Joseph Sabin [and Wilberforce Eames], *A Dictionary of Books Relating to America* (29 vols., New York, 1868–1936), XX, 254–55; and, on Watson and Bingley, numerous references in the *Calendar of State Papers, Domestic,* 1603–10, 1611–18, and 1619–23, consult indexes.

On Sir Thomas Smythe and the launching of the *Trade's Increase,* "the largest merchantman yet constructed in an English dockyard," see Sir William Foster, *England's Quest of Eastern Trade* (London, 1933), 194. On Harcourt, see *Colonising Expeditions to the West Indies and Guiana,* ed. V. T. Harlow (Hakluyt Society, 2nd ser., LVI [1925]), lxxi–lxxii, and *A Relation of a Voyage to Guiana by Robert Harcourt, 1613,* ed. Sir C. Alexander Harris (Hakluyt Society, 2nd ser., LX [1928]), 7–8.

The *Instructions* to Lord [De] La Warr are reprinted in Bemiss, *Charters,* 70–75 (from Kingsbury, *Records,* III, 24–29). There is a brief life of him in the *DNB* and another in Brown, *Genesis,* 1048. Lord De La Warr's family connections are to be found in any standard English peerage.

The known tie between John Smith and the Earl of Hertford consists of an "inserted leaf of address signed John Smith, presenting the book 'To the Right Honourable Sr. Edward Semer [Seymour] Knight, Baron Beauchamp, Earle of Hartford,' etc.," in a copy of Smith's *Map of Virginia* in the New York Public Library. The route which I have proposed, for John Smith to reach the Earl, is pure conjecture. He could, as a more remote possibility, have been referred directly to Seymour by Robert Bertie. (Bertie's father had been a sort of stepbrother of the Earl's first mother-in-law.) The sole reason for the conjecture has been to show that Smith always had a channel to the nobility through the Berties.

The phrase from Virgil is in the *Aeneid,* VII, 587–88.

4. Francis West's unauthorized and surreptitious departure from Jamestown in the *Swallow* has been glossed over by most historians. The facts as seen by those in Virginia are unemotionally stated in Smith, *Works,* 170. George Percy explained the matter thus: "And Capt. West I sent to Potomac with about thirty-six men to trade for maize and grain, where he in short time loaded his pinnace sufficiently . . . And coming by Algernon's Fort Captain Davis did call unto them . . . exhorting them to make all the speed they could to relieve us, upon which report Capt. West, by the persuasion or rather by the enforcement of his company, hoisted up sails and shaped their course directly for England, and left us in that extreme misery and want" (*Tyler's Quarterly,* III [1922], 266). It is hard to believe that the men could

have moved West to sail away had he not been willing. (I have omitted as irrelevant the gruesome details of his treatment of the Indians while he was gathering the maize.)

On the return of Richard Potts, David Wiffin, and Post Ginnat, the *Instructions* of May, 1609, required Gates "to give them their licence to come back" (Bemiss, *Charters*, 67). If the three did come back to England, it could not have been before the return of the *Blessing* and the *Hercules*, which arrived in London on August 22, 1610 (Brown, *Genesis*, I, 418). David Wiffin is known to have been in London on January 7, 1618 (Kingsbury, *Records*, III, 59). And although Ginnat disappears from the scene, Richard Potts appears as one of the authors of the *Map of Virginia* (1612), which requires that he have returned before that volume was published. (His name appears on the title pages of both parts [*Works*, 41, 85], in the heading of the second part [*ibid.*, 89], and as co-author of most [or all] of Chapter XII [*ibid.*, 169, 488].) Unless we deny the authenticity of the whole make-up of the *Map*, including the note by Symonds at the end of the book (*ibid.*, 174), Richard Potts must have come back to England. In my reconstruction of the events, admittedly hypothetical, I have postulated Potts's return on one of the two ships mentioned, since that would have been in line with the license granted him. The crux of the matter, then, is whether the *form* of the 1612 account is a hoax, *twice* permitted by the Reverend William Symonds.

Raleigh Crashaw is provokingly puzzling. It seems almost unthinkable that he should not have been related to the preacher, and it is possible that he may even have been a younger brother. For that reason I have not hesitated to suggest that Raleigh Crashaw was the contact through whom Smith got to know the clergymen (see also "Virginia Gleanings in England," by Reginald M. Glencross, *VMHB*, XXX (1922), 275–79, with mention of a Crashaw connection with Sir Thomas Metham, connected in turn with Smith's onetime guardian).

For the message from Philip's ambassador, Don Alonso de Velasco, see Brown, *Genesis*, I, 392.

For a parallel, and independent, analysis of the book on which Smith, Potts, and others were working, see E. G. R. Taylor, *Late Tudor and Early Stuart Geography, 1583–1650* (London, 1934), 164–65.

With regard to Hakluyt and Purchas, George Bruner Parks and E. G. R. Taylor have somewhat divergent views. I am inclined to agree with Parks.

5. I do not believe that any question has been raised seriously on the ethnological value of Smith's writings (unless Alexander Brown has somewhere included that in his blind denunciation of the man).

Strachey, whose *Historie* was largely (one-third of Book I) based on Smith, is virtually the only independent contemporary authority on the Indians and things American generally. (S. G. Culliford's *William*

*Strachey, 1572–1621,* a thesis [University of London, 1950], has unfortunately remained in typescript — a copy of which I have consulted in the Folger Library, Washington.) The only other "authority" (obviously secondary) is a recently discovered MS (Bodleian Library, Oxford [Ashmole MSS, H 171–5]), labeled Simon Forman's "Of the Country of Virginia," a transcript of which was kindly given me by Professor David B. Quinn. It merely "confirms" Smith and Strachey. A century later, Robert Beverley supplied further information, but still used John Smith as a basic guide (see *The History and Present State of Virginia,* ed. Louis B. Wright [Chapel Hill, 1947]). The brief notes of Gabriel Archer and Henry Spelman (the latter in Smith, *Works,* ci–cxiv) add a few details to Smith and Strachey, but Spelman particularly is not always to be trusted.

While a complete study of John Smith's vocabulary of Indian words has not yet been made, it can be stated that practically all of Smith's words appear in Strachey's much larger vocabulary, also not thoroughly analyzed. A baker's dozen of Smith's words have been incorporated in the English language, including "moccasins," "hickory" and "hominy." Finally, Smith's illustrative sentences in the Powhatan language have been scanned and "readily recognized" as to sense by Fr. Mercredi, O.M.I., a native Cree Indian (personal communication from Jean Lessard, O.M.I., Edmonton, Canada, October 15, 1962).

As to the shipwreck of Gates and Somers on the Bermuda reefs, see Purchas, *Pilgrimes,* XIX, 5–72, for the Strachey account, and Silvester Jourdain, *A Discovery of the Barmudas* (London, 1610), for further details.

On Richard Martin's plea for "the truth" from Strachey, see *Historie,* xxv.

6. The most readable account of early publishing in England which I have run across is in Frank A. Mumby, *Publishing and Book-selling* (London, 1930 and 1934), where the presses outside London are described in Chapter 18, "The Learned Presses."

Philip Fote (or Foote) still remains a mystery. An address by him to Watson and Bingley is mentioned in Sabin (Eames), *Dictionary,* XX, 247, a photostatic copy of which is inserted in the New York Public Library copy of the *Map of Virginia* mentioned above. Beyond this, the only mention of the gentleman I have seen is in *CSP, Dom., 1611–1618,* p. 557, where it is stated: "Licence to Philip Foote to sell clay for making tobacco pipes, for twenty-one years." The date is July 24, 1618.

Two discussions of the map may be mentioned here: Ben C. McCary, *John Smith's Map of Virginia* (Jamestown Booklet, 1957), and Coolie Verner, "The First Maps of Virginia, 1590–1673," in *VMHB,* LVIII (1950), 3–15. William Hole has a brief biography in the *DNB,* and is discussed in a number of general works, such as A. M. Hind's *Engraving in England,* recently (1963) completed by Michael Norton and Margery Corbett. I have borrowed the descriptive adjective "refined" from Malcolm C. Salaman, in the Special Spring Number, 1908, of *The Studio,* "Art in England . . ." ed. Aymer Vallance, p. 110. On John White's drawings, see Quinn, *Roanoke,* I, 390–464.

Robert Tindall's *Draught* of the James and York Rivers, 1608, was redrawn for and printed in Strachey's *Historie,* to face p. 31. It is a good example of what such an engraver as Hole had to go by.

For Sir Thomas Smythe's forgetfulness, see H. S. Vere Hodges, *Sir Andrew Judde* (privately printed, Tonbridge, Kent, 1953), 68.

On Strachey and George Percy, see Strachey, *Historie,* xiii–xiv, xv–xvii, xxvii–xxix, 49–50.

## CHAPTER 21

1. The scandal attached to Robert Carr's name had to do with Carr, his wife, and a Sir Thomas Overbury. It ruined Carr. (For a full discussion, strikingly written, see Edward Abbott Parry, *The Overbury Mystery* [London, 1925].)

The phrase "the Jacobean Pageant" I have borrowed from the title of G. P. V. Akrigg's *Jacobean Pageant: The Court of King James I* (London, 1962). As for *Gold* and *Power,* considerable light is thrown on these matters by L. C. Knights's *Drama and Society in the Age of Jonson* (London, 1937, reprinted by Penguin Books, 1962).

As for Sir Thomas Dale, there can be little question that his strictness was necessary (Wesley Frank Craven, *The Southern Colonies in the Seventeenth Century, 1607–1689* [Baton Rouge, La., 1949], 116), but the sober judgment of the historian cannot wipe out the odium heaped on the man in his own day (see Alexander Whitaker's letter of June 18, 1614, in Ralph Hamor's *A True Discourse of the Present State of Virginia* [reprinted from the London, 1615, edition, Richmond, Va., 1957], p. 60). Further light is thrown on Dale in Darrett B. Rutman's "The Historian and the Marshall, A Note on the Background of Sir Thomas Dale," *VMHB,* LXVIII (1960), 284–94, which, incidentally, invalidates much of Alexander Brown's overimaginative biography in the *Genesis,* 869–74.

John Chamberlain's letter of July 9, 1612, to Sir Dudley Carleton, is in Chamberlain, *Letters,* I, 366–67.

On Marmaduke Rawdon, see *The Life of Marmaduke Rawdon of York,* ed. Robert Davies (Camden Society, No. 85 [1863]), especially pp. xvi–xvii. Rawdon's marriage license is in *Caribbeana,* V, 121, with other information in the pages following. It is also probable that Rawdon was somehow connected with Sir Thomas Smythe and the Virginia Company. A document dated May, 1623, refers to "the Discoverie of the fishinge in newe England found out dureinge S^r Tho: Smiths government at the Charge of the Company by S^r Samuell Argall, Capteyne John Smith and others" (Kingsbury, *Records*, IV, 150).

The document of uncertain authorship referring to a trip by Smith to Plymouth is a letter (B.M., Cotton MSS, Otho, E. VIII, f. 240), somewhat damaged by fire, and signed only *Smythe*. Although the signature bears little resemblance to a signature of Smith's in an autographic inscription at the front of a copy of his *Generall Historie* now in the Huntington Library, San Marino, California, the partially burnt letter has been regarded as Smith's and tentatively dated as of 1606 (surely wrong), and 1615 or 1616 (Preston, *Gorges*, 401). If the letter is Smith's, which I doubt, it would rather belong to the period before his voyage of 1614, since it says, "I would . . . one voyage," not "I would . . . *another voyage.*" (The letter is available, reprinted, in *NEGHR*, XXVIII [1874], 248–51, and in Levermore, *Forerunners*, II, 570.)

On Sir Ferdinando Gorges and John Smith at this time, see Preston, *Gorges*, 149–62.

For Rawdon's interests, see the *Life* mentioned above, p. xvii. It is worth noting that Rawdon's nephew, also named Marmaduke (a common Yorkshire name), specifies that the older Marmaduke was "something lower [in stature] than the middle sort of men," and adds a note that such a height would be five feet four inches (p. 196). Since Smith has been described somewhat similarly, we may hazard a guess that Smith was also only a very few inches over five feet tall.

2. The story of Smith's New England voyage is based on his *Description of New England* (London, 1616), additional comments in *New Englands Trials* (London, 1620, 2nd ed., 1622), Book Six of the *General History* (London, 1624), and a few references in his *Advertisements For the unexperienced Planters of New-England* (London, 1631). Outside sources are mentioned below.

The identity of Samuel Cramton has not been found, although the name Crampton is known in Norfolk and Suffolk. Whaling was not yet greatly developed among the English, which may explain Cramton's lack of specialized knowledge. If Cramton was a Frenchman (Smith met him later in Bordeaux), I can only wonder what his name was.

On the *jubartes* whale, see *Encyclopaedia Britannica*, XXVIII (11th ed.), 573.

I have taken the phrase "gold and bounty" from Shakespeare's *Merry Wives of Windsor*, I, iii, 76: "she is a region in Guiana, all gold and bounty."

On Hakluyt and the translation of Lescarbot's *Histoire*, see Parks, *Hakluyt*, 221, with full details on pp. 266–67. The text as translated by Pierre Erondelle is in Purchas, *Pilgrimes*, XVIII, 228–88. The reference to gold versus tilling the soil is on p. 232.

There is a good account of John Smith in Maine waters in Henry S. Burrage, *The Beginnings of Colonial Maine, 1602–1658* (Portland, Me.,

1914), 123–32. The reference to Popham's ship is on p. 126, and the name of the captain is given in Smith, *Works*, 697. As to the Indian who may or may not have been with Smith at the time, he was added to the story in 1624, but it is my opinion that the addition may be dismissed as spurious.

For Argall's destruction of the French settlement, see Burrage, *Colonial Maine*, 109–17. For the identification of Castine, *ibid.*, 127.

The passages referring to Smith's map-making are in *Works*, p. 190, repeated on p. 703, with some elaboration continuing onto p. 704.

On the Micmacs and Mecaddacut, see Fannie Hardy Eckstorm, *Indian Place-Names of the Penobscot Valley and the Maine Coast* (Orono, Me., 1941), xxvii, 74–75.

On the meaning of Massachusetts, see Mitford M. Mathews, *A Dictionary of Americanisms* (2 vols., Chicago, 1951), II, 1033.

On Quonahasset, see William Bradford's history *Of Plimoth Plantation* (Boston, 1899), 442. This quotation from Smith, along with the following one, is taken from *Works*, 205. The aside on hurly-burly is from Shakespeare's *Macbeth*, I, i, 3.

On Accomack versus Patuxet as the site of Plymouth, see Mourt's *Relation* (Edward Arber, *Story of the Pilgrim fathers*), 452, and W. T. Davies's comments in Arber, footnote to p. 260 and under "Patuxet" in the Index, p. 624.

On the results of Smith's trip, see the brief but pointed comment in John A. Goodwin, *The Pilgrim Republic* (Boston, 1920), 149, with the concluding statement, "this map [of Smith's] was used by the Pilgrims." On p. 397 of the same work there are some figures regarding later trade in beaver and other skins which will give an idea of the value of Smith's cargo.

3. Thomas Hunt's name seems generally to have been execrated, yet I have been unable to find out much about the man. He is mentioned in Mourt's *Relation*, 453, 456, 475, and in Bradford's *Plimoth*, 115–16. See also *Sir Ferdinando Gorges and his Province of Maine*, ed. James Phinney Baxter (The Prince Society, Boston, 3 vols., 1890), I, 96–106, with details, including a long footnote on the Indian Tisquantum or Squantum.

For Gorges and his relations with John Smith, see Preston, *Gorges*, 151–59. Smith's own account is in *Works*, 219–21.

Smith's story of his second projected voyage to New England is told more fully in the 1624 account than in the first version, of 1616. Reference is therefore made to the *Works*, 731–34. See also Baxter, *Gorges*, I, 98.

The death of Captain Rowcroft, alias Stallings (Stallenge), is mentioned in Kingsbury, *Records*, III, 242.

On the Cage family, see the *Visitation of Buckinghamshire* (Harleian Society, LVIII, 1909), 22.

4. During all of John Smith's adulthood, pirates swarmed the seas, in

bands and singly. There are many mentions of attacks in contemporary documents, the gist of which can be found in C. D. Penn, *The Navy under the Early Stuarts* (Leighton Buzzard and Manchester, 1913), particularly Chs. IV and V.

For the investigation of Smith's case, see *Works*, 221–23 (1616), reprinted on pp. 734–36 (1624). The opening of the reprint hints that the copy is not verbatim, and there is no knowing which copy is closer to the official records — and these have not survived.

Although the story depends entirely on Smith's own account, in the *Works* as above and the pages immediately following, documentary evidence supporting the latter part of the story has been found in the archives of La Rochelle, France (see the Commentary on the next chapter).

CHAPTER 22

1. The chapter title is taken from a message sent by Sir Francis Walsingham early in February, 1583, to Sir Humphrey Gilbert, who was then planning to sail for America. He wrote "that the Queen desired him not to accompany his expedition, on the grounds that he was 'a man noted of not good happ by sea.' " See Quinn, *Gilbert*, I, 82.

Documentary evidence of John Smith's encounter with Captain du Poiron was discovered by me in the Archives at La Rochelle, thanks to the interest and zeal of M. Marcel Delafosse, Directeur des Services d'Archives. In all, there are two long documents and one very brief reference. The matter is discussed in detail in my article, "A French Account of Captain John Smith's Adventures in the Azores, 1615," scheduled for publication in *VMHB*, LXXII (1964).

On the pirate Barra, it is perhaps worth mentioning that the engraver of the "ingenious" title page to John Smith's *General History* (1624) was John Barré, or Jan Barrà, probably of Middelburg, Holland, only four or five miles from Flushing, which was not without pirates who were citizens (see, *e.g.*, a letter of Sir John Throckmorton to Viscount Lisle, dated May 7, 1612, Flushing, in Hist. MSS Comm., *De L'Isle and Dudley MSS*, V [1961], 49–50).

On Brouage, see for example Marcel Delafosse, *La Rochelle et la côte charentaise* (La Rochelle, 1960), 73–79.

On the Ile de Ré, see René James and Louis Suire, *L'Ile de Ré d'autrefois et d'aujourd'hui* (La Rochelle, 1959).

On "Madam Chanoyes," M. Delafosse writes: "I wonder if it isn't a matter of the Chaurroy family, which was a family of lawyers of La Rochelle living at that time. But this is a mere hypothesis" (personal communication, dated June 6, 1963).

For the story of Bordeaux late in 1615, see Louis Vaunois, *Vie de*

*Louis XIII* (Paris, 1961), 189–94, 198. There are adequate biographies of Sir Thomas Edmondes in the *DNB* and Brown's *Genesis*.

On Cramton, see the preceding chapter. The fact is that nothing is known about him beyond what Smith has written.

2. There are account books of nobles and gentry alike, though few of them have survived. For two recently published examples, see: *Household Papers of Henry Percy, ninth earl of Northumberland*, ed. G. R. Batho (Camden Society, 3rd ser., XCIII [1962]); and *The Wealth of the Gentry 1540–1660*, by Alan Simpson (Cambridge, England, 1961).

As for Prince Charles and his alteration of the names of a number of Indian villages, see Sabin (Eames), *Dictionary*, XX, 223.

I am indebted to the Chief of the Geophysics Division of the Coast and Geodetic Survey, U.S. Department of Commerce, Washington, for information regarding magnetic declination in Lower Chesapeake Bay and Cape Cod regions in the early 17th century. The Division's personal communication to me is dated August 31, 1962. I take advantage of this opportunity to express my thanks.

Simon van de Passe did an engraving of the painting of Pocahontas (the latter now in the National Gallery of Art, Washington) by an unknown artist about the same time — 1616. A color reproduction of the portrait adorns the cover of *American Heritage*, IX, No. 6 (Oct., 1958). A comparison of the van de Passe engraving with the original portrait gives some idea of the extent to which van de Passe's engraving of John Smith reflects that gentleman's appearance.

The "investment" of Lownes and Low in the Virginia Company was only indirect, yet it showed an interest. They were among the stationers who contributed to the £125 invested by the Stationers' Company (Brown, *Genesis,* I, 292–93).

With regard to Gunnell, or Gonneld, the name (spelled either way) was sufficiently uncommon for me to have little doubt that the Cambridge scholar and Smith's friend were relatives — brothers or cousins.

George Wither and John Davies of Hereford are both in the *DNB,* with more extensive information in Douglas Bush, *English Literature in the Earlier Seventeenth Century* (Oxford, reprinted 1959), consult Index.

As for Nicholas Smith, it would seem on the surface that this is the same man who wrote ten commendatory lines for *Coryat's Crudities,* by Thomas Coryate (1611, reprinted in 2 vols., Glasgow, 1905). The matter of his specific identity is more difficult. The N. Smith who wrote for John Smith states that he was a cousin. Strachan, in his *Life and Adventures of Thomas Coryate* (London, 1962), p. 288, suggests that Coryate's Smith was either Nicholas, son of Sir George of Exeter, or Nicholas, son of Nicholas of Theddlethorpe, Lincolnshire, nine miles east of Louth, where John Smith went to school. The latter Nicholas would seem to be the one who honored both John Smith and Tom Coryate with verses.

It is worth noting that "John Smith, his New England" is mentioned in 1624 by Richard Eburne among the books "describing and commending this country" — *i.e.*, the coast of North America (*A Plain Pathway to Plantations*, ed. Louis B. Wright [Ithaca, New York, 1962], 7).

3. For Governor Dale's letter of June 3, from Plymouth, see Brown, *Genesis, II*, 783–84. For the details of Pocahontas's kidnapping, see Hamor's *True Discourse*, 4–7.

For the story of Rolfe, see Hamor's work, pp. 10–11, 55–56, and 59–61, which ends with Pocahontas's departure for England. Edward D. Neill has elaborated on this in *Pocahontas and her Companions* (Albany, 1869), but source references are scanty. Rolfe's letter to Governor Dale is quoted in full in *Rolfe Family Records*, by R. T. and A. Günther, II (Heacham, Norfolk, London and Aylesbury, 1914), 15–20.

That John Smith ever wrote a letter to Queen Anne regarding Pocahontas has been doubted by the hyperskeptic. The fact that it was not published until after both ladies were dead does not prove it was not written.

The *True Declaration of the Estate of the Colonie in Virginia* (London, 1610), p. 11, published by the Virginia Council, states: "Powhatan, their chiefe King, received voluntarilie a crowne and a scepter, with a full acknowledgement of dutie and submission." The truth of the matter seems to be in the account of 1612, which states: "But a foul trouble there was to make him kneel to receive his crown . . . At last, by leaning hard on his shoulders, he a little stooped, and Newport put the Crown on his head . . ." (Smith, *Works*, 125). Smith's comment on this, in his 1608 letter to the Company, is: "For the Coronation of Powhatan, by whose advice you sent him such presents, I know not; but this give me leave to tell you, I fear they will be the confusion of us all ere we hear from you again . . ." (*Ibid.*, 443).

Before the Rolfe family moved to Brentford, there is a record of their staying at an inn in Ludgate Hill called the "Belle Sauvage" — a name dating back to 1453. (See *An Encyclopedia of London*, ed. William Kent [London, 1937], 6–7, 395; and Purchas, *Pilgrimes*, XIX, 117–19.) For further bits on Pocahontas, see Chamberlain's *Letters*, I, 470–71 (for an account of her capture), and ii, 12, 50, 57, and 66. Chamberlain sent a picture of Pocahontas to Sir Dudley Carleton at the Hague on February 22, 1617, with this comment: "Here is a fine picture of no fair Lady and yet with her tricking up and high style and titles you might think her and her worshipful husband to be somebody, if you do not know that the poor company of Virginia out of their poverty are fain to allow her four pound a week for her maintenance" (*op. cit.*, II, 57).

4. On Gorges and Richard Vines, see Preston, *Gorges*, consult Index.

While it is true that the years 1617 and 1618 seemed to point to better things for Virginia, Argall's behavior and Dale's reputation for running what amounted to a "penal colony" would have been a matter of concern to John Smith. That something was in the air is proven by the sudden election of Sir Edwin Sandys to take Sir Thomas Smythe's place, April 28, 1619. The end of Smythe's twelve years in office cannot have come without omens perceptible to such men as Captain John Smith. (See Wesley Frank Craven, *The Virginia Company of London* [Jamestown Booklet, 1957], 33-45, from which I have borrowed the phrase, "penal colony" [p. 38]; and Kingsbury, *Records*, I, 211-14.)

On Drake and the contrary winds, see the vivid account in E. F. Benson, *Sir Francis Drake* (London, 1927), 241-43.

On the southwesters which plagued Gilbert, see Quinn, *Gilbert*, II, 339; on the Queen's opposition to his personal sailing, see *ibid.*, I, 82.

On Smith and Gorges in those days, see Preston, *Gorges*, 161.

### CHAPTER 23

1. On the date of Pocahontas's death, see Chamberlain's *Letters*, II, 66–67: "The Virginian woman (whose picture I sent you) died this last week at Gravesend as she was returning homeward . . . From London, this [Saturday] 29th of March, 1617."

   For the quotation from Sir Francis Bacon, see the *Essays*, "Of Seditions and Troubles" (Everyman's Library ed., 44).

   On Ralegh and his Guiana Venture, see Quinn's *Raleigh and the British Empire*, especially pp. 187–208.

   On the willingness of Basque and other traders to help Smith, see the note in *VMHB*, XXII (1914), 199: "1616, December — Letters to the city of San Sebastian from Don Diego Sarmiento de Acuña, ambassador from Spain in London, giving notice that the King of Denmark has conceded licence that the Guipuzcoan vessels can fish for whales in the region of the North, and that the Englishman John Smith proposes to accompany, with two or three vessels of his, those of Guipúzcoa for the examination of those places, and that he sends a book arranged by him [*Description of New England*?] to facilitate the operations of the said examination" (quoted and translated from Cesáreo Fernández Duro, *Disquisiciones Náuticas*, VI, 415).

   With regard to my suggestion that another Lord Chancellor might have befriended Smith, I have in mind Sir Thomas Egerton, who occupied that post from 1603 to 1617 (see Campbell, *Lives of the Lord Chancellors*, II, 380).

2. No trace of Rowcroft-Stallings's letter to Smith seems to have survived. There is a good deal about Rowcroft in Purchas, *Pilgrimes*, XIX, 275-77 (abstracted from Gorges's *Brief Relation* of 1622).

The "anonymous voice" cried out, of course, at the execution of Sir Walter Ralegh. See Edward Edwards, *Ralegh*, I, 705. The phrase "guilty of corruption" is Bacon's own, in a document addressed to the House of Lords (quoted in Catherine Drinker Bowen, *The Lion and the Throne* [London, 1957], 373).

My account of James's troubles is based largely on David Harris Willson's *King James VI & I* (London, 1956), Ch. XXI, "The Crisis of the Reign" (pp. 399–424). The opinion of the French Ambassador, Tillières, is on p. 412; James's anguished cry, on p. 415.

There is a sketch biography of Samuel Argall in Brown, *Genesis*, 815–16. It is possible that Argall was knighted for his services in the Mediterranean in 1620–21, but the cries against him in Virginia were almost universal. (See also Seymour Connor's "Sir Samuel Argall: A Biographical Sketch," *VMHB*, LIX [1951], 162–75.)

The significance of the Virginia general assembly of 1619 has been widely discussed. There is a brief account in Charles E. Hatch, Jr., *The First Seventeen Years: Virginia, 1607–1624* (Jamestown Booklet, 1957), 23–24, but for fuller treatment of the matter see: Charles M. Andrews, *Colonial Period*, I, 180–88, and Craven, *Southern Colonies*, 134–36. For a presentation of the factors which brought about the different growth of Virginia from that of New England see Louis B. Wright, *The Colonial Civilisation of North America, 1607–1763* (London, 1949), especially 1–122.

For a description of Smith's *New England Trials* (1620), see Sabin (Eames), *Dictionary*, XX, 248–49. It should be added relative to both this book and its 1622 revised edition that Captain (later Sir) Richard Whitbourne of Devonshire had published *A Discourse and Discovery of Newfoundland* in 1620, with a second edition dated 1622. It may be surmised that these, coupled possibly with a little book by a friend of Smith's associate Dermer, published in 1620, had some bearing on the urgency with which Smith put out the two editions of *New Englands Trials*. (See the Introduction to *A Plain Pathway to Plantations*, by Eburne, pp. xi–xxi.)

3. The bases for my account of the Pilgrims are: Edward Arber, *The Story of the Pilgrim Fathers* (London, Boston, and New York, 1897); *Bradford's History "Of Plimoth Plantation"* (Boston, 1899); John A. Goodwin, *The Pilgrim Republic* (Boston, 1920). There are other works, of course, which have been consulted, but they are too numerous for inclusion here.

On the region available for settlement in South America, see *Colonising Expeditions to the West Indies and Guiana, 1623–1667*, ed. V. T. Harlow (Hakluyt Society, 2nd ser., LVI [1925], lxxii).

For the Articles sent from Leiden to England in 1618, see Goodwin, *Pilgrim Republic*, 41. The signers were John Robinson, the pastor, and William Brewster, the elder of the church (but in name "William the younger").

For a brief discussion of Sandys and King James, see Craven, *Virginia Company*, 41-48. George Abbot, Archbishop of Canterbury, was Puritan in instinct, but was as harsh with separatists as he was with papists.

On King James's refusal to permit Sandys to be Treasurer (or Governor) of the Virginia Company, see Brown, *First Republic*, 366-67. The official accounts of the election are in Kingsbury, *Records*, I, 356-87, with much extraneous matter. For further reading, consult Wesley Frank Craven, *The Dissolution of the Virginia Company*.

On the troubles of the Pilgrims, see Goodwin, *Pilgrim Republic*, 44-46.

Governor Bradford refers to John Smith but three times in his *Of Plimoth Plantation* (pp. 94, 117, 441). That the Pilgrims named their settlement Plymouth is because of Smith's map, however, not because of Plymouth, England (Goodwin, *Pilgrim Republic*, 91). Smith's influence is felt, rather than stated.

4. On the Pilgrims, the chartering of the Council for New England, and a dash of John Smith, see Preston, *Gorges*, 197-200, with pertinent footnotes on p. 415. On the date of the charter, see *Gorges*, 170.

As for the arrival date of the Pilgrims, see the discussion in Goodwin, *Pilgrim Republic*, 59-60.

John Smith's personal trials, as quoted, are in *Works*, p. 243. His petition, as quoted, is in Kingsbury, *Records*, I, 474. A petition of one Richard Markham is referred to on p. 440 of the same.

The motion of John Smyth of Nibley is in Kingsbury, I, 451-52. It has been misassigned to Captain John Smith, and otherwise misjudged. That it was, directly or indirectly, responsible for John Smith's *General History*, I believe there can be little doubt, since John Smyth of Nibley apparently made no effort at all to do the job himself. In any case, the motion, followed in relatively short order by the known beginning of John Smith's work on his book, seems to point to an influence of the prior fact on the later one.

5. John Smith's visit to Fishmongers' Hall is described by Bradford Smith, *Captain John Smith*, 246-47. The date was July, 1621, and the Fishmongers considered the matter until mid-November. I cannot entirely agree, however, that the Company's refusal to help Smith unless others joined with them was "a polite brush-off." The first patent making the Pilgrim settlement at Plymouth (New England) legal was not dispatched until the end of June. There was confusion in Virginia, and a new governor was being sent out in August. Then, the Virginia and New England companies had recently signed an agreement on fishing. It was logical that the Fishmongers would proceed cautiously, particularly at that time. (See Brown, *First Republic*, 422-30, for a story of events — remembering that Brown's dates are all *new style*.) Smith's other visit of which there is record, was to the brown bakers (see Sylvia Thrupp, *A Short History of the Worshipful Company of*

*Bakers of London* [Croydon, 1933?], 150–51 — first noticed also by Bradford Smith, *op. cit.,* 245–46).

For Gorges and his idea of fishing licenses, see Preston, *Gorges,* 213–15. If there was anything in the wind about this development when Smith visited the Fishmongers, there is even less reason to be surprised that he got a temporary refusal.

Samuel Purchas reprinted a portion of the *Brief Relation of the Discovery and Planting of New England* in his *Pilgrimes,* XIX, 269–84. On John Smith's book, reprinted at the same time as Gorges's, see Sabin (Eames), *Dictionary,* XX, 249, for a description.

Smith refers to Dr. Dee and the Royal Navy, and the potential raw material for shipbuilding in New England in *Works,* 269–71. His quotation from Richard Hakluyt is just before, on p. 267. There has been doubt that this quotation is from Hakluyt himself (see Parks, *Hakluyt,* 259) — with which I concur. I believe that no one has noticed before, however, that the quotation, which is printed as prose, is (with extremely minor alterations) good blank verse. I have therefore copied it in verse form, and only regret that so far I have not been able to trace the source, despite help from a number of specialists both in the east of the United States and in England.

## CHAPTER 24

1. According to a "Relation from Master John Rolfe, June 15, 1618" (Smith, *Works,* 539), Powhatan died in April. He was succeeded by his "brother" Itoyatin (or Taughaiten) — which was a new name for Opitchapam (Smith, *Works,* 539, 570, 591; Strachey, *Historie,* 69). But Opitchapam within a short time retired in favor of Opechancanough, who was clearly the most defiant of the whole family. This characteristic may be at the root of rumors and theories that he was not Powhatan's half brother at all, but some strayed Indian from the South (Florida, or even Mexico!). Thomas J. Wertenbaker, in his *Virginia under the Stuarts* (repr., New York, 1958), p. 89, believes that evidence shows that Opechancanough "belonged to a foreign tribe." To me, the evidence is highly suspect.

The passion vine, noted for its extraordinary flowers, grows wild in the southeast of the United States (see Beverley, *History,* 142–43). It is sturdy, but will not endure the cold of the north.

As to Itoyatin-Opitchapam, I have purposely left his fate unspecified. He was not young, certainly; but when he died cannot be determined, so far as I can see.

As for Yeardley's wardrobe, John Chamberlain wrote to Sir Dudley Carleton on November 28, 1618: "Here be two or three ships ready for Virginia, and one Captain Yardley a meane fellow by way of provision goes as governor, and to grace him the more the King knighted him this weeke at Newmarket; which hath set him up so high that he flaunts yt up and downe the streets in extraordinarie braverie [ostentation], with fowrteen or fifteen fayre liveries [servants in livery] after him" (Letters, II, 188). There is a highly favorable biography of Yeardley by Nora Miller Turman, George Yeardley, Governor of Virginia and Organizer of the General Assembly in 1619 (Richmond, Va., 1959).

The episode of Opechancanough and the poison is in Smith, Works, 578; that involving the murder of Savage, on p. 569. The whole story is told at considerable length by Jennings C. Wise in Ye Kingdome of Accawmacke; or, the Eastern Shore of Virginia in the Seventeenth Century (Richmond, Va., 1911). See also Raphael Semmes, Captains and Mariners of Early Maryland (Baltimore, 1937), 381.

There is an excellent biography of Sandys by Richard Beale Davis, George Sandys: Poet-Adventurer (London and New York, 1955); consult Index. On Sir Francis Wyatt, there is about as much in Davis's book as anywhere, but see the DNB for a brief biography.

On Wyatt's messenger to Opechancanough, see Kingsbury, Records, III, 550 f.

There is as good an account of the massacre in Davis's Sandys as I have found (see Index and Ch. VI, pp. 119–62). Waterhouse's Declaration is in Kingsbury, Records, III, 541–71. The date of July 3 is obtained from a statement at a court held on July 17, 1622: "Sir Edw. Sackvill beinge entreated by the former Court [July 3] to acquaint the Lords of his Majesties Counsell with the Massacre . . ." But the news was kept as "dark" as possible. (See Kingsbury, Records, II, 96.) For the Council's letter to Virginia, see Kingsbury, Records, III, 666–73.

John Smith's project, or proposal, is in Works, 588–90. George Sandys's letter to his brother, Sir Myles, is in Davis, Sandys, 144 ff., with the statement (contrasting strongly with Smith's ideas) that the Indians are "not to be destroyed but by surprize or famine," and that he and his associates "will trie if wee can make them [the Indians] as secure as wee were, that wee may followe their example in destroying them." (Sandys himself underlined the passage printed in italics.)

2. On Samuel Purchas in general, apart from the DNB, see E. G. R. Taylor, Late Tudor and Early Stuart Geography (London, 1934), Ch. V, pp. 53–66; on his major work, ibid., 59 ff.

As to Smith's statement in Book One of the General History implying that he had written so much by a given date, his own words are: ". . . we met with many of the Queen's ships . . . the 23. of September 1590. And thus we left seeking our Colony, that was never any of them found, nor seen to this day 1622." (See Works, 331.) This, to my mind, does not necessarily mean that he completed the passage on that same date, although Arber assumes that he did.

On Strachey, see *Historie,* p. 3, for the quote, and the Introduction for background.

Smith's definition of history is on p. 948 of the *Works.* I am indebted to A. L. Rowse's *Ralegh and the Throckmortons* (London, 1962), 271, for the reference to Ben Jonson's. For an illuminating discussion, see *English Historical Scholarship in the Sixteenth and Seventeenth Centuries,* ed. Levi Fox (The Dugdale Society, 1956). The quotation from John Selden is to be found on p. 4 of that work.

On the stationers — Smith's map of Virginia, which had been engraved by 1612, shows the addition of a place-name *Bollers Bush* (quickly, and clumsily, altered to *Boolers*) for the *General History* (Sabin [Eames], *Dictionary,* XX, 229). James Boler (or Bowler) seems to be the only "candidate" (see Arber's *Stationers,* Vols. III and IV [consult Index]). He is mentioned as a possibility, nothing more. For the rest, the "mere stationers," see Frank A. Mumby, *Publishing and Bookselling* (London, 1934), especially pp. 120–23. For Ben Jonson's Maecenases and John Minsheu's troubles, see the same, pp. 116–17.

3. Purchas's ideas about geography are to be found in Taylor, *Stuart Geography,* 56. He sprinkled as many maps as he could afford through his *Pilgrimes.* Dr. Taylor (*ibid.,* 65) refers to the high cost of engravings, and to what Purchas would have liked to do.

My reference to John Smith "with paste and shears" is more figurative than factual. Undoubtedly, most of his assembling of material was done by the tedious process of copying. Nevertheless, the fact that so very few original MSS for writings incorporated in Smith (and Purchas) survive may be a hint that the originals were put in their proper place in Smith (and Purchas) and sent to the printer's. (It is unlikely that *printed* works were clipped and pasted.)

The first real evidence of Smith's definite dislike for Archer appears in his account of Archer's attitude when he returned from captivity, January 2, 1608 (*Works,* 22).

Smith's admiration for Sandy's *Relation,* is reflected in what seems a clear case of emulation-cum-imitation, although there are a number of other contemporary authors who also illustrated their narratives with more or less pertinent quotations from the ancients.

On Smith's borrowings from Bishop Fotherby, see my "Captain John Smith and the Bishop of Sarum," *The Huntington Library Quarterly,* XXVI (1962–63), 11–29.

As to some connection between John Smith and Thomas Adams, Smith inscribed an "Adams Sound" in his *Map of Ould Virginia,* along with the names of other divines, such as the Archbishop of Canterbury, the Bishop of London, and Samuel Purchas. That he should have honored so outstanding a preacher as Adams would not be at all puzzling — and there is no other Adams who seems to merit Smith's attention. (On Thomas Adams, see *DNB,* and Millar MacLure,

*The Paul's Cross Sermons 1634–1642* [Toronto, 1958], consult Index.)

The soldier who fought under Smith in Transylvania was Thomas Carlton, an ensign (second- or sub-lieutenant), who contributed a poem placed at the end of Smith's *Description of New England* (*Works*, 231, 692) and is mentioned in his *True Travels* (*ibid.*, 852).

On Palingenius, see *Shakespeare's England* (Oxford, 1917), I, 233. For Hariot's text, see Quinn, *Roanoke*, I, 382. For Fotherby, see my *Smith and the Bishop*, p. 15.

4. John Smith's prospectus has been preserved in a single copy, in the collection of the Society of Antiquaries, London. It is described in Sabin (Eames) *Dictionary*, XX, 225–26.

On Frances Howard, daughter of Thomas, Viscount Bindon, nothing less than a full-length biography could do her justice. Unfortunately, that seems to be lacking. Outside of occasional references in John Chamberlain's *Letters*, the most readily available account of the lady appears to be that in John Heneage Jesse's *Memoirs of the Court of England during the Reign of the Stuarts, Including the Protectorate* (new ed., London, 1893), I, 173–76, from which I have quoted. (On the "double Duchess," see the *Letters*, II, 499.)

In addition to the engravings of Frances Howard made by van de Passe and Delaram, there is a full-length portrait by Marc Gheeraerts the younger (which certainly does not reflect any "beauty"); and a miniature done by Nicholas Hilliard.

5. On Robert Vaughan, see Sidney Colvin, *Early Engraving and Engravers in England: 1545–1695* (London, 1905), 126, who had a low opinion of Vaughan. John Herbert Slater expresses a slightly better one in his *Engravings and Their Value*, in connection with Vaughan's engraving of James Stuart (*q.v.*), but there is little pertinent to the Vaughan whom Smith knew as a person. This man is brought out in Isaac J. Williams's "Early Welsh Line and Mezzotint Engravers," *Archaeologia Cambrensis*, LXXXVIII, Part 1 (June, 1933), p. 1 *et seq.*, and T. A. Glenn's "Robert Vaughan of Hengwrt and Robert Vaughan the London Engraver," *ibid.*, LXXXIX, Part 2 (Dec., 1934), 291–301. Much more recent is M. Norton and M. Corbett, *Engraving in England in the Sixteenth and Seventeenth Centuries*, Vol. III (London, 1963), which I have not yet seen in print.

For the reasons which led me to surmise that Vaughan and Purchas were responsible for some of the "exotic" place-names mentioned in Smith's *True Travels*, east European chapters, see Chapter 25, Commentaries.

For a discussion of the place-names on Smith's maps and the additions made in their various "states," see Sabin (Eames) *Dictionary*, XX, 227–31. In addition there is the specialized study by Coolie Verner, "The First Maps of Virginia," *VMHB*, LVIII (1950), 3–15. See also Ben C. McCary, *John Smith's Map of Virginia* (Jamestown Booklet, 1957).

Verner has recently found evidence of an additional state (or states) of the map of Virginia, the supporting arguments being on file in the John Carter Brown Library, Providence, R.I. (summer, 1962).

On the identity of the Gordon honored on Smith's map, I am indebted to Mr. John Imrie, of the Scottish Record Office, Edinburgh, for guidance. The basic source-book here was Sir William Fraser, *The Sutherland Book* (3 vols., Edinburgh, 1892), especially I, 192–205 and 506–11.

On Towneraw, see *Lincolnshire Pedigrees* (Harleian Society, LII), 1007–8. A Steven Townerowe was employed by the Levant Company in Istanbul sometime very early in the 17th century (*The Travels of John Sanderson in the Levant 1584–1602* [Hakluyt Society, 2nd ser., LXVII (1931)], 250).

On John Murray, the basic material is in Sir Robert Douglas, *The Peerage of Scotland* (2nd ed., 2 vols., Edinburgh, 1813), 66–69, and *The Scots Peerage*, founded on Douglas's, ed. Sir James Balfour Paul (Edinburgh, 1904–14), I, 219, 227–28. Murray was created Earl of Annandale, March 13, 1625. There are many references to him in such collections as the *C.S.P., Domestic* for the appropriate years.

Chamberlain's letter on the behavior of the Duchess of Richmond and Lennox is in *Letters,* II, 545–46.

The details on the Virginia Company are in Kingsbury, *Records,* IV, 575 ff., and consult Index.

For John Smith's relation to the Commissioners, etc., see *Works,* 610–20.

6. That the *General History* was hurriedly farmed out to two printers was first suggested (and demonstrated) by Henry Stevens. See Arber's comment in Smith, *Works,* 274, with a fuller explanation in Sabin (Eames) *Dictionary,* XX, 233–34. It should be noted that the printer of the first three books is assumed to have been the same as the printer of the prospectus.

A detail of purely academic interest is the original (and since perpetuated) misprint of the Greek word *Anonymos* as *Agogymos,* with *gamma's* for the letter *nu.*

On the general style of the *General History,* Charles M. Andrews's *Colonial Period of American History,* I, footnote 1, p. 58: "It must be remembered that language of this sort was due in part to the inflated style of the day and in part to a desire to make an impression for propagandistic purposes."


CHAPTER 25


1. The chapter title is taken from the poem, "Character of a Happy Life," by Sir Henry Wotton, the last stanza of which reads:

— This man is freed from servile bands
Of hope to rise, or fear to fall;
Lord of himself, though not of lands;
And having nothing, yet hath all.

George Percy's letter to his brother was printed in *Tyler's Quarterly Historical and Genealogical Magazine*, III (1922), 259–82. Percy went to the Netherlands in 1625, where he had a finger shot off in 1627. He died in 1632.

On the death rate in Virginia, see Craven, *Southern Colonies*, 147, where I have also found the phrase "disappointment and disgust."

The laws and orders promulgated by the Council are to be found in Kingsbury, *Records*, IV, 580–85, under date of March 5, 1623/4. The one I have quoted is No. 34, on p. 584.

On James's virtual abdication to Buckingham (and Prince Charles) there is evidence in all accounts of the period. See, for example, Willson, *James VI & I*, 441–45, and, more pointedly, Gardiner, *History of England*, V, 184. The important period from 1623 to 1625 in fact is covered by Gardiner in Vol. 5 of his detailed history, to which reference may be had for background on my account of the happenings. (I have labeled Buckingham "premier peer" for want of a better phrase of equal brevity. Richmond was created Duke before Buckingham, but was of royal blood; Buckingham was the only other Duke in England. The *richest* peer was the Earl of Pembroke.)

2. Purchas's version of Smith's travels is in *Pilgrimes*, VIII, 321–42. Smith's accurate reference to the *Pilgrimes* is in *Works*, 770; the passage to which he referred, in *Pilgrimes*, XIX, 129 ff., modern edition.

In 1617, a trick had been played on Segar and Ralph Brooke which resulted in their giving the hangman of London a "fair coat of arms," and both landed in the Marshalsea for a short time (Chamberlain, *Letters*, II, 48). Segar apparently continued to be somewhat gullible. But this need not be interpreted to mean either that Smith had no document (which is virtually impossible) or that it was not genuine.

As for possible damage to Smith's patent, I have personally experimented with a document signed by Zsigmond Báthory, dated December 26, 1597, which was picked for me at random by one of the staff in the State Archives in Vienna, and which had originally been folded and sealed. I had this document photographed, and then wrote out the Latin text of Smith's patent in handwriting of the same size as that in the genuine document. Rather strikingly, Smith's "doubtful titles" corresponded generally in position to the damages from folding and sealing in the document photographed.

On the basis of this experiment, and lumping together the doubtful names with a few other curiosities in his *True Travels*, I believe the following hypothesis to be sound:

Purchas or Vaughan, or perhaps Sir William Segar himself, tried to help with the undecipherable names on Smith's pass. Smith may have made suggestions where his memory preserved a clue: Meldrich for Modrusch (pronounced Mödritsch), Anchard for Ecsed (pronounced "atshad"), Growenda for Grosswardein. Elsewhere, it is difficult to guess (Salmaria and Peldoia might possibly have something to do with St. Marein and Pölland-Tal in the Krain, near Ljubljana, but Salford is an English city!). Modrusch's personal name, on the other hand, seems pretty clearly to have been borrowed from (William) Henry Volda or Faldo, the Swiss in whom Smith placed so much trust in Virginia. Whether this was Smith's idea, we cannot tell. Almost certainly, however, Smith picked his own motto, *Vincere est vivere*, from Spanish sources (see my note in *VMHB*, LXVIII [1960], 273), and Vaughan redesigned Zsigmond Báthory's seal, possibly on hints from Smith. (It bears no resemblance to any seal known to have been used by the volatile prince.) In short, without going into further detail, the faded and maimed document was properly repaired and replenished so that Smith's story could be related with all semblance of completeness.

3. As to the George Burton who went to Virginia in 1608, judging by two late additions to Smith's Map of Virginia, he must have been the brother of the famous Robert Burton.

On Charles I's proclamation and Gervase Markham, see D. W. Waters, *Art of Navigation*, 467–77; with comments on John Smith, to boot. On Markham, see Bush, *English Literature*, 44–45, and *English Literature in the Seventeenth Century*, a guide to an exhibition (Bodleian Library, Oxford, 1957), 96–97.

On the "present occasion," see Gardiner, *History*, VI, 131–33.

The reference to the copy of the *Accidence* inscribed to Sir Robert Heath is in Sabin (Eames) *Dictionary*, XX, 219. Heath was on the Virginia Commission, and in 1629 received a grant to what is now North and South Carolina, which was not, and could not be, followed up at that time (Craven, *Southern Colonies*, 188).

On Trinity House, "a fraternity of pilots, seamen, and mariners," see *An Encyclopaedia of London*, ed. William Kent (London, 1937), 686. The home of the fraternity has been moved and rebuilt several times in the past 500 years, for the latest time since World War Two (see *The Buildings of England: London*, I, by Nikolaus Pevsner [Penguin Books, 1962], 265–66).

On the Saltonstall family, there is a pedigree in the Davy MSS (British Museum, Add. MSS, 19148), information on Wye Saltonstall is available with the *DNB* biography as a springboard, and there are scattered references in Alfred B. Beaven, *The Aldermen of The City of London* (London, 2 vols., 1908 and 1913), concerning Sir Richard, the *pater familias*, who died in 1601; but there does not seem to be any full study of either Sir Samuel or Wye, or of the family (except for genealogical purposes). The biography of John Hagthorpe in the *DNB* supplies the basic material for studying the relationship between him and Wye Saltonstall.

I have mentioned Sir Samuel's half sister, Abigail, only because of the puzzling appearance of *Abigail's Isle* as one of the place-names in the first state of Smith's *Map of Ould Virginia*. The name Abigail was not overcommon in the 1620's, and the only person of that name I have run across who has any connection with John Smith at all is Abigail Baker. She would have been about ten to twelve years Smith's junior, and it is known that she was unmarried in 1631. The clue is slim indeed, but it is worth noting that the only "real-life" woman mentioned by John Smith was Abigail — all the others were so many protectresses, benefactresses, and guardian angels. Someday, someone may stumble upon Smith's Abigail's identity. Until then, I can only suggest the remote possibility of Saltonstall's half sister, who was ignored by the legitimate children with studied care.

The identification of the Edward Jorden who wrote verses for John Smith is based on the slim evidence that the style is that of a cultured man and that the physician is the only person of that name possessed of such culture.

The "modern authority" quoted is again Waters, *Art of Navigation,* 474.

4. Samuel Purchas's will was dated May 31, 1625, and was probated October 21, 1626 (*Pilgrimes,* I, XXIX). He appears to have been buried on September 30 (Taylor, *Stuart Geography,* 66).

The guess as to life expectancy in the days of James I is taken from G. P. V. Akrigg, *Jacobean Pageant* (London, 1962), 259.

On Causey's return, see Smith, *Works,* 885, 888. He had remained in Virginia almost 20 years, surviving the massacre, although wounded. There are a few details of his life in Charles E. Hatch, Jr., *The First Seventeen Years* (Jamestown Booklet, 1957), 46–47.

On the word "hominy" and its derivation, see Smith, *Works,* 63; 886; Strachey, *Historie,* 81; and W. R. Gerard, "Some Virginia Indian Words," *American Anthropologist,* new ser., VII (1905), 222–49.

For Smith's comments on New England, see *Works,* 892.

For Sir Robert Bruce Cotton's career, see the biography, *A Fly in Amber,* by Hope Mirrlees (London, 1962). The tangle of Cottons and Montagus is clearly brought out in scattered passages (consult Index). For Cotton and Parliament, see also Hulme, *Sir John Eliot* (consult Index). Robert Bertie's activities appear here and there in Gardiner's *History* (e.g., VI, 133). Bertie had been created Earl of Lindsey in 1626, the year he received the post of Lord High Chamberlain, but he seems to have continued to be a remarkably self-effacing man (see Lady Cecilie Goff, *Three Generations of a Loyal House* [privately printed, 1957], 95–156).

William Camden, in his *Britannia,* laid the basis for linking the

Britain of his own day with the classic past. (See Fox, *Historical Scholarship,* various passages listed under Camden in Index.) Antonio Bòsio laid the basis for linking the Rome of his day with the Christian Rome of antiquity by his investigations of the newly discovered Catacombs. His great work, *Roma sotterranea,* was published in 1632, three years after his death.

Cotton's interest in John Smith could have been inspired by Pliny the Younger, in whose *Epistles* (Book V, 8) is the statement: "I believe it fundamentally right not to suffer those to be forgotten to whom immortality is due . . ."

Smith's allusion to those who acted his "fatal tragedies" on the stage is in *Works,* 809. The mention of the "blessed Pocahontas" in the same, p. 276. The passage from the *Staple of News* is quoted from Act II, almost the end.

5. On the illustrations, an engraver of great potentialities named John Payne "extracted" them, but he left the task of engraving to Martin Droeshout, famous now for his *First Folio* engraving of William Shakespeare.

As to the poets who contributed verses to Smith's new book, Brathwait's identity has been known for a long time. His *Barnabae Itinerarium* (London, 1638) has won him a certain amount of fame.

The commendatory verses signed Ma. Hawkins (Smith, *Works,* 816–17) I have attributed to William Hawkins as being almost the only possible author. Hawkins, who is little known, achieved at least contemporary recognition with his *Corolla Varia.* A few years later, Dr. Goad, Rector of Hadleigh, who had "allowed" the publication of Smith's *General History,* appointed Hawkins his curate (post-1634). See the brief biography in *Parnassian Molehill,* by the Earl of Cranbrook (John David Gathorne-Hardy) (Ipswich, 1953).

On Brian O'Rourke, see John O'Hart, *Irish Pedigrees* (Dublin, 1887), I, 749–51. There are a few references to him in Fynes Moryson's *Itinerary* (4 vols., Glasgow, 1907–8), II, 212, III, 185, 237, 258, 273, and 312, the first of which in all probability refers rather to his father. But the significant material is for the most part scattered through the C.S.P. Ireland, 1603–6 and subsequent volumes (see Indexes), and the C.S.P. Domestic, 1627–28, p. 457. There is also a reference in Frederick Devon, *Issues of the Exchequer* ("Pell Records") (London, 1836), p. 296.

On Captain Callice, see A. L. Rowse, *The Expansion of Elizabethan England* (London, 1955), 64.

Smith's peroration is in *Works,* 916.

### CHAPTER 26

1. John Haviland was "free" of the Stationers' Company June 25, 1613; his publishing career may be said to have begun about eight years later.

Made master printer in 1632, he soon became one of the biggest publishers in London. This, of course, is of interest in John Smith's case only "for the record." What is most noteworthy is that John Haviland certainly printed John Smith's *Sea Grammar* and *Advertisements* (discussed a little later in the text), and almost certainly did the *True Travels* and the second half of the *General History*. This would seem to hint that Haviland was personally interested in John Smith. Why the book was delayed remains unknown.

For Gorges and his troubles with the Virginia Company, and the fishing licenses, see Preston, *Gorges,* 170 f. and 233–45. In fact, the whole account from p. 170 to p. 293 has bearing on John Smith.

There is a full biography of John White in Frances Rose-Troup, *John White, the Patriarch of Dorchester [Dorset] and the Founder of Massachusetts 1575–1648* (New York and London, 1930).

On the Puritans, there are countless works. Among the old-timers, I have found two to be of interest and suggestive: Peter Oliver's *The Puritan Commonwealth,* with a long subtitle (Boston, 1856); and Douglas Campbell, *The Puritan in Holland, England, and America* (2 vols., New York, 1892). Three other, more recent, works have been valuable: Thomas Jefferson Wertenbaker, *The Puritan Oligarchy* (New York, 1947), which is a broad study of the "Massachusetts Bible State"; Louis B. Wright, *The Colonial Civilisation of North America 1607–1763* (London, 1949); and Samuel Eliot Morison's "The Plymouth Colony and Virginia," *VMHB,* LXII (1954), pp. 147–65. Charles M. Andrews's *The Colonial Period of American History* (4 vols., New Haven, 1934) is, of course, virtually indispensable.

John Smith's mention of the departure of the Puritans is in *Works,* 893. The actual number of ships was five, not six. See *Winthrop Papers,* published by the Massachusetts Historical Society (5 vols., 1929–47), II, 157, for the news of their safe arrival in Massachusetts.

On the Mildmays, there are two worth-while works: H. A. St. John-Mildmay, *A Brief Memoir of the Mildmay Family* (London, 1913); and Philip Lee Ralph, *Sir Humphrey Mildmay: Royalist Gentleman* (New Brunswick, N.J., 1947). The latter presents a picture of Smith's host based on that gentleman's diary — which unfortunately does not begin until two years after John Smith's death. The diary nevertheless confirms Mildmay's hospitality, and frequently refers to his guests at Danbury.

2. On the importance of religion in the planting of colonies, see Louis B. Wright, *Religion and Empire* (Chapel Hill, N. Car., 1943). That all was not *pure* religion, however, is pointed out in George L. Mosse, *The Holy Pretence* (Oxford, 1957), which puts a pinch of salt in what might otherwise be a rather flat stew. For the development of religion outside the Puritan belt, see George Maclaren Brydon, *Virginia's Mother Church and The Political Conditions Under Which It Grew* (Richmond, 1947).

John Smith's personal attitude toward religion is clearly shown in his list of sects whose tenets are distasteful to him (see *Works,* 926), and it is remarkable that he should not have sensed the puritanism of the men who led the Puritans. Perhaps his friendship for Sir Samuel Saltonstall veiled his normally perceptive sight.

The reference to the Massachusetts Colony being responsible for its own success or failure is in *Works,* 927; the thirty pages following in the original edition are comprised in *Works,* 927–57.

Smith's account of October, 1622, is in *Works,* 265; the later one, *ibid.,* 929.

Smith's full explanation on history, mentioned already in Chapter 24, is in *Works,* 948, while the later quotations are from the same, 956, 959, and 966. Besides the acknowledgment that he wrote the *Advertisements* "with his owne hand" (p. 966), there are only three other like statements: at the end of Book Two of the *General History* (p. 380); at the end of the rewritten *Description of New England* (1616), in Book Six of the *General History* (p. 742); and at the end of the rewritten *New Englands Trials* (1622), in the same (p. 776).

3. On the division of the Council's territory, see Preston, *Gorges,* 231; Smith's reference to what he got is in *Works,* 947.

Much of the information from here to the end is taken from Smith's will, in *Works,* 969–71. On Hinde, the Clerk of the Salters' Company sent me, under date of December 16, 1960, transcripts of the only two references in the Minute Books, neither of which is of direct significance to Smith's life.

I take this opportunity to thank the Clerk of the Salters' Company for his efforts in my behalf.

On John Tradescant, see Kingsbury, *Records,* III, 58, for his shares in the Virginia Company. There is a brief biography of him in Brown, *Genesis,* II, 1032, and there are two references in Davis, *Sandys,* in the footnotes to pp. 66 and 193. There are a few of Tradescant's books in the Ashmolean collection in the Bodleian Library at Oxford, but a preliminary survey did not reveal any that appear to have belonged to John Smith, although Smith's will bequeathed half of his books to be shared between Richard Hinde and Tradescant (*Works,* 970).

For information on John Smith and the Packer family, I am indebted to Bradford Smith's investigations in London, the results of which are in his *Life of John Smith,* 291. (See also Part II, Chapter 18, Commentary 2.)

The detail of the alteration in the map of New England, with "Charles, nowe King," is described in Sabin (Eames) *Dictionary,* XX, 220–21.

The short lyric, "The Sea Marke," should probably be considered John Smith's until proven otherwise. I have found nothing quite like it in versification at the time, but there are two sad poems in almost identical verse-form by James Shirley, "Death's Emissaries" and "Death the Leveller," which were not printed until 1653 and 1659 (see William Stanley Braithwaite, *The Book of Elizabethan Verse* [Boston, 1907], 642–43, and notes on p. 766). I have modernized the spelling of "The Sea Marke" for greater facility in reading.

On the cost of John Smith's funeral, begrudged him by some modern critics, see the broad picture given in *Shakespeare's England* (Oxford, 1917), II, 148–52, with its mention of Sir Thomas Gresham's funeral costing £800. Of course, Sir Thomas was very rich. John Smith was poor. But was that a reason for going to face his Maker clad in pauper's rags?

On John Smith in legend, I hesitate to say anything. I should be forced to *defend* Smith, and my aim in this work has been merely to *present* him. Those interested can consult the bibliography (incomplete, I fear) of works on Smith which I have appended.

John Smith was buried in St. Sepulchre's Church, but the memorial tablet containing his epitaph was destroyed in the Great Fire of 1666. It has since been replaced, utilizing the text of the original given in Stow's *Survey of London*, edition of 1633. It is an appropriate conclusion to this work:

> To the living memory of his deceased friend
> Captain John Smith,
> sometime Governour of Virginia,
> and Admiral of New England,
> who departed this life the 21st of June 1631.
> ACCORDAMUS VINCERE EST VIVERE

Here lyes one conquered that hath conquered Kings.
Subdu'd large Territories, and done things
Which to the World impossible would seem,
But that the Truth is held in more esteem.
Shall I report his former Service done
In honour of his God and Christendom?
How that he did divide from Pagans three
Their Heads and Lives, Types of his Chivalry.
For which great Service in that Climate done,
Brave Sigismundus, King of Hungarion,
Did give him as a Coat of Armes to wear,
These Conquered Heads got by his Sword and Spear.
Or shall I tell of his Adventures since
Done in Virginia, that large Continent?
How that he subdu'd Kings unto his Yoke,
And made those Heathen flee, as Wind doth Smoke:
And made their land, being of so large a Station,
An Habitation for our Christian Nation,

Where God is glorify'd, their Wants supply'd;
Which else, for Necessaries must have dy'd.
But what avails his Conquests, now he lyes
Interr'd in Earth, a Prey to Worms and Flyes?
O! May his Soul in sweet Elysium sleep,
Until the Keeper that all Souls doth keep,
Return to Judgment; and that after thence,
With Angels he may have his Recompence.

# BIBLIOGRAPHY

# BIBLIOGRAPHY

A<small>NYONE</small> beginning to search for relevant material for a life of Captain John Smith is all but thwarted at the outset by his mere name. At least two other John Smiths (or Smyths) flourished with some prominence at the same time, while a dozen or more additional John Smiths flash for a moment in this or that historical document. Indeed, relatively few of the primary printed sources directly mentioned our Captain John. On the other hand, the amount of circumstantial evidence to be had for the looking is more than ample to document the story of his career. This circumstantial evidence, this body of indirect references, is scattered through a large portion of the documents and printed books of the period.

As for the documents, the vast store of available manuscripts in which some direct or circumstantial evidence of Smith might be found puts the searcher in mind of a couplet by Smith's contemporary, John Taylor, "The Water Poet":

> By wondrous accident perchance one may
> Grope out a needle in a load of hay.

Even if I have been fortunate in groping out a few needles, this does not mean that I must catalogue the hay. Yet some reference must be made to such sources, and I trust that the list of works supplied below may prove useful. It will at least indicate how wide a net the biographer of John Smith must cast.

To save space, I have first listed five already published bibliographies of special value, either for thoroughness or pertinence, or both. Then follow the works of greatest utilitarian value, in the usual order of manuscript sources, primary printed works, and secondary references, the last mentioned being subdivided for convenience. Titles abbreviated in the Commentaries appear only in their proper alphabetical order, but will, I believe, be readily identifiable. The same applies to the *short titles* I have used in the text as well, in place of the long *full titles* in such common use in John Smith's day.

Common Abbreviations

AA     American Anthropologist, new series.
BAE    Bureau of American Ethnology, Smithsonian Institution.
DNB    Dictionary of National Biography.
NEHGR   New England Historical and Genealogical Register.
OED    Oxford English Dictionary.
Tyler's Quarterly   Tyler's Quarterly Historical and Genealogical Magazine.
VMHB   Virginia Magazine of History and Biography.
WMQ    William and Mary Quarterly.

## BIBLIOGRAPHICAL REFERENCES

For the earliest period of English colonization: *The Roanoke Voyages 1584–1590*, edited by David Beers Quinn (see under The Hakluyt Society below), Appendix IV, "Sources," II, 911–46.

Supplementary thereto: Wesley Frank Craven, *The Southern Colonies in the Seventeenth Century 1607–1689* (A History of the South, vol. 1, Louisiana State University Press, 1949), "Critical Essay on Authorities," pp. 417–33.

Catalogue of state and private papers: E. L. C. Mullins, *Texts and Calendars: An analytical guide to Serial Publications* (Royal Historical Society, London, 1958). Almost all of the calendars, etc., covering the years 1580–1631 contain something of value or interest.

For John Smith in eastern Europe: Bradford Smith, *Captain John Smith: His Life and Legend* (Philadelphia, 1953), Appendix I, Laura Polanyi Striker, "Sources and Notes," pp. 333–35. Basic but incomplete.

For Smith's career generally: The same, Appendix V, Bradford Smith's "References," pp. 351–63. Random, but valuable.

## MANUSCRIPT SOURCES CONSULTED

Since only the first of these contains any reference to John Smith at all, I have mentioned only the location of the deposits.

The *Ancaster* deposits, Lincolnshire Archives Committee, Lincoln. (See Bradford Smith, *Life*, p. 355. This huge collection had not yet been completely surveyed in the spring of 1962, and further information may someday be found there.)

The *Davy* manuscripts, in the British Museum (Add. MSS 19114–19156), and scattered *Cottonian* MSS, specifically mentioned in the Commentaries.

The *Records of the Goldsmiths' Company*, Goldsmiths' Hall, London.

*Wills* and *Feet of Fines* in the County Records Offices of Ipswich, Chelmsford, and Hertford.

The surviving *Records* in the Departmental Archives, La Rochelle, France.

*Archives* of the Haus-, Hof- und Staatsarchiv, Vienna. (Section *Ungarische Akten* and *Kriegsakten*.)

*Archives* of the K. K. Kriegs-Archiv, Vienna. (Section *Geschichte*.)

*Archives* of the Landesarchiv, Graz, Austria.

*Archives* of the Landesarchiv, Klagenfurt, Austria.

Many other manuscripts were consulted in London, Rennes (France), Siena, Rome, and elsewhere, either personally or through the courteous cooperation of the archivists on duty, but the negative results of my inquiries make more detailed mention idle. In addition, a careful scanning of about three quarters of the Survey Reports of the Colonial Records Project, Colonial Williamsburg and the Virginia State Library, Richmond, failed to produce anything new. In some instances the microfilms available through this project provided verification of printed copies or, more often, correct readings; and it is possible that some unexpected curiosity will someday be found. In my opinion, however, that will be by accident, not by systematic search.

### PRIMARY PRINTED WORKS

*in addition to those mentioned in the Bibliographical References*

#### PUBLICATIONS OF THE HAKLUYT SOCIETY

*chronologically arranged*

#### General

*The Journal of Christopher Columbus*, trans. by Cecil Jane, revised and annotated by L. A. Vigneras, with appendix by R. A. Skelton. Extra ser., 38.

*A Brief Summe of Geographie*, by Roger Barlow, ed. E. G. R. Taylor. 2nd ser., Vol. 69.

*A Regiment for the Sea . . .* , by William Bourne, ed. E. G. R. Taylor. 2nd ser., Vol. 121.

*The Principal Navigations Voyages Traffiques & Discoveries of the English Nation*, by Richard Hakluyt. 12 vols., extra ser., 1–12. (Referred to as Hakluyt, *Voyages*.)

*The Original Writings and Correspondence of the two Richard Hakluyts*, ed. E. G. R. Taylor. 2nd ser., Vols. 76–77.

*Hakluytus Posthumus, or Purchas His Pilgrimes,* by Samuel Purchas. 20 vols., extra ser., 14–33. (Referred to as Purchas, *Pilgrimes.*)

### Caribbean Voyages

*English Voyages to the Caribbean . . . 1527–1568,* ed. Irene A. Wright. 2nd ser., Vol. 62.

*English Voyages to the Spanish Main . . . 1569–1580,* ed. Irene A. Wright. 2nd ser., Vol. 71.

*Further English Voyages to Spanish America, 1583–1594,* ed. Irene A. Wright. 2nd ser., Vol. 99.

*English Privateering Voyages . . . 1588–1595,* ed. Kenneth R. Andrews. 2nd ser., Vol. 111.

*A Relation of a Voyage to Guiana, by Robert Harcourt, 1613,* ed. Sir C. Alexander Harris. 2nd ser., Vol. 60.

*Colonising Expeditions to the West Indies and Guiana, 1623–1667,* ed. Vincent T. Harlow. 2nd ser., Vol. 56.

### Voyages to "Virginia"

*The Cabot Voyages and Bristol Discovery under Henry VII,* ed. J. A. Williamson. 2nd ser., Vol. 120.

*The Voyages and Colonising Enterprises of Sir Humphrey Gilbert,* ed. David Beers Quinn. 2nd ser., Vols. 83–84.

*The Roanoke Voyages, 1584–1590,* ed. David Beers Quinn. 2nd ser., Vols. 104–5.

*The Historie of Travaile into Virginia Britannia, by William Strachey,* ed. Richard Henry Major. 1st ser., Vol. 6.

*The Historie of Travell into Virginia Britannia (1612), by William Strachey,* eds. Louis B. Wright and Virginia Freund. 2nd ser., Vol. 103.

*The History of the Bermudas or Summer Islands, attributed to Captain Nathaniel Butler,* ed. Sir John Henry Lefroy. 1st ser., Vol. 61 (an old work, containing a few untenable suggestions).

Three further volumes on English voyages to and colonization of North America are announced but not yet published.

### CONTEMPORARY BOOKS, PERTINENT TO THE VIRGINIA VENTURE

*in addition to the foregoing*

The early works on colonization and exploration are listed in the "Short Chronological List of English books, co-ordinate, or supplementary to the present Text," in the *Travels and Works of Captain John Smith . . . ,* ed. Edward Arber, new edition with introduction by A. G. Bradley (Edinburgh, 1910, in 2 vols.), pp. cxxxii–cxxxiii, which is virtually identical with the original edition by Arber (Birmingham, 1884, in one vol.). To these may be added:

*A Briefe and true Relation of the Discoverie of the North part of Virginia* . . . , by John Brereton. 2nd ed., London, 1602.
*The Description of the now-discovered river and country of Virginia* . . . (*1607*), anonymous MS in Lambeth Palace Library, London; printed in *Archaeologia Americana*, IV (Boston), 1860.
*A Brief Description of the People (1607); ibid.*
*Of the Country of Virginia*, by Simon Forman (*ca.* 1610). MS in Bodleian Library, Oxford, now in process of editing by David B. Quinn.
*A Discovery of the Barmudas*, by Silvester Jourdain; London, 1610.
*A Trewe Relatyon of the Procedeinges and Ocurrentes of Momente* $w^{ch}$ *have hapned in Virginia from* . . . *1609 untill* . . . *1612*, by George Percy. Printed in *Tyler's Quarterly*, III (1922), 259–82.
*A Plain Pathway to Plantations* (1624), by Richard Eburne, ed. Louis B. Wright. Cornell Univ. Press, 1962.

OTHER PRIMARY PRINTED WORKS

Alberti, L. de, and Chapman, A. B. Wallis, eds. *English Merchants and the Spanish Inquisition in the Canaries*. Vol. 23. Camden Society, London, 1912.
Arbaleste, Charlotte de, Mlle. du Plessis. *Memoirs of Philippe de Mornay* . . . , abr. and trans. by Lucy Crump as *A Huguenot Family*. Broadway Translations, n.d.
Arber, Edward, ed. *The Story of the Pilgrim Fathers, 1606–1623 A.D.* . . . London, 1897.
Bacon, Nathaniel. *The Annalls of Ipswiche* . . . , ed. William H. Richardson. Ipswich, 1884.
*Battle of Nieuport, 1600*. Shakespeare Association Facsimiles, no. 9. London, 1935.
Baudier, Michel. *Inventaire de l'histoire generale des Turcs*. Paris, 1628.
Baxter, James Phinney. *Sir Ferdinando Gorges and His Province of Maine*. 3 vols. Prince Society, Boston, 1890.
Bell, Robert, ed. *Extract from the Despatches of M. Courcelles*. Bannatyne Club, Edinburgh, 1828.
Biringuccio. *The Pirotechnia of Vannoccio Biringuccio*, trans. by Cyril Stanley Smith and Martha Teach Gnudi. New York, 1942.
Bohun, Edmund. *Geographical Dictionary*. London, 1693.
Botero, Giovanni. *Relations of the Most Famous Kingdoms and Commonweales Thorough the World*, trans. by Robert Johnson. London, 1608.
Bradford, William. *Bradford's History "Of Plimoth Plantation."* Boston, 1899.

---

Brown, Alexander. *The Genesis of the United States.* 2 vols. Boston, 1890.

Browne, J[ohn], merchant. *The Marchants Aviso* (1589), ed. Patrick McGrath. Baker Library, Harvard Univ., 1957.

Bry, Theodore de. *Pannoniae Historia Chronologica.* Frankfurt a/M., 1596. (Other works listed in Quinn's *Roanoke Voyages*, II, 922–23.)

Bullock, William. *Virginia Impartially Examined.* . . . London, 1649.

Buckminster, Thomas. *An Almanack and Prognostication for the Year 1598.* Shakespeare Association Facsimiles, no. 8. London, 1935.

Carew of Anthony, Richard. *The Survey of Cornwall,* ed. F. E. Halliday. London, 1953.

Carrillo. *Epistolae et Acta P. Alfonsi Carrilli, S.J.,* ed. Dr. Endre Veress. Magyar Történelmi Emlékek, Budapest, 1906.

Cartier. *The Voyages of Jacques Cartier,* ed. by H. P. Biggar. Ottawa, 1924.

Chamberlain. *The Letters of John Chamberlain,* ed. Norman Egbert McClure. Philadelphia, 1939.

Champlain. *Voyages of Samuel de Champlain,* ed. and trans. by Edmund F. Slafter. 3 vols. Boston, 1880–82.

—— *The Works of Samuel de Champlain,* ed. Henry Perceval Biggar. 6 vols. Toronto, 1922–36.

Churchill, Awnsham and J., eds. *A Collection of Voyages and Travels.* . . . 3rd ed., London, 1744.

Dee, [Dr.] John. *General and rare memorials pertayning to the Perfect Arte of Navigation . . . , by John Dee.* London, 1577. (Called by John Smith, "Master Dee's *British Monarchie.*")

Devereux, Walter Bourchier. *Lives and Letters of the Devereux, Earls of Essex.* London, 1853.

Donne, John. *A Sermon upon the viii Verse of the I Chapter of the Acts of the Apostles,* preached to the Hon. Company of the Virginian Plantations. London, 1622.

*Egerton Papers.* A Collection of Public and Private Documents . . . the property of the Right Hon. Lord Francis Egerton. Camden Society, London, 1840.

Ens, Gaspar. *Rerum Hungaricarum Historia.* Cologne, 1604.

Fotherby, Martin. *Atheomastix: Clearing foure Truthes, Against Atheists and Infidels.* London, 1622.

Giraldus de Barri, Cambrensis. *Itinerarium Cambriae* and *Cambriae Descriptio.* London, 1585.

Gooss, Roderich, ed. *Österreichische Staatsvorträge: Fürstentum Siebenbürgen.* Komm. für neuere Geschichte Österreichs, Veröffentlichungen, 9, Vienna, 1911.

Gouyon, Charles, Baron de la Moussaye. *Mémoires,* eds. G. Vallée and P. Parfouru. Paris, 1901.

Guevara, Antonio de. *The Diall of Princes,* Englished by Thomas North. London, 1582 (partial reprint, London, 1919).

Guevara, John. "A Declaration of my prociedings after the late Lord Wyllughby his decease," *Lincolnshire Historian*, II, no. 3 (1955–56), 23–26.

Guillim, John: *A Display of Heraldrie*. London, 1610.

Harrison, William. *Description of England in Shakspere's Youth*, ed. Frederick J. Furnival. 3 vols. London, 1877–81.

Hiltebrandt, Conrad Jacob. *Dreifache Schwedische Gesandtschaftsreise nach Siebenbürgen, der Ukraine und Constantinopel (1656–1658)*, ed. Franz Babinger. Leiden, 1937.

Hondius, Jodocus, ed. *Historia Mundi, or Mercator's Atlas*, trans. by Wye Saltonstall. London, 1635.

Illésházy, István. *Följegyzése* [Writings]. Monumenta Hungariae Historica, Pest, 1963.

Istvanffi, Nikolaus. *Historiarum de Rebus Ungaricis Libri IV*. Cologne, 1622.

Julien, Ch.-André, René Herval, and Th. Beauchesne, eds. *Les Français en Amérique pendant la première moitié du XVI* e *siècle*. Paris, 1946.

Kingsbury, Susan Myra, ed. *The Records of the Virginia Company of London*. 4 vols. Washington, 1906–35.

Knolles, Richard. *The Turkish History . . . with a Continuation . . . by Sir Paul Rycaut*. 6th ed., 3 vols. London, 1687–1700.

Laughton, John Knox. *State Papers Relating to the Defeat of the Spanish Armada, Anno 1588*. Navy Records Society, London, 1894.

Lawson, John. *Lawson's History of North Carolina*, ed. Frances Latham Harriss. Richmond, 1951.

Lazius, Wolfgang. *Reipublicae Romanae in Exteris Provinciis, Bello acquisitis, constitutae, commentariorum Libri duodecim*. Frankfurt a/M., 1598.

L'Estoile, Pierre de. *Journal de L'Estoile pour le règne de Henri IV*, eds. Louis-Raymond Lefèvre and André Martin. 3 vols. Paris, 1948–60.

Levermore, Charles Herbert, ed. *Forerunners and Competitors of the Pilgrims and Puritans*. 2 vols. Brooklyn, N.Y., 1912.

Lewkenor, Sir Lewis. *The Estate of English Fugitives under the King of Spain and his Ministers*. London, 1595.

Lewkenor, Samuel. *A Discourse not altogether unprofitable nor unpleasant for such as are desirous to know the situation and customes of forraine cities without travelling to see them*. London, 1600.

Lloyd, David. *Memoires of the Lives, Actions, Sufferings & Deaths of . . . Excellent Personages . . . 1637–1660*. London, 1668. (Far from trustworthy.)

Llwyd [Lloyd], Humfrey. *The breviary of Britayne*, trans. by Thomas Twyne. London, 1573.

——— *The historie of Cambria, now called Wales . . .* [by Caradog of Llancarvan], trans. by H. Lhoyd, and continued by David Powel, D.D. London, 1584.

*Louth Old Corporation Records,* compiled by R. W. Goulding. Louth, 1891.

Lussagnet, Suzanne, ed. *Les Français en Amérique pendant la deuxième moitié du XVIᵉ siècle.* 2 vols. Paris, 1953, 1958.

Machiavelli, Niccolò. *The Art of War,* trans. by Peter Whitehorne, 1560. The Tudor Translations, London, 1905.

Magini, Ioannis Antonii. *Geographiae, tum veteris, tum novae, volumina duo.* Arnhem, 1617.

Marcus Aurelius. *The Golden Book of Marcus Aurelius Emperour and eloquente oratour,* trans. by John Bourchier, 2nd Baron Berners. London, 1546. (Cf. Guevara, Antonio de, whose *Diall of Princes* is also translated from Marcus Aurelius.)

Mead, Joseph. "The Indian Massacre of 1622: Some Correspondence of the Reverend Joseph Mead," ed. Robert C. Johnson. *VMHB,* LXXI (1963), 408–10.

Meteren, Emanuel van. *Historie der Neder-landscher ende haerder Naburen Oorlogen en geschiedenissen, tot den Iare M.VI ᶜ.XII.* The Hague, 1614.

*Minutes of the Council and General Court, 1622–1624, Virginia Company,* from the originals in the Library of Congress, *VMHB,* XVII (1909), 149–57.

Moryson, Fynes. *An Itinerary. Containing His Ten Yeeres Travell. . . .* 4 vols. Glasgow, 1907–8.

——— *Shakespeare's Europe,* unpublished chapters of Fynes Moryson's *Itinerary.* London, 1903.

Naima. *Annals of the Turkish Empire from 1591 to 1659, by Naima,* trans. by Charles Fraser. Vol. I, London, 1832. (The complete work was published in Istanbul, in Turkish, 1864–65.)

Ortelius, Abraham. *Abrahami Ortelii Antverpiani Synonymia Geographica.* Antwerp, 1578.

——— *Theatrum Orbis Terrarum.* Antwerp, 1597.

Ortelius, Hieronymus. *Ortelius Redivivus et Continuatus . . . Mit einer Continuation . . . durch Martin Meyern . . . aussgezieret.* Frankfurt a/M., 1665.

Perrot, Sir James. *The Chronicle of Ireland, 1584–1608,* ed. Herbert Wood. Irish MSS Comm., Dublin, 1933.

Pory. *John Pory's Lost Description of Plymouth Colony,* ed. Champlin Burrage. Boston, 1918.

Quadt, Matthias. *Geographisch Handtbuch. . . .* Cologne, 1600.

Rawdon, Marmaduke. *The Life of Marmaduke Rawdon, by his nephew of the same name,* ed. Robert Davies. Camden Society, London, 1863.

*Respublica et Status Regni Hungariae,* ex officina Elzeveriana. Leiden, 1634.

Rosier, James. *A true relation of the most prosperous voyage made . . . by Captaine George Waymouth . . .* London, 1605.

Rubens. *The Letters of Peter Paul Rubens,* trans. and ed. by Ruth Saunders Magurn. Cambridge, Mass., 1955.

Sackville. "Lord Sackville's Papers Respecting Virginia, 1613–1631," *American Historical Review,* XXVII (1921–22), 493–538 and 738–65.

Sandys, George. *A Relation of a Journey begun An. Dom. 1610.* . . . London, 1615.

Schwandner, Johann Georg. *Scriptores Rerum Hungaricarum veteres ac genuini.* 3 vols. Vienna, 1746–48.

Smyth of Nibley, John. *The Berkeley Manuscripts. The Lives of the Berkeleys* . . . *From 1066 to 1618.* 3 vols. Gloucester, England, 1883–85.

Spedding, James. *The Letters and the Life of Francis Bacon.* 7 vols. London, 1861–74.

Stow, John. *Annales,* continued and augmented by Edmund Howes. London, 1631.

———— *A Survey of London.* London, 1603 (repr. in Everyman's Library, 1956).

Szamosközy, István. *Történeti Maradványai* [Historical Notes], ed. Szilágyi Sándor, in *Monumenta Hungariae Historica, Scriptores,* Vols. 21, 28–30. Budapest, 1876–80.

Thévenot, Melchisédech: *Relations de divers voyages curieux.* . . . 2 vols. Paris, 1683.

Thevet, André. *La Cosmographie Universelle de André Thevet.* 2 vols. Paris, 1575.

Thwaites, Reuben Gold, ed. *The Jesuit Relations and Allied Documents.* 73 vols. Cleveland, 1896–1901.

Vaughan, William. *Cambrensium Caroleia* . . . *reportata a Colchide Cambriola.* London, 1625.

Vere. *The Commentaries of Sir Francis Vere.* Cambridge, 1657.

Wadding, Luke. *Annales Minorum.* 2nd ed., 25 vols. Rome, 1731–1886.

Weldon, Sir Anthony. *The Court and Character of King James.* London, 1650.

*Winthrop Papers.* Massachusetts Historical Society, 5 vols. 1929–47.

Winwood, Sir Ralph. *Memorials of Affairs of State in the Reigns of Queen Elizabeth and King James I.* 3 vols. London, 1725.

Young, Alexander. *Chronicles of the Pilgrim Fathers.* Boston, 1841.

Zeiller, Martin. *Beschreibung des Koenigreichs Ungarn / und dazu gehoeriger Landen / Staedte / und vornehmster Oerter.* Ulm, 1664.

## SECONDARY AUTHORITIES

### DICTIONARIES, ENCYCLOPAEDIAS, INDEXES, AND THE LIKE

Aubert de la Chesnaye des Bois, François Alexandre. *Dictionnaire de la noblesse.* 12 vols. Paris, 1864.

Bartholomew, John. *The Survey Gazetteer of the British Isles.* 9th ed., Edinburgh, n.d. [post-1951].

Battisti, Carlo, & Giovanni Alessio. *Dizionario Etimologico Italiano.* 5 vols. Florence, 1950–57.

Bense, J. F. *A Dictionary of the Low-Dutch Element in the English Vocabulary.* The Hague, 1939.

Bernardo, M. R. P. F. *Vocabulario Italiano Turchesco.* Rome, 1665.

*Biographia Britannica.* 2nd ed., with corrections by Andrew Kippis. 5 vols. London, 1778–93.

Black, William Henry. *A Descriptive, Analytical, and Critical Catalogue of the Manuscripts Bequeathed unto the University of Oxford by Elias Ashmole. . . .* Oxford, 1845.

*Bol'shaya Sovyetskaya Entsiklopediya* [Great Soviet Encyclopaedia]. 2nd ed., 51 vols. Moscow, 1949–58.

Collins, Arthur. *Peerage of England.* 9 vols. London, 1812.

Dargan, Marion. *Guide to American Biography: Part I, 1607–1815.* Univ. of New Mexico Press, 1949.

Deschamps, P[ierre]. *Dictionnaire de géographie ancienne et moderne.* Paris, 1870.

*Dictionary of American Biography.* 22 vols. New York, 1928–44.

*Dictionary of National Biography.* 63 vols. Oxford Univ. Press, 1885–1900.

*Eerste Nederlandse Systematisch Ingerichte Encyclopedie.* 12 vols. Amsterdam, 1946–60.

Ekwall, Eilert. *The Concise Oxford Dictionary of English Place-Names.* Oxford, 1936.

*Enciclopedia Italiana di Scienze, Lettere ed Arti.* 36 vols. Imprint varies, 1930–50.

*Enciclopedia Universal Ilustrada Europeo-Americana, Espasa-Calpe.* 70 vols. in 72. Imprint varies, c. 1907–30. (Referred to as *Esp.-Cal.*)

*Encyclopaedia Britannica.* 11th ed., 29 vols. Cambridge, England, 1910–11.

*Entsiklopedicheskiĭ Slovar',* ed. I. E. Andreyevskiĭ. Published by Brockhaus-Efron, St. Petersburg, 1890–1904. 41 vols., usually bound in about 90, with supp.

Fennell, C. A. M., ed. *The Stanford Dictionary of Anglicised Words and Phrases.* Cambridge, 1892.

Foulché-Delbosc, R. "Bibliographie des Voyages en Espagne et en Portugal," *Revue Hispanique,* Vol. 3 (1896).

Friederici, Georg. *Amerikanistisches Wörterbuch.* Hamburg, 1937.

Girault de Saint Fargeau, A. *Dictionnaire géographique, historique, industriel et commercial de toutes les communes de la France.* Paris, 1844.

*Grande Encyclopédie, La.* 31 vols. Paris, c. 1886–1903.

Kent, William, ed. *An Encyclopaedia of London.* London, 1937.

Korabinsky, Johann Matthias. *Geographisch-Historisches und Produkten Lexikon von Ungarn.* Pressburg, 1786.

Marshall, George W. *The Genealogist's Guide.* Guildford, Surrey, 1903.
Mathews, Mitford M. *A Dictionary of Americanisms.* . . . Univ. of Chicago Press, 1951.
McKerrow, R. B., and others. *A Dictionary of Printers and Booksellers in England, Scotland and Ireland.* . . . London, 1910.
Metcalfe, Walter Charles. *A Book of the Knights Banneret, Knights of the Bath, and Knights Bachelor.* London, 1885.
*Meyers Konversations-Lexikon.* 5th ed., 19 vols. Leipzig/Vienna, 1894–99.
Mullins, E. L. C. *Texts and Calendars: An Analytical Guide to Serial Publications.* Royal Historical Society, London, 1958.
Nichols, Frances S. *Index to Schoolcraft's "Indian Tribes of the United States."* Bureau of American Ethnology, Bulletin 152, Washington, 1954.
Ogée, Jean. *Dictionnaire historique et géographique de la province de Bretagne.* 2 vols. Rennes, 1843.
Orgelbrand, S. L. *Encyklopedja Powszechna.* 16 vols. Warsaw, 1898–1904.
*Oxford English Dictionary.* 13 vols. Oxford, 1933.
Palmer, Henrietta R. *List of English Editions and Translations of Greek and Latin Classics Printed before 1641.* London, 1911.
Phillips, P. Lee. "List of Books Relating to America in the Register of the London Company of Stationers," *Annual Report of the American Historical Association,* I (1896), 1251–61.
Pollard, A. W., and Redgrave, G. R. *A Short-Title Catalogue* . . . *1475–1640.* London, 1926.
Polunin, Fyodor Afanasyevich. *Novy i polny geograficheskiĭ Slovar' rossiĭskago gosudarstva, ili Leksikon.* 5 vols. Moscow, 1788–89.
Radlov, V. V. *Opyt slovarya tyurkskikh narechii.* St. Petersburg, 1893–1911.
Ramstedt, G. J. *Kalmückisches Wörterbuch.* Helsinki, 1935.
Reaney, P. H. *A Dictionary of British Surnames.* 2nd impr., London, 1961.
*Révai Nagy Lexikona* [Hungarian Great Lexikon]. 20 vols., plus supp. Budapest, 1911–27.
*Ritters Geographisch-Statistisches Lexikon,* Joh. Pensler, ed. 9te Ausgabe, Leipzig/Vienna, 1910.
*Russko-Tatarskiĭ Slovar'.* Kazan, 1941.
Sabin, Joseph (et al.). *A Dictionary of Books Relating to America.* 29 vols. New York, 1868–1936. (Referred to in connection with John Smith as Sabin [Eames], *Dictionary.*)
Shaw, William A. *The Knights of England.* London, 1906.
Swem, Earl G. *Virginia Historical Index.* 2 vols. Roanoke, Va., 1934.
Vollmer, Hans. *Allgemeines Lexikon der bildenden Künstler.* 36 vols. Leipzig, 1907–47.
Whitmore, J. B. *A Genealogical Guide,* with Final Addenda (in 1 vol.). London, 1953.

Wing, Donald. *Short-Title Catalogue . . . 1641–1700.* New York, 1945–51.

*Winkler Prins Encyclopaedie.* 18 vols. plus supp. Amsterdam, 1947–54. (The foregoing list includes only those works most often consulted; it is pared to the bone on such subjects as British genealogy, since the Commentaries supply further indications of sources.)

GENERAL WORKS

Including only those which have not been mentioned in the Commentaries, yet contain pertinent information.

Anderson, William. *The Scottish Nation.* Edinburgh, 1864.

Andrews, William. *Bygone Lincolnshire.* Hull, 1891.

Atkins, Samuel Elliott, and Overall, William Henry, compilers. *Some Account of the Worshipful Company of Clockmakers of the City of London.* London, 1881.

*Atlas Geographus: or, A Compleat system of geography, ancient and modern.* 5 vols. London, 1711–17.

Baán, Kálmán. *Magyar Genealogiai és Heraldikai Forrásmunkák, 1561–1932.* Budapest, 1932.

Baker, William A. "Notes on a Shallop," *American Neptune,* XVII (1957), 105–13.

Bald, R. C. *Donne and the Drurys.* Cambridge, 1959.

Bedwell, C. E. A. *Brief History of the Middle Temple.* London, 1909.

Bense, J. F. *Anglo-Dutch Relations. . . .* The Hague, 1925.

Berkley, Dr. Henry J. "The Berkeley-Berkley Family and Their Kindred in the Colonization of Virginia and Maryland," *WMQ,* 2nd ser., III (1923), 180–99.

Biggar, H. P. *The Early Trading Companies of New France.* Toronto, 1901.

Blackham, Robert J. *Wig and Gown: The Story of the Temple, Gray's and Lincoln's Inn.* London, c. 1930.

Bodilly, Ralph Burland. *The Voyage of Captain Thomas James for the Discovery of the Northwest Passage, 1631.* London, 1928.

Bosch-Gimpera, P. "Les Mouvements Celtiques — Essai de Reconstitution," *Études Celtiques,* V, fascs. 1 and 2 (1950–51), 352–400; VI, fasc. 1 (1952), 72–126, and fasc. 2 (1953–54), 328–55.

Bourne, H. R. Fox. *English Merchants.* London, 1886.

Bratianu, G. I. *Recherches sur le commerce génois dans la Mer Noire au XIIIᵉ siècle.* Paris, 1929.

Braudel, Fernand. *La Méditerranée et le monde méditerranéen à l'époque de Philippe II.* Paris, 1949.

Brears, Charles. *Lincolnshire in the Seventeenth and Eighteenth Centuries.* London, 1940.

Brown, Alexander. Letter of May 3, 1901, to W. D. Chesterman. Brown Deposit, William and Mary College Library, Box 12.

—— *New Views of Early Virginia History.* Liberty, Va., 1886.

Bruce, John. *Annals of the Honourable East India Company.* London, 1810.

Burrage, Henry S. *Gorges and the Grant of the Province of Maine, 1622.* Printed for the State of Maine, 1923.

Busquet, Raoul. *Histoire de Marseille.* Paris, 1945.

*Cambridge Modern History*, eds. A. W. Ward, G. W. Prothero, and Stanley Leathes. 12 vols. and atlas. Cambridge, 1902–12. (The pertinent volumes [3 and 4] of the new edition had not appeared at the time of writing.)

Campbell, John, Lord. *The Lives of the Chief Justices of England.* 3rd ed., 4 vols. London, 1874.

—— *The Lives of the Lord Chancellors and Keepers of the Great Seal of England.* 5th ed., 10 vols. London, 1868.

Campbell, Mildred. *The English Yeoman.* Yale Univ. Press, 1942.

Casson, Lionel. "Speed under Sail of Ancient Ships," *Transactions and Proceedings of the American Philological Association*, LXXXII (1951), 136–48.

Castro, P. José de. *Dom Sebastião e Dom Henrique.* Lisbon, 1942.

Cecil, Algernon. *A Life of Robert Cecil, First Earl of Salisbury.* London, 1915.

Chapman, Hester W. *The Last Tudor King, A Study of Edward VI.* New York, 1959.

Christensen, Aksel E. *Dutch Trade to the Baltic about 1600.* Copenhagen/The Hague, 1941.

Collins, Arthur. *Historical Collections of the Noble Families of Cavendishe, Holles, Vere, Harley and Ogle.* London, 1757.

Cook, Minnie G. "The Susan Constant and the Mayflower." *WMQ*, 2nd ser., XVII (1937), 229–33 and 469–80.

Cooke, W. H., ed. *Students Admitted to the Inner Temple.* London, 1877.

Copinger, W. A. *County of Suffolk.* 5 vols. London, 1904; index, Manchester, 1907.

—— *The Manors of Suffolk.* 7 vols. Privately printed, 1905–11.

Corser, Rev. T., ed. *Iter Lancastrense.* Chetham Society, 1845.

Cotter, John L., and Hudson, J. Paul. *New Discoveries at Jamestown.* . . . National Park Service, Washington, 1957.

Craven, Wesley Frank. "The Earl of Warwick — A Speculator in Piracy," *Hispanic American Historical Review*, X (1930), 457–79.

—— "An Introduction to the History of Bermuda," *WMQ*, 2nd ser., XVII (1937), 176–215, 317–62, and 437–65, and XVIII (1938), 13–63.

Crouse, Nellis M. *In Quest of the Western Ocean.* New York, 1928.

Cumming, William P. *The Southeast in Early Maps.* Princeton Univ. Press, 1958.

Czvittinger, David. *Specimen Hungariae Literatae, virorum eruditione clarorum.* . . . Frankfurt a/M, 1740.

Davis, John. *Travels of four years and a half in the United States of America;* . . . with an introduction and notes by A. J. Morrison. New York, 1909.

Davis, Richard Beale. "The Devil in Virginia in the Seventeenth Century," *VMHB,* LXV (1957), 131–49.

—— "Volumes from George Sandys's Library now in America," *VMHB,* LXV (1957), 450–57.

Davis, Thomas Frederick. "Juan Ponce de Leon's Voyages to Florida," *Florida Historical Soc. Quarterly,* XIV (1935), 1–70.

Dawley, Powell Mills. *John Whitgift and the English Reformation.* New York, 1954.

Demidov, E. *After Wild Sheep in the Altai and Mongolia.* London, 1900.

Diamond, Sigmund. "Norumbega: New England Xanadu," *American Neptune,* XI (1951), 95–107.

Dinan, W. *Monumenta Historica Celtica.* London, 1911.

Droysen, Gustav. *Prof. G. Droysens Allgemeiner historischer Handatlas,* ed. Dr. Richard Andree. Bielefeld/Leipzig, 1886.

Dudding, Reginald Charles. *History of the Parish and Manors of Alford.* . . . Horncastle, 1930.

Ervin, Spencer. "The Establishment, Government, and Functioning of the Church in Colonial Virginia," *Historical Magazine of the Protestant Episcopal Church,* XXVI (1957), 65–107.

Falkiner, C. Litton. *Illustrations of Irish History and Topography.* . . . London, 1904.

Fiske, John. *The Historical Writings.* 12 vols. Boston and New York, 1902.

Forman, Henry Chandlee. "The Bygone 'Subberbs of James Cittie,'" *WMQ,* 2nd ser., XX (1940), 475–86.

Foss, Edward. *The Judges of England.* 6 vols. London, 1848–57.

Foster, Joseph. *Alumni Oxonienses, 1500–1714.* 4 vols. Oxford, 1891–92.

—— *The Register of Admissions to Gray's Inn.* London, 1889.

Fowke, Gerard. *Archeologic Investigations in James and Potomac Valleys.* BAE Bull. 23 (1894).

Ganong, W. F. "The Identity of Animals and Plants Mentioned in the Early Voyages to Eastern Canada and Newfoundland," *Proceedings and Transactions of the Royal Society of Canada,* 3rd ser., III (1909), Sec. ii, 197–242.

Goff, Lady Cecilie. *A Woman of the Tudor Age.* London, 1930.

Goodman, William. *The Social History of Great Britain during the Reigns of the Stuarts.* 2 vols. New York, 1847.

Granges de Surgères, Le Marquis de. *Iconographie Bretonne, ou Liste de Portraits.* Rennes/Paris, 1888.

Gritzner, M., and Hildebrandt, Ad. M. *Wappenalbum der Gräflichen Familien Deutschlands und Österreich-Ungarns.* 4 vols. Leipzig, 1885–90.

Harmsworth, Geoffrey. "Little Known Louth," *Country Life* (London, June 17, 1949), pp. 1428–31.

Harrison, Francis Burton. "Footnotes on Some XVII Century Virginians," *VMHB*, LI (1943), 27–35.

Harrison, G. B. *The Elizabethan Journals . . . 1591–1603.* 1-vol. ed. London, 1955.

—— *A Second Jacobean Journal . . . 1607–1610.* London, 1958.

Hart, Simon. *The Prehistory of the New Netherland Company.* Amsterdam, 1959.

Haslewood, Rev. Francis. "The Ancient Families of Suffolk," *Proceedings of the Suffolk Institute of Archaeology and Natural History,* VIII (1894), 121–214.

Hatch, Charles E., Jr. "Archer's Hope and the Glebe," *VMHB,* LXV (1957), 467–84.

—— "The Great Road," *VMHB,* LVII (1949), 14–21.

—— *Jamestown, Virginia: The Townsite and its Story.* National Park Service, Hist. Handbook Ser., no. 2, Washington, rev. 1957.

—— "Mulberry Trees and Silkworms," *VMHB,* LXV (1957), 3–61.

Hatch, Charles E., Jr., and Gregory, Thurlow Gates. "The First American Blast Furnace, 1619–1622," *VMHB,* LXX (1962), 259–96.

Haydn, Joseph. *Book of Dignities.* London, 1851.

Hayes-McCoy, Gerard A. *Scots Mercenary Forces in Ireland (1565–1603).* Dublin/London, 1937.

Herrgott, R. P. Marquardus. *Genealogia Diplomatica Augustae Gentis Habsburgicae.* Vienna, 1737.

Hiden, Martha Woodroof. *Adventures of Purse and Person, Virginia 1607–1625.* Privately printed, 1956.

Higham, Florence. *Lancelot Andrewes.* London, 1952.

Hill, Rev. George. *An Historical Account of the Plantation in Ulster at the Commencement of the 17th Century 1608–1620.* Belfast, 1877.

Hotten, John Camden. *The Original List of Persons of Quality . . . and others who went from Great Britain to the American Plantations, 1600–1700.* 2 vols. New York, 1880.

Hudson, J. Paul. *A Pictorial Story of Jamestown, Virginia. . . .* Richmond, 1957.

Hull, Felix. "The Tufton Manuscripts and the Virginia Connection," *VMHB,* LXV (1957), 313–27.

Iorga, Nicolae. "Socotelile Braşovului şi scrisorĭ către Sfat în secolul al xvii-lea," *Analele Academiei Romane, Memoriile Secţiuniĭ Istorice,* Ser. 2, XXI (1898–99), 109–270.

—— "Secotelile Sibiuluĭ," *ibid.,* 271–302.

Johnson, Francis R. *Astronomical Thought in Renaissance England . . . 1500–1645.* Baltimore, 1937.

Johnson, Robert C. "The 'Running Lotteries' of the Virginia Company," *VMHB,* LXVIII (1960), 156–65.

508        BIBLIOGRAPHY

Julien, Ch.-A. *Les voyages de découverte et les premiers établissements* (*XVe–XVIe siècles*). Paris, 1948.

Kretschmer, Konrad. *Die italienischen Portolane des Mittelalters.* Veröffentlichungen des Instituts für Meereskunde und des Geographischen Instituts an der Universität Berlin, Vol. 13 (February 1909).

Kurat, Akdes Nimet. *Türk-Ingiliz Münasebetlerinin Başlangici ve Gelişmesi* (*1553–1610*). Ankara, 1953.

Latimer, John. *The History of the Society of Merchant Venturers of the City of Bristol.* Bristol, 1903.

Lefroy, Sir John Henry. *Memorials of the Discovery and Early Settlement of the Bermudas or Somers Islands, 1515–1685.* 2 vols. London, 1877–85.

Lelewel, Joachim. *Géographie du moyen âge.* 4 vols. Brussels, 1852.

Lincoln's Inn. *The Black Books — The Records of the Honourable Society of Lincoln's Inn.* Published by the Society. 4 vols., 1897–1902.

Liske, Javier [Ksawery], ed. *Viajes de Extranjeros por España y Portugal en los siglos xv, xvi, y xvii.* Madrid, 1880.

Lysons, Daniel. *The Environs of London.* 4 vols. London, 1792–96.

Maclear, James Fulton. "Puritan Relations with Buckingham," *Huntington Library Quarterly,* XXI (1958), 111–32.

*Magyarország Helységeinek 1773-ban Kézült Hivatalos Összeirása* [Geographical Dictionary]. Budapest, 1920.

Manhart, George Born. *The English Search for the Northwest Passage;* with Albert Lindsay Rowland's *Studies in English Commerce and Exploration in the Reign of Elizabeth.* Univ. of Pennsylvania Press, 1924.

Marañón, Gregorio. *Antonio Pérez (El hombre, el drama, la época).* 2 vols. Madrid, 1958.

McGrath, Patrick, and Rowe, Joy. "The Recusancy of Sir Thomas Cornwallis," *Proceedings of the Suffolk Institute of Archaeology,* XXVIII (1960), 226–71.

McIntyre, Ruth A. *Debts Hopeful and Desperate.* Plymouth, Mass., 1963.

McJimsey, George Davis. *Topographic Terms in Virginia.* New York, 1940.

Meyer, Arnold Oskar. "Clemens VIII und Jakob I. von England," *Quellen und Forschungen aus ital. Archiven u. Bibliotheken,* herausg. v. K. Preuss. Hist. Institut in Rom, VII (1904), 268–306.

Miller, Perry. "The Religious Impulse in the Founding of Virginia," *WMQ,* Ser. 3, V (1948), 492–522, and VI (1949), 24–41.

Molinari, Diego Luis. *El Nacimiento del Nuevo Mundo.* Buenos Aires, 1945.

Mood, Fulmer. "The English Geographers and the Anglo-American Frontier in the Seventeenth Century," *Univ. of Calif. Publns. in Geography,* VI (1944), 363–96.

Morant, Philip. *The History and Antiquities of the County of Essex.* Chelmsford, 1816.

Motley, John Lothrop. *The Rise of the Dutch Republic.* 3 vols. London, 1856.

Müller, F. *Mappa novissima Regnorum Hungariae, Croatiae, Sclavoniae.* Vienna, 1792.

Munk, William. *The Roll of the Royal College of Physicians of London,* Vol. i, 1518–1700. London, 1878.

Muskett, Joseph James. *Suffolk Manorial Families.* Exeter, 1908.

Mžik, Hans von, ed. *Beiträge zur historischen Geographie, Kulturgeographie, Ethnogeographie und Kartographie vornehmlich des Orients.* Leipzig/Vienna, 1929.

Nagy, Ludovicus. *Notitiae Politico-Statisticae inclyti regni Hungarium, partiumque eidem adnexarum,* Tomus I. Buda, 1828.

Namitok, Aytek. *Origines des Circassiens,* Ire Partie. Paris, 1939.

Neill, Edward Duffield. *Early Settlement of Virginia and Virginiola as Noticed by Poets and Players.* Minneapolis, 1878.

—— *The English Colonization of America.* London, 1871.

—— *History of the Virginia Company of London.* Albany, 1869.

Nichols, John. *The Progresses, Processions and Magnificent Festivities of King James I.* . . . 4 vols. London, 1828.

Notestein, Wallace. *The English People on the Eve of Colonization, 1603–1630.* New York, 1954.

Oakeshott, Walter. *The Queen and the Poet.* London, 1960.

O'Brien, Terence H. "The London Livery Companies and the Virginia Company," *VMHB,* LXVIII (1960), 137–55.

Orend, Misch. *Zur Heimatfrage der Siebenbürgen Sachsen.* Marburg, 1927.

Osgood, Herbert L. *The American Colonies in the Seventeenth Century.* New York, 1930.

Palfrey, John Gorham. *History of New England.* 5 vols. Boston, 1858–90.

Pares, Richard. *Merchants and Planters.* Economic History Review Supplement 4. Cambridge Univ. Press, 1960.

Parkman. *Francis Parkman's Works.* 16 vols. Boston, 1902.

Parks, George B., compiler. *The Contents and Sources of Ramusio's 'Navigationi.'* New York, 1955.

Peck, Francis. *Desiderata Curiosa.* 2 vols. London, 1732, 1735.

Penrose, Boies. *Travel and Discovery in the Renaissance.* Cambridge, Mass., 1952.

Perry, William Stevens. "The Foundations of Church and State in Virginia," *Historical Magazine of the Protestant Episcopal Church,* XXVI (1957), 34–64.

Platonov, S[ergyei F.]: *Boris Godunov, Tsar de Russie (1598–1605).* Paris, 1929.

—— *Smutnoye Vremya* [Time of Troubles]. Prague, 1924.

Playfair, Sir Robert Lambert. *The Scourge of Christendom.* London, 1884.

Plomer, Henry R. *Short History of English Printing, 1476–1898.* London, 1900.

Porter, Harry Culverwell. "Alexander Whitaker: Cambridge Apostle to Virginia," *WMQ,* 3rd ser., XIV (1957), 317–43.

Potocki, Comte Jean. *Fragments Historiques et Géographiques sur la Scythie, la Sarmatie et les Slaves.* Brunswick [Lower Saxony], 1796.

Prideaux, Sir Walter Sherburne. *Memorials of the Goldsmiths' Company.* London, 1896–97.

Prinzivalli, Virginio. *Gli anni santi (1300–1925).* Rome [1924?].

Przezdziecki, Count Renaud. *Diplomatic Ventures and Adventures.* London, 1953.

Quinn, David Beers. "Christopher Newport in 1590," *North Carolina Historical Review,* XXIX (1952), 305–16.

――― "Notes by a Pious Colonial Investor 1608–1610," *WMQ,* 3rd ser., XVI (1959), 551–55.

Raach, John H. *A Directory of English Country Physicians, 1603–1643.* London, 1962.

Raleigh, Sir Walter (1861–1922). "The English Voyages of the Sixteenth Century," an essay published in Hakluyt's *Voyages,* XII, 1–120. (Do not confuse with the Elizabethan Sir Walter Ralegh.)

Ranke, Leopold von. *Die römische Päpste, ihre Kirche und ihr Staat, im 16ten und 17ten Jahrhundert.* 3 vols. Berlin, 1845.

Read, Evelyn. *Catherine, Duchess of Suffolk. A Portrait.* London, 1962.

Reichard, Christianus Theophilus. *Orbis Terrarum Antiquus.* Nuremberg, 1824.

Richardson, Ethel M. *The Lion and the Rose (The Great Howard Story).* . . . 2 vols. London, n.d.

Riesenfeld, Stefan A. "Law-Making and Legislative Precedent in American Legal History," *Minnesota Law Review,* XXXIII (1949), 103–44.

Rose-Troup, Frances. *The Massachusetts Bay Company and its Predecessors.* New York, 1930.

St. Maur, H. *Annals of the Seymours.* London, 1902.

Sams, Conway Whittle. *The Conquest of Virginia: The First Attempt.* Norfolk, 1924.

――― *The Conquest of Virginia: The Forest Primeval.* New York, 1916. (Two other volumes, *The Second Attempt* and *The Third Attempt,* appeared subsequently, but are vitiated by serious bias.)

Sanders, Charles Richard. "William Strachey, the Virginia Colony and Shakespeare," *VMHB,* LVII (1949), 115–32.

Schneider, Reinhold. *Philippe II, ou Pouvoir et Religion,* trans. from the German. Paris, 1943.

Schullerus, Adolf. *Siebenbürgisch-sächsische Volkskunde im Umriss.* Leipzig, 1926.

Shirley, John W. "George Percy at Jamestown," *VMHB,* LVII (1949), 227–43.

Simpson, Alan. *The Wealth of the Gentry.* Cambridge (Cambs.) and Chicago, 1961.

Skelton, R. A. "Ralegh as a Geographer," *VMHB,* LXXI (1963), 131–49.

Smirnov, N. A. "Rossiya i Turtsiya v xvi–xvii vv.," *Uchonye Zapiski,* Universitet, Moscow, XCIV (1946), parts i and ii.

Smith, G. C. Moore. *The Family of Withypoll*, rev. by P. H. Reaney. Walthamstow Antiquarian Soc., Official Pub. no. 34 (1936).

Sommi-Picenardi, Guido. "Don Giovanni de' Medici, Governatore dell'-esercito Veneto nel Friuli," *Nuovo archivio Veneto*, Vol. 13, n.s., Parts 1 and 2, 1907.

Squires, W. H. T. *The Days of Yesteryear*. Portsmouth, Va., 1928.

Stanard, W. G. "Abstracts of Virginia Land Patents," *VMHB*, I (1893–94), 84, and II (1894–95), 182–83.

Stevenson, Edward Luther, trans. and ed. *Geography of Claudius Ptolemy*. New York Public Library, 1932.

Stokes, Isaac Newton Phelps. *Iconography of Manhattan Island*. 6 vols. New York, 1915–28.

Stotz, J. L. *Neueste Statistisch-topographisches Darstellung des Gross-Fürstentums Siebenbürgen*. . . . Vienna, 1812.

Ströhl, Hugo Gerard. *Österreichisch-ungarische Wappenrolle*. Vienna, 1895.

Sturgess, H. A. C. *Register of Admissions to the Honourable Society of the Middle Temple*. 3 vols. London, 1949.

Sugden, Edward H. *A Topographical Dictionary to the Works of Shakespeare and his Fellow Dramatists*. Manchester Univ. Press, 1925.

Taylor, Raymond L. *Plants of Colonial Days*. Williamsburg, Va., 1952.

Traylor, Robert Lee. *Some Notes on the First Recorded Visit of White Men to the Site of the Present City of Richmond, Virginia*. Richmond, 1899.

Trevor-Roper, H. R. *The Gentry 1540–1640*. Economic History Review Supplement 1, Cambridge [1953?].

Tuttle, Charles Wesley. *Captain John Mason, The Founder of New Hampshire*. Prince Society, Boston, 1887.

Tyack, N. C. P. *Migration from East Anglia to New England before 1660*. Doctoral dissertation, in Essex County Record Office. Chelmsford, 1951.

Varga, Nicholas. "The English Parliament's Authority over Virginia before the Restoration," *VMHB*, LXII (1954), 281–88.

Vaughan, Dorothy Margaret. *Europe and the Turk*. Liverpool, 1954.

Vávra, Jaroslav. *5000 Years of Glass-Making: The History of Glass*. Prague, 1954.

Venn, J. A. *Alumni Cantabrigenses*. 10 vols. Cambridge, 1922–54.

Vere-Hodge, H. S. *Sir Andrew Judde*. Privately printed [1953?].

Veress, Andrei [Endre]. "Nunţii Apostolici in Ardeal," *Analele Academiei Romane, Memoriile Secţiunii Istorice*, Ser. 3, VIII (1927–28), 305–60.

Wadmore, James Foster. *Some Account of The Worshipful Company of Skinners of London*. London, 1902.

Wadsworth, Frank W. *The Poacher from Stratford*. Los Angeles, 1958.

Ward, John. *The Lives of the Professors of Gresham College*. . . . London, 1740.

Watson, Robert. *The History of the Reign of Philip the Third, King of Spain.* 2 vols. London, 1808.

Whitley, W. L. "The Colonising of America by the Owners of Leez Priory," *The Essex Review,* XLV (1936), 160–65.

Willan, T. S. *The Early History of the Russia Company, 1553–1603.* Manchester Univ. Press, 1956.

Willey, Basil. *The Seventeenth Century Background.* Repr. New York, 1953.

Williamson, Dr. G. C. *George, Third Earl of Cumberland (1558–1605), His Life and His Voyages.* Cambridge Univ. Press, 1920.

Willson, David Harris. *The Privy Councillors in the House of Commons.* Univ. of Minnesota Press, *c.* 1940.

Wilson, Elkin Calhoun. *Prince Henry and English Literature,* Cornell Univ. Press, 1946.

Winsor, Justin. *Narrative and Critical History of America.* 8 vols. Boston and New York, *c.* 1884–89.

Wood, Alfred C. *History of the Levant Company.* London, 1935.

Wood, Anthony à. *Athenae Oxonienses . . . to which are added the fasti. . . .* 2 vols. London, 1721.

Wright, Louis B. *The Atlantic Frontier.* New York, 1947.

Wroth, Lawrence C. *Tobacco or Codfish.* New York, 1954.

Yonge, Charlotte M. *History of Christian Names.* London, 1863.

Young, Alexander. *Chronicles of the First Planters of the Colony of Massachusetts Bay.* Boston, 1846.

—— *Chronicles of the Pilgrim Fathers of the Colony of Plymouth.* Boston, 1844.

Young, Sydney. *The Annals of the Barber-Surgeons of London. . . .* London, 1890.

THE JAMESTOWN 350TH ANNIVERSARY HISTORICAL BOOKLETS

*Editor, Dr. Earl G. Swem, Librarian Emeritus, College of William and Mary.* Williamsburg, 1957.

The following monographs in this series are of particular pertinence to the life of Captain John Smith:

1. *A Selected Bibliography of Virginia, 1607–1699,* by E. G. Swem and John M. Jennings, with James A. Servies
2. *A Virginia Chronology 1585–1783,* by William W. Abbot
3. *John Smith's Map Of Virginia . . . ,* by Ben C. McCary
4. *The Three Charters Of The Virginia Company Of London With Seven Related Documents, 1606–1621,* introd. by Samuel M. Bemiss
5. *The Virginia Company of London, 1606–1624,* by Wesley Frank Craven
6. *The First Seventeen Years: Virginia, 1607–1624,* by Charles E. Hatch, Jr.

7. *Virginia under Charles I and Cromwell, 1625–1660,* by Wilcomb E. Washburn
10. *Religious Life of Virginia in the Seventeenth Century . . . ,* by George MacLaren Brydon
12. *Mother Earth: Land Grants in Virginia, 1607–1699,* by W. Stitt Robinson, Jr.
13. *The Bounty of the Chesapeake: Fishing in Colonial Virginia,* by James Wharton
18. *Indians in Seventeenth-Century Virginia,* by Ben C. McCary
21. *Medicine in Virginia, 1607–1699,* by Thomas P. Hughes
23. *A Pictorial Booklet on Early Jamestown Commodities and Industries,* by J. Paul Hudson.

## WORKS PERTINENT TO THE INDIANS

### Primitive Society Generally

NOTE: The following list does not include such classics as Morgan's *Ancient Society,* Tylor's *Primitive Culture,* or Frazer's *The Golden Bough.* Neither does it attempt to compete with such bibliographies as those in Radin's *Primitive Religion* or Birket-Smith's *Primitive Man and his Ways* (see below). The choice of works listed has been purely personal, and for reasons of space I have included only books which I have found particularly helpful in guiding me toward some understanding of the Indians Smith encountered.

Allier, Raoul. *Le non-civilisé et nous.* Paris, 1927.
Birket-Smith, Kaj. *Histoire de la civilisation.* Paris, 1955.
―――― *Primitive Man and His Ways.* London, 1960.
Eliade, Mircea. *Le chamanisme.* Paris, 1951.
―――― *Mythes, rêves et mystères.* Paris, 1957.
Findeisen, Hans. *Schamanentum.* Stuttgart, 1957.
Frobenius, Leo. *The Childhood of Man.* Repr. New York, 1960.
Garibay K., Angel María. *Vida Económica de Tenochtitlan.* Mexico, D.F., 1961.
Katz, Friedrich. "Vergleichsmomente zwischen der sozialen und wirtschaftlichen Organisation der Inka und der Azteken," *Estudios de Cultura Náhuatl,* II (1960), 59–76.
León Portilla, Miguel. *La filosofía náhuatl.* Mexico, D.F., 1956.
―――― "La Institución Cultural del Comercio Prehispánico," *Estudios de Cultura Náhuatl,* III (1962), 23–54.
León Portilla, Miguel, and Garibay K., Angel María, eds. *Visión de los Vencidos.* Mexico, D.F., 1961.
Leroy, Olivier. *La raison primitive.* Paris, 1927.
Levin, M. G., and Potapov, L. P. *Istoriko-etnograficheskiǐ atlas Sibiri.* Moscow/Leningrad, 1961. (See article "Shamans' Drums," pp. 435–90.)

Lévi-Strauss, Claude. *La pensée sauvage.* Paris, 1962.

Lévy-Bruhl, Lucien. *La mentalité primitive.* 15th ed., Paris, 1960.

Lopatin, Ivan A. "The Extinct and Near Extinct Tribes of Northeastern Asia as Compared with the American Indian," *American Antiquity,* V (1940), 202–8.

Maringer, Johannes. *Vorgeschichtliche Religion.* Einsiedeln (Switzerland), 1956.

Müller, Werner. *Die Religionen der Waldlandindianer Nordamerikas.* Berlin, 1956.

Radin, Paul. *Primitive Religion.* New York, 1957.

## The Indians

NOTE: This list does not pretend to be complete, long though it seems to be. These are works which I have consulted and found to be of use — directly or indirectly. Although three extensive bibliographies are mentioned, I have made no attempt to cover the field, or even to survey it thoroughly. Again, the choice of books listed has been purely personal, as explained above.

Battle, H. B. "The Domestic Use of Oil among the Southern Aborigines," *AA,* XXIV (1922), 171–82.

Barratt, Joseph. *The Indian of New England.* . . . Middletown, Conn., 1851.

Benedict, Ruth Fulton. *The Concept of the Guardian Spirit in North America.* Memoirs of the American Anthropological Assn., no. 29, 1923.

Bennett, M. K. "The Food Economy of the New England Indians," *Journal of Political Economy,* LXIII (1955), 369–97.

Birket-Smith, Kaj. "A Geographic Study of the Early History of the Algonquian Indians," *Internationales Archiv für Ethnographie,* XXIV (1916–18?), 174–222.

——— *The Origin of Maize Cultivation.* Copenhagen, 1943.

Bloomfield, Leonard. "The Word Stems of Central Algonquian," *Festschrift Meinhof.* 2 vols. Hamburg, 1927. (See also article in Hoijer's *Linguistic Structures,* cited below.)

Boas, Franz. *Handbook of American Indian Languages, Part I.* BAE Bull. 40, Washington, 1911.

Brinton, Daniel Garrison. "The Lenape and Their Legends," *Library of Aboriginal American Literature.* 8 vols. Philadelphia, 1882–90.

——— "A Vocabulary of the Nanticoke Dialect," *Proceedings of the American Philosophical Society,* XXXI (1893), 327–33.

Brinton, Daniel G., and Anthony, Albert Seqaqkind. *A Lenâpé-English Dictionary.* Philadelphia, 1888.

Bushnell, David I., Jr. "Evidence of Indian Occupancy in Albemarle County, Virginia," *Smithsonian Miscellaneous Collections,* Vol. 89, no. 7, 1933.

———— "The Five Monacan Towns in Virginia, 1607," *ibid.,* Vol. 82, no. 12, 1930.

———— "Indian Sites below the Falls of the Rappahannock," *ibid.,* Vol. 96, no. 4, 1937.

———— "The Manahoac Tribes in Virginia, 1608," *ibid.,* Vol. 94, no. 8, 1935.

———— "Virginia — From Early Records," *AA,* IX (1907), 31–44. (NOTE: For a full list of Bushnell's numerous monographs, see John R. Swanton, "David I. Bushnell, Jr.," *AA,* XLIV (1942), 104–10.)

Cadzow, Donald A. "Safe Harbor Report, No. 2," *Archaeological Studies of the Susquehannock Indians of Pennsylvania,* Vol. 3. Harrisburg (Pa.), 1936.

Campanius Holm, John. *Lutheri Catechismus öfwersatt på American-Virginiske språket, Vocabularium Barbaro-Virgineorum,* pp. 135–53. Stockholm, 1696.

Chamberlain, Alexander F. "Significations of Certain Algonkian Animal Names," *AA,* III (1901), 669–83.

*Comparative Vocabulary of Algonquin Dialects,* from Heckewelder's Manuscripts. Cambridge, Mass., 1887.

Cotterill, R. S. *The Southern Indians.* . . . Univ. of Oklahoma Press, 1954.

Culin, Stewart. "Games of the North American Indians," *24th Ann. Report of the BAE, 1902–1903,* especially pp. 697–99. Washington, 1907.

Day, Gordon M. "English-Indian Contacts in New England," *Ethnohistory,* IX (1962), 24–40.

Dockstader, Frederick J. *The American Indian in Graduate Studies: A Bibliography.* . . . Heye Foundation, New York, 1957.

Dunlap, A. R., and Weslager, C. A. *Indian Place-Names in Delaware.* Archaeol. Soc. of Del., Wilmington, 1950.

Eckstorm, Fannie Hardy. *Indian Place-Names of the Penobscot Valley and the Maine Coast.* Univ. Press, Orono (Maine), 1941, repr. 1960.

Evans, Clifford. *A Ceramic Study of Virginia Archeology.* BAE Bull. 160. Washington, 1955.

Faries, Ven. R., ed. *A Dictionary of the Cree Language.* Toronto, 1938.

Fenton, W. N. "Present Status of Anthropology in Northeastern North America," *AA,* L (1948), 494–515.

———— "Problems Arising from the Historic Northeastern Position of the Iroquois," *Smithsonian Misc. Collns.,* no. 100 (1940), especially pp. 117–252.

Fenton, William N., and Gulick, John, eds. *Symposium on Cherokee and Iroquois Culture.* BAE Bull. 180. Washington, 1961.

Flannery, Regina. *An Analysis of Coastal Algonquian Culture.* Catholic Univ. of America Press, Washington, 1939.

Gerard, William R. "Some Virginia Indian Words," *AA,* VII (1905), 222–49.

—— "The Tapehanek Dialect of Virginia," *AA*, VI (1904), 313–30.

—— "Virginia's Indian Contribution to English," *AA*, IX (1907), 87–112.

Gilliam, Charles Edgar. "Ethno-Historical Demurrers to General English Indictments of the Great Powhatan Confederacy of Virginia Algonkians," *Tyler's Quarterly*, XXVIII (1946–47), 139–62.

—— "Queen Opussoquionuske," *ibid.*, XXIII (1941–42), 148–54.

Hagan, William T. *American Indians*. Univ. of Chicago Press, 1961.

Hallowell, A. Irving. "The Impact of the American Indian on American Culture," *AA*, LIX (1957), 201–17.

Harrington, John P. "The Original Strachey Vocabulary of the Virginia Indian Language," in BAE Bull. 157, pp. 189–202. Washington, 1955.

Harrington, M. R. "A Preliminary Sketch of Lenâpé Culture," *AA*, XV (1913), 208–35.

—— *Religion and Ceremonies of the Lenape*. Indian Notes and Monographs, Misc. 19. Heye Foundation, New York, 1921.

Heckewelder, John. *Names Given by the Lenni Lenape or Delaware Indians to Rivers, Streams, and Places. . . .* Pennsylvania German Folklore Society, Vol. 5. Allentown (Pa.), 1940.

Hickerson, Harold. "Notes on the Post-Contact Origin of the Midewiwin," *Ethnohistory*, IX (1962), 404–23.

Hodge, Frederick Webb, ed. *Handbook of American Indians North of Mexico*. BAE Bull. 30, Parts 1 and 2. Washington, 1907 and 1910.

Hoijer, Harry, and others. *Linguistic Structures of Native America*. Viking Fund Pubs. in Anthropology, no. 6. New York, 1946.

Holmes, William Henry. *Aboriginal Pottery of the Eastern United States*. BAE Report 20. Washington, 1903.

Howse, Joseph. *A Grammar of the Cree Language*. London, 1865.

Hrdlička, Aleš. *The Anthropology of Florida*. Florida State Hist. Soc., DeLand (Fla.), 1922.

Huden, John C. *Indian Place Names of New England*. Heye Foundation, New York, 1962.

Hultkrantz, Ake. *Conceptions of the Soul among the North American Indians*. Stockholm, 1953.

Jenks, Albert Ernest. "The Wild Rice Gatherers of the Upper Lakes," in BAE Report 19, Part 2, pp. 1013–1137. Washington, 1900.

Joffe, Natalie F. "The Fox of Iowa," in Linton, *Acculturation* (see below), pp. 259–332.

Jones, William. "Some Principles of Algonquian Word Formation," *AA*, VI (1904), 369–412.

Kenny, Hamill. *The Origin and Meaning of the Indian Place Names of Maryland*. Baltimore, 1961.

—— *West Virginia Place Names, their Origin and Meaning*. Piedmont, W. Va., 1945.

Kenton, Edna, ed. *Black Gown and Redskins*. New ed., London, 1956.

Lindeström, Peter. *Geographia Americae with an Account of the Delaware Indians,* trans. and ed. by Amandus Johnson. Philadelphia, 1925.

Linton, Ralph, ed. *Acculturation in seven American Indian tribes.* New York [*c.* 1940].

Lokotsch, Karl. *Etymologisches Wörterbuch der amerikanischen (indianischen) Wörter im Deutschen.* Heidelberg, 1926.

MacLeod, William Christie. *The Origin of the State, reconsidered in the light of the date of aboriginal North America.* Univ. of Pennsylvania Press, Philadelphia, 1924.

—— "On the Significance of Matrilineal Chiefship," *AA,* XXV (1923), 495–524.

Maddox, John Lee. *The Medicine Man: A Sociological Study of the Character and Evolution of Shamanism.* New York, 1923.

Manakee, Harold R. *Indians of Early Maryland.* Maryland Hist. Soc., Baltimore, 1959.

Maxwell, Hu. "The Use and Abuse of Forests by Virginia Indians," *WMQ,* 1st ser., XIX (1910), 73–103.

Michelson, Truman. "The Linguistic Classification of Powhatan," *AA,* XXXV (1933), 549.

—— "Notes on Fox Mortuary Customs and Beliefs," *BAE, 40th Annual Report,* pp. 351–496. Washington, 1925.

—— "Preliminary Report on the Linguistic Classification of the Algonquian Tribes," *BAE, 28th Annual Report,* pp. 221–90. Washington, 1912.

Miller, Carl F. "Revaluation of the Eastern Siouan Problem with Particular Emphasis on the Virginia Branches — the Occaneechi, the Saponi, and the Tutelo," in BAE Bull. 164, pp. 115–211. Washington, 1957.

Mook, Maurice A. "The Aboriginal Population of Tidewater Virginia," *AA,* XLVI (1944), 193–208.

—— *Seventeenth-Century Southeastern Algonkian Ethno-History,* a doctoral dissertation presented at the Univ. of Pennsylvania (1943); the bulk published in the *William and Mary Quarterly,* 2nd ser., XXIII (1943), 27–40, 101–29, and 371–408.

Mooney, James. "The Powhatan Confederacy Past and Present," *AA,* IX (1907), 129–52.

Murray, Louise Welles, ed. *Selected MSS of General John S. Clark Relating to the Aboriginal History of the Susquehanna.* Athens, 1931.

Neill, Edward Duffield. *Effort and Failure to Civilize the Aborigines.* Washington, 1868.

Palmer, Rose A. *The North American Indians.* Smithsonian Scientific Ser., Vol. 4. New York, 1929.

Pargellis, Stanley. "An Account of the Indians in Virginia," an anonymous manuscript of 1689 in the Ayer Collection, Newberry Library, Chicago; *WMQ,* 3rd ser., XVI (1959), 228–43.

Pearce, Roy Harvey. *The Savages of America: A Study of the Indian.* . . . Baltimore, 1953.

Petrullo, Vincenzo. *The Diabolic Root: A Study of Peyotism.* . . . Philadelphia, 1934.

Rand, Silas Tertius. *Dictionary of the Language of the Micmac Indians.* Halifax (N.S.), 1888.

Rasles, Sebastian. *A Dictionary of the Abnaki Language in North America.* Cambridge, Mass., 1833.

Read, William Alexander. *Louisiana Place-Names of Indian Origin.* Baton Rouge, 1927. (With a few addenda in "Indian Place-Names in Louisiana," *Louisiana Hist. Quarterly,* for July, 1928.)

Rights, Douglas L. *The American Indian in North Carolina,* 2nd ed. The Wachovia Hist. Soc., Winston-Salem (N. Car.), 1957.

Speck, Frank Gouldsmith. "Algonkian Influence upon Iroquois Social Organization," *AA,* XXV (1923), 219–27.

—— *Chapters on the Ethnology of the Powhatan Tribes of Virginia.* Indian Notes and Monographs, Vol. 1, no. 5. Heye Foundation, New York, 1928.

—— "The Ethnic Position of the Southeast Algonkian," *AA,* XXVI (1924), 184–200.

—— "Penobscot Shamanism," *Memoirs of the Amer. Anthropological Assn.,* Vol. 6, No. 4 (1919).

—— *The Rappahannock Indians of Virginia.* Indian Notes and Monographs, Vol. 5, no. 3. Heye Foundation, New York, 1925.

—— "Siouan Tribes from the Carolinas as known from Catawba, Tutelo and Documentary Sources," *AA,* XXXVII (1935), 201–25.

—— "Some Outlines of Aboriginal Culture in the Southeastern States," *AA,* IX (1907), 287–95.

(NOTE: For a full list of Dr. Speck's numerous monographs and larger works, see the complete bibliography compiled by John Witthoft for A. Irving Hallowell's "Frank Gouldsmith Speck, 1881–1950," *AA,* LIII [1951], 67–87.)

Stern, Theodore. "Chickahominy: The Changing Culture of a Virginia Indian Community," *Proceedings of the American Philosophical Society,* XCVI (1952), 157–225. (Contains an extensive bibliography.)

Stiles, Martha Bennett. "Hostage to the Indians," *Virginia Cavalcade,* XII no. 1 (1962), 5–11.

Sturtevant, William C. "The Significance of Ethnological Similarities between Southeastern North America and the Antilles," Yale Univ. Pubs. in Anthropology, no. 64, 1960.

—— "Spanish-Indian Relations in Southeastern North America," *Ethnohistory,* IX (1962), 41–94. (Extensive bibliography.)

Swanton, John R. "Aboriginal Culture of the Southeast," *BAE, 42nd Annual Report,* pp. 673–726. Washington, 1928.

—— *The Indians of the Southeastern United States.* BAE Bull. 137. Washington, 1946.

—— The Indian Tribes of North America. BAE Bull. 145. Washington, 1952.

Tooker, William Wallace. "Algonkian Names of Some Mountains and Hills," Journal of American Folklore, XVII (1904), 171–79.

—— "Derivation of the Name Powhatan," AA, VI (1904), 464–68.

—— "The Powhatan Name for Virginia," AA, VIII (1906), 23–27.

—— "Some More about Virginia Names," AA, VII (1905), 524–28.

—— "Some Powhatan Names," AA, VI (1904), 670–94.

Toomey, Noxon. Proper Names from the Muskhogean Languages. Hervas Laboratories of American Linguistics, Bull. 3. St. Louis, 1917.

Trelease, Allen W. "Indian-White Contacts in Eastern North America: The Dutch in New Netherland," Ethnohistory, IX (1962), 137–46.

Trigger, Bruce Graham. "Trade and Tribal Warfare on the St. Lawrence in the Sixteenth Century," Ethnohistory, IX (1962), 240–56.

Trumbull, James Hammond. Natick Dictionary. BAE Bull. 25. Washington, 1903.

Underhill, Ruth Murray. Red Man's America: A History of Indians in the United States. Chicago, 1953.

Walam Olum, or Red Score; The Migration Legend of the Lenni Lenape or Delaware Indians; ed. by the Indiana Historical Soc. Indianapolis, 1954.

Weatherwax, Paul. Indian Corn in Old America. New York, 1954.

Weitenkampf, Frank. Early Pictures of North American Indians. New York, 1950.

Wentworth, Edward. "Dried Meat — Early Man's Travel Ration," Smithsonian Report for 1956, pp. 557–71. Washington, 1957.

Weslager, C. A. The Nanticoke Indians. Harrisburg, Pa., 1948.

Whitford, A. C. "Textile Fibers Used in Eastern Aboriginal North America," Anthropological Papers of the American Museum of Natural History, XXXVIII, Part 1 (1941), 5–22.

Williams, Roger. A Key into the Language of America. . . . London, 1643 (repr. in Collections of the Rhode Island Hist. Soc., Vol. 1 [1827]).

Willoughby, C. C. "Virginia Indians in the 17th Century," AA, IX (1907), 57–86.

Wissler, Clark. "General Discussion of Shamanistic and Dancing Societies," Anthropological Papers of the American Museum of Natural History, XI, Part 12 (1916), 853–76.

Witthoft, John, and Kinsey, W. Fred, III. Susquehannock Miscellany. Pennsylvania Hist. and Museum Comm., Harrisburg, Pa., 1959.

Indian-White Relations

Day, Gordon M. "English-Indian Contacts in New England," Ethnohistory, IX (1962), 24–40.

Fenton, William N., and others: American Indian and White Relations to

*1830.* Publ. for the Institute of Early American History and Culture, 1957.

Lurie, Nancy Oestreich. "Indian Cultural Adjustment to European Civilization," in *Seventeenth Century America,* publ. for the Institute of Early American History and Culture. Univ. of N. Car. Press, 1959.

Sturtevant, William C. "Spanish-Indian Relations in Southeastern North America," *Ethnohistory,* IX (1962), 41–94.

Trelease, Allen W. "Indian-White Contacts in Eastern North America: The Dutch in New Netherland," *Ethnohistory,* IX (1962), 137–46.

Trigger, Bruce Graham. "Trade and Tribal Warfare on the St. Lawrence in the Sixteenth Century," *Ethnohistory,* IX (1962), 240–56.

Washburn, Wilcomb E. "A Moral History of Indian-White Relations: Needs and Opportunities for Study," *Ethnohistory,* IV (1957), 47–61.

——— "The Moral and Legal Justifications for Dispossessing the Indians," in *Seventeenth Century America* (see above), pp. 15–32.

## BIBLIOGRAPHY OF JOHN SMITH'S WORKS

*(Based on the Sabin [Eames] Dictionary; first editions only)*

1608. *A True Relation of such occurrences and accidents of noate as hath hapned in Virginia since the first planting of that Collony. . . .* Printed for John Tappe, by W[illiam] W[elby].

1612. *A Map of Virginia. With a Description of the Countrey, the Commodities, People, Government and Religion.* Printed at Oxford by Joseph Barnes.

1616. *A Description of New England: or the Observations, and discoveries, of Captain John Smith. . . .* Printed by Humfrey Lownes, for Robert Clerke.

1620. *New Englands Trials.* Printed by William Jones.

1622. *New Englands Trials.* Printed by William Jones. (This edition, 12 pp. longer than that of 1620, carries the account into 1622.)

1623. [A four-page prospectus.] *The generall History of Virginia, the Somer Isles, and New England . . .* [probably printed by John Dawson].

1624. *The Generall Historie of Virginia, New-England, and the Summer Isles. . . .* Printed by I[ohn] D[awson] and I[ohn] H[aviland] for Michael Sparkes.

1626. *An Accidence [for the Sea], or The Pathway to Experience.* Printed for Jonas Man and Benjamin Fisher. (The words "for the Sea" were added in 1636.)

1627. *A Sea Grammar, With The Plaine Exposition of Smiths Accidence for young Sea-men, enlarged.* Printed by John Haviland. (This edition of the *Accidence* is rearranged as well as enlarged.)

1630. *The True Travels, Adventures, and Observations of Captaine John*

*Smith, In Europe, Asia, Affrica, and America, from Anno Domini 1593 to 1629.* Printed by J[ohn] H[aviland] for Thomas Slater.

1631. *Advertisements For the unexperienced Planters of New-England, or any where. Or, The Path-way to experience to erect a Plantation.* Printed by John Haviland.

#### PRINCIPAL MODERN EDITIONS

Smith, John. *Works,* ed. Edward Arber. The English Scholar's Library, No. 16. Birmingham, 1884. (What was apparently a remainder of this was issued in 2 vols., Westminster [London], 1895.)

Smith, John. *The Generall Historie of Virginia, New England & The Summer Isles. Together with The True Travels, Adventures and Observations, and A Sea Grammar.* 2 vols. Glasgow, 1907.

Smith, John. *Travels and Works . . . ,* ed. Edward Arber . . . A New Edition with a Biographical and Critical Introduction by A. G. Bradley. Edinburgh, 1910. (The 2 vols. have the same pagination as the one-vol. 1884 ed.)

## BIBLIOGRAPHY OF WORKS RELATING TO JOHN SMITH

*(No purely fictional works are listed; nor are histories of English or American literature which mention Smith)*

#### BIBLIOGRAPHICAL WORK

Eames, Wilberforce. *A Bibliography of Captain John Smith.* New York, 1927. (A reprint of J. Sabin's *Dictionary of works relating to America,* XX [1927], 218–65.)

#### ANONYMOUS

*A Congratulatory Poem upon the Noble Feast Made by the Ancient and Renouned Families of the Smiths.* Broadside, publ. London *c.* 1680–84.

"A Virginian." *The Lives of Sir Walter Raleigh and Capt. John Smith; with an account of the Governors of Virginia, to 1781.* Shepherd's-town, Va. (now Shepherdstown, W. Va.), 1817.

C. "Biographical Notice of Captain John Smith," *Stryker's American Register and Magazine,* VI (1851), 489–501.

"Family of Captain John Smith," *Tyler's Quarterly,* VII (1925–26), 118–19.

"Myths of American History," *Tyler's Quarterly,* VI (1924–25), 149–58. (Partly a reprint from the Baltimore *Evening Sun.*)

BOOKS, ARTICLES, MONOGRAPHS, ETC.

Adams, Henry. "Captain John Smith," *North American Review*, CIV (1867), 1–30. (A review of *Captain John Smith's "A true relation of Virginia*," ed. Charles Deane.)

Adams, James Truslow. "Smith, John," biographical notice in the *Dictionary of American Biography*, XVII, 294–96.

Adams, Randolph Greenfield. "Notes on the engraved portraits of Captain John Smith," *WMQ*, 2nd ser., XXI (1941), 27–28.

Addison, W. Meade, and others: "A Portrait of Captain John Smith," a letter conveying a portrait of John Smith to the State of Virginia, together with a letter concerning the authenticity of the portrait. [Richmond?], 1923.

Arber, Edward. *Introduction to Capt. John Smith . . . Works.* Birmingham (Warwickshire), 1884.

Armstrong, W. C. *The life and adventures of Captain John Smith: . . . Principally compiled from his own works.* New York, 1860.

Ashton, John. *The Life of Captain John Smith.* London, 1884.

Azulay, Fortunato. *Heróis da história norte-americana; estudos biograficos de Capitão John Smith. . . .* Rio de Janeiro, 1945.

Barbour, Philip L. "Captain John Smith and the Bishop of Sarum," *Huntington Library Quarterly*, XXVI (1962), 11–29.

——— "Captain John Smith's Observations on Life in Tartary," *VMHB*, LXVIII (1960), 271–83.

——— "Captain John Smith's Route through Turkey and Russia," *WMQ*, 3rd ser., XIV (1957), 358–69.

——— "Fact and Fiction in Captain John Smith's *True Travels*," *Bulletin of the New York Public Library*, LXVII (1963), 517–28; reprinted with minor changes in *Literature as a Mode of Travel: Five Essays and a Postscript*, pp. 101–14. The New York Public Library, New York, 1963.

——— "A French Account of Captain John Smith's Adventures in the Azores, 1615," scheduled for publication in *VMHB*, LXXII (1964).

——— "Smith, John," biographical notice in *The Encyclopedia Americana*, 1965 edition, XXV, scheduled to come off the press, January, 1965.

Basso, Hamilton. *Mainstream.* New York [1943].

Belknap, Jeremy. *The life and extraordinary adventures of Captain John Smith. . . .* London [1803]. (From the author's *American Biography.* Boston, 1794.)

Blackstock, Walter. "Captain John Smith: his role in American colonial history," *Florida State Univ. Studies, no. 6,* pp. 23–45. Tallahassee, 1952.

Blow, Mrs. A. Allmond. *An address delivered before the Daughters of the American Revolution,* at their Congress held in Washington, April, 1905; n.p., 1905.

Bradley, Arthur Granville. *Captain John Smith.* London, 1905.

——— "Introduction, Critical and Biographical" to *Travels and Works of Captain John Smith,* ed. Edward Arber. Edinburgh, 1910.

Brown, Alexander. "Some Notes on Smith's History — on The Virginia Company of London and the Managers thereof, followed by some Queries," NEHGR, XLVII (1893), 205–11.

Brown, Neal. "John Smith," in his *Critical Confessions*, pp. 116–70. Wausau, Wis., 1899.

Bruce, Philip A. *Virginia Plutarch*, I, 12–27. 2 vols. Univ. of N. Car. Press, 1929.

Chatterton, Edward Keble. *Captain John Smith*. London, 1927.

Childs, J. Rives. "The First Great American Boaster," *Foreign Service Journal*, IX (1932), 293–97 and 303.

Cohasset, Massachusetts. Addresses at the unveiling of a memorial, July 4, 1914, commemorating the discovery of Cohasset in 1614 by Captain John Smith. Cohasset, Mass., 1914.

Davis, Richard Beale. "The First American Edition of Capt. John Smith's True Travels and General Historie," *VMHB*, XLVII (1939), 97–108.

——— "The Gentlest Art in Seventeenth-Century Virginia," *Tennessee Studies in Literature*, II (1957), 51–63.

Doyle, John Andrew. "Smith, John," biographical notice in the *Dictionary of National Biography*, XVIII, 478–81.

Edmunds, Pocahontas Wight. *The Pocahontas-John Smith Story*. Richmond, 1956.

Eggleston, Edward, and Seelye, E. E. *Pocahontas: including an account . . . of the adventures of Captain John Smith*. Famous American Indians, New York, 1879. (See also under SEELYE for later edition.)

Fishwick, Marshall W. *American Heroes: Myth and Reality*. Washington, 1954.

——— *Gentlemen of Virginia*. New York, 1961.

——— "Virginians on Olympus: I. The Last Great Knight Errant," *VMHB*, LVIII (1950), 40–57; reprinted as "John Smith, the Virginian, as Colonist," in *Virginians on Olympus: a cultural analysis of four great men*. Richmond, 1951.

——— "Was John Smith a Liar?" *American Heritage*, IX, no. 6 (1958), 28–33 and 110–11.

Fletcher, John Gould. *John Smith — also Pocahontas*. New York, 1928. (See also under WROTH.)

Ford, Worthington Chauncey. "Captain John Smith's map of Virginia," *Geographical Review* [New York], XIV (1924), 433–43.

Fuller, Thomas. *The History of the Worthies of England* [1662]. Repr. London, 1840. (Contains a brief biographical note marred by at least one misstatement.)

Glenn, Keith. "Captain John Smith and the Indians," *VMHB*, LII (1944), 228–48.

Gooding, Elsie. *From Virginia to Willoughby to Remember The Great Capt. John Smith*. Alford (Lincs.), [1960].

Goodrich, Samuel Griswold. *Stories about Captain John Smith, of Virginia; for the instruction and amusement of children*. Hartford (Conn.), 1829.

Gookin, Warner F. "The First Leaders at Jamestown," *VMHB,* LVIII (1950), 181–93.

Granger, James. *A Biographical History of England,* pp. 399–400. London, 1779.

Groome, H. C. "The Finding of Fauquier [County]," *Tyler's Quarterly,* II (1920–21), 314–19.

Guss, Abraham L. *Early Indian history on the Susquehanna . . . Based on rare and original documents . . .* Harrisburg (Pa.), 1883.

Gwathmey, John Hastings. *The Love Affairs of Captain John Smith.* Richmond, 1935.

Harrison, Fairfax. *Landmarks of Old Prince William.* Richmond, 1924.

Hart, Albert Bushnell. "American historical liars: John Smith," *Harper's Magazine,* CXXXI (1915), 726–35.

[Hawks, Francis Lister]: *The Adventures of Captain John Smith, the founder of the Colony of Virginia,* by the Author of "Uncle Philip's Conversations." New York, 1843, and later eds. (Attributed in British Museum Catalogue to Hawks or William Dunlap.)

Haydon, Arthur Lincoln. *Captain John Smith: Soldier of Fortune and Pioneer.* London, 1907.

Hazard, Lucy. *The Frontier in American Literature,* pp. 49–55. New York, 1927.

Hemphill, William Edward. "Not born for ourselves," *Virginia Cavalcade,* VI, no. 4 (1957), 4–7. (On the statue of Smith by William Couper.)

Henderson, Brantley. *Being the Story of Fabulous John Smith, Virginia's First Explorer and Author.* Richmond, 1956.

Henry, William Wirt. "A Defence of Captain John Smith," *Magazine of American History,* XXV (1891), 300–313.

———— "Did (George) Percy Denounce Smith's History of Virginia?" *VMHB,* I (1893–94), 473–76.

———— "The rescue of Captain John Smith by Pocahontas," *Potters American Monthly,* IV (1875), 523–28, and V (1875), 591–97.

———— "The Settlement at Jamestown, with particular reference to the late attacks upon Captain John Smith, Pocahontas, and John Rolfe," *Proceedings of the Virginia Historical Society,* Annual meeting, Feb. 24, 1882 [Richmond].

Hill, George Canning. *Captain John Smith: a biography.* Boston, 1858.

Hillard, George Stillman. "The Life and Adventures of Captain John Smith," Jared Sparks's *The Library of American Biography,* II (1835), 171–407.

Hopkins, Samuel. *The Youth of the Old Dominion.* Boston and New York, 1856.

Howe, Henry F. *Prologue to New England.* New York and Toronto, 1943.

Hubbell, Jay Broadus. "The Smith-Pocahontas Story in Literature," *VMHB,* LXV (1957), 275–300.

Jalbert, H. H. "Captain John Smith, Jack of all Trades and Master of Most," *Mentor*, XIV (1926), 39–40.

Jenks, Tudor. *Captain John Smith*. New York, 1904.

Johnson, Rossiter [Edwin Rossiter]. *Captain John Smith (1579–1631)*. New York, 1915.

Kibler, J. Luther. "More about Smith and Pocahontas," *Tyler's Quarterly*, XXIX (1947–48), 84.

Kropf, Lewis L. "Notes [on Captain John Smith]," *Notes and Queries*, 7th ser., IX (1890), 1–2, 41–43, 102–04, 161–62, 223–24, 281–82.

Livingston, Luther Samuel, ed. *Captain John Smith's Circular or Prospectus of his Generall Historie of Virginia, New-England, and the Summer Isles* [1623, see Bibliography of Smith's Works, above], reproduced from the only known copy in the Collection of the Society of Antiquaries, London, with notes. Privately printed, Cambridge, Mass., 1914.

London. St. Sepulchre's Church . . . Commemoration service on the occasion of the tercentenary of the death of Captain John Smith. . . . London, 1931.

—— *A Short History of St. Sepulchre's Church . . . A.D. 1137–1931*. London, n.d.

Lukens, R. R. "Captain John Smith's Map," *Military Engineer*, XXIII (Sept.–Oct. 1931), pp. 435–38.

Marriott, Sir John Charles Oakes. *Admiral of New England: The exploits of John Smith, his London Epitaph*. London, n.d. (Repr. from *The Times*, June 19, 1931.)

McCabe, W. Gordon. "Captain John Smith's Travels," *Oxford and Cambridge Review*, 1907, no. 2, pp. 3–17.

McCary, Ben C. *John Smith's Map of Virginia*. Jamestown Booklet, 1957 (see above).

McDavid, Mittie Owen. *Princess Pocahontas*. New York, 1907.

Morison, Samuel Eliot. *Builders of the Bay Colony*, pp. 7–14. Boston, 1930.

Morse, Jarvis M. "John Smith and his critics: a chapter in colonial historiography," *Journal of Southern History*, I (1935), 123–37.

Neill, Edward Duffield. "Captain John Smith, adventurer and romancer," *Macalester College Contributions*, Ser. 1, no. 11 (St. Paul, Minn., 1891?), pp. 241–52.

—— "Captain John Smith, President of the Virginia Council, 1608–1609," a series of articles in the *Richmond Dispatch*, 1877.

—— *Pocahontas and her companions*. . . . Albany (N.Y.), 1869.

Palfrey, John Gorham. *History of New England* (5 vols.), I, 85–100. Boston, 1858–90.

Parker, Helen Eliza Fitch. *Discoverers and pioneers of America*. New York, 1856 and 1859.

Parsons, Harold G. "A Knight of the Sun," *Blackwood's Magazine*, CLXXIV (1903), 28–40.

Patterson, Dorothil Desmond. *Captain John Smith: An Analysis of his Ability as a Historian.* Unpublished M.A. thesis presented at Columbia University. New York, [May] 1942.

Phillips, P. Lee. "Some Early Maps of Virginia and the Makers . . ." *VMHB*, XV (1907), 71–81.

Pichler, J. Franz. "Captain John Smith in the Light of Styrian Sources," *VMHB*, LXV (1957), 332–54.

Poindexter, Charles. "Captain John Smith and his critics." A lecture before the Society for Geographical and Historical Study of Richmond College, Richmond (1893).

Quinn, Vernon. *The exciting adventures of Captain John Smith.* New York, 1928.

Randel, William. "Captain John Smith's Attitude toward the Indians," *VMHB*, XLVII (1939), 218–29.

Raup, George B. "Captain John Smith, Adventurer Extraordinary," *VMHB*, LXI (1953), 186–92.

Ristow, Walter W. "Captain John Smith's Map of Virginia." Brochure of the *Library of Congress,* with facsimile of the map. Washington, 1957.

Roberts, E. P. *The Adventures of Captain John Smith.* London, 1902.

Rowland, Kate Mason. "Captain John Smith, Soldier and Historian," *The Conservative Review,* I, no. 1 (Feb., 1899), 113–26.

Rozwenc, Edwin C. "Captain John Smith's Image of America," *WMQ,* 3rd ser., XVI (1959), 27–36.

Rutman, Darrett B. "The Pilgrims and their Harbor," *WMQ,* 3rd ser., XVII (1960), 164–82.

Scheibler, Carl Friedrich. *Reisen, Entdeckungen und Unternehmungen des Schifs-Capitain Iohan Schmidt.* Berlin, 1782.

Seelye, Elizabeth Eggleston, assisted by Edward Eggleston. *Pocahontas.* New York [1890?]. (New ed. of work listed under EGGLESTON.)

Shelley, Henry C. "American Shrines on English Soil: Memorials of Captain John Smith," *Book News Monthly,* XXXII (Philadelphia, 1914), 435–37.

Simms, William Gilmore. *The Life of Captain John Smith: The founder of Jamestown.* 7th ed., Philadelphia, 1866. (Apparently first published in New York, where it was copyrighted in 1846; I have not seen a copy of the first edition.)

Smith, Bradford. "Biographer's Notebook," *VMHB,* LXV (1957), 301–12.

——— *Captain John Smith: His Life and Legend.* Philadelphia, 1953.

——— "Captain Smith's Earl of Ployer," *VMHB,* LXII, (1954), 348–49.

Smith, Bradford, and Striker, Laura Polanyi. See STRIKER.

Smith, Elmer Boyd. *The Story of Pocahontas and Captain John Smith.* Boston and New York, 1906.

Smith, Justin Harvey. "Captain John Smith," an address at the dedication of a memorial to the Reverend John Tucke (1702–73), Star Island, Isles of Shoals, N.H., July 29, 1914. Concord (N.H.), 1914.

Smyth, Clifford. *Captain John Smith and England's first successful colony in America.* New York and London, 1931.

Southall, James P. C. "Captain John Smith (1580–1631) and Pocahontas (1595?–1617)," *Tyler's Quarterly,* XXVIII (1946–47), 209–25.

Squires, W. H. T. *Through Centuries Three.* Portsmouth, Va., 1929.

Striker, Laura Polanyi. "Captain John Smith's Hungary and Transylvania," in Bradford Smith's *Life and Legend,* above.

—— "The Hungarian Historian, Lewis L. Kropf, on Captain John Smith's *True Travels; a Reappraisal,*" *VMHB,* LXVI (1958), 22–43.

—— "Hungary's Role in the Life of Captain John Smith," *True Hungary,* no. 2–3 (New York, 1957), first article (no pagination).

Striker, Laura Polanyi, and Smith, Bradford. "The Rehabilitation of Captain John Smith," *Journal of Southern History,* XXVIII (1962), 474–81.

Sweetser, Kate Dickinson. *Ten Great Adventurers.* New York, 1915.

Syme, Ronald. *John Smith of Virginia.* New York, 1954.

Szerb, Anthony. "Captain John Smith in Transylvania," *Hungarian Quarterly,* VI (1940), 734–41.

Tyler, Lyon Gardiner. *England in America.* American Nation Series (New York), V (1904), 43–64 and 150–52.

Verner, Coolie. "The First Maps of Virginia," *VMHB,* LVIII (1950), 3–15.

Warner, Charles Dudley. *Captain John Smith (1579–1631).* Lives of American Worthies, New York, 1881.

Wecter, Dixon. *The Hero in American History.* New York, 1941.

Wharton, Henry. *The Life of John Smith, English Soldier;* trans. from the Latin MS with an essay on Captain John Smith in 17th-century literature by Laura Polanyi Striker. Univ. of N. Car. Press for the Va. Hist. Soc., 1957.

Woods, Katharine Pearson. *The True Story of Captain John Smith.* New York, 1901.

Wrench, Sir Evelyn. "Founders of Virginia," *National Geographic Magazine,* XCIII (1948), 433–63.

Wroth, Lawrence C. "Bibliographical Note," in John Gould Fletcher's ed. of Smith's *True Travels . . . ,* pp. 71–80. Repr. New York, 1930.

Yonge, Samuel H. "The Site of Old Jamestown," *VMHB,* XI (1903–4), 257–76 and 393–414, and XII (1904–5), 33–53 and 113–33.

# Index

Index

# INDEX

Nოᴛᴇ: The transliteration of Russian names is a compromise—there is no "standard" system.

The approximate locations of geographical features no longer on maps are indicated by reference to modern counties, etc., in square brackets. No reference has been made to the place-names added to Smith's maps to honor friends or cajole sponsors. Little-known places are supplied with district names. Abbreviations (n. for north; Mass. for Massachusetts) are self-explanatory.

Descriptive epithets have been limited to those needed for clarity. Noblemen are generally given their last title only. Married women and widows similarly appear under their last recorded married names.

To save space, the Index refers only to the text, variant spellings have rarely been indicated, the names of the various councils have been omitted, and Indian place-names refer to the tribe as well as the village.